Praise for *Stamped from the Beginning*

"An altogether remarkable thesis on history. . . . *Stamped from the Beginning* is a riveting (and often rivetingly written) work, well deserving of the National Book Award."
—*The Stranger*

"Kendi upends many commonly held beliefs about how racism works, exploring the ideas and thinkers behind our most intractable social and cultural problem."
—*Boston Globe*

"Essential reading."
—*Bustle*

"Ambitious, well-researched, and worth the time of anyone who wants to understand racism."
—*Seattle Times*

"I honestly wish every American would read this book, especially people who haven't been exposed to the history of blatant, transparent racism in our public policy."
—*Chicago Review of Books*, Best Books of 2016

"Perhaps the most significant book of 2016, this National Book Award winner is a lucid, highly readable look at the origins of racist ideas in the United States."
—*Daily Kos*

"Ambitious. . . . Kendi bases his exhaustive study in one central thought: Racist ideas . . . have historically sprung from racist policies, and self-preservation of the ruling class. The policy leads to the ideology, not vice versa."
—*Dallas Morning News*

"This book should be on every young leader's bookshelf. It's not pretty, but the truth often isn't."
—*Forbes Online*

"An accomplished history of racist thought and practice in the United States from the Puritans to the present. . . . In this tour de force, Kendi explores the history of racist ideas—and their connection with racist practices—across American history. . . . Racism is the enduring scar on the American consciousness. In this ambitious, magisterial book, Kendi reveals just how deep that scar cuts and why it endures, its barely subcutaneous pain still able to flare."

—*Kirkus Reviews*, starred review

"This heavily researched yet easily readable volume explores the roots and the effects of racism in America. The narrative smoothly weaves throughout history, culminating in the declaration that as much as we'd like it to be, America today is nowhere near the 'postracial' country that the media declared following the election of Barack Obama in 2008. The hope here is that by studying and remembering the lessons of history, we may be able to move forward to an equitable society."

—*Booklist*

"Kendi's provocative egalitarian argument combines prodigious reading and research with keen insights into the manipulative power of racist ideologies that suppress the recognition of diversity. This is a must for serious readers of American history, politics, or social thought."

—*Library Journal*

"Self-proclaimed as a definitive history of racist ideas in the United States, this exhaustive, encyclopedic opus lives up to that claim. Kendi's mighty tome is breathtaking in its scope. . . . Both worthwhile and extraordinary. . . . Essential."

—*CHOICE*

"A work as prodigious as the subtitle implies. . . . Had Kendi only provided history, *Stamped from the Beginning* would be a meaningful contribution to the literature, but it is so much more. It a call for all Americans to look inward."

—*Albany Times Union*

"In his relentless odyssey through the making of America's particular brand of prejudice . . . Kendi challenges our assumptions about racism by exposing the development of racist ideas—and their connection to racist actions and policies throughout our history."

—Stephenie Livingston, University of Florida

"*Stamped from the Beginning* is a history of how racist ideas are built, and how they are built to last. Understanding this history is essential if we want to have any hope of progress. This book will forever change the way we think about race."

—Touré, MSNBC contributor and author of
Who's Afraid of Post-Blackness

"In his ambitious, illuminating, and engaging book, Ibram X. Kendi seamlessly assembles sources from Cotton Mather to Angela Davis, the Great Awakening to Black Lives Matter, the *Birth of a Nation* to Hip Hop culture, to show how not only race but racist ideas are at the center of American thought."

—Paula J. Giddings, EA Woodson Professor,
Smith College, and author of *Ida: A Sword Among Lions:
Ida B. Wells and the Campaign Against Lynching*

"Both a penetrating treatise and a wonderfully accessible work of intellectual history, *Stamped from the Beginning* reveals the heritage of ideas behind the modern dialectic of race-denial and race-obsession. By historicizing our entrenched logic of racial difference, Kendi shows why 'I don't see color' and other professions of post-racialism remain inexorable alibis for white supremacy. *Stamped from the Beginning* has done the cause of anti-racism a great service."

—Russell Rickford, associate professor, Cornell University,
and author of *We Are an African People: Independent Education,
Black Power, and the Radical Imagination*

"Ibram X. Kendi is an important new voice in African American intellectual and social history. This book, an intellectual history of racist ideas, promises to break important new ground for scholarly and general audiences interested in the construction of racism in America."

—Peniel E. Joseph, author of
Stokely: A Life and *Waiting 'Til the Midnight Hour*

"Richly sourced and engaging, Ibram X. Kendi's *Stamped from the Beginning* is a highly accessible yet provocative study that seeks to complicate our understanding of racist ideas and the forces that produce them."

—Yohuru Williams, professor of history and dean of
the College of Arts and Sciences, Fairfield University

"*Stamped from the Beginning* delivers a timely and bold corrective to the history of racist and anti-racist ideas that explodes our understanding of the root of anti-black violence as we know it today. Kendi's deft analysis of key thinkers from Cotton Mather to Angela Davis illustrates how racial thought, specifically debates about racial difference, take shape across space and time and influence racial policies and the persistence of racial discrimination. This book is a must-read for those interested in working to unearth the foundational ideas and practices that hinder true racial progress."

—Keisha-Khan Y. Perry, associate professor,
Brown University, and author of
Black Women Against the Land Grab: The Fight for Racial Justice in Brazil

STAMPED FROM THE BEGINNING

STAMPED FROM THE BEGINNING

*The Definitive History of
Racist Ideas in America*

Ibram X. Kendi

BOLD TYPE BOOKS

New York

Bold Type Books
116 East 16th Street, 8th Floor New York, NY 10003
www.boldtypebooks.org
@BoldTypeBooks

Printed in the United States of America
Originally published in hardcover and ebook by Nation Books in 2016
First Trade Paperback Edition: August 2017
Published by Bold Type Books, an imprint of Perseus Books, LLC, a subsidiary of Hachette Book Group, Inc.
Bold Type Books is a co-publishing venture of the Type Media Center and Perseus Books.

The Hachette Speakers Bureau provides a wide range of authors for speaking events. To find out more, go to www.hachettespeakersbureau.com or call (866) 376-6591.
The publisher is not responsible for websites (or their content) that are not owned by the publisher.

Print book interior design by Jack Lenzo

Library of Congress Cataloging-in-Publication Data
Names: Kendi, Ibram X., author.
Title: Stamped from the beginning : the definitive history of racist ideas in America / Ibram X. Kendi.
Description: New York : Nation Books, 2016. | Includes bibliographical references and index.
Identifiers: LCCN 2015033671| ISBN 9781568584638 (hardcover : alk. paper) | ISBN 9781568584645 (ebook : alk. paper)
Subjects: LCSH: Racism—United States—History. | United States—Race relations.
Classification: LCC E185.61 .K358 2016 | DDC 305.800973—dc23
LC record available at http://lccn.loc.gov/2015033671

ISBN 978-1-56858-598-7 (paperback)

LSC-C

To the lives they said don't matter

Contents

Preface to the
Paperback Edition

I STARTED WORKING on this project squarely in the middle of the presidential age of Barack Obama. No one could fathom back in 2012 that the reality television star trolling Obama about the authenticity of his birth certificate would succeed him in the White House. But Donald Trump's "birther theory," as it came to be known, proved to be the beginning of his successful presidential campaign of bigotry. It proved to be the beginning of the end of the Obama era that was supposed to continue with the election of the first woman president of the United States.

Trump's election left many Americans in shock, in search of serious answers to their serious questions. How could a Donald Trump follow Barack Obama into the presidency? How could the candidate of angry bigots, the Klan's candidate, the stop-and-frisk candidate, the candidate of border walls, the candidate that said a Latino judge can't be objective and that "African Americans and Hispanics" live in "hell"— how could this birther theorist follow the first Black president? How could Trump rise when Obama's rise seemed to make it impossible?

Neither of the two popular Obama eras' racial histories prepared shocked Americans for the advent of Donald Trump. His election neither fit the Republicans' postracial narrative of the end of racial history nor the Democrats' narrative of the march of racial progress. His election neither fit the arrival narrative after the 1960s nor the progressive narrative that discriminatory policies have become more covert and racist ideas have become more implicit since the 1960s. Trump's election did not fit these historical narratives because they were grounded in political ideology—and racist ideas—not firm scholarly research.

The sudden storm of Trump has uprooted—should be uprooting—beliefs in these two tales. Americans need a new racial history, rooted in meticulous research, that explains this confusing present and prepares the nation and world for the racial future, after Trump.

Stamped from the Beginning presents this new history. It does not use terms like overt and covert, or explicit and implicit to describe the historical evolution of race. It does not present a postracial story that ends with the election of Obama. It does not present a story of racial progress, showing how far we have come, and the long way we have to go. It does not even present a story of racial progress of two steps forward—as embodied in Obama—and one step back—as embodied in Trump.

As I carefully studied America's racial past, I did not see a *singular* historical force arriving at a postracial America. I did not see a *singular* historical force becoming more covert and implicit over time. I did not see a *singular* historical force taking steps forward and backward on race. I saw *two* distinct historical forces. I saw a *dual* and *dueling* history of racial progress and the simultaneous progression of racism. I saw the antiracist force of equality and the racist force of inequality marching forward, progressing in rhetoric, in tactics, in policies.

When the Obamas of the nation broke through racial barriers, the Trumps of the nation did not retire to their sunny estates in Florida. They created and sometimes succeeded in putting new and more sophisticated barriers in place, like the great-grandchildren of Jim Crow voting laws—the new age-voter ID laws that are disenfranchising Black Americans in the twenty-first century. And the Trumps of the nation developed a new round of racist ideas to justify those policies, to redirect the blame for racial disparities away from those new discriminatory policies and onto the supposed Black pathology.

I AM WRITING this preface on the eve of Trump's 100th day in office as the forty-fifth president of the United States. But I am less concerned about Trump's first 100 days—or last 100 days for that matter—than what Trump's election reveals about America's racial history.

If Barack Obama came to embody America's history of racial progress, then Donald Trump should come to embody America's history of racist progress. And racist progress has consistently followed racial progress.

It is this dueling duality that I present in *Stamped from the Beginning*, taking away the shock of Trump's election, and showing its striking consistency within America's history. Trump was shocking for me, but then again not shocking at all. This history prepared me for Trump, and all the other Trumps that could rise one day on the timeworn back of bigotry.

Ibram X. Kendi
April 28, 2017

Prologue

EVERY HISTORIAN WRITES IN—and is impacted by—a precise historical moment. My moment, this book's moment, coincides with the televised and untelevised killings of unarmed human beings at the hands of law enforcement officials, and with the televised and untelevised life of the shooting star of #Black Lives Matter during America's stormiest nights. I somehow managed to write this book between the heartbreaks of Trayvon Martin and Rekia Boyd and Michael Brown and Freddie Gray and the Charleston 9 and Sandra Bland, heartbreaks that are a product of America's history of racist ideas as much as this history book of racist ideas is a product of these heartbreaks.

Young Black males were *twenty-one times* more likely to be killed by police than their White counterparts between 2010 and 2012, according to federal statistics. The under-recorded, under-analyzed racial disparities between female victims of lethal police force may be even greater. Federal data show that the median wealth of White households is a staggering *thirteen times* the median wealth of Black households—and Black people are *five times* more likely to be incarcerated than Whites.[1]

But these statistics should come as no surprise. Most Americans are probably aware of these racial disparities in police killings, in wealth, in prisons—in nearly every sector of US society. By racial disparities, I mean how racial groups are not statistically represented according to their populations. If Black people make up 13.2 percent of the US population, then Black people should make up somewhere close to 13 percent of the Americans killed by the police, somewhere close to 13 percent of the Americans sitting in prisons, somewhere close to owning 13 percent of US wealth. But today, the United States remains nowhere close to racial parity. African Americans own 2.7 percent of the nation's wealth, and make up 40 percent of the incarcerated population. These are racial disparities, and racial disparities are older than the life of the United States.[2]

In 2016, the United States is celebrating its 240th birthday. But even before Thomas Jefferson and the other founders declared independence, Americans were engaging in a polarizing debate over racial disparities, over why they exist and persist, and over why White Americans as a group were prospering more than Black Americans as a group. Historically, there have been three sides to this heated argument. A group we can call *segregationists* has blamed Black people themselves for the racial disparities. A group we can call *antiracists* has pointed to racial discrimination. A group we can call *assimilationists* has tried to argue for both, saying that Black people *and* racial discrimination were to blame for racial disparities. During the ongoing debate over police killings, these three sides to the argument have been on full display. *Segregationists* have been blaming the recklessly criminal behavior of the Black people who were killed by police officers. Michael Brown was a monstrous, threatening thief; therefore Darren Wilson had reason to fear him and to kill him. *Antiracists* have been blaming the recklessly racist behavior of the police. The life of this dark-skinned eighteen-year-old did not matter to Darren Wilson. *Assimilationists* have tried to have it both ways. Both Wilson and Brown acted like irresponsible criminals.

Listening to this three-way argument in recent years has been like listening to the three distinct arguments you will hear throughout *Stamped from the Beginning*. For nearly six centuries, antiracist ideas have been pitted against *two* kinds of racist ideas: segregationist and assimilationist. The history of racial ideas that follows is the history of these three distinct voices—segregationists, assimilationists, and antiracists—and how they each have rationalized racial disparities, arguing why Whites have remained on the living and winning end, while Blacks remained on the losing and dying end.

THE TITLE *STAMPED FROM THE BEGINNING* comes from a speech that Mississippi senator Jefferson Davis gave on the floor of the US Senate on April 12, 1860. This future president of the Confederacy objected to a bill funding Black education in Washington, DC. "This Government was not founded by negroes nor for negroes," but "by white men for white men," Davis lectured his colleagues. The bill was based on the false notion of racial equality, he declared. The "inequality of the white and black races" was "stamped from the beginning."[3]

It may not be surprising that Jefferson Davis regarded Black people as biologically distinct and inferior to White people—and Black skin as an ugly stamp on the beautiful White canvas of normal human skin—and this Black stamp as a signifier of the Negro's everlasting inferiority. This kind of segregationist thinking is perhaps easier to identify—and easier to condemn—as obviously racist. And yet so many prominent Americans, many of whom we celebrate for their progressive ideas and activism, many of whom had very good intentions, subscribed to assimilationist thinking that also served up racist beliefs about Black inferiority. We have remembered assimilationists' glorious struggle against racial discrimination, and tucked away their inglorious partial blaming of inferior Black behavior for racial disparities. In embracing biological racial equality, assimilationists point to environment—hot climates, discrimination, culture, and poverty—as the creators of inferior Black behaviors. For solutions, they maintain that the ugly Black stamp can be erased—that inferior Black behaviors can be developed, given the proper environment. As such, assimilationists constantly encourage Black adoption of White cultural traits and/or physical ideals. In his landmark 1944 study of race relations, a study widely regarded as one of the instigators of the civil rights movement, Swedish economist and Nobel Laureate Gunnar Myrdal wrote, "It is to the advantage of American Negroes as individuals and as a group to become assimilated into American culture, to acquire the traits held in esteem by the dominant white Americans." He had also claimed, in *An American Dilemma*, that "in practically all its divergences, American Negro culture is . . . a distorted development, or a pathological condition, of the general American culture."[4]

But there is, and has always been, a persistent line of antiracist thought in this country, challenging those assimilationist and segregationist lines, and giving the line of truth hope. Antiracists have long argued that racial discrimination was stamped from the beginning of America, which explains why racial disparities have existed and persisted. Unlike segregationists and assimilationists, antiracists have recognized that the different skin colors, hair textures, behaviors, and cultural ways of Blacks and Whites are on the same level, are equal in all their divergences. As the legendary Black lesbian poet Audre Lorde lectured in 1980: "We have no patterns for relating across our human differences as equals."[5]

THERE WAS NOTHING simple or straightforward or predictable about racist ideas, and thus their history. Frankly speaking, for generations of Americans, racist ideas have been their common sense. The simple logic of racist ideas has manipulated millions over the years, muffling the more complex antiracist reality again and again. And so, this history could not be made for readers in an easy-to-predict narrative of absurd racists clashing with reasonable antiracists. This history could not be made for readers in an easy-to-predict, two-sided Hollywood battle of obvious good versus obvious evil, with good triumphing in the end. From the beginning, it has been a three-sided battle, a battle of antiracist ideas being pitted against two kinds of racist ideas at the same time, with evil and good failing and triumphing in the end. Both segregationist and assimilationist ideas have been wrapped up in attractive arguments to seem good, and both have made sure to re-wrap antiracist ideas as evil. And in wrapping their ideas in goodness, segregationists and assimilationists have rarely confessed to their racist public policies and ideas. But why would they? Racists confessing to their crimes is not in their self-interest. It has been smarter and more exonerating to identify what they did and said as not racist. Criminals hardly ever acknowledge their crimes against humanity. And the shrewdest and most powerful anti-Black criminals have legalized their criminal activities, have managed to define their crimes of slave trading and enslaving and discriminating and killing outside of the criminal code. Likewise, the shrewdest and most powerful racist ideologues have managed to define their ideas outside of racism. Actually, assimilationists first used and defined and popularized the term "racism" during the 1940s. All the while, they refused to define their own assimilationist ideas of Black *cultural* and *behavioral* inferiority as racist. These assimilationists defined only segregationist ideas of Black *biological* inferiority as racist. And segregationists, too, have always resisted the label of "racist." They have claimed instead that they were merely articulating God's word, nature's design, science's plan, or plain old common sense.[6]

All these self-serving efforts by powerful factions to define their racist rhetoric as nonracist has left Americans thoroughly divided over, and ignorant of, what racist ideas truly are. It has all allowed Americans who think something is wrong with Black people to believe, somehow, that they are not racists. But to say something is wrong with a group is to say something is inferior about that group. These sayings are interlocked logically whether Americans realize it or not, whether Americans are willing to admit it or not. Any comprehensive history of racist ideas must grapple with the ongoing manipulation and confusion, must set the record straight on those who are espousing racist ideas and those who are not. My definition of a racist idea is a simple one: it is any concept that regards one racial group as inferior or superior to another racial group in any way. I define anti-Black racist ideas—the subject of this book—as any idea suggesting that Black people, or any group of Black people, are inferior in any way to another racial group.

Like the other identifiable races, Black people are in reality a collection of groups differentiated by gender, class, ethnicity, sexuality, culture, skin color, profession, and nationality—among a series of other identifiers, including biracial people who may or may not identify as Black. Each and every identifiable Black group has been subjected to what critical race theorist Kimberlé Crenshaw has called "intersectionality"—prejudice stemming from the intersections of racist ideas and other forms of bigotry, such as sexism, classism, ethnocentrism, and homophobia. For example, sexist notions of real women as weak, and racist notions of Black women as not really women, have intersected to produce the *gender racism* of the strong Black woman, inferior to the pinnacle of womanhood, the weak White woman. In other words, to call women as a group stupid is sexism. To call Black people as a group stupid is racism. To call *Black* women as a group stupid is gender racism. Such intersections have also led to articulations of class racism (demeaning the *Black* poor and *Black* elites), queer racism (demeaning *Black* lesbians, gays, bisexuals, transgender, and queer people), and ethnic racism (concocting a hierarchy of *Black* ethnic groups), to name a few. Sweeping histories of racist ideas have traditionally focused on racism toward Black people in general, neglecting intersecting conceptions of specific Black groups—or even of Black spaces, such as Black neighborhoods, Black schools, Black businesses, and Black churches. *Stamped from the Beginning* focuses its narration on both—on the general as well as specific forms of assimilationist and segregationist ideas.[7]

STAMPED FROM THE BEGINNING narrates the entire history of racist ideas, from their origins in fifteenth-century Europe, through colonial times when the early British settlers carried racist ideas to America, all the way to the twenty-first century and current debates about the events taking place on our streets. Five main characters, in particular, will serve as our tour guides as we explore the landscape of racial ideas through five periods in American history. During America's first century, racist theological ideas were absolutely critical to sanctioning the growth of American slavery and making it acceptable to the Christian churches. These ideas were featured in the sermons of early America's greatest preacher and intellectual, Boston divine Cotton Mather (1663–1728), our first tour guide. Cotton Mather was the namesake and grandson of two of New England's intellectual trailblazers, John Cotton and Richard Mather, Puritan preachers who helped carry two-hundred-year-old racist ideas from Europe across the Atlantic Ocean. To substantiate American slavery and win converts, Cotton Mather preached racial inequality in body while insisting that the dark souls of enslaved Africans would become White when they became Christians. His writings and sermons were widely read in the colonies and in Europe, where the progenitors of the scientific revolution—and then the Enlightenment—were racializing and whitening Europeans, freedom, civilization, rationality, and beauty. During the American Revolution and thereafter, years that saw the stunning growth of American slavery, politicians and secular intellectuals alike joined slavery's justifying fray. These justifiers included one of the most powerful politicians and secular intellectuals of the new United States—our second tour guide, the antislavery, anti-abolitionist Thomas Jefferson (1743–1826).

Jefferson died on the eve of the nineteenth century's movement for emancipation and civil rights, a movement partially spearheaded by the pulsating editor of *The Liberator*, William Lloyd Garrison (1805–1879), tour guide number three. Like his peers, Garrison's most instrumentally passionate antislavery ideas drawing Americans to the cause of abolition and civil rights were usually not antiracist ideas. He popularized the assimilationist idea that slavery—or racial discrimination more broadly—had "imbruted" Black people; this oppression had made their cultures, psychologies, and behaviors inferior. It is one antiracist thing to say discriminators treated Black people like they were barbarians. It is yet another racist thing to say the discrimination actually transformed Black people into barbarians. The nation's first great professionally trained Black scholar, W. E. B. Du Bois (1868–1963), our fourth tour guide, initially adopted Garrison's racist idea. But he also stood at the forefront of antiracist ideas, challenging Jim Crow's rise in the late nineteenth century. Over the course of his long and storied career into the twentieth century, Du Bois's double-consciousness of racist and antiracist ideas amazingly transfigured into a single consciousness of antiracism. In the process, however, his influence waned. In the 1950s and 1960s, racist arguments once again became the most influential ideas drawing Americans to the cause of civil rights. Later, civil rights and Black power advances—and the sensationalized "crises" of Black single-parent households, welfare "queens," affirmative action, and violent rebels and criminals—all fed a ravishing racist backlash to the racial progress of the 1960s, including the judicial persecution of antiracist activists, most famously a young philosopher from the University of California at Los Angeles. Exonerated of all capital charges in 1972, Angela Davis (1943–present) spent the next four decades opposing the racial discriminators who learned to hide their intent, denouncing those who promoted end-of-racism fairytales while advocating bipartisan tough-on-crime policies and a prison-industrial complex that engineered the mass incarceration, beatings, and killings of Black people by law enforcement. She will be our fifth and final tour guide.

These five main characters—Cotton Mather, Thomas Jefferson, William Lloyd Garrison, W. E. B. Du Bois, and Angela Davis—were arguably the most consistently prominent or provocative racial theorists of their respective lifetimes, writing and speaking and teaching racial (and nonracial) ideas that were as fascinating as they were original, influential, and/or contradictory. But *Stamped from the Beginning* is not a set of five biographies of these people. Their complex lives and influential ideas have sat at the apex of debates between assimilationists and segregationists, or between racists and antiracists, and thus provide a window to those debates, to this intricately woven history.

STAMPED FROM THE BEGINNING is not merely a history of overt racism becoming covert; nor is it a history of racial progress, or a history of ignorance and hate. *Stamped from the Beginning* rewrites the history of racist ideas by exposing the incompleteness of these three widely believed historical storylines. Racist intentions—not policies—became covert after the 1960s. Old and new racist policies remained as overt as ever, and we can see the effects of these policies whenever we see racial disparities in everything from wealth to health in the twenty-first century. That's not to say that antiracist reformers have not made progress in exposing and burying racist policies over the years. But racist reformers have made progress, too. The outlawing of chattel slavery in 1865 brought on racial progress. Then, the legalization of Jim Crow brought on the progression of racist policies in the late nineteenth century. The outlawing of Jim Crow in 1964 brought on racial progress. Then, the legalization of superficially unintentional discrimination brought on the progression of racist policies in the late twentieth century.

In order to fully explain the complex history of racist ideas, *Stamped from the Beginning* must chronicle this racial progress and the simultaneous progression of racist policies. Hate and ignorance have not driven the history of racist ideas in America. Racist policies have driven the history of racist ideas in America. And this fact becomes apparent when we examine the causes behind, not the consumption of racist ideas, but the production of racist ideas. What caused US senator John C. Calhoun of South Carolina in 1837 to produce the racist idea of slavery as a "positive good," when he knew slavery's torturous horrors? What caused Atlanta newspaper editor Henry W. Grady in 1885 to produce the racist idea of "separate but equal," when he knew southern communities were hardly separate or equal? What caused think tankers after the presidential election of Barack Obama in 2008 to produce the racist idea of a postracial society, when they knew all those studies had documented discrimination? Time and again, racist ideas have not been cooked up from the boiling pot of ignorance and hate. Time and again, powerful and brilliant men and women have produced racist ideas in order to justify the racist policies of their era, in order to redirect the blame for their era's racial disparities away from those policies and onto Black people.

I was taught the popular folktale of racism: that ignorant and hateful people had produced racist ideas, and that these racist people had instituted racist policies. But when I learned the motives behind the production of many of America's most influentially racist ideas, it became quite obvious that this folktale, though sensible, was not based on a firm footing of historical evidence. Ignorance/hate→racist ideas→discrimination: this causal relationship is largely ahistorical. It has actually been the inverse relationship—racial discrimination led to racist ideas which led to ignorance and hate. Racial discrimination →racist ideas→ignorance/hate: this is the causal relationship driving America's history of race relations.

Their own racist ideas usually did *not* dictate the decisions of the most powerful Americans when they instituted, defended, and tolerated discriminatory policies that affected millions of Black lives over the course of American history. Racially discriminatory policies have usually sprung from economic, political, and cultural self-interests, self-interests that are constantly changing. Politicians seeking higher office have primarily created and defended discriminatory policies out of political self-interest—not racist ideas. Capitalists seeking to increase profit margins have primarily created and defended discriminatory policies out of economic self-interest—not racist ideas. Cultural professionals, including theologians, artists, scholars, and journalists, were seeking to advance their careers or cultures and have primarily created and defended discriminatory policies out of professional self-interest—not racist ideas.

When we look back on our history, we often wonder why so many Americans did not resist slave trading, enslaving, segregating, or now, mass incarcerating. The reason is, again, racist ideas. The principal function of racist ideas in American history has been the suppression of resistance to racial discrimination and its resulting racial disparities. The beneficiaries of slavery, segregation, and mass incarceration have produced racist ideas of Black people being best suited for or deserving of the confines of slavery, segregation, or the jail cell. Consumers of these racist ideas have been led to believe there is something wrong with Black people, and not the policies that have enslaved, oppressed, and confined so many Black people.

Racist ideas have done their job on us. We have a hard time recognizing that racial discrimination is the sole cause of racial disparities in this country and in the world at large. I write *we* for a reason. When I began this book, with a heavy heart for Trayvon Martin and Rekia Boyd, I must confess that I held quite a few racist ideas. Even though I am an Africana studies historian and have been tutored all my life in egalitarian spaces, I held racist notions of Black inferiority before researching and writing this book. Racist ideas are ideas. Anyone can produce them or consume them, as *Stamped from the Beginning*'s interracial cast of producers and consumers show. Anyone—Whites, Latina/os, Blacks, Asians, Native Americans—anyone can express the idea that Black people are inferior, that something is wrong with Black people. Anyone can believe both racist and antiracist ideas, that certain things are wrong with Black people and other things are equal. Fooled by racist ideas, I did not fully realize that the only thing wrong with Black people is that we think something is wrong with Black people. I did not fully realize that the only thing extraordinary about White people is that they think something is extraordinary about White people.

I am not saying all individuals who happen to identify as Black (or White or Latina/o or Asian or Native American) are equal in all ways. I am saying that there is nothing wrong with Black people *as a group*, or with any other racial group. That is what it truly means to think as an antiracist: to think there is nothing wrong with Black people, to think that racial groups are equal. There are lazy and unwise and harmful individuals of African ancestry. There are lazy and unwise and harmful individuals of European ancestry. There are industrious and wise and harmless individuals of European ancestry. There are industrious and wise and harmless individuals of African ancestry. But no racial group has ever had a monopoly on any type of human trait or gene— not now, not ever. Under our different-looking hair and skin, doctors cannot tell the difference between our bodies, our brains, or the blood that runs in our veins. All cultures, in all their behavioral differences, are on the same level. Black Americans' history of oppression has made Black opportunities—not Black people—inferior.

When you truly believe that the racial groups are equal, then you also believe that racial disparities must be the result of racial discrimination. Committed to this antiracist idea of group equality, I was able to self-critique, discover, and shed the racist ideas I had consumed over my lifetime while I uncovered and exposed the racist ideas that others have produced over the lifetime of America. I know that readers truly committed to racial equality will join me on this journey of interrogating and shedding our racist ideas. But if there is anything I have learned during my research, it's that the principal producers and defenders of racist ideas will not join us. And no logic or fact or history book can change them, because logic and facts and scholarship have little to do with why they are expressing racist ideas in the first place. *Stamped from the Beginning* is about these closed-minded, cunning, captivating producers of racist ideas. But it is not for them.

My open mind was liberated in writing this story. I am hoping that other open minds can be liberated in reading this story.

PART I

Cotton Mather

CHAPTER 1

Human Hierarchy

THEY WEATHERED BRUTAL WINTERS, suffered diseases, and learned to cope with the resisting Native Americans. But nothing brought more destruction to Puritan settlements than the Great Hurricane of 1635. On August 16, 1635, the hurricane—today judged to be perhaps Category 3—thundered up the Atlantic Coast, brushing Jamestown and passing over eastern Long Island. The storm's eye glanced at Providence to the east and moved inland, snatching up thousands of trees like weeds. In the seven-year-old Massachusetts Bay Colony, the hurricane smashed down English homes as if they were ants, before reaching the Atlantic Ocean and swinging knockout waves onto the New England shores.

Large ships from England transporting settlers and supplies were sitting ducks. Seamen anchored one ship, the *James*, off the coast of New Hampshire to wait out the hurricane. Suddenly, a powerful wave sliced the ship's anchors and cables like an invisible knife. Seamen slashed the third cable in distress and hoisted sail to cruise back out to a safer sea. The winds smashed the new sail into "rotten rags," recorded notable Puritan minister Richard Mather in his diary. As the rags disappeared into the ocean, so did hope.

Abducted now by the hurricane, the ship headed toward a mighty rock. All seemed lost. Richard Mather and fellow passengers cried out to the Lord for deliverance. Using "his own immediate good hand," God guided the ship around the mighty rock, Mather later testified. The sea calmed. The crew hurriedly rigged the ship with new sails. The Lord blew "a fresh gale of wind," allowing the captain to navigate away from danger. The battered *James* arrived in Boston on August 17, 1635. All one hundred passengers credited God for their survival. Richard Mather took the deliverance as a charge "to walk uprightly before him as long as we live."[1]

As a Puritan minister, Richard Mather had walked uprightly through fifteen years of British persecution before embarking on the perilous journey across the Atlantic to begin life anew in New England. There, he would be reunited with his illustrious ministerial friend John Cotton, who had faced British persecution for twenty years in Boston, England. In 1630, Cotton had given the farewell sermon to hundreds of Puritan founders of New England communities, blessing their fulfillment of God's prophetic vision. As dissenters from the Church of England, Puritans believed themselves to be God's chosen piece of humanity, a special, superior people, and New England, their Israel, was to be their exceptional land.[2]

Within a week of the Great Hurricane, Richard Mather was installed as pastor of Dorchester's North Church near the renowned North Church of the new Boston, which was pastored by John Cotton. Mather and Cotton then embarked on a sacred mission to create, articulate, and defend the *New* England Way. They used their pens as much as their pulpits, and they used their power as much as their pens and pulpits. They penned the colonies' first adult and children's books as part of this endeavor. Mather, in all likelihood, steered the selection of Henry Dunster to lead colonial America's first college, Harvard's forerunner, in 1640. And Cotton did not mind when Dunster fashioned Harvard's curriculum after their alma mater, Cambridge, setting off an ideological trend. Like the founders of Cambridge and Harvard before them, the founders of William & Mary (1693), Yale (1701), the University of Pennsylvania (1740), Princeton (1746), Columbia (1754), Brown (1764), Rutgers (1766), and Dartmouth (1769)—the other eight colonial colleges—regarded ancient Greek and Latin literature as universal truths worthy of memorization and unworthy of critique. At the center of the Old and New England Greek library hailed the resurrected Aristotle, who had come under suspicion as a threat to doctrine among some factions in Christianity during the medieval period.[3]

In studying Aristotle's philosophy, Puritans learned rationales for human hierarchy, and they began to believe that some groups were superior to other groups. In Aristotle's case, ancient Greeks were superior to all non-Greeks. But Puritans believed they were superior to Native Americans, the African people, and even Anglicans—that is, all non-Puritans. Aristotle, who lived from 384 to 322 BCE, concocted a climate theory to justify Greek superiority, saying that extreme hot or cold climates produced intellectually, physically, and morally inferior people who were ugly and lacked the capacity for freedom and self-government. Aristotle labeled Africans "burnt faces"—the original meaning in Greek of "Ethiopian"—and viewed the "ugly" extremes of pale or dark skins as the effect of the extreme cold or hot climates. All of this was in the interest of normalizing Greek slaveholding practices and Greece's rule over the western Mediterranean. Aristotle situated the Greeks, in their supreme, intermediate climate, as the most beautifully endowed superior rulers and enslavers of the world. "Humanity is divided into two: the masters and the slaves; or, if one prefers it, the Greeks and the Barbarians, those who have the right to command; and those who are born to obey," Aristotle said. For him, the enslaved peoples were "by nature incapable of reasoning and live a life of pure sensation, like certain tribes on the borders of the civilized world, or like people who are diseased through the onset of illnesses like epilepsy or madness."[4]

By the birth of Christ or the start of the Common Era, Romans were justifying their slaveholding practices using Aristotle's climate theory, and soon the new Christianity began to contribute to these arguments. For early Christian theologians—whom Puritans studied alongside Aristotle—God ordained the human hierarchy. St. Paul introduced, in the first century, a three-tiered hierarchy of slave relations—heavenly master (top), earthly master (middle), enslaved (bottom). "He who was free when called is a slave of Christ," he testified in 1 Corinthians. "Slaves" were to "obey in everything those that are your earthly masters, not with eyeservice as men-pleasers, but in singleness of heart, fearing the Lord." In a crucial caveat in Galatians 3:28, St. Paul equalized the *souls* of masters and slaves as "all one in Christ Jesus."

All in all, ethnic and religious and color prejudice existed in the ancient world. Constructions of *races*—White Europe, Black Africa, for instance—did not, and therefore racist ideas did not. But crucially, the foundations of race and racist ideas were laid. And so were the foundations for egalitarianism, antiracism, and antislavery laid in Greco-Roman antiquity. "The deity gave liberty to all men, and nature created no one a slave," wrote Alkidamas, Aristotle's rival in Athens. When Herodotus, the foremost historian of ancient Greece, traveled up the Nile River, he found the Nubians "the most handsome of peoples." Lactantius, an adviser to Constantine I, the first Christian Roman emperor, announced early in the fourth century: "God who creates and inspires men wished them all to be fair, that is, equal." St. Augustine, an African church father in the fourth and fifth centuries, maintained that "whoever is born anywhere as a human being, that is, as a rational mortal creature, however strange he may appear to our senses in bodily form or colour or motion or utterance, or in any faculty, part or quality of his nature whatsoever, let no true believer have any doubt that such an individual is descended from the one man who was first created." However, these antislavery and egalitarian champions did not accompany Aristotle and St. Paul into the modern era, into the new Harvard curriculum, or into the New England mind seeking to justify slavery and the racial hierarchy it produced.[5]

When John Cotton drafted New England's first constitution in 1636, *Moses his judicials*, he legalized the enslavement of captives taken in just wars as well as "such strangers as willingly selle themselves or are sold to us." The New England way imitated the Old England way on slavery. Cotton reproduced the policies of his British peers close and far away. In 1636, Barbados officials announced that "*Negroes* and *Indians* that come here to be sold, should serve for Life, unless a Contract was before made to the contrary."[6]

The Pequot War, the first major war between the New England colonists and the area's indigenous peoples, erupted in 1637. Captain William Pierce forced some indigenous war captives onto the *Desire*, the first slaver to leave British North America. The ship sailed to the Isla de Providencia off Nicaragua, where "Negroes" were reportedly "being . . . kept as perpetuall servants." Massachusetts governor John Winthrop recorded Captain Pierce's historic arrival back into Boston in 1638, noting that his ship was hauling "salt, cotton, tobacco and Negroes."[7]

The first generation of Puritans began rationalizing the enslavement of these "Negroes" without skipping a Christian beat. Their chilling nightmares of persecution were not the only hallucinations the Puritans had carried over the Atlantic waters in their minds to America. From the first ships that landed in Virginia in 1607, to the ships that survived the Great Hurricane of 1635, to the first slave ships, some British settlers of colonial America carried across the sea Puritan, biblical, scientific, and Aristotelian rationalizations of slavery and human hierarchy. From Western Europe and the new settlements in Latin America, some Puritans carried across their judgment of the many African peoples as one inferior people. They carried across racist ideas—racist ideas that preceded American slavery, because the need to justify African slavery preceded colonial America.

AFTER ARAB MUSLIMS conquered parts of North Africa, Portugal, and Spain during the seventh century, Christians and Muslims battled for centuries over the prize of Mediterranean supremacy. Meanwhile, below the Sahara Desert, the West African empires of Ghana (700–1200), Mali (1200–1500), and Songhay (1350–1600) were situated at the crossroads of the lucrative trade routes for gold and salt. A robust trans-Saharan trade emerged, allowing Europeans to obtain West African goods through Muslim intermediaries.

Ghana, Mali, and Songhay developed empires that could rival in size, power, scholarship, and wealth any in the world. Intellectuals at universities in Timbuktu and Jenne pumped out scholarship and pumped in students from around West Africa. Songhay grew to be the largest. Mali may have been the most illustrious. The world's greatest globe-trotter of the fourteenth century, who trotted from North Africa to Eastern Europe to Eastern Asia, decided to see Mali for himself in 1352. "There is complete security in their country," Moroccan

Ibn Battuta marveled in his travel notes. "Neither traveler nor inhabitant in it has anything to fear from robbers or men of violence."[8]

Ibn Battuta was an oddity—an abhorred oddity—among the Islamic intelligentsia in Fez, Morocco. Hardly any scholars had traveled far from home, and Battuta's travel accounts threatened their own armchair credibility in depicting foreigners. None of Battuta's antagonists was more influential than the intellectual tower of the Muslim world at that time, Tunisian Ibn Khaldun, who arrived in Fez just as Battuta returned from Mali. "People in the dynasty (in official positions) whispered to each other that he must be a liar," Khaldun reported in 1377 in *The Muqaddimah*, the foremost Islamic history of the premodern world. Khaldun then painted a very different picture of sub-Sahara Africa in *The Muqaddimah*: "The Negro nations are, as a rule, submissive to slavery," Khaldun surmised, "because (Negroes) have little that is (essentially) human and possess attributes that are quite similar to those of dumb animals." And the "same applies to the Slavs," argued this disciple of Aristotle. Following Greek and Roman justifiers, Khaldun used climate theory to justify Islamic enslavement of sub-Saharan Africans and Eastern European Slavs—groups sharing only one obvious characteristic: their remoteness. "All their conditions are remote from those of human beings and close to those of wild animals," Khaldun suggested. Their inferior conditions were neither permanent nor hereditary, however. "Negroes" who migrated to the cooler north were "found to produce descendants whose colour gradually turns white," Khaldun stressed. Dark-skinned people had the capacity for *physical* assimilation in a colder climate. Later, cultural assimilationists would imagine that culturally inferior African people, placed in the proper European cultural environment, could or should adopt European culture. But first physical assimilationists like Khaldun imagined that physically inferior African people, placed in the proper cold environment, could or should adopt European physicality: white skin and straight hair.[9]

Ibn Khaldun did not intend merely to demean African people as inferior. He intended to belittle all the different-looking African and Slavic peoples whom the Muslims were trading as slaves. Even so, he reinforced the conceptual foundation for racist ideas. On the eve of the fifteenth century, Khaldun helped bolster the foundation for assimilationist ideas, for racist notions of the environment producing African inferiority. All an enslaver had to do was to stop justifying Slavic slavery and inferiority using climate theory, and focus the theory on African people, for the racist attitude toward dark-skinned people to be complete.

There was one enslavement theory focused on Black people already circulating, a theory somehow derived from Genesis 9:18–29, which said "that Negroes were the children of Ham, the son of Noah, and that they were singled out to be black as the result of Noah's curse, which produced Ham's colour and the slavery God inflicted upon his descendants," as Khaldun explained. The lineage of this curse of Ham theory curves back through the great Persian scholar Tabari (838–923) all the way to Islamic and Hebrew sources. God had permanently cursed ugly Blackness and slavery into the very nature of African people, curse theorists maintained. As strictly a climate theorist, Khaldun discarded the "silly story" of the curse of Ham.[10]

Although it clearly supposed Black inferiority, the curse theory was like an unelected politician during the medieval period. Muslim and Christian enslavers hardly gave credence to the curse theory: they enslaved too many non-Black descendants of Shem and Japheth, Ham's supposed non-cursed brothers, for that. But the medieval curse theorists laid the foundation for segregationist ideas and for racist notions of Black genetic inferiority. The shift to solely enslaving Black people, and justifying it using the curse of Ham, was in the offing. Once that shift occurred, the disempowered curse theory became empowered, and racist ideas truly came into being.[11]

CHAPTER 2

Origins of Racist Ideas

RICHARD MATHER AND John Cotton inherited from the English thinkers of their generation the *old* racist ideas that African slavery was natural and normal and holy. These racist ideas were nearly two centuries old when Puritans used them in the 1630s to legalize and codify New England slavery—and Virginians had done the same in the 1620s. Back in 1415, Prince Henry and his brothers had convinced their father, King John of Portugal, to capture the principal Muslim trading depot in the western Mediterranean: Ceuta, on the northeastern tip of Morocco. These brothers were envious of Muslim riches, and they sought to eliminate the Islamic middleman so that they could find the southern source of gold and Black captives.

After the battle, Moorish prisoners left Prince Henry spellbound as they detailed trans-Saharan trade routes down into the disintegrating Mali Empire. Since Muslims still controlled these desert routes, Prince Henry decided to "seek the lands by the way of the sea." He sought out those African lands until his death in 1460, using his position as the Grand Master of Portugal's wealthy Military Order of Christ (successor of the Knights Templar) to draw venture capital and loyal men for his African expeditions.

In 1452, Prince Henry's nephew, King Afonso V, commissioned Gomes Eanes de Zurara to write a biography of the life and slave-trading work of his "beloved uncle." Zurara was a learned and obedient commander in Prince Henry's Military Order of Christ. In recording and celebrating Prince Henry's life, Zurara was also implicitly

22

obscuring his Grand Master's monetary decision to exclusively trade in African slaves. In 1453, Zurara finished the inaugural defense of African slave-trading, the first European book on Africans in the modern era. *The Chronicle of the Discovery and Conquest of Guinea* begins the recorded history of anti-Black racist ideas. Zurara's inaugural racist ideas, in other words, were a product of, not a producer of, Prince Henry's racist policies concerning African slave-trading.[1]

The Portuguese made history as the first Europeans to sail along the Atlantic beyond the Western Sahara's Cape Bojador in order to bring enslaved Africans back to Europe, as Zurara shared in his book. The six caravels, carrying 240 captives, arrived in Lagos, Portugal, on August 6, 1444. Prince Henry made the slave auction into a spectacle to show the Portuguese had joined the European league of serious slave-traders of African people. For some time, the Genoese of Italy, the Catalans of northern Spain, and the Valencians of eastern Spain had been raiding the Canary Islands or purchasing African slaves from Moroccan traders. Zurara distinguished the Portuguese by framing their African slave-trading ventures as missionary expeditions. Prince Henry's competitors could not play that mind game as effectively as he did, in all likelihood because they still traded so many Eastern Europeans.[2]

But the market was changing. Around the time the Portuguese opened their sea route to a new slave export area, the old slave export area started to close up. In Ibn Khaldun's day, most of the captives sold in Western Europe were Eastern Europeans who had been seized by Turkish raiders from areas around the Black Sea. So many of the seized captives were "Slavs" that the ethnic term became the root word for "slave" in most Western European languages. By the mid-1400s, Slavic communities had built forts against slave raiders, causing the supply of Slavs in Western Europe's slave market to plunge at around the same time that the supply of Africans was increasing. As a result, Western Europeans began to see the natural Slav(e) not as White, but Black.[3]

THE CAPTIVES IN 1444 disembarked from the ship and marched to an open space outside of the city, according to Zurara's chronicle. Prince Henry oversaw the slave auction, mounted on horseback, beaming in delight. Some of the captives were "white enough, fair to look upon, and well proportioned," while others were "like mulattoes," Zurara reported. Still others were "as black as Ethiops, and so ugly" that they almost appeared as visitors from Hell. The captives included people in the many shades of the Tuareg Moors as well as the dark-skinned people whom the Tuareg Moors may have enslaved. Despite their different ethnicities and skin colors, Zurara viewed them as one people—one inferior people.[4]

Zurara made it a point to remind his readers that Prince Henry's "chief riches" in quickly seizing forty-six of the most valuable captives "lay in his own purpose; for he reflected with great pleasure upon the salvation of those souls that before were lost." In building up Prince Henry's evangelical justification for enslaving Africans, Zurara reduced these captives to barbarians who desperately needed not only religious but also civil salvation. "They lived like beasts, without any custom of reasonable beings," he wrote. What's more, "they have no knowledge of bread or wine, and they were without covering of clothes, or the lodgement of houses; and worse than all, they had no understanding of good, but only knew how to live in bestial sloth." In Portugal, their lot was "quite the contrary of what it had been." Zurara imagined slavery in Portugal as an improvement over their free state in Africa.[5]

Zurara's narrative covered from 1434 to 1447. During that period, Zurara estimated, 927 enslaved Africans were brought to Portugal, "the greater part of whom were turned into the true path of salvation." Zurara failed to mention that Prince Henry received the royal fifth (*quinto*), or about 185 of those captives, for his immense fortune. But that was irrelevant to his mission, a mission he accomplished. For convincing readers, successive popes, and the reading European world that Prince Henry's Portugal did not engage in the slave trade for money, Zurara was handsomely rewarded as Portugal's chief royal chronicler, and he was given two more lucrative commanderships in the Military Order of Christ. Zurara's bosses quickly reaped returns from their slave trading. In 1466, a Czech traveler noticed that the king of Portugal was making more selling captives to foreigners "than from all the taxes levied on the entire kingdom."[6]

Zurara circulated the manuscript of *The Chronicle of the Discovery and Conquest of Guinea* to the royal court as well as to scholars, investors, and captains, who then read and circulated it throughout Portugal and Spain. Zurara died in Lisbon in 1474, but his ideas about slavery endured as the slave trade expanded. By the 1490s, Portuguese explorers had crept southward along the West African coast, rounding the Cape of Good Hope into the Indian Ocean. In their growing networks of ports, agents, ships, crews, and financiers, pioneering Portuguese slave-traders and explorers circulated the racist ideas in Zurara's book faster and farther than the text itself had reached. The Portuguese became the primary source of knowledge on unknown Africa and the African people for the original slave-traders and enslavers in Spain, Holland, France, and England. By the time German printer Valentim Fernandes published an abridged version of Zurara's book in Lisbon in 1506, enslaved Africans—and racist ideas—had arrived in the Americas.[7]

IN 1481, THE PORTUGUESE began building a large fort, São Jorge da Mina, known simply as Elmina, or "the mine," as part of their plan to acquire Ghanaian gold. In due time, this European building, the first known to be erected south of the Sahara, became West Africa's largest slave-trading post, the nucleus of Portugal's operations in West Africa. A Genoese explorer barely three decades old may have witnessed the erection of Elmina Castle. Christopher Columbus, newly married to the daughter of a Genoese protégé of Prince Henry, desired to make his own story—but not in Africa. He looked instead to East Asia, the source of spices. After Portuguese royalty refused to sponsor his daring westward expedition, Queen Isabel of Spain, a great-niece of Prince Henry, consented. So in 1492, after sixty-nine days at sea, Columbus's three small ships touched the shores that Europeans did not know existed: first the glistening Bahamas, and the next night, Cuba.[8]

Almost from Columbus's arrival, Spanish colonists began to degrade and enslave the indigenous American peoples, naming them *negros da terra* (Blacks from the land), transferring their racist constructions of African people onto Native Americans. Over the years that followed, they used the force of the gun and the Bible in one of the most frightful and sudden massacres in human history. Thousands of Native Americans died resisting enslavement. More died from European diseases, from the conditions they suffered while forcibly tilling fields, and on death marches searching and mining for gold. Millions of Native Americans were driven off their land by Spanish settlers dashing into the colonies after riches. Spanish merchant Pedro de Las Casas settled in Hispaniola in 1502, the year the first enslaved Africans disembarked from a Portuguese slave ship. He brought along his eighteen-year-old son Bartolomé, who would play an outsized role in the direction slavery took in the so-called New World.[9]

By 1510, Bartolomé de Las Casas had accumulated land and captives as well as his ordination papers as the Americas' first priest. He felt proud in welcoming the Dominican Friars to Hispaniola in 1511. Sickened by Taíno slavery, the Friars stunned Las Casas and broke abolitionist ground, rejecting the Spanish line (taken from the Portuguese) that the Taíno people benefited, through Christianity, from slavery. King Ferdinand promptly recalled the Dominican Friars, but their antislavery sermons never left Bartolomé de Las Casas. In 1515, he departed for Spain, where he would conduct a lifelong campaign to ease the suffering of Native Americans, and, possibly more importantly—solve the settlers' extreme labor shortage. In one of his first written pleas in 1516, Las Casas suggested importing enslaved Africans to replace the rapidly declining Native American laborers, a plea he made again two years later. Alonso de Zuazo, a University of Salamanca–trained lawyer, had made a similar recommendation back in 1510. "General license should be given to bring negroes, a [people] strong for work, the opposite of the natives, so weak who can work only in undemanding tasks," Zuazo wrote. In time, some indigenous peoples had caught wind of this new racist idea, and they readily agreed that a policy of importing African laborers would be better. An indigenous group in Mexico complained that the "difficult and arduous work" involved in harnessing a sugar crop was "only for the blacks and not for the thin and weak Indians." Las Casas and company birthed twins—racist twins that some Native Americans and Africans took in: the myth of the physically strong, beastly African, and the myth of the physically weak Native American who easily died from the strain of hard labor.[10]

ALTHOUGH LAS CASAS'S IDEAS were at first discounted, his treatises soon became a useful tool for Spain's growing empire and its investment in American slavery. Bishop Sebastián Ramirez de Fuenleal reported in 1531 that the "entire population . . . of Espanola, San Juan and even Cuba are demanding that they should have negroes to mine gold" and produce crops. Las Casas led the charge for the historic passage in 1542 of the "New Laws of the Indies for the Good Treatment and Preservation of the Indians." That memorable year, he also finished and sent to Prince Philip II his classic, *A Short Account of the Destruction of the Indies*, and issued his third memorial recommending that enslaved Africans replace Native Americans.

At some point after that, Las Casas read Gomes Eanes de Zurara's book. The more he read, the less he could square the African slave trade with the teachings of Jesus Christ. In *History of the Indies* (1561), released five years before his death, Las Casas regretted "the advice he gave the king" to import enslaved Africans. He saw in Zurara's writing evidence revealing the slave trade to "be the horror that it is." Las Casas lamented Zurara's attempt "to blur [the slave trade] with the mercy and goodness of God." Las Casas tried to close the door on African slavery, after opening it for so many Spanish slaveholders. He failed. A powerful reformer labeled a radical extremist in his last days—like every antiracist who came after him—Las Casas was condemned in Spain after his death, and his works were practically banned there. Catholic Spain's Protestant rivals published and republished his devastating *Account of the Destruction of the Indies*—in Dutch (1578), French (1578), English (1583), and German (1599)—in their quest to label the Spanish Empire corrupt and morally repugnant, all in their quest to replace Spain as Europe's superpower.[11]

DESPITE SPAIN'S RISE, Portugal remained the undisputed power of the African slave trade. And Gomes Eanes de Zurara's racist ideas remained Europe's undisputed defenders of slave trading until another man, an African, rose up to carry on the legacy. Around 1510, Al-Hasan Ibn Muhammad al-Wazzan al-Fasi, a well-educated Moroccan, accompanied his uncle on a diplomatic mission down into the Songhay Empire. Eight years later, he was enslaved on another diplomatic voyage along the Mediterranean Sea. His captors presented the learned twenty-four-year-old to the scholarly Pope Leo X in Italy. Before dying in 1521, the pope freed the youngster, converted him to Christianity, renamed him Johannes Leo, and possibly commissioned him to write a survey of Africa. He became known as Leo the African, or Leo Africanus. He satisfied Italian curiosity in 1526 with the first scholarly survey of Africa in Europe, *Della descrittione dell'Africa* (*Description of Africa*).

Leo Africanus described the etymology of Africa and then surveyed African geography, languages, cultures, religions, and diseases. His summation: "There is no Nation under Heaven more prone to Venery [sexual indulgence]." The Africans "leade a beastly kind of life, being utterly destitute of the use of reason, of dexterities of wit, and of all arts," Africanus wrote. "They . . . behave themselves, as if they had continually lived in a Forrest among wild beasts."

Leo the African did not ignore the elephant in the room. How do "I my selfe write so homely of Africa," he asked, when "I stand indebted [to Africa] both for my birth" and education? He considered himself to be a "historiographer" charged with telling "the plaine truth in all places." Africanus did not mind if Africans were denigrated. He believed he was describing Africans accurately.[12]

Leo Africanus established himself through *Della descrittione dell'Africa* as the world's first known African racist, the first illustrious African producer of racist ideas (as Zurara was the first illustrious European producer of racist ideas). Anyone can consume or produce racist ideas of African inferiority—any European, any Asian, any Native American, any Latina/o, and any African. Leo's African ancestry hardly shielded him from believing in African inferiority and European superiority, or from trying to convince others of this plain racist "truth."

Leo Africanus may have never visited the fifteen African lands he claims to have seen. He could have paraphrased the notes of Portuguese travelers. But veracity did not matter. Once the manuscript was finished in 1526, once it was published in Italian in 1550, and once it was translated into French and Latin in 1556, readers across Western Europe were consuming it and tying African people to hypersexuality, to animals, and to the lack of reason. It is not known what happened to Leo the African, the author of the most widely read and most influential book on Africa—next to Zurara's—during the 1500s. He made countless Europeans feel that they knew him, or rather, knew Africa.

Around the time Leo the African's text was making its way through Europe, and around the time Richard Mather's parents were born, the British began their quest to break the Portuguese monopoly on African slave-trading, eager to reap the benefits and grow their empire. In 1554, an expedition captained by John Lok, ancestor of philosopher John Locke, arrived in England after traveling to "Guinea." Lok and his compatriots Robert Gainish and William Towerson docked with 450 pounds of gold, 250 ivory tusks, and five enslaved African men. These three Englishmen established themselves as the new authorities on Africa and African people among curious British minds. Their opinions seemed to be shaped as much by the Portuguese and French as by their own observations. Sounding like Leo Africanus or Zurara, Gainish labeled Africans a "people of beastly living, without a God, law, religions, or common wealth." The five "beasts" that he and his shipmates brought back to England all learned English and were sent back to Africa to serve as translators for English traders.[13]

As English contact with Africans matured, so did the desire to explain the radical color differences. Writers like Gainish applied climate theory to the dark skins of Africa and the light skins of Europe. The popular theory made sense when looking at Europe, the Mediterranean, and Africa. But what about the rest of the world? During the final decades of the sixteenth century, a new genre of British literature adopted a different theory. Writers brought amazing stories of the world into Anglican homes, into the Puritan homes of Richard Mather and John Cotton, and into the homes of other future leaders of colonial America. And these worldly stories were as racist as they were amazing.

CHAPTER 3

Coming to America

EXPLORERS WROTE ABOUT their adventures, and their tales fascinated Europeans. This new travel literature gave Europeans sitting by their firesides a window into faraway lands where different-looking people resided in cultures that seemed exotic and strange. But the literary glimpses that explorers provided of African lands were usually overshadowed by the self-interests of the backers of the expeditions, who aimed most of all to fulfill their colonizing and slave-trading desires. Even a lonely abolitionist, French philosopher Jean Bodin, found his thoughts bogged down by tales connecting two simultaneous discoveries: that of West Africans, and that of the dark, tailless apes walking around like humans in West Africa. Africa's heat had produced hypersexual Africans, Bodin theorized in 1576, and "intimate relations between the men and beasts . . . still give birth to monsters in Africa." The climate theory of Africa's hot sun transforming the people into uncivil beasts of burden still held the court of racist opinion. But not much longer.[1]

For English travel writer George Best, climate theory fell apart when he saw on an Arctic voyage in 1577 that the Inuit people in northeastern Canada were darker than the people living in the hotter south. In a 1578 account of the expedition, Best shied away from climate theory in explaining "the Ethiopians blacknesse." He found an alternative: "holy Scripture," or the curse theory that had recently been articulated by a Dominican Friar in Peru and a handful of French intellectuals, a theory more enticing to slaveholders. In Best's whimsical interpretation of Genesis, Noah orders his White and "Angelike" sons to abstain from sex with their wives on the Ark, and then tells them that the first child born after the flood would inherit the earth. When the evil, tyrannical, and hypersexual Ham has sex on the Ark, God wills that Ham's descendants shall be "so blacke and loathsome," in Best's telling, "that it might remain a spectacle of disobedience to all the worlde."[2]

The first major debate between racists had invaded the English discourse. This argument about the cause of inferior Blackness—curse or climate, nature or nurture—would rage for decades, and eventually influence settlers to America. Curse theorists were the first known segregationists. They believed that Black people were naturally and permanently inferior, and totally incapable of becoming White. Climate theorists were the first known assimilationists, believing Black people had been nurtured by the hot sun into a temporary inferiority, but were capable of becoming White if they moved to a cooler climate.

George Best produced his curse theory in 1578, in the era between Henry VII and Oliver Cromwell, a time during which the English nation was experiencing the snowballing, conflicting passions of overseas adventure and domestic control, or, to use historian Winthrop Jordan's words, of "voyages of discovery overseas" and "inward voyages of discovery." The mercantile expansion abroad, the progressively commercialized economy at home, the fabulous profits, the exciting adventure stories, and the class warfare all destabilized the social order in Elizabethan England, a social order being intensely scrutinized by the rising congregation of morally strict, hyper-dictating, pious Puritans.

George Best used Africans as "social mirrors," to use Jordan's phrase, for the hypersexuality, greed, and lack of discipline—the Devil's machinations—that he "found first" in England "but could not speak of." Normalizing negative behavior in faraway African people allowed writers to de-normalize negative behavior in White people, to de-normalize what they witnessed during intense appraisals of self and nation.

PROBABLY NO ONE in England collected and read travel stories more eagerly than Richard Hakluyt. In 1589, he published his travel collection in *The Principall Navigations, Voyages, and Discoveries of the English*

Nation. In issuing this monumental collection of nearly all the available documents describing British overseas adventures, Hakluyt urged explorers, traders, and missionaries to fulfill their superior destiny, to civilize, Christianize, capitalize, and command the world.[3]

The Puritans believed, too, in civilizing and Christianizing the world, but their approach to the project was slightly different from that of most explorers and expedition sponsors. For the others, it was about economic returns or political power. For Puritan preachers, it was about bringing social order to the world. Cambridge professor William Perkins rested at the cornerstone of British Puritanism in the late sixteenth century. "Though the servant in regard of faith and the inner man be equal to his master, in regard of the outward man . . . the master is above the servant," he explained in *Ordering a Familie*, published in 1590. In paraphrasing St. Paul, Perkins became one of the first major English theorists—or assimilationist theologians, to be more precise—to mask the exploitative master/servant or master/slave relationship as a loving family relationship. He thus added to Zurara's justifying theory of Portuguese enslavers nurturing African beasts. For generations to come, assimilationist slaveholders, from Richard Mather's New England to Hispaniola, would shrewdly use this loving-family mask to cover up the exploitation and brutality of slavery. It was Perkins's family ordering that Puritan leaders like John Cotton and Richard Mather used to sanction slavery in Massachusetts a generation later. And it was Perkins's claim of equal souls and unequal bodies that led Puritan preachers like Cotton and Mather to minister to African souls and not challenge the enslavement of their bodies.[4]

Richard Mather was born in 1596 in northeastern England at the height of William Perkins's influence. After Perkins died in 1602, Puritan Paul Baynes succeeded him at Cambridge. Richard Mather closely studied Baynes's writings, and he probably could quote his most famous treatise, *Commentary on Ephesians*. In the commentary, Baynes said slavery was partly a curse for sins and partly a result of "civil condition," or barbarism. "Blackmores" were "slavish," he said, and he urged slaves to be cheerfully obedient. Masters were to show their superiority through kindness and through a display of "a white sincere heart."[5]

AS RICHARD MATHER came of age, Richard Hakluyt was establishing himself as England's greatest promoter of overseas colonization. Hakluyt surrounded himself with a legion of travel writers, translators, explorers, traders, investors, colonizers—everyone who might play a role in colonizing the world—and began mentoring them. In 1597, he urged mentee John Pory, a recent Cambridge graduate, to complete a translation that may have been on Hakluyt's list for quite some time. Pory translated Leo Africanus's *Geographical Histories of Africa* into English in 1600. English readers consumed it as quickly as other Europeans had for decades, and they were just as impressed. In a long introduction, Pory argued that climate theory could not explain the geographical distinctions in color. They must be "hereditary," Pory suggested. Africans were "descended from Ham the cursed son of Noah."[6]

Whether they chose to illuminate the stamp of Blackness through curse theory or climate theory, the travel writers and translators of the time had a larger common goal, and they accomplished it: they ushered in the British age of adventure. They were soon followed by another group: the playwrights. With the English literacy rate low, many more British imaginations were churned by playwrights than by travel writers. At the turn of the century, a respected London playwright from Stratford-upon-Avon was escorting English audiences back into the ancient world and around modern Europe, from Scotland (*Macbeth*), to Denmark (*Hamlet*), to inferior Blackness and superior Whiteness in Italy (*The Tragedy of Othello, the Moor of Venice*). The racial politics of William Shakespeare's *Othello* did not surprise English audiences when it premiered in 1604. By the late 1500s, English dramatists were used to manufacturing Satan's Black agents on earth. Shakespeare's first Black character, the evil, oversexed Aaron in *Titus Andronicus*, first came to the stage in 1594. Down in Spain, dramatists frequently staged Black people as cruel idiots in the genre called *comedias de negros*.[7]

Shakespeare's Othello is a Moorish Christian general in the Venetian military, a character inspired by the 1565 Italian tale *Gli Hecatommithi*, and possibly by Leo Africanus, the Christian Moor in Italy who despised his Blackness. Othello's trusted ensign, Iago, resents Othello for marrying the Venetian Desdemona. "For that I do suspect the lusty Moor / Hath leaped into my seat," Iago explains. To Desdemona's father, Iago labels Othello "an old black ram / . . . tupping your white ewe." Iago manipulates Othello to make him believe his wife betrayed him. "Her name that was as fresh / as Dian's visage, is now begrim'd and black / As mine own face," Othello says before strangling Desdemona. At the play's climax, Othello realizes his dead wife's innocence and confesses to Emilia, Desdemona's maidservant. "O! the more angel she," Emilia responds. "And you the blacker devil." Othello commits suicide.[8]

The theater-loving Queen Elizabeth did not see *Othello*, as she did some of Shakespeare's earlier plays. She died in 1603. When the deadly plague of 1604 subsided, her successor, King James I, arrived in London, and started making plans for his grand coronation. King James I and his wife, Queen Anne of Denmark, saw *Othello*. But King James I commissioned Shakespeare's rival playwright, Ben Jonson, to produce an alluring international masque for his coronation, and to mark the end of Elizabethan self-isolation. Queen Anne proposed an African theme to reflect the new king's international focus. Leo Africanus, travel stories, and Othello had sparked the queen's interest in Africa. Satisfying his queen, Jonson wrote *The Masque of Blackness*.

Premiering on January 7, 1605, in the great hall of London's sparkling Whitehall Palace, which overlooks the snowy banks of the Thames River, *The Masque of Blackness* was the most expensive production ever presented in London. Its elaborate costumes, exciting dancing, sensational choirs, booming orchestras, exotic scenery, and a luxurious banquet caused all in attendance to marvel at the spectacle. Inspired by climate theory, it was the story of twelve ugly African princesses of the river god Niger who learn they can be "made beautiful" if they travel to "Britannia," where the sun "beams shine day and night, and are of force / To blanch an Æthiop, and revive a corpse." Queen Anne herself and eleven court ladies played the African princesses in blackface, inaugurating the use of black paint on the royal stage.[9]

The Masque of Blackness presented the imperial vision of King James I, Prince Charles, Richard Hakluyt, and a powerful lineup of English investors, merchants, missionaries, and explorers. And it helped renew British determination to expand Britannia to America. King James chartered the London Company in 1606 with his eyes on North America—one eye on Virginia, another on New England. Although misfortune plagued the New England undertakings, Virginia fared better. Captain John Smith, a mentee of Richard Hakluyt, helped command the expedition of roughly 150 volunteers on the three boats that entered the Chesapeake Bay on April 26, 1607. Against all odds— and thanks to the assistance of the indigenous Powhatan Americans— North America's first permanent English settlement survived. His mission accomplished, John Smith returned as a hero to England in October 1609.[10]

In colonizing Virginia (and later New England), the British had already begun to conceive of distinct races. The word *race* first appeared in Frenchman Jacques de Brézé's 1481 poem "The Hunt," where it referred to hunting dogs. As the term expanded to include humans over the next century, it was used primarily to identify and differenti- ate and animalize African people. The term did not appear in a dictio- nary until 1606, when French diplomat Jean Nicot included an entry for it. "Race . . . means descent," he explained, and "it is said that a man, a horse, a dog or another animal is from good or bad race." Thanks to this malleable concept in Western Europe, the British were free to lump the multiethnic Native Americans and the multiethnic Africans into the same racial groups. In time, Nicot's construction became as addictive as the tobacco plant, which he introduced in France.[11]

Captain John Smith never returned to Jamestown. He spent the rest of his life as the greatest literary mentee of Richard Hakluyt, pro- moting British migration to America. Thousands crossed the Atlantic moved by Smith's exhilarating travel books, which by 1624 included his tale of Pocahontas saving his life. Pocahontas, the "civilized sav- age," had by then converted to Christianity, married an Englishman, and visited London. The English approved. Black people did not fare so well, in Smith's estimation. Settlers read his worldly—or rather, racist—opinions, though, and adopted them as their own. In his final book, published the year of his death in 1631, Smith told "unexpe- rienced" New England planters that the enslaved Africans were "as idle and as devilish as any in the world." Apparently, Smith thought this knowledge would be useful to planters, probably knowing it was only a matter of time before enslaved Africans were brought to New England.[12]

But Smith was only recasting ideas he had heard in England between *The Masque of Blackness*, the founding of Virginia, and the founding of New England, ideas English intellectuals had probably learned from Spanish enslavers and Portuguese slave-traders. "Men that have low and flat nostrils are as Libidinous as Apes," cleric Edward Topsell explained in 1607 in *Historie of Foure-Footed Beastes*. King James made the common association of apes and devils in his 1597 book *Daemonologie*. In one of his last plays, *The Tempest* (1611), Shakespeare played on these associations of the ape and devil and African in crafting Caliban, the hypersexual bastard child of a demon and an African witch from a "vile race." In 1614, England's first famous working-class poet, John Taylor, said that "black nations" adored the "Black" Devil. In a 1615 address for the planters in Ireland and Virginia, the Reverend Thomas Cooper said that White Shem, one of Noah's three sons, "shall be Lord over" the "cursed race of Cham"—meaning Noah's son Ham—in Africa. Future Virginia politician George Sandys also conjured curse theory to degrade Blackness. In a 1620 paraphrase of Genesis, future politician Thomas Peyton wrote of Cain, or "the Southern man," as a "black deformed elf," and "the Northern white, like unto God himself." Five years later, Clergyman Samuel Purchas released the gargantuan four-volume *Hakluytus Posthumus* of travel manuscripts left to him by his mentor, Richard Hakluyt. Purchas blasted the "filthy sodomits, sleepers, ignorant, beast, disciples of Cham . . . to whom the blacke darknesse is reserved for ever." These were the ideas about African people circulating throughout England and the English colonies as African people were being hauled into Britannia on slave ships.[13]

IN 1619, RICHARD MATHER began ministering not far from the future center of the British slave trade, the port of Liverpool. In those days, the British slave trade was minuscule, and Africans hardly existed in Britannia. But that would soon change. The vessels of slave traders were cruising deeper and deeper into the heart of West Africa, especially after the Moroccans, armed with English guns, crushed the Songhay Empire in 1591. The vessels of English commerce were cruising deeper and deeper into Virginia, too, as English merchants competed with the Spanish, Portuguese, and rising Dutch and French empires.[14]

The first recorded slave ship to arrive in colonial America laden with African people was not originally intended for the English colonies. The Spanish ship *San Juan Bautista* departed Angola in July 1619 hauling 350 captives, probably headed for Vera Cruz, Mexico. Latin American slaveholders had used racist ideas to craft a permanent slavery for the quarter of a million Africans they held at that time. Two pirate ships probably attacked the Spanish ship in the Gulf of Mexico, snatching some 60 captives, and then headed east. Weeks later, in August 1619, the pirates sold 20 of their Angolan captives in Jamestown to Virginia governor George Yeardley, the owner of 1,000 acres.[15]

John Pory, the translator of Leo the African's book into English, was Yeardley's cousin, and he ventured to Jamestown in 1619 to serve as Yeardley's secretary. On July 30, 1619, Yeardley convened the inaugural meeting of elected politicians in colonial America, a group that included Thomas Jefferson's great-grandfather. These lawmakers named John Pory their speaker. The English translator of Leo the African's book, who had defended curse theory, thus became colonial America's first legislative leader.[16]

John Pory set the price of America's first cash crop, tobacco, and recognized the need for labor to grow it. So when the Angolans bound for slavery arrived in August, they were right on time. There is no reason to believe that George Yeardley and the other original enslavers did not rationalize their enslavement of African people in the same way that other British intellectuals did—and in the same way that Latin American slaveholders did—by considering these African people to be stamped from the beginning as a racially distinct people, as lower than themselves, and as lower in the scale of being than the more populous White indentured servants. The 1625 Virginia census did not list the ages or dates of arrival for most Africans. Nor did the census list any of them—despite in some cases the fact that they had resided in Virginia for six years—as free. Africans were recorded as distinct from White servants. When Yeardley died in 1627, he willed to his heirs his "goods debts chattles servants negars cattle or any other thynge." "Negars" were dropped below "servants" in the social hierarchy to reflect the economic hierarchy. And this stratification became clear in Virginia's first judicial decision explicitly referring to race. The court ordered a White man in 1630 "to be soundly whipt before an assembly of negroes & others for abusing himself to the dishonor of God and the shame of Christianity by defiling his body in lying with a negro." The court contrasted the polluted Black woman and the pure White woman, with whom he could lie without defiling his body. It was the first recorded instance of gender racism in America, of considering the body of the Black woman to be a tainted object that could defile a White man upon contact.[17]

Richard Mather never saw a slave ship leave the Liverpool docks during his ministerial tenure in Toxteth in the 1620s. Liverpool did not become England's main slave-ship station until the 1740s, succeeding London and Bristol. British slave-traders were slowly expanding their activities in the 1620s, unlike all those Anglican persecutors of Puritans. The death of King James and the coronation of his son, Charles I, in 1625 set off a persecuting stampede. William Ames, a disciple of William Perkins, who was exiled in Holland, steeled Richard Mather, John Cotton, and countless other Puritans with *The Marrow of Sacred Divinity*. Translated from Latin into English in 1627, the treatise described the sacred divinity of spiritual equality "between a free man and a servant"; the sacred divinity of "inferiors" owing "subjection and obedience" to their "superiors"; and the sacred divinity of "our blood kin" being "given more love than strangers." *The Marrow*'s explanation became a guiding principle for Mather's generation of Puritans settling the Massachusetts Bay area in the late 1620s and 1630s. Puritans used this doctrine when assessing Native American and African strangers, ensuring intolerance from the start in their land of tolerance.[18]

Beginning in 1642, Anglican monarchists and nonconforming parliamentarians locked arms in the English Civil War. As New England Puritans welcomed the nonconforming parliamentarians, Virginia's royalists prayed for their retreating King Charles I. But in 1649, he was executed. Three years later, Virginia was forced to surrender to the new ruling parliament.

The economic hierarchy that had emerged in Virginia resembled the pecking order that William Ames had proposed and that Puritans established in New England—although their political and religious allegiances differed. Large planters and ministers and merchants stood at the top—men like John Mottrom of Virginia's Northern Neck, who used his power to acquire fertile land, solicit trade, procure labor, and keep legally free people—like Elizabeth Key—enslaved.[19]

Elizabeth Key was the daughter of an unnamed African woman and Newport News legislator Thomas Key. Before his death, Thomas had arranged for his biracial daughter to be freed at age fifteen. Her subsequent masters, however, kept her enslaved. At some point, she adopted Christianity. She birthed a baby, whose father was William Greenstead, an English indentured servant and amateur lawyer on Mottrom's plantation. Upon Mottrom's death in 1655, Key and Greenstead successfully sued the estate for her and her child's freedom.

Virginia planters followed the Key case almost as closely as they followed the English Civil War. They realized that the English common laws regarding not enslaving Christians—and stipulating that the father's status determined the child's status—both superseded curse theory, climate theory, beast theory, evangelical theory, and every other racist theory substantiating Black and biracial enslavement. Elizabeth Key had ravaged the ties that planters had unofficially used to bind African slavery.[20]

For Virginia planters, the timing of the Key case could not have been worse. By the 1660s, labor demands had grown. Virginians had uprooted more indigenous communities to expand their farmlands. Landowners were looking increasingly to African laborers to do the work, since their lower death rates made them more valuable and more permanent than temporary indentures. At the same time, the bloody English Civil War that had driven so many from England to America had come to a close, and new socioeconomic opportunities in England slowed the flow of voluntary indentured migrants. The White servants still arriving partnered with the enslaved Africans in escapes and rebellions, possibly bonding on similar stories of apprehension—being lured onto ships on the western coasts of Africa or Europe.[21]

Planters responded to labor demands and laborers' unity by purchasing more African people and luring Whiteness away from Blackness. In the first official recognition of slavery in Virginia, legislators stipulated, in 1660 (and in stricter terms in 1661), that any White servant running away "in company with any negroes" shall serve for the time of the "said negroes absence"—even if it meant life. In 1662, Virginia lawmen plugged one of Key's freedom loopholes to resolve "doubts [that] have arisen whether children got by an Englishman upon a negro woman should be slave or free." They proclaimed that "all children borne in this country" derived their status from "the condition of the mother." Trashing English law, they dusted off the Roman principle of *partus sequitur ventrem*, which held that "among tame and domestic animals, the brood belongs to the owner of the dam or mother."[22]

With this law in place, White enslavers could now reap financial reward from relations "upon a negro woman." But they wanted to prevent the limited number of White women from engaging in similar interracial relations (as their biracial babies would become free). In 1664, Maryland legislators declared it a "disgrace to our Nation" when "English women . . . intermarry with Negro slaves." By the end of the century, Maryland and Virginia legislators had enacted severe penalties for White women in relationships with non-White men.[23]

In this way, heterosexual White men freed themselves, through racist laws, to engage in sexual relations with all women. And then their racist literature codified their sexual privileges. *The Isle of Pines*, a bizarre short story published in 1668 by former English parliamentarian Henry Neville, gave readers one such ominous account. The tale purposefully begins in 1589, the year the first edition of Richard Hakluyt's *Principal Navigations* appeared. Surviving a shipwreck in the Indian Ocean, George Pines finds himself alone on an uninhabited island with an English fourteen-year-old; a Welsh maidservant; another maidservant, whose Whiteness is clear and ethnicity is not; and "one Negro female slave." For Pines, "idleness and Fulness of every thing

begot in me a desire of enjoying the women." He persuades the two
maids to lie with him, and then reports that the English fourteen-year-
old was "content also to do as we did." The Negro woman, "seeing
what we did, longed also for her share." One night, the uniquely sexually aggressive Black woman makes her move in the darkness while
Pines sleeps.[24]

The Isle of Pines was one of the first portrayals in British letters of
aggressive hypersexual African femininity. Such portrayals served
both to exonerate White men of their inhuman rapes and to mask
their human attractions to the supposed beast-like women. And the
portrayals just kept coming, like the slave ships. Meanwhile, American enslavers publicly prostituted African women well into the eighteenth century (privately thereafter). In a 1736 exchange of letters on
the inextricable sexuality and service of "African Ladies," single White
men were counseled in the *South-Carolina Gazette* to "wait for the next
shipping from the Coast of Guinny": "Those African Ladies are of a
strong, robust Constitution: not easily jaded out, able to serve them
by Night as well as Day." On their isles of pines in colonial America,
White men continued to depict African women as sexually aggressive,
shifting the responsibility of their own sexual desires to the women.

Of the nearly one hundred reports of rape or attempted rape in
twenty-one newspapers in nine American colonies between 1728
and 1776, none reported the rape of a Black woman. Rapes of Black
women, by men of all races, were not considered newsworthy. Like
raped prostitutes, Black women's credibility had been stolen by racist beliefs in their hypersexuality. For Black men, the story was similar. There was not a single article in the colonial era announcing the
acquittal of a suspected Black male rapist. One-third of White men
mentioned in rape articles were acknowledged as being acquitted of
at least one charge. Moreover, "newspaper reports of rape constructed
white defendants as individual offenders and black defendants as representative of the failings of their racial group," according to journalism historian Sharon Block.[25]

Already, the American mind was accomplishing that indispens-
able intellectual activity of someone consumed with racist ideas:

individualizing White negativity and *generalizing* Black negativity. Negative behavior by any Black person became proof of what was wrong with Black people, while negative behavior by any White person only proved what was wrong with that person.

Black women were thought to aggressively pursue White men sexually, and Black men were thought to aggressively pursue White women sexually. Neither could help it, the racist myth posited. They naturally craved superior Whiteness. Black women possessed a "temper hot and lascivious, making no scruple to prostitute themselves to the Europeans for a very slender profit, so great is their inclination to white men," dreamt William Smith, the author of *New Voyage to Guinea* in 1744. And all of this lasciviousness on the part of Black men and women stemmed from their relatively large genitalia, the theory went. As early as 1482, Italian cartographer Jayme Bertrand depicted Mali emperor Mansa Musa almost naked on his throne with oversized genitals.[26]

SOME WHITE MEN were honest enough to broadcast their attractions, usually justifying them with assimilationist ideas. Royalist Richard Ligon, exiled from parliamentary England in Barbados, sat at a dinner adoring the "black Mistress" of the colony's governor. Barbados had become richer than all the other British colonies combined by the mid-1600s. Sugar was planted right up to the steps of homes, and the residents ate New England food instead of growing their own. To Ligon, the Black mistress had "the greatest beauty and majesty together: that ever I saw in one woman," exceeding Queen Anne of Denmark. Ligon presented her with a gift after the dinner. She responded with "the loveliest smile that I have ever seen." It was impossible for Ligon to tell what was whiter, her teeth "or the whites of her eyes."

This was one of the many small stories that made up Ligon's *A True and Exact Historie of the Island of Barbadoes* in 1657, the year Elizabeth Key's case was finally settled. In one story, a submissive slave named "Sambo" tells on his fellows who are planning a slave revolt and refuses his reward. In another, Ligon informs a "cruel" master of Sambo's desire to be "made a Christian." By English law, we cannot "make a Christian a Slave," the master responds. "My request was far different from that," Ligon replies, "for I desired him to make a Slave a Christian." If Sambo becomes a Christian, he can no longer be enslaved, the master says, and it will open "such a gap" that "all of the planters in the island" will be upset. Ligon lamented that Sambo was to be kept out of the church. But at the same time, he gave enslavers a new theory to defend their enterprise: Blacks were naturally docile, and slaves could and should become Christians. Planters had feared the conversion of slaves because they believed that if their slaves were Christian, they would have to be freed—and Elizabeth Key's successful suit showed that the laws supported this belief. Ligon's distinction between making "a Christian a slave" and "a slave a Christian" turned this idea on its head. Though it took time, eventually it became the basis for closing the religious loophole Key had exposed. Ligon lifted the biblical law of converting the unconverted over British law barring the enslavement of Christians. He promoted the idea of baptizing enslaved Africans through the docile figure of Sambo, and planters and intellectuals almost certainly got the point: submissive, confessing Sambo desired Christianity, and he should be permitted to have it. Indeed, Christianity would only make slaves more docile. Ligon's recommendation of Christianizing the slave for docility appeared during a crucial time of intellectual innovation. And as intellectual ideas abounded, justifications for slavery abounded, too.

ON NOVEMBER 28, 1660, a dozen men gathered in London and founded what became known as the Royal Society. Europe's scientific revolution had reached England. Italians initiated the Accademia dei Lincei in 1603, the French L'Academie française was founded in 1635, and the Germans established their national academy, Leopoldina, in 1652. King Charles II chartered the Royal Society as one of the first acts of his restored anti-Puritan monarchy in 1660. One of the early leaders of the Royal Society was one of England's most celebrated young scholars, the author of *The Sceptical Chymist* (1661) and the father of English chemistry—Robert Boyle. In 1665, Boyle urged his European peers to compile more "natural" histories of foreign lands and peoples, with Richard Ligon's *Historie of Barbados* serving as the racist prototype.[27]

The year before, Boyle had jumped into the ring of the racial debate with *Of the Nature of Whiteness and Blackness*. He rejected both curse and climate theorists and knocked up a foundational antiracist idea: "The Seat" of human pigmentation "seems to be but the thin *Epidermes*, or outward Skin," he wrote. And yet, this antiracist idea of skin color being only skin deep did not stop Boyle from judging different colors. Black skin, he maintained, was an "ugly" deformity of normal Whiteness. The physics of light, Boyle argued, showed that Whiteness was "the chiefest color." He claimed to have ignored his personal "opinions" and "clearly and faithfully" presented the truth, as his Royal Society deeded. As Boyle and the Royal Society promoted the innovation and circulation of racist ideas, they promoted objectivity in all their writings.[28]

Intellectuals from Geneva to Boston, including Richard Mather's youngest son, Increase Mather, carefully read and loudly hailed Boyle's work in 1664. A twenty-two-year-old unremarkable Cambridge student from a farming family copied full quotations. As he rose in stature over the next forty years to become one of the most influential scientists of all time, Isaac Newton took it upon himself to substantiate Boyle's color law: light is white is standard. In 1704, a year after he assumed the presidency of the Royal Society, Newton released one of the most eminent books of the modern era, *Opticks*. "*Whiteness* is produced by the Convention of all Colors," he wrote. Newton created a color wheel to illustrate his thesis. "The center" was "white of the first order," and all the other colors were positioned in relation to their "distance from Whiteness." In one of the foundational books of the upcoming European intellectual renaissance, Newton imaged "perfect whiteness."[29]

Robert Boyle would not live to read *Opticks*. He died, after a long and influential life, in 1691. During his lifetime, he did not merely found chemistry, whiten light, power the Royal Society, and inspire Isaac Newton, the Mather clan, and throngs of intellectuals on both sides of the Atlantic. Boyle sat on the original Council for Foreign Plantations in 1660, which was commissioned concurrently with the Royal Society to centralize and advise the vast empire that Charles II inherited.

In 1661, Boyle's council made its first formal plea to planters in Barbados, Maryland, and Virginia to convert enslaved Africans. "This Act . . . shall [not] . . . impead, restrain, or impair" the power of masters, the council made sure to note. The council's pleas resounded louder and louder each year as the plantation economy surged across the Western Hemisphere, as a growing flock of powerful British ministers vied for submission of African souls, and as planters vied for submission of their bodies. Missionaries endeavored to grow God's kingdom as planters endeavored to grow profits. The marriage of Christian slavery seemed destined. But enslaved Africans balked. The vast majority of Africans in early America firmly resisted the religion of their masters. And their masters balked, too. Enslavers would not, or could not, listen to sermons to convert their slaves. Saving their crops each year was more important to them than saving souls. But of course they could not say that, and risk angering their ministers. Enslavers routinely defended their inaction by claiming that enslaved Africans were too barbaric to be converted.

The racist debate over the cause of Blackness—climate or curse— had been joined by this new racist debate over Blacks' capability for Christianity. The segregationist belief that enslaved Africans should not or could not be baptized was so widespread, and so taboo to discuss—as Richard Ligon found in Barbados—that virtually no enslaver took to writing to defend it in a major piece in the 1600s. That did not stop the assimilationists, who believed that lowly enslaved Africans, practicing their supposed animalistic religions, were capable of being raised to Christianity. In the 1660s, there emerged a missionary movement to publicize this divine duty to resistant slaveholders and slaves. Richard Mather's grandson spent his adult life carrying this movement to the churches of New England. But Mather did not live to see it.

CHAPTER 4

Saving Souls, Not Bodies

WHEN CHARLES II restored the English throne in 1660, he restored the religious persecution of Puritans. Roughly 2,000 Puritan ministers were forced out of the Church of England during the Great Ejection. In New England, Richard Mather had lost some hearing and sight in one eye. But he was still as defiant to the crown as he had been as a younger man, and he steered New England nonconformists as adroitly as he had done for three decades. His fellow theological captain, John Cotton, had died in 1652. Mather's first wife had also died, and he had married Cotton's widow, Sarah Hankredge Story Cotton. His youngest son, Increase Mather, married Sarah's daughter—now his stepsister—Maria Cotton, further interlacing the ties between the famous Cottons and Mathers. As if to triple-knot the family tie, Increase and Maria named their first son, upon his birth on February 12, 1663, Cotton Mather.

Richard Mather lived six years after the birth of his grandson. When he died, Increase Mather honored his father by writing his biography, putting in print Richard Mather's providential deliverance from the Great Hurricane of 1635, a story as meaningful to the Mather lineage as any passage in the Bible. Increase Mather, who took the helm of John Cotton's famed North Church of Boston in 1664, taught all ten of his eventual children that they were regular receivers of divine providence like their grandfather. Increase especially expressed this exceptionality to Cotton Mather. In time, Cotton would make his father a prophet. He combined the best of the Cottons and Mathers, eclipsing them all in America's historical memory. By the century's end, African slavery sounded as natural to the colonists as the name "Cotton Mather," and hardly any intellectual was more responsible for this binding than Cotton Mather himself. Cotton Mather was not the sole progenitor of such ideas, however. He was influenced by the books he read by his contemporaries. And few, if any, books influenced Cotton Mather's racist ideas more than Richard Baxter's *A Christian Directory*.

From his British ministerial post in Kidderminster, Richard Baxter urged slaveholders across the ocean to follow God's law in making slaves into Christians in his well-traveled treatise *A Christian Directory* (1664–1665). He told them to "make it your chief end in buying and using slaves, to win them to Christ, and save their Souls." Be sure to "let their Salvation be far more valued by you than their Service." Although he was at the head of the missionary movement, Baxter was not alone in proselytizing to African people. As early as 1657, English Dissenter George Fox prevailed on his newly founded Religious Society of Friends, or Quakers, to convert the enslaved. Eschewing church hierarchies, and preaching that everyone had access to the "inward light of God," the Quakers seemed primed to one day produce abolitionists and antiracists.[1]

In an effort to square his Christian faith—or his nation's Christian faith—with slavery, Baxter tried to argue that some kind of benevolent slavery was possible and would be helpful for African people. These assimilationist ideas of Christianizing and civilizing enslaved Africans were particularly dangerous because they gave convincing power to the idea that slavery was just and should not be resisted. And so Baxter, a nonconforming Puritan, conformed—and conformed his Puritan readers—to most, though certainly not all, of the racist policies of Charles II's expanding slaveholding empire. People who have "forfeited life or liberty" can be enslaved, Baxter wrote. However, "to go as pirates and catch up poor negroes . . . is one of the worst kind of thievery in the world." Enslavers "that buy them and use them as beasts and . . . neglect their souls, are fitter to be called incarnate devils than Christians." Baxter naïvely believed there existed in bulk in the slave trade what he called a "voluntary-slave." He tried to will into existence a world where loving masters bought voluntary slaves to save their souls. Baxter's world remained a heavenly dream crafted long ago by Gomes Eanes de Zurara. But even that dream world was seen as a threat by enslavers. American enslavers were still afraid to baptize Africans, because Christian slaves, like Elizabeth Key, could sue for their freedom.[2]

The colonies moved quickly to legalize the proselytizing demands of missionaries like Richard Baxter, and to hush the freedom cries from Christian slaves. In 1667, Virginia decreed that "the conferring of baptisme doth not alter the condition of the person as to his bondage." New York did the same in 1664, as did Maryland in 1671. "May more" masters, the Virginia legislators inscribed, "carefully endeavor the propagation of Christianity" to slaves. Masters were supposed to care for the resisting souls of their captives. But what about their resisting bodies? In 1667, the English Parliament empowered masters to control the "wild, barbarous and savage nature" of enslaved Africans "only with strict severity." And in 1669, the personal physician of Lord Anthony Ashley Cooper, one of the Lords Proprietor of the Province of Carolina, in his draft of the original *Fundamental Constitution of the Carolinas*, awarded the founding planters of the province "absolute power and authority" over their captives.[3]

WHEN JOHN LOCKE moved to London in 1667 to become the personal physician of Lord Cooper, he had much more to offer the colonizing British politician than his medical expertise. He had studied at the feet of Robert Boyle after his educational tenure at Oxford, and he had ended up collecting more travel books than philosophy texts for his immense personal library. Lord Cooper asked Locke to draw up the Carolinas constitution and serve as the secretary of the Proprietors (and soon the Council of Trade and Plantations and the Board of Trade and Plantations). Not many Englishmen were more knowledgeable— or less compassionate—than Locke about British colonialism and slavery. "You should feel nothing at all of others' misfortune," Locke advised a friend in 1670.[4]

Between all his colonial and medical duties, by July 1671 Locke had written the first draft of his lasting philosophical monument, *An Essay Concerning Humane Understanding.* Over the next two decades, he revised and expanded the essay before its grand appearance in four books in 1689. That year, Locke also released his *Two Treatises of Government,* attacking monarchy, requesting a "government with the consent of the governed," and distinguishing between temporary "servants" and "slaves, who being captives taken in a just war, are by the right of nature subjected to the absolute dominion and arbitrary power of their masters." Just as Richard Baxter had pushed his "voluntary slave" theory to defend slavery in his free Christian society, John Locke pushed his "just war" theory to defend slavery in his free civil society.

In any society, the mind "at first . . . is rasa tabula," Locke famously wrote in *An Essay Concerning Humane Understanding.* If people are born without innate intelligence, then there cannot be a natural intellectual hierarchy. But Locke's egalitarian idea had a caveat. As Boyle and Newton painted unblemished light white, Locke more or less painted the unblemished mind white. Locke used the term "white paper" much more often than "blank slate" or "tabula rasa" to describe the child's "as yet unprejudiced Understanding."[5]

Locke also touched on the origin of species in *An Essay Concerning Humane Understanding.* Apes, whether "these be all *Men,* or no, all of human *Species,*" depended on one's "definition of the Word *Man,*" because, he said, "if History lie not," then West African women had conceived babies with apes. Locke thus reinforced African female hypersexuality in a passage sent round the English-speaking world. "And what real *Species,* by that measure, such a Production will be in Nature, will be a new Question." Locke's new "Question" reflected another new racist debate that most debaters feared to engage in publicly. Assimilationists argued monogenesis: that all humans were one species descended from a single human creation in Europe's Garden of Eden. Segregationists argued polygenesis: that there were multiple origins of multiple human species.

Ever since Europeans had laid eyes on Native Americans in 1492, a people unmentioned in the Bible, they had started questioning the biblical creation story. Some speculated that Native Americans had to have descended from "a different Adam." By the end of the sixteenth century, European thinkers had added African people to the list of species descended from a different Adam. In 1616, Italian freethinker Lucilio Vanini said—as Locke suggested later—that Ethiopians and apes must have the same ancestry, distinct from Europeans. But no one made the case for polygenesis as stoutly as French theologian Isaac La Peyrère in *Prae-Adamitae* in 1655. Translated into English in 1656, *Men Before Adam* was publicly burned in Paris and banned from Europe (after Locke secured a copy). Christians tossed La Peyrère in prison and burned Vanini at the stake for defying the Christian monogenesis story of Adam and Eve. But they could not stop the drift of polygenesis.

To justify Black enslavement, Barbados planters actually "preferred" the polygenesis theory over the curse theory of Ham, according to eyewitness Morgan Godwyn. Godwyn made this revelation in a 1680 pamphlet that criticized racist planters for making "those two words, *Negro* and *Slave*," synonymous, while "*White*" was "the general name for *Europeans*." This Anglican brought his missionary zeal from Virginia to Barbados in the 1670s. He stood at the forefront of his denomination's efforts to baptize enslaved Africans, aping a Quaker named William Edmundson.[6]

IN 1675, A WAR more destructive than the Great Hurricane of 1635 ravaged New England. Three thousand Native Americans and six hundred settlers were killed, and numerous towns and burgeoning economies were destroyed during King Philip's War. In the midst of the carnage, William Edmundson, who had founded Quakerism in Ireland, arrived in Rhode Island, reeling from his failure to convert enslaved Africans in Barbados. When his failures continued in Rhode Island, he began to understand that slavery was holding back his missions, and he told slave-owning Quakers as much in a letter in 1676. Edmundson had an assimilationist vision, a vision to "restrain and reclaim" African people from "their accustomed filthy, unclean practices" in defiling each other. Quakers' "self-denial" of human property could "be known to all."

Abolitionist ideas blossomed again a dozen years later among the Mennonite and Quaker founders of Germantown in Philadelphia, this time, without Edmundson's assimilationist ideas. Mennonites were an Anabaptist denomination born out of the Protestant Reformation in the German- and Dutch-speaking areas of Central Europe. During the sixteenth and early seventeenth centuries, orthodox authorities lethally persecuted the Mennonites. The Mennonites did not intend to leave behind one site of oppression to build another in America.

Mennonites therefore circulated an antislavery petition on April 18, 1688. "There is a saying, that we shall doe to all men like as we will be done ourselves; making no difference of what generation, descent or colour they are," they wrote. "In Europe there are many oppressed" for their religion, and "here those are oppressed" for their "black colour." Both oppressions were wrong. Actually, as an oppressor, America "surpass[ed] Holland and Germany." Africans had the "right to fight for their freedom."

The 1688 Germantown Petition Against Slavery was the inaugural antiracist tract among European settlers in colonial America. Beginning with this piece, the Golden Rule would forever inspire the cause of White antiracists. Antiracists of all races—whether out of altruism or intelligent self-interest—would always recognize that preserving racial hierarchy simultaneously preserves ethnic, gender, class, sexual, age, and religious hierarchies. Human hierarchies of any kind, they understood, would do little more than oppress all of humanity.

But powerful slaveholding Philadelphia Quakers killed the Germantown petition out of economic self-interest. William Edmundson had likewise suffered for promoting antislavery arguments a dozen years earlier. Slaveholding Quakers across New England had banished Edmundson from their meetings. The elderly founder of the American Baptist Church, Rhode Island's Roger Williams, called Edmundson "nothing but a bundle of ignorance." Not many New Englanders read Edmundson's letter to slaveholding Quakers, and not many noticed its significance. Everyone was focused on King Philip's War.[7]

In early August 1676, Increase Mather—the theological scion of New England with his father dead—implored God from sunup to sundown to cut down King Philip, or Metacomet, the Native American war leader. The conflict had been worsening for a little over a year, and the Puritans had lost homes and dozens of soldiers. Less than a week after Mather's prayer campaign, Metacomet was killed, more or less ending the war. Puritans cut up his body as if it were a hog's. A nearly fourteen-year-old Cotton Mather detached Metacomet's jaw from his skull. Puritans then paraded Metacomet's remains around Plymouth.[8]

Down in Virginia, Governor George Berkeley was trying to avoid a totally different war with neighboring Native Americans, in part to avoid disrupting his profitable fur trade. Twenty-nine-year-old frontier planter Nathaniel Bacon had other plans. The racial laws passed in the 1660s had done little to diminish class conflict. Around April 1676, Bacon mobilized a force of frontier White laborers to redirect their anger from elite Whites to Susquehannocks. Bacon's mind game worked. "Since my being with the volunteers, the discourse and earnestness of the people is against the Indians," Bacon wrote to Berkeley in triumph. Berkeley charged Bacon with treason, more worried about armed landless Whites—the "Rabble Crew"—than the Susquehannocks and nearby Occaneechees. But Bacon was not so easily stopped. By summer, the frontier war had quickly become a civil war—or to some, a class war—with Bacon and his supporters rebelling against Berkeley, and Berkeley hiring a militia of mercenaries.

By September 1676, a defiant Bacon had "proclaimed liberty to all Servants and Negroes." For Governor Berkeley's wealthy White inner circle, poor Whites and enslaved Blacks joining hands presaged the apocalypse. At the head of five hundred men, Bacon burned down Jamestown, forcing Berkeley to flee. When Bacon died of dysentery in October, the rebellion was doomed. Luring Whites with pardons and Blacks with liberty, Berkeley's forces persuaded most of Bacon's army to lay down their weapons. They spent the next few years crushing the rest of the rebels.

Rich planters learned from Bacon's Rebellion that poor Whites had to be forever separated from enslaved Blacks. They divided and conquered by creating more White privileges. In 1680, legislators pardoned only the White rebels; they prescribed thirty lashes for any slave who lifted a hand "against any Christian" (Christian now meant White). All Whites now wielded absolute power to abuse any African person. By the early eighteenth century, every Virginia county had a militia of landless Whites "ready in case of any sudden eruption of Indians or insurrection of Negroes." Poor Whites had risen into their lowly place in slave society—the armed defenders of planters—a place that would sow bitter animosity between them and enslaved Africans.[9]

COTTON MATHER WAS in college when he detached Metacomet's jaw from his skull and heard about Bacon's Rebellion. Back in the summer of 1674, Increase Mather crossed the Charles River to present an eleven-year-old Cotton Mather for admission as the youngest student in Harvard's history. He was already well known in New England as an intellectual prodigy—or, from the Puritans' standpoint, the chosen one. Cotton Mather was fluent in Latin, running through fifteen chapters of the Bible a day, and as pious as boys came.[10]

Smaller than a sixth-grade pupil, when Cotton Mather walked onto the tiny campus he was like a self-righteous politician entering a corrupted Congress. The dozen or so fifteen- to eighteen-year-olds schemed to break the eleven-year-old's moral backbone until Increase Mather complained about the hazing. The teenagers stopped prodding him to sin, but sin still bedeviled him. Sin was like the shadow he could never shake. The most trivial incident could explode into anxiety. One day, his tooth ached. "Have I not sinned with my Teeth?" his mind raced. "How? By sinful, graceless excessive Eating. And by evil Speeches." Cotton Mather had started stuttering, and the incessant self-searching and the burden of trying to live up to his two famous names may have worsened his condition. For the young minister-in-training, the soul-searching setback caused him to turn to his ink and quill.[11]

Insecure in speech, Cotton Mather seemed to be a different person as a writer—confident, brilliant, and artistic. His father allowed him to write up many important church and government documents. Cotton ended up writing 7,000 pages of sermons in his notebooks

between the ages of thirteen and thirty-two, far and away more ser-
monic pages than any other American Puritan. And his diary from
1681 to 1725 is the lengthiest available of any American Puritan.[12]

Cotton Mather had been encouraged by his anxious but reassuring
father. Sooner or later, Cotton steeled his determination to find a way
around the mighty rock. The youngster incessantly practiced away his
stammer by singing psalms and speaking slowly, and by the end of his
Harvard days he had learned to control it. He was delivered.

Cotton Mather cruised to the annual Boston Commencement
Day in 1678. Harvard president Urian Oakes called him to receive his
degree. "What a name!" Oakes smiled. "I made a mistake, I confess; I
should have said, what names!"[13]

THE FIFTEEN-YEAR-OLD COTTON MATHER graduated into a British world
that was developing more and more sophisticated racist ideas to rationalize African slavery. English scientists and colonizers seemed to
be trading theories. Around 1677, Royal Society economist William
Petty drafted a hierarchical "Scale" of humanity, locating the "Guinea
Negroes" at the bottom. Middle Europeans, he wrote, differed from
Africans "in their natural manners, and in the internal qualities of their
minds." In 1679, the British Board of Trade approved Barbados's bru-
tally racist slave codes, which were securing the investments of traders
and planters, and then produced a racist idea to justify the approval:
Africans were "a brutish sort of People."[14]

In 1683, Increase and Cotton Mather founded colonial America's
first formal intellectual group, the Boston Philosophical Society. Modeled after London's Royal Society, the Boston Society lasted only four
years. The Mathers never published a journal, but if they had, they
might have modeled it after the Royal Society's *Philosophical Transactions*, or the *Journal des Sçavans* in Paris. These were the organs of Western Europe's scientific revolution, and new ideas on race were a part
of that revolution. French physician and travel writer François Bernier,
a friend of John Locke's, anonymously crafted a "new division of the
earth" in the French journal in 1684.[15]

Through this essay, Bernier became the first popular classifier of all humans into races, which he differentiated fundamentally by their phenotypic characteristics. To Bernier, there existed "four or five Species or Races of men so notably differing from each other that this may serve as the just foundation of a new division of the world." As a monogenesist, he held that "all men are descended from one individual." He distinguished four races: the "first" race, which included Europeans, were the original humans; then there were the Africans, the East Asians, and the "quite frightful" people of northern Finland, "the Lapps." Bernier gave future taxonomists some revisionist work to do when he lumped with Europeans in the "first" race the people of North Africa, the Middle East, India, the Americas, and Southeast Asia.

The notion of Europeans—save the Lapps—as being in the "first" race was part of Western thought almost from the beginning of racist ideas. It sat in the conceptual core of climate theory: Africans darkened by the sun could return to their original White complexion by living in cooler Europe. In advancing White originality and normality, Bernier positioned the "first" race as the "yardstick against which the others are measured," as historian Siep Stuurman later explained. Bernier simultaneously veiled and normalized, screened and standardized White people—and he eroticized African women. "Those cherry-red lips, those ivory teeth, those large lively eyes . . . that bosom and the rest," Bernier marveled. "I dare say there is no more delightful spectacle in the world."

It was a subtle contradiction—the diminution of Black people's total (as racial) humanity in the midst of the elevation of their sexual humanity, a contradiction inherent in much of anti-Black racism. Bernier valued rationality, using it as a yardstick of superiority, irrespective of physicality. Superior physicality related Africans to those creatures containing the utmost physical prowess—animals. François Bernier posed the notion of two human souls: one hereditary, sensitive, nonrational, and animal-like; the other God-given, spiritual, and rational. "Those who excel in the powers of the mind . . . [should] command those who only excel in brute force," Bernier concluded, "just as the soul governs the body, and man rules animals."[16]

IT IS UNCLEAR whether Cotton Mather read Bernier's "new division of the earth." Next to his father, he was more likely than any other English-speaking New Englander to know a little French and read the *Journal des Sçavans*. In the years after his graduation, he amassed one of the largest libraries in New England. But the late 1670s and 1680s were a tense time for New England elites. It was difficult to maintain the peace of mind for leisurely reading.

In 1676, English colonial administrator Edward Randolph had journeyed to New England, and he had seen the devastation wrought by King Philip's War. Randolph, an advocate of stern royal control, informed King Charles II of New England's vulnerability and suggested that the time had come to snatch the royally appointed chair of autonomy for Massachusetts—the precious charter of 1629—out of colonial hands. In the coming years, while Cotton Mather finished college and prepared for the pulpit, Randolph journeyed back and forth over the Atlantic Ocean. Every trip stirred new rumors of the charter being pulled and a new round of debates on whether to submit, compromise, or defy the king. Some New Englanders were furious at the prospect of losing local rule. "God forbid, that I should give away the Inheritance of my Fathers," stormed Increase Mather at a town meeting in January 1684.

A year after Cotton Mather became co-pastor with his father of Boston's North Church, Randolph returned holding the royal revocation of the charter and the installation of a royal governor, Sir Edmund Andros. Much of New England despondently submitted on May 14, 1686. Not Increase Mather, the newly installed head of Harvard. By May 1688, he was in England lobbying the successor to Charles II, James II, who offered religious liberty to Catholics and nonconformists. But during the "Glorious Revolution" later in the year, James II was overthrown by William, the Dutch prince, and James's daughter, Mary. New Englanders did not sit by idly. In 1689, they raised the baton of revolt.

CHAPTER 5

Black Hunts

ON THE EVENING of April 17, 1689, the twenty-six-year-old Cotton Mather probably held a meeting at his house. These elite merchants and ministers plotted to seize the captain of the royal warship guarding Boston Harbor, arrest royalists, and compel the surrender of the royalist contingent on Fort Hill. They hoped to control and contain the revolt, avoid the bloodshed, and await instructions from England, where Increase Mather held his lobbying post before William and Mary. They did not want a revolution. They merely wanted their royally backed local power reestablished. But "if the Country people, by any unrestrainable Violences," pushed toward revolution, Cotton Mather explained, then to pacify the "ungoverned Mobile" they would present a *Declaration of Gentleman and Merchants*.

The next morning, conspirators seized the warship captain as planned. News of the seizure initiated rebellious seizures all over Boston, as the elite plotters feared would occur. A convulsed working-class crowd gathered at the Town House in the center of town, "driving and furious," avid for royal blood and independence. Mather rushed to the Town House. At noon, he probably read from the gallery a *Declaration of Gentleman and Merchants* to the revolutionaries. Mather's calm, assuring, ministerial voice "reasoned down the Passions of the Populace," according to family lore. By nightfall, Sir Edmund Andros, Edward Randolph, and other known royalists had been arrested, and Puritan merchants and preachers once again ruled New England.[1]

The populace remained unruly, however, over the next few weeks. Cotton Mather was tapped to preach at a May convention called to settle the various demands for independence, military rule, or the old charter. He did not see democracy in the different demands; he saw pandemonium. "I am old enough to cry *Peace!* And in the Name of God I do it," he preached at the convention. The next day, town representatives voted to return to the old charter and reappoint the old governor, Simon Bradstreet. Peace, or the old social order of the populace submitting to the ministers and merchants, did not reappear, as Mather had wished. Nearly everyone knew the Bradstreet government was unofficial, as it had not received royal backing. When the king recalled Andros, Randolph, and other royalists in July 1689, it did not calm the masses. "All confusion is here," one New Englander reported. "Every man is a Governor," another testified.[2]

THE *DECLARATION OF GENTLEMAN AND MERCHANTS*—most likely written by Mather—resembled another declaration by another prominent intellectual down in Virginia a century later. In the sixth article (of twelve), the writer declared, "The people of *New England* were all *slaves* and the only difference between them and slaves is their not being bought and sold." In unifying New Englanders, Mather tried to redirect the resistance of commoners from local elites to British masters. And in actuality, Mather saw more differences between Puritans and slaves, if his other published words in 1689 were any indication, than between local New Englanders and their British masters. In the collection of sermons *Small Offers Toward the Service of the Tabernacle in the Wilderness*, Mather first shared his racial views, calling the Puritan colonists "the English Israel"—a chosen people. Puritans must religiously instruct all slaves and children, the "inferiors," Mather pleaded. But masters were not doing their job of looking after African souls, "which are as white and good as those of other Nations, but are Destroyed for lack of Knowledge." Cotton Mather had built on Richard Baxter's theological race concept. The souls of African people were equal to those of the Puritans: they were *White* and good.[3]

Mather wrote of all humans having an unblemished *White* soul the same year John Locke declared all unblemished minds to be White. Robert Boyle and Isaac Newton had already popularized light as White. Michelangelo had already painted the original Adam and God as both being White in the Vatican's Sistine Chapel. And for all these White men, Whiteness symbolized beauty, a trope taken up by one of the first popular novels by an English woman.

Published in 1688, Aphra Behn's *Oroonoko: or, The Royal Slave*, was the first English novel to repeatedly use terms like "White Men," "White People," and "Negro." Set in the Dutch South American colony of Surinam, *Oroonoko* is the story of the enslavement and resistance of a young English woman and her husband, Oroonoko, an African prince. Oroonoko's "beautiful, agreeable and handsome" physical features looked more European than African ("His nose was rising and *Roman*, instead of *African* and flat"), and his behavior was "more civilized, according to the European Mode, than any other had been." Behn framed Oroonoko as a heroic "noble savage," superior to Europeans in his ignorance, in his innocence, in his harmlessness, and in his capacity for learning from Europeans. And in true assimilationist fashion, one of the characters insists, "A Negro *can change colour*; for I have seen 'em as frequently blush and look pale, and that as visibly as I ever saw in the most beautiful White."[4]

RICHARD BAXTER ENDORSED the London edition of Cotton Mather's other 1689 publication, his first book-length work, which became a best seller: *Memorable Providences, Relating to Witchcrafts and Possessions*. Baxter rejoiced, having influenced the young Mather, as someone "likely to prove so great a Master Building in the Lords Work." Mather's treatise, outlining the symptoms of witchcraft, reflected his crusade against the enemies of White souls. He could not stop preaching about the existence of the Devil and witches. Or perhaps the restlessness of the commoners in the aftermath of the 1689 revolt triggered the real obsession in Cotton Mather. The revolt, indeed, had fueled public strife against not only the faraway British king but also Puritan rulers of Mather's stature. Maybe Mather was consciously attempting to redirect the public's anger away from elites and toward invisible demons. He did regularly preach that anyone and anything that criticized his English Israel must be led by the Devil. Long before egalitarian rebels in America started to be cast off as extremists, criminals, radicals, outsiders, communists, or terrorists, Mather's community of ministers ostracized egalitarian rebels as devils and witches.[5]

"How many doleful Wretches, have been decoy'd into Witchcraft," Cotton Mather asked in 1691. His father, Increase, preached a lengthy series on devils in 1693 after returning from England with the new Massachusetts charter. Samuel Parris, a Salem minister, preached endlessly about the devils in their midst. And on one dismal day in February 1692, Parris anxiously watched his nine-year-old daughter and eleven-year-old niece suffer chokes, convulsions, and pinches. As their condition worsened each day, the minister's worsened, too. It dawned on Parris: the girls had been bewitched.[6]

While prayers rose up like kites in Salem and nearby towns, the Salem witch hunt began. The number of afflicted and accused spread over the next few months, swelling the public uproar and turning public attention from political to religious strife. And in nearly every instance, the Devil who was preying upon innocent White Puritans was described as Black. One Puritan accuser described the Devil as "a little black bearded man"; another saw "a black thing of a considerable bigness." A Black thing jumped in one man's window. "The body was like that of a Monkey," the observer added. "The Feet like a Cocks, but the Face much like a man's." Since the Devil represented criminality, and since criminals in New England were said to be the Devil's operatives, the Salem witch hunt ascribed a Black face to criminality—an ascription that remains to this day.[7]

Cotton Mather's friends were appointed judges, including merchant John Richards, who had just officiated at Mather's wedding. In a letter to Richards on May 31, 1692, Mather expressed his support for capital punishment. The Richards court executed Bridget Bishop on June 10, the first of more than twenty accused witches to die.[8]

The accused up north in Andover, Massachusetts, confessed that the Black Devil man compelled them to renounce their baptism and sign his book. They rode poles to meetings where as many as five hundred witches plotted to destroy New England, the accused confessed. Hearing about this, Cotton Mather sniffed out a "Hellish Design of Bewitching and Ruining our Land." Mather ventured to Salem for the first time to witness the executions on August 19, 1692. He came to see the killing of George Burroughs, the supposed general of the Black Devil's New England army of witches. Burroughs preached Anabaptist ideas of religious equality on the northern frontier, the kind of ideas that had bred antiracism in Germantown. Mather watched Burroughs plead his innocence at the execution site, and stir the "very great number" of spectators when he recited the Lord's Prayer, something the judges said witches could not do.[9]

"The black Man stood and dictated to him!" Burroughs's accuser shouted, trying and failing to calm the crowd. Mather heard the ticking time bomb of the spectators, sounding like the unruly masses during the 1689 revolt. As soon as Burroughs was hanged, Mather sought to quell the passions of the crowd by re-inscribing the executive policies of his ruling class into God's law. Remember, he preached, the Devil often transformed himself into an Angel of Light. Mather clearly believed in the power of religious (and racial) transformation, from Black devils to White angels, with good or bad intentions.

The fervor over witches soon died down. But even after Massachusetts authorities apologized, reversed the convictions, and provided reparations in the early 1700s, Mather never stopped defending the Salem witch trials, because he never stopped defending the religious, class, slaveholding, gender, and racial hierarchies reinforced by the trials. These hierarchies benefited elites like him, or, as he continued to preach, they were in accord with the law of God. And Cotton Mather viewed himself—or presented himself—as the defender of God's law, the crucifier of any non-Puritan, African, Native American, poor person, or woman who defied God's law by not following the rules of submission.[10]

Sometime after the witch trials, maybe to save their Black faces from accusations of devilishness and criminality, a group of enslaved

Africans formed a "Religious Society of Negroes" in Boston. It was one of the first known organizations of African people in colonial America. In 1693, Cotton Mather drew up the society's list of rules, prefaced by a covenant: "Wee, the miserable children of *Adam* and *Noah* . . . freely resolve . . . to become the *Servants* of that Glorious Lord." Two of Mather's rules were instructive: members were to be counseled by someone "wise and of English" descent, and they were not to "afford" any "Shelter" to anyone who had "Run away from their Masters." Meeting weekly, some members of the society probably delighted in hearing Mather cast their souls as White. Some probably rejected these racist ideas and used the society to mobilize against enslavement. The Religious Society of Negroes did not last. Few Africans wanted to be Christians at that time (though that would change in a few decades). And not many masters were willing to let their captives become Christians because, unlike in other colonies, there was no Massachusetts law stipulating that baptized slaves did not have to be freed.[11]

Throughout the social tumult of the 1690s, Mather obsessed over maintaining the social hierarchies by convincing the lowly that God and nature had put them there, whether it applied to women, children, enslaved Africans, or poor people. In *A Good Master Well Served* (1696), he presumed that nature had created "a conjugal society" between husband and wife; a "Parental Society" between parent and child; and, "lowest of all," a "herile society" between master and servant. Society, he said, became destabilized when children, women, and servants refused to accept their station. Mather compared egalitarian resisters to that old ambitious Devil, who wanted to become the all-powerful God. This line of thinking became Mather's everlasting justification of social hierarchy: the ambitious lowly resembled Satan; his kind of elites resembled God.

"You are better fed & better clothed, & better managed by far, than you would be, if you were your own men," Mather informed enslaved Africans in *A Good Master Well Served*. His insistence that urbane American slavery was better than barbaric African freedom was not unlike Gomes Eanes de Zurara's estimation that Africans were better off as slaves in Portugal than they had been in Africa. Do not partake in evil and "make yourself infinitely Blacker than you are all ready," Mather warned. By obeying, your "souls will be washed 'White in the blood of the lamb.'" If you fail to be "orderly servants," then you shall forever welter "under intolerable blows and wounds" from the Devil, "your overseer." In sum, Mather offered enslaved Africans two options: righteous assimilated Whiteness and slavery to God and God's minions, or segregated criminal Blackness and slavery to the Devil and the Devil's minions.[12]

Mather's writings on slavery spread throughout the colonies, influencing enslavers from Boston to Virginia. By the eighteenth century, he had published more books than any other American, and his native Boston had become colonial America's booming intellectual center. Boston was now on the periphery of a booming slave society centered in the tidewater region of Maryland, Virginia, and northeastern Carolina. The Mid-Atlantic's moderate climate, fertile land, and waterways for transportation were ideal for the raising of tobacco, and lots of it. Fulfilling the voracious European demand, tobacco exports from this region skyrocketed from 20,000 pounds in 1619 to 38 million in 1700. The imports of captives (and racist ideas) soared with tobacco exports. In the 1680s, enslaved Africans eclipsed White servants as the principal labor force. In 1698, the crown ended the Royal African Company's monopoly and opened the slave trade. Purchasing enslaved Africans became the investment craze.[13]

The economic craze did not yield a religious craze, though. Planters still shied away from converting enslaved Africans, ignoring Mather's arguments. One lady inquired, "Is it possible that any of my slaves should go to heaven, and must I see them there?" Christian knowledge, one planter complained, "would be a means to make the slave more . . . [apt] to wickedness." Cotton Mather's counterpart in Virginia, Scottish minister James Blair, tried to induce planters to realize the submission wrought by Christianity. The 1689 appointment of the thirty-three-year-old Blair as commissary of Virginia—the highest-ranking religious leader—reflected King William and Queen Mary's new interest in the empire's most populous colony. Blair used profits from slave labor to found the College of William & Mary in 1693, the colonies' second college.[14]

In 1699, Blair presented to the Virginia House of Burgesses "a Proposition for encouraging the Christian Education of Indians, Negroes, and Mulatto Children." Lawmakers responded, rather inaccurately, that the "negroes born in this country are generally baptised and brought up in the Christian religion." As for imported Africans, lawmakers announced, "the gross bestiality and rudeness of their manners, the variety and strangeness of their languages, and the weakness and shallowness of their minds, render it in a manner impossible to make any progress in their conversion." For the much more difficult commercial tasks, planters overcame the "strange" languages and had no problem teaching these "shallow-minded rude beasts" in other matters. Planters of impossibilities suddenly became planters of possibilities when instructing imported Africans on the complexities of proslavery theory, racist ideas, tobacco production, skilled trades, domestic work, and plantation management.[15]

As Maryland's commissary, the Oxford-educated Thomas Bray did not fare much better than Blair in converting Blacks during his tour of Maryland in 1700. Returning to London distressed in 1701, he organized the Society for the Propagation of the Gospel in Foreign Parts (SPG). King William approved, and an all-star cast of ministers signed up to become founding members of the Church of England's first systematic effort to spread its views in the colonies. Cotton Mather did not sign up for SPG, distrustful of Anglicans on every level. Even though Mather started mocking "the Society for the Molestation of the Gospel in foreign parts," he remained in solidarity with Anglican SPG missionaries—and Quaker missionaries—in trying to persuade resistant enslavers to Christianize resistant Africans. Persuading planters was extremely difficult. Then again, persuading them to Christianize their captives was much easier than what Mather's friend tried to persuade them to do in 1700.[16]

CHAPTER 6

Great Awakening

THE NEW CENTURY brought on the first major public debate over slavery in colonial America. New England businessman John Saffin refused to free his Black indentured servant named Adam after Adam served his contracted term of seven years. When Boston judge Samuel Sewall learned of Saffin's decision essentially to enslave Adam for the foreseeable future, Sewall was livid. Well known as one of the first Salem witch trial judges to publicly apologize, Sewall courageously took another public stand when he released *The Selling of Joseph* on June 24, 1700. "Originally, and Naturally, there is no such thing as Slavery," Sewall wrote. He shot down popular proslavery justifications, such as curse theory, the notion that the "good" end of Christianity justified the "evil" means of slavery, and John Locke's just war theory. Sewall rejected these proslavery theories from the quicksand of another kind of racism. New Englanders should rid themselves of slavery *and* African people, Sewall maintained. African people "seldom use their freedom well," he said. They can never live "with us, and grow up into orderly Families."[1]

Samuel Sewall could not be easily cast aside like those powerless Germantown petitioners. A close friend of Cotton Mather, Sewall had received an audience with the king in England, and he had served as judge on the highest court in Boston. He was on track to becoming the Puritans' chief justice in 1717. When Sewall judged slavery to be bad, he should have opened the minds of many. But proslavery racism had almost always been a close-minded affair. In place of open minds, closed-minded "Frowns and hard Words" bombarded the forty-six-year-old jurist.

John Saffin, in particular, was maddened by Sewall's attack on his business dealings. A judge himself, Saffin refused to disqualify himself from adjuring a freedom case for Adam. At seventy-five years old in 1701, his lifetime in the trenches of early American capitalism had nurtured his outlook on powerful people. "Friendship & Munificence are Strangers in this world," Saffin once opined. "Interest and profit are the Principles by [which] all are Sway'd." No one attacked Saffin, called him "manstealer," and got away with it.[2]

Before the end of 1701, John Saffin had printed *A Brief and Candid Answer, to a Late Printed Sheet, Entitled, The Selling of Joseph*. "God hath set different Orders and Degrees of Men in the World," Saffin declared. No matter what Sewall said, it was not an "Evil thing to bring [Africans] out of their own Heathenish Country" and convert them. Saffin, well known among literary historians as a leading seventeenth-century poet, ended his pamphlet in verse with "The Negroes Character": "*Cowardly and cruel are those* Blacks *Innate, Prone to Revenge, Imp of inveterate hate*."[3]

Samuel Sewall won the battle—Adam was freed in 1703 after a long and bitter trial—but he lost the war. America did not rid itself of slavery or of Black people. In the newspaper debate that trailed the Sewall-Saffin dispute, Bostonians seemingly found Saffin's segregationist ideas more persuasive than Sewall's. Sewall did get in the last volley in his lost war, prompted by the London Athenian Society questioning whether the slave trade was "contrary to the great law of Christianity." Sewall answered affirmatively in a fourteen-page pamphlet in 1705. He pointed out that the so-called just wars between Africans were actually instigated by European slave-traders drumming up demand for captives.[4]

Meanwhile, the enslaved population continued to rise noticeably, which led to fears of revolts and then, in 1705, new racist codes to prevent revolts and secure human property up and down the Atlantic Coast. Massachusetts authorities forbade interracial relationships, began taxing imported captives, and, over Samuel Sewall's objections, rated Indians and Negroes with horses and hogs during a revision of the tax code. Virginia lawmakers made slave patrols compulsory for non-slaveholding Whites; these groups of White citizens were charged with policing slaves, enforcing discipline, and guarding routes of escape. The Virginia legislature also denied Blacks the ability to hold office. Evoking repeatedly the term "christian white servant" and defining their rights, Virginia lawmakers fully married Whiteness and Christianity, uniting rich White enslavers and the non-slaveholding White poor. To seal the unity (and racial loyalty), Virginia's White lawmakers seized and sold all property owned by "any slave," the "profit thereof applied to the use of the poor of the said parish." The story would be told many times in American history: Black property legally or illegally seized; the resulting Black destitution blamed on Black inferiority; the past discrimination ignored when the blame was assigned. Virginia's 1705 code mandated that planters provide freed White servants with fifty acres of land. The resulting White prosperity was then attributed to White superiority.[5]

ON MARCH 1, 1706, Cotton Mather asked God whether, if he "[wrote] an Essay, about the Christianity of our *Negro* and other *Slaves*," God would bless him with "Good Servants." Mather hoped a pamphlet focusing exclusively on this topic would help to shift the minds of enslavers who refused to baptize their captives. By now, he was unquestionably America's foremost minister and intellectual, having just published his New England history, a toast of American exceptionalism, *Magnalia Christi Americana*, regarded as the greatest literary achievement of New England's first century.[6]

Mather released *The Negro Christianized* in June 1706. The "Providence of God" sent Africans into slavery and over to Christian America to have the capacity to learn from their masters the "Glorious Gospel." They "are *Men*, and not *Beasts*," Mather stressed, opposing segregationists. "Indeed their Stupidity is a Discouragement. It may seem, unto as little purpose, to Teach, as to wash" Africans. "But the greater their Stupidity, the greater must be our Application," he proclaimed. Don't worry about baptism leading to freedom. The "Law of

Christianity . . . allows Slavery," he resolved. He cited the writings of other Puritan theologians as well as St. Paul.[7]

On December 13, 1706, Mather believed wholeheartedly that God had rewarded him for writing *The Negro Christianized*. Members of Mather's church—"without any Application of mine to them for such a Thing"—spent forty or fifty pounds on "a very likely Slave," he happily noted in his diary. New England churches routinely gifted captives to ministers. Mather named "it" Onesimus, after St. Paul's adopted son, a converted runaway. Mather kept a close racist eye on Onesimus, constantly suspecting him of thievery.[8]

Mather's Christian slavery views were more representative in New England than Samuel Sewall's or John Saffin's ideas. But Samuel Sewall's views continued to echo in the writings of others. In 1706, John Campbell's first full-fledged essay in his *Boston News-Letter*, the second newspaper in colonial America, urged the importation of more White servants to reduce the colony's dependence on enslaved Africans, who were "much addicted to Stealing, Lying and Purloning." Americans reading early colonial newspapers learned two recurring lessons about Black people: they could be bought like cattle, and they were dangerous criminals like those witches.

From their arrival around 1619, African people had illegally resisted legal slavery. They had thus been stamped from the beginning as criminals. In all of the fifty suspected or actual slave revolts reported in newspapers during the American colonial era, resisting Africans were nearly always cast as violent criminals, not people reacting to enslavers' regular brutality, or pressing for the most basic human desire: freedom.[9]

As the sun fired up the sky on April 7, 1712, about thirty enslaved Africans and two Native Americans set fire to a New York building, ambushing the "Christians" who came to put it out, as the story was told. Nine "Christians" were slayed, five or six seriously wounded. The freedom fighters ran off into the nearby woods. Fear and revenge smoldered through the city. Within twenty-four hours, six of the rebels had committed suicide (believing they would return to Africa in death); the rest were "hunted out" by soldiers and publicly executed, mostly

burned alive. New York colonial governor Robert Hunter, who supervised the hunt, the trials, and the executions, was a member of Thomas
Bray's Society for the Propagation of the Gospel in Foreign Parts and
the Royal Society. He framed the slave revolt a "barbarous attempt of
some of their slaves." No matter what African people did, they were
barbaric beasts or brutalized like beasts. If they did not clamor for freedom, then their obedience showed they were naturally beasts of burden. If they nonviolently resisted enslavement, they were brutalized. If
they killed for their freedom, they were barbaric murderers.

Their "barbarism" occasioned a "severe" slave code, resembling the
laws passed by the Virginians and Puritans in 1705. New York lawmakers stripped free Blacks of the right to own property, and then they
denigrated "the free negroes of the colony" as an "idle, slothful people"
who weighed on the "public charge."[10]

IN THE MIDST of relentless African resistance and increasingly vocal
antislavery Quakers, British slave-traders were still doing quite well,
and they were primed for growth. In 1713, England won the *Assiento*,
the privilege of supplying captives to all those Spanish American colonies, allowing it to soon become the eighteenth century's greatest
slave-trader, following in the footsteps of France, Holland, and the
pioneers in Portugal. New England had become the main entryway
into the colonies for European and Caribbean goods. Ships setting out
from the colonies, mostly from Boston and Newport, Rhode Island,
carried the food that fed the British Caribbean's planters, overseers,
and laborers. Ships returned hauling sugar, rum, captives, and molas-
ses, all supplying New England's largest manufacturing industry before
the American Revolution—liquor.[11]

Boston's status as one of the key ports in the colonies left the city
vulnerable to disease. On April 21, 1721, the HMS *Seahorse* sailed into
Boston Harbor from Barbados. A month later, Cotton Mather logged
in his journal, "The grievous calamity of the smallpox has now entered
the town." One thousand Bostonians, nearly 10 percent of the town,
fled to the countryside to escape the judgment of the Almighty.[12]

Fifteen years prior, Mather had asked Onesimus one of the standard questions that Boston slaveholders asked new house slaves—Have you had smallpox? "Yes and no," Onesimus answered. He explained how in Africa before his enslavement, a tiny amount of pus from a smallpox victim had been scraped into his skin with a thorn, following a practice hundreds of years old that resulted in building up healthy recipients' immunities to the disease. This form of inoculation—a precursor to modern vaccination—was an innovative practice that prevented untold numbers of deaths in West Africa and on disease-ridden slave ships to ports throughout the Atlantic. Racist European scientists at first refused to recognize that African physicians could have made such advances. Indeed, it would take several decades and many more deaths before British physician Edward Jenner, the so-called father of immunology, validated inoculation.

Cotton Mather, however, became an early believer when he read an essay on inoculation in the Royal Society's *Philosophical Transactions* in 1714. He then interviewed Africans around Boston to be sure. Sharing their inoculation stories, they gave him a window into the intellectual culture of West Africa. He had trouble grasping it, instead complaining about how "brokenly and blunderingly and like Idiots they tell the Story."[13]

On June 6, 1721, Mather calmly composed an "Address to the Physicians of Boston," respectfully requesting that they consider inoculation. If anyone had the credibility to suggest something so new in a time of peril it was Cotton Mather, the first American-born fellow in London's Royal Society, which was still headed by Isaac Newton. Mather had released fifteen to twenty books and pamphlets a year since the 1690s, and he was nearing his mammoth career total of 388—probably more than the rest of his entire generation of New England ministers combined.[14]

The only doctor who responded to Mather was Zabadiel Boylston, President John Adams's great-uncle. When Boylston announced his successful inoculation of his six-year-old son and two enslaved Africans on July 15, 1721, area doctors and councilmen were horrified. It made no sense that people should inject themselves with a disease to save themselves from the disease. Boston's only holder of a medical degree, a physician pressing to maintain his professional legitimacy, fanned the city's flames of fear. Dr. William Douglass concocted a conspiracy theory, saying there was a grand plot afoot among African people, who had agreed to kill their masters by convincing them to be inoculated. "There is not a Race of Men on Earth more False Liars" than Africans, Douglass barked.[15]

Anti-inoculators like Dr. Douglass found a friendly medium in one of the colonies' first independent newspapers, the *New England Courant*, launched by twenty-four-year-old James Franklin in 1721. James Franklin's fifteen-year-old indentured servant and younger brother, Ben, worked as the typesetter for the newspaper. Feeling disrespected by the *Courant*, Cotton Mather demanded intellectual obedience like a tired college professor. The general public ignored him and withdrew. Bostonians' distaste for Mather and Boylston improved only when the epidemic that killed 842 people finally ended in early 1722.[16]

As April 1722 approached, Ben Franklin decided he wanted to do more than setting type for his brother's newspaper. He started anonymously penning letters with fascinating social advice, slipping them under the print shop door for his brother to print in the *Courant*. Signing the letters Silence Dogood, Ben was inspired by Mather's 1710 *Bonifacius, or Essays to Do Good*, on maintaining social order through benevolence. The book "gave me such a turn of thinking, as to have an influence on my conduct through life," Benjamin Franklin later explained to Mather's son. After publishing sixteen popular letters, Ben revealed the true identity of Silence Dogood to his jealous and overbearing brother. James promptly censured Ben. By 1723, all the ambitious Ben could think about was running away.[17]

Before fleeing to Philadelphia, Ben was summoned to a home on Ship Street. He nervously knocked. A servant appeared and led him to the study. Ben entered and beheld probably the largest library in North America. Cotton Mather forgave Ben for the war of words, as a father would a misbehaving child. No one knows what else the sixty-year-old and seventeen-year-old discussed.

Ben Franklin may have noticed Cotton Mather's melancholy. Mather's beloved father, then eighty-four, was ill. When Increase Mather died in his oldest son's arms on August 23, 1723, the tragedy topped off some weary years for Cotton Mather, who had weathered marital disputes, financial problems, disagreements with Anglican ministers, being passed over twice for the Harvard presidency, and the news that Isaac Newton's Royal Society would no longer publish his work. Despite all his successes, Mather had begun to worry about his intellectual legacy.

If Mather stayed abreast of current events in the colonies in the 1720s, then he had no reason to worry about his missionary legacy. More fervently than any American voice since the 1680s, Mather had urged slaveholders to baptize enslaved Africans, and enslaved Africans to leave the religions of their ancestors. Moving slowly and carefully uphill, he had made strides over the years. Like-minded Anglican missionaries, such as James Blair, Thomas Bray, and the agents of his Society for the Propagation of the Gospel in Foreign Parts, had taken this idea further. Whether he realized it or not, and whether he despised the Anglican missionaries or not, Mather's prayers finally began to be answered during his final years.

Edmund Gibson, the distinguished Anglican bishop of London, decided to eliminate any lingering doubt in planters as to whether they could hold Christian captives. In two letters to Virginians in 1727, he praised and authenticated the innovative statute of 1667 that denied freedom to baptized captives. Gibson talked about how conversion obligated captives to "the greatest Diligences and Fidelity," an idea that Mather had been stressing for years. The British crown and the aides of Sir Robert Walpole, the first prime minister of Great Britain, echoed the bishop. All of Britain's religious, political, and economic power now united to free missionaries and planters from having to free the converted, thus reinvigorating proselytizing movements and dooming calls for manumission.[18]

More and more enslavers began to listen to the arguments of missionaries that Christian submission could supplement their violence in subduing African people. Actually, the ministers focused on the submission and were mum on the violence. Minister Hugh Jones, a William & Mary professor, published his highly influential *Present State of Virginia* in 1724. "Christianity," Jones wrote, "encourages and orders" African people "to become more humble and better servants." They should not learn to read and write, though. They were "by Nature cut out for hard Labour and Fatigue." In his stunningly popular 1722 collection of sermons, James Blair proclaimed that the Golden Rule did not suggest equality between "superiors and inferiors." Order required hierarchy. Hierarchy required responsibility. Masters, Blair preached, were to baptize and treat their slaves kindly.[19]

Enslavers continued to become more open to these ideas right up until the First Great Awakening, which swept through the colonies in the 1730s, spearheaded by Connecticut native Jonathan Edwards. His father, Timothy Edwards, had studied under Increase Mather at Harvard, and he knew and venerated Cotton Mather. During Edwards's junior year at Yale in 1718, Cotton Mather had secured the donation from Welsh merchant Elihu Yale that had resulted in the name of America's third college (the Collegiate School) being changed.

Revivals at Edwards's Massachusetts church in Northampton jump-started the First Great Awakening around 1733. In awakening souls, passionate evangelicals like Edwards spoke about human equality (in soul) and the capability of everyone for conversion. "I am God's servant as they are mine, and much more inferior to God than my servant is to me," the slaveholding Edwards explained in 1741. But the proslavery Great Awakening did not extend to the South Carolina plantation of Hugh Bryan, who was awakened into antislavery thought. Bryan proclaimed "sundry enthusiastic Prophecies of the Destruction of Charles Town and Deliverance of the Negroes from servitude" in 1740. His praying captives stopped laboring. One woman was overheard "singing a spiritual at the water's edge," like so many other unidentified antiracist, antislavery Christian women and men who started singing in those years. South Carolina authorities reprimanded Bryan. They wanted evangelists preaching a racist Christianity for submission, not an antiracist Christianity for liberation.[20]

Hugh Bryan was an exception in the missionary days of the First Great Awakening, days Cotton Mather would not live to see. Though bedridden, he was happy he lived to see his sixty-fifth birthday on February 13, 1728. The next morning, Mather called his church's new pastor, Joshua Gee, into the room for prayer. Mather felt a release. "Now I have nothing more to do here," Mather told Gee. Hours later, Cotton Mather was dead.[21]

"He was perhaps the *principal Ornament* of this Country, and the greatest Scholar that was ever bred in it," praised the *New-England Weekly Journal* on February 19, 1728, the day of Mather's burial. It was an accurate eulogy for the grandson of John Cotton and Richard Mather. Cotton Mather had indeed overtaken the names of his grandfathers, two ministerial giants bred in an intellectual world debating whether Africa's heat or Ham's curse had produced the ugly apelike African beasts who were benefiting from enslavement. If his grandfathers consumed in England the racist idea of the African who can and should be enslaved, then Cotton Mather led the way in producing the racist idea of Christianity simultaneously subduing and uplifting the enslaved African. He joined with the producers of racist ideas in other colonial empires, from the mother countries in Europe, and normalized and rationalized the expansion of colonialism and slavery. Europeans were taking over and subduing the Western world, establishing their rightful ruling place as the very standard of human greatness, these racist producers proclaimed in a nutshell. By the time of Mather's death in 1728, Royal Society fellows had fully constructed this White ruling standard for humanity. Christianity, rationality, civilization, wealth, goodness, souls, beauty, light, Adam, Jesus, God, and freedom had all been framed as the dominion of White people from Europe. The only question was whether lowly African people had the capacity of rising up and reaching the standard. As America's first great assimilationist, Cotton Mather preached that African people could become White in their souls.

In 1729, Samuel Mather completed his esteeming biography of his deceased father, as Cotton Mather had done for his father, and as Increase Mather had done for Richard Mather. "When he *walked the streets,"* Samuel wrote of Cotton Mather, "he still blessed many persons who never knew it, with Secret Wishes." He blessed the Black man, dearly praying *"Lord, Wash that poor Soul, make him white by the Washing of thy SPIRIT."*[22]

PART II

Thomas Jefferson

CHAPTER 7

Enlightenment

NOTHING FAZED HIM. He carried tired mules. He pressed on while companions fainted. He cut down predators as calmly as he rested in trees at night. Peter Jefferson had a job to do in 1747: he was surveying land never before seen by White settlers, in order to continue the boundary-line between Virginia and North Carolina across the dangerous Blue Ridge Mountains. He had been commissioned to certify that colonial America's westernmost point had not become like Jamaica's Blue Mountains, a haven for runaways.[1]

In time, Peter Jefferson's mesmerizing stamina, strength, and courage on surveying trips became transfixed in family lore. Among the first to hear the stories was four-year-old Thomas, overjoyed when his father finally came home at the end of 1747. Thomas was Peter's oldest son, born on April 13 during the memorable year of 1743. Cotton Mather's missionary counterpart in Virginia, James Blair, died sixteen days after Thomas's birth, marking the end of an era when theologians almost completely dominated the racial discourse in America. The year also marked the birth of a new intellectual era. "Enlightened" thinkers started secularizing and expanding the racist discourse throughout the colonies, tutoring future antislavery, anti-abolitionist, and anti-royal revolutionaries in Thomas Jefferson's generation. And Cotton Mather's greatest secular disciple led the way.

"THE FIRST DRUDGERY of settling new colonies is now pretty well over," Benjamin Franklin observed in 1743, "and there are many in every province in circumstances that set them at ease, and afford leisure to cultivate the finer arts, and improve the common stock of knowledge." At thirty-seven, Franklin's circumstances certainly set him at ease. Since fleeing Boston, he had built an empire of stores, almanacs, and newspapers in Philadelphia. For men like him, who leisured about as their capital literally or figuratively worked for them, his observations about living at ease were no doubt true. Franklin founded the American Philosophical Society (APS) in 1743 in Philadelphia. Modeled after the Royal Society, the APS became the colonies' first formal association of scholars since the Mathers' Boston Society in the 1680s. Franklin's scholarly baby died in infancy, but it was revived in 1767 with a commitment to "all philosophical Experiments that let Light into the Nature of Things."[2]

THE SCIENTIFIC REVOLUTION of the 1600s had given way to a greater intellectual movement in the 1700s. Secular knowledge, and notions of the propensity for universal human progress, had long been distrusted in Christian Europe. That changed with the dawn of an age that came to be known as *les Lumières* in France, *Aufklärung* in Germany, *Illuminismo* in Italy, and the *Enlightenment* in Great Britain and America.

For Enlightenment intellectuals, the metaphor of light typically had a double meaning. Europeans had rediscovered learning after a thousand years in religious darkness, and their bright continental beacon of insight existed in the midst of a "dark" world not yet touched by light. Light, then, became a metaphor for Europeanness, and therefore Whiteness, a notion that Benjamin Franklin and his philosophical society eagerly embraced and imported to the colonies. White colonists, Franklin alleged in *Observations Concerning the Increase of Mankind* (1751), were "making this side of our Globe reflect a brighter Light." Let us bar uneconomical slavery and Black people, Franklin suggested. "But perhaps," he thought, "I am partial to the complexion of my Country, for such kind of partiality is natural to Mankind." Enlightenment ideas gave legitimacy to this long-held racist "partiality," the connection between lightness and Whiteness and reason, on the one hand, and between darkness and Blackness and ignorance, on the other.[3]

These Enlightenment counterpoints arose, conveniently, at a time when Western Europe's triangular transatlantic trade was flourishing. Great Britain, France, and colonial America principally furnished ships and manufactured goods. The ships sailed to West Africa, and traders exchanged these goods, at a profit, for human merchandise. Manufactured cloth became the most sought-after item in eighteenth-century Africa for the same reason that cloth was coveted in Europe—nearly everyone in Africa (as in Europe) wore clothes, and nearly everyone in Africa (as in Europe) desired better clothes. Only the poorest of African people did not wear an upper garment, but this small number became representative in the European mind. It was the irony of the age: slave traders knew that cloth was the most desired commodity in both places, but at the same time some of them were producing the racist idea that Africans walked around naked like animals. Producers of this racist idea had to know their tales were false. But they went on producing them anyway to justify their lucrative commerce in human beings.[4]

The slave ships traveled from Africa to the Americas, where dealers exchanged at another profit the newly enslaved Africans for raw materials that had been produced by the long-enslaved Africans. The ships and traders returned home and began the process anew, providing a "triple stimulus" for European commerce (and a triple exploitation of African people). Practically all the coastal manufacturing and trading towns in the Western world developed an enriching connection to the transatlantic trade during the eighteenth century. Profits exploded with the growth and prosperity of the slave trade in Britain's principal port, Richard Mather's old preaching ground, Liverpool. The principal American slave-trading port was Newport, Rhode Island, and the proceeds produced mammoth fortunes that can be seen in the mansions still dotting the town's historic waterfront.

In his 1745 book endorsing the slave-trading Royal African Company, famous economics writer Malachy Postlethwayt defined the British Empire as "a magnificent superstructure of American commerce and naval power, on an African foundation." But another foundation lay beneath that foundation: those all-important producers of racist ideas, who ensured that this magnificent superstructure would continue to seem normal to potential resisters. Enlightenment intellectuals produced the racist idea that the growing socioeconomic inequities between England and Senegambia, Europe and Africa, the enslavers and enslaved, had to be God's or nature's or nurture's will. Racist ideas clouded the discrimination, rationalized the racial disparities, defined the enslaved, as opposed to the enslavers, as the problem people. Antiracist ideas hardly made the dictionary of racial thought during the Enlightenment.[5]

Carl Linnaeus, the progenitor of Sweden's Enlightenment, followed in the footsteps of François Bernier and took the lead classifying humanity into a racial hierarchy for the new intellectual and commercial age. In *Systema Naturae*, first published in 1735, Linnaeus placed humans at the pinnacle of the animal kingdom. He sliced the genus *Homo* into *Homo sapiens* (humans) and *Homo troglodytes* (ape), and so on, and further divided the single *Homo sapiens* species into four varieties. At the pinnacle of his human kingdom reigned *H. sapiens europaeus*: "Very smart, inventive. Covered by tight clothing. Ruled by law." Then came *H. sapiens americanus* ("Ruled by custom") and *H. sapiens asiaticus* ("Ruled by opinion"). He relegated humanity's nadir, *H. sapiens afer*, to the bottom, calling this group "sluggish, lazy . . . [c]rafty, slow, careless. Covered by grease. Ruled by caprice," describing, in particular, the "females with genital flap and elongated breasts."[6]

Carl Linnaeus created a hierarchy within the animal kingdom and a hierarchy within the human kingdom, and this human hierarchy was based on race. His "enlightened" peers were also creating human hierarchies; within the European kingdom, they placed Irish people, Jews, Romani, and southern and eastern Europeans at the bottom. Enslavers and slave traders were creating similar ethnic hierarchies within the African kingdom. Enslaved Africans in North America were coming mainly from seven cultural-geopolitical regions: Angola (26 percent), Senegambia (20 percent), Nigeria (17 percent), Sierra Leone (11 percent), Ghana (11 percent), Ivory Coast (6 percent), and Benin (3 percent). Since the hierarchies were usually based on which ancestral groups were thought to make the best slaves, or whose ways most resembled those of Europeans, different enslavers with different needs and different cultures had different hierarchies. Generally, Angolans were classed as the most inferior Africans, since they were priced so cheaply in slave markets (due to their greater supply). Linnaeus classed the Khoi (or Hottentot) of South Africa as a divergent branch of humanity, *Homo monstrosis monorchidei*. Since the late seventeenth century, the Khoi people had been deemed "the missing link between human and ape species."[7]

Making hierarchies of Black ethnic groups within the African kingdom can be termed *ethnic racism*, because it is at the intersection of ethnocentric and racist ideas, while making hierarchies pitting all Europeans over all Africans was simply racism. In the end, both classified a Black ethnic group as inferior. Standards of measurement for the ethnic groups within the African hierarchies were based on European cultural values and traits, and hierarchy-making was wielded in the service of a political project: enslavement. Senegambians were deemed superior to Angolans because they supposedly made better slaves, and because supposedly their ways were closer to European ways. Imported Africans in the Americas no doubt recognized the hierarchy of African peoples as quickly as imported White servants recognized the broader racial hierarchy. When and if Senegambians cast themselves as superior to Angolans to justify any relative privileges they received, Senegambians were espousing ethnically racist ideas, just like those Whites who used racist ideas to justify their White privileges. Whenever a Black person or group used White people as a standard of measurement, and cast another Black person or group as inferior, it was another instance of racism. Carl Linnaeus and company crafted one massive hierarchy of races and of ethnic groups within the races. The entire ladder and all of its steps—from the Greeks or Brits at the very top down to the Angolans and Hottentots at the bottom—everything bespoke ethnic racism. Some "superior" Africans agreed with the collection of ethnocentric steps for Africans, but rejected the racist ladder that deemed them inferior to White people. They smacked the racist chicken and enjoyed its racist eggs.[8]

Every traded African ethnic group was like a product, and slave traders seemed to be valuing and devaluing these ethnic products based on the laws of supply and demand. Linnaeus did not seem to be part of a grandiose scheme to force-feed ethnic racism to enslaved peoples to divide and conquer them. But whenever ethnic racism did set the natural allies on American plantations apart, in the manner that racism set the natural allies in American poverty apart, enslavers hardly minded. They were usually willing to deploy any tool—intellectual or otherwise—to suppress slave resistance and ensure returns on their investments.

VOLTAIRE, FRANCE'S ENLIGHTENMENT GURU, used Linnaeus's racist ladder in the book of additions that supplemented his half-million-word *Essay on Universal History* in 1756. He agreed there was a permanent natural order of the species. He asked, "Were the flowers, fruits, trees, and animals with which nature covers the face of the earth, planted by her at first only in one spot, in order that they might be spread over the rest of the world?" No, he boldly declared. "The negro race is a species of men as different from ours as the breed of spaniels is from that of greyhound. . . . If their understanding is not of a different nature from ours it is at least greatly inferior." The African people were like animals, he added, merely living to satisfy "bodily wants." However, as a "warlike, hardy, and cruel people," they were "superior" soldiers.[9]

With the publication of *Essay on Universal History*, Voltaire became the first prominent writer in almost a century daring enough to suggest polygenesis. The theory of separately created races was a contrast to the assimilationist idea of monogenesis, that is, of all humans as descendants of a White Adam and Eve. Voltaire emerged as the eighteenth century's chief arbiter of segregationist thought, promoting the idea that the races were fundamentally separate, that the separation was immutable, and that the inferior Black race had no capability to assimilate, to be normal, or to be civilized and White. The Enlightenment shift to secular thought had thus opened the door to the production of more segregationist ideas. And segregationist ideas of permanent Black inferiority appealed to enslavers, because they bolstered their defense of the permanent enslavement of Black people.

Voltaire was intellectually at odds with naturalist Georges Louis Leclerc, who adopted the name Buffon. Buffon headed the moderate mainstream of the French Enlightenment through his encyclopedic *Histoire naturelle* (Natural history), which appeared in forty-five volumes over fifty-five years beginning in 1749. Nearly every European intellectual read them. And while Voltaire promoted segregationist thinking, Buffon remained committed to assimilationist ideas.

The argument over Voltaire's multiple human species versus Buffon's single human species was one aspect of a larger scientific divide during the Enlightenment era. Their beloved Sir Isaac Newton envisioned the natural world as an assembled machine running on "natural laws." Newton did not explain how it was assembled. That was fine for Voltaire, who believed the natural world—including the races—to be unchangeable, even from God's power. Buffon instead beheld an ever-changing world. Buffon and Voltaire did agree on one thing: they both opposed slavery. Actually, most of the leading Enlightenment intellectuals were producers of racist ideas *and* abolitionist thought.[10]

Buffon defined a species as "a constant succession of similar individuals that can reproduce together." And since different races could reproduce together, they must be of the same species, he argued. Buffon was responding to some of the first segregationist denigrations of biracial people. Polygenesists were questioning or rejecting the reproductive capability of biracial people in order to substantiate their arguments for racial groups being separate species. If Blacks and Whites were separate species, then their offspring would be infertile. And so the word *mulatto*, which came from "mule," came into being, because mules were the infertile offspring of horses and donkeys. In the eighteenth century, the adage "black as the devil" battled for popularity in the English-speaking world with "God made the white man, the devil made the mulatto."[11]

Buffon distinguished six races or varieties of a single human species (and the Khoi people of South Africa he placed with monkeys). He positioned Africans "between the extremes of barbarism and of civilization." They had "little knowledge" of the "arts and sciences," and their language was "without rules," said Buffon. As a climate theorist and monogenesist, Buffon did not believe these qualities were fixed in stone. If Africans were imported to Europe, then their color would gradually change and become "perhaps as white as the natives" of Europe. It was in Europe where "we behold the human form in its greatest perfection," and where "we ought to form our ideas of the real and natural colour of man." Buffon sounded like the foundational thinker of modern European art history, Johann Joachim Winckelmann of Germany. "A beautiful body will be all the more beautiful the whiter it is," Winckelmann said in his disciplinary classic, *Geschichte der Kunst des Alterthums* (*History of the Art of Antiquity*) in 1764. These were the "enlightened" ideas on race that Benjamin Franklin's American Philosophical Society and a young Thomas Jefferson were consuming and importing to America on the eve of the American Revolution.[12]

PETER JEFFERSON ACQUIRED around twelve hundred acres in Virginia's Albemarle County and went on to represent the county in the House of Burgesses, Virginia's legislative body. Shadwell, his tobacco plantation, sat about five miles east of the current center of Charlottesville. The Jefferson home was a popular rest stop for nearby Cherokees and Catawbas on their regular diplomatic journeys to Williamsburg. The young Thomas Jefferson "acquired impressions of attachment and commiseration for them which have never been obliterated," he reminisced years later.[13]

While Thomas was raised on the common sight of distinguished Native American visitors, he commonly saw African people as house workers tending to his every need as well as field workers tending to tobacco. In 1745, someone brought a two-year-old Thomas Jefferson out of Shadwell's big house. Thomas was held up to a woman on horseback who placed him on a pillow secured to the horse. The rider, who was a slave, took the boy for a ride to a relative's plantation. This was Thomas Jefferson's earliest childhood memory. It associated slavery with comfort. The slave was entrusted with looking after him, and on his soft saddle he felt safe and secure, later recalling the woman as "kind and gentle."[14]

When he played with African boys years later, Thomas learned more about slaveholding. As he recalled, "The parent storms, the child looks on, catches the lineaments of wrath, puts on the same airs in the circle of smaller slaves, gives a loose to his worst passions, and thus nursed, educated, and daily exercised in tyranny, cannot but be stamped by it with odious peculiarities."[15]

In his home, no one around him saw anything wrong with the tyranny. Slavery was as customary as prisons are today. Few could imagine an ordered world without them. Peter Jefferson had accumulated almost sixty captives by the 1750s, which made him the second-largest slaveholder in Albemarle County. Peter preached to his children the importance of self-reliance—oblivious of the contradiction—to which he credited his own success.

Peter did not, however, preach to his son the importance of religion. In fact, when Virginia's First Great Awakening reached the area, it bypassed the Shadwell plantation. Peter did not allow Samuel Davies, who almost single-handedly brought the Awakening to Virginia, to minister to his children or his captives. It is likely that Peter believed— like many of his slaveholding peers—"that Christianizing the Negroes makes them proud and saucy, and tempts them to imagine themselves upon an equality with the white people," as Davies reported in his most celebrated sermon in 1757. Some American planters had been sold on Davies's viewpoint that "some should be Masters and some Servants," and more were open to converting their captives than ever before. But not enough of them to satisfy Cotton Mather's likeminded missionaries, who agreed with Davies that "a *good Christian* will always be a *good Servant*." Enslavers commonly "let [slaves] live on in their Pagan darkness," fearing Christianity would incite their resistance, observed a visiting Swede, Peter Kalm, in the late 1740s. Twenty years later, irritable Virginia planter Landon Carter fumed about Blacks being "devils," adding, "to make them otherwise than slaves will be to set devils free."[16]

Not all Christian missionaries were protecting slavery by preaching Christian submission in the mid-eighteenth century. In 1742, New

Jersey native John Woolman, a store clerk, was asked to write a bill of sale for an unnamed African woman. He began to question the institution and soon kicked off what became a legendary traveling ministry, spreading Quakerism and antislavery. After his first Quaker mission in the harrowing slaveholding South in 1746, Woolman jotted down *Some Considerations on the Keeping of Negroes.*[17]

"We are in a high Station, and enjoy greater Favours than they," Woolman theorized. God had endowed White Christians with "distinguished Gifts." By sanctioning slavery, America was "misusing his Gifts." Woolman planted his groundbreaking abolitionist tree in the same racist soil that proslavery theologians like Cotton Mather— preaching divine slavery—had used a century ago. Their divergences over slavery itself obscured their parallel political racism that denied Black people self-determination. Mather's proslavery theological treatises proclaimed masters divinely charged to care for the degraded race of natural servants. Woolman's antislavery treatise proclaimed Christians to be divinely charged with "greater Favours" to emancipate, Christianize, and care for the degraded slaves. But whether they were to be given eternal slavery or eventual emancipation, enslaved Africans would be acted upon as dependent children reliant on White enslavers or abolitionists for their fate.[18]

John Woolman bided his time before submitting his essay to the press of the Philadelphia Yearly Meeting. Woolman knew the history of Quakers quarreling over slavery, of abolitionists disrupting meetings and being banished. He cared just as much about his Quaker ministry and Quaker unity as he did antislavery. In 1752, when abolitionist Anthony Benezet was elected to the press's editorial board, Woolman knew the time was right to publish his eight-year-old essay. By early 1754, Benjamin Franklin's *Pennsylvania Gazette* was advertising the new publication of *Some Considerations on the Keeping of Negroes.*

By the end of the year, some Quakers had started to move like never before against slavery, pushed by Benezet and Woolman and the contradictions of Christian slavery. Benezet had edited Woolman's essay. If Woolman thrived in privacy, Benezet thrived in public, and the two reformers made a dynamic duo of antislavery activists. In

September 1754, the Philadelphia Yearly Meeting approved for publication the *Epistle of Caution and Advice Concerning the Buying and Keeping
of Slaves*. In the *Epistle*, antislavery reformers struck a compromise, urging Quakers to buy no more slaves. The writers evoked the Golden
Law on the sixty-sixth uncelebrated anniversary of the Germantown
Petition. Benezet initiated the writing of the *Epistle* and incorporated
input from Woolman. Hundreds of copies were shipped to the quarterly meetings in the Delaware Valley. The front door of American
Quakerism had officially been opened to antislavery. But Quaker masters quickly slammed the doors to their separate rooms. Seventy percent refused to free their captives. Woolman learned firsthand of their
dogged refusal when he ventured into Maryland, Virginia, and North
Carolina in 1757.[19]

Slavery's defenders spewed many racist ideas, ranging from Blacks
being a backward people, to them living better in America than in
Africa, to the curse of Ham. It "troubled" Woolman "to perceive the
darkness of their imagination." He never faltered in shooting back,
in his calm, compassionate way. No one is inferior in God's eyes,
he stressed. They had not imported Africans for their own good,
as demonstrated by their constant abuse, overwork, starvation, and
scarce clothing.[20]

In 1760, Woolman traveled to the Rhode Island homes of some
of colonial America's wealthiest slave-traders. Their "smooth conduct"
and "superficial friendship" nearly lured him away from antislavery. He
ventured back home to New Jersey as he had done from the South
years earlier—dragging a heavy bag of thoughts. In arguing against
slavery over the years, he found himself arguing against African inferiority, and thus arguing against himself. He had to rethink whether
White people were in fact bestowed a "high Station." In 1762, he
updated *Considerations on Keeping Negroes*.[21]

We must speak out against slavery "from a love of equity," Woolman avowed in the second part of the pamphlet. He dropped the
rhetoric of greater "Favours" in a racial sense, although it remained
in a religious sense. His antiracism shined. "Placing on Men the igno-
minious Title SLAVE, dressing them in uncomely Garments, keeping

them to servile Labour . . . tends gradually to fix a Nation in the mind, that they are a Sort of People below us in Nature," stated Woolman. But Whites should not connect slavery "with the Black Colour, and Liberty with the White," because "where false Ideas are twisted into our Minds, it is with Difficulty we get fair disentangled." In matters of right and equity, "the Colour of a Man avails nothing."[22]

Woolman's antiracism was ahead of its time, like his passionate sermons against poverty, animal cruelty, military conscription, and war. But Woolman's antislavery in the 1750s and 1760s was right on time for the American Revolution, a political upheaval that forced freedom fighters of Thomas Jefferson's generation to address their relationships with slavery.[23]

DR. THOMAS WALKER'S remedies did not work, and when his patient, the forty-nine-year-old father of Thomas Jefferson, died on August 17, 1757, it was an unbelievable sight for all who had heard the family lore of Peter Jefferson's strength. The fourteen-year-old Thomas had to run his own life. As the oldest male, he now headed the household, according to Virginia's patriarchal creed. But by all accounts, the thirty-seven-year-old Jane Randolph Jefferson did not look to her fourteen-year-old son for guidance, or to Dr. Walker, the estate's overseer. She became the manager of eight children, sixty-six enslaved people, and at least 2,750 acres. Jane Jefferson was sociable, fond of luxury, and meticulous about keeping the plantation's records—traits she bestowed upon Thomas.[24]

In 1760, Thomas Jefferson enrolled in the College of William & Mary, where he thoroughly immersed himself in Enlightenment thought, including its antislavery ideas. He studied under the newly hired twenty-six-year-old Enlightenment intellectual William Small of Scotland, who taught that reason, not religion, should command human affairs, a lesson that would inform Jefferson's views about government. Jefferson also read Buffon's *Natural History*, and he studied Francis Bacon, John Locke, and Isaac Newton, a trio he later called "the three greatest men the world has ever produced."

When Jefferson graduated in 1762, he entered the informal law school of Virginia's leading lawyer, George Wythe, well known for his legal mind and taste for luxury. Admitted to the bar at twenty-four years old in 1767, Jefferson stepped into the political whirlwind of the House of Burgesses, representing Albemarle County like his father had. The Burgesses protested England's latest imposition of taxes, prompting Virginia's royal governor to close their doors on May 17, 1769. Jefferson had been seated all of ten days.[25]

Even after he lost his seat, Jefferson actively participated in the growing hostilities to England and to slavery. He took the freedom suit of twenty-seven-year-old fugitive Samuel Howell. Virginia law prescribed thirty years of servitude for first-generation biracial children of free parents "to prevent that abominable mixture of white man or women with negroes or mulattoes." Howell was second generation, and Jefferson told the court that it was wicked to extend slavery, because "under the law of nature, all men are born free." Wythe, the opposing attorney, stood up to start his rejoinder. The judge ordered Wythe back down and ruled against Jefferson. The law in the colonies was still staunchly proslavery, and racial laws were becoming staunchly segregationist. But then, suddenly, a Boston panel of judges reversed the ideological trend.[26]

CHAPTER 8

Black Exhibits

AS THOMAS JEFFERSON supervised the building of his plantation near Charlottesville in October 1772, an enslaved nineteen-year-old woman up the coast gazed anxiously at eighteen gentlemen who identified publicly "as the most respectable characters in Boston." They all had been instructed to judge whether she had actually authored her famous poetry, especially its sophisticated Greek and Latin imagery. She saw familiar faces: Massachusetts governor Thomas Hutchinson, future governor James Bowdoin, mega-slaveholder John Hancock, and Cotton Mather's son Samuel, who is remembered as the last in the line of illustrious Mathers after Richard, Increase, and Cotton. Phillis Wheatley, the poet making her case before Samuel Mather and the other Bostonians, is now remembered as the first in the line of illustrious African American writers.[1]

Her enslavement story did not begin like that of many other African people. In 1761, Susanna Wheatley, the wife of tailor and financier John Wheatley, visited the newest storehouse of chained humanity in southwest Boston, not far from where Cotton Mather used to live. Captain Peter Gwinn of the *Phillis* had just arrived in Boston with seventy-five captives from Senegambia. Looking for a domestic servant, Susanna Wheatley scanned past the "several robust, healthy females" and laid her eyes on a sickly, naked little girl, covered by a dirty carpet. Some of the seven-year-old captive's front baby teeth had come out, possibly reminding Wheatley of her seven-year-old daughter, who had died. Susanna Wheatley was mourning the ninth anniversary of Sarah Wheatley's tragic death.[2]

Well before she became the most famous Black exhibit in the Western world, the young African girl was most likely purchased by Susanna and John to serve as a living reminder of Sarah Wheatley. Whatever name her Wolof relatives had given her, it was now lost to gray chains, bloody blue waters, and scribbled history. The Wheatleys renamed her after the slave ship that had brought her to them. From the beginning, Phillis Wheatley "had a child's place," suggested an early biographer, in the Wheatley's "house and in their hearts." Home-schooled, Phillis "never was looked on as a slave," explained Hannah Mather Crocker, the granddaughter of Cotton Mather.[3]

About four years after her arrival, eleven-year-old Phillis jotted down her first poem in English. It was a four-line tribute to the 1764 death (from smallpox) of the seventeen-year-old daughter of the Thachers, a distinguished Puritan family. Phillis was moved to write the poem after overhearing the Wheatleys lament the tragic death of Sarah Thacher.

By age twelve, Phillis had no problem reading Latin and Greek classics, English literature, and the Bible. She published her first poem, "On Messrs. Hussey and Coffin," in a December 1767 issue of the *Newport Mercury*. A storm had almost caused two local merchants to shipwreck off the Boston coast. The Wheatleys had one or both of the merchants over for dinner. Phillis listened intently as the merchant(s) told the story of "their narrow Escape."

In 1767, the fifteen-year-old composed "To the University of Cambridge," a poem that signified her longing to enter the all-White, all-male Harvard. She had already consumed the assimilationist ideas about her race that had probably been fed to her by the Wheatley family, saying, for instance, "'Twas but e'en now I left my native Shore / The sable Land of error's darkest night." Assimilationists were producing the racist idea of unenlightened Africa, and telling Wheatley and other Blacks that the light of America was a gift. The next year, Wheatley continued to marvel in her assimilation—and attack segregationist curse theory—in the poem, "On Being Brought from Africa to America."

Some view our sable race with scornful eye,
"Their coulour is a diabolical die,"
Remember, Christians, Negros, black as Cain,
May be refin'd, and join th' angelic train.

In 1771, Phillis Wheatley began assembling her work into a collection, including a number of inspirational poems on the increasing tensions between Britain and colonial America in the 1760s, which became her claim to fame. The Wheatleys figured that prospective publishers and buyers would need to be assured of Phillis's authenticity. This is why John Wheatley assembled such a powerhouse of Boston elites in 1772.[4]

Hardly believing an enslaved Black woman could fathom Greek and Latin, the eighteen men probably asked her to unpack the classical allusions in her poems. Whatever their questions were, Wheatley dazzled the skeptical tribunal of eighteen men. They signed the following assimilationist attestation: "We whose Names are under-written do assure the World, that the Poems specified in the following Page, were (as we verily believe) written by Phillis, a young Negro Girl, who was but a few Years since, brought an uncultivated Barbarian from Africa."[5]

The Wheatleys were delighted. But even with this attestation in hand, no American publisher was willing to alienate slaveholding consumers by publishing her by now famous poems, which were entering the abolitionist literature of the Revolutionary era. Phillis Wheatley had auditioned and proven the capability of Black humanity to the assimilationist scions of Boston. But unlike the publishers, these men did not have much to lose.

PHILLIS WHEATLEY WAS not the first so-called "uncultivated Barbarian" to be examined and exhibited. Throughout the eighteenth century's race for Enlightenment, assimilationists galloped around seeking out human experiments—"barbarians" to civilize into the "superior" ways of Europeans—to prove segregationists wrong, and sometimes to prove slaveholders wrong. As trained exotic creatures in the racist circus,

Black people could showcase Black capacity for Whiteness, for human equality, for something other than slavery. They could show they were capable of freedom—someday. Few worked as passionately to provide this human evidence, or put up as much money to experiment, as John Montagu, England's Second Duke of Montagu.

Early in the 1700s, the duke experimented on the youngest son of Jamaica's first freed Blacks to see if he could match the intellectual achievements of his White peers. The duke sent Francis Williams to an English academy and Cambridge University, where Francis equaled in intellectual attainments his peers who were similarly educated.

Sometime between 1738 and 1740, Williams returned home, probably donning a white wig of curls over his dark skin and assimilated mind. He opened a grammar school for slaveholders' children and penned fawning Latin odes to every colonial governor of Jamaica. His 1758 anti-Black poem to Governor George Haldane read: "Tho' dark the stream on which the tribute flows, / Not from the skin, but from the heart it rose."[6]

Celebrity Scottish philosopher David Hume learned about the Cambridge-trained Francis Williams. But neither Williams, nor the growing fashion of having Black boys as servants in England, nor Buffon's climate theory could change his mind about natural human hierarchy and Blacks' incapability for Whiteness. Hume declared his segregationist position emphatically. In 1753, he updated his popular critique of climate theory, "Of Natural Characters," adding the most infamous footnote in the history of racist ideas:

> I am apt to suspect the negroes and in general all the other species of men (for there are four or five different kinds) to be naturally inferior to the whites. There never was a civilized nation of any other complexion than white, nor even any individual eminent either in action or speculation. On the other hand, the most rude and barbarous of the Whites . . . have still something eminent about them. . . . Such a uniform and constant difference could not happen, in so many countries and ages, if nature had not made an original distinction between these breeds of men. . . . In Jamaica, indeed,

they talk of one Negro as a man of parts and learning; but it is likely
he is admired for slender accomplishments, like a parrot who speaks
a few words plainly.[7]

Hume strongly opposed slavery, but like many other abolitionists
of the Enlightenment period, he never saw his segregationist thinking
as contradicting his antislavery stance. Ignoring his antislavery position, proslavery theorists over the next few decades used David Hume
as a model, adopting his footnote to "Of Natural Characters" as their
international anthem.[8]

SIMILAR EXPERIMENTS OF educating young Black males were carried out
in America, and while some segregationists began to accept assimilationist ideas and even oppose slavery, few White Americans rejected
racist thinking altogether. On a visit home in 1763 during his nearly
two decades of residence in Europe, Benjamin Franklin saw some Black
exhibits at a Philadelphia school run by the Associates of Dr. Thomas
Bray. The London-based educational group had been named in 1731
after the deceased organizer of the Society for the Propagation of the
Gospel in Foreign Parts. Assessing the pupils, Franklin gained "a higher
opinion of the natural capacities of the black Race." Some Blacks could
"adopt our Language or Customs," he admitted. But that seemed to be
all Franklin could concede, probably recognizing that the production
of racist ideas was essential to substantiating slavery. Seven years later,
in lobbying the crown for Georgia's harsh slave code, Franklin argued
that the "majority" of slaves was "of a plotting Disposition, dark, sullen,
malicious, revengeful, and cruel in the highest Degree."[9]

For racists like Franklin, it proved difficult to believe that many
Blacks were capable of becoming another Francis Williams or Phillis Wheatley. Racists often understood this capable handful to be
"extraordinary Negroes." Joseph Jekyll actually began his 1805 biography of popular Afro-British writer and Duke of Montague protégé
Ignatius Sancho identifying him as "this extraordinary Negro." These

extraordinary Negros supposedly defied the laws of nature or nurture that standardized Black decadence. They were not ordinarily inferior like the "majority." This mind game allowed racists to maintain their racist ideas in the midst of individual Africans defying its precepts. It doomed from the start the strategy of exhibiting excelling Blacks to change racist minds. But this strategy of persuasion endured.[10]

After the Duke of Montagu died in 1749, Selina Hastings, known as the Countess of Huntingdon, replaced him as the principal shepherd of Black exhibits in the English-speaking world. If she had been a Puritan male, Cotton Mather would have adored this Methodist trailblazer, who promoted the writings of Christian Blacks as a testament of Black capability for conversion. Two years before her death, the countess sponsored Olaudah Equiano's aptly titled *Interesting Narrative* of his Nigerian birth, capture, enslavement, education, and emancipation in 1789. Her first and potentially most rewarding campaign was shepherding the inaugural slave narrative of Ukawsaw Gronniosaw (James Albert) into print in 1772. The countess almost certainly adored Gronniosaw's assimilationist plot: the more he conformed to slavery, superior European culture, and Christianity, and left behind his heathen, inferior upbringing in West Africa, the happier and holier he became. Since freedom had been colored white, Gronniosaw believed that in order to be truly free, he had to abandon his Nigerian traditions and become White.[11]

Britain's chief justice, Lord Mansfield, went further than the Duke of Montagu and Selina Hastings and freed a Virginia runaway, James Somerset, overshadowing Gronniosaw's pioneering slave narrative and Wheatley's tribunal in Boston in 1772. No one could be enslaved in England, Mansfield ruled, raising antislavery English law over proslavery colonial law. Fearing Mansfield's ruling could one day extend to the British colonies, the Somerset case prodded proslavery theorists out into the open and roused the transatlantic abolitionist movement. University of Pennsylvania professor and pioneering American physician Benjamin Rush anonymously issued a stinging antislavery pamphlet in Philadelphia in February 1773, using Phillis Wheatley's work to push the abolitionist case in America.

Rush praised the "singular genius" of Wheatley (without naming her). All the vices attributed to Black people, from idleness to treachery to theft, were "the offspring of slavery," Rush wrote. In fact, those unsubstantiated vices attributed to Black people were the offspring of the illogically racist mind. Were captives really lazier, more deceitful, and more crooked than their enslavers? It was the latter who forced others to work for them, treacherously whipping them when they did not, and stealing the proceeds of their labor when they did. In any case, Rush was the first activist to commercialize the persuasive, though racist, abolitionist theory that slavery made Black people inferior. Whether benevolent or not, any idea that suggests that Black people as a group are inferior, that something is wrong with Black people, is a racist idea. Slavery was killing, torturing, raping, and exploiting people, tearing apart families, snatching precious time, and locking captives in socioeconomic desolation. The confines of enslavement were producing Black people who were intellectually, psychologically, culturally, and behaviorally different, not inferior.

Benjamin Rush whacked down curse theory and pushed against a century of American theology, from Cotton Mather to Samuel Davies, in his pamphlet. "A Christian slave is a contradiction in terms," he argued, demanding that America "put a stop to slavery!" Reprinted and circulated in New York, Boston, London, and Paris, Rush's words consolidated the forces that in 1774 organized the Pennsylvania Abolition Society, the first known antislavery society of non-Africans in North America.[12]

TO FIND A publisher for her *Poems on Various Subjects*, Wheatley had to journey to London in the summer of 1773—where she was greeted and paraded and exhibited like an exotic rock star. There, she secured the financial support of the Countess of Huntingdon. In thanks, Wheatley dedicated her book, the first ever by an African American woman and the second by an American woman, to the countess. The publication of her poems in September 1773, a year after slavery had been outlawed in England and a few months after Rush's abolitionist pamphlet reached England, set off a social earthquake in London. Londoners condemned American slavery, and American slaveholders resisted the Londoners. And then abolitionists on both sides of the Atlantic more firmly resisted the rule of slaveholders in the colonies. In December 1773, the Boston Tea Party set off a political earthquake, and then England's Coercive Acts, and then the Patriots' resistance to British rule in the colonies. As the American Revolution budded, British commentators slammed the hypocrisy of Bostonians' boasts of Wheatley's ingenuity while keeping her enslaved. The poet was quickly freed.[13]

George Washington praised the talents of Phillis Wheatley. In France, Voltaire somehow got his hands on *Poems on Various Subjects.* Wheatley proved, Voltaire confessed, that Blacks could write poetry. This from a man who a few years prior had not been able to decide whether Blacks had developed from monkeys, or monkeys had developed from Blacks. Still, neither Wheatley nor Benjamin Rush nor any Enlightenment abolitionist was able to alter the position of proslavery segregationists. So long as there was slavery, there would be racist ideas justifying it. And there was nothing Wheatley and Rush could do to stop the production of racist proslavery ideas other than end slavery.

In September 1773, Philadelphia-based Caribbean absentee planter Richard Nisbet attacked Benjamin Rush for peddling "a single example of a negro girl writing a few silly poems, to prove that the blacks are not deficient to us in understanding." On November 15, 1773, a short, satirical essay appeared in the *Pennsylvania Packet* containing a rewritten biblical passage as evidence that God had fitted Africans for slavery. A few weeks later, someone released *Personal Slavery Established.* In attacking Rush (or satirizing Nisbet), the anonymous author plagiarized David Hume's footnote and wrote of the "five classes" of "Africans": "1st, Negroes, 2d, Ourang Outangs, 3d, Apes, 4th, Baboons, and 5th Monkeys."[14]

THOMAS JEFFERSON WAS spending even more time away from law in 1773 to oversee the building of his plantation, Monticello. But his mind, like the minds of many rich men in the colonies, remained on building a new nation. They were reeling from British debt, taxes, and mandates to trade within the empire. They had the most to gain in independence and the most to lose under British colonialism. Politically, they could not help but fear all those British abolitionists opposing American slavery, toasting Phillis Wheatley, and freeing the Virginia runaways. Financially, they could not help but salivate over all those non-British markets for their goods, and all those non-British products they could consume, like the world-renowned sugar that French enslavers forced Africans to grow in what is now Haiti. Rebel Virginia legislators met in Williamsburg in 1774.

One of Virginia's staunchest rebel legislators sent in a scorching freedom manifesto, *A Summary View of the Rights of British America*. "Can any one reason be assigned why 160,000 [British] electors" should make laws for 4 million equal Americans? His majesty, said the author, had rejected our "great object of desire" to abolish slavery and the slave trade, and thus disregarded "the rights of human nature, deeply wounded by this infamous practice." Some politicians folded over in disgust as they took in Thomas Jefferson's rhetorical gunshot at slavery. But "several of the author's admirers" loved his clever turn: he had blamed England for American slavery. Printed and circulated, *Summary View* piloted Jefferson into the clouds of national recognition.[15]

The British (and some Americans) immediately began questioning the authenticity of a slaveholder throwing a freedom manifesto at the world. No one could question the authenticity of Phillis Wheatley's 1774 words—"in every human Breast, God has implanted a Principle which we call love of freedom"—or the Connecticut Blacks, who a few years later had proclaimed, "We perceive by our own Reflection, that we are endowed with the same Faculties with our masters, and there is nothing that leads us to a Belief, or Suspicion, that we are any more obliged to serve them, than they us." All over Revolutionary America, African people were rejecting the racist compact that asserted that they were meant to be enslaved.[16]

Edward Long watched the rising tidal wave of abolitionism and antiracism from his massive sugar plantation in Jamaica. He realized that a new racial justification was badly needed to save slavery from being abolished. So, in 1774, he breathed new life into polygenesis by issuing his massive book *History of Jamaica*. Why did it remain so difficult to see that Black people constituted "a different species"? he asked. The ape had "in form a much nearer resemblance to the Negroe race, than the latter bear to White men." Just as Black people conceived a passion for White people, apes "conceive[d] a passion for the Negroe women," Long reasoned, as John Locke once had.

Long dedicated a full chapter to discrediting the ability of Jamaica's old Francis Williams, with, he assured, "the impartiality that becomes me." Williams's talents were the result of "the Northern air" of Europe, he said. Long then contradictorily questioned Williams's talents, quoting Hume's footnote. Long assailed Williams for looking "down with sovereign contempt on his fellow Blacks," as if Long did not share that contempt. Williams self-identified as "a *white* man acting under a *black* skin," as Long described it. Williams's proverbial saying, he said, was, "Shew me *a Negroe*, and I will shew you *a thief*."[17]

Later that year, Lord Kames, a Scottish judge and philosopher and one of the engines of the Scottish Enlightenment, followed Long's *History* with *Sketches of the History of Man*. The devastating treatise attacked assimilationist thinking and tore apart monogenesis, which assumed that all the races were one species. Kames's book carried more force than Long's. Few thinkers in the Western world had the intellectual pedigree of Lord Kames in 1774. He paraphrased Voltaire, another supporter of polygenesis, explaining, "There are different [species] of men as well as of dogs: a mastiff differs not more from a spaniel, than a white man from a negro." Climates created the species, but they could not change one color to another, Kames maintained. Dismissing Adam and Eve, Kames based his multiple creations on the Tower of Babel story in Genesis.[18]

Polygenesists loved *Sketches*. Christian monogenesists bristled at its blasphemy. But the concept of different creation stories and different species started making sense to more and more people in the late eighteenth century as they tried to come to grips with racial difference. How else could they explain such glaring differences in skin color, in culture, in wealth, and in the degree of freedom people enjoyed?

If someone had told Lord Kames that a German doctoral student, fifty-six years his junior, would lead the initial charge against his theory of polygenesis, the old jurist would probably have laughed. And he was known for his sense of humor. Unlike Lord Kames, "I have written this book quite unprejudiced," the audacious young Johann Friedrich Blumenbach claimed in On the Natural Variety of Mankind. Environment—not separate creations—caused the "variety in humans," the German wrote in 1775. Blumenbach followed Linnaeus in allotting four "classes of inhabitants," or races. "The first and most important to us . . . is that of Europe," he theorized. "All these nations regarded as a whole are white in colour, and if compared with the rest, beautiful in form."[19]

A full-blown debate on the origins of humans had exploded into the European world during the American Revolution. Backing up Blumenbach against Long and Lord Kames was none other than the German philosopher Immanuel Kant, soon to be widely heralded for his legendary Critique of Pure Reason. Kant lectured on "the rule of Buffon," that all humans were one species from the "same natural genus." Europe was the cradle of humanity, "where man . . . must have departed the least from his original formation." The inhabitant of Europe had a "more beautiful body, works harder, is more jocular, more controlled in his passions, more intelligent than any other race of people in the world," Kant lectured. "Humanity is at its greatest perfection in the race of whites."[20]

American intellectuals followed this debate between monogenesis and polygenesis in the same way students would follow the debates of their professors. And in following the racist debate, American intellectuals followed the racist debaters. American enslavers and secular intellectuals most likely lined up behind Lord Kames and other polygenesists. Abolitionists and theologians more likely lined up behind Immanuel Kant and other monogenesists. But these American polygenesists and monogenesists had no problem coming together to inflame public sentiment against England and dismiss their own atrocities against enslaved Africans.

One man, Samuel Johnson, had no problem calling out Americans on this hypocrisy. Johnson was perhaps the most illustrious literary voice in British history. When he opined about public debates, intellectuals in America and England alike paid attention. George Washington, Thomas Jefferson, and Benjamin Franklin were among those who admired Johnson's writings. Johnson did not return the admiration. He loathed Americans' hatred of authority, their greedy rushes for wealth, their dependence on enslavement, and their way of teaching Christianity to make Blacks docile: "I am willing to love all mankind, except an American," he once said.[21]

Benjamin Franklin had spent years across the water lobbying English power for a relaxation of its colonial policies. He was arguing that England was enslaving Americans, and regularly using the analogy that England was making "American whites black." All along, Samuel Johnson hated this racist analogy. As Franklin sailed back to America at the outbreak of the American Revolutionary War in 1775, Johnson released *Taxation No Tyranny*. He defended the Coercive Acts, judged Americans as inferior to the British, and advocated the arming of enslaved Africans. "How is it," Johnson asked, "that we hear the loudest yelps for liberty among the drivers of negroes?" Someone in the colonies had to officially answer the great Samuel Johnson. That someone was Thomas Jefferson.[22]

CHAPTER 9

Created Equal

ON JUNE 7, 1776, the delegates at the Second Continental Congress in Philadelphia decided to draft an independence document. The task fell to a thirty-three-year-old marginal delegate, who distinguished himself as a willing and talented writer as he carried out their instructions. The older and more distinguished delegates felt they had more important things to do: addressing the convention, drafting state constitutions, and wartime planning.[1]

For years, European intellectuals like France's Buffon and England's Samuel Johnson had projected Americans, their ways, their land, their animals, and their people as naturally inferior to everything European. Thomas Jefferson disagreed. At the beginning of the Declaration of Independence, he paraphrased the Virginia constitution, indelibly penning: "all Men are created equal."

It is impossible to know for sure whether Jefferson meant to include his enslaved laborers (or women) in his "all Men." Was he merely emphasizing the equality of White Americans and the English? Later in the document, he did scold the British for "exciting those very *people* to rise in arms among us"—those "people" being resisting Africans. Did Jefferson insert *"created* equal" as a nod to the swirling debate between monogenesis and polygenesis? Even if Jefferson believed all groups to be "created equal," he never believed the antiracist creed that all human groups *are* equal. But his "all Men are created equal" was revolutionary nonetheless; it even propelled Vermont and Massachusetts to abolish slavery. To uphold polygenesis and slavery, six

104

southern slaveholding states inserted "All *free*men are created equal" into their constitutions.[2]

Continuing the Declaration, Jefferson maintained that "Men" were "endowed by their creator with inherent and inalienable rights; that among these are life, liberty, & the pursuit of happiness." As a holder of nearly two hundred people with no known plans to free them, Thomas Jefferson authored the heralded American philosophy of freedom. What did it mean for Jefferson to call "liberty" an "inalienable right" when he enslaved people? It is not hard to figure out what Native Americans, enslaved Africans, and indentured White servants meant when they demanded liberty in 1776. But what about Jefferson and other slaveholders like him, whose wealth and power were dependent upon their land and their slaves? Did they desire unbridled freedom to enslave and exploit? Did they perceive any reduction in their power to be a reduction in their freedom? For these rich men, freedom was not the power to make choices; freedom was the power to create choices. England created the choices, the policies American elites had to abide by, just as planters created choices and policies that laborers had to follow. Only power gave Jefferson and other wealthy White colonists freedom from England. For Jefferson, power came before freedom. Indeed, power creates freedom, not the other way around—as the powerless are taught.

"To secure these rights," Jefferson continued, "it is the right of the people . . . to institute a new government . . . organizing its powers in such form, as to them shall seem most likely to effect their safety & happiness." As Jefferson sat forward on his Windsor chair and penned this thrilling call for revolutionary action, thousands of Africans were taking matters into their own hands, too, running away from their plantations, setting up their own governments on the frontier, or fighting with the British—all to "effect their safety & happiness." In South Carolina, there emerged a three-sided conflict, with as many as 20,000 Africans asserting their own interests. An estimated two-thirds of enslaved Africans in Georgia ran away. According to Jefferson's own calculations, Virginia lost as many as 30,000 enslaved Africans in a single year. Of course, racist planters could not admit that Black runaways were self-reliant enough to effect their own safety and happiness—to be free. South Carolina planters blamed British soldiers for "stealing" Blacks or persuading them to "desert" their masters.[3]

Thomas Jefferson only really handed revolutionary license to his band of wealthy, White, male revolutionaries. He criminalized runaways in the Declaration of Independence, and he silenced women. Boston delegate John Adams sent a letter home to his wife, Abigail, to "laugh" at her strivings for women's rights. White "children and Apprentices were disobedient" as a result of "our struggle," Adams said the delegates had been told. "Indians slighted their guardians and Negroes grew insolent to their Masters." Now she had informed him that women were also "discontented."[4]

After outlining more justifications for independence in his Declaration, Jefferson listed the "long train of abuses & usurpations" by the British monopolists, like "cutting off our trade with all parts of the world." The inability of American merchants and planters to do business with merchants and planters outside the British Empire had checked their freedoms in buying and selling African people to and from anyone, in buying cheaper or better products from non-British sources, in selling their slave-grown crops and manufactured goods outside of Britannica, and in escaping the subjugation of British merchants and banks. Jefferson and his freedom-fighting class of aspiring international free traders gained a powerful ally in 1776. Scottish philosopher Adam Smith condemned England's trade acts for constraining the "free" market in his instant best seller, *The Wealth of Nations*. To this founding father of capitalist economics, the wealth of nations stemmed from a nation's productive capacity, a productive capacity African nations lacked. "All the inland parts of Africa," he scripted, "seem in all ages of the world to have been in the same barbarous and uncivilized state in which we find them at present." Meanwhile, Smith praised Americans for "contriving a new form of government for an extensive empire, which . . . seems very likely to become, one of the greatest and most formidable that ever was in the world." The founding fathers beamed reading Adam Smith's prediction. Jefferson later called *Wealth of Nations* "the best book extant" on political economy.[5]

Jefferson saved the worst of the king's abuses for last in his Declaration. Ever the lawyer, ever the wordsmith, he fought back against Samuel Johnson's charge of American hypocrisy. The English crown, Jefferson wrote, which had prevented Americans from abolishing slavery, was now freeing and arming enslaved Africans to maintain British enslavement over Americans, "thus paying off former crimes committed against the LIBERTIES of one people, with crimes which [the king] urged them to commit against the LIVES of another."[6]

Rhode Island pastor Samuel Hopkins, an antislavery Puritan, would have found Jefferson's passage laughable. He had just sent the congress *A Dialogue concerning the Slavery of the Africans*. Americans' so-called enslavement to the British was "lighter than a feather" compared to Africans' enslavement to Americans, Hopkins argued. The electrifying antiracist pamphlet nearly overshadowed the Quakers' demand in 1776 for all Friends to manumit their slaves or face banishment. "Our education has filled us with strong prejudices against them," Hopkins professed, "and led us to consider them, not as our brethren, or in any degree on a level with us; but as quite another species of animals, made only to serve us and our children." Hopkins became the first major Christian leader outside of the Society of Friends to forcefully oppose slavery, but he sat lonely on the pew of antislavery in 1776. Other preachers stayed away from the pew, and so did the delegates declaring independence. No one had to tell them that their revolutionary avowals were leaking in contradictions. Nothing could persuade slaveholding American patriots to put an end to their inciting proclamations of British slavery, or to their enriching enslavement of African people. Forget contradictions. Both were in their political and economic self-interest.[7]

By July 2, 1776, the resolution to declare independence had passed. The delegates then peered over Jefferson's draft like barbers over a head of hair. Every time they trimmed, changed, or added something, the hypersensitive Jefferson sank deeper into his chair. Benjamin Franklin, sitting next to him, failed to cheer him up. The delegates cut Jefferson's long passage calling the English hypocrites. Apparently, delegates from South Carolina and Georgia disliked

Jefferson's characterization of slavery as a "cruel war against human nature"; that language threatened the foundation of their vast estates. The delegates finished making their revisions of the Declaration of Independence on July 4, 1776.[8]

OVER THE NEXT five years, the fighting remained pitched. But the British failed to crush the revolt. On January 5, 1781, in one of their last-ditch efforts, the Redcoats reached the outskirts of Richmond. British soldiers were hunting Virginia's governor as if he were a runaway. With 10,000 acres of land in his possession to choose from, Governor Thomas Jefferson hid his family on an inherited property about ninety miles southwest of Monticello. There, in hiding, Jefferson finally found the time to answer the twenty-three "Queries" that French diplomat François Barbé-Marbois had sent to the thirteen American governors in 1780.

The Frenchman asked for information on each state's history, government, natural resources, geography, and population. Only a few responded, none as comprehensively as Thomas Jefferson. A new member of Philadelphia's American Philosophical Society, Jefferson had collected thousands of books for his Monticello library and enjoyed a scholarly challenge. He titled his book of answers *Notes on the State of Virginia*. He wrote for French diplomats and intellectuals as well as close friends in America. He sent Barbé-Marbois the manuscript by the end of 1781.

With no intention to publish, Jefferson unabashedly expressed his views on Black people, and in particular on potentially freed Black people. "Incorporating the [freed] blacks into the state" was out of the question, he declared. "Deep rooted prejudices entertained by the whites; ten thousand recollections, by the blacks, of the injuries they have sustained; new provocations; the real distinctions which nature has made; and many other circumstances, will divide us into parties, and produce convulsions, which will probably never end but in the extermination of the one or the other race." This hodgepodge of thoughts was classic Jefferson, classically both antislavery and anti-abolition—with a segregationist dose of nature's distinctions, and an antiracist dose acknowledging White prejudice and discrimination.[9]

Revolutionary War general George Washington had a different take on the prejudices. When asked to join an antislavery petition campaign in 1785, he did not think the time was right. "It would be dangerous to make a frontal attack on a prejudice which is beginning to decrease," Washington advised. Prejudice beginning to decrease in 1785? However General Washington came to this conclusion, the soon-to-be first president sounded one of the first drumbeats of supposed racial progress to drown out the passionate arguments of antiracism.[10]

Thomas Jefferson did propose a frontal attack on slavery in *Notes on the State of Virginia*, a plan he would endorse for the rest of his life: the mass schooling, emancipation, and colonization of Africans back to Africa. Jefferson, who enslaved Blacks at Monticello, listed "the real distinctions which nature has made," that is, those traits that he believed made free Black incorporation into the new nation impossible. Whites were more beautiful, he wrote, as shown by Blacks' "preference of them." He was paraphrasing Edward Long (and John Locke) in the passage—but it was still ironic that the observation came from the pen of a man who may have already preferred a Black woman.[11]

Black people had a memory on par with Whites, Jefferson continued, but "in reason [were] much inferior." He then paused to mask his racist ideas in scientific neutrality: "It would be unfair to follow them to Africa for this investigation. We will consider them here, on the same stage with the whites, and where the facts are not apocryphal on which a judgment is to be formed." On this "same stage," he could "never . . . find that a black had uttered a thought above the level of plain narration; never saw an elementary trait of painting or sculpture." "Religion," he said, "indeed has produced a Phyllis Wheatley; but it could not produce a poet."[12]

With *Notes on the State of Virginia*, Thomas Jefferson emerged as the preeminent American authority on Black intellectual inferiority. This status would persist over the next fifty years. Jefferson did not mention the innumerable enslaved Africans who learned to be highly intelligent blacksmiths, shoemakers, bricklayers, coopers, carpenters, engineers, manufacturers, artisans, musicians, farmers, midwives, physicians, overseers, house managers, cooks, and bi- and trilingual translators—all of the workers who made his Virginia plantation and many others almost entirely self-sufficient. Jefferson had to ignore his own advertisements for skilled runaways and the many advertisements from other planters calling for the return of their valuable skilled captives, who were "remarkably smart and sensible," and "very ingenious at any work." One wonders whether Jefferson really believed his own words. Did Jefferson really believe Black people were smart in slavery and stupid in freedom?[13]

Notes on the State of Virginia was replete with other contradictory ideas about Black people. "They are at least as brave, and more adventuresome" than Whites, because they lacked the forethought to see "danger till it be present," Jefferson wrote. Africans felt love more, but they felt pain less, he said, and "their existence appears to participate more of sensation than reflection." That is why they were disposed "to sleep when abstracted from their diversions, and unemployed in labour. An animal whose body is at rest, and who does not reflect, must be disposed to sleep of course." But on the previous page, Jefferson cast Blacks as requiring "less sleep. A black, after hard labour through the day, will be induced by the slightest amusements to sit up till midnight." In Jefferson's vivid imagination, lazy Blacks *desired* to sleep more than Whites, but, as physical savants, they *required* less sleep.[14]

While Jefferson confidently labeled enslaved Africans as inferior to Roman slaves, for Native Americans he cried that the comparison "would be unequal." While confidently making distinctions between Blacks and Whites, Jefferson equated Native Americans and Whites. As he told François-Jean de Chastellux, who served as liaison between the French and American militaries during the Revolutionary War, Native Americans were "in body and mind equal to the whiteman." He "supposed the blackman in his present state, might not be so": "But it would be hazardous to affirm that, equally cultivated for a few generations, he would not become so." For Jefferson, clarity always seemed to be lacking when it came to racial conceptions. This note proved to be the clearest expression of his assimilationist ideas.

The reason for Native Americans having fewer children than Whites was "not in a difference of nature, but of circumstance," Jefferson argued. For Black people, the opposite was true. "The blacks," he said, "whether originally a distinct race, or made distinct by time and circumstances, are inferior to the whites in the endowments both of body and mind." The ambitious politician, maybe fearful of alienating potential friends, maybe torn between Enlightenment antislavery and American proslavery, maybe honestly unsure, did not pick sides between polygenesists and monogenesists, between segregationists and assimilationists, between slavery and freedom. But he did pick the side of racism.[15]

IN 1782, JEFFERSON had no plans to publish *Notes on the State of Virginia*. He was busy putting his life back together, a life torn apart by thirteen years of public service, and by months of being hunted by the British. War had shattered Jefferson's past. Martha Jefferson's death on September 6 of that year shattered his future. He had planned to retire and grow old as a planter and scholar in the seclusion of Monticello next to his wife. Overnight, the sanctuary of Monticello became the caged pen of Monticello, bordered by bars of wounding memories. He had to escape. His friends in Congress found a solution.[16]

On August 6, 1784, Jefferson arrived in Paris for a new diplomatic stint eager to take advantage of the shopping, the shows, the culture, and the trading prospects. The same week that he made contact with the French foreign minister, Jefferson sent instructions to Monticello to speed up production. He figured that his own captives, and his nation's captives, would be tasked for the foreseeable future with producing enough tobacco for French merchants to pay back British creditors. At the same time, Jefferson was busy telling abolitionists, "Nobody wishes more ardently [than me] to see an abolition." Jefferson loathed slavery almost as much as he feared losing American freedom to British banks, or losing his pampered lifestyle in Monticello.

He liked and disliked both freedom and slavery, and he never divorced himself from either.[17]

Economic diplomacy was Jefferson's official job. His hobby was science, and he partnered with Benjamin Franklin, who was also in Paris, to defend America from French onslaughts of American inferiority. Jefferson brought his still unpublished *Notes on the State of Virginia* and "an uncommonly large panther skin" in his baggage. He had two hundred English copies of his *Notes* printed in Paris in 1785. He sent the manuscript to French intellectuals, to Benjamin Franklin, and to John Adams, James Madison, and James Monroe. A copy reached a devious printer who without Jefferson's approval translated it into French in 1786. Jefferson arranged for an English edition to be released in London on his own terms in the summer of 1787. Thereafter, *Notes on the State of Virginia* would become the most consumed American nonfiction book until well into the mid-nineteenth century.

Count Constantine Volney, known in France as Herodotus's biographer, was putting his finishing touches on *Travels in Syria and Egypt* when he read *Notes* and befriended its author. When Volney first saw the Sphinx in Egypt, he remembered Herodotus—the foremost historian in ancient Greece—describing the "black and frizzled hair" of the ancient Egyptians. Making the connection to the present, Volney mused, "To the race of negroes, at present our slaves, and the objects of our extreme contempt, we owe our arts, sciences, and even the use of speech itself." American racists ridiculed Volney as an ignorant worshiper of Black people when he visited the United States in 1796. Not Jefferson. He invited Volney and his antiracist ideas and his history of Black ancient Egypt to Monticello. How could Jefferson—the authority of Black intellectual inferiority—look to Volney as the authority of ancient Egypt? Clearly, scientific truths were forever tugging at his self-interests.[18]

Thomas Jefferson visited southern France and northern Italy in February 1787. "If I should happen to die in Paris I will beg of you to send me here," Jefferson wrote in awe of the beautiful countryside of Aix-en-Provence. When he returned to Paris in June, he may have noticed a copy of the year's annual oration of the American

Philosophical Society (APS), which had been delivered by Princeton theologian Samuel Stanhope Smith. The annual APS oration was the most heralded scholarly lecture in the new nation, and APS members were a who's who of American power: men like Ben Franklin of Pennsylvania, Alexander Hamilton of New York, and Virginia's Jefferson, James Madison, and George Washington. Smith's oration before APS stood for all intents and purposes as the first great domestic challenge to Jefferson's *Notes*.[19]

Smith had been pondering assimilationist climate theory for some time. He may have learned it first from Buffon, or from James Bowdoin's opening oration of the newly established American Academy of Arts and Sciences in Boston on May 4, 1780. As the founder and first president of the Academy, as one of Massachusetts' political leaders, Bowdoin's address to some of the nation's leading intellectuals and politicians in Boston probably circulated down to Smith's New Jersey. If the "natural faculties" of Europeans and Africans were "unequal, as probably is the case," Bowdoin proclaimed, then we know the reason: climate. Hot climates destroyed the mind and body. In moderate climates in northern America and Europe, humankind would be "capable of greater exertions of both mind and body." Samuel Stanhope Smith may also have learned climate theory from John Morgan, the founder of the University of Pennsylvania's medical school. Morgan exhibited two whitening two-year-olds to APS members in 1784. "We meet with few negroes of so beautiful a form," Morgan said at the time.[20]

Samuel Stanhope Smith titled his 1787 lecture "An Essay on the Causes of the Variety of Complexion and Figure in the Human Species." He described two causes of human variety: climate and state of society. Hot weather bred physical disorders—like kinky hair, which was "the farthest removed from the ordinary laws of nature." Cold weather was "followed by a contrary effect": it cured these ailments, Smith suggested, leaning on Buffon.

In addition to changing climate, a change in the state of society could remove the stamp of Blackness, Smith maintained. Just look at the house slaves. In their nearness to White society, they were acquiring "the agreeable and regular features" of civilized society—light complexion, straight hair, thin lips. "Europeans, and Americans are, the most beautiful people in the world, chiefly, because their state of society is the most improved." In the end, this assimilationist made sure to disassociate himself from Lord Kames and polygenesis. From only "one pair"—Adam and Eve in Europe—"all of the families of the earth [have] sprung," Smith closed.[21]

Using European features as the standard of measurement, Smith judged light skin and thin lips on Blacks to be more beautiful than dark skin and full lips. He also distinguished between "good hair"—the straighter and longer the better—and "bad hair," the kinkier and shorter the worse. He positioned biracial people as superior to African people.

In slavery and freedom, as usually the offspring of planters, biracial people oftentimes benefited from a higher social status than people of only African descent, and often they experienced less discrimination as well. Biracial people were probably more likely to have to perform the backbreaking tasks of the household, and they were often under closer supervision by planters than the slaves in the field, which could be just as backbreaking in a way, if not sexually abusive. Despite their elevated status, they still felt the terror of the enslavers, and some anti-racist biracial people partnered with Africans to resist White supremacy. Others were no different from White racists in their thinking, discriminating against dark-skinned Blacks, and rationalizing the discrimination, and their elevated status, through notions of their own superiority. In the late eighteenth century, biracial people in Charleston barred dark-skinned people from their business network, the Brown Fellowship Society. In response, the Society of Free Dark Men appeared in that South Carolina town.[22]

The American Philosophical Society thanked Samuel Stanhope Smith for "his ingenious and learned Oration" in the minutes. After outlining the position of climate theorists—seemingly the dominant strain of racial thought among northern elites—Smith added a long appendix to the published pamphlet attacking Lord Kames and polygenesis. Races were not fixed and "fitted for different climates," Smith argued. "The Goths, the Mogus, the Africans have become infinitely meliorated by changing those skies, for which it is said they were peculiarly fitted by nature." Smith breathlessly asserted that the slave trade—the cause of millions of deaths—had substantially improved the African condition.[23]

Samuel Stanhope Smith joined those preeminent intellectuals in Boston's American Academy of Arts and Sciences and Philadelphia's American Philosophical Society in attacking polygenesists, in reviving climate theory in America. His scholarly defense of scripture was quickly printed in Philadelphia, in London, and in Lord Kames's backyard, Edinburgh. By the time he sat down in Princeton's presidential chair in 1795, he had amassed an international scholarly reputation.

FROM HIS HOME in Paris, Jefferson was closely following—but not closely influencing—the events of the Constitutional Convention. It had begun in Philadelphia on May 25, 1787, months after Samuel Stanhope Smith had addressed some of the delegates on race. Jefferson's powerful Declaration of Independence had resulted in years of violent struggle against the British, and then in a weak and powerless Confederation of states. Faced with an empty national treasury, erratic trade policies, international disrespect, and fears of the union falling apart, American leaders returned to the nation-building table. If it was left up to the delegates, some of whom were APS members, Smith's annual oration would have been the Philadelphia convention's only serious discussion of race and slavery that year.

In fact, delegates made it clear that slavery would be left out of the conversation. Antislavery discussions were disallowed in drawing up what the writers were pegging as humankind's ultimate constitution of freedom. It only took a few weeks, though, for slavery and its baggage to creep into the constitutional deliberations. Once opened, the question of slavery never left.

The constitutional debate centered on the issue of the states' representation in the federal legislature. On a scorching hot June 11, 1787, South Carolina delegate John Rutledge rose at Independence Hall. The former South Carolina governor and future chief justice of the US Supreme Court motioned once again for representation based on taxes (since slaveholding states paid disproportionately high taxes, and thus would monopolize political power). Rutledge was seconded once more by fellow South Carolinian Major Pierce Butler, owner of five hundred people by 1793. Pennsylvania's James Wilson, another future Supreme Court justice, practically forecasted Rutledge's motion and had a plan. Rutledge may have been in on that plan.

Wilson offered an alternative: "representation in proportion to the whole number of white & other free Citizens & inhabitants . . . and three-fifths of all other persons not comprehended in the foregoing description, except Indians not paying taxes." The only delegate who pounced on the three-fifths "compromise" was Massachusetts abolitionist and future vice president Elbridge Gerry. "Blacks are property, and are used [in the South] . . . as horses and cattle are [in the North]," Gerry stammered out. So "why should their representation be increased to the southward on account of the number of slaves, [rather] than [on the basis of] horses or oxen to the north?"

Gerry looked around. Silence looked back. No one was prepared to answer the unanswerable. A vote sprung from the quietness: 9–2 in favor of the three-fifths clause. A deadlocked Massachusetts abstained. Only New Jersey and Delaware voted against Wilson's compromise.[24]

Equating enslaved Blacks to three-fifths of all other (White) persons matched the ideology of racists on both sides of the aisle. Both assimilationists and segregationists argued, yet with different premises and conclusions, that Black people were simultaneously human and subhuman. Assimilationists stridently declared the capability of sub-White, sub-human Blacks to become whole, five-fifths, White, one day. For segregationists, three-fifths offered a mathematical approximation of inherent and permanent Black inferiority. They may have disagreed on the rationale and the question of permanence, but seemingly all embraced Black inferiority—and in the process enshrined the power of slaveholders and racist ideas in the nation's founding document.

By September 17, 1787, delegates in Philadelphia had extracted "slave" and "slavery" from the signed US Constitution to hide their racist enslavement policies. These policies hardly fit with securing "the Blessing of Liberty to ourselves and our Posterity." Then again, for the delegates, slavery brought freedom. And other policies of the US Constitution, such as empowering federal troops to suppress slave revolts and deliver up runaways like "criminals," ensured slavery's continuance. The language was taken from the Northwest Ordinance, which had been issued earlier in the year. It forbade Blacks, slave or free, in territories north of Ohio and east of Mississippi. After a bitter debate, the delegates in Philadelphia put in place provisions for eliminating the slave trade in twenty years, a small triumph, since only Georgia and North Carolina allowed slave imports in the summer of 1787.[25]

ON JULY 15, 1787, eight-year-old Polly Jefferson and fourteen-year-old Sally Hemings reached Jefferson's Paris doorstep. Sally Hemings had come to Monticello as an infant in 1773 as part of Martha Jefferson's inheritance from her father. John Wayles had fathered six children with his biracial captive Elizabeth Hemings. Sally was the youngest. By 1787, she was reportedly "very handsome, [with] long straight hair down her back," and she accompanied Polly to Paris instead of an "old nurse."[26]

As his peers penned the US Constitution, Jefferson began a sexual relationship with Sally Hemings. Her older brother James, meanwhile, was training as a chef in Paris to satisfy Jefferson's gustatory desires. Hemings was more or less forced to settle for the overtures of a sexually aggressive forty-four-year-old (Jefferson also pursued a married local Frenchwoman at the time). Jefferson pursued Hemings as he arranged for the publication of Notes in London. He did not revise his previously stated opinions about Blacks; nor did he remove the passage about Whites being more beautiful than Blacks.[27]

Jefferson had always assailed interracial relationships between White women and Black or biracial men. Before arriving in Paris, he had lobbied, unsuccessfully, for Virginia's White women to be banished (instead of merely fined) for bearing the child of a Black or biracial man. Even after his measure was defeated, even after his relations with Hemings began, and even after the relations matured and he had time to reflect on his own hypocrisy, Jefferson did not stop proclaiming his public position. "Amalgamation with the other color, produces degradation to which no lover of his country, no lover of excellence in the human character, can innocently consent," he wrote in 1814, after he had fathered several biracial children. Like so many men who spoke out against "amalgamation" in public, and who degraded Black or biracial women's beauty in public, Jefferson hid his actual views in the privacy of his mind and bedroom.[28]

In 1789, Jefferson had a front-row seat to the anti-royal unrest in Paris that launched the French Revolution. He assisted his friend the Marquis de Lafayette in writing the Declaration of the Rights of Man and of the Citizen, adopted in August, weeks before his departure. But while putting the starting touches on the French Revolution and the finishing touches on the American Revolution, Jefferson had to deal with a revolt from sixteen-year-old Sally Hemings. She was pregnant with his child, refused to return to slavery, and planned to petition French officials for her freedom. Jefferson did the only thing he could do: "He promised her extraordinary privileges, and made a solemn pledge that her children should be freed," according to an account Hemings told their son Madison. "In consequence of his promise, on which she implicitly relied, she returned with him to Virginia," Madison wrote in his diary. Hemings gave birth to at least five and possibly as many as seven children from Jefferson, a paternity confirmed by DNA tests and documents proving they were together nine months prior to the birth of each of Sally's children. Some of the children died young, but Jefferson kept his word and freed their remaining children when they reached adulthood.[29]

Upon his return from Paris, Jefferson agreed, after some wavering, to become the first US secretary of state in George Washington's inaugural administration. Beginning his tenure on March 22, 1790, Jefferson quickly felt uncomfortable surrounded by all those aristocratic, anti-republican cabinet members in America's first political party, the Federalists. Vice President John Adams was questioning the effectiveness of "equal laws." Secretary of the Treasury Alexander Hamilton was quietly calling for a monarchy; he wanted to hand control of the economy over to financiers, and he pushed for close (or, in Jefferson's conception, *subordinate*) economic ties to Britain. Jefferson took solace watching the French Revolution. That is, until it spilled over into Haiti. In 1790, Haiti's enslavers saw the Declaration of the Rights of Man (Article 1: "Men are born and remain free and equal in rights") as a green light for their independence drive and for their demands for new trade relations to increase their wealth. Free and affluent biracial activists numbering almost 30,000 (slightly less than the White population) started driving for their civil rights. Close to half a million enslaved Africans, who were producing about half the world's sugar and coffee in the most profitable European colony in the world, heard these curious cries for rights and liberty among the island's free people. On August 22, 1791, enslaved Africans revolted, inspired in more ways than one by Vodou priest Dutty Boukman. They emerged as the fourth faction in the civil war between White royalists, White independence seekers, and free biracial activists.[30]

It was a civil war that no slaveholder, including Thomas Jefferson, wanted enslaved Africans to win. If these Black freedom fighters could declare their independence and win it on the richest soil of the Americas, then their nation would become the hemispheric symbol of freedom, not Jefferson's United States. Enslaved peoples everywhere would be inspired by that symbol and fight for their freedom, and there was nothing that racist ideas could do anymore to stop them.

CHAPTER 10

Uplift Suasion

AS FREED PEOPLE in Haiti were warring against French re-enslavers, a prominent free Black man in Maryland sat down to write to Thomas Jefferson. The man's grandmother, Mary Welsh, had come to Maryland in the 1680s as an indentured servant. After finishing her indenture, she acquired some land and two Black captives, freed them, and married one, named Bannaka. This interracial family defied White males' insistence that White women not marry Black men. Their biracial daughter, Mary, married an enslaved man named Robert. Mary and Robert birthed a free son in 1731 and named him Benjamin. As Benjamin came of age, "all he liked was to dive into books," remembered an observer. Friendly White neighbors were constantly loaning him books. Proceeds from growing tobacco on his inherited farm—he was as adept a farmer as anything else—gave Benjamin Banneker the time to read and think and write.[1]

Few free Blacks had the leisure time to read and write in Banneker's day. As soon as they shook off slavery's shackles, the shackles of discrimination clamped down on them. Northern states, in gradually eliminating slave labor during the Revolutionary era, made almost no moves—gradual or otherwise—to end racial discrimination and thereby racist ideas. Proposals to ensure the manageability of African people by former masters, as if they were more naturally slave than free, shadowed abolition proposals. Discriminatory policies were a feature of almost every emancipation law.[2]

Debates about the future of slavery and the characteristics of enslaved Blacks, both in Congress and between prominent intellectuals, only reinforced the climate of racism and discrimination that plagued free Blacks like Banneker. Benjamin Franklin, who had become head of the Pennsylvania Abolition Society, spent some of his last days trying to resolve the world's greatest political contradiction: America's freedom and slavery. In early 1790, the eighty-four-year-old trudged before Congress to give what one narrator called "a memorial." Christianity and the "political creed of Americans" demand the removal of this "inconsistency from the land of liberty," Franklin implored. He conceded that Blacks too often fell below "the common standard of the human species," but he urged his peers to "step to the very verge of the power vested in you."

Franklin's speech and a torrent of Quaker emancipation petitions aroused a bitter boxing match over slavery in the First US Congress. It carried on for months after Franklin's death on April 17, 1790. Black people were "indolent, improvident, averse to labor; when emancipated, they would either starve or plunder," one congressman argued, defending the interests of southern planters who were dependent on slave labor. Blacks were "an inferior race even to the Indians," another insisted. A northern congressman held that southerners would never submit to a general emancipation without civil war. As they argued over slavery, congressmen paused to unite for the first Naturalization Act on March 26, 1790, which limited citizenship to "free white persons" of "good character."[3]

The congressional slavery debate dribbled into the rest of society. Assimilationists challenged segregationists, stressing Black *capability* for equality if Blacks were not under the imbruting boot of slavery. Critiquing David Hume, citing Samuel Stanhope Smith, and parading out a line of Black exhibits, from Sancho to Phillis Wheatley, Pennsylvania abolitionist Charles Crawford asserted that the "Negro is in every respect similar to us." In 1791, Quaker Moses Brown pointed to Black exhibits from his Providence school as proof of "their being Men capable of Every Improvement with ourselves where they [are] under the Same Advantages." Benjamin Rush, perhaps the nation's leading abolitionist after Franklin's death, presented adult exhibits: New Orleans physician James Derham and Thomas "Negro Calculator" Fuller of Maryland. Legend has it that it took Fuller only a few minutes to calculate the number of seconds a man aged seventy years, seventeen days, and twelve hours had lived. But these remarkable exhibits of remarkable Black adults and children did little to sway the proslavery mind. Enslavers probably knew more than anyone about Black capabilities in freedom. But they only cared about Black capabilities to make them money.[4]

As quite possibly the most remarkable exhibit of them all, Benjamin Banneker was literally in the middle of these debates between assimilationist abolitionists and segregationist enslavers. And so was Thomas Jefferson, agreeing and disagreeing with both sides. Early in 1791, months before writing to Jefferson, Banneker had helped survey the nation's new capital, Washington, DC.

Banneker began his letter "freely and cheerfully" acknowledging that he was "of the African race." If Jefferson was flexible in his sentiments of nature, friendly to Black people, and willing to aid in their relief, Banneker wrote, then "I apprehend you will embrace every opportunity, to eradicate that train of absurd and false ideas and opinions." Jefferson and his slaveholding countrymen who were "detaining by fraud and violence so numerous a part of my brethren," but who assailed against British oppression, were walking, talking contradictions. Banneker closed the letter by introducing his enclosed unpublished almanac, "in my own hand writing." Banneker's letter was staunchly antiracist, a direct confrontation to the young country's leading disseminator of racist ideas.[5]

Nearly two weeks later, on August 30, 1791, Thomas Jefferson sent Banneker his standard reply to antislavery and antiracist letters. "No body wishes more than I," he said, to see the end of prejudice and slavery. He informed Banneker that he had sent the almanac to Monsieur de Condorcet, the secretary of the Academy of Science in Paris, because "your whole colour had a right for their justification against the doubts which have been entertained of them." Jefferson sidestepped his contradiction. But what could he say? In his letter to Condorcet, Jefferson called Banneker a "very respectable mathematician." In Notes, he claimed that Black people did not think "above the level of plain narration." Did Banneker change Jefferson's mind? Yes and no. Jefferson branded Banneker an extraordinary Negro. "I shall be delighted to see these instances of moral eminence so multiplied," he told Condorcet.[6]

FROM THE PERSPECTIVE of the enslaved, the most profound instance of moral eminence was evolving in Haiti. Jefferson learned of the Black revolt on September 8, 1791. Within two months, a force of 100,000 African freedom-fighters had killed more than 4,000 enslavers, destroyed almost 200 plantations, and gained control of the entire Northern Province. As historian C. L. R. James explained in the 1930s, "they were seeking their salvation in the most obvious way, the destruction of what they knew was the cause of their sufferings; and if they destroyed much it was because they had suffered much."[7]

What Jefferson and every other holder of African people had long feared had come to pass. In response, Congress passed the Fugitive Slave Act of 1793, bestowing on slaveholders the right and legal apparatus to recover escaped Africans and criminalize those who harbored them. Thomas Jefferson, for one, did not view the Haitian Revolution in the same guise as the American or French Revolutions. "Never was so deep a tragedy presented to the feelings of man," he wrote in July 1793. To Jefferson, the slave revolt against the enslavers was more evil and tragic to the feelings of man than the millions of African people who died on American plantations. Jefferson would soon call General Toussaint L'Ouverture and other Haitian leaders "Cannibals of the terrible Republic."[8]

That year, Jefferson's troubles over revolting Haitians also hit closer to home. A ship or two of distressed masters and slaves from Haiti arrived in Philadelphia in late July. Philadelphians started dying a week later. By August 20, 1793, Benjamin Rush had fatefully noticed the pattern of the contagion of yellow fever. But it was not yet an epidemic, so Rush had time in the late summer to attend to other matters. He possibly sent off letters to abolitionists around the nation. The next year, he welcomed to Philadelphia twenty-two delegates from abolitionist societies across the United States as they arrived for the

"American Convention for promoting the Abolition of Slavery and Improving the Condition of the African Race." The convention met over the next few years and then sporadically over the next three decades, pressing for gradual emancipation, anti-kidnapping legislation, and civil rights for alleged runaways.

As freed Blacks proliferated in the 1790s and the number of enslaved Blacks began to decline in the North, the racial discourse shifted from the problems of enslavement to the condition and capabilities of free Blacks. The American Convention delegates believed that the future advance of abolitionism depended on how Black people used their freedom. Periodically, the convention published and circulated advice tracts for free Blacks. Abolitionists urged free Blacks to attend church regularly, acquire English literacy, learn math, adopt trades, avoid vice, legally marry and maintain marriages, evade lawsuits, avoid expensive delights, abstain from noisy and disorderly conduct, always act in a civil and respectable manner, and develop habits of industry, sobriety, and frugality. If Black people behaved admirably, abolitionists reasoned, they would be undermining justifications for slavery and proving that notions of their inferiority were wrong.[9]

This strategy of what can be termed *uplift suasion* was based on the idea that White people could be persuaded away from their racist ideas if they saw Black people improving their behavior, uplifting themselves from their low station in American society. The burden of race relations was placed squarely on the shoulders of Black Americans. Positive Black behavior, abolitionist strategists held, undermined racist ideas, and negative Black behavior confirmed them.

Uplift suasion was not conceived by the abolitionists meeting in Philadelphia in 1794. It lurked behind the craze to exhibit Phillis Wheatley and Francis Williams and other "extraordinary" Black people. So the American Convention, raising the stakes, asked *every* free Black person to serve as a Black exhibit. In every state, abolitionists publicly and privately drilled this theory into the minds of African people as they entered the ranks of freedom in the 1790s and beyond.

This strategy to undermine racist ideas was actually based on a racist idea: "negative" Black behavior, said that idea, was partially or totally responsible for the existence and persistence of racist ideas. To believe that the negative ways of Black people were responsible for racist ideas was to believe that there was some truth in notions of Black inferiority. To believe that there was some truth in notions of Black inferiority was to hold racist ideas.

From the beginning, uplift suasion was not only racist, it was also impossible for Blacks to execute. Free Blacks were unable to always display positive characteristics for the same reasons poor immigrants and rich planters were unable to do so: free Blacks were human and humanly flawed. Uplift suasion assumed, moreover, that racist ideas were sensible and could be undone by appealing to sensibilities. But the common political desire to justify racial inequities produced racist ideas, not logic. Uplift suasion also failed to account for the widespread belief in the extraordinary Negro, which had dominated assimilationist and abolitionist thinking in America for a century. Upwardly mobile Blacks were regularly cast aside as unique and as different from ordinary, inferior Black people.

Still, from the perspective of White and Black abolitionists alike, uplift suasion seemed to be working in the 1790s. It would always seem to be working. Consumers of racist ideas sometimes changed their viewpoints when exposed to Black people defying stereotypes (and then sometimes changed back when exposed to someone confirming the stereotypes). Then again, upwardly mobile Blacks seemed as likely to produce resentment as admiration. "If you were well dressed they would insult you for that, and if you were ragged you would surely be insulted for being so," one Black Rhode Island resident complained in his memoir in the early 1800s. It was the cruel illogic of racism. When Black people rose, racists either violently knocked them down or ignored them as extraordinary. When Black people were down, racists called it their natural or nurtured place, and denied any role in knocking them down in the first place.[10]

UPLIFT SUASION MOVED neither segregationist enslavers nor assimilationist abolitionists away from their racist ideas. Not even Benjamin Rush, the scion of abolitionism, could be moved. By the end of August 1793, he was up to his neck in yellow fever cases and using racist ideas to solicit assistance. Rush inserted a note in Philadelphia's *American Daily Advertiser* in September telling Black people they had immunity to yellow fever, a conclusion he had reached based on his belief in their animal-like physical superiority. Quite a few Black nurses suffered horribly before Rush realized his gross error. In all, 5,000 people perished before the epidemic subsided in November and federal officials returned to the city.[11]

Thomas Jefferson used his time away from Philadelphia during the epidemic to spend money on scientific devices that he planned to use in retirement. His agony over Treasury Secretary Alexander Hamilton's wheeling toward monarchy and financial speculation had set him to packing. We are "daily pitted in the Cabinet like two cocks," Jefferson sobbed. In one of his last days as secretary of state, Jefferson received a patent application from Eli Whitney, a Yale-educated Massachusetts native looking for his fortune in Georgia. Whitney had invented a high-quality cotton gin that quickly separated cotton fibers from their seeds. Jefferson knew about the growing demand for American cotton abroad and the costly, labor-intensive process of manually removing the seeds. The introduction of steam power in England and waterpower in the northeastern United States drastically lowered the cost of making cotton into yarn and making yarn into fabric. Forward us a model of the gin and you will receive your patent "immediately," Jefferson wrote to Whitney. Jefferson had retired by the time Whitney received his patent in 1794.[12]

Enthroning King Cotton, the cotton gin made the value of southern lands skyrocket and quickly dethroned rice and tobacco. King Cotton incessantly demanded more and more to stabilize its reign: more enslaved Africans, more land, more violence, and more racist ideas. Annual cotton production slammed through the ceiling of about 3,000 bales in 1790, reaching 178,000 bales in 1810 and more than 4 million bales on the eve of the Civil War. Cotton became America's leading export, exceeding in dollar value all exports, helping to free Americans from British banks, helping to expand the factory system in the North, and helping to power the Industrial Revolution in the United States. Cotton—more than anyone or anything else— economically freed American enslavers from England and tightened the chains of African people in American slavery. Uplift suasion had no chance of dethroning King Cotton.[13]

IN 1796, BEFORE the cotton gin had taken hold—feeding cotton production and the demand for more enslaved Africans—Benjamin Rush thought he had found the ultimate abolitionist cure. The good doctor believed he had found a way to cure captives of their abnormal Blackness. The two presidential candidates—Thomas Jefferson and incumbent vice president John Adams—shared the Philadelphia sunlight that summer with a free "white black man." Henry Moss, unbeknownst to Americans, was suffering from vitiligo, a skin disease that causes the loss of skin color, making one's dark skin lighten. Moss exhibited his forty-two-year-old whitened body in Philadelphia taverns and before members of the American Philosophical Society. Long before "Black-faced" White entertainers enthralled Americans, "White-faced" Blacks enthralled American believers and skeptics of the theory that Black skin could change to White. Moss became "almost as familiar to the readers of newspapers and other periodicals . . . as . . . John Adams, Thomas Jefferson, or Madison," according to one observer. Like John "Primrose" Boby, who showcased his whitening body in the United Kingdom around the same time, Moss was a freak to some, but to others, such as Benjamin Rush, he was the future of racial progress. After 1796, history loses Henry Moss until 1803, when Providence abolitionist Moses Brown carefully examined him and saw "evidence of the sameness of human nature." In 1814, Moss resurfaced again in the *New England Journal of Medicine and Surgery*, where he is described as a Black man "whose skin has nearly lost its native colour and become perfectly white."[14]

President George Washington, Samuel Stanhope Smith, Benjamin Rush, and other dignitaries viewed Moss in the summer of 1796. "The parts that were covered and sweated advanced most rapidly in whiteness, his face slowest," Rush jotted down in his notes. "His skin was exactly like a white man. No rubbing accelerated it. The black skin did not come off, but changed." Thomas Jefferson, apparently, did not see Moss. Jefferson did own a few "white Negroes," and he called them an "anomaly of nature" in *Notes on the State of Virginia*. They were all "born of parents who had no mixture of white blood," Jefferson wrote, careful to exonerate his peers and uphold his false stand against interracial sex. Jefferson probably knew the term "albino" came from the Latin *albus*, meaning an animal, plant, or person lacking pigment. But their skin color—"a pallid cadaverous white"—was different, Jefferson wrote, and their "curled" hair was "that of the negro." No wonder Jefferson never took aim at physical assimilationists. He did not even concede the color change from Black to White.[15]

To Jefferson's dismay, other American intellectuals did take whitening Blacks very seriously. On February 4, 1797, Benjamin Rush, the APS's vice president, informed Jefferson that he was "preparing a paper in which I have attempted to prove that the black color . . . of the Negroes is the effect of a disease in the skin." Rush gave the paper at a special APS meeting on July 14, 1797. He praised the "elegant and ingenious Essay" of fellow assimilationist Samuel Stanhope Smith, given a decade prior. Rush, however, disagreed with Smith on how to make Black people White again. He proclaimed that all Africans were suffering from leprosy. This skin disease explained why they all had ugly Black skin, Rush told APS members. And the whiter their skins became, the healthier they became.[16]

This skin disease was brought on by poor diet, he theorized, along with "greater heat, more savage manners, and bilious fevers." He then listed other side effects of the skin disease: Blacks' physical superiority, their "wooly heads," their laziness, their hypersexuality, and their insensitivity to pain. "They bear surgical operations much better than white people," Rush quoted a doctor as saying. "I have amputated the legs of many negroes, who have held the upper part of the limb themselves."

Benjamin Rush projected himself as a friend of the Philadelphia Negro, a racial egalitarian, and an abolitionist. He attempted to uphold his persona at the end of his address. "All the claims of superiority of the whites over the blacks, on account of their color, are founded alike in ignorance and inhumanity," he stressed. "If the color of the negroes be the effect of a disease, instead of inviting us to tyrannise over them, it should entitle them to a double portion of our humanity." Rush was upbeat about Black capability, about the future, and about potential remedies: Nature had begun to cure Black people. The famous assimilationist mentioned Henry Moss and his glorious "change from black to a natural white flesh color." His "wool," Rush announced with satisfaction, "has been changed into hair."[17]

Benjamin Rush's leprosy theory and Samuel Stanhope Smith's climate theory were as popular among northern assimilationists and abolitionists as Thomas Jefferson was unpopular. Jefferson had lost the presidential election to Adams in 1796, but ran for president again in 1800. Federalist operatives and journalists tried to convince voters of Jefferson's atheism and anti-Black views, using his *Notes* as evidence, just as they had done during the previous election. "You have degraded the blacks from the rank which God hath given them in the scale of being!" wrote one Federalist pamphleteer. Some of Jefferson's defenders during the campaign were jailed by the Adams administration under the 1798 Sedition Act—namely, James Callender. Pardoned by Jefferson when he won the presidency in 1800, Callender apparently requested patronage as retribution for his services. President Jefferson refused. Incensed, Callender exposed Jefferson's secret.[18]

On September 1, 1802, Richmond's *Recorder* readers learned about the relationship between President Thomas Jefferson and Sally Hemings. "By this wench Sally, our president has had several children," Callender wrote. The arrangement had begun in France, "when he endeavored so much to belittle the African race." (Callender, ironically, belittled the African race too. "Wench" oftentimes meant a promiscuous woman, connoting the common idea that African women pursued White men.)[19]

If Callender thought his series of articles would destroy Jefferson's political fortunes, then he was wrong. Callender's reports did not surprise many White male voters, either in Virginia or around the nation.

If anything, Callender upset them, because some of them were having their own secretive affairs with Black women—or raping them—and they did not want such things publicly aired. Nationally, White male voters bolstered Jefferson's party in Congress in the 1802 midterm elections, and they overwhelmingly supported his presidential reelection in 1804.

When Jefferson's daughter Patsy showed him Callender's article, Jefferson laughed. No words came from his lips to give the matter any credence. John Adams privately called it a "blot on his character" and the "natural and almost unavoidable consequence of that foul contagion in the human character, Negro slavery." Jefferson may have privately justified his relations with Sally Hemings by reminding himself that everyone did it, or tried to do it. From teens ending their (and their victims') virginity, to married men sneaking around, to single and widowed men having their longtime liaisons—master/slave rape or intercourse seemed "natural," and enslaving one's children seemed normal in slaveholding America.

Even Jefferson's old law teacher, his "earliest and best friend," engaged in an interracial liaison. Widower George Wythe had lived for some time in Williamsburg with the young, biracial Michael Brown and a Black "housekeeper," Lydia Broadnax. Wythe willed his house to Broadnax, and he asked Jefferson to oversee Brown's education. Perhaps angry about this arrangement, Wythe's White grandnephew, George Sweeney, probably poisoned Wythe, Broadnax, and Brown one day in 1806. Only Broadnax survived. In his second presidential term, Jefferson publicly avoided the Wythe scandal, trying to create as much "imaginative distance," to use his biographer's term, as possible.[20]

Master/slave sex fundamentally acknowledged the humanity of Black and biracial women, but it simultaneously reduced that humanity to their sexuality. In the Christian world, sexuality was believed to be the animal trait of humans. Fast becoming the iconic image of a Black woman at this time was the 1800 *Portrait d'une negresse* (*Portrait of a Negress*) by French painter Marie-Guillemine Benoist. An African woman sits staring at the viewer with her head wrapped and breast exposed. The white cloth wrapping her head and lower body contrasts vividly with the darkness of her skin. The portrait is thought to be the first painting of a Black woman by a European woman.[21]

It is not surprising that Jefferson's career survived Callender's scandalous revelation. During his presidency, many Americans came to understand slavery (and its sexual politics) as an immutable fact of their lives and their economy. The nation that Jefferson had called "the world's best hope" and "the strongest government on earth" in his First Inaugural Address in 1801 was not hopefully anticipating the end of slavery. The antislavery refrains first heard from the mouths of the Germantown Petitioners reached a crescendo during the American Revolution, but then started to trail off. And the remaining abolitionists, such as Benjamin Rush and company, who were urging uplift suasion hardly had as large an audience as John Woolman and Samuel Hopkins had enjoyed a generation prior. King Cotton was on the march. And the slaveholding producers of racist ideas had convinced legions of Americans to see slavery as a necessary evil to pay off their debts and build their nation. Besides, it seemed better than the supposed horrific barbarism bound to arise, they argued, from Black freedom.[22]

More than anything else, the Haitian Revolution and the slave rebellions it inspired across the Americas made White Americans fearful of race war and, even more worrying, a potential Black victory. Southern congressmen and newspaper editors did what they could to silence dissent and stoke White fears, claiming that public discussion of slavery and the presence of free Blacks were inciting slaves to rebel. And there were more free Blacks than ever before, because of wartime runaways and the outbreak of manumissions following the Revolution. The free Black population in Virginia, for instance, leaped from 1,800 in 1782 to 12,766 in 1790 and then to 30,570 in 1810.[23]

Then there was the sudden expansion of the cotton kingdom. Napoleon's defeat at the hands of Haitian revolutionaries—free Black Haiti declared independence in 1804—required him to reimagine the French Empire. Holding and defending faraway colonies had become too costly and too bothersome. The vast Louisiana Territory did not fit in his new leaner, stronger empire. "I renounce Louisiana,"

Napoleon said on April 11, 1803. By April 30, the Jefferson administration had purchased the territory from France for $15 million, or three cents per acre. Jefferson learned of the purchase on the eve of Independence Day. "It is something larger than the whole U.S.," he wrote with happiness.

Over the next few decades, slaveholders marched their captives onto the new western lands, terrorizing them into planting new cotton and sugar fields, sending the crops to northern and British factories, and powering the Industrial Revolution. Southern planters and northern investors grew rich. With so much money to make, antislavery and antiracist ideas were whipped to the side like antislavery, antiracist Africans.[24]

THE NEW LIFE and lands of slavery, and the new crops and cash from slavery, sucked the life out of the antislavery movement during Jefferson's presidency in the early 1800s. Assimilationist ideas, especially monogenesis, also faded. Theologians like Princeton's president, Samuel Stanhope Smith, the most eminent scholar on race in the United States in that era, seeing the loss of their cultural power, grew to hate Jefferson's disregard for religious authority. Jefferson questioned the orthodox Christian belief that all humans descended from Adam and Eve, and articulators of separately created human species nagged Smith like an incessantly barking dog.[25]

English physician Charles White, the well-known author of a treatise on midwifery, entered the debate over species in 1799. Unlike Scotland's Lord Kames, White circled around religion and employed a new method of proving the existence of separate race species—comparative anatomy. He did not want the conclusions in his *Account on the Regular Gradation in Man* to "be construed so as to give the smallest countenance to the pernicious practice of enslaving mankind." His only objective was "to investigate the truth." White disputed Buffon's legendary contention that since interracial unions were fertile, the races had to be of the same species. Actually, orangutans had been "known to carry off negro-boys, girls, and even women," he said, sometimes enslaving them for "brutal passion." On the natural scale, Europeans were the highest and Africans the lowest, approaching "nearer to the brute creation than any other of the human species." Blacks were superior in areas where apes were superior to humans— seeing, hearing, smelling, memorizing things, and chewing food. "The PENIS of an African is larger than that of an European," White told his readers. Most anatomical museums in Europe preserved Black penises, and, he noted, "I have one in mine."[26]

Science had been too religious in the days of Voltaire for discussions of separate species to catch on. Too much freedom and Revolutionary rhetoric clouded the words of Edward Long and Lord Kames. By the period of Charles White's publication, the debate was on. In 1808, New York physician John Augustine Smith, a disciple of Charles White, rebuked Samuel Stanhope Smith as a minister dabbling in science. "I hold it my duty to lay before you all the facts which are relevant," John Augustine Smith announced in his circulated lecture. The principal fact was that the "anatomical structure" of the European was "superior" to that of the other races. As different species, Blacks and Whites had been "placed at the opposite extremes of the scale." The polygenesis lecture launched Smith's academic career: he became editor of the *Medical and Physiological Journal*, tenth president of the College of William & Mary, and president of the New York College of Physicians and Surgeons.[27]

The advance of slavery, possibly more than the persuasive arguments of Lord Kames, Charles White, and John Augustine Smith, caused intellectuals long committed to monogenesis to start changing their views. Watching the Christian world unravel, Samuel Stanhope Smith made one last intellectual stand for theology, for assimilationists, and for monogenesis. He released an "enlarged and improved" second edition of *Essay on the Causes of Variety of Complexion and Figure in the Human Species* in 1810, pledging to appeal "to the evidence of facts." Nothing in the past twenty years had changed his position: racial difference resulted from climate and the state of a society. If anything, Smith asserted it more forcefully. And he introduced "another fact" in the climate section: Henry Moss's skin had changed, and his new "fine, straight hair" had replaced "the wooly substance." In a hard-hitting appendix, Smith responded to "certain strictures made on the first edition of this essay," the polygenesis of Charles White, Thomas Jefferson, and John Augustine Smith. "Let infidels appear in their true form," Smith roared in closing. "If they seek the combat, we only pray, like Ajax, to see the enemy in open day."[28]

Thomas Jefferson did not publicly respond to Samuel Stanhope Smith in 1810. He refused to come out into open day altogether. He had retired from public life.

CHAPTER 11

Big Bottoms

LESS THAN THIRTY years earlier, Thomas Jefferson had been anxious to leave Monticello and to be free from the sorrow of his wife's passing. After France, three years as US secretary of state, four years as vice president, and eight years as president, he wanted to return to his home in Virginia. "Never did a prisoner, released from his chains, feel such as I shall on shaking off the shackles of power," he informed a French businessman on March 4, 1809, days before his release from the presidency.

After rooming for years in earsplitting Washington, Jefferson longed for quiet seclusion to read, write, and think in private. "But the enormities of the times in which I have lived," he said, "have forced me to take part in resisting them." No foreign enormity was greater than the wars raging in the early 1800s between France and England. Jefferson kept the United States neutral, ignoring war hawks, but he could not ignore the violations on the high seas of American neutrality. He proposed (and Congress adopted) a general embargo of US trade with France and England in 1807. Congress repealed the controversial embargo during the final days of Jefferson's presidency on March 1, 1809. Jefferson's neutral doctrine delayed the inevitable. Three years after he had left the presidency, the United States faced off with England in the War of 1812.[1]

Presiding over the American Philosophical Society from 1797 to 1815, Jefferson did remain neutral in the war between monogenesis and polygenesis. He rarely even struck back at the Federalist offensive against his *Notes on the State of Virginia* in the presidential campaigns. In 1804, printer William Duane offered Jefferson the opportunity to respond in a new edition. Jefferson balked. He did not have time. But he did plan to revise and enlarge *Notes* when he left Washington in 1809.[2]

Weeks before leaving office, Jefferson thanked abolitionist and scientist Henri Gregoire for sending him a copy of *An Enquiry Concerning the Intellectual and Moral Faculties, and Literature of Negroes* on February 25. Gregoire offered travel "testimony" of glorious Black nations to refute what "Jefferson tells us, that no nation of them was ever civilized," he wrote. "We do not pretend to place the negroes on a level" with Whites, Gregoire explained in assimilationist form, but only to challenge those who say "that the negroes are incapable of becoming partners in the store-house of human knowledge."[3]

After years of apologizing for American slavery, Jefferson probably finally felt good about responding to Henri Gregoire. He was in a better position now to write to the famed abolitionist. In his Annual Message to Congress three years earlier, Jefferson had condemned the "violations of human rights" enabled by the slave trade and urged Congress to abolish it. Congress followed his lead in 1807, after a contentious debate over how illegal slave traders would be punished. Traders, they decided, would be fined under the Slave Trade Act of 1807. But Congress did nothing to ensure the act's enforcement.

It was an empty and mostly symbolic law. The act failed to close the door on the ongoing international slave trade while flinging open the door to a domestic one. Violations of human rights continued when children were snatched from parents, and slave ships now traveled down American waters in a kind of "middle passage" from Virginia to New Orleans, which took as many days as the transatlantic "middle passage" had. Jefferson and like-minded planters of the Upper South started deliberately "breeding" captives to supply the Deep South's demand. "I consider a woman who brings a child every two years as more profitable than the best man on the farm," Jefferson once explained to a friend. A year after the Slave Trade Act, a South Carolina court ruled that enslaved women had no legal claims on their children. They stood "on the same footings as other animals."[4]

Ending the international slave trade was in reality a boon for the largest American slave-owners, as it increased the demand and value of their captives. And so the largest slave-owners and the gradual-emancipation advocates joined hands in cheering on the legal termination of the international slave trade on January 1, 1808. Massachusetts clergyman Jedidiah Morse deemed it a victory. He spoke for most northern assimilationist evangelicals when he proclaimed that since Christianity was finally lighting up the "heathenish and Mahometan darkness" of Africa, "its natives have no need to be carried to foreign lands." Morse believed that slavery would be gradually abolished, too.[5]

Thomas Jefferson must have relied on this widespread support for the Slave Trade Act when he finally replied to Henri Gregoire in stock fashion in 1809. "No person living wishes more sincerely than I do," he said, to see racial equality proven. "On this subject [Black people] are gaining daily in the opinions of nations," Jefferson wrote, "and hopeful advances are making towards their re-establishment of an equal footing with the other colors of the human family."[6]

In fact, Black people were losing ground daily in the opinions of European nations. Not long after Gregoire and Jefferson exchanged letters, London was blitzed with a broadsheet picturing a seminude African woman standing sideways to the viewer, her oversized buttocks exposed on one side, the unseen side draped in animal skin. A headband wraps her forehead, and she holds a body-sized stick. Whitening Blacks, Black exhibits, and "converted Hottentots," sharing their supposed journeys from savagery to civilization, were becoming less remarkable with each passing year. But Londoners were captivated by Sarah Baartman, or rather, her enormous buttocks and genitalia.

Baartman's Khoi people of southern Africa had been classified as the lowest Africans, the closest to animals, for more than a century. Baartman's buttocks and genitals were irregularly large among her fellow Khoi women, not to mention African women across the continent, or across the Atlantic on Jefferson's plantation. And yet Baartman's enormous buttocks and genitals were presented as regular and authentically African. She was billed on stage in the fashionable West End of London as the "Hottentot Venus," which tightened the bolt on the racist stereotype linking Black women to big buttocks. Polygenesist Charles White had already tightened the bolt linking Black men with big genitalia.

Retiring colonial official Alexander Dunlop and Baartman's South African master Hendrik Cesars brought Baartman to London in July 1810. Upon Dunlop's death in 1814, exhibiter Henry Taylor brought the thirty-six or thirty-seven-year-old Baartman to Paris for another round of shows. Papers rejoiced over her arrival. She appeared in the grand Palais-Royal, the centerfold of Parisian debauchery, where prostitutes mixed with printers, restaurants with gambling houses, coffee gossipers with drunk dancers, beggars with elites. On November 19, 1814, Parisians strolled into the Vaudeville Theater across from the Palais-Royal to view the opening of *La Venus Hottentote, ou Haine aux Francais (or the Hatred of French Women)*. In the opera's plot, a young Frenchman does not find his suitor sufficiently exotic. When she appears disguised as the "Hottentot Venus," he falls in love. Secure in his attraction, she drops the disguise. The Frenchman drops the ridiculous attraction to the Hottentot Venus, comes to his senses, and the couple marries. The opera revealed Europeans' ideas about Black women. After all, when Frenchmen are seduced by the Hottentot Venus, they are acting like animals. When Frenchmen are attracted to Frenchwomen, they are acting rationally. While hypersexual Black women are worthy of sexual attraction, asexual Frenchwomen are worthy of love and marriage.

In January 1815, animal showman S. Reaux obtained Baartman from Henry Taylor. Reaux paraded her, sometimes with a collar around her neck, at cafés, at restaurants, and in soirées for Parisian elites—wherever there was money. One day in March 1815, Reaux shepherded Baartman to the Museum of Natural History in Paris, which housed the world's greatest collection of natural objects. They had a meeting with Europe's most distinguished intellectual, the comparative anatomist Georges Cuvier.

That rare segregationist who rejected polygenesis, Cuvier believed that all humans descended from Europe's Garden of Eden. A catastrophic event 5,000 years earlier had sent the survivors fleeing to Asia and Africa; three races had emerged and had started passing on unchangeable hereditary traits. "The white race" was the "most beautiful of all" and was "superior," according to Cuvier. The African's physical features "approximate[d] it to the monkey tribe."

In his lab, Cuvier asked Baartman to take off her long skirt and shawl, which she had worn to ward off the March wind. Baartman refused. Startled, Cuvier did all he could to document her with her clothes on over the next three days, measuring and drawing her body.

Sometime in late December 1815, Baartman died, perhaps of pneumonia. No Black woman was the subject of more obituaries in Parisian newspapers in the nineteenth century than Sarah Baartman. Cuvier secured her corpse and brought her to his laboratory. He removed her clothes, cracked open her chest wall, removed and studied all of her major organs. Cuvier spread her legs, studied her buttocks, and cut out her genitals, setting them aside for preservation. After Cuvier and his team of scientists finished their scientific rape, they boiled off the rest of Baartman's flesh. They reassembled the bones into a skeleton. Cuvier then added her remains to his world-famous collection. In his report, he claimed to have "never seen a human head more resembling a monkey's than hers." The Khoi people of South Africa, he concluded, were more closely related to the ape than to the human.[7]

Parisians displayed Baartman's skeleton, genitals, and brain until 1974. When President Nelson Mandela took office in 1994, he renewed South Africans' calls for Baartman's return home. France returned her remains to her homeland in 2002. After a life and afterlife of unceasing exhibitions, Baartman finally rested in peace.[8]

Baartman's fate was particularly horrific in the early 1810s, and Cuvier's conclusions about Black bodies were consumed with little hesitation by those seeking evidence of Black inferiority to justify their commerce on both sides of the Atlantic, a commerce taking root in the wombs of Black women.

NO MATTER WHAT Thomas Jefferson said to Henri Gregoire in 1809, Black people were not gaining daily in the opinions of those Choctaws and Chickasaws who started acquiring them (or were re-enslaving runaways). While these indigenous southern slaveholders rejected ideas of White superiority and Native American inferiority, they embraced associations of Blackness with slavery. Enslaved Africans in Jefferson's Louisiana Territory were not gaining daily in the opinions of their French and American masters, either. And these captives refused to wait until their French and American masters gained an emancipatory opinion of them, knowing they could be waiting forever for their freedom. On January 8, 1811, about fifteen captives on a sugar plantation in an area known as the German Coast wounded a planter, Major Manuel Andry, and killed his son. Bearing military uniforms and guns, cane knives, and axes while beating drums and waving flags, they started marching from plantation to plantation, swelling their numbers and the dead bodies of enslavers. In time, between two hundred and five hundred biracial and African people had joined the thirty-five-mile freedom march to invade New Orleans. Led by Asante warriors Quamana and Kook, along with biracial men Harry Kenner and Charles Deslondes—and inspired by the Haitian Revolution— these revolutionaries waged the largest slave revolt in the history of the United States.[9]

On January 10, 1811, the poorly armed band of freed people was defeated by a well-armed band of four hundred militiamen and sixty US army troops. In the end, almost one hundred former captives were killed or executed. Louisiana provided reparations for the planters—$300 (about $4,200 in 2014) for each captive killed. Authorities whacked off their heads and strung them up for all to see at intervals from New Orleans to Andry's plantation."[10]

Hoping for assurances of federal protection in case of future rebellions, Louisiana sugar planters voted to join the union in 1812. With the addition of Louisiana, another slave state, it became clear that slavery was expanding, not contracting, as Jefferson left office. The number of enslaved Africans swelled 70 percent in twenty years, increasing from 697,897 in the first federal census of 1790 to 1,191,354 in 1810, before tripling over the next fifty years. The escalation of slavery and the need to defend it against anti-American abolitionists in Europe generated one of the first waves of proslavery thought after the Revolution.

Even northerners, or native northerners living in the South, defended it. In 1810, future Pennsylvania congressman Charles Jared Ingersoll released *Inchiquin, the Jesuit's Letters*, refuting the aspersions cast upon slavery "by former residents and tourists." A few years later, New York antislavery novelist James Kirke Paulding tried to defend his nation and the slow pace of change. Freeing happy Africans could endanger the community, undermine property rights, and render them "more wretched" than they already were, Paulding wrote.[11]

Philadelphia Federalist Robert Walsh published *An Appeal from the Judgments of Great Britain Respecting the United States of America* in 1819. "Your work will furnish the first volume of every future American history," Thomas Jefferson accurately predicted. Though Walsh blamed the British for slavery, he said the institution endeared masters with "sensibility, justice and steadfastness." For the African, whose "colour is a perpetual momento of their servile origin," their enslavement is *"positively good."* The slave was "exempt from those racking anxieties" experienced by the English.[12]

If Jefferson truly desired to see a refutation of his racist ideas in *Notes*, as he told Gregoire, then he had made no moves in that direction during his presidency, neither politically nor in print. His most pressing personal concern in 1809 was moving back home, to the comfort of Monticello and Sally Hemings, and away from the ongoing political parade in Washington.

Jefferson left Washington a week after his close friend and mentee James Madison was installed as the fourth president of the United States on March 4, 1809. Jefferson's presidential reign did not end with his departure from Washington. Until 1841, a series of self-described disciples of Jefferson served as US presidents, the lone exception being John Quincy Adams in the late 1820s.[13]

In 1809, Jefferson estimated his net worth to be $225,000 (roughly $3.3 million in 2014) based on 10,000 acres of land, a manufacturing mill, 200 slaves, and a mountain of debt. Whether he was proslavery or antislavery, Jefferson needed slavery in 1809 to maintain his financial solvency and life of luxury. In the initial years of his retirement, Jefferson finally finished his 11,000-square-foot, 33-room mansion displaying all the things he had collected: the animal specimens and Native American objects, the medals and maps, the portraits and sculptures of Jesus, Benjamin Franklin, John Locke, Sir Isaac Newton, Christopher Columbus, and Voltaire, and the painting of himself, drawn by Boston painter Mather Brown, a descendant of Cotton Mather.[14]

Loving retirement, Jefferson placed books on top of newspapers. He did not have to leave Monticello, and he rarely did. He had a plantation to run, which relied on slave labor to pay off his debts, or rather, pay for the luxuries he loved. He put science, not politics, at the center of his affairs, emerging as America's celebrity scholar in the 1810s. The requests for advice and data and the reviewing of manuscripts seemed endless. "From sunrise to one or two o'clock, and often from dinner to dark, I am drudging at the writing table," Jefferson complained to John Adams. He was not updating *Notes*, though. By 1813, he had lost all drive to reproduce his ideas.[15]

Jefferson had also lost all drive to support the cause of antislavery. In 1814, Edward Coles, the personal secretary of President James Madison, asked Jefferson to arouse public sentiment against slavery. Jefferson balked, using the excuse of old age. The seventy-one-year-old advised Coles to reconcile himself with enslavement and only promote emancipation in a way that did not offend anyone.[16] Ironically, the inoffensive solution that Jefferson offered in *Notes*, and that he tried to execute once as president, was about be adopted by a new generation.

CHAPTER 12

Colonization

ONE OF THOMAS JEFFERSON'S most enduring legacies was a race relations effort that spanned the course of the nineteenth century. It all began in the spring of 1800 in Jefferson's home state. Two captives, Gabriel and Nancy Prosser, were organizing a slave rebellion. Standing well over six feet tall, with dark skin, penetrating eyes, and bulging scars, the twenty-four-year-old Gabriel Prosser caught people's attention wherever he went. He won converts by reminding them of the Haitian armies that had turned back the armies of Spain, England, and France. The Prossers planned to have hundreds of captives march on Richmond, where they would seize 4,000 unguarded muskets, arrest Governor James Monroe, hold the city until reinforcements arrived from surrounding counties, and negotiate the end of slavery and equal rights. The lives of friendly Methodists, Quakers, and French people were to be spared, but racist Blacks would be killed. Allies were to be recruited among Virginia's poor whites and Native Americans.

The revolt failed to materialize on the planned date of Saturday, August 30, 1800. Two cynical slaves begging for their master's favor betrayed what would have been the largest slave revolt in the history of North America, with as many as 50,000 rebels joining in from as far as Norfolk, Virginia. Given notice that afternoon, Governor James Monroe dispatched Richmond's defenses and informed every militia commander in Virginia. Wind and rain stormed through the Virginia Tidewater. A capsized bridge halted the march of a thousand armed rebels into the city. The liberating army disbanded, dripping

143

in disgust. The enslaving army stayed intact, over the next few weeks invading communities and arresting rebel leaders. Gabriel Prosser fled to Norfolk, where he was betrayed and captured on September 25. Dragged back to Richmond, he was hanged along with his comrades, but they appeared defiant until the end. "The accused have exhibited a spirit, which, if it becomes general, must deluge the Southern country in blood," said an eyewitness.[1]

A rebellious slave was extraordinary—real, but not really representative. During the final months of 1800, enslavers blasted this racist mantra of contented slaves and then hypocritically demanded more weapons, more organization, and more sophisticated laws to restrain them. On December 31, 1800, the Virginia House of Delegates secretly instructed Governor James Monroe to correspond with the incoming President Jefferson on finding lands outside of Virginia where "persons . . . dangerous to the peace of society may be removed." Jefferson requested clarity on their desires on November 24, 1801. He suggested colonization in the Caribbean or Africa to the Virginia delegates, expressing the improbability of securing lands within the continental United States.[2]

Virginia lawmakers again gathered in secret in 1802 to respond to their native son. Slavery had to continue, and its natural by-product—resistance—had to stop. So Virginia lawmen took Jefferson up on his proposal, asking him to find a foreign home for the state's free Blacks. Jefferson went to work, inquiring through intermediaries about West Africa's Sierra Leone, England's colony for freed people since 1792. England spurned Jefferson, as did other European nations. Breaking the bad news to Monroe on December 27, 1804, Jefferson assured him he would "keep it under my constant attention."[3]

Virginia lawmakers swore themselves to secrecy, agreeing to never reveal their maneuvers for colonization; they did not even inform the next generation of lawmakers. But in 1816, Charles Fenton Mercer, a member of the House of Delegates since 1810, learned of Jefferson's plan. He uncovered the correspondence between Monroe and Jefferson, and he was inspired by the Jeffersonian rationale for sending Blacks abroad. Mercer was an antislavery, anti-abolitionist slaveholder like Jefferson. Although "slavery is wrong," he later wrote, emancipa-tion "would do more harm than good."[4]

Mercer wanted to remake his region's agrarian, slave-labor econ-omy into a free-labor, industrial economy. He dreaded the working-class revolts that were picking up steam in Western Europe, but had faith in the ability of a public education system to placate lower- and middle-income Whites. Yet he recognized that the rampant racial dis-crimination in America would fashion free Blacks into a perpetually rebellious working class. He wanted to expel Blacks from the United States before it was too late.

Colonization seemed like a godsend to Mercer. It also appealed to Robert Finley, who learned about the cause from his brother-in-law, Mercer's old friend Elias B. Caldwell, the longtime clerk of the US Supreme Court. An antislavery clergyman, Finley had already taken an interest in the plight of low-income free Blacks, and to him, colo-nization seemed to be the perfect solution to their problems. Mercer, Finley, and the colonizationists they inspired ended up being the ideo-logical children of an odd couple who had disliked each other: Thomas Jefferson and Samuel Stanhope Smith. The latter endorsed the cause before his 1819 death. While Smith believed that Black people were capable of Whiteness, Jefferson insisted that they were incapable of achieving Whiteness in the United States. Colonization offered an alternative that both men could embrace.[5]

In 1816, Finley sat down and wrote the colonization movement's manifesto, *Thoughts on the Colonization of Free Blacks*. "What shall we do with the free people of color?" he began the pamphlet. Free Blacks must be trained "for self-government" and returned to their land of ori-gin, he wrote. For the enslaved, "the evil of slavery will be diminished, and in a way so gradual as to prepare the whites for the happy and progressive change."[6]

Carrying this literary cannonball of racist ideas, Finley invaded Washington, DC, in late November 1816. He lobbied journalists, poli-ticians, and President James Madison, whose views on Blacks mirrored Jefferson's. Finley and his powerful associates called an organizational meeting for colonizationists on December 21, 1816. Presiding was

Kentucky representative Henry Clay, whose early life had resembled Thomas Jefferson's. Born to Virginia planters, Clay had become a lawyer, a Kentucky planter, and then a politician. He had expressed an early abolitionism that had faded with time. Clay had just finished his second stint as Speaker of the House when he presided over the colonization meeting that birthed the American Colonization Society. Slaveholder and Supreme Court Justice Bushrod Washington—the nephew of George Washington—was elected president of the society, and the vice presidents included Finley, Clay, General Andrew Jackson, and Mercer's Princeton schoolmate Richard Rush, the son of Benjamin Rush, who had pledged his support for colonization before his death in 1813.

At the inaugural meeting, Finley's gradual abolitionism took a back seat to the demands of the slaveholders. The society would ignore the "delicate question" of abolition and only promote the deportation of free Blacks, Henry Clay said. "Can there be a nobler cause than that which, whilst it proposed to rid our country of a useless and pernicious, if not dangerous portion of its population, contemplates the spreading of the arts of civilized life, and the possible redemption from ignorance and barbarism of a benighted quarter of the globe?" Newspapers around the nation reprinted his words.

In Philadelphia, at least 3,000 Black men packed into Mother Bethel A.M.E. Church on January 15, 1817, to discuss the ACS's formation. Longtime colonization supporter James Forten, A.M.E. church founder Richard Allen, and two other Black ministers pledged their support for colonization and its missionary potential. Speeches concluded, Forten stepped to the pulpit to gauge the crowd. Those in favor? Forten asked. No one spoke. No one raised a hand. Nothing. All opposed? Forten nervously asked. Everything. A booming "no" rang out, shaking the walls of the church.

These Black men had walked into the church fuming. Their wives, girlfriends, sisters, and mothers were probably angry, too (but were disallowed from proclaiming it at the male-only meeting). The meeting attendees audaciously denounced the "unmerited stigma" that Henry Clay had "cast upon the reputation of the free people of color."

They did not want to go to the "savage wilds of Africa," the attendees resolved, demonstrating that they had already consumed those racist myths. But at the same time, they were expressing their commitment to enslaved people and America and demanding recognition for their role in the nation's growth. It was "the land of our nativity," a land that had been "manured" by their "blood and sweat." "We will never separate ourselves voluntarily from the slave population of this country," they resolved.[7]

American-born descendants of Africa judged the continent based on the standards they had learned from the very people who were calling them inferior and trying to kick them out of the United States. Africans in America had received their knowledge of Africa and their racist ideas from White Americans. And White Americans' racist ideas had been procured from a host of European writers—everyone from Sarah Baartman's dissector, Georges Cuvier of France, to philosopher Georg Wilhelm Friedrich Hegel of Germany.

Around the time of the American Colonization Society's founding, European nations were increasingly turning their capital and guns from the slave trade to the cause of colonizing Africa (as well as Asia). English, French, German, and Portuguese armies fought African armies throughout the nineteenth century, trying to establish colonies in order to exploit Africa's resources and bodies more systematically and efficiently. This new racist drive required racist ideas to make sense of it, and Hegel's pontifications about backward Africans arrived right on time. Racist ideas always seemed to arrive right on time to dress up the ugly economic and political exploitation of African people.

Ironically, back in 1807, Hegel had expressed a very antiracist idea in his classic book *Phenomenology of Spirit*, condemning "the overhasty judgement formed at first sight about the inner nature and character" of a person. He revolutionized European philosophy and history in many important matters in the nineteenth century. Legions of philosophy chairs across Europe became Hegelians, and the philosophers he influenced—including men like Søren Kierkegaard, Karl Marx, and Friedrich Engels—constitute a who's who of European intellectuals. But before his death in 1831, Hegel failed to free himself and

Europe from the Enlightenment era's racist ideas. "It is . . . the concrete universal, self-determining thought, which constitutes the principle and character of *Europeans*," Hegel once wrote. "God becomes man, revealing himself." In contrast, African people, he said, were "a nation of children" in the "first stage" of human development: "The negro is an example of animal man in all his savagery and lawlessness." They could be educated, but they would never advance on their own. Hegel's foundational racist idea justified Europe's ongoing colonization of Africa. European colonizers would supposedly bring progress to Africa's residents, just as European enslavers had brought progress to Africans in the Americas.[8]

IN THEIR RESOLUTION against the American Colonization Society, Philadelphia Blacks noted the "unmerited stigma" that had been "cast upon the reputation of the free people of color." The death of Robert Finley later in the year strained the ACS, and it struggled to attract federal funding and the support of slaveholders, especially in the Deep South. The slaveholders would never accept colonization unless they were convinced that it would allow slavery to endure. Free Blacks would never sign on unless emancipation was promised. Neither group was satisfied.[9]

Still, the society was persistent. In terms of federal funding, Charles Fenton Mercer steered the next offensive after joining the House of Representatives. On January 13, 1819, Mercer introduced the Slave Trade Act, which allocated $100,000 to send "negroes" back to Africa. Signing the bill into law was the old Virginia governor sympathetic to colonization: James Monroe, who had been elected to the US presidency weeks before the formation of the ACS. Almost immediately, debates sprang up as to whether the bill authorized Monroe to acquire land in Africa. By 1821, Monroe had dispatched US naval officer Robert Stockton, as an agent of the society, to West Africa. With a drawn pistol in one hand and a pen in the other, Stockton embezzled—some say for $300—a strip of Atlantic coastal land south of Sierra Leone from a local ruler, who probably did not hold title to his people's land.

The United States thus joined the growing band of nations seeking to colonize Africa. By 1824, American settlers had built fortifications there. They renamed the settlement "Liberia," and its capital "Monrovia," after the US president. Between 1820 and 1830, only 154 Black northerners out of more than 100,000 sailed to Liberia.[10]

THE NINETEENTH CENTURY had begun with a slave rebellion plot that had caused Virginia enslavers and President Jefferson to think seriously of sending free and enslaved Blacks back to Africa. The slave rebellions kept coming, and nothing accelerated enslavers' support for the colonization movement more than actual or potential slave rebellions.

In 1818, a fifty-one-year-old free carpenter named Denmark Vesey started recruiting the thousands of slaves in and around Charleston that would form his army—one estimate says 9,000. Vesey was well known locally as one of the founders of Emmanuel A.M.E. Church, the first African Methodist Episcopal church in the South. Before receiving his freedom in 1800, Vesey had traveled the Atlantic with his seafaring owner, acquiring a tremendous pride in the agency, culture, and humanity of African people. He had also been inspired by the American, French, and Haitian revolutions. Vesey likely spent time teaching, motivating, and encouraging fellow enslaved Blacks and challenging the racist ideas they had consumed, perhaps regularly reciting the biblical story of the Israelites' deliverance from Egyptian bondage. He set the revolt for July 14, 1822, the anniversary of the French Revolution. Trusted house servants were to assassinate top South Carolina officials as they slept. Six infantry and cavalry companies were to invade the city and kill every White and Black antagonist they encountered on sight. Arsonists were to burn the city to the ground. Spared captains of ships were to bring the rebels to Haiti or Africa—not as colonizers, but as immigrants.

House slave Peter Prioleau betrayed the plot in late May; he received a reward of freedom and later became a slaveholder himself. Prioleau had no desire to abolish slavery, and he probably did not question the racist ideas behind it. In four long years of recruiting

thousands of rebels, no mistakes had been made by Vesey's lieuten-
ants; no one betrayed the plot—an amazing organizational feat—until
Prioleau opened his mouth. By late June, South Carolina authorities
had destroyed Vesey's army, banished thirty-four of Vesey's soldiers,
and hanged thirty-five men, including Denmark Vesey himself, who
was defiant to the very end.[11]

The vast Vesey conspiracy provoked fear in Charleston and beyond.
Slaveholders began to contemplate the end of slavery, and ejecting
the Black people seemed like an attractive option. In the words of one
writer, "the whole United States [should] join in a Colonization Society."
Another Charleston essayist who endorsed colonization pledged that he
was ready to help "free the country of so unwelcome a burden." Instead,
new laws tightening the noose on enslaved Blacks soothed the raw fear.
Officials stipulated that enslaved Blacks should only wear "negro cloth,"
a cheap, coarse cotton sometimes mixed with wool. "Every distinction
should be created between the whites and the negroes," a jurist said,
" . . . to make the latter feel the superiority of the former."[12]

Until 1822—until Denmark Vesey—northerners had produced
most of the racist books and tracts defending slavery. Writers like
Charles Jared Ingersoll, James Kirke Paulding, and Robert Walsh—
all from the North—defended slavery from British onslaughts in the
1810s. On October 29, 1822, *Charleston Times* editor Edwin Clifford
Holland released the first proslavery treatise by a native southerner.
Enslaved Africans, he said, could never "affect any revolution" because
of "their general inferiority in the gifts of nature." He was trying to
calm his worried fellows. But they could disrupt society, he said, and
Whites should always be on guard. "Let it never be forgotten, that
our NEGROES . . . are the anarchists and the domestic enemy; the
common enemy of civilized society, and the barbarians who would, IF
THEY COULD, become DESTROYERS OF OUR RACE." Holland
did not include the "industrious, sober, hardworking," and free biracial people in this denunciation. In the event of a rebellion, Holland
believed they would form "a *barrier* between our own color and that of
the black," because they were "more likely to enlist themselves under
the banners of the whites."[13]

THOMAS JEFFERSON PROBABLY expected rebellions like Denmark Vesey's, and he probably expected grandiose betrayals like Peter Prioleau's. He did not expect the Missouri Question. Weeks after Charles Fenton Mercer introduced the Slave Trade Act, which led to America's first colony in Africa, his New York colleague James Tallmadge Jr. tacked an amendment onto a bill admitting Missouri to the Union. The bill would have barred the admission of enslaved Africans into the new state. The Tallmadge Amendment sparked a smoldering fire of debate that burned for two years. Ultimately, it was tempered—but not extinguished—by the Missouri Compromise of 1820. Congress agreed to admit Missouri as a slave state and Maine as a free state, and to prohibit the introduction of slavery in the northern section of the vast Louisiana Territory, which Jefferson had purchased from France.

Thomas Jefferson did not make much of the early Missouri Question debate. He expected it to pass "like waves in a storm pass under the ship." When the storm did not pass, he became worried, and he soon described the storm as "the most portentous one which ever yet threatened our Union." By 1820, he was warning of a civil war that could become a racial war, and that could then develop into "a war of extermination toward the African in our land."

The Missouri Question had roused Jefferson "like a fire bell in the night," as he told Massachusetts congressman John Holmes on April 22, 1820. "I considered it at once," he wrote, "the knell of the union." He gave Holmes his stump speech on emancipation: no man wanted it more than him, but no workable plan for compensating owners and colonizing the freed had been put forth. "As it is," he said, "we have the wolf by the ears, and we can neither hold him, nor safely let him go." What could be done? "Justice is in one scale and self-preservation in the other."

Jefferson, the nation's most famous antislavery anti-abolitionist, longed for the Louisiana Territory, which he purchased in 1803, to become the republic's hospital, the place where the illnesses of the original states could be cured—most notably, the illness of slavery. Enslaved Africans would be spread out in the vast Louisiana Territory (if not sent to Africa). The "diffusion [of enslaved Africans] over a greater surface would make them individually happier, and proportionally facilitate the accomplishment of their emancipation, by dividing the burden on a great number of coadjutors." Jefferson dreamed that the vast Louisiana Territory could swallow slavery. Spread enslaved Africans out, and they will go away?[14]

Jefferson adamantly came to believe that Black freedom should not be discussed in the White halls of Congress, and that southerners should be left alone to solve the problem of slavery at their own pace, in their own way. In his younger years, he had considered gradual emancipation and colonization to be the solution. His gradualism turned into procrastination. In his final years, Jefferson said that "on the subject of emancipation I have ceased to think because [it is] not to be the work of my day." Slavery had become too lucrative, to too many slaveholders, for emancipation to be Jefferson's work of those days.[15]

For Jefferson, the Missouri Question was personal. If slavery could not continue its western expansion, his finances might be affected by the decreased demand for enslaved Africans in the domestic slave trade. As he agonized over the future livelihood of the United States and his own economic prospects, Jefferson could not have helped but think of the nation's past and his own past—and how both had reached this point of no return. Seventy-seven years old in 1821, Jefferson decided to "state some recollections of dates and facts concerning myself." *The Autobiography of Thomas Jefferson* runs less than one hundred pages and ends when he becomes US secretary of state in 1790. In this work, Jefferson attempted once again to secure his antislavery credentials, after training for a lifetime as a slaveholder: "Nothing is more certainly written in the book of fate than that these people are to be free," he wrote. "Nor is it less certain that the two races, equally free, cannot live in the same government. Nature, habit, opinion has drawn indelible lines of distinction between them." In forty years, nothing had diminished his need to produce racist ideas—not the Black exhibits, uplift suasion, letters from abolitionists, Sally Hemings, or the loyalty or the resistance of enslaved Africans. Jefferson shared the same view in his *Autobiography* in 1821 that he had in *Notes* in 1781. He promoted the colonization idea, that freed Blacks be hauled away to Africa in the same manner that enslaved Blacks had been hauled to America.[16]

IN THE 1820S, the American Colonization Society grew into the preeminent race-relations reform organization in the United States. Jefferson was again endorsing colonization, and calculating segregationists were beginning to see it as a solution to Black resistance. Altruistic assimilationists figured that it was a way to develop Black people in both America and Africa. In 1825, a twenty-eight-year-old Yale alumnus, Ralph Gurley, became the new ACS secretary. He held the position until his death in 1872, while also serving twice as the chaplain of the House of Representatives. Gurley had a vision: he believed that to win the minds and souls of Americans to the colonization cause, it had to be linked to the Protestant movement. His timing was good, because the Second Great Awakening was at hand as he began his ACS post.

The American Bible Society, the American Sunday School Union, and the American Tract Society were all established in this period, and they each used the printing press to besiege the nation with Bibles, tracts, pictures, and picture cards that would help to create a strong, unified, Jesus-centered national identity. A good tract *"should be entertaining,"* announced the American Tract Society in 1824. "There must be something to allure the listless to read." Allurement—those pictures of holy figures—had long been considered a sinful trick of Satan and "devilish" Catholics. No more. Protestant organizations started mass-producing, mass-marketing, and mass-distributing images of Jesus, who was always depicted as White. Protestants saw all the aspirations of the new American identity in the White Jesus—a racist idea that proved to be in their cultural self-interest. As pictures of this White Jesus started to appear, Blacks and Whites started to make connections, consciously and unconsciously, between the White God the Father, his White son Jesus, and the power and perfection of White people. "I really believed my old master was almighty God," runaway Henry Brown admitted, "and that his son, my young master, was Jesus Christ."[17]

As the revived Protestant movement ignited the enthusiasm of students, professors, clergymen, merchants, and legislators in New England, the American Colonization Society drew more people into its fold. While southern colonizationists sought to remove free Blacks, northerners sought to remove all Blacks, enslaved and freed. Northern race relations had grown progressively worse since the 1790s, defying uplift suasion. Each uplifting step of Black people stoked animosity, and runaways stoked further animosity. Race riots embroiled New York City, New Haven, Boston, Cincinnati, and Pittsburgh in the 1820s. As racial tensions accumulated, the ACS continued to gain adherents to the cause. Its agents argued forcefully that White prejudice and Black slavery would be eternal, and that freed Blacks must use the talents they had acquired from Whites to go back and redeem unenlightened Africa. By 1832, every northern state legislature had passed resolutions of endorsement for the colonization idea.[18]

Free Blacks remained overwhelmingly against colonization. Their resistance to the concept partly accounted for the identifier "Negro" replacing "African" in common usage in the 1820s. Free Blacks theorized that if they called themselves "African," they would be giving credence to the notion that they should be sent back to Africa. Their own racist ideas were also behind the shift in terminology. They considered Africa and its cultural practices to be backward, having accepted racist notions of the continent. Some light-skinned Blacks preferred "colored," to separate themselves from dark-skinned Negroes or Africans.[19]

For many, the colonization movement gave a new urgency to the idea of uplift suasion. Racist free Blacks thought uplift suasion offered Black people a way to prove their worthiness to White elites. In 1828, Boston preacher Hosea Easton urged a Thanksgiving Day crowd of Rhode Island Black folk to "come out of this degrading course of life." By uplifting themselves, they would "demand respect from those who exalt themselves above you."[20]

As part of the renewed effort to promote uplift suasion, a group of free Blacks established the nation's first Black newspaper, *Freedom's Journal*, with its headquarters in New York City. The two editors were both biracial: Samuel Cornish, a Presbyterian preacher, and John Russwurm, the third African American college graduate in the United States. Their mission was to chronicle the uplift of the North's 500,000 free Blacks in order to reduce prejudice. "The further decrease of prejudice, and the amelioration of the condition of thousands of our brethren who are yet in bondage greatly depend on our conduct," the *Freedom's Journal* said in its opening editorial on March 16, 1827. "It is for us to convince the world by uniform propriety of conduct, industry and economy, that we are worthy of esteem and patronage."[21]

The editors and the elite Blacks they represented often focused, however, on the conduct of the "lower classes of our people," whom they blamed for bringing the race down. Class racism dotted the pages of the *Freedom's Journal*, with articles pitting lower-income Blacks against upper-income Blacks, and the former being portrayed as inferior to the latter. Cornish and Russwurm did sometimes defend low-income Blacks. As New York planned to emancipate its remaining captives on July 4, 1827, the mainstream newspapers announced their disapproval. Freed Africans would "increase" the city's "criminal calendar, pauper list and *dandy* register," stammered the *Morning Chronicle*. Cornish and Russwurm admonished the newspaper for its "vulgar" attack while agreeing with much of the reasoning behind it. The Africans about to be freed were "an injured people," the editors pleaded, "and we think it beneath the character of a public Editor, to add insult to injury."[22]

Cornish and Russwurm eventually split on colonization, prompting Cornish's resignation. Russwurm decided to endorse the American Colonization Society in 1829, dooming his newspaper in anti-colonizationist Black America. After putting the first Black newspaper to bed, Russwurm departed for Liberia, convinced that he had given his all, but he nevertheless had lost the battle against America's racist ideas. He failed to realize that he had contributed to the racist ideas. He had used the first African American periodical to circulate the ideas of class racism. He had said that lower-income Blacks had an inferior work ethic, inferior intelligence, and inferior morality compared to White people and Black elites like him. One reason poor Blacks were discriminated against, he expressed, was that they were inferior. Russwurm had used his paper to circulate the enslaving strategy of uplift suasion, a strategy that compelled free Blacks to worry about their every action in front of White people, just as their enslaved brethren worried about their every action in front of their enslavers.[23]

THE AGENTS OF the American Colonization Society practically ignored the ire of most free Blacks, and they could afford to do so. Donations streamed into the national office. The society's annual income leaped from $778 in 1825 (about $16,000 in 2014) to $40,000 a decade later (about $904,000 in 2014). State colonization societies sprang up in nearly every western and northern state. But the ACS never attracted its greatest patron saint: Thomas Jefferson. The former president only tracked the development of the ACS from afar. He was suspicious of the organization because he could not stand the Federalists and the Presbyterians behind it.[24]

Jefferson may not have supported the ACS, but he never wavered in his support for the colonizationist idea during his final years. Establishing a colony in Africa "may introduce among the aborigines the arts of cultivated life, and the blessing of civilization and science," he wrote to historian and future Harvard president Jared Sparks on February 4, 1824. Apparently, Black Americans would civilize the continent under the tutelage of those White Americans who had civilized them. It would compensate for "the long course of injuries" they had endured, Jefferson said, such that in the end, America "[would] have rendered them perhaps more good than evil."[25]

A string of illnesses slowed Jefferson down in 1825. He still read, and he may have perused the first issue of the society's *African Repository and Colonial Journal* in March. The issue opened with a history of the ACS, which gave a nod to Jefferson, and ended by speaking of the four hundred settlers in Liberia "standing in lonely beauty." In another piece, entitled "Observations on the Early History of the Negro Race," a writer identified as "T.R." took aim at polygenesists who spoke of Black people as a separate species, incapable of civilization, or "the connecting link between men and monkies." The polygenesists must not know, T.R. wrote, "that the people who they traduce, were for more than a thousand years . . . the most enlightened on the globe."

T.R. cited Jefferson's old friend Count Constantine Volney, the French historian who forty years earlier had said the ancient Egyptians were of African descent. After several pages passionately demonstrating that the ancient Egyptians were African, T.R. declared that America should "carry back by colonies to Africa, now in barbarism, the blessings which . . . were received from her." Civilization was supposedly exhausted in Africa, but awakened in Europe, T.R. stated. But how did the originators of civilization produce such a region of ignorance and barbarism? How did they forget the arts and sciences? These questions were not asked, and they went unanswered. As assimilationists, the only point colonizationists like T.R. tried to make was that since Africans had been civilized in an earlier time, they could be civilized once again.[26]

By the time the ACS released the second volume of its periodical in the spring of 1826, Jefferson's health had deteriorated to the point that he could not leave home. By June, he could not leave his bed. Late that month, writer Henry Lee IV—known to Jefferson as the grandson of a Revolutionary War hero—desired a meeting with him. When the bedridden Jefferson learned of Lee's presence, he demanded to see him. The half-brother of future Confederate general Robert E. Lee was Jefferson's last visitor.

Jefferson had to decline an invitation to Washington to attend the fiftieth anniversary of the Declaration of Independence. He sent a celebratory statement to Washington instead, saying: "The general spread of the light of science has already laid open to every view the palpable truth that the mass of mankind has not been born with saddles on their backs, nor a favored few booted and spurred, ready to ride them legitimately, by the grace of God." His last public words— so sweet to every free person, so bitter to the enslaved.[27]

Aside from his Hemings children (and Sally Hemings), Jefferson did not free any of the other enslaved people at Monticello. One historian estimated that Jefferson had owned more than six hundred slaves over the course of his lifetime. In 1826, he held around two hundred people as property and he was about $100,000 in debt (about $2 million in 2014), an amount so staggering that he knew that once he died, everything—and everyone—would be sold.

On July 2, 1826, Jefferson seemed to be fighting to stay alive. The eighty-three-year-old awoke before dawn on July 4 and beckoned his enslaved house servants. The Black faces gathered around his bed. They were probably his final sight, and he gave them his final words. He had come full circle. In his earliest childhood memory and in his final lucid moment, Jefferson rested in the comfort of slavery.[28]

PART III

William Lloyd Garrison

CHAPTER 13

Gradual Equality

IT WAS THE STORY of the age—Thomas Jefferson and John Adams dying on July 4, 1826, the fiftieth anniversary of the Declaration of Independence. No other headline had ever before caused such amazement. Many thought the twin deaths on Freedom Day must have been an act of divine will, an undeniable sign that the United States had the blessing of God Almighty. Newspapers could not print enough eulogies, anecdotes, letters, statements, and biographical pieces on the two men whom Benjamin Rush had once called "the North and South Poles of the American Revolution."[1]

John Adams died in his home in Quincy, due south of the overgrown maritime city of Boston. By the time of Adams's death, Boston had grown to nearly 60,000 people and was fully immersed in New England's industrial revolution, which ran on the wheels of southern cotton. The odd collection of philosophies, business dealings, denominations, interest groups, and moral movements visitors encountered in the seaside city might have been enough to make them dizzy. But none of the moral movements were trying to stamp out the nation's most immoral institution. The Revolutionary-era abolitionist movement was pretty much dead. Jefferson's fatalism about the difficulty of solving the problem of evil slavery, and his habit of deflecting blame for it onto the British, had become entrenched across the nation. The convention of abolitionist societies that Benjamin Rush had gathered together in 1794 still existed, but it was no longer much of a force for change. Tiny antislavery societies in the Upper South and in the

North were being swallowed up by colonizationists and their racist ideas.[2]

Every moral cause seemed to have its day on the annual giving schedule for New England philanthropists. The American Colonization Society imprinted its cause onto America's greatest national holiday, Independence Day. On July 4, 1829, the ACS invited a young newcomer to give the Fourth of July Address at the distinguished Park Street Church in Boston. Since arriving in the city in 1826, the twenty-three-year-old William Lloyd Garrison had amassed a reputation as a reform-minded, pious, and passionate editor, the usual characteristics of a forthright champion of colonization.

His mother, Frances Maria Lloyd, was the source of his piety. She had raised him and his two siblings as a single mother in Newburyport, Massachusetts. They had been poor, but her Baptist faith had brought them through the rough times. He remembered the poverty and her maternal lessons like it was yesterday. When he and his older brother had come home carrying food from their mother's employers or the town's soup kitchen, they had endured a gauntlet of taunts from the richer kids on the street. But Frances Maria Lloyd preached to them about human worth: though they were low on funds, they were not low as people.

His older brother had been a difficult boy to raise, but William Lloyd was a model child, seeking only to please his mother. In 1818, when he was twelve, he had begun a seven-year indenture to Ephraim W. Allen, the talented editor of the *Newburyport Herald*. When he was not busy learning the printing trade or writing letters to his mother, who had moved to Baltimore, he was usually intent on educating himself through reading. He devoured the works of Cotton Mather and tracts by politicians and other clergyman proclaiming New England's peculiar destiny to civilize the world. He especially enjoyed the novels of Sir Walter Scott, whose heroes changed the world through the might of their character and their readiness to sacrifice their blood for human justice. He also admired the work of the English poet Felicia Hemans, which was praised for its moral purity.

William Lloyd Garrison's mother died before his indenture ended in 1825. In one of her final requests to her son that did not involve religion, Frances pleaded with him to "remember[,] . . . for your poor mother's sake," the Black woman, Henny, who had kindly cared for her. "Although a slave to man," Frances wrote her son, she is "yet a free-born soul by the grace of God."

Freed of his indenture, and now skilled in the printing trade, Garrison moved to Boston and secured an editorship at a temperance paper. He had a personal interest in the temperance movement. His absent father had never left liquor, and his older brother had been seduced by it. Garrison probably would have become one of the most notable voices for temperance of the age. But a year before his Independence Day Address for the American Colonization Society, an itinerant abolitionist came along to change the course of his life.[3]

Garrison first met the Quaker founder and editor of the *Genius of Universal Emancipation* on March 17, 1828. He sat next to eight esteemed Boston clergymen listening to Benjamin Lundy in the parlor of his boardinghouse, which was owned by a local Baptist minister. Up from Baltimore, Lundy was in town raising money for his newspaper and raising support for emancipation. The wrongs of enslavement Lundy spoke about that night wrenched Garrison's heart. And Lundy's activist's life, no doubt inspired by John Woolman, thrilled Garrison. The man seemed to be straight out of a Walter Scott novel—he had given speeches in nineteen of the twenty-four states, traveled 12,000 miles, engaged in marathon debates with slave owners, been beaten in Baltimore for his beliefs. Authorities had attempted to suppress his paper, but he had kept saying what he believed: "Nothing is wanting . . . but the *will*." He had continued to publish his crude sketches of slave coffles under the title "Hail Columbia!" and a stinging demand: "LOOK AT IT, *again* and *again!*" While Garrison sat on the edge of his seat, the eight ministers sat back. They politely listened, but only one offered to help. The others saw nothing to gain and a lot to lose in the cause of emancipation. They feared that a push for emancipation would only cause social disorder.

Before the meeting, Garrison—like the lazy ministers sitting beside him—probably thought nothing could be done about the evil institution of slavery. It's not that they were in favor of it, but that they thought trying to abolish it was a hopeless cause. As Garrison listened to Lundy, everything changed. Garrison crawled into bed that night enthusiastic about working toward Lundy's aim of provoking "gradual, though total, abolition of slavery in the United States." Soon after Lundy's visit, Garrison resigned from his temperance newspaper and thrust himself into the antislavery cause. Little did he know that almost four decades would pass before he could stop pressing America to free itself of slavery.[4]

ALMOST FROM HIS first words in 1829, agents of the American Colonization Society knew they had selected the wrong Independence Day speaker. "I am sick of . . . our hypocritical cant about the rights of man," Garrison bellowed, making the church crowd uncomfortable. We should be demanding "a gradual abolition of slavery," not promoting colonization. It was a "pitiful subterfuge" to say that liberation would hurt the enslaved. If enslavement had reduced Blacks to "brutes," then was it "a valid argument to say that therefore they must remain brutes?" Freedom and education would "elevate [Blacks] to a proper rank in the scale of being."[5]

Ten days later, Garrison attended a Black Baptist church and participated in the annual celebration of England's abolition of the slave trade. A White clergyman addressed the largely Black crowd, lecturing them that emancipation was neither wise nor safe without a long period qualifying Blacks for freedom. A murmur of disgust shot from the crowd, and an ACS agent leaped to the speaker's defense.

The murmur rang in Garrison's ears as he walked home that night. In the Independence Day Address, he had called immediate emancipation a "wild vision." But was it really wild? Or was it wilder to stand on some middle ground between sinful slavery and righteous freedom? "I saw there was nothing to stand upon," Garrison admitted. In August,

Garrison moved to Baltimore to join Benjamin Lundy and co-edit the *Genius of Universal Emancipation*.[6]

FROM THE EDITORIAL page of the *Genius of Universal Emancipation*, Garrison called for immediate emancipation in September 1829. This new position was not only a change from his own view of two months earlier, but a stance more bold than even Benjamin Lundy's. "No valid excuse can be given for the continuance of the evil [of slavery] a single hour," he wrote—not even colonization. Colonization could be used to relieve some enslaved Africans, of course, but as a solution to the problem of slavery it was "altogether inadequate."[7]

A disciple of Denmark Vesey agreed, and he let the world know it about two months later, in November, when he published his *Appeal . . . to the Colored Citizens of the World*. Antislavery activist David Walker was part of the Black community in Boston, and Garrison may have already crossed paths with him. The Whites, raged Walker in the pamphlet, were "dragging us around in chains" to enrich themselves, "believing firmly" that Black people had been made to serve them forever. "Did our Creator make us to be slaves?" he asked. "Unless we try to refute Mr. Jefferson's arguments respecting us, we will only establish them." Walker appealed for Black people to refute and resist racism, and he had the antiracist foresight to see that racism would only end when slavery ended. Walker told enslaved Blacks to mobilize themselves for the second American revolutionary war.

No Black person could have read Walker's intoxicating *Appeal* without being moved. And yet Walker watered down his appeal by disparaging the very people he was calling upon to resist. Blacks were "the most degraded, wretched, and abject set of beings that ever lived since the world began," he proclaimed. He cited the "inhuman system of slavery," Black ignorance, preachers, and colonizationists as all being responsible for their present plight. In doing so, he regurgitated the theory of how slavery had made Black people inferior. Walker repeated popular racist contrasts of "enlightened Europe" and wretched Africa, contrasts that had been reproduced by the gradual abolitionists, col-onizationists, and the very enslavers he so fervently opposed. Walker did not, however, share his opponents' imaginative version of how enlightened Europe had civilized Africa. He spoke instead of "enlightened . . . Europe" plunging the "ignorant" fathers of Black people into a "wretchedness ten thousand times more intolerable."

In Walker's historical racism, Africa was the place where "learning [had] originated" in antiquity. It had become a land of "ignorance" since that time, however, because African people had been disobedient to their Maker. Cursed by God, Black people lacked political unity, and that lack of unity had enabled their "natural enemies" in the United States "to keep their feet on our throats." David Walker was hardly the first, and he was certainly not the last, Black activist to complain about political disunity as a uniquely Black problem—as if White abolitionists were not betraying White enslavers, and as if White people were more politically unified, and therefore superior politically and better able to rule. Voting patterns never did quite support complaints of Black disunity and White unity. In the late 1820s, Black male voters in the Northeast typically supported the fading Federalists, while White male voters were split between the two major parties. (Although the parties have changed, similar voting patterns persist today.)

These racist ideas diluted Walker's message, and yet it was still intoxicatingly antiracist. Walker identified and decried America's favorite racist pastime: denying Blacks access to education and jobs and then calling their resultant impoverished state "natural." In closing, Walker addressed enslaving America, courageously booming that he was prepared to die for the "truth": "For what is the use of living, when in fact I am dead." Give us freedom, give us rights, or one day you will "curse the day that you ever were born!" He then reprinted parts of Jefferson's Declaration of Independence, imploring Americans to "See your Declaration!" Finally, he asked Americans to compare the "cruelties" England had inflicted on them to those they had inflicted on Black people.[8]

Walker's *Appeal* spread quickly, forcing racial commentators like Garrison to respond to its arguments. Garrison's philosophical commitment to nonviolence caused him to deplore it as a "most injudicious publication." But he did concede in early 1830 that the *Appeal* contained "many valuable truths and seasonable warnings." By then, the South had begun a dogged political and legal battle to suppress the pamphlet. The North Carolina governor called the *Appeal* "totally subversive of all subordination in our slaves"—a proclamation Walker enjoyed reading. In the midst of (and probably because of) the commotion over Walker's pamphlet, Baltimore authorities jailed Garrison on April 17, 1830. Garrison did not seem to mind his seven weeks of imprisonment. "A few white victims must be sacrificed to open the eyes of this nation," he declared upon his release in June, when a wealthy abolitionist paid his fine.

David Walker died weeks later of tuberculosis. But the force of his opposition to racism and slavery—save the part about violent resistance—lived on in the pens and voices of his friends, especially the firebrand abolitionist and feminist Maria Stewart. "It is not the color of the skin that makes the man or the woman, but the principle formed in the soul," Stewart told Bostonians. Stewart's four public lectures in 1832 and 1833 are known today as the first time an American-born woman addressed a mixed audience of White and Black men and women. And she was a pioneering Black feminist, at that. But some called the idea of a mixed audience "promiscuous."[9]

Lundy continued to publish the *Genius*, though irregularly, after that, but he and Garrison parted ways. Garrison needed a new medium to continue his antislavery advocacy. He headed north on an antislavery lecture tour, where his opponents denigrated him as "a second Walker," and where he encountered "prejudice more stubborn" than anywhere else. It was a sentiment Frenchman Alexis de Tocqueville would echo after he toured the United States in 1831. "The prejudice of race appears to be stronger in the states that have abolished slavery than in those where it still exists," Tocqueville shared in his instant political-science classic, *Democracy in America* (1835). Tocqueville described the vicious cycle of racist ideas, a cycle that made persuading or educating racist ideas away nearly impossible. In "order to induce whites to abandon" their opinions of Black inferiority, "the negroes must change," he wrote. "But, as long as this opinion persists, to change is impossible." The United States faced two options: colonization or the eradication or extinction of African Americans—since uplift suasion, Tocqueville felt, would never work. Tocqueville labeled colonization a "lofty" idea, but an impractical one. Extinction remained the only option.[10]

Garrison had a different option in mind when he settled back in Boston: immediate abolition and gradual equality. On Saturday, January 1, 1831, he published the first issue of *The Liberator*, the organ that relaunched an abolitionist movement among White Americans. In his first editorial manifesto, "To the Public," Garrison made a "full and unequivocal" recant of the "popular but pernicious doctrine of *gradual* abolition."[11]

For the rest of his abolitionist life, Garrison never retreated on immediate emancipation. He rebuked any talk of gradual abolition—of preparing society and enslaved Africans for emancipation one day. But he did make clear his preference for gradual equality, retreating on immediate equality and outlining a process of civilizing Black people to be equal one day. Garrison and his band of assimilationists would stridently fight for gradual equality, calling antiracists who fought for immediate equality impractical and crazy—just as segregationists called him crazy for demanding immediate emancipation.

Black subscribers were the early lifeblood of *The Liberator*. Garrison spoke to Black people in his newspaper and in speeches in New York and Philadelphia. He pressed for free Blacks to challenge "every law which infringes on your rights as free native citizens," and to "respect yourself, if you desire the respect of others." They had "acquired," and would continue to acquire, "the esteem, confidence and patronage of the whites, in proportion to your increase in knowledge and moral improvement." Garrison urged Blacks to acquire money, too, because "money begets influence, and influence respectability."

Garrison believed that the nearer Blacks "approached the whites in their habits the better they were," according to an early biographer. "They always seemed to him a social problem rather than simply people." When Blacks were seen as a social problem, the solution to racist ideas seemed simple. As Blacks rose, so would White opinions. When Blacks were seen as simply people—a collection of imperfect individuals, equal to the imperfect collection of individuals with white skins—then Blacks' imperfect behavior became irrelevant. Discrimination was the social problem: the cause of the racial disparities between two equal collections of individuals.[12]

In emphasizing Black self-improvement to ward off racism, Garrison was reflecting the views of the elite Black activists who invited him to their cities and subscribed to his newspaper. Black activists in many cases saw each other as social problems that needed to be fixed. "If we ever expect to see the influence of prejudice decrease and ourselves respected, it must be by the blessings of an enlightenment education," resolved the attendees of Philadelphia's Second Annual Convention for the Improvement of Free People of Color in 1831.[13]

GARRISON WAS WRITING in response to the racial disparities and discrimination he witnessed in the North, where Blacks were free. His calls for an "increase in knowledge and moral improvement" among free Blacks was an effort in uplift suasion not unlike the avowals of the editors of the first Black newspaper, the *Freedom's Journal*. Of course, recent history had not shown a proportional relationship between Black uplift and White respect. The existence of upwardly mobile Blacks did not slow the colonization movement, the spread of enslaved Africans into the southwestern territories, or the unification of White commoners and enslavers in the new anti-Black Democratic Party. When Tennessee enslaver and war hero Andrew Jackson became the new president as the hero of democracy for White men and autocracy for others in 1829, the production and consumption of racist ideas seemed to be quickening, despite recent Black advances. When Kentucky senator Henry Clay organized aristocrats, industrialists, moralists, and colonizationists into the Whig Party in 1832 to oppose Jackson's Democratic Party, racist ideas were spreading on pace within the United States.

In the early 1830s, the new urban penny press turned away from the "good" news and printed more eye-catching "bad" news, sensationalizing and connecting crime and Blackness and poverty. Free Blacks had been forced into the shacks, cellars, and alleys of segregated "Nigger Hill" in Boston, "Little Africa" in Cincinnati, or "Five Points" in New York—"the worst hell of America," wrote a visitor. Black behavior—not the wrenching housing and economic discrimination—was blamed for these impoverished Black enclaves. As early as 1793, a White minister protested that "a Negro hut" had depreciated property values in Salem. Similar protests surfaced in New Haven and Indiana, and they had become commonplace in Boston by the time Garrison settled there. The vicious housing cycle had already begun. Racist policies harmed Black neighborhoods, generating racist ideas that caused people not to want to live next to Blacks, which depressed the value of Black homes, which caused people not to want to live in Black neighborhoods even more, owing to low property values.[14]

Millions of the poor European immigrants pouring into northern port cities after 1830 further amplified the housing discrimination and threatened free Blacks' hold on menial and service jobs. Native Whites swung their rhetorical tools, long used to demean Blacks, and hit Irish immigrants, calling them "white niggers." Some Irish struck back at this nativism. Others channeled—or were led to channel—their economic and political frustrations into racist ideas, which then led to more hatred of Black people.

It was in this environment of entrenched racism that America's first minstrel shows appeared, and they began attracting large audiences of European immigrants, native Whites, and sometimes even Blacks. By 1830, Thomas "Daddy" Rice, who learned to mimic African American English (today called "Ebonics"), was touring the South, perfecting the character that thrust him into international prominence: Jim Crow. Appearing in blackface, and dressed in rags, torn shoes, and a weathered hat, Jim Crow sang and danced as a stupid, childlike, cheerful Black field hand. Other minstrel characters included "Old darky," the thoughtless, musical head of an enslaved family, and "Mammy," the hefty asexual devoted caretaker of Whites. The biracial, beautiful, sexually promiscuous "yaller gal" titillated White men. "Dandy," or "Zip Coon," was an upwardly mobile northern Black male who mimicked—outrageously—White elites. Typically, minstrel shows included a song-and-dance portion, a variety show, and a plantation skit. In the decades leading up to the Civil War, blackface minstrelsy became the first American theatrical form, the incubator of the American entertainment industry. Exported to excited European audiences, minstrel shows remained mainstream in the United States until around 1920 (when the rise of racist films took their place).[15]

Amid the illogic and perpetual challenges to racist ideas over the course of the nineteenth century, superior Whiteness found a normalizing shield in blackface minstrelsy. In 1835 and 1836, those who did not like minstrel shows could see the "Greatest Natural and National Curiosity in the World." A bankrupt twenty-five-year-old, P. T. Barnum, started showing off Joice Heth, who he claimed was 161 years old. What's more, he said, she was the former mammy of George Washington. And she looked the part, with her skeletal frame, paralyzed arm and legs, deeply wrinkled skin, toothless grin, "talons" for nails, and nearly blind eyes. Most of all, Heth's dark skin made her longevity believable. Longevity was common in Africa, the *Evening Star* told its readers. P. T. Barnum, of course, would go on to become one of the greatest showmen in American history, exhibiting all kinds of "freaks," including whitening Blacks. Physical assimilationists continued to view them with pleasure, declaring that skin-color change was what would eventually cure the nation's racial ills.[16]

In addition to minstrel shows and "freak" shows, a series of novels and children's books produced racist ideas to inculcate younger and younger children. John Pendleton Kennedy's novel *Swallow Barn* (1832) inaugurated the plantation genre that more or less recycled minstrel-show mammies and Sambos as characters in inebriating novels. Boston-born South Carolina enslaver Caroline Gilman wrote the plantation genre into *The Rose Bud*, the South's first weekly magazine for children, established in 1832. Reading Gilman (but more often, simply observing their parents), southern White children played master, or worse, overseer, with enslaved Black playmates, ordering them, ridiculing them, and tormenting them. Enslaved children took solace in outwitting their free playmates in physical games, such as anything involving running, jumping, or throwing. "We was stronger and knowed how to play, and the white children didn't," recalled one ex-slave. In slavery, both Black and White children were building a sense of self on a foundation of racist ideas.[17]

This was the America that *The Liberator* entered in the 1830s, a land where Black people were simultaneously seen as scary threats, as sources of comedy, and as freaks. In their totality, all these racist ideas—emanating from minstrel shows, from "freak" shows, from literature, from newspapers, and from the Democrats and Whigs—looked down upon Black people as the social problem. Garrison loathed the shows and the literature, and he loathed those politicians, too. And yet he also crafted Black people as the social problem.

ONE ENSLAVED VIRGINIAN did not share Garrison's view that enslaved Africans should wait while White abolitionists and refined free Blacks solved the problem through nonviolent tactics of persuasion. This preacher rejected uplift suasion, and he rejected racist talk of Black behavior as part of the problem. On the evening of August 21, 1831, Nat Turner and five of his disciples, believing they had been given a task by God, began their fight against the problem in Southampton County. Turner killed his master's family, snatched arms and horses, and moved on to the next plantation. Twenty-four hours later, about seventy freed people had joined the crusade.

After two days, seventy Black soldiers had killed at least fifty-seven enslavers across a twenty-mile path of destruction before the rebellion was put down. Panic spread as newspapers everywhere blared the gory details of the "Southampton Tragedy." Before his hanging, Turner shared his liberation theology with a local lawyer named Thomas Gray. "I heard a loud noise in the heavens, and the Spirit instantly appeared to me and said the Serpent was loosened, and Christ had laid down the yoke he had borne for the sins of men, and that I should take it on and fight against the Serpent, for the time was fast approaching, when the first should be the last and the last should be the first."

"Do you find yourself mistaken now?" Gray had flatly asked. "Was not Christ crucified?" Turner replied.[18]

"We are horror-struck," Garrison wrote of the rebellion. In America's "fury against the revolters," who would remember the "wrongs" of slavery? Garrison would, and he listed them. But he could not condone the strategy of violence. He did not realize that some, if not most, enslavers would die rather than set their wealth free. Garrison pledged his undying commitment to his philosophy: that the best way to "accomplish the great work of national redemption" was "through the agency of moral power," that is, of moral persuasion.

If Blacks did not violently resist, then they were cast as naturally servile. And yet, whenever they did fight, reactionary commentators, in both North and South, classified them as barbaric animals who needed to be caged in slavery. Those enslavers who sought comfort in myths of natural Black docility hunted for those whom they considered the real agitators: abolitionists like Garrison. Georgia went as far as offering a reward of $5,000 (roughly $109,000 today) for anyone who brought Garrison to the state for trial. But the ransom did not stop Garrison from issuing weekly reports and antislavery commentary in *The Liberator* on the debates that raged in response to the Nat Turner Rebellion.

The newspaper had just expanded its number of pages, thanks to funds from the newly formed New England Anti-Slavery Society, the first non-Black organization committed to immediate emancipation. In response to *The Liberator's* expansion, a Connecticut editor scoffed, Georgia legislators ought "to enlarge their reward" for Garrison's head "accordingly." Georgia legislators ought to put out rewards for Virginia's legislators, Garrison shot back. They were "seriously talking of breaking the fetters of their *happy* and *loving* slaves."[19]

After Turner's rebellion, Virginians started seriously contemplating the end of slavery. It was not from the moral persuasion of nonviolent abolitionists, but from the fear of slave revolts, or the "smothered volcano" that could one day kill them all. During the winter of 1831–1832, undercover abolitionists, powerful colonizationists, and hysterical legislators in Virginia raised their voices against slavery. In the end, proslavery legislators batted away every single antislavery measure, and ended up pushing through an even more harrowing slave code than the one that had been in place. Proslavery legislators repressed the very captives they said were docile, and restricted the education of the very people they argued could not be educated. Racist ideas, clearly, did not generate these slave codes. Enslaving interests generated these slave codes. Racist ideas were produced to preserve the enslaving interests.[20]

William Lloyd Garrison did not realize this. But he did realize that these enslaving interests were, in fact, not emancipation's greatest foe. On June 1, 1832, Garrison offered his thoughts on the matter in his first and only book. "Out of thine own mouth will I condemn thee," he wrote, and he went on to lace the book with quotations from colonizationists proving that they were proslavery, enemies of "immediate abolition" who aimed "at the utter expulsion of the Blacks," and who denied "the possibility of elevating the blacks in this country." Garrison concluded with seventy-six pages of anticolonization proclamations from "people of color." The book, entitled *Thoughts on African Colonization*, was a devastating assault on what had become one of the country's most powerful racial reform organizations. With Garrison's book in hand, abolitionists declared war on the American Colonization Society. It was an assault from which the society never recovered.[21]

It was not the only devastating assault the society bore in 1832. Representing southern slaveholders opposed to colonization, College of William & Mary professor Thomas Roderick Dew released his *Review of the Debate in the Virginia Legislature of 1831 and 1832* within a month of *Thoughts*. Dew was the child of Virginia planters and had been profoundly influenced by Adam Smith's *Wealth of Nations*. "The plantations at the south" should "be cultivated" by enslaved Africans who can "resist the intensity of a southern sun" and "endure the fatigues attendant on the cultivation of rice, cotton, tobacco and sugar-cane, better than white labourers." Therefore, the "banishment of one-sixth of our population . . . would be an act of suicide." Thomas Roderick Dew—actually William Lloyd Garrison wrote this bigoted statement in *Thoughts on African Colonization*. Dew agreed in his book. These anti-slavery and proslavery advocates agreed on much more. Like Garrison, Dew considered colonization to be an evil and impractical idea. Black people, "though vastly inferior in the scale of civilization," and though unable to work "except by compulsion," still constituted the cheap labor force that the southern economy needed, Dew wrote.[22]

The US Senate's Foreign Relations Committee had offered the same reasoning in rejecting the American Colonization Society's latest plea for funds in 1828. Since Blacks performed "various necessary menial duties," the committee members concluded, colonization would create a vacuum in cheap labor in seaboard cities, thus increasing labor costs. These various menial and service duties included the work done by day laborers, mariners, servants, waiters, barbers, coachmen, shoe-shiners, and porters for men, and washers, dressmakers, seamstresses, and domestics for the women. "We see them engaged in no business that requires even ordinary capacity," a commentator from Pennsylvania observed. "The mass are improvident, and seek the lowest avocations." Racist policies forcing free Blacks into menial jobs were being defended by racist claims that lazy and unskilled Black people were best for those positions. Racial discrimination was off the hook, and cities received the assurance that their menial labor pools, which the US Senate found so essential to the economy, were safe.[23]

Thomas Roderick Dew's *Review* accomplished in enslaving circles what Garrison's *Thoughts* accomplished in abolitionist circles. "After President Dew," who became president of the College of William & Mary in 1836, "it is unnecessary to say a single word on the practicability of colonizing our slaves," said one South Carolinian. The ACS did its best to fight back. In November 1832, ACS secretary Ralph Gurley argued that "it is not right that men should possess freedom, for which they are entirely unprepared, [and] which can only prove injurious to themselves and others." Gurley's piece, in the ACS's journal, was the opening volley in a nasty ACS counteroffensive against immediate abolitionists that took place on the lecture circuit, from the pulpits, in the colleges, in the newspapers, and in the streets with mobs. Still trying to woo enslavers over to the cause, the ACS did not wage a similar offensive against Thomas Roderick Dew or the slave-holders he represented.[24]

While White mobs made some hesitate, sixty-six abolitionists, fearing only the threat of apathy, gathered in Philadelphia on December 4, 1833, to form the American Anti-Slavery Society (AASS). They believed in the radical idea of "immediate emancipation, without expatriation." The AASS was led by America's most illustrious philanthropist, New Yorker Arthur Tappan, and his rich brothers, future Ohio US senator Benjamin Tappan and abolitionist Lewis Tappan, best known for working to free the illegally enslaved Africans on the *Amistad* ship. The impracticable strategy of uplift suasion was written into the AASS constitution. "This Society shall aim to elevate the character and conditions of the people of color, by encouraging their intellectual, moral and religious improvement, and by removing public prejudice."[25]

Garrison received a minor AASS post, as the relatively cautious Tappan brothers and their friends were attempting to wrest control of the abolitionist movement from Bostonians. More paternalistically and brazenly than Garrison, the Tappan brothers instructed AASS agents to instill in free Blacks "the importance of domestic order, and the performance of relative duties in families; of correct habits; command of temper and courteous manners." Their mission: uplift the inferior free Blacks to "an equality with whites." And yet, AASS agents and supporters were cautioned not to adopt Black children, encourage interracial marriages, or excite "the people of color to assume airs." Blacks were to assume "the true dignity of meekness" in order to win over their critics.

At the annual meeting of the AASS in May 1835, members resolved to use new technologies to spread their gospel to potential abolitionist converts. They relied on the mass printing machinery of stereotyped plates, on cheap rag paper, on steam presses, and on new railroads and an efficient postal service to overwhelm the nation with 20,000 to 50,000 copies a week of abolitionist tracts. The aim: "to awaken the conscience of the nation to the evils of slavery." Slaveholders had no clue what was coming.[26]

CHAPTER 14

Imbruted or Civilized

AS ENSLAVERS CALMLY discussed profits, losses, colonization, torture techniques, and the duties of Christian masters, they felt the spring drizzle of abolitionist tracts. By the summer of 1835, it had become a downpour—there were some 20,000 tracts in July alone, and over 1 million by the year's end. Presenting slaveholders as evil, the literature challenged some racist ideas, such as the Black incapacity for freedom, yet at the same time produced other racist ideas, such as Africans being naturally religious and forgiving people, who always responded to whippings with loving compassion. The movement's ubiquitous logo pictured a chained African, kneeling, raising his weak arms up in prayer to an unseen heavenly God or hovering White savior. Enslaved Africans were to wait for enslavers to sustain them, colonizationists to evacuate them, and abolitionists to free them.[1]

Enraged enslavers viewed the American Anti-Slavery Society's postal campaign as an act of war. Raging to defend "our sister states" against abolitionists, White male thugs roamed northern Black neighborhoods in the summer and fall of 1835, looting and destroying homes, schools, and churches. They shouted about their mission to protect White women from the hypersexual Black-faced animals that, if freed, would ravage the exemplars of human purity and beauty. In fact, after 1830, young, single, and White working-class women earning wages outside the home were growing less dependent on men financially and becoming more sexually free. White male gang rapes of White women began to appear around the same time as the gang assaults by White men on Black people. Both were desperate attempts to maintain White male supremacy.[2]

The most fearless and astute defender of slavery to emerge in the wake of abolitionist pressures was Senator John C. Calhoun of South Carolina, the son of rich planters who had served as vice president under two presidents, John Quincy Adams and Andrew Jackson. Even those who hated him could not deny his brilliance as a strategist and communicator. Calhoun shared his latest and greatest proslavery strategy on the Senate floor on February 6, 1837. Agitated by a Virginia senator's earlier reference to slavery as a "lesser evil," Calhoun rose to "take higher ground." Once and for all, Calhoun wanted to bury that old antislavery Jeffersonian concept. "I hold that . . . the relation now existing in the slaveholding States between the two [races], is, instead of an evil, a good—a positive good," he said. Calhoun went on to explain that it was both a positive good for society and a positive good for subordinate Black people. Slavery, Calhoun suggested, was racial progress.[3]

In a way, William Lloyd Garrison respected Calhoun, preferring him and his bold proslavery candor over politicians like the timid Henry Clay, who still believed in gradual abolitionism and colonization. Nevertheless, he said Calhoun was "the champion of hell-born slavery": "His conscience is seared with a hot iron, his heart is a piece of adamant." For advocates of gradual emancipation, Garrison was a radical because of his belief in immediate emancipation, whereas Calhoun was a radical for his support of perpetual slavery. Both Garrison and Calhoun regarded the other as the fanatical Devil Incarnate, the destroyer of America, the decimator of all that was good in the world and the keeper of all that was evil. Garrison needed more courage than Calhoun. While Calhoun was the loudest voice in a national choir of public figures shouting down Garrison, Garrison was nearly alone among White public figures shouting down Calhoun.[4]

But neither Calhoun's claims about slavery as a positive good nor the threat of roving White mobs could stop the growing appeal of abolitionism. Garrison had responded to a Boston mob in October 1835 with majestic nonviolent resistance, and his conduct had pushed thousands of northerners toward his personage and the cause of antislavery. As many as 300,000 had joined the movement by the decade's end.

As new converts rushed into the movement in the late 1830s, abolitionist splits widened. There were the Garrisonians, who refused to participate in the "corrupt" political parties and churches, and the abolitionists, trying to bring the cause into these parties and churches. Splits had grown apparent among Black abolitionists as well. No longer would antiracists calmly listen to people call Black behavior a source of White prejudice. Peter Paul Simons, known for criticizing the *Colored American* editor for believing that biracial people had "the most talent," became one of the first African Americans to publicly attack the idea of uplift suasion. Before the African Clarkson Society in New York City on April 23, 1839, Simons said the strategy reeked of a conspiracy that put "white men at the head of even our private affairs." The "foolish thought of moral elevation" was "a conspicuous scarecrow." Blacks were already a moral people, the antiracist said. "Show up to the world an African and you will show in truth morality." Simon demanded protest, calling for "ACTION! ACTION! ACTION!"[5]

But antiracists had to contend against both powerful antislavery assimilationists and the even more powerful proslavery segregationists. Whig evangelist Calvin Colton demanded action against antislavery in *Abolition a Sedition* and *A Voice from America to England* in 1839. "There is no such thing as equality among men, nor can there be," Colton wrote. "Neither God nor man ever instituted equality." Science affirmed Colton's view. There was a virtual consensus among scholars—from Cambridge in Massachusetts to Cambridge in England—that racial equality did not exist. The debate in 1839 still swirled around the origin of the races: monogenesis versus polygenesis.[6]

THE FOUNDER OF anthropology in the United States, Dr. Samuel Morton, jumped into the origins debate on September 1, 1839, when he published *Crania Americana*. He had made use of his famous "American Golgotha" at Philadelphia's Academy of Natural Sciences, the world's largest collection of human skulls. Morton wanted to give scholars an objective tool for distinguishing the races: mathematical comparative anatomy. He had made painstaking measurements of the "mean internal capacity" of nearly one hundred skulls in cubic inches. Finding that the skulls from the "Caucasian Race" measured out the largest in that tiny sample, Morton concluded that Whites had "the highest intellectual endowments" of all the races. He relied on an incorrect assumption, however: the bigger the skull, the bigger the intellect of the person.[7]

Loving reviews from distinguished medical journals and scientists came pouring into Philadelphia about Morton's "immense body of facts." Not from everyone, though. German Friedrich Tiedemann's skull measurements did not match Morton's hierarchy. So Tiedemann concluded there was racial equality. Like the Germantown petitioners in the 1600s, and John Woolman in the 1700s, Tiedemann showed that racists were never simply products of their time. Although most scholars made the easy, popular, professionally rewarding choice of racism, some did not. Some made the hard, unpopular choice of antiracism.[8]

One of the first major scientific controversies in the United States began with what seemed like a simple observation. Harvard-trained, antislavery psychiatrist Edward Jarvis reviewed data from the 1840 US Census and found that northern free Blacks were about ten times more likely to have been classified as insane than enslaved southern Blacks. On September 21, 1842, he published his findings in the *New England Journal of Medicine*, which was and remains the nation's leading medical journal. Slavery must have had "a wonderful influence upon the development of the moral faculties and the intellectual powers" of Black people, Jarvis ascertained.[9]

A month later, in the same journal, someone anonymously published another purportedly scientific study, "Vital Statistics of Negroes and Mulattoes." Biracial people had shorter life spans than Whites and "pure Africans," the census apparently also showed. The writer called for an investigation into "the cause of such momentous effects." Dr. Josiah C. Nott of Mobile, Alabama, came to the rescue in the *American Journal of Medical Science* in 1843. In "The Mulatto—A Hybrid," the distinguished surgeon contended that biracial women were "bad breeders," because they were the product of "two distinct species," the same way the mule was "from the horse and the ass." Nott's contention was as outrageous as the insanity figures, but scientists reproduced it.[10]

When Jarvis looked more closely at the 1840 census data, he found errors everywhere. Some northern towns reported more Black lunatics than Black residents. Jarvis and the American Statistical Association asked the US government to correct the census. On February 26, 1844, the House of Representatives asked Secretary of State Abel Upshur to investigate. He never had the opportunity. Two days later, Upshur was among the six people killed on the warship USS *Princeton*. President John Tyler named none other than John C. Calhoun as Upshur's replacement. Calhoun saw two matters on Upshur's desk: the census issue and an antislavery letter from the British foreign secretary, Lord Aberdeen. The Brit expressed hope for universal emancipation and a free and independent Texas.[11]

Slaveholders' pursuit of Texas's annexation as a slave state was guiding the 1844 election. Tennessee slaveholder James K. Polk, a Democrat, narrowly defeated Whig Henry Clay, who lost swing votes to James Birney of the new antislavery Liberty Party. Refusing to vote, Garrison leaned on the American Anti-Slavery Society to adopt a new slogan: "NO UNION WITH SLAVEHOLDERS!" He was trying—and failing—to stop the drift of the movement toward politics. Antislavery voting blocs had arisen in the 1840s. They were sending antislavery congressmen to Washington—from John Quincy Adams of Massachusetts to Joshua Reed Giddings of Ohio, and soon Thaddeus Stevens of Pennsylvania, Owen Lovejoy of Ohio, and Charles Sumner of Massachusetts. These congressmen were openly debating slavery and emancipation after 1840, to the horror of John C. Calhoun.[12]

In April 1844, months after withdrawing his own presidential candidacy, Secretary Calhoun informed the British foreign secretary that the treaty of annexation was a done deal. Slavery in Texas was a concern of neither England nor the US government. The United States must not emancipate its slaves because, as the census had proved, "the condition of the African" was worse in freedom than in slavery.

Needing more data to defend US slavery before Western Europe, Calhoun sought out the latest scientific information on the races. He summoned pioneering Egyptologist George R. Gliddon, who had just arrived in Washington as part of his national speaking tour on the wonders of ancient "White" Egypt. Gliddon sent Calhoun copies of Morton's *Crania Americana* and Morton's newest, acclaimed bombshell, *Crania Aegyptiaca*, which depicted ancient Egypt as a land of Caucasian rulers, Hebrews, and Black slaves. Morton's research, Gliddon added in a letter to Calhoun, proved that "Negro-Races" had always "been *Servants* and *Slaves*, always distinct from, and subject to, the Caucasian, in the remotest times." Bolstered by Gliddon's "facts," Calhoun defended American domestic policy before antislavery Europe. The "facts" of the 1840 census were never corrected—and slavery's apologists never stopped wielding its "unquestionable" proof of slavery's positive good. They continued to assert that slavery brought racial progress—almost certainly knowing that this proof was untrue. "It is too good a thing for our politicians to give [up]," a Georgia congressman reportedly confessed. On the eve of the Civil War, a Unitarian clergyman said it best: "It was the census that was insane, and not the colored people."[13]

THE FIRM POLITICAL and scientific support for slavery made it all the more difficult for the abolitionists to change the minds of the consumers of slavery's "positive good." Would the voice of a runaway, expressing his or her own horrific experience, be more convincing? In 1841, William Lloyd Garrison spent three joyous days with abolitionists on the nearby island of Nantucket. As the August 11 session came to a close, a tall twenty-three-year-old runaway mustered the courage to request the floor. This was the first time many White abolitionists had ever heard a runaway share his experience of the grueling trek from slavery to freedom. Impressed, the Massachusetts Antislavery Society (MAS) offered Frederick Douglass a job as a traveling speaker. Douglass then emerged as America's newest Black exhibit. He was introduced to audiences as a "chattel," a "thing," a "piece of southern property," before he shared the brutality of slavery. Though he understood the strategy of shocking White Americans into antislavery, Douglass grew to dislike the regular dehumanization. Whether enslaved or free, Black people were people. Although their enslavers tried, they had never been reduced to things. Their humanity had never been eliminated—a humanity that made them equal to people the world over, even in their chains. Douglass was and always had been a man, and he wanted to be introduced as such.

Douglass also grew tired of merely telling his story over and over again. He had honed his speaking ability and developed his own ideas. Whenever he veered off script into his philosophy, he heard a whisper: "Tell your story, Frederick." Afterward, White abolitionists would say to him, "Give us the facts, we will take care of the philosophy." And do not sound like that when you give the facts: "Have a *little* of the plantation manner of speech than not; 'tis not best that you seem too learned." Douglass knew exactly why they said that. Usually, minutes into his speeches, Douglass could hear the crowd grumbling, "He's never been a slave." And that reaction made sense. Racist abolitionists spoke endlessly about how slavery had made people into brutes. Douglass was clearly no brute.[14]

When Douglass was finally able to tell his story and philosophy in full in his own words, it offered perhaps the most compelling counterweight yet to the 1840 census and the positive good theory. In June 1845, Garrison's printing office published *The Narrative of the Life of Frederick Douglass, an American Slave*. In five months, 4,500 copies were sold, and in the next five years, 30,000. The gripping best seller garnered Douglass international prestige and forced thousands of readers to come to grips with the brutality of slavery and the human desire of Black people to be free. No other piece of antislavery literature had such a profound effect. Douglass's *Narrative* opened the door to a series of slave narratives. For anyone who had the courage to look, they showed the absolute falsity of the notion that enslavement was good for Black people.

William Lloyd Garrison penned the preface to Douglass's 1845 *Narrative*. Enslavement had "degraded" Black people "in the scale of humanity," Garrison claimed. "Nothing has been left undone to cripple their intellects, darken their minds, debase their moral nature, obliterate all traces of their relationship to mankind." Though starting at different places and taking different conceptual routes, Garrison kept arriving in the same racist place as his enslaving enemies—subhuman Black inferiority. But if you let Garrison tell it in Douglass's preface, antislavery had "wholly confounded complexional differences." Garrison chose not to highlight the chilling physical battle with a slave-breaker that thrust Douglass on his freedom course. Garrison enjoyed presenting two types of Black people: degraded or excelling. He hoped the narrative elicited White "sympathy" and "untiring" efforts "to break every yoke." The narrative did do that, and the many slave narratives that followed it attracted White antislavery sympathy, too, especially in New England and Old England. But these narratives did not attract nearly as much White antiracist sympathy. After all, Garrison had packaged the book in his assimilationist idea of the enslaved or free African as actually subpar, someone "capable of high attainments as an intellectual and moral being—needing nothing but a comparatively small amount of cultivation to make him an ornament to society and a blessing to his race."[15]

Garrison's own preface—though powerfully persuasive, as his readers expected—was a compellingly racist counterweight to Douglass's *Narrative*. Another compelling counterweight was Alabama surgeon Josiah Nott's *Two Lectures on the Natural History of the Caucasian and Negro Races* in 1845. He had moved from racist biracial theory to polygenesis, once again using the faulty census data as evidence. As a separate species, "nature has endowed" Black people "with an inferior organization, and all the powers of earth cannot elevate them above their destiny." Nott's polygenesis had become "not only the science of the age," declared one observer, but also "an America science." Popular northern children's books were speaking of the "capacity of the cranium." Best-selling New England author Samuel Goodrich wrote, in *The World and Its Inhabitants*, that "Ethiopians" ranked "decidedly lowest in the intellectual scale."[16]

Douglass's *Narrative* had to contend with the rapidly changing news media as well. In early 1846, the newly formed Associated Press used the newly invented telegraph to become the nation's principal filter and supplier of news. The rapid speed of transmission and monopoly pricing encouraged shorter and simpler stories that told and did not explain—that sensationalized and did not nuance, that recycled and did not trash stereotypes or the status quo. News dispatches reinforcing racist ideas met these demands. In January 1846, New Orleans resident James D. B. De Bow met the demand for a powerful homegrown southern voice, launching *De Bow's Review*. It struggled early on, but by the 1850s it had become the preeminent page of southern thought— the proslavery, segregationist counterpoint to the antislavery, assimilationist *The Liberator*.[17]

Regular contributors drove the expansion of *De Bow's Review*, writers like Louisiana physician Samuel A. Cartwright, a former student of Benjamin Rush. Cartwright wrote about healthy Black captives laboring productively and loving enslavement. Whenever they resisted on the plantation, Cartwright wrote in 1851, they were suffering from what he called *dysesthesia*. "Nearly all" free Blacks were suffering from this disease, because they did not have "some white person" to "take care of them." When enslaved Blacks ran away, they were suffering from insanity, from what he called *drapetomania*. "They have only to be . . . treated like children," Cartwright told slaveholders, "to prevent and cure them" of this insane desire to run away.[18]

Southern medical experiments found an airing in *De Bow's Review*. Researchers routinely used Black subjects. In 1845, Alabama's J. Marion Sims horrifically started experimenting on the vaginas of eleven enslaved women for a procedure to heal a complication of childbirth called *vesicovaginal fistula*. The procedures were "not painful enough to justify the trouble" of anesthesia, he said. It was a racist idea to justify his cruelty, not something Sims truly knew from his experiments. "Lucy's agony was extreme," Sims later noted in his memoir. After a marathon of surgeries into the early 1850s—one woman, Anarcha, suffered under his knife thirty times—Sims perfected the procedure for curing the fistula. Anesthesia in hand, Sims started healing White victims, moved to New York, built the first woman's hospital, and fathered American gynecology. A massive bronze and granite monument dedicated to him—the first US statue depicting a physician—now sits at Fifth Avenue and 103rd Street, across from the Academy of Medicine.[19]

VULNERABLE NOW TO recapture by his former master as a publicly known runaway, Frederick Douglass embarked in 1845 on an extended lecture tour in Great Britain. John O'Sullivan, editor of the *Democratic Review*, was irate that the "black vagabond Douglass" was spending "his time in England propagating his filthy lies against the United States." Douglass sent a crushing reply. Like other followers of national politics in America, Douglass probably knew O'Sullivan as a rabid fan of the annexation of Texas (and all points west). Texas had been admitted as a slave state on December 29, 1845. Expansionists—and especially slavery's expansionists—were clamoring for more: for California, for New Mexico, for Oregon. As the first copies of the *Narrative* went out, O'Sullivan wrote of White Americans' "manifest destiny . . . to possess the whole of the continent which Providence has given us."[20]

In May 1846, President James K. Polk ordered troops over the disputed Texas boundary. When Mexican troops defended themselves, Polk painted Mexicans as the aggressors and publicized his war cause. The ploy worked. The fight against Mexico helped rally North and South alike to the cause of national expansion. But the question of whether the expansion of the nation would mean an expansion of slavery divided northerners and southerners. In August 1846, Democratic representative David Wilmot of Pennsylvania stapled onto an appropriations bill a clause barring slavery in any territory Polk obtained from the Mexican-American War. Wilmot represented the newest political force in the United States: the antislavery, anti-Black Free-Soil movement. What Polk called "foolish," what historians call the Wilmot Proviso, what Wilmot called the "white man's proviso," never passed.[21]

Over the years, William Lloyd Garrison and John C. Calhoun had done their best to polarize the United States into rival camps: those favoring immediate emancipation versus those insisting on permanent slavery. The colonizationists' middle ground of gradual emancipation had capsized by the late 1830s. In 1846, the new Free Soilers rebuilt that middle ground, primarily, but not exclusively, in the North. When Richmond's Tredegar Iron Works placed enslaved Blacks in skilled positions to cut labor costs, White workers protested. In the only protracted urban industrial strike in the pre–Civil War South, they demanded pay raises and the removal of "the negroes" from skilled work. If the striking ironworkers thought enslavers really cared more about racism than profit, or that they would not abandon, out of self-interest, their promotions of a unified White masculinity, then they were in for a long and tortured lesson about power and profit and propaganda. Richmond elites banded together. They viewed the anti-Black strikers as being equivalent to abolitionists because they were trying to prevent them "from making use of slave labor," as the local newspaper cried. In the end, the White strikers were fired.[22]

THE "SLAVE POWER" had declined in the past ten years, leading to a "gradual abatement of the prejudice which we have been deploring," William Lloyd Garrison wrote in *The Liberator* in the summer of 1847. But it remained a "disgusting fact, that they who cannot tolerate the company or presence of educated and refined colored men, are quite willing to be surrounded by ignorant and imbruted slaves, and never think of objecting to the closest contact with them, on account of their complexion! The more of such the better!" Though Garrison was constrained by the bigoted idea of "ignorant and imbruted slaves," and was completely wrong that the western-marching slave power had declined, he had a point. "It is only as they are free, educated, enlightened, that they become a nuisance," he wrote. He realized why uplift suasion was unworkable, but nothing would shake his faith in the strategy.[23]

When General Zachary Taylor began his tenure as the twelfth US president in 1849, Free Soilers were demanding slavery's restriction; abolitionists were demanding the closure of the slave market in Washington, DC; and enslavers were demanding the expansion of slavery and a stricter fugitive slave law to derail the Underground Railroad and its courageous conductors, such as Harriet "Moses" Tubman. Henry Clay, the old architect of the Missouri Compromise of 1820, came out of the gloom of his failed presidential runs to engineer a "reunion of the Union." In January 1850, he proposed satisfying enslavers by denying Congress jurisdiction over the domestic slave trade and instituting a stronger Fugitive Slave Act. To satisfy antislavery or Free Soil northerners, slave trading would be banned in the nation's capital, and California would be admitted to the Union as a free state. Admitting California as a free state gave the balance of power to the North. And with that power, the North could eradicate slavery. Calhoun and teeming numbers of southerners balked at submitting, or even at compromising for a second. Calhoun fumed, and he mustered the forces of secession.[24]

In March 1850, a horde of northern scientists trotted onto Calhoun's turf to attend the third meeting of the American Association for the Advancement of Science (AAAS) in Charleston. Samuel Morton, Josiah C. Nott, and Harvard polygenesist Louis Agassiz were some of the association's first members. Charleston prided itself on its nationally lauded scientists, its natural history museum, and a medical school that boasted plenty of available cadavers and "interesting cases." Weeks before the conference, Charleston's own John Bachman, the undisputed king of southern Lutherans, issued *The Doctrine of the Unity of the Human Race* and an article in the highly respectable *Charleston Medical Journal*. Noah's son Shem was the "parent of the Caucasian race— the progenitor of . . . our Savior." Ham was the parent of Africans, whose "whole history" displayed an inability to self-govern. Bachman's monogenesis made a controversial splash at the meeting. But northern and southern minds were made up for polygenesis in 1850.[25]

Louis Agassiz and Josiah Nott came and gave their papers on polygenesis on March 15, 1850. Philadelphian Peter A. Browne, who helped found the science-oriented Franklin Institute in honor of Benjamin Franklin, presented his comparative study of human hair. Not far from the world's largest collections of skulls, Browne showed off the world's largest collection of hair, a collection he studied to pen

The Classification of Mankind, By the Hair and Wool of Their Heads in 1850. Since Whites had "hair" and Blacks "wool," Browne had "no hesitancy in pronouncing that they *"belong[ed] to two distinct species."* As for the hair properties, Browne declared that "the hair of the white man is more perfect than that of the negro." According to Browne's study, in which he deemed Blacks a separate and inferior animal-like species, straight hair was "good hair" and the "matted" hair of African people was bad. But he was hardly saying something new. So many Black people, let alone White people, had consumed this assimilationist idea that in 1859 an *Anglo-African Magazine* writer complained of Black parents teaching their children "that he or she is pretty, just in proportion as the features approximate to the Anglo-Saxon standard." Black parents must, the writer pleaded, stop characterizing straight hair as "good hair" or Anglo-Saxon features as "good features."[26]

Proud of its scientists, the city of Charleston picked up the tab for the AAAS meeting and the publication of the proceedings. Entire families in all of their gentility attended the sessions. The meeting diverted them from rapid-fire telegraphic news reports on the frenzied debate over the Compromise of 1850. The AAAS conference in the home of proslavery thought demonstrated the crossroads of American science and politics. As enslavers angrily followed northern political developments, Charleston's scientists eagerly followed northern scientific developments, especially the development of polygenesis as the mainstream of racial science.

Days after the AAAS conference ended in Charleston, South Carolina's "town bell" toiled "with sad news." After a long battle with tuberculosis, John C. Calhoun died on March 31, 1850. The hard-lined anti-secessionist President Taylor died months later. Millard Fillmore, an intuitive compromiser, took the presidential office in the aftershock of the deaths of these two rigid giants. By September, Henry Clay's Compromise of 1850 had passed. "There is . . . peace," Clay happily announced. "I believe it is permanent."[27]

The compromise's signature measure, the Fugitive Slave Act, handed enslavers octopus powers, allowing their tentacles to extend to the North. The Act criminalized abettors of fugitives, provided north-erners incentives to capture them, and denied captured Blacks a jury trial, opening the door to mass kidnappings. To William Lloyd Garri-son, the act was "so coldblooded, so inhuman and so atrocious, that Satan himself would blush to claim paternity to it."[28]

CHAPTER 15

Soul

THERE WAS NO customary public outlet for a Maine woman's rage against the Fugitive Slave Act of 1850. This daughter of a famous clergyman, who was also the wife of a famous professor, knew men made the laws, and she knew men reacted publicly to laws. But Harriet Beecher Stowe was not a man, so her choices were limited. She was not the only woman who was frustrated. As Stowe's biographer explained, "The political impotence Stowe felt in the face of unjust laws was building up like water behind a dam for many middle-class women."[1]

The first major collective strike against the dam had come two years earlier at the first women's rights convention, held in Seneca Falls, New York, on July 19 and 20, 1848. Local Quaker women organized the convention alongside Elizabeth Cady Stanton, who penned the meeting's Declaration of Sentiments. The declaration pleaded for gender equality and women's suffrage, desires considered as radical as racial equality and immediate emancipation. Many of the early White women suffragists had spent years in the trenches of abolitionism, oftentimes recognizing the interlocking nature of American racism and sexism.

The Seneca Falls Convention set off a series of local women's rights conventions over the next few years, especially along the northern abolitionist belt from New England to upstate New York and to the state where Harriet Beecher Stowe had lived before moving to Maine: Ohio. Suffragist and abolitionist Frances Dana Gage, one of the first Americans to call for voting rights for all citizens regardless of gender or race, helped organize women's rights conferences across Ohio during the early 1850s.

Gage's most memorable conference took place at a church in Akron, Ohio, in 1851. But she was not the only celebrity there. A tall, thin, fifty-something-year-old lady adorned by a gray dress, white turban, and sunbonnet walked into the church "with the air of a queen up the aisle," an observer recorded. As White women buzzed for her to turn back around and leave, Sojourner Truth defiantly took her seat and bowed her head in disgust. She may have thought back to all the turmoil she had experienced, which she had described in *The Narrative of Sojourner Truth*, printed by Garrison the year before.

On May 29, 1851, day two of the meeting, men came in full force to berate the resolutions. The convention turned into a bitter argument over gender. Male ministers preached about superior male intellect, the gender of Jesus, Eve's sin, the feebleness of women, all to counter the equal rights resolutions. The women were growing weary when Sojourner Truth, who had kept her head bowed almost the whole time, raised her head up. She lifted her body slowly and started walking to the front. "Don't let her speak!" some women shouted.

Before the audience now, she laid her eyes on the convention organizer. Gage announced her and begged the audience for silence. Quiet came in an instant as all the eyes on White faces became transfixed on the single dark face. Truth straightened her back and raised herself to her full height—all six feet. She towered over nearby men. "Ain't I a Woman? Look at me! Look at my arm!" Truth showed off her bulging muscles. "Ain't I a Woman? I can outwork, outeat, outlast any man! Ain't I a Woman!" Sojourner Truth had shut down and shut up the male hecklers.

As she returned to her seat, Truth could not help but see the "streaming eyes, and hearts beating with gratitude" from the women, the muddled daze from the men. Truth imparted a double blow in "Ain't I a Woman": an attack on the sexist ideas of the male disrupters, and an attack on the racist ideas of females trying to banish her. "Ain't I a Woman" in all of my strength and power and tenderness and intelligence. "Ain't I a Woman" in all of my dark skin. Never again would anyone enfold more seamlessly the dual challenge of antiracist feminism.[2]

Harriet Beecher Stowe no doubt heard about Sojourner Truth's speech in Garrison's *The Liberator*, or through correspondence with Ohio suffragists and abolitionists. But the attention of this gifted writer was not on the awakening suffrage movement. It was on the outrages of the Fugitive Slave Act, which was sending fugitives and free Blacks to the cotton fields. And Stowe learned about these outrages from letters that her younger sister, Isabella, was sending her from Connecticut. The letters were often read aloud in the parlor for Harriet's seven children to hear. "Now Hattie," Isabella wrote her big sister in one such letter, "if I could use a pen as you can, I would write something that would make this whole nation feel what an accursed thing slavery is." Harriet Beecher Stowe rose from her chair. "I will write something," she declared. "I will write if I live."[3]

Titled *Uncle Tom's Cabin*, Stowe's "living dramatic reality" entered bookstores on March 20, 1852. "The scenes of this story," she opened the novel's preface, "lie among . . . an exotic race, whose . . . character" was "so essentially unlike the hard and dominant Anglo-Saxon race." In Black people's "lowly docility of heart, their aptitude to repose on a superior mind and rest on a higher power, their childlike simplicity of affection, and facility of forgiveness," she wrote, "[i]n all these they will exhibit the highest form of the peculiarly *Christian life*." Only enslavement was holding them back.[4]

In one novel, Stowe ingeniously achieved what Garrison had been trying to do for roughly two decades in article after article in *The Liberator*. For the cosmic shift to antislavery, Stowe did not ask Americans to change their deep-seated beliefs. She asked only for them to alter the implications, the *meaning* of their deep-seated beliefs. Stowe met Americans where they were: in the concreteness of racist ideas. She accepted the nationally accepted premise of the enslaver. Naturally docile and intellectually inferior Black people were disposed to their enslavement to White people—and, Stowe crucially tacked on—to God. Stowe inverted Cotton Mather and all those preachers after him who had spent years trying to convince planters that Christianity made Blacks better slaves. She claimed that since docile Blacks made the best slaves, they made the best Christians. Since domineering Whites made the worst slaves, they made the worst Christians. Stowe offered Christian salvation to White America through antislavery. In order to become better Christians, White people must constrain their domineering temperament and end the evil outgrowth of that temperament: slavery.

Uncle Tom's Cabin was a powerfully effective tool for Stowe's racist abolitionism because it was such an awesome page turner. An indebted Kentucky slaveholder plans to sell the enslaved religious leader Uncle Tom and the young son of Eliza Harris. Eliza grabs her son, flees, and reunites in northern freedom with her fugitive husband, George Harris. Tom stays and is sold South. Heading downriver on a boat, Tom saves a pious little White girl, Eva, who had fallen in the river. Grateful, her father, Augustine St. Clare, buys Tom.

The relations of Tom and Eva sit at the novel's thematic center. Stowe created the double-character—the naturally Christian Tom/Eva—to highlight her conception of Blacks being more feminine, "docile, child-like and affectionate," which allows Christianity to find a "more congenial atmosphere" in Black bodies. In a major proselytizing battle, Stowe pits the *soulful* Christian Black slave, Tom, against the *mindful* un-Christian White master, St. Clare. "Thou hast hid from the wise and prudent, and revealed unto babes," Tom says in biblical style. Blacks were spiritually superior because of their intellectual inferiority, Stowe maintained. This spiritual superiority allowed Blacks to have soul.[5]

Stowe's popularization of spiritually gifted Black people quickly became a central pillar of African American identity as Black readers consumed the book and passed on its racist ideas. Racist Whites, believing themselves to be void of soul, made it their personal mission to find soul through Black people. Racist Blacks, believing themselves to be void of intellect, made it their personal mission to find intellect through White people. Black Americans almost immediately made Uncle Tom the identifier of Black submissiveness, while accepting Stowe's underlying racist idea that made Uncle Tom so submissive: Blacks were especially spiritual; they, especially, had soul.

And these Black people were inferior to biracial people, in Stowe's reproduction of biracial racism. The only four adult characters who run away are the novel's four biracial captives, the "tragic mulattos." Though appearing and acting White, they are tragically imprisoned by Blackness. And yet in their intellectual and aesthetic superiority, in their active resistance to enslavement, Stowe distinguishes the mulattos from the "full black."[6]

In the novel's "concluding remarks," Stowe called for northerners to teach Blacks until they reached "moral and intellectual maturity, and then assist them in their passage" to Africa, "where they may put into practice the lessons they have learned in America." Her call was a godsend to the vanishing American Colonization Society. *Uncle Tom's Cabin* and Blacks fed up with the United States revitalized the colonization movement in the 1850s. President Fillmore intended to endorse colonization in his 1852 Message to Congress. "There can be no well-grounded hope," he was going to say, "for the improvement of either [Blacks'] moral or social condition, until they are removed from a humiliating sense of inferiority in the presence of a superior race." Although they were omitted in the speech itself, these remarks found their way into newspapers.[7]

Garrison revered Uncle Tom in his book review of March 26, 1852. But he was virtually alone in his antiracist questioning of Stowe's religious bigotry. "Is there one law of submission and non-resistance for the black man, and another law of rebellion and conflict for the white man? Are there two Christs?" Garrison also regretted seeing the "sentiments respecting African colonization." His antiracist religiosity hardly made waves like his critique of Stowe's endorsement of colonization.[8]

Frederick Douglass was also wary of Stowe's embrace of colonization, though he did not criticize her portrait of the "soulful" Uncle Tom. He sent off an assimilationist, anti-Indian letter to Stowe explaining why Blacks would never accept colonization. "This black man (*un*like the Indian) loves civilization," Douglass wrote. "He does not make very great progress in civilization himself, but he likes to be in the midst of it." In not totally rebuking Stowe and her novel, the most influential Black man in America hardly slowed the consumption of the novel's racist ideas.[9]

No one came closer to totally trashing *Uncle Tom's Cabin* than a Black writer and physician named Martin R. Delany. He had become disillusioned about abolitionism because its proponents had not come to his aid when he had been ejected from Harvard Medical School in 1850. He had been accepted, along with two other Black students, but when they arrived, White students had called for their dismissal. In 1852, Delany released his largely antiracist *The Condition, Elevation, Emigration, and Destiny of the Colored People of the United States, Politically Considered*. Antislavery societies, Delany charged, "presumed to *think* for, dictate to, and *know* better what suited colored people, than they know for themselves." Black people had two choices: continued degradation in the United States, or establishment of a prosperous community elsewhere—meaning colonization on Black terms. Even on Black terms, Black people still mostly opposed colonization.[10]

While splitting on colonization in the 1850s, Black male activists seemingly united in their distaste of Uncle Tom for disseminating the stereotype of the weak Black male. For some time, racist Black patriarchs had been measuring their masculinity off of the perceived controlling masculinity of White men, and they found Black masculinity to be lacking. They demanded control of Black women, families, and communities to redeem their masculinity from the "weak Black male" stereotype. As antislavery Black patriarchs petitioned in 1773, in Massachusetts, "How can the wife submit themselves to [their] husbands in all things" if Blacks remained enslaved? And then, at the male-dominated National Convention of Colored Citizens in Syracuse in 1864, they complained, "We have been denied ownership of our bodies, our wives, home, children and the products of our own labor." These Black men resolved to "vindicate our manhood," as if it needed any vindication. It could not have been a coincidence that while women like Sojourner Truth were asserting their right to gender equity in the 1850s and early 1860s, Black (and White) men were asserting their right to rule women.[11]

The sexist opposition seemed wrapped up in the proslavery opposition, especially since a woman had penned *Uncle Tom's Cabin*. Southerners hailed the publication of Caroline Lee Hentz's *The Planter's Northern Bride*, and William Gilmore Simms's *The Sword and the Distaff*, the most prominent of the more than twenty plantation-school novels published in the reactionary aftermath of *Uncle Tom's Cabin*. In these books, professorial planters, and their pure and upright wives, civilized their animal-like or childlike contented captives on their family farms. These plantation novelists could write up some fiction. Although *Uncle Tom's Cabin* may not have spread among southerners as widely as the plantation-school books, a large number of southerners did get their hands on it. "Mrs. Stowe says that the . . . chief wrong in the catalogue of sins against the negro, is the prejudice of caste, the antipathy of race, the feeling we crush into their souls that they are 'nothing but niggers,'" wrote a Georgia "lady" in *De Bow's Review*. But Mrs. Stowe was forgetting, she said, "the fact that their Maker created them 'nothing but niggers.'"[12]

NEITHER THE FREE-SOIL upsurge nor the antislavery upsurge from the Fugitive Slave Act and *Uncle Tom's Cabin* could overcome the political parties' overwhelming propaganda or the sectional and slavery tensions during the presidential election of 1852. New Hampshire's flamboyant Mexican-American War general, Franklin Pierce, ready to turn the nation's attention from slavery toward national expansion, won in a rout for the Democrats. "The question is at rest," Pierce proclaimed in his First Inaugural Address in 1853. Abolitionists will never rest until "the eternal overthrow" of slavery, the forty-seven-year-old Garrison shot back.[13]

In 1853, the American Anti-Slavery Society refused to admit defeat in the wake of Franklin Pierce's victory. Members celebrated their twentieth anniversary by celebrating Garrison, in order to put him before as many eyes as possible. It mirrored the international effort in 1853 to put the recently deceased University of Pennsylvania polygenesist Samuel Morton before the public and hail him as the exemplary pioneer. Josiah C. Nott and George Gliddon published, on April 1, 1853, the monumental *Types of Mankind*, eight-hundred pages of polygenesis, dedicated "to the Memory of Morton." For visual learners, they inserted an illustration of two columns of faces adjoining skulls: the "Greek" at the top, the "ape" at the bottom, the "Negro" in the middle. The debate over "the primitive origin of the races" was the "last grand battle between science and dogmatism." Who would win? "Science must again, and finally, triumph!"[14]

Types of Mankind appeared during a crowded 1853, a critical year for segregationist ideas making the case for permanent Black inferiority while assimilationist abolitionists advanced. Democrats welcomed the publication of New York editor John H. Van Evrie's *Negroes and Negro Slavery*. Van Evrie ran at the front of a stampede of northern proslavery, pro-White pamphleteers chasing down the abolitionist movement in the 1850s. "God has made the negro an inferior being not in most cases, but in all cases," Van Evrie declared. "The same almighty creator made all white men equal." Over in France in 1853, aristocratic royalist Arthur de Gobineau released his four-volume *Essai sur l'inégalité des races humaines* (*An Essay on the Inequality of the Human Races*). Gobineau's demand for France's return to aristocracy included an analysis of the "colossal truth" of racial hierarchy, of polygenesis. The intelligent White lovers of liberty were at the top; the yellow race was the "middle class"; and at the bottom were the greedy, sexual Black people. Blacks' abnormal physical traits had developed to compensate for their stupidity, Gobineau wrote. Within the White species, the Aryan was supreme—and was the supreme maker of all great civilizations in history the world over. Germans embraced Gobineau, especially since he said Aryans were "la race germanique." In 1856, Josiah C. Nott arranged for the translation of Gobineau's book into English.[15]

Though the book was expensive and had a lot of competition for readers' attention, *Types of Mankind* sold out almost immediately. It was "handsomely welcomed" in Europe, and well regarded as an excellent treatment of the "pre-eminently . . . American science" of polygenesis, as the *New York Herald* wrote. The reviewer for *Putnam's Monthly* accepted polygenesis, too, explaining that "the nations are of one blood, therefore, not genealogically, but spiritually." Cotton Mather's old case of spiritual equality (and bodily inequality) to square slavery and Christianity was now squaring polygenesis and Christianity.

In *Putnam's* competitor, *Harper's Magazine*, Herman Melville, who had just authored *Moby-Dick*, issued "The 'Gees." The antiracist satire relentlessly mocked the contradictions of polygenesis. The fictional 'Gees are a people "ranking pretty high in incivility, but rather low in stature and morals." They have "a great appetite, but little imagination; a large eyeball, but small insight. Biscuit he crunches, but sentiment he eschews." Meanwhile, the character of Queequeg in *Moby-Dick* gave Melville a chance to challenge racial stereotypes.[16]

Types of Mankind was so popular and so influential that it compelled the first major response to polygenesis by an African American. The Reverend Martin B. Anderson, the first president of the University of Rochester, loaned the book to his friend Frederick Douglass. Anderson also handed over works by Nott, Gliddon, and Morton. Douglass used his first formal address before a college audience—Cleveland's Case Western Reserve on July 12, 1854—to mount a spirited rebuttal. The address was published that year in Rochester, and Douglass recycled the message in other speeches for years.[17]

"Before the Notts, the Gliddens, the Agassiz, the Mortons made their profound discoveries," speaking "in the name of *science*," Douglass said, humans believed in monogenesis. Nearly all advocates of polygenesis "hold it be the privilege of the *Anglo-Saxon* to enslave and oppress the African," he went on. "When men oppress their fellow-men, the oppressor ever finds, in the character of the oppressed, a full justification for his oppression." Douglass, amazingly, summed up the history of racist ideas in a single sentence.

After effortlessly proving the ancient Egyptians were Black, labeling *Types of Mankind* the most "compendious and barefaced" attempt ever to "brand the negro with natural inferiority," and rooting all human differences in environment, Douglass turns from his antiracist best to his racist worst. He references the work of biracial physician James McCune Smith of New York, who had the single greatest influence on Douglass's life—more than Garrison. At Scotland's University of Glasgow in the 1830s, Smith had earned bachelor's, master's, and medical degrees—the first American of African descent to do so. The hair of Black people was "growing more and more straight," Smith once rejoiced. "These influences—climate and culture—will ultimately produce a uniform" American of White skin and straight hair.[18]

Leaning on Smith's climate theory and cultural racism, Douglass asked the students in Cleveland, "Need we go behind the vicissitudes of barbarism for an explanation of the gaunt, wiry, apelike appearance of some of the genuine Negroes? Need we look higher than a vertical sun, or lower than the damp, black soil [of West Africa] . . . for an explanation of the Negro's color?" While Douglass beat the vicissitudes of barbarism into Africa, he ascribed "the very heart of the civilized world" into England. He had emerged as the most famous Black male abolitionist *and* assimilationist in the United States.[19]

The cutting up of the Bible, "root and branch," in Gobineau's *Types of Mankind* did not sit well with the most famous White male abolitionist and assimilationist either. William Lloyd Garrison reviewed the segregationist book on October 13, 1854, in his first bout, too, with polygenesis. Garrison took aim, in particular, at Josiah C. Nott, who had said that he "looked in vain, during twenty years for a solitary exception" to Jefferson's verdict of never finding "a black had uttered a thought above the level of plain narrative." This is "something extraordinary," said Garrison sardonically, "that Jefferson should beget so many stupid children."[20]

THOUGH THEY WERE firmly united against *Types of Mankind*, against segregationist ideas, and against slavery, Douglass and Garrison eventually grew apart. When Frederick Douglass attacked the paternalism of White abolitionists and recognized the need for Black organizing, interracial organizers lashed back, Garrison included. By the summer and fall of 1853, invective filled the pages of *Frederick Douglass' Paper* and *The Liberator*. Garrison issued his most damning comment in *The Liberator* on September 23, 1853: "The sufferers from American slavery and prejudice, as a class," were unable "to perceive" the demands of the movement "or to understand the philosophy of its operations."[21]

All along, mutual friends tried to stop the quarrel. Before the year expired, Harriet Beecher Stowe stepped between Douglass and Garrison. She achieved what others could not. After all, the best-selling *Uncle Tom's Cabin* had catapulted Stowe to the pinnacle of the abolitionist movement overlooking both Douglass and Garrison. Her novel was drawing more northerners to the movement than the writings and speeches of Douglass and Garrison—especially, and crucially, the women who were firing the nation up for their rights. Stowe's letters to both men held them back. The bitter warfare tailed off and stopped. They each forgave, but did not forget. They each turned their attention to the controversy that undermined the "finality" platform of the Pierce administration in 1854.[22]

CHAPTER 16

The Impending Crisis

US SENATOR STEPHEN A. DOUGLAS of Illinois desired to give statehood to the territories of Nebraska and Kansas in order to build through these states a transcontinental railroad. Douglas and his benefactors envisioned this railroad transforming the flourishing Mississippi Valley into the nation's epicenter. To secure crucial southern support, the Kansas-Nebraska Act in 1854 left the slavery question to be settled by the settlers, thus repealing the Missouri Compromise.

Stephen Douglas knew the bill would produce "a hell of a storm," but his forecast underestimated northern ire. Slavery seemed officially on the national march, and the days of Free Soil seemed numbered. And fears of this future caused northerners to speak out against the march of slavery, including a politically ambitious Illinois lawyer who had served one term, from 1847 to 1849, as an Illinois congressman. Abraham Lincoln took an antislavery stand, reviving his dead political career as he vied for Illinois's second US Senate seat across from Stephen Douglas in 1854. He scolded the "monstrous injustice" in a long speech in Peoria, Illinois, on October 16, 1854. But he did not know what to do "as to the existing institution," adding, "My first impulse would be to free all the slaves, and send them to Liberia." But that was impossible. "What then? Free them all, and keep them among us as underlings? . . . Free them, and make them politically and socially, our equals? My own feeling will not admit this; and if mine would, we well know that those of the great mass of white people will not."[1]

Abraham Lincoln was a political disciple of Henry Clay, the Great Compromiser, who had just engineered compromises of 1820 and 1850. One of the great causes of Clay's political life was colonization. He spoke at the founding meeting of the American Colonization Society and presided over the organization from 1836 to 1849. When Henry Clay died in 1852, he became the first American to lie in state at the US Capitol. Not many abolitionists joined in the mourning. No man was a greater enemy to Black people, William Lloyd Garrison insisted. Lincoln called Clay "my ideal of a great man."[2]

Abraham Lincoln gave Clay's eulogy in the Illinois capitol in 1852, and for the first time in his public life endorsed returning both free and freed Blacks to their "long-lost fatherland" in Africa. Lincoln hailed from Kentucky like Clay, and some of his relatives owned people. His parents did not, showing an aversion to slavery. Lincoln did not like the domestic slave trade, and yet he had no problem advocating against Black voting rights early in his career as an Illinois state legislator. In 1852, the forty-three-year-old had settled for practicing law, believing his political career in the Whig Party had ended before he resurfaced to run for a Senate seat in 1854.[3]

THE KANSAS-NEBRASKA ACT split open Abraham Lincoln's Whig Party along regional lines and killed Henry Clay's baby. Two new parties emerged in time for the 1856 presidential election: the Know-Nothings, calling immigrants and Catholics the enemy, and the Republican Party, calling the expanding "slave power" the enemy. Neither could outduel the Democrats, who united in opposition to abolitionism. On March 4, 1857, Democrat James Buchanan took the presidential oath of office as the fifteenth president of the United States. The "difference of opinion" in Congress and in America over slavery's expansion should and would be "speedily and finally settled" by the US Supreme Court, he announced. Buchanan had insider information of the Supreme Court's impending decision on the differences, but he feigned ignorance. "All good citizens" should join him, Buchanan said, in "cheerfully" submitting to the Court's decision.[4]

All of two days later, on March 6, 1857, the Supreme Court submitted its decision, but not many antislavery northerners cheerfully submitted. In *Dred Scott v. Sandford*, the Court rejected the freedom suit of Dred Scott, who had been taken to free states and territories. Five southerners (Democrat and Whig) and two northerners (both Democrats) had ruled the Missouri Compromise unconstitutional, questioned the constitutionality of northern abolition, stripped Congress of its power to regulate slavery in the territories, and stated that Black people could not be citizens. An Ohio Republican and a New England Whig had dissented.

Chief Justice Roger B. Taney issued the stingingly controversial majority opinion. A steadfast Jacksonian Democrat from Maryland who had emancipated his captives long ago, he had made a career out of defending the property rights of slaveholders, his right to emancipate, and his friends' rights to enslave. About to turn eighty years old, Taney refused to bury slavery (as it turned out, Taney died the day Maryland abolished slavery in 1864). When he finished his fifty-five-page majority opinion, Taney hoped that Blacks, Free Soilers, and abolitionists would have no constitutional life to fortify their freedom fights against slaveholders. Since Black people had been excluded from the American political community when the nation was founded, the United States could not now extend them rights, Taney reasoned. "They had for more than a century been regarded as beings of an inferior order, and altogether unfit to associate with the white race, either in social or political relations, and so far unfit that they had no rights which the white man was bound to respect."[5]

Although Taney was absolutely right about the founding fathers regarding Blacks as inferior, he was absolutely wrong that Black men had been excluded from the original political community. Dissenting Justice Benjamin Curtis revealed that upon the nation's founding, Black men had possessed voting rights in at least five states—almost half the Union—sinking Taney's argument against Black citizenship rights. But Curtis's history lesson made no headway upon Taney, his other colleagues on the Court, or the residents of the White House or the US Capitol, who applauded the *Dred Scott* decision. They probably already knew the history. They seemed not to care about the crippling effects of the Court's racist decision. All they seemed to care about was maintaining their nation's enriching economic interests. And nothing enriched northern investors and factory owners and southern landowners and slaveholders in 1857 as much as the nation's principal export: cotton.[6]

Democratic senator Stephen Douglas rejoiced over the Taney decision, speaking for enslavers and their northern defenders alike. Abraham Lincoln, who was now campaigning for Douglas's Senate seat in 1858, opposed the decision, speaking for the Free Soilers and abolitionists in the fledgling Republican Party. Abraham Lincoln and Stephen Douglas agreed to a series of seven debates from late August to mid-October 1858 in Illinois. Thousands showed up to watch them, and millions read the transcripts. The candidates became household names. The tall, slight, poorly dressed, and unassuming Lincoln quietly arrived alone to the debates, ready to stand on the defensive. The short, stocky, custom-suit-clad, and arrogant Douglas arrived with his young wife, Adele, in a private railcar to the firing of cannons, ready to go on the offensive. The visual and audio contrasts were tailor-made for a technology that did not yet exist.

"If you desire negro citizenship," said Douglas, "then support Mr. Lincoln and the Black Republican party." Douglass kept race baiting, manipulating the racist ideas of voters to turn them off of Republicans. In the decades before the Civil War, race baiting had become a crucial campaign ploy, especially for the dominant Democratic Party. Douglas went on to say that America "was made by white men, for the benefit of white men and their posterity forever," warning that a Lincoln presidency would lead to integrated communities. As the race baiting from Douglas intensified, the stream of letters urging Lincoln to separate Republicans from racial equality intensified, too. By the fourth debate in Charleston in central Illinois, Lincoln had had enough. "I am not nor ever have been in favor of making [Black people] voters or jurors," or politicians or marriage partners, Lincoln insisted. "There is a physical difference between the white and black races which I believe will for ever forbid the two races living together on terms of social and political equality. And inasmuch as they cannot live, while they do remain together there must be the position of superior and inferior, and I as much as any other man am in favor of having the superior position assigned to the white race."

Abraham Lincoln threw Stephen Douglas on the defensive. Douglas charged Lincoln with changing his views on race to fit the audience: "jet black" in the northern abolitionist part of the state, the "color of a decent mulatto" in the antislavery, anti-abolitionist center, and "almost white" in proslavery southern Illinois. Douglas wanted to keep the discussion on race. Putting race behind him, Lincoln went on the offensive in the last three debates and steered the discussion toward slavery. In the final debate, in Alton, Illinois, the home of assassinated abolitionist editor Elijah P. Lovejoy, Lincoln declared that a vote for Douglas was a vote for expanding slavery, and a vote against "free white people" finding homes and improving their lives by moving west.[7]

Illinois Democrats won control of both houses and reelected Douglas in the 1858 midterm elections. Illinois Republicans learned that being branded pro-Black was more politically crippling than being branded proslavery. But in the rest of the North, Republicans did much better. Abraham Lincoln, in Springfield, Illinois; William Lloyd Garrison one thousand miles away in Boston; and other watchers of American politics saw the same obvious results of the elections. In addition to seizing power in the swing states of New York, Pennsylvania, and Indiana, Republicans had won big in abolitionist country: small-town New England, "the Yankee West," and the northern counties along the Great Lakes. They had differing vantage points, differing ideologies, and differing personal and national ambitions, so it is not surprising that Lincoln and Garrison responded differently to the same results.[8]

Garrison tamed his criticism of a major political party for the first time in almost thirty years, recognizing that America's antislavery voters had flocked to the Republican fold. He envisioned its coalition of "incongruous elements" breaking up after losing the 1860 election and the genuinely antislavery politicians taking over. In the meantime, it was his job—it was the job of the movement—to "distinguish the shortcomings of the Republican platform from the promise of the

Republican constituency," that is, to persuade this constituency that there could be no compromise with slavery, and no union with slave-holders. Garrison's biographer termed this new strategy "political sua-sion." Old friends committed to keeping the movement out of politics admonished him, generating heated debates at abolitionist meetings in the late 1850s.[9]

In contrast, Lincoln turned away from the Republicans' anti-slavery-expansion base and reached for the independents. Republicans in swing states like Illinois started focusing on the much more popu-lar rights of "free labor," a topic inspired by the 1857 best seller *The Impending Crisis of the South* by North Carolinian Hinton Rowan Helper. Slavery needed to end because it was retarding southern economic progress and the opportunities of non-slaveholding Whites, who were oppressed by wealthy enslavers. Helper didn't "believe in the unity of races." But he refused to accept the doctrine of polygenesis as a justifi-cation to continue slavery. Emancipated Africans, he wrote, should be sent to Africa.[10]

Horace Greeley, the nation's most famous editor, promoted Help-er's book in the nation's leading newspaper, the *New York Tribune*. Helper and Greeley partnered in soliciting funds and Republican endorse-ments to produce a small, more inexpensive *Compendium* version of *The Impending Crisis of the South* to distribute during the upcoming election. Widely endorsed and published in July 1859, the *Compendium* became an instant best-seller in Republican circles, but an instant dartboard in enslaving circles. Helper's free White labor, antislavery message was everything the Republicans—and Lincoln—were looking for: a way to oppose slavery without being cast as pro-Black.[11]

Enslavers were furious about the implications of Helper's book, which practically called for a united front made up of Free Soilers, abolitionists, and former slaves. That unholy alliance became a reality in October 1859, when abolitionist John Brown and his nineteen-man interracial battalion captured the federal armory at Harpers Ferry, West Virginia, sixty miles northwest of Washington, DC. "General" Harriet Tubman was unable to come as planned, probably because she was suffering one of her recurring fevers. Brown could have used her ingenuity. He selected an area of small-scale farms instead of massive gang-scale plantations, where he could have armed thousands and plotted the next stage of his revolt. Marines led by Colonel Robert E. Lee crushed the rebellion instead and apprehended Brown. Seventeen people perished.

Although enslavers had fought off larger Black slave revolts throughout the tumultuous 1850s, Brown's revolt affected them deeply. The growing breach in White unity unsettled them into delirium. William Lloyd Garrison initially described the revolt as an "insane," though "well-intended," attempt. But in the weeks after the conflict, he joined with abolitionists in transforming John Brown in the eyes of antislavery northerners from a madman to a "martyr." Countless Americans came to admire his David-like courage to strike at the mighty and hated Goliath-like slave power. The disdain for violent Black revolutionaries lurked in the shadow of the praises for John Brown, however. Black slave rebels never became martyrs and remained madmen and madwomen. Never before had the leader of a major slave uprising been so praised. Not since Bacon's Rebellion had the leader of a major antislavery uprising been White.

Millions read John Brown's final court statement. Brown presented himself as a righteous Christian shepherd who was willing to follow the Golden Rule—willing to lead the dependent sheep out of slavery. On the day of his hanging, December 2, 1859, White and Black northerners mourned to the sounds of church bells for hours.[12]

ON FEBRUARY 2, 1860, Jefferson Davis, a senator from Mississippi, presented the southern platform of unlimited states' rights and enslavers rights to the US Senate. The South needed these resolutions to be passed if they were going to remain in the Stephen Douglas–led Democratic Party and in the Union. Davis could have easily added that southerners believed the federal government should not use its resources to assist Black people in any way. On April 12, 1860, Davis objected to appropriating funds for educating Blacks in Washington, DC. "This Government was not founded by negroes nor for negroes," he said, but "by white men for white men." The bill was based on the false assertion of racial equality, he stated. The "inequality of the white and black races" was "stamped from the beginning."

Adam had driven away the first White criminal, his son Cain, who was "no longer the fit associate of those who were created to exercise dominion over the earth," Davis lectured the senators. Cain had found in the "land of Nod those to whom his crime had degraded him to an equality." Apparently, Blacks had lived in the Land of Nod among the "living creatures" God had created before humans. Blacks were later taken on Noah's ark with other animals. Their overseer: Ham.[13]

On the lips of one of America's most renowned politicians, it looked as if polygenesis had finally become mainstream. In actuality, the days of the notion of separately created human species were numbered. Another pernicious theory of the human species was about to take hold, one that would be used by racist apologists for the next one hundred years.

In August 1860, polygenesist Josiah C. Nott took some time away from raising Alabama's first medical school (now in Birmingham). He skimmed through a five-hundred-page tome published the previous November in England. It had a long title, *On the Origin of Species by Means of Natural Selection, or the Preservation of Favoured Races in the Struggle for Life*. Nott probably knew the author: the eminent, antislavery British marine biologist Charles Darwin.

"The view which most naturalists entertain, and which I formerly entertained—namely, that each species has been independently created—is erroneous," Darwin famously declared. "I am fully convinced that species are not immutable." Recent discoveries were showing, he explained, that humans had originated much earlier than a few thousand years ago. Darwin effectively declared war on biblical chronology *and* the ruling conception of polygenesis, offering a new ruling idea: natural selection. In the "recurring struggle for existence," he wrote, "all corporeal and mental endowments will tend to progress towards perfection."

Darwin did not explicitly claim that the White race had been naturally selected to evolve toward perfection. He hardly spent any writing time on humans in *The Origin of Species*. He had a grander purpose: proving that all living things the world over were struggling, evolving, spreading, and facing extinction or perfection. Darwin did, however, open the door for bigots to use his theory by referring to "civilized" states, the "savage races of man," and "half-civilized man," and calling the natives of southern Africa and their descendants "the lowest savages."[14]

Over the course of the 1860s, the Western reception of Darwin transformed from opposition to skepticism to approval to hailing praise. The sensitive, private, and sickly Darwin let his many friends develop his ideas and engage his critics. The mind of English polymath Herbert Spencer became the ultimate womb for Darwin's ideas, his writings the amplifier of what came to be known as Social Darwinism. In *Principles of Biology* in 1864, Spencer coined the iconic phrase "survival of the fittest." He religiously believed that human behavior was inherited. Superior hereditary traits made the "dominant races" better fit to survive than the "inferior races." Spencer spent the rest of his life calling for governments to get out of the way of the struggle for existence. In his quest to limit government, Spencer ignored the discriminators, probably knowing they were rigging the struggle for existence. Longing for ideas to justify the nation's growing inequities, American elites firmly embraced Charles Darwin and fell head over heels for Herbert Spencer.[15]

Charles Darwin's scholarly circle grew immeasurably over the 1860s, encircling the entire Western world. *The Origin of Species* even changed the life of Darwin's cousin, Sir Francis Galton. The father of modern statistics, Galton created the concepts of correlation and regression toward the mean and blazed the trail for the use of questionnaires and surveys to collect data. In *Hereditary Genius* (1869), he used his data to popularize the myth that parents passed on hereditary traits like intelligence that environment could not alter. "The average intellectual standard of the negro race is some two grades below our own," Galton wrote. He coined the phrase "nature versus nurture," claiming that nature was undefeated. Galton urged governments to rid the world of all naturally unselected peoples, or at least stop them from reproducing, a social policy he called "eugenics" in 1883.[16]

Darwin did not stop his adherents from applying the principles of natural selection to humans. However, the largely unknown co-discoverer of natural selection did. By 1869, British naturalist Alfred Russel Wallace professed that human spirituality and the equal capacity of healthy brains took humans outside of natural selection. Then again, as Wallace made a name for himself as the most egalitarian English scientist of his generation, he still professed European culture to be superior to any other.[17]

Darwin attempted to prove once and for all that natural selection applied to humans in *Descent of Man*, released in 1871. In the book, he was all over the place as he related race and intelligence. He spoke about the "mental similarity between the most distinct races of man," and then claimed that "the American aborigines, Negroes and Europeans differ as much from each other in mind as any three races that can be named." He noted that he was "incessantly struck" by some South Americans and "a full-blood negro" acquaintance who impressed him with "how similar their minds were to ours." On racial evolution, he said that the "civilized races" had "extended, and are now everywhere extending, their range, so as to take the place of the lower races." A future evolutionary break would occur between "civilized" Whites and "some ape"—unlike like the present break "between the negro or Australian and the gorilla." Both assimilationists and segregationists hailed *Descent of Man*. Assimilationists read Darwin as saying Blacks could one day evolve into White civilization; segregationists read him as saying Blacks were bound for extinction.[18]

IN APRIL 1860, *De Bow's Review* printed the results of a "search [for] a moral, happy, and voluntarily industrious community of free negroes." The reporter apparently surveyed Jamaica, Haiti, Trinidad, British Guiana, Antilles, Martinique, Guadeloupe, St. Thomas, St. John, Antigua, Peru, Mexico, Panama, Mauritius, England, Canada, Sierra Leone, and Liberia, but found that "no such community exists upon the face of the earth."[19]

The proslavery magazine's lead story that April 1860 spoke of "the Secession of the south and a new confederation necessary to the preservation of constitutional liberty and social morality." Not yet ready to secede from the Union, southern Democrats seceded from the Democratic Party and fielded Vice President John C. Breckinridge of Kentucky as their presidential nominee for the 1860 election.[20]

Northern and southern Democrats came to their nominating conventions unwilling to moderate their views for the sake of victory, but moderation for victory headlined the Republican convention. Delegates came ready to erase the "Black Republican" label once and for all. Abraham Lincoln helped them do just that. His humble life appealed to working-class voters, his principled stance against slavery appealed to radicals, and his principled stance against Black voting and racial equality appealed to anti-Black Free Soilers. With their man in place, Republicans passed a platform that pledged *not* to challenge southern slavery. The pavement of the platform, what the Republicans intended to run on, was the declaration of freedom as "the normal condition of all the territories."

Praising Lincoln as "a man of will and nerve," Frederick Douglass refused to vote for him, knowing his horrible Illinois record on Black rights. William Lloyd Garrison ignored the promoters playing up Lincoln's antislavery credentials. Lincoln would "do nothing to offend the South," Garrison scoffed.[21]

Days before the November 1860 election, 30,000 Democrats processed through New York City carrying torches, placards, and banners that blared: "No Negro Equality" and "Free Love, Free Niggers, and Free Women." But the Republicans managed to convince enough northerners that the party stood against extending slavery and Black civil rights. Garrison spoke for many when he hoped that the election of Abraham Lincoln as the sixteenth president of the United States signified a "much deeper sentiment" in the North, which "in the process of time must ripen into more decisive action" against slavery. It was exactly what enslavers feared.[22]

In an open letter to a southerner on December 15, 1860, Lincoln tried to stop the secession talk. There was only one "substantial difference" between the North and the South, Lincoln wrote. "You think slavery is right and ought to be extended; we think it is wrong and ought to be restricted." Proslavery southerners were unlikely to listen to Lincoln on this question. They heard the secessionist talk from their preachers, from their church bodies, from their periodicals, from their politicians—nowhere more so than in South Carolina, the only state with a Black majority. Enslavers knew that abolitionism—and the loss of federal power, White proslavery unity, and the ability to spread out their enslaved population—all hindered their ability to control the teeming slave resistance that had not relented in 1860. South Carolina secessionists only had to utter one word to induce fear—Haiti—its meaning well known. While Garrison considered secession to be suicidal, some enslavers considered remaining in the Union to be suicidal. In the final week of 1860, South Carolina enslavers took drastic steps to ensure their safety.[23]

CHAPTER 17

History's Emancipator

ON DECEMBER 24, 1860, South Carolina legislators alluded to the Declaration of Independence when stating their reasons for secession. Abolitionists were "inciting" contented captives to "servile insurrection," and "elevating to citizenships" Blacks who constitutionally were "incapable of becoming citizens." South Carolina's secession from the United States did not just mean the loss of a state, and soon a region, but the loss of the region's land and wealth. The South had millions of acres of land that were worth more in purely economic terms than the almost 4 million enslaved human beings who were toiling on its plantations in 1860. With their financial investments in the institution of slavery and their dependence on its productivity, northern lenders and manufacturers were crucial sponsors of slavery. And so, they pushed their congressmen onto their compromising knees to restore the Union. Garrison called all the "Union-saving efforts" of December 1860 and January 1861 "simply idiotic." Whether smart or idiotic, they failed. The rest of the Deep South seceded in January and February 1861. Florida's secessionists issued a Declaration of Causes maintaining that Blacks must be enslaved because everywhere "their natural tendency" was toward "idleness, vagrancy and crime."[1]

In February 1861, Jefferson Davis took the presidential oath of the new Confederate States of America in Montgomery, Alabama. In his Inaugural Address in March, Lincoln did not object to the proposed Thirteenth Amendment, which would make slavery untouchable and potentially reunite the union. But Lincoln did swear that he would never allow the extension of slavery. On March 21, the Confederacy's vice president, Alexander Stephens, responded to Lincoln's pledge in an extemporaneous speech. The Confederate government, he declared, rested "upon the great truth that the negro is not equal to the white man; that slavery subordination to the superior race is his natural and normal condition. This, our new government, is the first, in the history of the world, based upon this great physical, philosophical, and moral truth." This "great . . . truth," Stephens said, was the "corner-stone" of the Confederacy. The speech became known as his "Cornerstone Speech."[2]

In the new literature or propaganda for southern adults and children, Confederates built upon this cornerstone with two stock characters: returning runaways who realized slavery was better than freedom; and heroic Black Confederates defending slavery. There have always been individual truths to support every generalized racist lie. It is true that some Black opportunists sought favor if slavery persisted by supporting the Confederate cause. It is true that some starving free Blacks supported the rebels for lifesaving provisions. It is true that Black racists who believed that Black people were better off enslaved sometimes voluntarily aided the Confederacy. The number of voluntary Black Confederates? Probably not many. But no one can say for sure.[3]

Three weeks after Alexander Stephens laid the cornerstone, the Confederates fired on Fort Sumter. On April 15, 1861, Lincoln raised the Union Army to put down the "insurrection," which, by the end of May, included Virginia, North Carolina, Tennessee, and Arkansas. No matter what Lincoln did not say about slavery, and no matter what blame the Democrats put on abolitionists, to Black people and to abolitionists the Civil War was over slavery and enslavers were to blame. On the Fourth of July at the annual abolitionist picnic in Framingham, Massachusetts, William Lloyd Garrison repudiated "colorphobia" for holding back northerners from supporting a war of emancipation. "Let us see, in every slave, Jesus himself," Garrison cried out.[4]

The *Weekly Anglo-African* forecasted that the millions of enslaved Africans would not be "impassive observers." Lincoln might deem it "a white man's war," but enslaved Africans had "a clear and decided idea of what they want—Liberty."[5]

The *Weekly Anglo-African* was right. First dozens, then hundreds, then thousands of runaways fled to Union forces in the summer of 1861. But Union soldiers enforced the Fugitive Slave Act with such an iron fist that, according to one Maryland newspaper, more runaways were returned in three months of the war "than during the whole of Mr. Buchanan's presidential term." Northerners listened uneasily to these reports of returning runaways side by side with reports of southern Blacks being thrust into work for the Confederate military.[6]

After the Confederates humiliated Union soldiers in the First Battle of Bull Run in northern Virginia on July 21, 1861, proposals about enslaved Africans' potential war utility besieged Congress and the Lincoln administration. Initially, Congress passed a resolution emphatically declaring that the war was not "for the purpose of overthrowing or interfering with the rights and or established institutions of these states." But war demands soon changed their calculations. In early August, the Republican-dominated Congress was forced to pass the Confiscation Act over the objections of Democrats and border-state Unionists. Lincoln reluctantly signed the bill, which said that slaveholders forfeited their ownership of any property, including enslaved Africans, used by the Confederate military. The Union could confiscate such people as "contraband." Legally, they were no longer enslaved; nor were they freed. They could, however, work for the Union Army for wages and live in the abysmal conditions of the contraband camps. One out of every four of the 1.1 million men, women, and children in the contraband camps died in one of the worst public health disasters in US history. Only 138 physicians were assigned to care for them. Some physicians called contrabands "animals" and blamed their mass deaths on inherent Black debilities, not the extreme inadequacies of sanitation, food, and medical care.[7]

Despite the horrendous conditions, the number of Black contrabands increased every month. Slaves were running from the abysmal conditions of the plantations, particularly after Union soldiers moved into the more densely populated Deep South. The *New York Times* reported at the end of 1861 that enslaved Africans were "earnestly desirous of liberty." The growing number of runaways proved that Confederate reports of contented captives was mere propaganda. This form of Black resistance—not persuasion—finally started to eradicate the racist idea of the docile Black person in northern minds. President Lincoln did not encourage the runaways in his December 1861 Message to Congress. But he did request funding for colonizing runaways and compensating Unionist emancipators to ensure that the war did not "degenerate" into a "remorseless revolutionary struggle." Furious, Garrison shrieked in a letter that Lincoln did not have "a drop of anti-slavery blood in his veins."[8]

Every week in the spring of 1862, thousands of fugitives were cutting through forests, reaching the southern Union lines, and leaving behind paralyzed plantations and an increasingly divided Confederacy. Some soldiers deserted the Confederate Army. Some of the Confederate deserters joined enslaved Africans to wage revolts against their common enemies: wealthy planters. And some upcountry non-slaveholding Whites had already become disillusioned fighting this slaveholders' war. Alexander H. Jones of eastern North Carolina helped organize the 10,000-man Heroes of America, which laid an "underground railroad" for White Unionists in Confederate territories to escape. "The fact is," Jones wrote in a secret antiracist circular, referring to the rich planters, that "these bombastic, highfalutin aristocratic fools have been in the habit of driving negroes and poor helpless white people until they think . . . that they themselves are superior; [and] hate, deride and suspicion the poor."[9]

Up north, Radical Republicans pushed through a horde of anti-slavery measures that southerners and their northern defenders had opposed for years. By the summer of 1862, slavery was prohibited in the territories, the ongoing transatlantic slave trade had been suppressed, the United States recognized Haiti and Liberia, abolition had arrived in Washington, DC, and the Union Army was forbidden from returning fugitives to the South. The Fugitive Slave Act had been effectively repealed. And then came the kicker: the Second Confiscation Act, passed and sent to Lincoln on July 17. The bill declared all Confederate-owned Africans who escaped to Union lines or who resided in territories occupied by the Union to be "forever free of their servitude." The *Springfield Republican* realized the bill's power, stating that enslaved Africans would become free "as fast as the armies penetrate the South section." But they were not penetrating the South fast enough, and Union casualties were piling up. Confederate generals Robert E. Lee and Stonewall Jackson appeared to be headed for sparsely defended Washington, DC, scaring Lincoln to death.

The Second Confiscation Act was a turning point, setting Union policy on the road leading to emancipation. The war and the failure to convince border states about the benefits of a gradual, compensated emancipation had sapped Lincoln's patience and the patience of Congress. Lincoln had finally opened up to the idea of proclaiming emancipation because it would save the Union (not because it would save Black people). Cries of Unionist planters to salvage slavery amid the war increasingly rankled him. "Broken eggs cannot be mended," he snapped to a Louisiana planter.

On July 22, 1862, five days after signing the Second Confiscation Act, Lincoln submitted to his cabinet a new draft order, effective January 1, 1863. "All persons held as slaves within any state [under rebel control] shall then, thenceforward, and forever, be free." Lincoln's staff was stunned and became quickly divided over the Preliminary Emancipation Proclamation. The cabinet made no immediate decision, but word got out. Not many Americans took the proclamation seriously.[10]

Talk of runaways and contrabands and emancipation in the spring and summer of 1862 invariably led to talk about colonization. Northern racists started looking to colonization as the only possibility for freed Blacks. They feared Black people sprinting north, invading their communities and becoming "roaming, vicious vagabonds," as the *Chicago Tribune* put it. Colonization provisions were stapled onto the Second Confiscation Act and the 1862 decree abolishing slavery in the nation's capital. Colonization designs were behind the United States opening diplomatic relations with Haiti and Liberia that year. In their allocation measures in 1862, Congress set aside $600,000 (about $14 million today) to eject Black people from the country.

Black people made their opposition to colonization loud and clear in the summer of 1862. Lincoln, desiring their support, welcomed five

Black men to the President's House on August 14, 1862. The delegation was led by the Reverend Joseph Mitchell, the commissioner of emigration for the Interior Department. The discussion quickly turned into a lecture. The Black race could never "be placed on an equality with the white race" in the United States, Lincoln professed. Whether this "is right or wrong I need not discuss," he said. Lincoln then blamed the presence of Blacks for the war. If Blacks leave, all will be well, Lincoln touted. "Sacrifice something of your present comfort," Lincoln advised, asking the group to press their fellow Blacks to make the trek to Liberia and start anew. To refuse would be "extremely selfish."

Although the five Black men apparently found Lincoln's views persuasive, Lincoln could not persuade the women and men who read his lecture in the nation's newspapers. William Lloyd Garrison angrily tossed Lincoln's words into *The Liberator*'s "Refuge of Oppression" section, where he often put the words of slaveholders. It was not their color that made "their presence here intolerable," Garrison declared. It was "their being free!" To Frederick Douglass, Lincoln showed "his contempt for Negroes and his canting hypocrisy!"[11]

SIX DAYS AFTER meeting with the Black delegation, Lincoln gained an opportunity to emphatically declare his views on war, emancipation, and Black people. The nation's most powerful editor, Horace Greeley, inserted an open letter to the president in his leading *New York Tribune* on August 20, 1862. Greeley had been as responsible for Lincoln's election as anyone. He urged Lincoln to enforce the "emancipation provisions" of the Second Confiscation Act.[12]

"My paramount object in this struggle is to save the Union, and is not either to save or to destroy slavery," Lincoln replied in Greeley's rival paper, Washington's *National Intelligencer*. "If I could save the Union without freeing any slave I would do it, and if I could save it by freeing all the slaves I would do that. What I do about slavery, and the colored race, I do because I believe it helps to save the Union." In the *New York Tribune*, rising abolitionist Wendell Phillips hammered Lincoln's remarks as "the most disgraceful document that ever came from the head of a free people."[13]

With the war looking like a never-ending highway, the midterm elections approaching, and runaways crippling Confederates faster than Union bullets, Lincoln gathered his cabinet on September 22, 1862. After laying his poker face on Americans for months, he finally showed his cards—cards William Lloyd Garrison never believed he had. Lincoln issued the Preliminary Emancipation Proclamation. For slaveholding Union states and any rebel state wishing to return, Lincoln once again offered gradual, compensated emancipation and colonization. For those states remaining in rebellion on January 1, 1863, Lincoln proclaimed that "all persons held as slaves . . . shall be then, thenceforward, and forever free."[14]

"Thank God!" blared the *Pittsburgh Gazette*. "We shall cease to be hypocrites and pretenders," proclaimed Ralph Waldo Emerson. William Lloyd Garrison enjoyed the sound of "forever free," but little else. Lincoln, he fumed in private, could "do nothing for freedom in a direct manner, but only by circumlocution and delay."[15]

In his Message to Congress on December 1, 1862, Lincoln laid out a more detailed plan for gradual, compensated emancipation and colonization. Any slave state could remain or return to the Union if it pledged loyalty and a willingness to abolish slavery at any time before January 1, 1900. The US government would compensate such states for freeing their human property, but if they decided to reintroduce or tolerate enslavement, they would have to repay the emancipation compensation. "Timely adoption" of gradual, compensated emancipation and colonization "would bring restoration," Lincoln pleaded. The Confederate leaders largely rejected Lincoln's proposals, emboldened by their stunning war victories in mid-December.[16]

Abraham Lincoln retired to his office on the afternoon of January 1, 1863. He read over the Emancipation Proclamation, "a fit and necessary war measure for suppressing said rebellion," as he termed it, that emancipated "all persons held as slaves" and allowed Black men to join the Union Army. As Lincoln read the final statement, his abolitionist treasury secretary, Salmon B. Chase, suggested that he add some morality. Lincoln acquiesced, adding, "Upon this act, sincerely believed to be an act of justice, warranted by the Constitution, upon military necessity, I invoke the considerate judgment of mankind, and the gracious favor of Almighty God."

In the next two years, Lincoln made himself available to writers, artists, photographers, and sculptors who memorialized him for the historical record as the Great Emancipator. With his proclamation, Lincoln emancipated about 50,000 Black people in the Union-occupied Confederate areas that January. He kept enslaved the nearly half-million African people in border states, in order to maintain their owners' loyalty. He also kept enslaved the roughly 300,000 African people in the newly exempted formerly Confederate areas, in order to establish their owners' loyalty. More than 2 million African people on Confederate plantations remained enslaved because Lincoln had no power to free them. Democrats mocked Lincoln for "purposefully" making "the proclamation inoperative in all places where . . . the slaves [were] accessible," and operative "only where he has notoriously no power to execute it," as the *New York World* put it.

But enslaved Africans now had the power to emancipate themselves. By the end of 1863, 400,000 Black people had escaped their plantations and found Union lines, running toward the freedom guaranteed by the proclamation.[17]

SOME BLACK CHRISTIANS had long prayed for a Great Emancipator, and they believed they had found him in Abraham Lincoln. Upper-crust Bostonians erupted in pandemonium when news of Lincoln's signature reached the afternoon Grand Jubilee Concert at Music Hall on January 1, 1863. After the hat throwing, the handkerchief waving, the hugging, the shouting, the stomping, the crying, the smiling, and the kissing, the attendees began their own jubilee concert. "Three cheers for GARRISON!" someone roared. Six thousand eyes turned and searched out the fifty-seven-year-old editor who had prayed so many times for this day to come. He leaned over the balcony wall, waved, and beamed a smile that warmed New England.

Garrison praised the Emancipation Proclamation as a "turning point." From that day forward, Garrison became a "tenacious Unionist," as ardent a defender and deifier of Abraham Lincoln as any Republican. Whereas before he had slammed Lincoln for his sluggishness and indecision, Garrison now began to praise Lincoln's "cautious" and "considerate" manner.[18]

Some people did not worship Lincoln that night, and were especially critical of the very same cautiousness that Garrison praised. The Black-owned San Francisco *Pacific Appeal* detested this "halfway measure," insisting that "every bondsman" should have been emancipated, and "every chain . . . broken."[19]

CHAPTER 18

Ready for Freedom?

IN LATE APRIL 1863, Willie Garrison, the editor's second-oldest son, brought home an acquaintance: German immigrant Henry Villard, one of the war's most talented young journalists. Villard had just come from the Sea Islands of South Carolina, where he had observed the war's first emancipated people and the first regiments of Black troops. Villard shared with the Garrisons his racist observations of the "half-heathenish blacks" in coastal South Carolina. As he did so, he condemned the Blacks' "savage superstitions" and described their "fetish worship" in ways that showed he did not understand their African religions or the ways in which they were remolding Christianity to suit their cultures. Villard derisively called their Gullah language "jargon" and looked down on them for not comprehending "our English." Using the same line of thinking, the Sea Island Blacks could have called Villard's language "jargon" and his religion "savage" and looked down on him for not comprehending their "Gullah" or their gods. Nevertheless, Villard's observations confirmed what Garrison had long believed, that "nothing else could be expected, indeed, from creatures who had been purposely kept in the conditions of brutes," as Villard said.[1]

For years, northern racists had agreed, almost religiously, that enslaved Africans were like brutes. They disagreed, among themselves, about the capacity of Black people for freedom, independence, and civilization. This racist northern debate—segregationists adamant about Black brutes' incapacity, assimilationists like Garrison and Villard adamant about Black brutes' capacity—became the primary conversation in the wake of emancipation. Hardly anyone in a position of authority—whether in the economic elite, the political elite, the cultural elite, or the intellectual elite—brought antiracist ideas of equal Black people into this conversation.[2]

During his Boston stay, Villard accompanied the Garrisons about thirteen miles south to watch the drilling exercises of the 54th Massachusetts Volunteer Infantry. In January 1863, Lincoln had asked the Massachusetts governor to organize a Black regiment. "Men of Color, to Arms!" became the rallying point for Black male leaders. By fighting in the army, Black men were made to believe that they could earn their right to citizenship—as if Black men had to—or could—earn their rights. Black male leaders spoke endlessly of soldiers vindicating Black manhood, which itself rested on the racist assumption that there was something truly lacking in Black manhood that could only be ameliorated by killing or being killed by Confederates. At the same time, some White Unionists posed having to fight "shoulder to shoulder, with this seething, sooty negro," as a threat to their superior manhood, as New York City's Democratic congressman James Brooks complained. It was a nasty convergence of racist and sexist ideas on the part of both Black and White men. By the war's end, almost 200,000 Black men had served in the war. They had been killed by the thousands and had killed thousands of Confederates. So much death as the weak Black male stereotype lived on.[3]

When Indiana's governor commended Black troops for bringing back their equipment when White troops did not, the Indianapolis State Sentinel registered an all-out effort to "disparage the white soldiers and elevate the negro soldiers." White soldiers never reported to Black officers, they faced more combat, were rarely enslaved or killed when captured, and were paid more money. Still, the accusation of Black favoritism was unending.

Racist ideas were easy to revise, especially as the demands of discriminators changed. Democrats changed their racist ideas to properly attack Black soldiers. While before the war they had justified slavery by stressing Black male physical superiority, during the war they promoted White soldiers and stressed White male physical superiority.

While before the war they had justified slavery by deeming Blacks naturally docile and well equipped to take orders, during the war they stressed that Blacks were uncontrollable brutes, arguing against the Republicans, who said that naturally docile Blacks made great soldiers. Republicans often credited superb Black performances on the battlefield to their superb submissiveness and to their excellent White commanders. Both sides used the same language, the same racist ideas at different points, to make their case, reinforcing the language and ideas with plausible examples on the battlefield.[4]

After the Union's excitement over winning at Gettysburg in early July 1863, and the success at Vicksburg, which divided the Confederacy into two, depressing war news came from South Carolina. On July 18, 1863, almost half of the Black 54th Massachusetts had been killed, captured, or wounded while leading the failed assault on Fort Wagner. The beachhead fortification defended the southern approach to the citadel of the South, Charleston. Six hundred tired and hungry Blacks had sprinted in a twilight of bullets and shells toward "maddened" Confederates and engaged in ferocious hand-to-hand combat. The stories of this battle shot through the North almost as quickly as the Confederacy murdered the captured. The *New York Tribune* accurately predicted that the battle would be the decisive turning point in the northern debate over Blacks' capacity to fight. As it turned out, the battle was decisive in more ways than one.[5]

Catholic publicist Orestes A. Brownson had been one of many powerful Americans advocating emancipation as a war measure and colonization as a postwar measure, and he had advised Lincoln accordingly in 1862. After Fort Wagner, Brownson had to admit that the "negro, having shed his blood in defense of the country, has the right to regard it as his country. And hence deportation or forced colonization is henceforth out of the question."[6]

President Lincoln still held out hope for colonization early in 1863. He advanced money to a Black minister establishing a settlement in Liberia, and he complained to an Ohio congressman that he did not "know what we should do with these people—Negroes—after peace came." War demands for able-bodied soldiers, and the postwar demands for able-bodied and loyal southern labor and voters, had begun to shift public opinion away from colonization. The debacle of the Lincoln administration's colonization schemes sealed the movement's fate. By July 1863, Lincoln was speaking about the "failure" of colonization. In 1864, Congress froze its appropriation for colonization, and Lincoln abandoned it as a potential postwar policy. The *Chicago Tribune* confidently declared "The End of Colonization." But it was not the end of racism. The Lincoln administration's progression of racism meant confining these loyal Black voters and laborers to the South, away from the northern and western free White soil.[7]

The reconstruction of the Union seemed to be on everyone's mind, including abolitionists. In late January 1864, Garrison challenged an anti-Lincoln resolution at the Massachusetts Anti-Slavery Society meeting. Garrison's longtime friend Wendell Phillips, primed to take the helm of abolitionism from his old friend and mentor, labeled Lincoln "a half-converted, honest Western Whig, trying to be an abolitionist." As Garrison stared down emancipation, Phillips looked past emancipation at the reconstruction of the United States. Back in December 1863, Lincoln had announced his Proclamation of Amnesty and Reconstruction, which offered restoration of rights (except slaveholding) to all Confederates taking the loyalty oath. When loyalty levels reached 10 percent, states could establish governments that restricted civil rights for Black residents, Lincoln had proposed. But this proposal "frees the slave and ignores the negro," Phillips snapped. The sizable free biracial community of New Orleans snapped, too, demanding voting rights. These biracial activists separated "their struggle from that of the Negroes," said an observer. "In their eyes, they were nearer to the white man; they were more advanced than the slave in all respects." Overtures to Louisiana Whites failed, and biracial activists had no choice but to swallow their racist pride and ally with emancipated Blacks by the end of 1864.[8]

Garrison's principled courage, which had made him a legend when emancipation seemed so far away, had been replaced by practical fear in 1864 when abolition seemed so close. Garrison feared Democrats gobbling up enough war-weary and anti-emancipation voters to seize presidential power, negotiate a war settlement, and maintain slavery. "Let *us* possess our souls in patience," he wrote. William Lloyd Garrison—the longtime evangelist of immediate emancipation—counseled patience.[9]

Maryland Unionists went ahead with plans to reconstruct their state without slavery. To encourage them, Lincoln made the short trip to Baltimore and gave one of the most insightful abolitionist speeches of his career on April 18, 1864. He answered the enduring American paradox: How could the land of freedom also be the land of slavery? "With some the word liberty may mean for each man to do as he pleases with himself, and the product of his labor," he said, "while with others the same word may mean for some men to do as they please with other men, and the product of other men's labor." Lincoln used an analogy for clarification. "The shepherd drives the wolf from the sheep's throat, for which the sheep thanks the shepherd as a liberator, while the wolf denounces him for the same act as the destroyer of liberty, especially as the sheep was a black one," he said. "Hence we behold the processes by which thousands are daily passing from under the yoke of bondage, hailed by some as the advance of liberty, and bewailed by others as the destruction of all liberty." Lincoln's freedom analogy, vividly evocative of his self-identity as the Great Emancipator, rewrote current events. Most enslaved Africans were hardly sheep, waiting on the Union shepherds to come to their plantations and lead them to freedom. The Union lines proved, if anything in this analogy, to be the stable of freedom. While Lincoln emancipated a minority of sheep, most fought off or slipped away from the Confederate wolves on their plantations on their own, and then ran to freedom on their own, and then into the Union Army on their own to put down the Confederate wolves.[10]

Since issuing the Emancipation Proclamation, Lincoln had begun to imagine himself (as Garrison long had) as the liberating shepherd of Black people, who were in need of civilizing direction. On November 1, 1864, Maryland's emancipation day, the freed people paraded to the President's House. Lincoln addressed them, urging them to "improve yourself, both morally and intellectually," while supporting Maryland's new constitution, which prevented them from improving themselves socioeconomically. Maryland's constitution barred Blacks from voting and from attending public schools. The constitution also sent thousands of Black children into long-term indentures to their former masters, against their parents' objections. Lincoln seemed to follow in the footsteps of Thomas Jefferson. Pay lip service to the cause of Black uplift, while supporting the racist policies that ensured the downfall of Black people.[11]

In setting out the terms of emancipation, Maryland (and Louisiana) ignored the recommendations of the American Freedmen's Inquiry Commission (AFIC), which had been authorized by the War Department at the request of Massachusetts senator Charles Sumner. In its widely publicized final report in May 1864, the commission called for equal rights, laws allowing Blacks to purchase land, and the creation of a temporary Bureau of Emancipation to shepherd freed people toward self-reliance. One commissioner, Boston abolitionist James McKaye, advocated redistributing confiscated Confederate land to landless Whites and emancipated people.

In promoting equal rights, McKaye and the other two commissioners, Indiana reformer Robert Dale Owen and New England abolitionist Dr. Samuel Gridley Howe, never entertained the idea that Blacks and Whites were truly equal. They had been charged with answering questions regarding the "condition and capacity" of Blacks for freedom and free labor, a task whose real aim was assuaging Whites who feared the effects of emancipation. Are Blacks naturally lazy? Would Blacks invade and ruin the North? Could Black labor be more profitable in freedom than in slavery? In his AFIC report on runaways in Canada, Howe forecasted that Blacks "will co-operate powerfully with whites from the North in re-organizing the industry of the South." However, "they will dwindle," this Social Darwinist made sure to note, "and gradually disappear from the peoples of this continent." Commissioner Owen eased fearful northerners' anxieties by speaking more to the potential contributions of African Americans in AFIC's final report. Their "softening influence," drawn from their "womanly" disposition, would one day improve the hardened "national character." The

Anglo-Saxon "head predominates over the heart," he wrote. "The African race is in many respects the reverse of this." A decade after Stowe's *Uncle Tom's Cabin*, abolitionists still viewed Black people through its racist lens.[12]

The AFIC reports were the most popular works to appear amid the sudden rush of emancipation literature about the future of Black people. Observations noting that slavery had not turned Blacks into brutes had a home in the post-emancipation reports, for anyone willing to wade through all of the racist testimonies to reach them. Before supervising the contrabands of Virginia, one Union Army captain, C. B. Wilder, admitted, "I did not think [Black people] had so much brain." His experiences had taught him that "they have got as many brains as you or I have, though they have an odd way of showing it." At the end of 1864, 78 percent of the contrabands under Wilder's supervision were "independent of assistance." A superintendent of contrabands in the Mississippi Valley described Black intelligence to be "as good as that of men, women & children anywhere, of any color, who cannot read."[13]

William Lloyd Garrison was *not* among those who questioned the brutishness of former slaves. For thirty years, Garrison had moved northerners toward abolitionism by sensationalizing the idea that slavery made people into brutes. Like any racist, he dismissed the evidence that undermined his theory, and hardened his theory with evidence that supported it. In July 1864, Garrison defended Lincoln's support of laws that restricted the citizenship rights of Blacks. "According to the laws of development and progress, it is not practicable," Garrison said, to give undeveloped Black men the vote.[14]

GARRISON HAD A difficult time defending Lincoln in the summer of 1864. Democratic editors and politicians were blitzing voters on the dangers of continued war, emancipated Black people invading the North, and Republican-supported miscegenation. War morale had dropped to its lowest level. A Confederate regiment neared Washington, DC, and Union armies were hardly winning battles. The war news got so bad that on August 22, 1864, the Republican National Committee determined that Lincoln could not be reelected. No one had to tell that to Lincoln.

"I am a beaten man, unless we can have some great victory," Lincoln reportedly said on August 31. Two days later, General William T. Sherman sacked Atlanta. Subsequent victories boosted voter support for the Republicans, and they consolidated their support by matching the Democrats' anti-Black ire. Repulsed, Black Americans came together for their first national convention in a decade. They blasted Republicans for remaining "largely under the influence of the prevailing contempt for the character and rights of the colored man." In spite of—or maybe because of—Black Americans' rebuke of Republicans, roughly 55 percent of Unionist Americans voted for Lincoln, and his party claimed three-quarters of the Congress. Forty-five percent of Unionist Americans voted for the Democrats to restore a union with slaveholders.[15]

A week after Lincoln's reelection, General Sherman departed captured Atlanta and steered 60,000 Union soldiers in the fabled March to the Sea. Sherman put his total war policies into full effect. The soldiers scorched the Confederate earth—the military installments, communications networks, plantations—everything in their path. Twenty thousand runaways joined the March to the Sea. Reporters telegraphed news of his successful victories to thoroughly pleased Unionist northerners. By Christmas, Sherman and his tens of thousands of soldiers and runaways had entered Savannah—and the hearts of millions.

Secretary of War Edwin McMasters Stanton arrived in Savannah after the New Year and urged General Sherman to meet with local Blacks over their future. Meeting with twenty leaders, mostly Baptist and Methodist ministers, on January 12, 1865, General Sherman received a crash course on their definitions of slavery and freedom. Slavery meant "receiving by irresistible power the work of another man, and not by his consent," said the group's spokesman, Garrison Frazier (*The Liberator* editor's name was everywhere). Freedom was "placing us where we could reap the fruit of our own labor." To accomplish this—*to be truly free*—we must "have land." When asked whether they desired interracial communities, Frazier shared their preference "to live by ourselves." There was "a prejudice against us in the South that will take years to get over."

Black people all over the South were saying this to Union officials: Do not abolish slavery and leave us landless. Do not force us to work for our former masters and call that freedom. They distinguished between *abolishing slavery* and *freeing people*. You can only set us free by providing us with land to "till . . . by our own labor," they declared. In offering postwar policy, Black people were rewriting what it meant to be free. *And*, in antiracist fashion, they were rejecting integration as a race relations strategy that involved Blacks showing Whites their equal humanity. They were rejecting uplift suasion—rejecting the job of working to undo the racist ideas of Whites by not performing stereotypes. Racist ideas, they were saying, were only in the eyes of the beholder, and only the beholders of racist ideas were responsible for their release.[16]

Savannah Blacks did not mention this, but millions of White settlers who had acquired western land, confiscated from rebel native communities over the years, had been freed. These Savannah Blacks— their peers across the South—were only asking for the same from rebel Confederate communities. But racist ideas rationalized the racist policy. White settlers on government-provided land were deemed receivers of American freedom; Black people, receivers of American handouts. Whenever talks earlier in the war touched on distributing land to Black people, Americans showed a respect for the landed rights of warring Confederates that they rarely showed for the landed rights of peaceful Native Americans. Since the federal government had started selling confiscated and abandoned southern land to private owners in 1863, more than 90 percent had gone to northern Whites over the widespread protests of local Blacks.[17]

Four days after he met with Savannah Blacks, General Sherman issued Special Field Order No. 15 to rid his camps of runaways and punish Confederates. He opened settlements for Black families on forty-acre plots of land on the Sea Islands and a large slice of the coastal areas of South Carolina and Georgia. By June 1865, 40,000 people had been settled on the plots and had been given old army mules. Sherman's field order was not the first of its kind. Black squatters on the Mississippi land of Jefferson Davis's family had formed their own government and swung a cotton profit of $160,000. "Davis Bend" became a testament of what Savannah Blacks were saying in those days: all Black people needed was to be left alone, secure on their own lands and guaranteed their own rights.

And yet, for so many racist Americans, it was inconceivable that Black people had not been damaged by slavery: that Black people could dance into freedom without skipping a beat. General John C. Robinson worried about landowning "sluggish" Blacks preventing "the energy and industry of the North" from utilizing the valuable acreage. Assimilationists Frederick Douglass and Horace Greeley rebuked Sherman's order, calling for interracial communities and ignoring the desires of local Blacks. Greeley wrote in his *New York Tribune* on January 30, 1865, that southern Blacks, "like their fellows at the North," must be "aided by contact with white civilization to become good citizens and enlightened men."[18]

President Lincoln did not overturn Sherman's field order; nor did he offer his public support or disapproval. At the time, Lincoln was busy expending his political energy on the House of Representatives. It paid off. On January 31, 1865, House members passed the Thirteenth Amendment abolishing slavery. The eruption of Republicans on the House floor—all the hugging, and dancing, and crying, and smiling, and shouting—foreshadowed emancipation parties and meetings across the United States that night and for nights to come.

The Thirteenth Amendment brought comfort to a weary emancipation-centered activist who was bickering with abolitionists pressing for Black civil rights. Days before the amendment's passage, Frederick Douglass and Wendell Phillips had passionately objected to readmitting Louisiana at the Massachusetts Anti-Slavery Society meeting. To deny Blacks in Louisiana voting rights was "to brand us with the stigma of inferiority," Douglass intoned. Defending Louisiana's readmission and Lincoln, William Lloyd Garrison argued back that suffrage was a "conventional right . . . not to be confused with the natural right" to liberty. Political equality was bound to come someday, he explained, but only after Black "industrial and educational development."[19]

On March 3, 1865, Congress established the Bureau of Refugees, Freedmen, and Abandoned Lands, or the Freedmen's Bureau, heeding the principal recommendation of the American Freedmen's Inquiry Commission. Quite possibly the most difficult duty the bureau had been given was to establish racial equality before the law in places where "to kill a negro they do not deem murder; to debauch a negro woman they do not think fornication; to take the property away from a Negro, they do not consider robbery," as one Union colonel observed. Another Union general, Oliver Otis Howard, was given charge of the Freedmen's Bureau. The New England native believed that emancipated Blacks wished to be dependent on government because they were used to being dependent on their masters. When the bureau was dissolved in 1869, General Howard bragged that his agency had not been a "pauperizing agency," since so "few" had been assisted. Officials of an assisting agency bragging about not assisting people? It only made sense in the context of racist ideas. But the fact that the bureau did help some people, and created some semblance of equal opportunity, was too much for segregationists like Dr. Josiah C. Nott. In an 1866 open letter to Howard, Nott stammered, "All the power of the Freedmen's Bureau or 'gates of hell' cannot prevail" against the permanent natural laws that kept Black people from creating civilization.[20]

ON APRIL 3, 1865, Robert E. Lee's army stopped defending Richmond. The next day, President Lincoln walked those same streets. Black people who had freed themselves ran up to him, fell on their knees, kissed his hands, and lifted Lincoln up as their "Messiah." Massachusetts senator Charles Sumner hoped their outpouring of praise would finally convince Lincoln to support Black suffrage. Black people had loftier goals: "All was equal," someone said. "All the land belongs to the Yankees now and they gwine divide it out among de colored people."[21]

On April 9, Lee's army surrendered, ending the Civil War. "Slavery is dead," announced the *Cincinnati Enquirer.* "The negro is not, there is our misfortune." On April 11, Lincoln delivered his reconstruction plans before a sizable crowd in front of the President's House. In defending the readmission of Louisiana, the president recognized that it "was unsatisfactory to some that the elective franchise is not given to the colored men." He expressed his preference for bestowing voting rights on "the very intelligent" Blacks and Black "soldiers."[22]

Never before had an American president expressed his preference for even limited Black suffrage. "That means nigger citizenship," murmured a twenty-six-year-old actor, from a family of famous thespians in Maryland. John Wilkes Booth and his Confederate conspirators had planned to kidnap Lincoln and demand the release of Confederate troops. "Now, by God," Booth reportedly said, staring savagely at Lincoln, "I'll put him through." On April 14, Mary and Abraham Lincoln took in a play, *Our American Cousin,* from his presidential booth at Ford's Theatre. When Lincoln's bodyguard stepped away sometime after 10 p.m., Booth crept up behind Lincoln and shot a bullet into Lincoln's skull.[23]

It was Good Friday, 1865, and Lincoln passed the next morning as the crucified Great Emancipator. "Lincoln died for us," remarked a Black South Carolinian. "Christ died for we, and me believe him de same mans."[24]

With emancipation assured, William Lloyd Garrison retired three weeks after Lincoln's death. "My vocation, as an Abolitionist, thank God, is ended," he said. Other abolitionists refused to retire with him. American Anti-Slavery Society (AASS) members refused Garrison's request to dissolve, gave his presidential chair to Wendell Phillips, and remade their new slogan: "No Reconstruction without Negro Suffrage." AASS members had high expectations for Lincoln's replacement: a Tennessee Democrat born into poverty, who had once signaled to Blacks, "I will indeed be your Moses," and who had once stammered to planters, "Tall poppies must be struck down."[25]

CHAPTER 19

Reconstructing Slavery

PRESIDENT ANDREW JOHNSON issued his Reconstruction proclamations on May 29, 1865, deflating the high hopes of civil rights activists. He offered amnesty, property rights, and voting rights to all but the highest Confederate officials (most of whom he pardoned a year later). Feeling empowered by President Johnson, Confederates barred Blacks from voting, elected Confederates as politicians, and instituted a series of discriminatory Black codes at their constitutional conventions to reformulate their state in the summer and fall of 1865. With the Thirteenth Amendment barring slavery "except as a punishment for crime," the law replaced the master. The postwar South became the spitting image of the prewar South in everything but name.

Of course, lawmakers justified these new racist policies with racist ideas. They proclaimed that the Black codes—which forced Blacks into labor contracts, barred their movement, and regulated their family lives—were meant to restrain them because they were naturally lazy, lawless, and oversexed. "If you call this Freedom," a Black veteran asked, "what do you call Slavery?"

Southern Blacks defended themselves in the war of re-enslavement, lifted up demands for rights and land, and issued brilliant antiracist retorts to the prevailing racist ideas. If any group should be characterized as "lazy," it was the planters, who had "lived in idleness all their lives on stolen labor," resolved a Petersburg, Virginia, mass meeting. It had always been amazing to enslaved people how someone could lounge back, drink lemonade, and look out over their fields, and call

235

the bent-over pickers lazy. To the racist forecasts that Blacks would not be able to take care of themselves, one emancipated person replied, "We used to support ourselves and our masters too when we were slaves and I reckon we can take care of ourselves now." When President Johnson evicted Blacks from their forty-acre plots in the summer and fall of 1865, Black people protested. "We has a right to the land we are located," Virginia's Bayley Wyatt griped. "Our wives, our children, our husbands, has been sold over and over again to purchase the lands we now locates upon."[1]

In September 1865, Pennsylvania congressman Thaddeus Stevens, arguably the most antiracist of the "Radical Republicans" favoring civil rights, proposed (and did not get approval for) the redistribution of the 400 million acres held by the wealthiest 10 percent of southerners. Every adult freedman would be granted forty acres, and the remaining 90 percent of the total would be sold in plots to the "highest bidder" to pay for the war and retire the national debt. Congress forced only one group of slaveholders to provide land to their former captives—the Confederacy's Native American allies.

The most popular defense against land redistribution was that it would "ruin the freedmen" by leading them to believe they could acquire land without "working for it," as the antislavery cotton manufacturer Edward Atkinson suggested. Did Atkinson really believe his own argument? This rich entrepreneur knew more than anyone that many rich men had not been ruined when they had inherited land without "working for it." Most Republicans wanted the government to create equality before the law, with all men having the same constitutional and voting rights. After that, they believed the government was finished. "The removal of white prejudice against the negro, depends almost entirely on the negro himself," declared *The Nation*, a periodical devoted to equal rights founded in July 1865, with Garrison's third-oldest son, Wendell, as assistant editor.[2]

William Lloyd Garrison and so many of the abolitionists he inspired chose not to engage in the political struggle against racial discrimination. Garrison failed to realize that it was his genius that had transformed abolitionism from a complex, multi-issue political project with unclear battle lines and objectives into a simple, single-issue moral project: slavery was evil, and those racists justifying or ignoring slavery were evil, and it was the moral duty of the United States to eliminate the evil of slavery. Garrison did not use his genius again for antiracism, in declaring that racial disparities were evil, and that those racists justifying or ignoring disparities were evil, and that it was the moral duty of the United States to eliminate the evil of racial disparities. He was too bogged down by the assimilationist idea that Black people needed to be developed by northerners. In the final months of *The Liberator*, Garrison allocated substantial space and praise to the northern missionaries' project of building southern schools for emancipated people. Never mind that the northern missionaries were not just handling the building and fund-raising but also planning to control and staff the schools and "civilize" the students.

Antiracist southern Blacks were not waiting on northern assimilationists. "Throughout the entire South an effort is being made by the colored people to educate themselves," reported the Freedmen's Bureau's superintendent of schools, John W. Alvord, in early 1866, after touring the South. These emancipated people were neither looking at the White missionaries as superior nor considering them their saviors. Black Georgia educators, for instance, said in February 1866 that they hoped White teachers were not in the South "in any vain reliance on their superior gifts . . . or in any foolish self-confidence that they have a special call to this office, or special endowments to meet its demands."[3]

On December 18, 1865, the United States officially added the Thirteenth Amendment to its Constitution. "At last, the old 'covenant with death' is annulled," Garrison wrote in the second-to-last issue of the voice of abolitionism. *The Liberator* had been established to destroy chattel slavery, he said in the final issue, on December 29, 1865. Now that slavery was dead and buried, it seemed only fitting to let *The Liberator*'s "existence cover the historic period of the great struggle."[4]

Without *The Liberator*, Garrison soon felt "like a hen plucked of its feathers." After two bad falls in early 1866 took him out of commission, he largely watched Reconstruction from the sidelines. He watched

Frederick Douglass head a delegation of Black male suffragists into the President's House on February 7, 1866. The meeting quickly turned combative when President Andrew Johnson said state majorities should decide voting rights. When someone retorted that Blacks were a majority in South Carolina, a miffed Johnson elaborated on his true fear: that Black voters looked down on poor Whites and would forge a political alliance with planters to rule them. When Douglass proposed "a party . . . among the poor," Johnson was disinterested.[5]

Whether Douglass admitted it or not, some—perhaps most—Blacks *did* look down on poor Whites. They denigrated the Whites who did *not* enslave them as "White trash." Actually, some uncorroborated reports suggest that enslaved Blacks created that term. Blacks had seen poor Whites doing the master's dirty work, as overseers, or on slave patrols, while clinging to the stinking fallacy that the lowest of them was still better than the highest Black person. And if poor Whites were "White trash," then what were elite Whites? Black consumers of racist ideas had come to associate Whiteness with wealth and power, and education and slaveholding. Only through the "White trash" construction could ideas of superior Whiteness be maintained, as it made invisible the majority of White people, the millions in poverty, by saying they were not ordinary Whites: they were "White trash." Similarly, the upwardly mobile Blacks were not really Black: they were extraordinary. At some point, racist and classist White elites started embracing the appellation to demean low-income Whites. "White trash" conveyed that White elites were the ordinary representatives of Whiteness.[6]

AS IT WAS, Black people no longer needed Andrew Johnson to secure some of their postwar rights. Republican senator Lyman Trumbull of Illinois stayed true to his 1862 Free Soil word: "Our people want nothing to do with the negroes." He felt the fervid panic that Blacks would flood the North in reaction to the violence, the Black codes, and the reelection of Confederates in 1865. To secure Black people in the South, Senator Trumbull and his anti-Black Republican comrades allied with the Radical Republicans in February 1866 to extend the Freedmen's Bureau. The "immense patronage" would hinder the "character" and "prospects" of emancipated Blacks who caused the South's problems by desiring to lead a "life of indolence," President Johnson responded in his stunning veto of the Freedmen's Bureau bill on February 19, 1866 (Congress overrode the veto in the summer).[7]

Senator Trumbull and company moved on to pass the Civil Rights Act of 1866 in March. The bill bestowed citizenship rights on all born in the United States and barred the "deprivation" of "any right secured or protected by this act" on the account of one's "color or race." Congress did not consider voting to be an essential right of US citizenship. Though aimed at southern Black codes, the act also invalidated northern Black codes that had discriminated against Blacks for decades. But the bill was limited in that it did not target private, local, or race-veiled laws of racial discrimination. Discriminatory racial language (not racial inequities) became the proof of racism for the federal courts—the apparatus charged with the huge burden of enforcing equal treatment. It was like writing laws for premeditated murders and not writing manslaughter laws for murders that the state could not prove were premeditated. The shrewdest discriminators switched tactics, and simply avoided using racial language to veil their discriminatory intent, to get away with racial murder.

President Johnson vetoed the Civil Rights Act of 1866 even in its limited, moderate form. Only from the perspective of someone who refused to acknowledge discrimination in racial disparities, who wanted to maintain White privileges and the power to discriminate, could this bill be seen as "in favor of the colored and against the white race," to use Johnson's words. Johnson came from a Democratic Party busily shouting that to give Blacks voting rights would result in "nigger domination." If there was any semblance of equal opportunity, these racists argued, then Blacks would become dominators and Whites would suffer. This was—and still is—the racist folklore of reverse discrimination. Andrew Johnson crafted this form of racism. And long after Congress impeached him, he still topped lists of the worst US presidents.[8]

In early April 1866, Congress overrode the presidential veto, turned its back on the president, and strode toward the Radical Reconstruction of the South. Southern violence against Blacks made congressmen move more quickly and forcefully to stop Blacks from coming north. In early May 1866, White mobs in Memphis killed at least forty-eight Black people, gang-raped at least five Black women, and looted or destroyed $100,000 worth of Black-owned property. Federal authorities slyly blamed nearby Black troops for provoking the violence, and they used their lies to substantiate redeploying them as "Buffalo Soldiers" out West. As southern Black citizens were killed over the next few decades to make way for Jim Crow, Buffalo Soldiers killed indigenous communities in the West to make way for White settlers.[9]

The irony was cruel—as cruel as the elite Blacks who blamed rural migrants for the race riot and urged their removal from Memphis. During and after the war, rural Blacks across the South had fled to southern cities and heard racist southerners—many Black elites included—predicting that the migrants would descend into idleness and criminality. It was said that God had made Black people to cultivate the soil (actually, Black elites diverged on this point). Black urbanites, new and old, were resisting discrimination and building schools, churches, and associations, achieving a modicum of economic security. And yet, their uplift did not improve race relations. Their uplift—and activism and migration—only fueled the violence in Memphis and beyond.[10]

As White southern violence spread, Democratic newspapers published stories arguing that masters' loss of control was energizing the *Black* crime wave. Southerners also read stories of the "murder and mutilation" of Whites in Jamaica by "infuriated negro savages, bent on destroying the civilization which surrounds and vexes them." Jamaica's 1865 revolt was, in fact, a freedom fight against British slavery in everything but name. So it made sense that those who were trying to re-enslave the emancipated in the United States feared another Jamaica. They used any opportunity to attack Black communities to prevent it, and every racist idea to justify their attacks.[11]

DAYS BEFORE THE Memphis riot, a compromise proposal appeared before Congress that incorporated all of the divergent postwar issues into a single constitutional amendment, including denying Confederates the ability to hold office and placing Confederate war debt on southern laps. The Fourteenth Amendment's first clause pleased the Radical Republicans: "No State shall make or enforce any law which shall abridge the privileges or immunities of citizens of the United States; nor shall any State deprive any person of life, liberty, or property, without due process of law, nor deny to any person within its jurisdiction the equal protection of the laws." For the sake of the amendment's passage, most Republicans rejected demands to define this statement's terms. Republicans did not deny Democrats' charges that the amendment was "open to ambiguity and . . . conflicting constructions." The ambiguity effectively ensured that both antiracists and racists would vie for the amendment's power. Indeed, both the defenders of equal opportunity and the defenders of White "privileges or immunities" would vie for the riches of the Fourteenth Amendment after its passage on June 13, 1866 (and ratification in 1868).[12]

For not guaranteeing Black male suffrage, Wendell Phillips blasted the Fourteenth Amendment as a "fatal and total surrender." Republicans argued that omitting suffrage was strategically necessary. They told Black male suffragists that "'the negro must vote,' but the issue must be avoided now so as 'to keep up a two thirds power in Congress."[13]

Suffragists Susan B. Anthony and Elizabeth Cady Stanton believed the woman must vote, too, and they joined Black male suffragists in founding the American Equal Rights Association (AERA) in 1866. "I would not trust [a Black man] with my rights; degraded, oppressed, himself, he would be more despotic . . . than ever our Saxon rulers are," Stanton said at the AERA's first annual meeting in 1867. With the "elevation of women," it would be possible to "develop the Saxon race into a higher and nobler life and thus, by law of attraction, to lift all races," she added. Stanton offered an enduring rationalization for the racist idea of the hypersexist Black male, of Black men being *more* sexist than White men. It was the consequence of his racial oppression; the abused becoming the abuser.[14]

Sojourner Truth rose to defend Stanton's opposition to the Fifteenth Amendment. "White women are a great deal smarter," Truth said, "while colored women do not know scarcely anything." After wielding racist ideas against colored women, the eighty-year-old legend turned her racist ideas onto colored men. Colored women "go out washing . . . and their men go about idle," she said. "And when the women come home, they ask for money and take it all, and then scold because there is no food."[15]

WHEN MIDTERM ELECTORS in 1866 sent the two-thirds majority of Republicans necessary to override presidential vetoes back to Congress, President Johnson was not dismayed. If Republicans brought Black male suffrage before Americans, a Johnson aide said, then "we can beat them at the next Presidential election." Republican congressmen and their voters were a motley crew: it included segregationists, who were seeking to confine Black "brutes" to the South by eliminating racial discrimination; assimilationists, who wanted to humanize the "imbruted" Blacks and eliminate racial discrimination; and a handful of antiracists, who wanted to eliminate racial discrimination and afford equal Blacks equal opportunities.[16]

Nowhere was opportunity as unequal as in work, where rural Blacks' desires for secure land and urban Blacks' desires for secure jobs hardly registered in the political discourse. Every union should promote "one dividing line—that which separates mankind into two great classes," said labor editor Andrew Carr Cameron at the 1867 convention of the newly founded National Labor Union (NLU). Cameron obscured the color line in the first-ever national labor agenda. From then on, this denial of racism allowed racist laborers to join with racist capitalists in depressing Black wages, in shoving Black workers into the nastiest jobs, in driving up their rates of unemployment, and in blaming the racial disparities they helped create on Black stupidity and laziness.[17]

African Americans and their allies tried to create their own opportunities by establishing dozens of historically Black colleges and universities (HBCUs) in the late 1860s. Antiracist educators and philanthropists who viewed southern Black students as intellectually equal to White students were almost certainly involved, but they were not nearly as numerous or as powerful as the assimilationist educators and philanthropists. These assimilationists commonly founded HBCUs "to educate . . . a number of blacks," and then "send them forth to regenerate" their people, who had been degenerated by slavery, as one philanthropist stated. Black and White HBCU founders assumed New England's Latin and Greek curriculum to be the finest, and they only wanted the finest for their students. Many founders assumed "white teachers" to be "the best," as claimed in the New York National Freedman's Relief Association in its 1865–1866 annual report. HBCU teachers and students worked hard to prove to segregationists that Blacks could master the "high culture" of a Greco-Latin education. But the handful of "refined," often biracial HBCU graduates were often dismissed as products of White blood, or as extraordinary in comparison to the ordinarily "unrefined" poor Blacks.

Not all the HBCUs founded in the aftermath of the Civil War adopted the liberal arts curriculum. African Americans "had three centuries of experience in general demoralization and behind that, paganism," the 1868 founder of the Hampton Institute in Virginia once said. Samuel Chapman Armstrong, the former Union officer and Freedmen's Bureau official, offered teaching and vocational training that tutored acceptance of White political supremacy and Blacks' working-class position in the capitalist economy. Hampton had a trade component that aimed to work its aspiring teachers hard so that they would come to appreciate the dignity of hard labor and go on to impress that dignity—instead of resistance—onto the toiling communities where they established schools.[18]

For all their submission schooling, Hampton-type HBCUs were less likely than the Greco-Roman-oriented HBCUs to bar darkskinned applicants. By the end of the century, a color partition had emerged: light-skinned Blacks tended to attend the schools with

Greco-Roman curricula, training for leadership, and darker-skinned Blacks ended up at industrial schools, training for submission. In 1916, one estimate found that 80 percent of the students at the HBCUs offering a Greco-Roman education were light-skinned or biracial. The racist colorism separating HBCUs was reflected in Black social clubs, in housing, and in the separate churches being built. Across postwar America, there emerged Black churches subjecting dark-skinned visitors to paper-bag tests or painting their doors a light brown. People darker than the bag or door were excluded, just as light-skinned Blacks were excluded from White spaces.[19]

CONGRESS PASSED FOUR Reconstruction Acts between March 2, 1867, and March 11, 1868, that laid the groundwork for the new state constitutions and for readmission of ten of the eleven southern states into the Union. Confederates were forced to accept Black male suffrage, while northern Free Soilers soundly rejected Black suffrage on their ballots in the fall of 1867. Confederates roared hypocrisy at these northerners, who were "seeking to fasten what they themselves repudiate with loathing upon the unfortunate people of the South." Republicans stripping the vote away from "respectable" southern Whites and handing it to the "unrespectable" southern Blacks was "worse than madness," President Johnson said in his Third Annual Message to Congress on December 3, 1867. "No independent government of any form has ever been successful in [Black] hands," he added. With voting power, Blacks would cause "a tyranny such as this continent has never yet witnessed." Johnson engaged in a debate that was over before it began. Since the very presence of Blacks was deemed to be tyrannical, racists would only see tyranny no matter what Black voters and politicians accomplished in the coming years.[20]

During the 1868 elections, Democrats pledged to free White southerners from the "semi-barbarous" Black male voters who longed to "subject the white women to their unbridled lust," as stated by a vice presidential candidate, the fanatical Missouri politician and Union general Francis P. Blair Jr. The Democratic platform attacked

Republicans for subjecting the South, "in time of profound peace, to military despotism and negro supremacy." The Ku Klux Klan, founded originally in 1865 as a social club in Tennessee, made a charade of the "profound peace." With Johnson's anti-Black military appointments looking away, the Klan commenced a "reign of terror," assassinating Republicans and barring Blacks from voting.

Millions of Blacks voted for president for the first time in armed southern Black counties that the Klan would not dare to enter, swinging the 1868 presidential election to a Republican war hero, General Ulysses S. Grant. Blacks voted into life what segregationists would begin their struggle to kill—the Black politician. "Nigger voting, holding office, and sitting in the jury box, are all wrong," blared Mississippi's *Columbus Democrat*. "Nothing is more certain to occur than these outrages upon justice and good government will soon be removed."[21]

Numerous Republican congressmen, such as Ohio's James A. Garfield, were privately expressing "a strong feeling of repugnance" about Blacks being "made our political equal." But when these racist Republicans calculated the serious advantages the "loyal" Black vote could give them in swing states, they finally gave their support to Black suffrage. As with the Thirteenth and Fourteenth Amendments, these powerful congressmen had not been morally persuaded to open the door to Black rights. It was about self-interests. On February 27, 1869, the Republican-dominated Congress passed the Fifteenth Amendment to the US Constitution. It forbade the United States and each state from denying or abridging voting rights "on account of race, color, or previous condition of servitude." Congress empowered itself to "enforce this article by appropriate legislation," but refused to go any further. Protections for Black politicians, uniform voting requirements, and the prohibition of race-veiled measures to exclude Blacks, however, were denied.[22]

Denied, too, was any serious discussion of enfranchising women. This issue caused dissension between White and Black suffragists at the American Equal Rights Association (AERA) meeting on May 12, 1869, weeks after Congress passed the Fifteenth Amendment. It stung leading suffragist Susan B. Anthony to think the Constitution had "recognized" Black men "as the political superiors of all the noble women." They had "just emerged from slavery," and were "not only totally illiterate, but also densely ignorant of every public question." Ironically, sexist men were using similar arguments about women's illiteracy, women's ignorance of public questions, and noble men—as the natural political superiors of all women—to oppose Anthony's drive for suffrage rights.[23]

For instance, George Downing, a Black activist and businessman who attended the meeting, spoke of women's obedience being God's will. The AERA meeting went from bad to worse. Feminists challenged him. Downing and other organizers of the Colored National Labor Union (CNLU) came under fire again for this view at their founding meeting later in the year. A Black woman from Downing's home state of Rhode Island expressed her disappointment that "poor women's interests were not mentioned." In the end, the CNLU admitted its "mistakes." It would have been wholly hypocritical for the CNLU to refuse to address gender discrimination, after developing in reaction to the National Labor Union's refusal to address racial discrimination. Then again, hypocrisy had normalized in the American reform movements. Racial, gender, ethnic, and labor activists were angrily challenging the popular bigotry targeting their own groups at the same time they were happily reproducing the popular bigotry targeting other groups. They did not realize that the racist, sexist, ethnocentric, and classist ideas were produced by some of the same powerful minds.

The National Labor Union welcomed Black delegates to its 1869 convention and proclaimed that it "knew neither color nor sex on the question of the rights of labor." Antiracists and feminists would have preferred for the NLU to accept neither racism nor sexism on the question of the rights of labor. But that was hardly forthcoming.[24]

After George Downing's debacle, Frederick Douglass tried to smooth things over by suggesting that AERA members support any measure that extended "suffrage to any class heretofore disenfranchised, as a cheering part of the triumph of our whole idea." Stanton and Anthony rejected the resolution. Poet Frances Harper, representing the guns of Black feminism, chastised "white women" for only going "for sex, letting race occupy a minor position." Sojourner Truth had come to agree with Harper and Douglass. "If you bait the suffrage-hook with a woman, you will certainly catch a black man," Truth advised, as only the Truth could. The division over the Fifteenth Amendment dissolved the AERA and severed the suffrage movement. The suffrage struggle limped into the 1870s and would not be resolved for women until nearly half a century later.

If it had been left up to the first generation of Black male politicians, women may have received voting rights in the 1870s. All six Black Massachusetts legislators, and six of seven Black US representatives from South Carolina, for example, supported women's suffrage. Susan B. Anthony may have privately realized that Black men were not "densely ignorant of every public question," including her right to vote.[25]

Democrats tried to block the ratification of the Fifteenth Amendment, demeaning it as a "nigger superiority bill" meant to establish horrific and barbaric Black supremacy. They had no luck. The amendment was ratified on February 3, 1870. Black people from Boston to Richmond to Vicksburg, Mississippi, planned grand celebrations after the ratification. For their keynote speaker, several communities invited a living legend.[26]

CHAPTER 20

Reconstructing Blame

WILLIAM LLOYD GARRISON decided to stay home and witness the magnificent two-hour procession of dignitaries, especially the veterans of the 54th and 55th Massachusetts regiments. When Garrison stepped to the podium of Faneuil Hall at the close of the celebration of the passage of the Fifteenth Amendment, he looked older than his sixty-four years, tired and ready to step fully out of public life. He regarded the Fifteenth Amendment as a "miracle." The members of the American Anti-Slavery Society, meanwhile, felt that their work was finished. They officially disbanded on April 9, 1870.

"The Fifteenth Amendment confers upon the African race the care of its own destiny. It places their fortunes in their own hands," imagined Ohio congressman James A. Garfield. An Illinois newspaper proclaimed, "The negro is now a voter and a citizen. Let him hereafter takes his chances in the battle of life."[1]

The passage of the Fifteenth Amendment caused Republicans to turn their backs on the struggle against racial discrimination. After refusing to redistribute land, and giving landless Blacks the ability to choose their own masters, and calling that freedom; after handing poor Blacks an equal rights statement they could use in the expensive courts, and calling that equality; they put the ballot in the Black man's hand and called that security. "The ballot is the citadel of the colored man's safety," parodied one Black southerner, "the guarantor of his liberty, the protector of his rights, the defender of his immunities and privileges, the savior of the fruits of his toil, his weapon of offense and defense, his peacemaker, his Nemesis that watches and guards over him with sleepless eye by day and by night." As this Black southerner knew so well, the ballot never did stop all those hooded night riders.[2]

Klan violence was needed to "keep the niggers in their place," explained Confederate general Nathan Bedford Forrest, the Klan's first honorary "Grand Wizard." To the Klan, the only thing worse than a Negro was "a white Radical." But the worst offender was a suspected Black rapist of a White woman. Klansmen glorified White womanhood as the epitome of honor and purity (and asexuality) and demeaned Black womanhood as the epitome of immorality and filth (and sex). Some Black men demeaned Black women, too. "Lord, sar!" said a prosperous Black Kansan. "You not think I marry a black nigger wench?" Klansmen religiously believed that Blacks possessed supernatural sexual powers, and this belief fueled their sexual attraction to Black women and their fear of White women being attracted to Black men. It became almost standard operating procedure to justify Klan terrorism by maintaining that southern White supremacy was necessary to defend the purity of White women. Black women's bodies, in contrast, were regarded as a "training ground" for White men, or a stabilizing "safety valve" for White men's "sexual energies" that allowed the veneration of the asexual pureness of White womanhood to continue.[3]

The other threat to White male dominance was upwardly mobile Black people. Klan terrorism showed the charade that was always the strategy of uplift suasion. The Klan did "not like to see the negro go ahead," reported a White Mississippian. Landless Blacks were terrorized by landowners. Landowning Blacks were terrorized by the Klan. In March 1870, President Grant sent to Congress documentary evidence of more than 5,000 cases of White terrorism. Between May 1870 and April 1871, Congress passed three poorly funded Enforcement Acts that dispatched election supervisors to the South, criminalized interference with Black voting, and turned a wide range of Klan-type terrorist acts into federal offenses. As a result, the Klan had "nominally dissolved" by 1871, but the train of terror still rushed down the tracks under new names. It became clear to all, as a northern transplant explained, that only "steady, unswerving power from without" could guarantee peace and the survival of southern Republicanism. A steady, unswerving Black power from within could have done so, too, but Republicans remained unwilling to fortify Blacks with Buffalo Soldiers and land.[4]

The vote was supposed to make miracles, and in some ways it did. Southern constitutional conventions from 1867 to 1869 were a revolutionary sight to behold. They included northern transplants, southern Republicans, and southern Black delegates, about half of whom had been born in slavery. For all their lack of political experience, wealth, and schooling—or rather because of it—these delegates produced alluringly democratic constitutions. They instituted the South's first publicly funded educational systems, penitentiaries, orphanages, and insane asylums; expanded women's rights and guaranteed Black rights; reduced the number of crimes; and reorganized local governments to eliminate dictatorships. Initially, however, Black politicians usually stepped aside when the positions of power were divided up because they did not want to lend credibility to persistent Democratic charges of "black supremacy," as if the charge had some logic to it.

While Blacks rarely benefited from Reconstruction's economic policies, growing corporations did. Facing war-torn communities and treasuries, the same Reconstruction politicians who refused to hand out land and aid to landless Blacks, on the pretext that it would ruin them, handed millions out to railroad companies, on the pretext that railroads would develop the South by bringing new jobs, factories, and towns; allow for transport of untapped minerals; and extend agriculture. By 1872, most of the South only had debt and poverty to show for the incredible amounts of welfare handed out to railroad corporations. Bribed politicians happily gave away these funds. Only a small number of Black politicians sat in senior positions of power, and thus their share of the corruption paled in comparison to that of White politicians.[5]

Every dollar taken from southern treasuries heightened southern reliance on cheap labor. President Grant figured that maybe if Blacks had somewhere else to go, planters would value Black labor more. (Actually, planters did value cheap labor, and they used their guns and racist ideas to keep Black labor as cheap as possible.) In early 1870, Grant began a presidential push for the annexation of the Dominican Republic to provide a haven for "the entire colored population of the United States, should it choose to emigrate." He sent Frederick Douglass on a fact-finding mission in 1871. The DR could not only become a Black haven, the impressed Douglass reported, but by "transplanting within her tropical borders the glorious institutions" of the United States, the Blacks who moved there could uplift the impoverished and backward Dominican people. Douglass seemed unaware that he was recycling against Dominicans the very same racist ideas that had been used against African Americans. And if the US institutions were so "glorious," then why did African Americans need a foreign haven?[6]

Assimilationists like Douglass encouraged American expansion, while segregationists and antiracists discouraged it, bringing the ongoing racial dispute into foreign policy. The US Senate voted down the annexation treaty in June 1871. Tired of Grant's preoccupation with annexation, and his openness to using federal power to protect southern Black lives, Republican dissidents broke away. In May 1872, *New York Tribune* editor Horace Greeley and Illinois senator Lyman Trumbull, central forces in the passage of the Reconstruction Amendments, headlined an assembly of "Liberal Republicans" in Cincinnati. "Reconstruction and slavery we have done with," declared E. L. Godkin, the editor of *The Nation*, speaking for the Liberal Republicans. They pledged amnesty and voting rights for ex-Confederates, the end of federal southern intervention, welfare for the rich in the form of tax breaks, and nothing for the poor.[7]

Greeley emerged as their presidential candidate. The arch-enemy of the Confederacy became the arch-friend of the Confederacy, similar to the nation's most famous preacher, whom Frederick Douglass sarcastically called the "apostle of forgiveness." Seeking to reunite White northerners and southerners through Christian Whiteness, Henry Ward Beecher published the first American biography of Jesus, *The Life of Jesus, the Christ*, in 1871. "There is absolutely nothing to determine the personal appearance of Jesus," wrote Harriet Beecher Stowe's brother. And yet Beecher included in the book five depictions of the perfect God-man named Jesus, and they all depicted a White man. Henry Ward Beecher gave White Americans a model for embedding Whiteness into their religious worldviews of Jesus Christ without ever saying so out loud, just as southern and northern Whites were doing with their political worldviews. It went without saying for racists that White people were the best equipped to rule the United States under the heavenly guidance of the White Father and Son.[8]

Horace Greeley had long been associated with emancipation and equality, but he made himself over in order to campaign as the Democratic candidate for president in 1872. "Political equality is far off," he lectured Blacks. "Social equality will remain forever out of reach. Don't expect free gifts of land. Segregate yourself; employ each other. Who are your best friends?—Sound, conservative, knowing white Southerners." These "knowing white Southerners" made it known to Black people, as one South Carolinian observed, that "to vote against the wishes of their white employers and neighbors was to risk death." Congress issued a report in the spring of 1872 condemning southern violence, but it only went so far. The report even adopted the segregationists' position, arguing that Blacks were the cause. The violence, the report explained, was a response to the "bad legislation, official incompetency, and corruption" of Black politicians. It hardly mattered that southern White politicians sat in the overwhelming majority of the powerful and corruptible positions. The truth hardly mattered to the producers of these racist ideas who were seeking to defend the racist policies of buckling Black political power. Grant's former secretary of the interior, Jacob Cox, said southerners could "only be governed through the part of the community that embodies the intelligence and the capital." *The Nation* put it more bluntly: Reconstruction had "totally failed."[9]

Enough Blacks and Republican Whites risked death to win most of the South and President Grant's reelection in 1872. On southern streets, armed Republicans had to defend their reelected politicians. In Colfax, Louisiana, sixty-one armed Blacks barricaded themselves inside a courthouse on Easter Sunday, 1873. Democrats shelled the courthouse with artillery, snatched out the thirty-seven survivors, and executed them in the town square. The day after the Colfax

Massacre, the US Supreme Court, including Grant's four corporate lawyer appointees, massacred the civil rights protections of the Fourteenth Amendment in the *Slaughterhouse Cases*. White New Orleans butchers felt their economic "privileges and immunities" were being denied by the bribe-instigated 1869 Louisiana statute requiring them to do business at the Slaughterhouse Company. Writing for the majority, Justice Samuel Miller upheld the monopoly on April 14, 1873, distinguishing between national and state citizenship and citing Roger B. Taney's *Dred Scott* opinion. The Fourteenth Amendment only protected the relatively few rights of national citizens, Miller stated. Three years later, this doctrinaire split between national and state citizenship allowed a unanimous Supreme Court to reverse the convictions of the perpetrators of the Colfax Massacre (murder prosecutions "rests alone with the States"), thus giving Louisiana the freedom to exonerate them. The Court also voided the Enforcement Acts and encouraged White terrorist organizations just in time for the election of 1876.[10]

None of the four *Slaughterhouse* dissenters objected to the most far-reaching part of Justice Miller's majority opinion: "We doubt very much whether any action of a state not directed by way of discrimination against the negroes as a class, or on account of their race, will ever come within the purview of this provision." To this day, the Supreme Court still uses Miller's doctrine to shield private and race-veiled discriminators, those who veil policies intended to discriminate against Black people by not using racial language.[11]

Neither ex-Confederates voting again nor the *Slaughterhouse* ruling could compare to the destructive force of the Panic of 1873. It was the first major economic depression of American industrial capitalism and lasted the rest of the decade. Southern Democrats declared their ability to restore order, just as the oil man John D. Rockefeller and the steel man Andrew Carnegie declared their ability to monitor their industries. By the end of the century, the Rockefeller and Carnegie monopolies reflected the White political monopolies steering the South.

As the poorest of the poor, southern Blacks were the most devastated of the devastated by the Panic of 1873. The Panic halted the modest postwar ascent of Black landowners, snatching their land and their freedom. When legions of small White landowners lost their land, too, they felt as if they were losing their Whiteness and freedom. Whites "must have small plots of land," one planter complained, "and prefer tending them, poor as may be the return, to lowering themselves, as they think it, by hiring to another."[12]

Holding out hope for redistributed land as long as they could, rural southern Blacks walked backward into sharecropping, meaning they handed the landowner a share of the crop as payment for the ability to farm there. Crooked landowners maneuvered sharecroppers into debt, and laws prevented sharecroppers from leaving landowners to whom they owed money. Blacks who were able to leave a bad situation took to the road, looking endlessly for ethical landowners. Landowners called this annual movement a sign of Black shiftlessness. Stuck between racist policies and ideas, sharecroppers could not win. Staying often meant servitude, but leaving meant shiftlessness.[13]

Nothing seemed to dent racist ideas, not even upwardly mobile urban Blacks. In 1874, Nashville's White-owned *Republican Banner* praised the "thrifty and cleanly" Blacks. But they could not "be taken as the representative of the indolent and shiftless hundreds of thousands," the *Banner* opined. They were extraordinary.[14]

BY THE EARLY 1870s, given the snatching away from Blacks' civil rights, William Lloyd Garrison had no choice but to make his voice heard once again. He ridiculed the abandonment of Reconstruction in essay after essay in *The Independent,* and in open letter after open letter in the *Boston Journal.* Vice President Henry Wilson complained to Garrison of a "Counter-Revolution" overtaking Reconstruction. "Our Anti-slavery veterans must again speak out," Wilson urged. Some failed to speak out because they were too busy blaming Black people for the failures of Reconstruction. And how could they not? Northern press reports regularly depicted Black voters and politicians as self-destructively stupid and corrupt. The Associated Press relied on anti-Black, anti-Reconstruction southern papers for daily dispatches. *New York Tribune* reporter James S. Pike blanketed northerners with racist fairytales of corrupt, incompetent, lazy Black politicians who conquered and deprived White South Carolinians during the "tragedy" of Reconstruction. These claims were published in his widely circulated newspaper articles in 1873, republished as *The Prostrate State, South Carolina Under Negro Government* in 1874. Pike's Democratic sources were happy to blame the southern corruption on Black people, as it diverted attention from their principal role in the corruption. Pike's well-written novel passed as eyewitness journalism. "In the place of this old aristocratic society stands the rude form of the most ignorant democracy that mankind ever saw," Pike wrote. "It is barbarism overwhelming civilization" and "the slave rioting in the halls of his master, and putting that master under his feet."[15]

The *Prostrate State* caused pro-Reconstruction periodicals—*Scribner's, Harper's, The Nation,* and *The Atlantic Monthly*—to pummel Black legislators even more and demand a national reunion of White rule. A New York Democrat read from *The Prostrate State* on the House floor. Where's your book on New York corruption? asked Black South Carolina congressman Robert Small. Though the bribers and the bribed knew corruption was a national affair, primarily among White politicians, racist ideas never did quite subscribe to the magazine of reality. Black corruption was a ready-made excuse to abandon the increasingly difficult, expensive, disordering, and divisive Reconstruction policies. Every time Grant's administration intervened to protect Black lives, he alienated northern and southern Whites from the Republican Party. During the 1874 midterm elections, Democrats knocked Republicans out of control of the House of Representatives and out of power in every southern state except Mississippi, Louisiana, South Carolina, and Florida. White terrorist organizations warred with armed and unarmed Black voters across the South. President Grant had to send troops to prevent an army of 3,500 Democrats from forcing out elected Republicans in New Orleans in September 1874. Wendell Phillips was jeered off a Boston stage for trying to defend Grant. The *New York Times* reported that "Wendell Phillips and William Lloyd Garrison are not exactly extinct from American politics, but they represent ideas in regard to the South which the majority of the Republican party have outgrown."[16]

The final bill of Radical Reconstruction was pushed through Congress in early 1875 before the new Democrats took office. The Civil Rights Act of 1875 was a legislative memorial to Senator Charles Sumner, who died in 1874 after decades in the antislavery and civil rights trenches. The bill outlawed racial discrimination in jury selection, public transportation, and public accommodations, but it required Blacks to seek redress in the expensive and hostile courts. The bill hardly stopped the terror campaign against Mississippi's Black voters that allowed Democrats to gain state control in the fall 1875 election. Mississippi's embattled Republican governor, Adelbert Ames, declared that "a revolution is taking place—by force of arms—and a race are disenfranchised—they are to be returned to a condition of serfdom—an era of second slavery." A southern newspaper declared that the Fourteenth and Fifteenth Amendments "may stand forever; but we intend . . . to make them dead letters."[17]

With Reconstruction of southern democracy on life support, the United States celebrated the one hundredth anniversary of the Declaration of Independence. From May to November 1876, roughly one-fifth of the US population attended the first of the official "world fairs," Philadelphia's Centennial Exposition. "A band of old-time plantation 'darkies'" singing songs at the Southern Restaurant was the only display depicting Black people. In Boston, William Lloyd Garrison gave an Independence Day address for the ages. The shift in public opinion away from Reconstruction was the consequence of emancipating Black people as a military necessity rather than as "an act of general repentance," he said. In his last major public speech, Garrison recognized racist ideas as the core of the problem. "We must give up the spirit of complexional caste," Garrison declared, "or give up Christianity."[18]

In Hamburg, South Carolina, the local Black militia celebrated the July 4 centennial with a parade. Area racists hated the militia for maintaining Blacks' ability to control the majority Black town. During the parade, harsh words were exchanged when a local White farmer ordered militia members to move aside for his carriage. The farmer appealed to former Confederate general Matthew C. Butler, the area's most powerful Democrat. On July 8, Butler and a small posse ordered the militia head, Union Army veteran Dock Adams, to disarm the Hamburg militia. Adams refused, and fighting broke out. The militiamen retreated to their armory. Butler dashed off for nearby Augusta, but returned with hundreds of reinforcements and cannon. Butler's contingent executed five militiamen and looted and destroyed the undefended homes and shops of Hamburg.

When southerners complained of their lost cause, an appalled President Grant realized they were complaining of their lost freedom "to kill negroes and Republicans without fear of punishment and without loss of caste or reputations." General Butler made a mockery of the congressional investigation, capitalizing on the attention by being elected to the US Senate in 1877. He blamed the massacre on innate Black criminality. Blacks, he said, possessed "little regard for human life."[19]

General Butler was invoking Blacks' natural proclivity for violence and criminality to avoid punishment for the massacre he had carried out. But hardly any congressional investigators questioned his motive for expressing these racist ideas, which at the time were being codified by a prison doctor in Italy. Cesare Lombroso "proved" in 1876 that non-White men loved to kill, "mutilate the corpse, tear its flesh and drink its blood." His *Criminal Man* gave birth to the discipline of criminology in 1876. Criminals were born, not bred, Lombroso said. He believed that born criminals emitted physical signs that could be studied, measured, and quantified, and that the "inability to blush"—and therefore, dark skin—had "always been considered the accompaniment of crime." Black women, in their close "degree of differentiation from the male," he claimed in *The Female Offender* in 1895, were the prototypical female criminals. As White terrorists brutalized, raped, and killed people in communities around the Black world, the first crop of Western criminologists were intent on giving criminals a Black face and the well-behaved citizen a White face. Lombroso's student, Italian law professor Raffaele Garofalo, invented the term "criminology" (*criminologia*) in 1885. British physician Havelock Ellis popularized Lombroso in the English-speaking world, publishing a compendium of his writings in 1890.[20]

The Hamburg perpetrators kept shouting: "This is the beginning of the redemption of South!" Indeed, it was. When the election of 1876 came in November, it was war at the polls, and Democrats stuffed ballot boxes across the South. By the morning of November 8, 1876, Democratic New York governor Samuel J. Tilden and Republican Ohio governor Rutherford B. Hayes were virtually tied in the electoral college. The presidential election's outcome rested in the contested election returns of Louisiana and South Carolina. When a fifteen-member electoral commission handed Republicans the presidency, Democrats were outraged. In early 1877, both parties, and both regions, began planning for another Civil War.

The parties and regions remained united on one issue. Blacks must quell their "new kindled ambition" and recognize their lack of Whites' "hereditary faculty of self government," said former Ohio governor Jacob D. Cox. Outgoing president Grant privately told his cabinet that giving Black men the ballot had been a mistake, and so did Republican presidential hopeful Rutherford B. Hayes. While a consensus formed on who should govern the South, division intensified over who should govern in Washington, DC.

The nation on the brink, Hayes's representatives met with Democrats at the Wormly House, a hotel owned by the capital's richest African American. No one ever revealed the exact terms of the "Bargain of 1877." But Democrats handed Republican Rutherford B. Hayes the presidency, while Hayes ended Reconstruction for the Democrats. Hayes recognized the stolen Democratic governments in Louisiana and South Carolina. He withdrew federal troops from the South and used those troops to crush the Great Strike of 1877. (As capital regained control of labor, the Knights of Labor materialized as the principal national labor organization. Knights head Terence V. Powderly demanded unions' desegregation to control the competition. He considered Blacks a "lazy" reservoir of "cheap labor" that could easily be used against White labor.)[21]

The Nation made the Bargain of 1877 plain. The time had come for "the negro to disappear from the field of national politics," said the newsmagazine. "Henceforth, the nation, as a nation, will have nothing more do with him." Meanwhile, William Lloyd Garrison labeled the Bargain "an abomination" amounting to the old "covenant with death." When troops departed Shreveport, Louisiana, a Black man grieved about his people being back in "the hands of the very men that held [them] as slaves," so that "there was no way on earth they could better [their] condition."[22]

"Not one single right enjoyed by the colored people shall be taken from them," pledged the new Democratic South Carolina governor, Wade Hampton. "As the negro becomes more intelligent," Hampton added, "he naturally allies himself with the more conservative whites, for his observation and experience both show him that his interests are identified with those of the white race here." Hampton opened two doors for Blacks in post-Reconstruction South Carolina: naturally submissive intelligence, or naturally rebellious stupidity.[23]

The Reconstruction era—the dozen or so years following the end of the Civil War in 1865—had been a horrific time for southern White men like Wade Hampton who were used to ruling *their* Black people and *their* women. They faced and beat back with violence and violent ideas a withering civil rights and Black empowerment movement— as well as a powerful women's movement that failed to grab as many headlines. But their supposed underlings did not stop rebelling after the fall of Reconstruction. To intimidate and reassert their control over rebellious Blacks and White women, White male redeemers took up lynching in the 1880s. Someone was lynched, on average, every four days from 1889 to 1929. Often justifying the ritualistic slaughters on a false rumor that the victim had raped a White woman, White men, women, and children gathered to watch the torture, killing, and dismemberment of human beings—all the while calling the victims savages. Hate fueled the lynching era. But behind this hatred lay racist ideas that had evolved to question Black freedoms at every stage. And behind these racist ideas were powerful White men, striving by word and deed to regain absolute political, economic, and cultural control of the South.[24]

SOUTHERN BLACK PEOPLE felt a range of emotions as they trekked from slavery to war to emancipation to Radical Reconstruction to Black Redemption to White Redemption. Their feelings seem to have resembled the range of emotions a parent might feel living through the exciting birth, hopeful growth, and tragic death of a beloved child. Some Blacks, angry over Reconstruction's demise, felt the need to run away from their second slavery. "It is impossible for us to live with these slaveholders of the South," said one Louisiana organizer, representing more than 60,000 "hard-laboring people" eager to flee the South. Resettlement to Africa or the North or far West was not nearly as popular in the late 1870s as the "Exodus" to Kansas. The "Exodusters" ignored the opposition of Frederick Douglass and increased Kansas's Black population by 150 percent. Northern allies did all they could to fund-raise for Exodusters. William Lloyd Garrison, at seventy-four years old, exhausted himself raising money for hundreds of Black Exodusters fleeing Mississippi and Louisiana.

On April 24, 1879, Garrison had hoped to address a rally for the Exodusters at Boston's Faneuil Hall, but he was too weak to attend. Still, he made sure his voice was heard, sending a reverberating statement. "Let the edict go forth, trumpet-tongued, that there shall be a speedy end put to all this bloody misrule; that the millions of loyal colored citizens at the South, now under ban and virtually disfranchised, shall be put in the safe enjoyment of their rights—shall freely vote and be fairly represented—just where they are located. And let the rallying-cry be heard from the Atlantic to the Pacific coast, 'Liberty and equal rights for each, for all, and forever, wherever the lot of man is cast without our broad domains!'" He had hoped for immediate emancipation when all hope had been lost. He now hoped for immediate equality when all hope had been lost. The thrilling statement of hope on April 24, 1879, proved to be the last will and testament of William Lloyd Garrison. Four weeks later, he was dead.[25]

PART IV

W. E. B. Du Bois

CHAPTER 21

Renewing the South

"THE SLAVE WENT FREE; stood a brief moment in the sun; then moved back again towards slavery." W. E. B. Du Bois had lived almost seven decades before he gave this classic summation of the Reconstruction era. He was born under the sun on February 23, 1868, the day before the impeachment of President Andrew Johnson. While Garrison applauded Johnson's impeachment from the eastern end of Massachusetts, "Willie" Du Bois came into being on the western end of Massachusetts in the small town of Great Barrington. He grew up between two encircling mountain ranges: the Berkshires to the east and the Taconic chain to the west, assimilationist ideas to the north and segregationist ideas to the south.[1]

Mary Silvina Burghardt raised Willie. Alfred Duboise, Willie's Franco-Haitian father, had left his wife and child for Connecticut by 1870. Burghardt became the single mother of two boys. She had already birthed the only out-of-wedlock child in recent family memory, Willie's older half-brother, Adelbert. In a way, Burghardt resembled Garrison's mother, Frances Maria Lloyd, who had defied her family, lived on the social edge, married a rover, and, after being deserted and devastated, poured what was left of herself into her children. And their prized youngest sons wanted nothing more than to make their distressed mothers happy.

Willie gleaned his first sense of racial difference on an interracial playground at ten years old in 1878. The exchange of "gorgeous visiting-cards . . . was merry, till one girl, a tall newcomer, refused my card—refused it peremptorily, with a glance. Then it dawned upon me with a certain suddenness that I was different from the others," he later wrote. From then on, Willie Du Bois fiercely competed with his White peers in the game of uplift suasion, in an attempt to prove "to the world that Negroes were just like other people." He would go on to hike and reach the summit of the European intellectual world. However, he did not like what he saw when he reached the top.[2]

IN THE 1870S and 1880s, no matter what Willie and other young Blacks like him achieved in school and in life, they were not changing the minds of the discriminators. The discriminators were subscribing to Social Darwinism and to the idea that Blacks were losing the racial struggle for existence. For ages, enslavers had pictured Black people as physically hardy, hardy enough to survive the heat of southern enslavement. With emancipation, racist ideas progressed to suit this new world. Discriminators started picturing Blacks as weak, too weak to survive in freedom, beings that desperately needed to learn to be strong without their masters and government assistance.[3]

In 1883, the US Supreme Court declared the Civil Rights Act of 1875 unconstitutional. Civil rights activists loudly protested the funeral of the Reconstruction era, but not loud enough for a fifteen-year-old lad in Great Barrington. Willie Du Bois launched his publishing career, complaining about local indifference to the Court ruling in T. Thomas Fortune's immensely popular Black newspaper, the *New York Globe*.[4]

Drowning out the young Willies and the older Fortunes in 1883, the united North and South hailed the decision to trash the 1875 Civil Rights Act. The *New York Times* applauded the Supreme Court's "useful purpose in . . . undoing the work of Congress." In the majority opinion, Justice Joseph Bradley wrote that the Thirteenth and Fourteenth Amendments did not bestow on Congress any power to prohibit discrimination in privately run public accommodations, but only "state action" that denied equal protection of the laws. "When a man has emerged from slavery and with the aid of beneficent legislation has

shaken off the inseparable concomitants of that state," Bradley concluded, "there must be some stage in the progress of his elevation
when he takes the rank of a mere citizen, and ceases to be a special
favorite of the laws, and when his rights . . . are to be protected in the
ordinary modes by which other men's rights are protected." A mere
citizen without special favors protected in the ordinary modes? Did
Justice Bradley not understand that Black people only wanted to be
mere citizens? Did Justice Bradley not understand that their rights
were not being protected from planters and Klansmen?[5]

Maybe the New York–born Bradley was indeed in the dark, especially if he believed the optimistic propaganda of what was being billed
as the "New South." *Atlanta Constitution* editor Henry W. Grady was the
chief propagandist of the New South in the 1880s. "The friendliness
that existed between the master and slave . . . has survived war, and
strife, and political campaigns," Grady imagined. Methodist bishop
and Emory College president Atticus Haygood also marketed the New
South in speeches across the country, and in his popular 1881 book,
Our Brother in Black. The "great majority of the slaves did truly love the
white people," Haygood presumed. White enslavers taught them labor
habits, English, the principles of free institutions, and Christianity.
Whites must continue the elevating legacy of slavery in a nicely segregated free labor society, Haygood instructed. How could wise Whites
teach unwise Blacks if the races were separated? Haygood disregarded
the contradiction.[6]

But an Episcopal bishop, Thomas U. Dudley, could not. He
opposed racial "separation" because it would mean "continued and
increasing degradation and decay" for Blacks. Their hope for salvation
must come from association "with White people," Dudley stressed. A
famous New Orleans novelist of prewar Creole life, George Washington Cable, also challenged these New South segregationists, inviting
their wrath. In April 1885, Grady issued his "official" reply in *Century
Magazine* to Cable and other assimilationist and antiracist critics: "The
assortment of races is wise and proper, and stands on the platform of
equal accommodations for each race but separate." With that statement, Grady birthed the New South's defense of racial segregation.

The system of separation had been created to ensure racial inequality, yet Grady propagated the notion that it was intended to ensure racial equality and bring racial progress. Truth never did stop the concocters of racist ideas. Grady had a separate-but-equal brand to invent, to defend, and to sell to the American mind. And millions of Americans bought it in the 1880s.[7]

In buying this New South, Americans had adopted a new tool for blaming racial disparities on Black people: faith in racial progress (and ignoring the simultaneous progression of racism). It was being taught that American slavery had developed those backward people who had been brought over from the wilds of Africa. Northern missionaries and New South stalwarts, it was said, were developing those backward people who were now freed from the wilds of slavery. And the Reconstruction Amendments, claimed the proponents of the New South, had indeed lessened racial discrimination and brought on equal opportunity. All this racist propaganda coalesced into an indelible postwar faith in racial progress, specifically, that "prejudice against color is slowly but surely dying out," as a Philadelphia newspaper reported in 1888. An aversion "to industry and frugality"—not discrimination—caused the socioeconomic disparities between the races, the newspaper stated. "Racial progress" became the most powerful racist rejoinder to antiracists, who were still pointing out discrimination and disparities. The New South really became the New America of racial progress.[8]

Social Darwinists, conjuring Black regression since slavery, and Confederate holdovers of the Old South rejected the New South's racial progress brand and the separate-but-equal formulation. The Reverend Robert L. Dabney, one of southern Presbyterianism's most influential intellectuals and an old Confederate Army chaplain, argued that only enslavement could provide Black people with a civilizing education. Lawyer-turned-writer Thomas Nelson Page spent his writing career sharply contrasting what he considered the hard, industrializing capitalism and the disobedient African of the New South with the soft, agricultural capitalism and the obedient African of the Old South. Through his short story collection *In Ole Virginia, or Marse Chan and Others* (1887), Page pioneered the postwar plantation school of fiction—a carbon copy of the prewar idyllic plantation fiction—reimagining his lovely childhood days surrounded by happy captives on his Virginia plantation. And then, in 1889, the most popular anti–New South book appeared, *The Plantation Negro as a Freeman*. Harvard alumnus Philip Alexander Bruce, Page's brother-in-law, claimed that Black people, "cut off" from their civilizing White masters, had degenerated back into the "African type," leading to "bold and forward" Black women advancing on White men, Black male criminals raping White women (compelling White men to lynch them), and Black parents producing problem children who were "less inclined to work."[9]

AS A TEENAGER, Willie Du Bois had dreamed of going to Harvard. Charitable local Whites, unwilling to send their town's extraordinary Negro to the nation's best historically White college, raised funds in 1885 to send him to the nation's best historically Black college: Fisk University of Nashville. Controlled by White philanthropists and instructors, Fisk was one of the nation's preeminent factories of uplift suasion and assimilationist ideas. Du Bois consumed these ideas like his peers and started reproducing them when he became the editor of Fisk's student newspaper, *The Herald*. In one of his published pieces, he eagerly reviewed the first full-length history of African Americans, George Washington Williams's *History of the Negro Race in America from 1619 to 1880*. "At last," Du Bois rejoiced, Black people "have a historian"![10]

Other reviews of the book, which was first released in 1883, were also favorable. But one critique from the *Magazine of American History*—saying that Williams was "not sufficiently restrained"—signified the conundrum that many Black revisionist scholars would face in future decades. When Black revisionists chose not to revise, then they seemingly allowed racist studies excluding or denigrating Blacks to stand for truth. When they did revise racist scholarship, they apparently lacked objectivity. Only White scholars apparently could be "sufficiently restrained" to write on race: only racist studies reflected scholarly truth.[11]

Williams's major antiracist (and sexist) historical revision had been to show that Black (male) Americans had played an integral part in US history. He challenged the racist ideas of scholars arguing that Black people had regressed since slavery with his own racist ideas of the "weak Black man" and the "strong Black woman." Williams liberally cited from the 1864 tract *Savage Africa*. "If the women of Africa are brutal," he wrote, "the men of Africa are feminine." According to Williams's assimilationist reading of history, freedom had facilitated Black adoption of civilized values and norms, of "better and purer traits of character." Black women "have risen to take their places in society." Black men were again becoming "enduring in affection, and benevolent to a fault."[12]

Du Bois embraced Williams's *History* and seemed to have been influenced by the book's assimilationist ideas and gender racism. In his Fisk graduation speech in June 1888, Du Bois offered the founder and first chancellor of Germany, Otto von Bismarck, as a model for Black leadership. Bismarck was well known for bringing together dozens of communities to form the mighty Germany in 1871. Du Bois said that Bismarck's Second Reich "should serve as a model for African-Americans 'marching forth with strength and determination under trained leadership.'" He did not mind that Bismarck had hosted the Berlin Conference in 1885, where European colonizers had partitioned Africa on the dishonest pretext that they were bringing civilization to the continent. "I did not understand at all, nor had my history courses led me to understand," he later admitted, that colonialism had so viciously exploited African raw materials and labor. "I was blithely European and imperialistic in outlook."[13]

After Fisk, Du Bois was able to pursue his dream to attend Harvard. He left for the North in 1888 at a time when racist southerners were calmly debating two paths for the Negro—Should they be carefully civilized, or rigidly segregated from Whites? As the New South Democrats tried to hold off Jim Crow Democrats, Republicans regained the President's House and Congress in the 1888 elections. In his First Message to Congress in 1889, President Benjamin Harrison asked, "When is [the Negro] in fact to have those full civil rights which have so long been his in law?"[14]

Never—as far as Jim Crow segregationists were concerned.

CHAPTER 22

Southern Horrors

SOUTH CAROLINA SENATOR Matthew Butler and Alabama senator and former Ku Klux Klan Grand Dragon John Tyler Morgan introduced a congressional bill on January 7, 1890, to fund Black emigration to Africa. It was an ingenious solution to the class and racial problems of big southern landowners. Withering under a southern agricultural depression, many White "dirt farmers" were raging against the Black farmers; others were joining with Blacks to rage against White landowners in the rising interracial, antiracist populist movement. The colonization bill was a deflective measure. It pointed White farmers to southern Blacks—and not rich White landowners—as the chief cause of the southern agrarian depression. White farmers could easily see how the mass ejection of southern Blacks would increase their own labor value.[1]

Americans were probably more open to colonization in 1890 than at any time since Abraham Lincoln's urgings during the Civil War. Caribbean-born Liberian diplomat Edward Wilmot Blyden was touring the United States proclaiming that African Americans had been schooled and preserved by slavery for their divine mission to redeem Africa. "God has a way of salting as well as purifying by fire," Blyden wrote in the American Colonization Society's journal in 1890. The writings of Henry Morton Stanley, the nineteenth century's most famous English-speaking explorer of Africa, were in mass circulation. Nearly every English speaker interested in Africa read Stanley's *Through the Dark Continent* (1878), and nearly everyone who read Stanley came away viewing African people as savages, including novelist

Joseph Conrad, who authored the classic *Heart of Darkness* in 1899. The White character's journey up the Congo River "was like traveling back to the earliest beginning of the world"—not back in chronological time, but back in evolutionary time.[2]

In his January 1890 speech before the Senate to push the colonization bill, John Tyler Morgan read from Henry Morgan Stanley. Under White tutelage, African Americans had been civilized to a level from which they could now pull Africa out of the depths of barbarism, Morgan said. He hoped that potential Black emigrants would "be as kind and patient and generous towards their own kindred as we [White southerners] have been to them." Although millions of American citizens supported the bill, the austere opposition held the day, and it never became law.[3]

Watching this colonization debate unfold only emboldened a zealous Democrat in Omaha, Nebraska. Walter Vaughan, the son of Alabama slaveholders, believed that his scheme would benefit the "tattered condition" of the emancipated people who, in his mind, had been well cared for during slavery. The business owner proposed that the federal government provide pensions for ex-slaves (who would then spend their money buying things from struggling White southern businesses). Vaughan convinced his congressman, Republican William J. Connell, to introduce the ex-slave pension bill in 1890. With Frederick Douglass as one of the few supportive Black elites, the reparations bill died a quiet death.

And yet, Vaughan continued to press for ex-slave pensions. He published the pamphlet *Freedmen's Pension Bill: A Plea for American Freedmen*, and soon, 10,000 worn copies of it were being passed from hand to hand in poor Black communities in the South and Midwest. Callie House, an ex-slave and washerwoman in Tennessee, came across the pamphlet in 1891, and then she helped formulate the National Ex-Slave Mutual Relief, Bounty and Pension Association, based in Nashville, Tennessee. Claiming hundreds of thousands of members, this organization gave birth to the reparations movement of the 1890s, a movement demanding restitution for the unpaid labors of American slavery. The movement was furiously supported by antiracist poor Blacks, and furiously opposed by the same class racism that had prevented Congress from giving Blacks their forty acres and a mule after the Civil War. Black elites, joining their White peers, typically ignored or castigated reparations bills. Economic injustices affecting low-income Blacks took a back seat to education and voting injustices among Black elites. "The most learned negroes," Callie House scolded, "have less interest in their race than any other negro as many of them are fighting against the welfare of their race."[4]

ON JUNE 25, 1890, W. E. B. Du Bois spoke at his Harvard graduation ceremony. He had now excelled, and had graduated from the most prestigious historically Black college *and* the most prestigious historically White college in the United States. He felt he was showing off the capability of his race. Du Bois's "brilliant and eloquent address," as judged by the reporters, was on "Jefferson Davis as Representative of Civilization." In Du Bois's rendering, Jefferson Davis, who had died the year before, represented the rugged individualism and domineering European civilization, in contrast to the rugged "submission" and selflessness of African civilization. The European "met civilization and crushed it," Du Bois concluded. "The Negro met civilization and was crushed by it." According to Du Bois's biographer, the Harvard graduate contrasted the civilized European "Strong Man" to the civilized African "Submissive Man."[5]

Du Bois had clearly been influenced by Harriet Beecher Stowe's postwar New England, where ideas on race seemed to start and end in *Uncle Tom's Cabin*. At Harvard, he had also been influenced by one of the professors, the historian Albert Hart, a hard-line moralist who deemed character—the "inner man not the outer"—as the key to social change. Du Bois consumed from Hart and other assimilationists the racist idea that African Americans had been socially and morally crippled by slavery (and Africa). Du Bois had more faith in future development than his professor did. In his 1910 travel book *The Southern South*, Hart claimed that "the Negro is inferior, and his past history in Africa and in America leads to the belief that he will remain inferior." Thinking about Du Bois specifically, Hart reduced his talents to his European ancestry. Du Bois was "living proof," Hart wrote confidentially, "that a mulatto may have as much power and passion as any white man."[6]

In the fall of 1890, Du Bois entered Harvard's history doctoral program to study under Hart and continue to prove Black capability. Soon, though, he would have the opportunity to provide even greater proof. Around the time he entered graduate school, former president Rutherford B. Hayes, the director of the Slater Fund for the Education of Freedmen, offered to underwrite the European education of "any young colored man" talented enough for the undertaking, if such a person existed. "Hitherto," Hayes told a Johns Hopkins audience, "their chief and almost only gift has been that of oratory." Du Bois stepped up to the intellectual challenge. Two years later, he enrolled at the University of Berlin, which at the time was the most distinguished university in the European world.[7]

THE DAY BEFORE Du Bois's Harvard commencement address, a young Massachusetts congressman, Henry Cabot Lodge, introduced the Federal Elections Bill. Unlike reparations, this bill garnered the support of Black elites. Its purpose was to mandate federal supervision of elections when local voters petitioned Washington about voter fraud. Also called the "Force Bill," the proposed legislation infuriated the southern segregationists who were listening to Lodge's speech at the US Capitol. Lodge questioned the wisdom of the Fifteenth Amendment but said it was still a "federal responsibility to protect it." "If any State thinks that any class of citizens is unfit to vote through ignorance, it can disqualify them," he said. "It has but to put an educational qualification into this constitution." House Republicans banged their hands together, and Lodge felt pleased as the applause guided him to his seat. House Democrats were silent, some probably jotting down and storing away his final statement. The *Atlanta Constitution* blasted the proposed voting rights bill as the "stillborn child of hate!" Segregationists were clearly already classing bills *against* racial discrimination as hateful.

Mississippi Democrats remembered Lodge's closing statement when they gathered for their constitutional convention on August 12, 1890. Surprising Lodge, Mississippi Democrats adapted the North's anti-poor literacy test, reformulating it into an anti-Black and anti-poor literacy test for their fourth constitution. The highly subjective "understanding clause" asked for someone to interpret something in the Mississippi constitution, allowing racist registrars to pass ignorant Whites into voting, and fail knowledgeable Blacks into not voting. When the new constitution went into effect on November 1, 1890, antiracist White lawyer and activist Albion Tourgee immediately recognized it as "the most important event" in American history since South Carolina had seceded from the Union. Over the next decade, the progression of racism came to all the former Confederate states and even several border states. They all followed Mississippi's example, instituting race-veiled voting restrictions, from literacy tests to poll taxes, that would purge their voting rolls of the remaining Black (and many poor White) voters without saying a racial word. The South, once again, defied the US Constitution—this time, without firing a single shot, and without northern retaliation.[8]

Blocked by a filibuster of Democratic senators, the Force Bill never passed, angering Frederick Douglass. But Du Bois remained calm and focused on the moral struggle of uplift suasion. "When you have the right sort of black voters, you will need no election laws," Du Bois wrote in the *New York Age*. "The battle of my people must be a moral one, not a legal or physical one." Black Americans were hardly losing any moral or cultural battles. They were being violently and nonviolently defeated in political and economic battles, as Du Bois would soon learn.[9]

The defeat of the Force Bill ended Republican efforts to enforce the Thirteenth (emancipation) and Fourteenth (civil rights) and Fifteenth (voting) Amendments. If the Bargain of federal noninterference was consummated in 1876, then after years of northern and southern reticence, it became the undisputed national policy in the 1890s and in the first decade of the twentieth century. A series of separate but (un)equal laws was instituted, segregating nearly every aspect of southern life, from water fountains, to businesses, to transportation—all to ensure White solidarity and Black submission and to ensure cheap Black labor. These separate and inferior Black facilities fed Whites and Blacks alike the segregationist idea of Blacks being a fundamentally separate and inferior people.

Segregationist ideas and organizing became a fact of American life in everything from the women's movement, where segregationist women were welcomed into the new National American Woman Suffrage Association in 1890, to the nation's newest leading labor association, the American Federation of Labor (AFL), which was a hotbed of discriminators. AFL president Samuel Gompers lectured Black workers that "organized labor" was not "antagonistic to the colored race." He claimed to know of only a "few instances . . . where colored workers are discriminated against." Gompers increasingly blamed Black workers for their depressed economic condition in order to exonerate the discriminatory actions of his unions.[10]

Black people did not sit idly by during this segregationist organizing. Black resistance caused lynchings to spike in the early 1890s. However, the White lynchers justified the spike in lynchings as corresponding to a spike in Black crime. This justification was accepted by a young W. E. B. Du Bois, by the middle-aged, ambitious principle of Alabama's Tuskegee Institute, Booker T. Washington, and by a dying Frederick Douglass. It took a young antiracist Black woman to set these racist men straight. Mississippi-born Memphis journalist Ida B. Wells recoiled from the lynching of friends and the sheer number of lynchings during the peak of the era in 1892, when the number of Blacks lynched in the nation reached a whopping 255 souls. She released a blazing pamphlet in 1892 called *Southern Horrors: Lynch Law in All Its Phases*. From a sample of 728 lynching reports in recent years, Wells found that only about a third of lynching victims had "ever been *charged* with rape, to say nothing of those who were innocent of the charge." White men were lying about Black-on-White rape, and hiding their own assaults of Black women, Wells raged.[11]

Wells knew that immoral constructions about Black women hindered them from fully engaging in the burgeoning women's club moral movement that cascaded across the 1890s. "I sometimes hear of a virtuous Negro woman, but the idea is absolutely inconceivable to me," wrote an anonymous "southern White woman" in *The Independent*. Oberlin graduate and teacher Anna Julia Cooper took it upon herself to defend Black womanhood and encourage Black women's education in *A Voice from the South* in 1892. Like Wells, Cooper wrote in the anti-racist feminist tradition. "The colored woman of to-day occupies, one may say, a unique position in this country," Cooper explained. "She is confronted by both a woman question and a race problem, and is as yet an unknown or unacknowledged factor in both." And yet, Cooper did espouse some class racism. She praised, for instance, the "quiet, chaste dignity and decorous solemnity" of the Protestant Episcopal Church, while demeaning the "semi-civilized religionism" of low-income Black southerners.[12]

SOUTHERN WHITE MEN were "shielding" themselves "behind the plausible screen of defending the honor" of their women through lynchings in order to "palliate" their record of hate and violence, Ida B. Wells maintained in *Southern Horrors*, and again during her 1893 anti-lynching tour of England. Her speaking tour was an embarrassment to White Americans. In her work, Wells more or less condemned the strategy of uplift suasion and championed armed Black self-defense to stop lynchings. "The more the Afro-American yields and cringes and begs," she declared, "the more he has to do so, the more he is insulted, outraged, lynched."[13]

The pro-lynching president of the Missouri Press Association, James Jacks, published an open letter to attack Wells—and all Black women, who, in his view, were nothing but thieves and prostitutes. If Jacks hoped to silence Wells and her sisters, then his plan backfired. By the summer of 1896, inflamed Black club women had united under the banner of the National Association of Colored Women (NACW) to defend Black womanhood, challenge discrimination, and lend power to self-help efforts. But some, if not most, of the self-help efforts of these mostly elite reformers encouraged the assimilation of White women's mores. They were based on the same old historical racism that said that low-income Black women had been morally and culturally ruined by slavery. "Lifting As We Climb" became the NACW motto.[14]

AFTER TWO YEARS of study abroad in Germany, W. E. B. Du Bois returned to the United States in 1894. Slater Fund officials declined to extend funding for his study abroad, which would have enabled him to defend his economics doctoral thesis. Though he intended to prove Black educational capacity, to Slater Fund officials, he looked like a special education teacher pursuing a physics doctorate. No matter what Du Bois did, he could not persuade away racist ideas. If Blacks pursued the European world's most prestigious degree, they were looked upon as stupid for doing so. If they did not pursue it, then they did not have the natural talent, as Rutherford B. Hayes said in 1890, provoking Du Bois. Even Du Bois's settling for being the first African American to earn a Harvard history doctorate in 1895 brought on racist ridicule. In elite White circles, Du Bois became known as one of those "half dozen Negroes" who had allowed Harvard "to make a man out of semi-beast," as New Yorker Franklin Delano Roosevelt exulted as a Harvard freshman in 1903.[15]

Though Du Bois's educational success in Germany did not prove much of anything to American producers and consumers of racist ideas, Du Bois did prove something to himself. He had grown more accustomed to meeting "not white folks, but folks." He mentally climbed in Germany and stood on an equal plane with White people. But his new antiracist mind-set of not looking up at White people did not stop him from looking down at supposedly low-class Black people. It would take Du Bois much longer to see not low-class Black folks, but folks on an equal human plane with him and the rest of the (White) folks.[16]

Du Bois accepted a position in 1894 teaching Greek and Latin at the A.M.E. Church's flagship college in Ohio, Wilberforce. He was determined "to begin a life-work, leading to the emancipation of the American Negro." Somehow, some way, he maintained his faith that

American racism could be persuaded and educated away. "The ultimate evil was stupidity" about race by "the majority of white Americans," he theorized. "The cure for it was knowledge based on scientific
investigation."[17]

Whereas Du Bois wanted to educate Americans about the capacity of Black people for the higher pursuits, Booker T. Washington, the
calculating thirty-eight-year-old principal of Tuskegee, wanted Black
people to publicly focus on the lower pursuits, which was much more
acceptable to White Americans. Booker T. Washington claimed the
vacancy of race leadership that had been vacated upon Frederick Douglass's death in 1895. Ida B. Wells would have been a better replacement, but she was a woman, and too antiracist for most Americans. In
private, Washington supported civil rights and empowerment causes
across the South throughout his career. In public, his talking points
reflected the New South racism that elites enjoyed hearing.[18]

At the opening of the Cotton States International Exposition on
September 18, 1895, Washington delivered the "Atlanta Compromise." He asked southern Whites to stop trying to push Blacks out
of the house of America, and to allow them to reside comfortably in
the basement—to help them to rise up, knowing that when they rose,
the whole house would rise. Many of the landowners in the Atlanta
audience had spent their lifetimes trying to convince their Black sharecroppers "to dignify and glorify common labour." So when Washington beckoned to them with the words, "It is at the bottom of life we
must begin, and not at the top," they were overjoyed. Rest assured,
Washington said, "the wisest among my race understand that the agitation of questions of social equality is the extremest folly."[19]

Amid the excited applause from thousands, the waving handker-
chiefs, the flowers pulled from White women's bosoms that showered
Washington when he finished, New South editor Clark Howell of the
Atlanta Constitution sprinted up to the speakers' platform. He shouted,
"That man's speech is the beginning of a moral revolution in Amer-
ica!" Washington's words were telegraphed to every major newspaper
in the nation. Editors published raving reviews. Democratic president
Grover Cleveland arrived in Atlanta and called Washington the "new

hope" for Black people. "Let me heartily congratulate you upon your phenomenal success at Atlanta," W. E. B. Du Bois glowed in a telegram on September 24, 1895. "It was a word fitly spoken."[20]

Not every Black commentator was like Du Bois, applauding Washington, however. Calvin Chase of the *Washington Bee* did not see compromise, but "death to the Afro-American and elevating to white people." Death or not, Booker T. Washington grasped the national acclaim, attracted philanthropists like Andrew Carnegie, and built the "Tuskegee Machine," an institution that over the next decade ruled Black colleges, businesses, newspapers, and political patronage. And a year after Washington had loudly issued the Atlanta Compromise with southern segregationists, the US Supreme Court quietly followed suit.[21]

For years, the US Supreme Court had been stuffed with northern-born corporate lawyers happily wielding the Fourteenth Amendment to cut down laws violating the "liberty" and "civil rights" of capital to dictate the wages and working conditions of labor. The Court provided no such protections for the liberty and civil rights of workers, women, immigrants, and Black people. On May 18, 1896, the Court ruled 7–1 in *Plessy v. Ferguson* that Louisiana's Separate Car Act—and other new Jim Crow laws—violated neither the Thirteenth nor the Fourteenth Amendments. The biracial Homer Plessy had challenged the law requiring Louisiana railroads to provide "equal but separate accommodations" for White and Black passengers. New Orleans judge John H. Ferguson had claimed that the "foul odors of blacks in close quarters" made the law reasonable. The Louisiana Supreme Court and the US Supreme Court upheld Ferguson's ruling.

In his majority opinion, Supreme Court Justice Henry Billings Brown relied on racist ideas to support a policy that was clearly discriminatory in intent. It was his job to obscure those intentions. Justice Brown evaded the politics of the Louisiana Separate Car Act, evaded the discriminatory intent, and evaded the obvious shoddiness of the railcars for Blacks, and instead semantically classed it a "social law" that merely recognized the social "distinction" between the races. "If one race be inferior to the other socially, the Constitution of the

United States cannot put them upon the same plane," wrote the former Detroit corporate lawyer. The lone dissenting voice to the *Plessy* ruling was hardly an antiracist voice. Though he did not doubt that Whites would forever be "the dominant race in this country," Justice John Harlan of Kentucky wrote, "in the view of the Constitution, in the eye of the law, there is in this country no superior, dominant, ruling class of citizens. Our Constitution is color-blind and neither knows nor tolerates classes among citizens."

On May 18, 1896, the *New York Times* buried the *Plessy* decision in a third-page column focusing on railroad news, reflecting the case's marginal news coverage and the nation's marginal awareness of its significance. The *Plessy* decision legalized what was already assumed by the New South and America: separate but unequal, and branded it equal for courts and consciences to stop antiracist resistance. The social conscience of America was a significant political factor during this period. It was the beginning of the Progressive era.[22]

Though it is popularly remembered as a time of heartfelt social concern and awareness, in reality the Progressive era was rigged by elite White men and women. It was dominated, at least from the standpoint of its elite funders and organizers, by a desire to end the social strife caused by industrialization, urbanization, immigration, and inequality in the 1880s and 1890s. Cotton Mather's blessings of order through benevolence still held the philanthropist's ear from Boston to Atlanta after all these years. The projected benevolence of the *Plessy* ruling and the Atlanta Compromise seemed to bring a finality to the disorder of the "Negro problem." Indeed, the finality of the "Negro problem" as the nineteenth century closed meant a United States dead set on playing down the southern horrors of discrimination and playing up what was wrong with Black people.[23]

CHAPTER 23

Black Judases

AFTER *PLESSY V. FERGUSON* reportedly solved the "Negro problem," British physician Havelock Ellis proclaimed that a new question had presented itself. "The question of sex," he said, "with the racial questions that rest on it—stands before the coming generations as the chief problem for solution." It was an overly ambitious prediction in the first medical treatise on homosexuality, *Studies in the Psychology of Sex* (1897). Western nations were still not ready to sufficiently deal with the reality of multiple sexualities, at least not in public. Ellis nevertheless tried to put sexuality on the Progressive era's agenda. This self-described friend of the yet unnamed LGBT community popularized the term "homosexual," classifying it as a congenital physiological abnormality (or "sexual inversion"). Ellis aimed to defend homosexuality against the "law and public opinion" that regarded homosexuals as criminals in the late nineteenth-century English-speaking world.[1]

Similarly, racist scholars had long conceived of Blacks as criminals, and of Blackness as a physiological abnormality, debating all along about whether it was congenital. "Sexologists," inspired by scholars of race, were already using the comparative anatomy of women's bodies to concoct biological differences between sexualities at the turn of the century. While racist scholars were distinguishing between the "free" and prominent clitorises of "negresses" and the "imprisonment" of the clitoris of the "Aryan American woman," homophobic scholars started claiming that lesbians "will in practically every instance disclose an abnormally prominent clitoris. This is particularly so in colored women."[2]

To sexist thinkers in the late nineteenth century, the more prominent the clitoris, the less chaste the woman, and the less chaste the woman, the lower the woman on the hierarchical scale of womanhood. Hence the convergence of racist, sexist, and homophobic ideas that deemed both White lesbians and Black heterosexual women to be more chaste, and higher on the scale of womanhood, than Black lesbians, who reportedly had the largest clitorises. When men, Black heterosexual women, or White lesbians viewed *Black* lesbians, bisexuals, or transgender women as biologically or socially inferior, as less chaste, they were speaking at the intersection of racist, sexist, and homophobic ideas. They were articulating queer racism.

But it was difficult to find a scholar willing to engage sexuality, let alone sexuality and race—and increasingly, even race. W. E. B. Du Bois had begun his career trying to present solutions to the "Negro problem" to White intellectuals. But many of these intellectuals now felt it had been solved by *Plessy*—or it would be solved, by the natural selection of evolution or extinction. A statistician for the Prudential Insurance Company predicted the imminent extinction of Black people in his epic book that relied on the 1890 census figures. Unlike the *Plessy* ruling, Frederick Hoffman's *Race Traits and Tendencies of the American Negro* received plenty of attention in 1896. Packed with statistical tables and published by the American Economic Association, the book was a pioneering work in American medical research, and it catapulted Hoffman into scientific celebrity in the Western world as the heralded father of American public health. At "the time of emancipation," he wrote, southern Blacks were "healthy in body and cheerful in mind." "What are the conditions thirty years after?" Well, "in the plain language of the facts," free Blacks were headed toward "gradual extinction," pulled down by their natural immoralities, law-breaking, and diseases. Hoffman supplied his employer with an excuse for its discriminatory policies concerning African Americans—that is, for denying them life insurance. White life insurance companies refused to insure a supposedly dying race. Yet another racist idea was produced to defend a racist policy.[3]

In a critical book review, W. E. B. Du Bois argued that Frederick Hoffman had manipulated statistics to present his prediction of

Black extinction. Hoffman's native Germany, Du Bois pointed out, had death rates that matched or exceeded that of African Americans. Were Germans headed toward extinction? Du Bois mockingly asked, before rejecting Hoffman's supposition that higher Black death rates indicated imminent Black extinction. But Du Bois could not reject Hoffman's supposition that higher Black arrest and prison rates indicated that Blacks actually committed more crimes. Not Hoffman, not Du Bois, no one really knew the actual crime rates—all of the instances of Americans breaking the law, whether caught or not. But the higher Black arrest and prison rates substantiated the racist ideas of more Black crime. And these racist ideas spun the cycle of racial discrimination in the criminal justice system, more suspicions of Black people, more police in Black neighborhoods, more arrests and prison time for Black people, and thus more suspicions, and on and on.

In all of his intellectual power, Du Bois proved unable to stop the cycle of racial profiling and crime statistics and racist ideas. He substantiated the disparities in arrest and prison rates through both antiracist ("dogged Anglo-Saxon prejudice" had "subjected [Blacks and Whites] to different standards of justice") and racist explanations (the "dazed freedman" lacked a moral foundation). Du Bois was far from alone. None of the scholars who became members of the first national Black intellectual group, the American Negro Academy, formed in 1897, could reject the statistics, or refute them as indicators of greater Black crime. Instead, they accepted the numbers as fact and tried to push against the stereotypes of criminal Blacks through education and persuasion, thus reproducing the racist ideas they were working to eliminate.[4]

For instance, in his 1897 address for the opening meeting of the American Negro Academy, entitled "The Conservation of Races," Du Bois put forth the argument of biologically distinct races with distinct histories, characteristics, and destinies. African Americans were "members of a vast historic race that from the dawn of creation has slept, but half awakening in the dark forests of its African fatherland," he said. "The first and greatest step toward the settlement of the present friction between the races," that is, toward social equilibrium, he said, "lies in the correction of the immorality, crime, and laziness among the Negroes themselves, which still remains as a heritage of slavery." The speech was hastily published, circulated, and acclaimed. Du Bois and the American Negro Academy hoped the pamphlet would refute the popular conception of the destructive, decaying, dying African in the post-*Plessy*, post-Hoffman era. But it was riddled with racist ideas, speaking of "blood" races, race traits, backward Africa, imbruting enslavement, criminally minded and effeminate African American men, strong Europeans, and the idea that African Americans were superior to continental Africans. Du Bois reinforced as much racism as he struck down.[5]

Du Bois was also working on a more antiracist tome, however. As a visiting researcher at the University of Pennsylvania in 1896 and 1897, he worked on *The Philadelphia Negro*, a thoroughly antiracist "social study" about racism being "the spirit that enters in and complicates all Negro social problems." And yet, he was unrestrained in his moral attacks on the poor, on Black criminals, and on women, saying, for example, that it was "the duty of Negroes" to "solve" the problem of Black female "unchastity." Though the book is now regarded as a classic sociological text, only a few academic journals reviewed it upon its release in 1899. One anonymous reviewer, in the leading *American Historical Review*, commended Du Bois for "laying all necessary stress on the weakness of his people," and then ridiculed him for believing that these supposed weaknesses could be cured. Reading this review, Du Bois should have gathered that when he tried directing his readers from the crossroads of racist and antiracist ideas, they oftentimes would not reach his desired antiracist destination. Then again, Du Bois, like his elite Black peers, hardly considered their attacks on the *Black* poor and *Black* women to be racist.[6]

Whatever Du Bois achieved, whatever he published, he failed to gain the following—or the financial support—of northern philanthropists that Booker T. Washington enjoyed. On his fund-raising travels, Washington had a knack for putting White audiences at ease by sharing his famously funny (or infamously offensive) southern "darky" jokes. Washington gave wealthy Whites what they wanted—a one-man minstrel show—and they gave him what he wanted—a check for Tuskegee. Washington somehow demeaned Black people as stupid for an hour and then received donations to educate those same stupid people.[7]

Washington was ingeniously playing the racial game, but it was a dangerous game to play at the end of the nineteenth century. A surge of racist violence to snatch Black economic and political power spread from North Carolina in 1898 to Georgia in 1899. Du Bois witnessed some of this violence in Georgia. He had taken a professorship at Atlanta University in 1897, and had started spearheading annual scientific studies on all aspects of southern Black life. But in April 1899, he became heartbroken over his inability to prevent the infamous lynching near Atlanta of Sam Hose, who had killed an oppressive White employer in self-defense. In August, armed Blacks in coastal Georgia's McIntosh County drove back a lynching mob. "One could not be a calm, cool, and detached scientist while Negroes were lynched, murdered and starved; and secondly, there was no such demand for scientific work of the sort that I was doing as I had confidently assumed would be easily forthcoming," Du Bois later wrote. Firmly believing "that the majority of Americans would rush to the defense of democracy . . . if they realized how race prejudice was threatening it," Du Bois adopted a more aggressive commitment to educational persuasion.[8]

In July 1900, he attended the First Pan-African Conference in London, sponsored by Booker T. Washington. "To be sure, the darker races are today the least advanced in culture according to European standards," said Du Bois in assimilationist style. But they had the "capacity" to one day reach those "high ideals." And so, "as soon as practicable," Du Bois proclaimed, there should be decolonization in Africa and the Caribbean.[9]

Du Bois's rationale for gradual decolonization—Black nations were not ready for independence—echoed the old racist rationales for gradual emancipation—Black people were not ready for freedom. Du Bois echoed those proclaiming in 1899 that Cuba, Guam, Puerto Rico, and the Philippines, the colonies the United States had received from winning the 1898 Spanish-American War, were not ready for independence. Segregationists and antiracists opposed, while assimilationists supported, the formal launching of the American Empire. In a poem printed in *McClure's Magazine* in 1899, the literary prophet of British imperialism, Rudyard Kipling, urged Americans to "Take up the White Man's burden— / Send forth the best ye breed— / Go send your sons to exile / To serve your captives' need / To wait in heavy harness / On fluttered folk and wild— / Your new-caught, sullen peoples / Half devil and half child."[10]

Imperial assimilationists won the debate among the mostly White male electorate, if President William McKinley's successful reelection campaign in 1900 was any indication. His running mate, Theodore Roosevelt, declared, in 1901, "It is our duty toward the people living in barbarism to see that they are freed from their chains, and we can free them only by destroying barbarism itself." While US leaders publicly debated the colonial peoples' capacity for civilization and assimilation, they privately debated military bases, puppet politics, natural resources, foreign markets, and war costs. This public humanitarian debate, which was also a private political-economic debate, became a twentieth-century staple as the American Empire publicly and privately warred to extend its sphere of influence. At home and abroad, a profound political racism cast non-Whites as incapable of self-rule, or capable of self-rule one day—in order to justify both their subjection and the resulting socioeconomic disparities. Some Black newspaper editors saw through the mask, connecting the nation's foreign racial policy to its domestic racial policy. They blasted the "robbers, murderers, and unscrupulous monopolists," to quote the Salt Lake City *Broad Ax* in 1899. The federal government "could not deal justly with dark-skinned peoples," another paper blared, "as evidenced by its do-nothing record at home."[11]

In this new American Empire, American racist ideas went through what seemed very much like a revolving door, constantly going out into the colonizing world and then coming back into the country after conditioning the immigrant minds of the people arriving in the United States in the early 1900s. When Irish, Jewish, Italian, Asian, Chicana/o, and Latina/o people in America were called anti-Black racial epithets like "greasers" or "guineas" or "White niggers," some resisted and joined in solidarity with Black people. But most probably consumed the racist ideas, distancing themselves from Black people. Blacks in the early twentieth century would joke that the first English word immigrants learned was "nigger."[12]

ON JANUARY 29, 1901, the lone Black representative, George H. White of North Carolina, gave his farewell address to Congress. About 90 percent of the nation's Black people resided in the South, but they were no longer represented by Black politicians in the state legislatures and in Congress. Their mass disenfranchisement, and charges of incompetency leveled against Black politicians by White ones, had made sure of that. "This, Mr. Chairman, is perhaps the negroes' temporary farewell to the American Congress," said White, "but let me say, Phoenix-like he will rise up someday and come again." Not many believed him. As White trotted out of the hall, the leading American historians and political scientists looked upon him as the Reconstruction era's final defective product in the nation's capital.[13]

At the time, William Archibald Dunning reigned as the director of Columbia University's preeminent Dunning School of Reconstruction history. The school was at the forefront of an academic revolution highlighting the "objective" use of the scientific method in the humanities. "For the first time meticulous and thorough research was carried on in an effort to determine the truth rather than to prove a thesis," was how one historian described the impact of the Dunning School in the *American Historical Review* in 1940. The "truth," though, meant Dunning school historians of the Reconstruction era chronicling the White South as victimized by the corrupt and incompetent Black politicians, and the North mistakenly forcing Reconstruction before quickly correcting itself and leaving the noble White South to its own wits. "All the forces that made for civilization were dominated by a mass of barbarous freedmen," Dunning supposed in his 1907 classic, *Reconstruction: Political and Economic, 1865–1877.*[14]

Dunning trained a generation of influential southern historians who became department chairs and dominated the discipline of history for decades in the twentieth century. His most notable student was Georgia native Ulrich Bonnell Phillips. In *American Negro Slavery* (1918), along with eight more books and a duffel bag of articles, Phillips erased the truth of slavery as a highly lucrative enterprise dominated by planters who incessantly forced a resisting people to labor through terror, manipulation, and racist ideas. Instead he dreamed up an unprofitable commerce dominated by benevolent, paternalistic planters civilizing and caring for a "robust, amiable, obedient and content" barbaric people. Phillips's pioneering use of plantation documents legitimated his racist dreams and made them seem like objective realities. Phillips remained the most respected scholarly voice on slavery until the mid-twentieth century.[15]

Until midcentury, the Dunning School's fables of slavery and Reconstruction were transferred into schoolbooks, or at least into those that mentioned Black people at all. Most textbook writers excluded Black people from schoolbooks as deliberately as southern Democrats excluded them from the polls. But the greatest popularizer of the Dunning story of Reconstruction was none other than a novelist, Thomas Dixon Jr. In one of his earliest memories, Dixon witnessed a lynching in his North Carolina town. "The Klan are . . . guarding us from harm," his mother told him that night, indoctrinating him into the racist justification for White terror. When he came of age, Dixon wept at the "misrepresentation of southerners" inflicted by northerners upon seeing a theatrical version of *Uncle Tom's Cabin*. Vowing to share the "true story," he composed a "Reconstruction Trilogy" of best-selling novels—*The Leopard's Spots: A Romance of the White Man's Burden—1865–1900* (1902), *The Clansman: An Historical Romance of the Ku Klux Klan* (1905), and *The Traitor: A Story of the Fall of the Invisible Empire* (1907). His goal was "to teach the North . . . what it has never known— the awful suffering of the white man during the dreadful Reconstruction period[,] . . . [and] to demonstrate to the world that the white man must and shall be supreme." In the fictional trilogy, which was taken as historical fact by millions, Dixon posed Reconstruction as a period when corrupt, incompetent northerners and Black legislators ruled, terrorized, disenfranchised, and raped southern Whites until they were redeemed by the might and virtue of the Ku Klux Klan. Nothing arrested the national mind in the hazards of Black voting, nothing justified the do-nothing attitude, better than this racist fiction of Reconstruction, whether it was written by novelists or by scholars.[16]

AS THE ALL-WHITE, all-male Congress settled into Washington in 1901, these White men were able to ease any twinges of guilt they may have felt by reading Booker T. Washington's hit autobiography, *Up from Slavery*. Washington expressed faith in God, took personal responsibility, worked mightily hard, overcame incredible hardship, and saw racial progress and "White saviors" at every turn. "White Savior" stories were fast becoming a fixture in American memoirs, novels, and theatrical productions. They were enjoyed by Americans of all races as hopeful signs of racial progress. Individual stories either reflected or deflected common realities. The individual White Savior stories cleverly deflected the reality of White saviors for a few, and White discriminators for the many, along with the reality of racial progress for a few, and deferred progress for the many.[17]

The release of *Up from Slavery* in February 1901 allowed Booker T. Washington to stand at the height of his career. W. E. B. Du Bois watched the national ovation for Washington's memoir. As the praise carried on into the summer of 1901, and as Du Bois looked up at Washington on the White pedestal of Black leadership, it all started to become too much for him to bear in silence. In his review of *Up from Slavery* in *Dial* on July 16, 1901, Du Bois fired the first shot in the civil war between Washington's Tuskegee Machine and Du Bois's elite civil rights activists.

In addition to scolding Washington for his "accommodation," Du Bois scolded those leaders "who represent the old ideas of revolt and revenge, and see in migration alone an outlet for the Negro people." A.M.E. bishop Henry McNeal Turner had for years preached that

God was a "Negro," but he urged African Americans to migrate to Africa so that they could leave all the discriminatory policies behind. Du Bois reduced all back-to-Africa efforts, including those on Black terms, and violent protests against enslavers and re-enslavers to revenge and hate. Antiracists were not defending Black humanity and freedom, he said, as Ida B. Wells had so eloquently advocated doing. It was customary for assimilationists to charge antiracists as being like segregationists—all hate-filled and irrational. These fabricated labels would marginalize antiracists throughout the twentieth century, would one day even marginalize the elderly antiracist Du Bois. But in 1901, Du Bois began to criticize the accommodators and the antiracists in part for his own purposes: in order to set the stage for his "large and important group" opposing the Tuskegee Machine, those reformist assimilationists seeking "self-development and self-realization in all lines of human endeavor" in order to allow Blacks, eventually, to take their place alongside the people of other races.[18]

Washington's *Up from Slavery* remains an American classic. However, in 1901, another book, released weeks before *Up from Slavery*, received much more praise: *The American Negro: What He Was, What He Is, and What He May Become*. For years, William Hannibal Thomas had tried to desegregate White institutions; he had preached, taught, and written to uplift Blacks, eliminate racial distinctions, and forge a world where Black people would be accepted by White people as their own. And yet, according to a prerelease preview by the *New York Times*, Thomas had presented "his subject without an atom of sentimentality."

Thomas described a Black "record of lawless existence, led by every impulse and passion," especially immorality and stupidity. Ninety percent of Black women, he said, were "lascivious by instinct and in bondage to physical pleasure"; they were living lives of filth "without parallel in modern civilization."

Thomas thought at the junction between assimilationist and segregationist ideas. He argued that a minority of Blacks—by which he meant himself and his kind—had overcome their inferior biological inheritance. These extraordinary Negroes showed that "the redemption of the negro [was] . . . possible and assured through a thorough assimilation of the thought and ideals of American civilization." Thomas advocated restricting the voting rights of naturally corrupt Blacks, policing naturally criminal Blacks, placing Black children with White guardians, and pursuing uplift suasion. Blacks should conduct themselves "so worthily as to disarm racial antagonism," he advised.[19]

As Thomas tried to distance himself from Blackness through *The American Negro*, it was, ironically, his very Blackness that caused White Americans to shower him with the adoration he so desired. Since racist ideas deemed every individual Black person an expert and representative of the race, Black people like Thomas had always proved to be the perfect dispensers of racist ideas. Their Blackness made them more believable. Their Blackness did not invite defensive mechanisms to guard against their racist ideas about Black inferiority.

Racist Americans, from the nation's most eminent sociologists to ordinary readers, hailed *The American Negro* as the most authoritative, believable, and comprehensive tract ever published on the subject, better than Du Bois's *The Philadelphia Negro*. William Hannibal Thomas was placed "next to Mr. Booker T. Washington" as "the best American authority on the negro question," said the *New York Times*. Within Black America, however, Thomas became known as "Black Judas." Activist Addie Hunton actually classed Thomas a "Judas Iscariot" in her piece "Negro Womanhood Defended." Booker T. Washington and W. E. B. Du Bois hated the book. "Mr. Thomas's book," Du Bois charged in his review, was a "sinister symptom" of the age, which desired nothing more for "the Negro" than to "kindly go to the devil and make haste about it," so that the "American conscience [could] justify three centuries of shameful history." After Black leaders dug up dirt on Thomas and destroyed his credibility, he fell into obscurity. He passed away as a Black man in 1935. He never did become White.[20]

ON OCTOBER 16, 1901, the newly sworn-in President Theodore Roosevelt, hearing that Booker T. Washington was in town, invited "the most distinguished member of his race in the world" over to the President's House for family supper. Roosevelt did not think much of the

invite, clearly unaware of the mood of segregationists. When Roosevelt's press secretary casually notified Americans the next day of
Washington's visit, the social earthquake was immediate and loud.
Black Americans were beside themselves in glee, and many fell in
love with Theodore Roosevelt. But to segregationists, Roosevelt had
crossed the color line. "When Mr. Roosevelt sits down to dinner with
a negro he declares that the negro is the social equal of the white
man," stammered a restrained New Orleans newspaper. South Carolina senator Ben "Pitchfork" Tillman was not restrained: "The action of
President Roosevelt in entertaining that nigger," he said, "will necessi-
tate our killing a thousand niggers in the South before they will learn
their place again." Tillman showed in this statement the real purpose
of lynchings: if racist ideas won't subdue Blacks, then violence will.
Roosevelt learned his lesson, and he never invited a Black person to
the President's House again. But he failed to quiet segregationists by
officially naming the president's residence the "White House." Blacks
were beasts—segregationist books were declaring in the early years
of the twentieth century, starting with Mississippi professor Charles
Carroll's *The Negro a Beast* (1900)—and beasts should not be dining at
the "White House."[21]

In the midst of this overpowering segregationist discourse, W. E. B.
Du Bois had the audacity to publish the most acclaimed book of his
career. Released on April 18, 1903, the book title decreed in profoundly
antiracist fashion that Blacks were not soulless beasts. Black folk were
fully human, and Du Bois made Americans "listen to the strivings in
the souls of black folk." Decades later, James Weldon Johnson, the
composer of the "Black National Anthem," sang the praises of Du Bois's
The Souls of Black Folk for having more impact "upon and within the
Negro race than any other single book published in this country since
Uncle Tom's Cabin." It was a perfect comparison. Like *Uncle Tom's Cabin*,
Du Bois's fourteen essays drilled much deeper into the American mind
the racist construction of complementary biological race traits, of the
humble, soulful African complementing the hard, rational European.
Blacks should be fostering and developing "the traits and talents of the
Negro," Du Bois proposed, "in order that some day on American soil

two world-races may give each to each those characteristics both so sadly lack." Black people were "the sole oasis of simple faith and reverence in a dusty desert of dollars and smartness."[22]

It was a racist idea to suppose that the racial groups were not equal, and that a racial group lacked certain human characteristics. In 1903, White people did not lack "simple faith and reverence," and Black people did not lack materialism and "smartness." Ironically, many of the northern defenders of slavery and abolition, and now Jim Crow and civil rights, had attested to the "simple faith" of humble Blacks and the "smartness" of strong Whites. In *The Souls of Black Folk*, Du Bois tried to revolutionize the dividing ideal of race into the "unifying ideal of race."

This "unifying ideal of race" would not only heal the United States, he argued, but also heal the souls of Black folk. In the book's most memorable passage, he explained further:

> This American world . . . yields [the Negro] no true self-consciousness, but only lets him see himself through the revelation of the other world. It is a peculiar sensation, this double-consciousness, this sense of always looking at one's self through the eyes of others, of measuring one's soul by the tape of a world that looks on in amused contempt and pity. One ever feels his two-ness,—an American, a Negro; two souls, two thoughts, two unreconciled strivings; two warring ideals in one dark body, whose dogged strength alone keeps it from being torn asunder.

Blacks must therefore reckon with the fact that "the history of the American Negro is the history of this strife—this longing to attain self-conscious manhood, to merge his double self into a better and truer self," Du Bois wrote. "He simply wishes to make it possible for a man to be both a Negro and an American."[23]

It was as if many of his Black readers had been straining all these years to do precisely what he had described. Du Bois's theory of double-consciousness finally gave many of them the glasses they needed to see—to see themselves, to see their own inner struggles. Just as Harriet Beecher Stowe's book met many White folk where they

were, at the warring crossroads between segregationist and assimilationist ideas, Du Bois met many Black folk where they were, at the warring crossroads between assimilationist and antiracist ideas. Du Bois
believed in both the antiracist concept of cultural relativity—of every
person looking at the self from the eyes of his or her *own* group—and
the assimilationist idea of Black individuals seeing themselves from the
perspective of White people. In Du Bois's mind, and for so many like-
minded people, this double-desire, or double-consciousness, yielded
an inner strife, a conflict between pride in equal Blackness and assimilation into superior Whiteness.

While his opening essay was timeless, his timely case against "Mr.
Booker T. Washington and Others" carried the book into controversy
in 1903. Du Bois had given his opening argument against the Tuskegee Machine two years earlier, and there was no leaving the courtroom now. After again disparaging Washington's accommodators, and
then the singly conscious antiracists, Du Bois asserted the standing of
his doubly-conscious group, which he named the Talented Tenth—
the top 10 percent of Black America. They knew "that the low social
level of the mass of the race is responsible for much discrimination
against it," but they also knew, along with the nation, "that relentless
color-prejudice is more often a cause than a result of the Negro's degradation." The Talented Tenth sought "the abatement of this relic of
barbarism and not its systematic encouragement."[24]

Du Bois identified the Talented Tenth in another published piece
in 1903 that was riddled with more assimilationist ideas and class racism. "There are in this land a million men of Negro blood . . . [who]
have reached the full measure of the best type European culture," Du
Bois judged. It was the duty of this "aristocracy of talent and character" to lead and civilize the masses, to filter culture "downward," and
to show "the capability of Negro blood." However, he complained,
"as this Talented Tenth is pointed out, the blind worshippers of the
Average cry out in alarm: 'These are exceptions, look here at death,
disease and crime—these are the happy rule.' Of course they are the
rule, because a silly nation made them the rule." Du Bois fumed about
the extraordinary-Negro conception, this "silly" conceptual loophole

to uplift suasion. But, somehow, he kept his own faith in the potential of the silly strategy of uplift suasion.[25]

Du Bois's call to arms in *The Souls of Black Folk* to strike down those accommodating to Jim Crow was as insightful and impassioned (and racist) as William Lloyd Garrison's call to arms to strike down the colonizationists accommodating slavery. And segregationists and accommodators instantly knew it. "This book is indeed dangerous for the negro to read," admitted the *Nashville American*. *The Outlook* chided Du Bois, rather accurately, for being "half ashamed of being a negro." Then the reviewer held up Booker T. Washington, rather inaccurately, as unashamed. The Tuskegee Machine tried to suppress the book, to no avail. Black newspapers, free of Washington, usually shouted the same thing: "SHOULD BE READ AND STUDIED BY EVERY PERSON, WHITE AND BLACK," as the *Ohio Enterprise* put it in a headline. University of Pennsylvania sociologist Carl Kelsey, speaking for racist White scholars, admonished Du Bois for emphasizing "the bad," the discrimination. Prejudice "will cease," Kelsey wrote, "when the blacks can command the respect and sympathy of the whites."[26]

In the aftermath of *The Souls of Black Folk* and Du Bois's Talented Tenth essay, racial reformers and scholars of race, whether White or Black, whether applauding or critiquing Du Bois, seemed to have formed a consensus on the solution to the "Negro problem." They spoke of the need for more strident uplift suasion, for upwardly mobile Talented Tenths persuading away the racist ideas of White folk. The strategy remained deeply racist. Black people, apparently, were responsible for changing racist White minds. White people, apparently, were not responsible for their own racist mentalities. If White people were racist and discriminated against Blacks, then Black people were to blame, because they had not commanded Whites' respect? Uplift suasion had been deployed for more than a century, and its effect in 1903? American racism may have never been worse. But neither its undergirding racist ideas, nor its historical failure, nor the extraordinary Negro construction ensuring its continued failure had lessened the faith of reformers. Uplift suasion had been and remained one of the many great White hopes of racist America.

CHAPTER 24

Great White Hopes

IN MAY 1906, W. E. B. Du Bois welcomed to Atlanta University the nation's most eminent anthropologist, a Columbia University professor who was actually questioning segregationist ideas of Blacks as beasts. Franz Boas had emigrated from Germany in 1886, when American racial classifiers were almost uniformly identifying the "organic inferiority," or Blackness, of his Jewish people. The "predominant mouth of some Jews," one anthropologist maintained, was "the result of the presence of black blood." Boas's own experiences with anti-Semitism had shaped his hostility to segregationist ideas of biologically distinct races (and ethnicities), of the natural human hierarchy of racial and ethnic groups—that is, ideas positioning Whites over Blacks, and further positioning lily-White Anglo-Saxons over semi-White Jews.[1]

Franz Boas attended Du Bois's Atlanta University conference on "The Health and Physique of the Negro-American." Scholars questioned or rejected the widely held impression that races were biologically distinct, and that cardiologists could actually distinguish "Black blood," and that below the skin and hair, doctors and scientists could actually distinguish a Black body, or a "Black disease." Du Bois presented, but he also learned about the absence of scientific proof for his long-held biological race concept.[2]

Two days after the May 1906 conference, Boas delivered Atlanta University's commencement address. "To those who stoutly maintain a material inferiority of the Negro race," he proclaimed, "the past history of your race does not sustain [that] statement." Boas then astonished

Du Bois and probably many of his Black students by recounting the glories of precolonial West African kingdoms like those of Ghana, Mali, and Songhay. Boas awakened Du Bois from the paralysis of his historical racism, or, as Du Bois explained it, "from the paralysis of the commonly held judgement taught to me in high school and in two of the world's great universities": that Africans had "no history."[3]

Du Bois's intellectual high, that May, came crashing down with Black America by the end of the year. The day after Republicans used Black votes to regain the House in the 1906 midterm elections, President Theodore Roosevelt ordered the dishonorable discharge (and loss of pensions) of 167 Black soldiers in the 25th Infantry Regiment, a Black unit that had been a huge source of Black pride. A dozen or so members of the regiment had been falsely accused of murdering a bartender and wounding a police officer in the horrifically racist town of Brownsville, Texas, on August 13, 1906. Overnight, the most popular US president in Black communities since Abraham Lincoln became the most unpopular. "Once enshrined in our hearts as Moses," shouted out a Harlem pastor, the Reverend Adam Clayton Powell Sr., Roosevelt was "now enshrouded in our scorn as Judas." In the final days of 1906, it was hard to find an African American who was not spitting ire at the Roosevelt administration. Roosevelt's efforts to regain Black support with new Black federal appointments failed. Sounding the indignation of the observant press, the *New York Times* reported that "not a particle of evidence" had been given to prove the men were guilty. Roosevelt was defiant in his Annual Message to Congress on December 3, 1906 (defiant in his crude attempts to gain southern White voters). He warned "respectable colored people . . . not to harbor criminals," meaning the criminals of Brownsville. And then he turned to lynchings: "The greatest existing cause of lynching is the perpetration, especially by black men, of the hideous crime of rape."[4]

President Roosevelt was speaking to a national choir of scholars. In *Pure Sociology* (1903), Brown sociologist and former abolitionist Lester Ward had claimed that Black men who lusted after and raped White women *and* the White mobs who lynched them in retaliation were both ordered by their racial nature to do so. In *Lynch Law* (1905), Wellesley economist James Elbert Cutler argued that in executing criminals, the White mobs were "merely [acting] in their sovereign capacity." Even Du Bois complained, in a 1904 Atlanta University study ("Some Notes on Negro Crime, Particularly in Georgia"), that there were "enough well authenticated cases of brutal assaults on women by black men" to "make every Negro bow his head in shame." Negroes must recognize, he said, their responsibility for their own so-called worst classes.[5]

When Black criminality ceased, lynchings would cease, and Black criminality could cease through education at "schools like Hampton and Tuskegee," President Roosevelt suggested. While in past years Booker T. Washington had rejoiced when Roosevelt had promoted his program, this time he probably felt uneasy. Given advance notice, Washington begged Roosevelt to reconsider the discharge, knowing the Tuskegee Machine would also feel the wrath of Black America. As Washington fell with Roosevelt, Du Bois's Talented Tenth rose in influence.[6]

THEODORE ROOSEVELT DID not become toxic in White communities. His groomed presidential successor, William Howard Taft, cruised to victory, weeks before African Americans lauded a victory of their own on December 26, 1908. At the center of the victory was a Texas-born colored heavyweight champion, the first counterpunching boxer in a sport of brawlers, who had finally received his shot at the heavyweight championship and knocked out Tommy Burns in Sydney, Australia. "No event in forty years has given more satisfaction to the colored people of this country than has the signal victory of Jack Johnson," reported the *Richmond Planet*. Almost immediately, the cry for a "Great White Hope" went up to redeem Whiteness. All eyes turned to retired heavyweight champion James J. Jeffries.

When the freely smiling Jack Johnson stepped from the Canadian-Australian liner onto the docks of Vancouver on March 9, 1909, American reporters peppered him with questions about whether he would fight Jeffries. And then they noticed the most newsworthy element of all for racist America: the champion's "white wife, a former

Philadelphia woman who threw in her lot with him," as newspaper readers found out in the Associated Press dispatch.

Jack Johnson's earlier "heartaches" with two Black women had caused him to date primarily White women. Johnson loathed that "no matter how colored women feel toward a man, they don't spoil him and pamper him and build up his ego." White women did, and thus they were superior partners, in Johnson's version of gender racism. In actuality, some White women refused to build up their man's ego, while some Black women catered to their man's ego. But by 1909, the gender racism of the submissive White woman and the hard Black woman was attracting patriarchal Black men to White women—just as the gender racism of the weak Black man being unable to handle the hard Black woman had attracted some Black women to the strong White man; and just as the gender racism of hypersexual Black people, embodied in the large penis or buttocks, attracted some White people to Black people; and just as the assimilationist belief that the Whiter and straighter the skin and hair, the more beautiful a person was, attracted Black people to (light and) White people. All these racist myths only hardened over the next century as Americans became better able to act on their interracial attractions in public. What did love have to do with those interracial attractions based in racist ideas? Only the couples knew. There were many interracial relationships *not* based in racist ideas. But how many were, and how many were not? Only the couples knew.

The most famous Black man in America quickly became the most hated Black man in America. By 1908, Johnson had won three of the four greatest prizes of patriarchal White masculinity—wealth, the heavyweight title, and the White woman. Taft winning the White House hardly could calm the fury of White men, especially when Jack Johnson went on to flaunt his White woman, his wealth, and his title.[7]

"If the black man wins, thousands and thousands of his ignorant brothers will misinterpret his victory as justifying claims to much more than mere physical equality with their white neighborhoods," predicted a writer in the *New York Times* months before the biggest sporting event in American history on July 4, 1910. It was the first to be reported live through wireless telegraphy. The former heavy-weight champion, the mammoth Jim Jeffries, dubbed the "Great White Hope," came out of retirement to seek the heavyweight title for the White race and win it back from the nation's most hated and beloved man, Jack Johnson. The match was held in Reno, Nevada, before 12,000 raging White spectators. Johnson knocked Jeffries out in the fifteenth round, sending a surge of excitement through Black America and a surge of fury through racist America. Racist mobs tried to beat Black bodies back down, and racist writers tried to beat Black minds back down. "Do not swell your chest too much," warned the *Los Angeles Times*. "No man will think a bit higher of you because your com-plexion is the same as that of the victor at Reno." Later, in *Knuckles and Gloves* (1922), London boxing aficionado John Gilbert explained that White men were "at a disadvantage" in boxing because of their "phys-ical inequality." The US government soon accomplished what White boxers failed to do: knocking out Jack Johnson, though only in a met-aphorical sense. He was arrested on trumped-up charges of transport-ing a prostitute (or rather a White woman) across state lines. After skipping bail, he lived abroad for seven years before turning himself in, and then he spent almost a year in jail.[8]

WITH RACIST AMERICANS hungry for the restoration of superior White masculinity after Johnson knocked it down and out, a pulp fiction writer served them what they needed. Edgar Rice Burroughs, who lived in Johnson's stomping ground of Chicago, had been moved by Henry Morgan Stanley's nineteenth-century productions of Africa's savagery. In *All-Story Magazine* in October 1912, Americans first tasted Burroughs's novel *Tarzan of the Apes*.

Tarzan tells the story of an orphan infant of White parents aban-doned in Central Africa who is raised by the she-ape Kala in a com-munity of apes. The orphan, John Clayton, is named "Tarzan" by the apes; it means "White skin" in their language. As he grows up, Tar-zan becomes the community's most skilled hunter and warrior, more skilled than any of the nearby ape-Africans. He eventually finds his parents' cabin and teaches himself to read. In subsequent stories, Tarzan protects a White woman named Jane from ravishing Black men and apes all around her. Tarzan goes on to teach his children, the Africans, how to fight and grow food.

It is hard to imagine a more famous fictional character during the twentieth century than Tarzan—and it is hard to imagine a more racist plot than what Burroughs wrote up in the Tarzan adventure series books, which he was writing and publishing almost up until his death in 1950. The plot became a Hollywood staple, reappearing again and again, most recently in the 2009 blockbuster *Avatar*. Burroughs made the association between animals, savages, and Africa permanent in the American mind. The defining message of the Tarzan series was clear: whether on Wall Street or in the forests of Central Africa, swinging through Greek literature or swinging from trees, White people will do it better than the African apelike children, so much better that Whites will always, the world over, become teachers of African people. Forget Jack Johnson's heavyweight title, White men had something better now. They had Tarzan, the instant sensation, a cultural icon for the ages, the character that inspired comic strips, merchandise, twenty-seven sequels, and forty-five motion pictures, the first appearing in 1918.[9]

W. E. B. DU BOIS couldn't have cared less about Jack Johnson and boxing in 1909. He was worried about his biography of the antislavery activist John Brown. The darling of White liberal America—the publisher of the *Evening Post* and *The Nation* and the grandson of William Lloyd Garrison—had also published a biography of Brown that year. Oswald Garrison Villard's biography was widely hailed as definitive and it sold well. Du Bois's sales were as disappointing as the reviews. Black scholars were routinely ignored by the White media and by White readers, even when they had nationally recognizable names, like Du Bois. "We rated merely as Negroes studying Negroes," Du Bois recalled, "and after all, what had Negroes to do with America or science?" What did science have to do with the fierce fight against the Tuskegee Machine and Jim Crow segregation? "What with all my dreaming, studying, and teaching was I going to do in this fierce fight?" Du Bois asked. Losing faith in scientific persuasion, he decided to "lead and inspire and decide." He left Atlanta University in the summer of 1910 and moved to New York to become the founding editor of *The Crisis*, the organ of the recently founded National Association for the Advancement of Colored People (NAACP).[10]

At the NAACP, Du Bois butted heads with Oswald Garrison Villard, who along with Du Bois was one of the co-founders of the new organization. Like his grandfather, Villard was more of an assimilationist than an antiracist, and he looked upon Black people as social problems. Then again, while his grandfather had loved aggressive antiracist Blacks, such as early Black feminist Maria Stewart, Villard "naturally expected" African Americans "to be humble and thankful or certainly not assertive and aggressive," Du Bois accurately noted. For instance, Villard tried, unsuccessfully, to push Ida B. Wells-Barnett out of the Committee of Forty, which had been responsible for organizing the NAACP.[11]

Assimilationists and antiracists launched the NAACP at a crucial moment. Segregationists had just launched their eugenics movement, demonstrating the progression of their racist policies and the racist ideas to justify them. Social Darwinism had fully immigrated to the United States. In 1910, former University of Chicago biologist Charles Davenport secured some financial support from a railroad heiress to establish the Eugenics Record Office at the nation's first center dedicated to improving the nation's genetic stock, the Cold Spring Harbor Laboratory in New York. Davenport was the son of an abolitionist and had studied at Harvard during Du Bois's tenure. Davenport sought to prove one of the most oppressive figments of the human imagination: that personality and mental traits were inherited, and that superior racial groups inherited superior traits.

"So you see that the seed sown by you is still sprouting in distant countries," Davenport wrote to England's pioneering eugenicist Frances Galton, Darwin's cousin, in 1910. And the vines of eugenics surely sprouted after 1910, watered incessantly by Davenport and the

250 eugenicists whom he trained. "Permanent advance" would only come about by "securing the best 'blood,'" he wrote in the movement's manifesto, *Heredity in Relation to Eugenics* (1911). The eugenics movement quickly rushed into American popular culture: in Better Babies contests, in magazines, in college courses, in popular lectures, and in a society assessing moguls and criminals as having good or bad genes, good or bad "blood." It did not matter that people did not change after blood transfusions. Nor did it matter that eugenicists never uncovered any evidence proving that heredity shaped behavior. The eugenics movement created believers, not evidence. Americans wanted to believe that the racial, ethnic, class, and gender hierarchies in the United States were natural and normal. They wanted to believe that they were passing their traits on to their children.[12]

As eugenics gained ground, Du Bois used *The Crisis* to combat the movement and to publicize "those facts and arguments which show the danger of race prejudice." As part of that agenda, he printed a piece by Franz Boas, prepping readers for Boas's 1911 magnum opus, *The Mind of Primitive Man*. Boas echoed the old creed of assimilationists in *The Mind of Primitive Man*: rejection of the segregationist "theory of hereditary inferiority" and belief that the "complete loss" of African cultures and the pressures of slavery and discrimination had made Black people inferior. "In short, there is every reason to believe that the negro when given facility and opportunity, will be perfectly able to fulfill the duties of citizenship as well as his white neighbor," Boas wrote. "It may be that he will not produce as many great men as the white race, and that his average achievement will not quite reach the level of the average achievement of the white race; but there will be endless numbers who will be able to outrun their white competitors."[13]

"North American negroes . . . in culture and language," Boas said, were "essentially European." Boas was "absolutely opposed to all kinds of attempts to foster racial solidarity," including among his own Jewish people. He, like other assimilationists, saw the United States as a melting pot in which all the cultural colors became absorbed together (into White Americanness). Ironically, assimilationists like Boas hated racial solidarity, but kept producing racist ideas based on racial solidarity.[14]

Boas composed a preface for another popular book in 1911, *Half a Man: The Status of the Negro in New York*, by NAACP co-founder and scholar Mary White Ovington. While pointing out some racial discrimination, she put a new statistical spin on the old racist stereotype of the oversexed, irresponsible Black woman. The higher the ratio of Black women to men, she said, made these "surplus women" prone to prostitution and prone to playing "havoc with their neighbors' sons, even with their neighbors' husbands." Along the same lines, social-work forerunner Jane Addams alleged, in *The Crisis*, that Black mothers were less able than Italian mothers to control their girls' sexual behavior. Ida B. Wells-Barnett could not let these attacks from White women go by unchecked. Black women, she wrote, had the "same love for husbands and children, the same ambitions for well-ordered families that white women have."[15]

As part of his effort to expand readership and demonstrate the capability of Black folk, Du Bois unveiled a popular section in *The Crisis* on Black firsts in June 1911—those individual Black professionals breaking through racial barriers. As America desegregated over the next century, praises rained down on Black firsts, such as hair industry mogul Madame C. J. Walker, and *Chicago Defender* founder Robert Abbott, who became the first Black millionaires. At their antiracist best, praises for Black firsts turned into demonstrations against racial discrimination, and demands for Black seconds and tenths and thirtieths. At their racist worst, Americans held up Black firsts as extraordinary Negroes, or as signposts of racial progress. As more Blacks broke free from the discriminatory barriers, society could find more ways to ignore the barriers themselves, and could even argue that something else was holding Black people back. With every Black first, the blame shifted to those Black people who failed to break away. Du Bois's *The Crisis* tried to assign blame to both: the Black have-nots, and the discriminatory barriers. But accommodating Black firsts advocated for a greater Black work ethic as a better social policy than action against discriminatory bars. If some could break away, the logic went, then all could, if they worked hard enough. Racist logic didn't have to be logical; it just had to make common sense. And so, as much as Black firsts broke racial barriers, the publicity around Black firsts sometimes, if not most times, reinforced racist ideas blaming Blacks and not the remaining discriminatory barriers.[16]

BY 1913, THE CRISIS had accumulated a captivated audience: captivated by the leadership of the Talented Tenth and the NAACP, captivated by popular sections of the publication, such as Black firsts, and captivated, more than anything else, by the brilliant editorial pen of W. E. B. Du Bois. In March, Du Bois joined the rest of the publishing nation in reporting on the first major suffrage parade in Washington, DC, organized by the segregated National American Woman Suffrage Association. In their march down Pennsylvania Avenue, 5,000 suffragists faced a funnel of White male policemen and hecklers. In The Crisis, Du Bois reported the "remarkable" contrast between the nasty White male opposition and the reportedly respectful Black male observers. In a rush of biting anti-assimilationist sarcasm, he asked his Black male readers: "Does it not make you burn with shame to be a mere black man when such mighty deeds are done by the Leaders of Civilization? Does it not make you 'ashamed of your race'? Does it not make you 'want to be white'?"[17]

A few years later, Du Bois published a forum on women's suffrage, particularly for the Black woman. Not many of the Black contributors advanced the popular (and sexist) argument of White suffragists: that women's innate (childlike) morality gave them a distinct entitlement to the vote. But educator Nannie H. Burroughs took this argument and refashioned it. She was one of the more articulate and hard-nosed leaders of her time. Back in 1904, Burroughs had indicted racist colorism in "Not Color But Character." There were legions of Black men "who would rather marry a woman for her color than her character," Burroughs charged. And so, Black women went about trying to change their appearance, straightening their hair and bleaching their skin to look like White women. "What every woman who . . . straightens out needs, is not her appearance changed but her mind changed," Burroughs charged. "If Negro women would use half of their time they spend on trying to get White, to get better, the race would move forward."[18]

On the suffrage issue in *The Crisis* forum, Burroughs skipped over into racist ideas, and especially into the idea of the weak Black male selling out his vote (and the strong Black woman not selling out hers). This gender racism had been articulated by everyone from Anna Julia Cooper to Frances Ellen Harper, W. E. B. Du Bois, and southern segregationists James K. Vardaman and Ben "Pitchfork" Tillman. Immoral, corrupt, and weak Black men had "bartered and sold" the vote, Burroughs argued. "The Negro woman . . . needs the ballot to get back, by the wise *use* of it, what the Negro man has lost by the *misuse* of it," Burroughs argued. In claiming that Black women would not have sold out their votes, Burroughs was simultaneously rewriting history and regarding Black women as politically superior to Black men. She was ignoring the history of Black male and female resistance to the ambush of laws, violence, and economic intimidation that forcibly stole Black male voting power.[19]

Then again, Burroughs may have still been upset about that loud minority of Black male voters who went for the Democrat in the 1912 presidential election. Though Woodrow Wilson, a Virginia-born Democrat, was a former Princeton political scientist who had made a name for himself conjuring up the Black terrors of Reconstruction and defending the re-enslaving White South, he had secured Du Bois's vote and the votes of thousands of other Black men by pledging moderation on race. Once in office, Wilson gave southern segregationists a dominant influence in his administration, while encouraging Blacks to focus on uplift suasion. W. E. B. Du Bois felt hoodwinked. An American politician had once again played Black voters like a drum, and forced them to hear the deadening beat of segregation in Washington, DC, and federal offices across the South.[20]

During his first term, Wilson enjoyed the first-ever film screening at the White House, and the selection was a stark symbol of his ideas about race. The 1915 film was Hollywood's first feature-length studio production, D. W. Griffith's *The Birth of a Nation*, based on Thomas Dixon's popular novel *The Clansmen*. The film signaled the birth of

Hollywood and of the motion-picture industry in the United States. It became the newest visual medium by which to circulate racist ideas, eclipsing the fading minstrel shows. The silent film depicted Reconstruction as an era of corrupt Black supremacists petrifying innocent Whites. At the climax, a Black male rapist (played by a White actor in blackface) pursues a White woman into the woods until she leaps to her death. "Lynch him! Lynch him!" moviegoers shouted in Houston, and nearly one hundred Blacks were actually lynched in 1915. In the end, the victim's brother in the film organizes Klansmen to regain control of southern society. A White Jesus—brown-haired, brown-eyed, and white-robed—appears to bless the triumph of White supremacy as the film concludes.[21]

"It is like writing history with lightning," Wilson reportedly said after the film. "And my only regret is that it is all so terribly true." Millions of White northerners and southerners packed movie houses beginning on February 8, 1915, to watch the widely believed truth of the Reconstruction era. By January 1916, more than 3 million people had viewed the film in New York alone. It was the nation's highest-grossing film for two decades, and it enabled millions of Americans to feel redeemed in their lynchings and segregation policies. The film revitalized the Ku Klux Klan, drawing millions of Americans by the 1920s into the club that terrorized Jews, immigrants, socialists, Catholics, and Blacks.

Angry at its terrible lies, Black communities everywhere protested *The Birth of a Nation*. In the final days of his life, Booker T. Washington tried to accomplish behind the scenes what the NAACP and other civil rights groups were trying to do openly: block its showing. They failed. Du Bois took a different approach, challenging the film's historical racism in his sweeping history *The Negro*, published right on time in 1915. He tore up the fairytales of the non-African ancient Egypt, the absence of sophisticated pre-modern African states, the horrors of Reconstruction, and so on. He had seemingly dropped his biological concept of race. But he had not dropped his racist notions about the traits of the Negro, whom he termed "the most lovable of men."[22]

For all the northern activists' efforts to block *The Birth of a Nation*— or to rewrite the history it depicted, or to challenge the mass disenfranchisement of Black men that it endorsed—southern Black activists did infinitely more. They protested southern segregationists with their feet. By the time they finished, they had indeed given birth to a new nation.

CHAPTER 25

The Birth of a Nation

"WAR IS HELL but there are things worse than Hell, as every Negro knows." W. E. B. Du Bois had a knack for packaging the complex feelings of Black folk into words. After World War I cut off immigration from Europe, labor recruiters from northern industries headed into southern towns searching for a new labor supply. Even if *The Birth of a Nation* had never appeared before excited southern audiences, southern Blacks would probably have still been all ears to northern industrial recruiters.[1]

Then again, southern Blacks did not need these recruiters to entice them to escape a place that in some ways was worse than hell. During the Great War, Black people once again used their legs as activism, escaping from rural towns to southern cities, from southern cities to border-state cities, and from border-state cities to northern cities in what became known as the "Great Migration." In the first mass antiracist movement of the twentieth century, migrants eschewed beliefs in the New South's racial progress, in the notion of Jim Crow being better than slavery, and in the claim that Blacks' political-economic plight was their fault. Segregationists tried to slow the migration through racist ideas, ideas put into action when they terrorized northern labor recruiters, when they arrested migrants, and even when they tried to improve labor conditions. But nothing and no one could stop this movement.

When migrants reached northern cities, they faced the same discrimination they thought they had left behind, and they heard the same racist ideas. The Black and White natives of northern cities looked down on the migrants and their different (though equal) south-ern or rural cultural ways as culturally backward. They looked at their families as dysfunctional. And they called these migrants, who had moved hundreds of miles seeking work and a better life, lazy.

In 1918, Harvard-trained historian Carter G. Woodson, who had just founded the first Black history journal and professional associa-tion, correctly predicted that "the maltreatment of Negroes will be nationalized." Migrants faced segregation in the northern "receiving stations," as journalist Isabel Wilkerson termed them in 2010. Racist Harlemites, for instance, organized to fight off what they called the "a growing menace" of "black hordes," and ended up segregating their communities. Over the course of six decades, some 6 million Black southerners left their homes, transforming Black America from a pri-marily southern population to a national and urban one, and segrega-tionist ideas became nationalized and urbanized in the process.[2]

The Great Migration overshadowed a smaller migration of people from the Caribbean and Africa to the United States. A young, well-read, charismatic Jamaican with a passion for African people and an understanding of racism arrived in New York in March 1916 to raise funds for a school in Jamaica. Seeking out Du Bois, the stocky, dark-skinned Marcus Mosiah Garvey visited the New York offices of the NAACP. Du Bois was absent, and Garvey was "unable to tell whether he was in a white office or that of the NAACP." The plethora of White and biracial assimilationists on the NAACP's staff, and all the biracial assimilationists in leadership positions in Black America, no doubt con-tributed to Garvey's decision to remain in Harlem and build his Uni-versal Negro Improvement Association (UNIA) there. His organizing principles were global African solidarity, the beauty of dark skin and African American culture, and global African self-determination. "Africa for the Africans," he liked to say. His UNIA quickly attracted antiracists, Black working people, and Black migrants and immigrants who did not like the colorism, class racism, assimilationism, and nativ-ism of the NAACP and the Talented Tenth.[3]

Marcus Garvey and his admirers were not the only people observing the growing population and power of biracial Americans.

Scholars were taking note. Two years after Garvey's jarring visit to the NAACP's headquarters, sociologist and eugenicist Edward Bryon Reuter finished *The Mulatto in the United States* (1918). From his base at the University of Iowa, Reuter made a name for himself arguing that anything Black people achieved was in fact the achievement of biracial people. He situated biracial people as a sort of racial middle class, below superior Whites, but above inferior "full Blacks," as they were called. (Biracial people often rejected the racist idea of their inferiority to Whites, but some consumed and reproduced the racist idea of their superiority to Blacks.) Reuter stamped biracial people as a "peculiar people"—despite their success—around the same time that homosexuals were being marked as a "peculiar people."[4]

Reuter reinforced the fundamentally racist idea that biracial people were *abnormal*. Homosexuals, like biracial people, also were considered abnormal, and the two were sometimes considered in the same breath as "peculiar people" situated in an in-between state. "Between the whitest of men and the blackest negro stretches out a vast line of intermediary races," proclaimed one of the earlier advocates of homosexual rights, Xavier Mayne, in *The Intersexes* (1908). "Nature abhors the absolute, delights in . . . the half-steps, the between-beings." Passing bisexuals and biracial people quietly disrupted the so-called normality of heterosexuality and racial purity.[5]

Eugenicists promoting the need for maintaining the purity of the White race endlessly berated interracial reproduction. In an explosive wartime book published in 1916 called *The Passing of the Great Race*, New York lawyer Madison Grant constructed a racial-ethnic ladder with Nordics (the new term for Anglo-Saxons) at the top and Jews, Italians, the Irish, Russians, and all non-Whites on lower rungs. He reconstructed a world history of rising and falling civilizations based on the "amount of Nordic blood in each nation." "[The] races vary intellectually and morally just as they do physically," Grant suggested. "It has taken us fifty years to learn that speaking English, wearing good clothes and going to school and church does not transform a Negro into a white man." This segregationist passionately told assimilationists that their efforts were bound to fail. Black people were incapable of development and could not become White. Grant revised and reissued his book three times in five years and it was translated into several foreign languages. Publishers were barely able to supply the voracious demand for segregationist ideas and for the dashing eugenicist movement as White theorists attempted to normalize the social inequities of the day.[6]

When Germany surrendered in the Great War, an embittered Austrian soldier sprinted into German politics, where he gained some cheers for his nasty speeches against Marxists and Jews. In 1924, Adolf Hitler was jailed for an attempted revolution. He used the time in prison—and Madison Grant's book—to write his magnum opus, *Mein Kampf*. "The highest aim of human existence is . . . the conservation of race," Hitler famously wrote. The Nazi czar later thanked Grant for writing *The Passing of the Great Race*, which Hitler called "my Bible."[7]

Eugenicist ideas also became part of the fledgling discipline of psychology and the basis of newly minted standardized intelligence tests. Many believed these tests would prove once and for all the existence of natural racial hierarchies. In 1916, Stanford eugenicist Lewis Terman and his associates "perfected" the IQ test based on the dubious theory that a standardized test could actually quantify and objectively measure something as intricate and subjective and varied as intelligence across different experiential groups. The concept of general intelligence did not exist. When scholars tried to point out this mirage, it seemed to be as much in the eye of the beholder as general beauty, another nonexistent phenomenon. But Terman managed to make Americans believe that something that was inherently subjective was actually objective and measurable. Terman predicted that the IQ test would show "enormously significant racial differences in general intelligence, differences which cannot be wiped out by any scheme of mental culture." Standardized tests became the newest "objective" method of proving Black intellectual inferiority and justifying discrimination, and a multimillion-dollar testing industry quickly developed in schools and workplaces.[8]

IQ tests were administered to 1.75 million soldiers in 1917 and 1918. American Psychological Association president and Princeton psychologist Carl C. Brigham used the results of the army intelligence tests to conjure up a genetic intellectual racial hierarchy, and a few years later, he constructed the SAT test for college admissions. White soldiers scored better, and for Brigham that was because of their superior White blood. African Americans in the North scored better than African Americans in the South, and Brigham argued that northern Blacks had a higher concentration of White blood, and that these genetically superior African Americans had sought better opportunities up North because of their greater intelligence.[9]

AN ARMISTICE SIGNED on November 11, 1918, ended the fighting in World War I. It took six months of negotiations at the Paris Peace Conference for colonial powers to come to an agreement on the Treaty of Versailles. W. E. B. Du Bois ventured to Paris in 1918 and sent back gripping letters and editorials to *The Crisis*. He shared the racism faced by Black soldiers, adding to the wartime press reports filled with stories of Black heroism. But this storyline of Black heroism changed in White newspapers to the storyline of Black deficiency when the officers, who were disproportionately White and southern, returned to the United States and began telling their own war stories to reporters. As a collection, Du Bois's Parisian dispatches and activities displayed his lingering double-consciousness of assimilationism and antiracism. Du Bois witnessed steadily fierce opposition among the victors at the Paris Peace Conference to granting independence to colonial peoples. In "Reconstruction and Africa," published in the February 1919 issue of *The Crisis*, Du Bois rejected, in antiracist fashion, the notion that Europe was the "Benevolent Civilizer of Africa." He declared, "White men are merely juggling with words—or worse—when they declare that the withdrawal of Europe from Africa will plunge the continent into chaos." On the other assimilationist hand, Du Bois helped organize the First Pan-African Congress that month in Paris, which called on the Paris Peace Conference to adopt "gradual" decolonization and civil rights. Du Bois desired a "chance for peaceful and accelerated development of black folk."[10]

At long last, the parties signed the Treaty of Versailles on June 28, 1919. The massive German state was forced to pay reparations. France, Belgium, South Africa, Portugal, and England received Germany's prized African colonies. The League of Nations was created to rule the world. The Wilson administration joined with England and Australia in rejecting Japan's proposal that the League's charter confess a commitment to the equality of all peoples. At least President Wilson was being honest. He feared that the relatively good treatment Black soldiers had received in France had "gone to their heads." To Wilson's racist Americans, there was nothing more dangerous than a self-respecting Black person with antiracist expectations of immediate equality, rather than the gradual equality of assimilationists or the permanent inequality of segregationists. In 1919, many Black soldiers returned to their towns, with antiracist expectations, as *New* Negroes. And they were greeted by New Negroes, too.[11]

These New Negroes heeded Du Bois's plea. "By the God of Heaven, we are cowards and jackasses if now that the war is over, we do not marshal every ounce of our brain and brawn to fight a sterner, long, more unbending battle against the forces of hell in our own land," Du Bois wrote in "We Return Fighting," in *The Crisis* of May 1919. The same US Postal Service that for decades had delivered White newspapers doused in lynching kerosene refused to deliver this *Crisis*, judging Du Bois's words as "unquestionably violent and extremely likely to excite a considerable amount of racial prejudice (if that has not already reached its maximum amongst the Negroes)." Du Bois's own false 1901 construction of antiracists as being filled with revenge and anger against White people—instead of anger against racist ideas and discrimination—had finally come back to bite him. He had spent his early years urging Black people to calmly focus their efforts on their own moral uplift, on uplift suasion, to change racist minds. He had tried to provide White Americans with the scientific facts of racial disparities, and he had believed that producers of racist ideas and policies could be persuaded through reason to end their production. He had spent his early years ridiculing leaders like Ida B. Wells-Barnett and Bishop Henry McNeal Turner as unwise, as violent, and as prejudiced when they had passionately called on Black people to fight. But every year, as the failures of education and persuasion and uplift piled up, Du Bois's urgings for Black people to protest and fight became stronger and more passionate. But then, he had to face the same criticism and censorship that he had dished out to others earlier in his career. After a week's delay, postal officials finally delivered *The Crisis*. They had found there were even more dangerous antiracist and socialist publications being edited by New Negroes, including Marcus Garvey's *The Negro World*.

How did those Americans still packing movie houses to watch *Tarzan* and *The Birth of a Nation*, who were still spending their afternoons reading *The Passing of the Great Race*, or attending Klan events, or trying to segregate away Black migrants, respond to the New Negro? James Weldon Johnson described their response during that year of 1919 as the "Red Summer" for all the blood that spilled in the deadliest series of White invasions of Black neighborhoods since Reconstruction. Since racist ideas were not working on New Negroes, violence came rushing forth in at least twenty-five US cities, as if to remind the assertive New Negro of White rule. "If we must die, let it not be like hogs," Claude McKay's booming poem of self-defense shouted in July. "Like men we'll face the murderous, cowardly pack, / Pressed to the wall, dying, but fighting back!"[12]

Racist White newspapers, as was customary then as it is today, tended to depict the Black victims as criminals, and the White criminals as victims. Black newspapers, as was also customary after dramatic shows of self-defense, tended to play up the redemption of Black masculinity. "At last our men had stood like men, struck back, were no longer dumb driven cattle," one Black woman rejoiced in *The Crisis*. For racist White commentators, the Black men who supposedly instigated the Red Summer were beastly cattle; to racist Black commentators, these formerly beastly cattle, by striking back, had proven themselves to be men after all. Racist ideas inflamed both sides in the Red Summer, and gender racism came out of the smoke, especially the horrible coughing silence about all those courageous Black women who had defended their men and children and communities.[13]

The Wilson administration somehow conflated the Red Summer with the postwar Red Scare, blaming anticapitalists for the carnage instead of violent White racists. On September 27, 1919, 128 alienated White socialists, inspired by the recent Russian Revolution, gathered in Chicago to form the Communist Party of the United States of America (CPUSA). "The racial oppression of the Negro is simply the expression of his economic bondage and oppression, each intensifying the other," the CPUSA's program declared, sounding eerily like the founding racial program of the Socialist Party of America (SPA) in 1903. Since then, SPA leaders, such as the party's five-time presidential candidate, Eugene V. Debs, had tended to say that there was "no negro question outside of the labor question." Like their SPA predecessors, CPUSA officials would also go on to raise capitalist exploitation over racial discrimination, instead of leveling and challenging them both at once. In their incomplete reading of the world's political economy, racism emerged out of capitalism, and therefore the problem of capitalism came before the problem of racism. The Communists theorized that if they killed capitalism, racism would die, too—not knowing that capitalism and racism had both emerged during the same long fifteenth century, and that since then, they had been mutually fortifying each other while developing separately. *The Communist* of the CPUSA admonished Blacks (and Whites) during the Red Summer to "realize their misery is not due to race antagonism, but the CLASS ANTAGONISM" between big business and labor.[14]

Big business was certainly producing and reproducing racist policies and ideas to divide and conquer the working class, decrease its labor costs, and increase its political power. However, the CPUSA downplayed or ignored the ways in which White laborers and unions were discriminating against and degrading Black laborers to increase their own wages, improve their own working conditions, and bolster their own political power. And why would White labor not continue ruling Black labor if labor gained political and economic control over capital in the United States? The Communists did not address that;

nor did they address their own racist ideas during these formative years, which were pointed out by the antiracist Blacks joining their ranks. In seeking to unify the working class, CPUSA leaders focused their early recruiting efforts on racist White laborers. They refused to update Karl Marx's scriptures to account for their deeply racialized nation in 1919. CPUSA officials typically stayed silent on what it might mean for the future of racism if a Communist revolution took place that did not simultaneously support a revolution against racism.[15]

W. E. B. Du Bois was inspired by the red hot summer like never before, and not just because he was excited about the New Negro, or because he started closely reading (and updating) Karl Marx. In February 1920, he put out the searing essays of *Darkwater: Voices from Within the Veil*. Du Bois had wearily come to realize that the segregationist "belief that black folk are sub-human" was not based on any lack of knowledge: "It is simply passionate, deep-seated heritage, and as such can be moved by neither argument nor fact." In moving away from educational persuasion, Du Bois finally began to turn instead toward a singly antiracist consciousness. But he did not quite reach it. Instead he wrote: "European culture—is it not better than any culture that arose in Africa or Asia? It is."[16]

After relegating modern African and Asian cultures, Du Bois spoke out against "The Damnation of Women." In *Darkwater*, Du Bois did something for Black women that was rarely done: for "their worth" and "their beauty" and "their promise, and for their hard past, I honor the women of my race," he said. But in honoring the Black woman, he dishonored non-Black women and Black men, especially in their roles as mothers and fathers. He described one global unhappy family. "The father and his worship is Asia; Europe is the precocious, self-centered, forward-striving child; but the land of the mother is and was Africa," he wrote. Nowhere was a mother's love stronger and deeper than in Africa. W. E. B. Du Bois—the son of a single mother—not surprisingly declared, "It is mothers and mothers of mothers who seem to count, while fathers are shadowy memories."[17]

Du Bois followed in the long line of reformers who played up in Black people what racists played down—in his case, he turned the global projection of the Black woman as the immoral anti-mother, the anti-woman, into the global projection of the Black woman as the moral super-mother, the super-woman. But whether redeeming or degrading Black women, such projections spun reality, generalizing the behavior of immoral individuals or motherly individuals, and in the process propagating racist ideas. An antiracist sketch of Black women would have depicted the same diversity of motherly and un-motherly behavior found in all equally imperfect female racial groups.

For decades, diverse sketches of Black feminine behavior had swayed heads and hips, minds and hearts, in buoyant juke joints. Months after the release of Du Bois's *Darkwater*, Mamie Robinson brought out the first recording of the great antiracist art form of the 1920s. "Crazy Blues" became a best seller. Record companies capitalized on the blues craze among Black and White listeners alike. Robinson, "Ma" Rainey, Ida Cox, and Bessie Smith sang about Black women as depressed and happy, as settling down and running around, as hating and loving men, as gullible and manipulative, as sexually free and sexually conforming, as assertive and passive, as migrating and staying, as angels and as "Wild Women." Blueswomen and their male counterparts embraced African American cultural ways, despised the strategy of trying to persuade Whites that Blacks were okay, and were therefore despised by Talented Tenth assimilationists.[18]

FOR ALL ITS assimilationist ideas, Du Bois's *Darkwater: Voices from Within the Veil* was still too well spiced with antiracism for the bland tastes of racist readers. Northern, southern, and foreign racist reviewers almost unanimously condemned the book as a bitter madman's "hymn of racial hate," or "what the southerner would write if he turned negro," as the socialist Harold Laski of the London School of Economics put it. Meanwhile, the overwhelming response of Black readers, including the legions of common sharecroppers and domestics, was that it was "a milestone in the history of the Negro race," as the *Washington Bee* attested. Some antiracist New Negroes did not like some of the bland moralizing and class racism of *Darkwater*. Yale alumnus William Ferris, the editor of Garvey's *The Negro World*, said Du Bois looked down on the Black masses and their ailments "from the heights of his own greatness."[19]

It was a charge hardly anyone could deny, especially after Du Bois's views on Marcus Garvey became known. Garvey's movement would collapse "in a short time," Du Bois had allegedly said, and "his followers are the lowest type of Negroes, mostly from the West Indies." The reporter who published this quotation exhibiting class and ethnic racism probably caught Du Bois in a rancorous mood that August 1920. All month long, Du Bois had had to watch and listen to the massive parades and meetings of the first international convention of Garvey's UNIA. "We shall now organize the 400,000,000 Negroes of the world into a vast organization to plant the banner of freedom on the great continent of Africa," Garvey had blared on August 2, 1920, to the UNIA convention's 25,000 enraptured delegates at Madison Square Garden. The bombastic convention left the activist African world in wondrous awe for months. Du Bois and the Talented Tenth, however, felt deeply threatened by Garvey's exposure of the touchy reality of light skin privilege. "Garvey is an extraordinary leader of men," Du Bois admitted in *The Crisis* at the end of 1920. But it had been a mistake for him to try to bring Caribbean color politics to the United States. "American Negroes recognized no color line in or out of the race," Du Bois said, "and they will in the end punish the man who attempts to establish it."[20]

It was probably the silliest statement of Du Bois's serious career. He sounded as oblivious as the racists who had angered him for decades by discounting the existence of the racial line. In denying the color line, Du Bois discounted the existence of color discrimination, in effect blaming darker Blacks for their disproportionate poverty. Du Bois had eyes. He knew light skins dominated the most desirable political and economic positions available to Blacks. In his own Talented Tenth essay in 1903, he had mentioned twenty-one present and past Black leaders, and all of them except Phillis Wheatley had been biracial. No Ida B. Wells-Barnett or Callie House appeared. He probably heard the circulating Black children's rhyme: "If you're white, you're

right / If you're yellow, you're mellow / If you're brown, stick around /
If you're black, get back." Du Bois knew that elite, light-skinned folks
were still using brown paper bags and rulers to bar dark-skinned folks
from churches, jobs, civic groups, historically Black colleges, Black
fraternities and sororities, and even neighborhoods and other types of
gatherings.[21]

Du Bois was probably not oblivious. More likely, he and his light-
skinned peers felt their color privilege was threatened by discussions
of colorism and color equality, not unlike Whites who felt their racial
privilege threatened by discussions of racism and racial equality. And
so, Du Bois copied his enemies: he used racist ideas and his punishing
power to silence the antiracist challenge to color discrimination.

THE CONFLICT BETWEEN Du Bois and Garvey reached its peak in the early
1920s, when they sparred over the question of interracial relations. In
October 1921, President Warren G. Harding went to Birmingham to
hunt up southern support, and he insisted that "racial amalgamation
there cannot be." While *The Crisis* reprimanded Harding for rejecting
interracial relations, Garvey hailed the president for his endorsement
of racial separatism. In contrast to Madison Grant's eugenicists, who
were advocating White racial purity, and opposing interracial reproduction due to the intrusion of *inferior* Black blood, Garvey advocated
Black racial purity, opposing interracial reproduction due to the intrusion of *different* White blood. Assimilationists often erroneously confused Garvey's separatists, who actually believed in separate but equal,
with segregationists, who really believed in separate but unequal. It
was Garvey's assimilationist opponents who were constructing Black
integration into White spaces as progress. And these assimilationists
also were conjoining Garvey's separatist efforts of racial solidarity
with segregationist efforts to maintain the racial exclusion of inferior
peoples. Garvey's assimilationist opponents failed to realize that there
was nothing inherently tolerant or intolerant about Americans voluntarily separating themselves or integrating themselves. Americans
routinely did separate and integrate themselves, voluntarily, based on

religion, gender, ethnicity, sexuality, profession, class, race, and social interests. Separatist organizing can be racist (and when it is, it turns into segregation), if the emphasis is on excluding inferior peoples. Interracial organizing can be racist (and when it is, it turns into assimilation), if the emphasis is on elevating inferior Blacks by putting them under the auspices of superior Whites. That was Garvey's somewhat false impression of the interracial program of the NAACP.[22]

Du Bois and Garvey represented a larger and nastier battle within Black America among assimilationists, antiracists, and separatists, between the classes, between natives and West Indians, between nationalists and Pan-Africanists, and between light skins and dark skins. But Garvey had a much bigger enemy trying to silence him: the US government. In June 1923, he was convicted of mail fraud. Out on bail, he ventured to Liberia—as did Du Bois. Upon his return, Du Bois's anger and sense of privilege got the better of him when in May 1924 he called Garvey the "most dangerous enemy of the Negro race in America and in the world." With his days of freedom numbered, Garvey struck back against Du Bois and the Talented Tenth when he presided over the UNIA convention that August. His antiracist affirmations had turned to blisteringly racist ridicule. Black people were "the most careless and indifferent people in the world," Garvey proclaimed to thousands at Madison Square Garden. Appeals exhausted, six months later Garvey walked into federal prison, only to be deported three years later.[23]

Weeks before Garvey's final UNIA convention, delegates gathered for the Democratic National Convention of 1924 at that very same Madison Square Garden. The Democrats came within a single vote of endorsing the anti-Black, anti-Catholic, anti-Semitic platform promulgated by the powerful Ku Klux Klan. The platform would have been anti-immigrant, too, if Congress had not passed the Immigration Act on a bipartisan vote earlier in the year. It was authored by Washington State Republican Albert Johnson, who was well-schooled in anti-Asian racist ideas and well-connected to Madison Grant. Politicians seized on the powerful eugenicist demands for immigration restrictions on people from all countries outside of Nordic northwestern

Europe. President Calvin Coolidge, the Massachusetts Republican who replaced Harding after his sudden death in 1923, happily signed the legislation before his reelection. "Biological laws tell us that certain divergent people will not mix or blend," Coolidge wrote as vice-president-elect in 1921. "The Nordics propagate themselves successfully. With other races, the outcome shows deterioration on both sides."[24]

After passage of the Immigration Act of 1924, eugenicists quickly turned back to focusing on the segregation of non-Nordics in the United States. Ironically, the act's side effects slowed the pace of the eugenic agenda. The act reduced Nordic fears of non-Nordics taking over the country, and it energized the intellectual struggle of the assimilationists to get non-Whites to comply with White ideals of American homogeneity. The Catholic, pro-immigrant Knights of Columbus Historical Commission even financed the publication of several books focusing on the contributions of different racial and ethnic groups. These included *The Germans in the Making of America* (since the Germans were hated in the interwar period), *The Jews in the Making of America*, and Du Bois's *The Gift of Black Folk: The Negro in the Making of America* (1924).

Unlike eugenicists and assimilationists, Du Bois desired a multiracial pluralism, where differences were acknowledged, embraced, and equalized in antiracist fashion, not graded, suppressed, and ignored. But instead of merely sharing the cultural differences of African American spirituality, artistry, and music, Du Bois graded Black people himself in racist fashion, echoing the view of the nation's leading urban sociologist, Robert Park of the University of Chicago. The Negro was "primarily an artist, loving life for its own sake," Park wrote. "He is, so to speak, the lady among races," and was interested in "physical things rather than . . . subjective states and objects of introspection." Du Bois likewise said the Negro had an unmatched sense of "sound and color," along with "humility" and "a certain spiritual joyousness: a sensuous, tropical love of life, in vivid contrast to the cool and cautious New England reason." After all these years, Du Bois was still helping to reinforce Harriet Beecher Stowe's ideas on the soft Black soul and the hard

White mind. It seemed that nothing could erase this wholeheartedly racist idea from the mind of W. E. B. Du Bois. And when he attended a historic event in March 1924, Du Bois probably felt that his longtime advocacy of Blacks' superior artistic gifts was finally paying off. He had hoped that Black artists could use the media and their creativity to persuade away racist ideas. Yet another faint hope in persuasion was about to fail another test.[25]

CHAPTER 26

Media Suasion

ON THE EVENING of March 21, 1924, W. E. B. Du Bois walked into a dazzling artistic gathering at Manhattan's Civic Club. Howard University philosopher Alaine LeRoy Locke was master of ceremonies. Cultural advancement would "prove the key to that reevaluation of the Negro which must precede or accompany any considerable further betterment of race relationships," Locke prophesied in the era's definitive anthology, *The New Negro* (1925). He proposed media suasion by "our talented groups" to persuade away racist ideas. Twenty-year-old New York University student and poet Countee Cullen, who was also committed to media suasion, was one of more than a dozen Black artists—most notably novelist Jessie Fauset—present to meet and receive advice from the Talented Tenth and the White publishers in attendance that evening. Cullen, who was dating Du Bois's daughter, Yolande, ended the Harlem Renaissance's coming-out party in a flurry of poems and ovations.[1]

Du Bois helped rouse the Harlem Renaissance artistic movement and was even more instrumental in rousing the activism of New Negro students. They protested against the remnants of the Tuskegee approach to schooling and against the efforts of all historically Black colleges that had been set up to "train servants and docile cheap labor," as Du Bois said in a critique published in *The American Mercury* in October 1924. Striking first at Florida A&M in 1923, and then Fisk in 1924, Howard in 1925, and Hampton in 1927, and dozens of other HBCUs in between, New Negro campus activists also protested the rules of morality imposed by the colleges to regulate and civilize the supposed barbaric, oversexed, undisciplined Black students (and keep them out of harm's way of Klansmen). On February 4, 1925, more than one hundred Fisk strikers ignored curfew and stormed through campus chanting "Du Bois! Du Bois!" and "Before I'll be a slave, I'll be buried in my grave!" By the time the protest fever subsided at the end of the decade, many of the rules had been expunged, and HBCU curricula, aside from a handful of Negro Studies courses, were hardly distinguishable from the curricula at historically White colleges and universities (HWCUs). Accommodators and antiracists were upset, but assimilationists were delighted.[2]

A CADRE OF Harlem's young and talented Black artists refused to take direction from W. E. B. Du Bois. They called themselves the "Niggerati" in 1926, clearly showing little interest in assimilation or in media suasion. The Niggerati included novelist Wallace Thurman, who was best known for his fictional tribute to dark beauty, *The Blacker the Berry* (1929), and Florida native Zora Neale Hurston, who would study with Franz Boas, reject his assimilationism, and become the penultimate antiracist mouthpiece of rural southern Black culture. These youngsters were formulating a literary and social space of total artistic freedom and tolerance for differences in culture, color, class, gender, race, and sexuality. The Niggerati was quite possibly the first known fully antiracist intellectual and artistic group in American history. Its members rejected class racism, cultural racism, historical racism, gender racism, and even queer racism, as some members were homosexual or bisexual. Not that they were bold enough to come out as such: Alaine LeRoy Locke, Bessie Smith, and Ma Rainey were among the many Harlem Renaissance headliners leading double lives in closeted homophobic America, privately affirming negated Black sexualities as they publicly affirmed Black negated artistry.[3]

In *The Nation* in June 1926, a twenty-four-year-old poetic sensation—another headliner who was quite possibly in the sexual closet—laid out the Niggerati's antiracist philosophy in "The Negro Artist and the Racial Mountain." The "urge within the race towards whiteness . . . and to be as little Negro and as much American as possible" was the "mountain standing in the way of any true Negro art," wrote Langston Hughes. Hughes was reacting to the words of another poet who had told him "I want to be a poet—not a Negro poet," probably referring to Countee Cullen, Du Bois's future son-in-law. Hughes went on to describe the upbringing of the "young poet" in a typical Black middle-income home, where the mother often told misbehaving children, "Don't be like niggers," and the father married the "lightest woman he could find" and told them, "Look how well a white man does things." In the home, they read White newspapers; they attended White theaters and schools; and they favored churches for light-skinned blacks. They aspired to "Nordic manners, Nordic faces, Nordic hair, Nordic art," said Hughes, as "the whisper of 'I want to be white' runs silently through their minds." This was "a very high mountain indeed for the would-be racial artist to climb in order to discover himself." It stopped the Negro artist from seeing the "beauty of his own people," Hughes added.

In the lives of the "low-down folks," who did not "particularly care whether they are like white folks," there was "sufficient matter to furnish a black artist," as his friend Zora Neale Hurston's career would show. The Negro artist did not have to touch "on the relations between Negroes and whites." The only duty Hughes dropped onto the "younger Negro artist" was to "change through the force of his art that old whispering 'I want to be white,' hidden in the aspirations of his people, to 'Why should I want to be white? I am a Negro—and beautiful'—*and* "ugly too."[4]

If Langston Hughes focused his antiracist creative energy on persuading Black people away from assimilationist ideas, and if Countee Cullen focused his assimilationist creative energy on persuading White people away from segregationist ideas, then Du Bois remained doubly focused on both. But in 1926, Du Bois's attention veered much more into persuading White people. And so Du Bois viewed Hughes's essay, and then his endorsement of Carl Van Vechten's *Nigger Heaven*, released in August 1926, as utterly traitorous.

Van Vechten was the Harlem Renaissance's most ubiquitous White patron, a man as curiously passionate about being around and showing off Black people as zookeepers are about being around and showing off their exotic pets. In the past few years, European artists arriving in New York had been calling on Van Vechten to take them on the "safari" of Harlem, as the tourists and tour guide more or less understood it. Now, Van Vechten gave them the tour in a book, *Nigger Heaven*.

Van Vechten's novel is a melodramatically tragic love story of boy meets girl, but with all that genre's affection, seduction, obstruction, betrayal, and death winding through the pitfalls of racial discrimination. It portrays the vivaciously lurid debauchery of the jazz clubs and cabarets of Black commoners; the solemn pretentiousness of the finely lit homes of educated, assimilated Black elites; and the politically correct intellectuals who debated "the race problem." The bitter racial line of negative Black reviews and positive White reviews could not have been starker. *Nigger Heaven*—from its outrageous title to the outrageous extremes of Black decadence and pomposity it delineated—felt like "a blow in the face" to W. E. B. Du Bois and the Talented Tenth. It was nearly as powerful a blow as the one that had been delivered by William Hannibal Thomas's *The American Negro* in 1901. A Black professorial character in *Nigger Heaven* claims, in a dig at media suasion, that the advance of Black artists in White circles will not change White opinions: "Because the white people they meet will regard them as geniuses, in other words, exceptions."[5]

Nothing worse rained down from *Nigger Heaven* than Van Vechten's outrageously untrue indictment of assimilated Blacks as spoiled, along the same line of thought that globe-trotting racists like to frame tropical "exotic" lands as being spoiled by White developers. The virginal and pure (and assimilated) gospel singer Mary Love, for example, had "lost or forfeited her birthright, this primitive birthright . . . that all civilized races were struggling to get back to," Van Vechten narrated in *Nigger Heaven*. She mourned that loss and yearned to rediscover it: "This love of drums, of exciting rhythms . . . this warm, sexual emotion. . . . We are all savages, she repeated to herself, all, apparently, but me!"[6]

In reducing Negro artists' gifts to their racial nature, Van Vechten was implying that there was no intellectual ingenuity, or constant rehearsing, or endless refinement of the ear, needed to master the sophisticated grandeur of music and dance performance in blues and jazz. Blacks were natural singers and dancers and musicians (and all those Black people who could not sing, dance, and play were apparently not really Black). It was an idea later reinforced by John Martin, who became America's first major dance critic when he joined the *New York Times* in 1927. He reasoned that for Blacks, the ability to dance was "intrinsic" and "innate." They had natural "racial rhythm," and struggled to learn the more technical dance styles, such as ballet. What Van Vechten and Martin posed as assimilated Blacks' tragic dilemma was stingingly racist: they could never quite reach the greatness of White civilization, but they were running away from the greatness of their natural savagery.[7]

Van Vechten made Harlem seem so exciting and exotic that White readers made *Nigger Heaven* a runaway best seller. Whites started pouring into Harlem—into Black America—to see, hear, and touch the supposed primitive superior birthright of Black artistry and sexuality. They flooded into clubs like Harlem's "Jungle," or went over to watch an exhibition of the newly established Harlem Globetrotters. In 1927, these Black showmen started running up and down the basketball court in a "natural rhythm," emitting jungle sounds and wild bursts of laughter like frivolous, dishonest, lazy children in need of "mature white handling." They found that handler in the club's founder, Abe Saperstein.[8]

In *Nigger Heaven* and in the blues art form in general, Black commoners were sometimes portrayed before White Americans as sexual, uneducated, lazy, crude, immoral, and criminal. This image brought on more debates about uplift and media suasion. Many Black elites agonized every time they saw "negative" Black portrayals in the media, convinced that these portrayals were reinforcing stereotypes and constituted the lifeblood of racist ideas. They religiously believed that if only Whites saw more "positive" Black portrayals, ones that were chaste, educated, refined, moral, and law-abiding, then racist ideas would wither away and die. And although Black elites did not want Whites to view the negative media portrayals of Black commoners as representative of Black elites like them, they themselves often viewed such portrayals as representative of Black commoners.[9]

Black commoners and their elite antiracist defenders, in contrast, saw the diverse truth of Black people in the portrayals and in their artistry. They cared little about the impact on racist ideas and enjoyed *Nigger Heaven* and the blues. And they should not have cared. The Americans who were generalizing the "negative" behavior of the individual Black characters in *Nigger Heaven* or the blues were showing that they had already consumed racist ideas. The Talented Tenth's attempt at media suasion was a lost cause from the start. While "negative" portrayals of Black people often reinforced racist ideas, "positive" portrayals did not necessarily weaken racist ideas. The "positive" portrayals could be dismissed as extraordinary Negroes, and the "negative" portrayals could be generalized as typical. Even if these racial reformers managed to one day replace all "negative" portrayals with "positive" portrayals in the mainstream media, then, like addicts, racists would then turn to other suppliers. Before *Nigger Heaven* and the blues, racists found their supply of reinforcing drugs in the minstrel shows, in science, in generalizing any negativities they saw in their interactions with any Black person.

The cross-class, cross-generational, cross-ideological portrayals debate was on in the 1920s, and it was centered in the portrayals of blues and then jazz, in *Nigger Heaven,* and then in Claude McKay's *Home to Harlem* in 1928. *Home to Harlem,* the first Black-authored best seller, made Du Bois feel "distinctly like taking a bath." Raging, Du Bois released his own *Dark Princess: A Romance* that year, portraying strong, intelligent women and sensitive, intelligent men, as he always did in his fiction, seemingly unaware that he, too, was reinforcing racist ideas.[10]

Du Bois was reinforcing assimilationist ideas, and in the 1920s these ideas were advancing on American northern minds—particularly among intellectuals. The acceptance of those ideas appeared to be the by-product of the ongoing Great Migration of Black folk out of the segregated South, the ongoing activism of New Negroes to desegregate the North and northern scholarship, and the ongoing reproduction of Black folk. The advance was not the by-product of Talented Tenth activists successfully persuading racist Americans that Black domestics and farmers could live and work in the industrial North. Migrants to the North were forcibly breaking out of the confines of agricultural and domestic labor in the segregated South, and thus the racist ideas justifying those confines. In 1928, some of the leading race scholars came together to publish a landmark special issue on "The Negro" in the prestigious *Annals of the American Academy of Political and Social Science*. Over the past fifteen years, the *Annals* editor wrote, "students of race as well as laymen have had to discard or even reverse many of their theories." The Great Migration had "upset" the "widely accepted theory" that segregating Blacks in their "tropical nature" would solve the Negro problem. Black people "of both sexes" had demonstrated their ability to work in industrial occupations formerly thought to be beyond them. And the theory of poor Black health causing "extinction through degeneracy," the editor said, had "suffered severe shocks": "The old theories concerning absorption through biological assimilation have been unable in their original form to withstand the tests of research." Moreover, "[Black] ethical and moral standards are developing," the editor beamed, in assimilationist fashion. In short, the most prestigious social scientific journal in American academia symbolically announced the retreat of segregationist ideas. Segregationists had dominated American academe for nearly a century, since the pre–Civil War days of Samuel Morton and the polygenesists.[11]

The special issue comprised a star-studded lineup of Black and White male scholars, including W. E. B. Du Bois, Robert Park, and esteemed University of Pennsylvania sociologist Thorsten Sellin. Sellin disclosed the "unreliability" of racial crime statistics for assessing actual levels of crime. "The colored criminal does not as a rule enjoy the racial anonymity which cloaks the offenses of individuals of the white race," Sellin wrote. "In setting the hall-mark of his color upon him, his individuality is in a sense submerged, and instead of a mere thief, robber, or murderer, he becomes a representative of his race."

And yet Sellin could not go as far as antiracist New Negro criminologists and concede that the "Negro's *real* criminality is lower or as low as the white's."[12]

Walter White, who on several occasions in the 1920s courageously "passed" to conduct brilliant NAACP investigations of southern lynching parties, suggested that the "color line" existed not only in America, but also in Europe and South Africa, and in "approximately the same proportions." Possibly to remain politically correct, he did not mention Communist Russia, where state views on race did not approximate the other colonizing European nations. In the summer of 1928, the Sixth Congress of the Soviet Comintern declared that "the Party must come out openly and unreservedly for the right of Negroes to national self-determination in the southern states, where the Negroes form a majority of the population."[13]

American Communists were stirred to action. The "central slogan" of the party should be: *"Abolition of the whole system of race discrimination,"* blared *The Communist.* For Black labor activists, the Comintern's 1928 statement (and expanded version in 1930) sounded like a lifeline for drowning Black labor. When American Federation of Labor head Samuel Gompers died in 1924, William Green continued his policy of saying Blacks were welcome in the AFL and denying the existence of racial discrimination in the ranks of labor unions. In doing so, Green effectively blamed Blacks for segregated unions and for their disproportionate placement at the bottom of labor pools.[14]

CLAUDE G. BOWERS probably did not read the essays in the special issue of *Annals.* His attention was focused elsewhere in November 1928—on the election returns. Bowers was the editor of the *New York Post,* a prominent biographer of Thomas Jefferson, and as aggressively loyal to the Democratic Party as anyone. Angrily watching the GOP snatch southern states in the presidential election, he decided to remind White southerners that the Republicans had been responsible for the horror of Reconstruction. His best-selling book, published in 1929, was called *The Tragic Era: The Revolution After Lincoln.* "Historians have shrunk from the unhappy tasks of showing us the torture chambers," he said, where guiltless southern Whites were "literally" tortured by vicious Black Republicans. We will never know just how many Americans read *The Tragic Era*, and then saw *The Birth of a Nation* again at their local theaters, and then pledged never to vote again for the Republican Party, never to miss a lynching bash, and never to consider desegregation—in short, never to do anything that might revive the specter of Blacks voting on a large scale and Whites being tortured. But there were many of them. More than any other book in the late 1920s, *The Tragic Era* helped the Democratic Party keep the segregationists in power for another generation.[15]

"It seems to me that the *Tragic Era* should be answered—adequately, fully, ably, finally[,] & again it seems to me Thou art the Man!" Du Bois received this encouragement to answer the book from the legendary Black educator Anna Julia Cooper. Du Bois dove into his research for the book he later considered to be his best, better even than *The Souls of Black Folk*. America could never have a truthful history "until we have in our colleges men who regard the truth as more important than the defense of the white race," Du Bois concluded in *Black Reconstruction in America: 1860–1880*, published in 1935. Far from a tragic era, Du Bois argued, Reconstruction was the first and only time the United States had ever truly tasted democracy. After the Civil War, Black and White commoners came together to build democratic state governments providing public resources for the masses of southerners. White elites overthrew these governments by securing the loyalty of White commoners, a feat accomplished not by offering them higher wages, but by holding up the rewards of the lucrative "public and psychological wage." From Du Bois, historians now term these rewards the "wages of whiteness": they were the privileges that would accrue to Whites through application of racist ideas and segregation. And to receive them, White laborers needed only stand shoulder to shoulder with White elites on lynched and raped and exploited Black bodies.[16]

To a *New Yorker* reviewer, Du Bois took the "odd view, in distinction to most previous writers, that the Negro is a human being." Du Bois's Reconstruction history "changed or swept away" our "familiar scenes and landmarks," wrote the reviewer for *Time*. But Du Bois did not blunt the appeal of *The Tragic Era* among southern segregationists. It is unlikely that racist readers would have their minds changed by a Black scholar. Indeed, it would take the legitimacy of a White historian and native southerner, historian Howard K. Beale of the University of North Carolina at Chapel Hill, to break the consensus of Columbia's Dunning School in 1940.[17]

THOUGH HIS BOOK certainly helped, Claude Bowers did not necessarily need to write *The Tragic Era* to break the back of the Republican Party. On October 29, 1929, the stock market crashed, ending the decades-long dominion of the pro-business GOP. The Great Depression hit the South and Black America particularly hard. "No jobs for niggers until every white man has a job," became the Deep South's slogan. In the North, Black migrants and natives were often found standing on "slave markets," as these street corners were called in northern cities. White employers would come by and choose the cheapest day laborers. Sexual and fiscal exploitation were rampant.[18]

In the midst of the Great Depression, with so many Americans suffering, it became harder to embrace eugenics—harder to blame one's economic plight on hereditary factors. Assimilationists took advantage of this lull and continued to assume control of the scientific community. Franz Boas blasted segregationists in his presidential address before the American Association for the Advancement of Science in 1931. Princeton psychologist Carl C. Brigham confessed in 1932 that his earlier findings about IQ tests determining genetic Black inferiority were "without foundation" (although the use of Brigham's SAT test only expanded). Scientific disciplines split into bickering factions, with geneticists distancing themselves from eugenicists. Meanwhile, eugenics was kept afloat by Nazi Germany and by the American birth control movement, the latter run by Margaret Sanger and her American Birth Control League.[19]

Physical anthropology, a discipline studying biological racial distinctions, had split off from cultural anthropology, which studied cultural distinctions. Boas was at the helm of cultural anthropology; the anthropologists at the helm of physical anthropology were Earnest A. Hooton and Carleton S. Coon at Harvard. In 1931, Hooton authored *Up from the Ape*, which became a staple in physical anthropology courses over the next few decades. "Physical characteristics," Hooton explained, "which determine race are associated, in the main, with specific intangible and non-measurable but nevertheless real and important, temperamental and mental variations."[20]

Many of Hooton's students entered the health-care sector, where segregationist ideas of biological races were rampant, and where workers were still treating diseases differently by race. Syphilis harmed Blacks much more than it did Whites, argued syphilis "expert" Thomas Murrell in *Journal of the American Medical Association* in 1910. But this theory had never been definitively proven. So in 1932, the US Public Health Service began its "Study of Syphilis in the Untreated Negro Male." Government researchers promised free medical care to six hundred syphilis-infected sharecroppers around Tuskegee, Alabama. They secretly withheld treatment to these men and waited for their deaths, so they could perform autopsies. Researchers wanted to confirm their hypothesis that syphilis damaged the neurological systems of Whites, while bypassing Blacks "underdeveloped" brains and damaging their cardiovascular systems instead. The study was not halted until the press exposed it in 1972.[21]

Hooton's *Up from the Ape* received a complement when *King Kong* appeared on the big screen in 1933. The film shares the adventure tale of a colossal, primordial, island-dwelling ape who dies attempting to possess a young and beautiful White woman. Americans scraped their pennies together, took their minds off the Depression, and gave the film stunning box-office sales. Reviewers were captivated. "One of the most original, thrilling and mammoth novelties to emerge from a movie studio," radiated the *Chicago Tribune*. Actually, *King Kong* was nothing but a remake of *The Birth of a Nation*, set in the island scenery of *Tarzan*, and then New York. But *King Kong* did not invite the controversy of *The Birth of a Nation*. The filmmakers had veiled the physically powerful Black man by casting him as the physically powerful ape. In both films, the Negro-Ape terrorizes White people, tries to destroy White civilization, and pursues a White woman before a dramatic climax—the lynching of the Negro-Ape. *King Kong* was stunningly original for showing images of racist ideas—without ever saying a word about Black people, like those southern grandfather clauses, poll taxes, and understanding clauses that had disenfranchised Black people.[22]

Black critics struggled to condemn *King Kong*, but they had no trouble launching an attack on NBC's radio comedy program *Amos 'n' Andy*. More than 40 million White and Black listeners tuned in nightly in the 1930s to hear "The Perfect Song" from the score of *The Birth of a Nation*, and then Amos and Andy came on. The stereotypical characters included Coons, Toms, Mammies, and even a nagging, assertive, emasculating Sapphire—the first major media representation of an angry Black woman. While racist listeners laughed *at* the characters, antiracist listeners laughed *with* them, especially the profoundly likeable and imperfectly human main characters played by two White minstrel-show veterans, who shared the relatable troubles, fears, frustrations, and restrictions of urban Black life in the Great Depression. Those African Americans who turned up their noses at *Amos 'n' Andy* usually also despised Hollywood's first Black celebrity: Stepin Fetchit, who played a series of roles depicting the "laziest man in the world." Stepin Fetchit starred in *Hearts in Dixie* (1929), the first studio production to boast a majority Black cast. He was clever, for in all of his laziness, Fetchit's characters hardly ever did any work, and the exasperated White characters were compelled to do the work themselves. Antiracist Blacks loved Fetchit's character. He was a trickster of racists, harkening back to slavery's tricksters.[23]

Economically depressed Black folk had to find some way to eat, some way to lessen their oppressive workloads in the nastiest and most taxing jobs, even if it meant feigning laziness. They did not find much help from the government, receiving the same Old Deal of racial discrimination. NAACP chapters tried to assist, but their membership and resources took a drastic plunge. And the association's national office was busy heading away from Du Bois and the struggles of poor Black folk.

CHAPTER 27

Old Deal

W. E. B. DU BOIS did not share the vision of the new executive secretary of the NAACP in 1933, Walter White. Du Bois envisioned an association of common people like the Scottsboro Boys, the nine Black teenagers falsely convicted in 1931 by an all-White Alabama jury of gang-raping two young White women on a train. These poor, dark, unschooled, unassimilated teens—whom activists around the world rallied to free—did not necessarily suit Walter White's vision. He wanted to transform the NAACP into a top-down litigating and lobbying outfit that put "refined" folks like himself before courts and politicians to persuade the White judges and legislators to end racial discrimination. Walter White, who sometimes passed as White, envisioned what a young, doubly-conscious Du Bois had envisioned. But in 1933, a sixty-five-year-old Du Bois had almost completely turned to antiracism.[1]

Du Bois escaped the internal battles of the NAACP offices for a five-month visiting professorship at his old stomping ground, Atlanta University. With the Great Depression spinning nearly every thinker onto economic matters, Du Bois taught two courses that spring semester of 1933 and mailed off two pieces to *The Crisis* on Marxism and the Negro. Howard's orthodox Marxist economist Abram Harris begged Du Bois to reconsider his intertwining of Marxist and antiracist ideas, saying that Marx had not fully addressed the racial issue, despite his famous declaration that "labor in a white skin can never be free as long as labor in a black skin is branded." But the present depressing reality, not an old theory, convinced Du Bois it was time to break ground on the ideology of antiracist socialism. In one of the 1933 articles, he described the United States as a "post-Marxian phenomenon" with a White "working-class aristocracy." At the end of the decade, Du Bois would expound on his antiracist socialism in *Dusk of Dawn* (1940). "Instead of a horizontal division of classes, there was a vertical fissure, a complete separation of classes by race, cutting square across the economic layers," Du Bois put forward. The vertical cutting knife was constructed of centuries of racist ideas. "This flat and incontrovertible fact, imported Russian Communism ignored, would not discuss."[2]

Du Bois's antiracist socialism reflected his disenchantment with not just capitalism, but assimilationist thinking. In June 1933, Du Bois challenged those HBCU educators who were copying White college curricula during a commencement address at his alma mater, Fisk. Du Bois knew Thurgood Marshall's class of 1929 at Lincoln University, in Pennsylvania, had overwhelmingly voted against the acquisition of Black professors and "Negro Studies," explaining their votes through racist ideas. The antiracist calls for Negro Studies at Negro colleges kept coming from Du Bois, from Langston Hughes, and from the 1926 architect of the popular Negro History week, Carter G. Woodson. In his 1933 book, Woodson called attention to the subject. In his title, he called it *The Mis-Education of the Negro*. "It was well understood that . . . by the teaching of history the white man could be further assured of his superiority," Woodson wrote. "If you can control a man's thinking you do not have to worry about his action. . . . If you make a man feel that he is inferior, you do not have to compel him to accept an inferior status, for he will seek it himself"; and "if there is no back door, his very nature will demand one." And so assimilationist Black scholars were demanding the back door, decelerating the advance of Negro Studies in the 1930s.[3]

The more antiracist W. E. B. Du Bois became, the more he realized that trying to persuade powerful racists was a waste of time, and the more certain he felt that Black people must rely on each other. What probably solidified the need for Black solidarity in Du Bois's mind the most was studying the remedies for the Great Depression coming out of Washington. After taking office, President Franklin D. Roosevelt powered through what he called the "New Deal," the flurry of government relief programs, job programs, labor rights bills, and capitalism-saving bills passed from 1933 to 1938. To secure the congressional votes of southern Democrats, Roosevelt and northern Democrats crafted these bills such that, to southern Blacks, they seemed more like the Old Deal. Just like in the old days before Roosevelt, segregationists were given the power to locally administer and racially discriminate the relief coming from these federal programs. And segregationists made sure that farmers and domestics—Blacks' primary vocations—were excluded from the laws' new job benefits, like minimum wage, social security, unemployment insurance, and unionizing rights. Not to be denied, Black southerners secretly joined sharecropper and industrial unions organized inside and outside of the CPUSA to fight for their own New Deal in the 1930s. Alabama Blacks during the Depression blended their homegrown antiracist socialism and Christian theology in a popular saying: "And the day shall come when the bottom rail shall be on top and the top rail on the bottom. The Ethiopians will stretch forth their arms and find their place under the sun."[4]

Northern Blacks joined the Congress of Industrial Organizations (CIO), which emerged in 1935. Some unions supported them in their dual fight against capitalism and racism. Other unions handed Black workers the Old Deal: in order to join the unions, "the Negroes will have to forget they are Negroes" and stop talking about that race stuff. These racist unions refused to do what could bring that about, eliminating racial discrimination.[5]

Next to employment, there may have been no more devastating area of discrimination than housing. The Roosevelt administration's new Home Owners Loan Corporation (HOLC) and the Federal Housing Administration (FHA) handed Black residents the Old Deal when these agencies drew "color-coded" maps, coloring Black neighborhoods in red as undesirable. The maps caused brokers to deny residents new thirty-year mortgages and prevented Black renters from purchasing a home and acquiring wealth. But, of course, the discrimination was ignored or discounted, and the fiscal habits of Black people were blamed for the growing fiscal inequities and segregation created by the policies. Discrimination for Blacks and government assistance for Whites usually won the day.[6]

Although they received disproportionately less than Whites, Black Americans, especially northerners, did receive some assistance from the New Deal, more than they had from any other federal government program in recent memory. Grateful Black Republicans flocked to Roosevelt's Democratic Party. They were enticed also by Roosevelt's famed "Black cabinet" of forty-five Blacks in his administration. But no one endeared Black Americans more to the Roosevelt administration, and thereby to the Democratic Party, than FDR's wife, Eleanor Roosevelt. In 1934, the First Lady publicly endorsed the anti-lynching measure lying in Congress's intensive care unit. She befriended the only woman in the "Black cabinet," Mary McLeod Bethune, and the NAACP's Walter White, and rejoiced about the Black gifts "of art and of music and of rhythm" that "come by nature to many of them."[7]

President Roosevelt made 1933 a pivotal year in the economic history of the United States, pushing through a series of economy-jump-starting bills during his first one hundred days in office. It could have also been a pivotal year in the racial history of the United States, but Roosevelt was too beholden to his party's segregationists. Meanwhile, powerful Blacks were too beholden to assimilationists or persuasion tactics for Du Bois's igniting articles to spark an antiracist movement. In the September 1933 issue of *The Crisis*, Du Bois published "On Being Ashamed," a look back at the lifelong course of his own thinking, which he generalized as Black America's thinking. From emancipation to around 1900, the "upper class of colored Americans," he said, had striven "to escape into the mass of Americans," practically "ashamed" of those who were not assimilating. But since then, "colored America has discovered itself," and Du Bois had discovered himself and his singular antiracist consciousness. Again in the November *Crisis*, Du Bois admonished the "large number of American Negroes who in all essential particulars conceive of themselves as belonging to the white race." And then, in the January 1934 issue, he surprised readers who were used to his integrationist politics by publishing "Segregation." Following Marcus Garvey, Du Bois distinguished between voluntary and nondiscriminatory separation and involuntary and discriminatory segregation. Opposition to voluntary Black separation should not come from racist ideas, he insisted, or from "any distaste or unwillingness of colored people to work with each other, to cooperate with each other, to live with each other."[8]

Scores of Black newspapers reported reactions to the pieces, which ranged from approval to confusion to rage. Assimilationists who finally felt they were making some headway desegregating northern White America, religious believers in uplift suasion, and those who were stubbornly committed to the political racism that Black advancement could only come from White hands all looked upon Du Bois as a traitor. "The vast majority of the Negroes in the United States are born in colored homes, educated in separate colored schools, attend separate colored churches, marry colored mates, and find their amusements in colored YMCA's and YWCA's," Du Bois went on to argue in 1934. Instead of using our energy to break down the brick walls of White institutions, why not use our energy refurbishing our own? Du Bois's bosses at the NAACP and the presiding officers of the National Association of Colored Women did not agree. Among the older or richer or more assimilated or more doctrinaire voices of the Talented Tenth, Du Bois was "slipping," as the *Philadelphia Tribune* editorialized.[9]

But with each essay, Du Bois was winning the respect of a new generation. Carter G. Woodson, Zora Neale Hurston, Mary McLeod Bethune, and Langston Hughes all agreed with his assessments. And to the unionized southern sharecroppers, the migrants laughing at *Amos 'n' Andy* and Stepin Fetchit, and the workers and students preparing to organize the National Negro Congress and its youth offshoot, the Southern Negro Youth Congress, Du Bois had never been better. Bolstered by this support, Du Bois swung back at the critics who believed that assimilation and "accomplishment by Negroes [could] break down prejudice." "This is fable," Du Bois thundered in the April 1934 *Crisis.* "I once believed it passionately. It may become true in 250 or 1,000 years. Now it is not true." Du Bois never again seriously promoted uplift suasion.[10]

W. E. B. DU BOIS knew he was "entering the eye of one of the deadliest political storms in modern times" when his train rolled into Berlin on June 30, 1936. The new Atlanta University professor was on a research trip after being pushed out of the NAACP for advocating Black empowerment instead of integration and assimilation. It did not take long for Du Bois to write home that the Jew was the Negro in Germany's second year of Adolf Hitler's chancellorship.[11]

Eleven days before Du Bois's arrival, the German-born Max Schmeling had squared off at Yankee Stadium against the pride of African America—and the scorn of segregationist America—the undefeated Brown Bomber, Joe Louis. Since the days of Jack Johnson, White masculinity had attempted to redeem itself not just through Tarzan, but by classing Black boxers like Joe Louis as "the magnificent animal," as the *New York Daily News* dubbed him before the bout. Stunningly, Schmeling knocked Louis out, inspiring the cheers of White supremacists from Brooklyn to Berlin. Two years later, Louis avenged the loss in the racial "Fight of the Century."[12]

Hitler aimed to project the supremacy of Aryan athleticism through hosting the 1936 Summer Olympics. The disinterested Du Bois remained away from Berlin for much of August, but Jesse Owens, a little-known son of Alabama sharecroppers, made history at the games. He sprinted and leaped for four gold medals and received several stadium-shaking ovations from viewers, Nazis included. When Owens arrived back in the states to a ticker tape parade, he hoped he had also managed to change Americans' racist ideas. That was one race he could not win. In no time, Owens was running against horses and dogs to stay out of poverty, talking about how the Nazis had treated him better than Americans.[13]

If anything, Jesse Owens's golden runs deepened the color line, and especially the racist ideas of animal-like Black athletic superiority. Racist Americans refused to acknowledge the extraordinary opportunities Blacks received in sports like boxing and track, and the fact that a disciplined, competitive, and clever mind, more than a robust physique, was what set the greatest athletes apart. Instead, athletic racists served up an odd menu of anatomical, behavioral, and historical explanations for the success of Black sprinters and jumpers in the 1932 and 1936 Olympics. "It was not long ago that his ability to sprint and jump was a life-and-death matter to him in the jungle," explained University of Southern California legend Dean Cromwell, Owens's Olympic track coach. But Jesse Owens did not possess the "Negroid type of calf, foot and heel bone" that supposedly gave Blacks a speed advantage, Howard anthropologist W. Montague Cobb found in 1936. Since some track stars could pass for White, "there is not a single physical characteristic, including skin color, which all the Negro stars have in common which definitely classify them as Negroes." Cobb did not receive many admirers in a United States where people were convinced about the benefits of natural Black athleticism and biological distinctions. Almost everyone still believed that different skin colors actually meant something more than different skin colors.[14]

HIS SIX MONTHS of cultural sightseeing, of learning about the political economies of Germany, Japan, China, and Russia, came to an end. In the second week of January 1937, W. E. B. Du Bois set his eyes on San Francisco Bay from the deck of the *Tatsuta Mara*. He once again entered the United States, where Franklin D. Roosevelt had forged a commanding coalition of liberals, labor, enfranchised northern Blacks, and southern segregationists to win the most lopsided presidential election in history. Fearful of alienating segregationists, Roosevelt did not use his power to ram the anti-lynching bill, which was still on life support, through Congress. "If you succeed in the passage of this bill," Mississippi senator Theodore Bilbo resounded on January 21, 1938, in opposition, then "raping, mobbing, lynching, race riots, and crime will be increased a thousandfold; and upon your garments . . . will be the blood of the raped" and the lynched. Bilbo proposed Black colonization abroad and praised the doctrines of Nazi Germany. But it was those very Nazi doctrines—and the mass murders of German Jews, which began in 1938—that were enraging White intellectuals and turning them off from Jim Crow. In December 1938, in a unanimous resolution, the American Anthropological Association denounced biological racism.[15]

In denouncing racism, scholars first had to define it. Beginning around 1940, Columbia anthropologist Ruth Benedict, a student of Franz Boas, dropped the term "racism" into the national vocabulary. "Racism is an unproved assumption of the biological and perpetual superiority of one human group over another," she wrote in *Race: Science and Politics* (1940). She excused her class of assimilationists from her definition, though, all those women and men who assumed the cultural and temporary superiority of one human group over another. As assimilationists took the helm of racial thought, their racist ideas became God's law, nature's law, scientific law, just like segregationist ideas over the past century. Assimilationists degraded and dismissed the behaviors of African people and somehow projected the idea that they were not racist, since they did not root those behaviors in biology, did not deem them perpetual, spoke of historical and environmental causes, and argued that Blacks were capable of being civilized and developed.[16]

Aside from Benedict's *Race: Science and Politics*, the most influential assimilationist scientific text of the era came from E. Franklin Frazier, the former student of assimilationist Robert Park. In 1939, the Howard University sociologist published a definitive study entitled *The Negro Family in the United States*. In his introduction, Frazier expressed a debt to Du Bois's Atlanta University Study on the Negro American Family thirty years prior, when Du Bois had concluded that "sexual immorality is probably the greatest single plague spot among Negro Americans." Du Bois returned the compliment by praising Frazier's brilliance as a Black sociologist, showing some of the holdover of his assimilationist ideas.[17]

Frazier painted broad strokes of the urban, non-elite Black family as an ugly, disordered, matriarchal albatross. He described absent fathers and unmarried working mothers leaving their children alone, sons growing into criminals, and daughters learning to imitate "the loose behavior of their mothers" and transmitting "moral degeneracy" from one generation to the next. In Frazier's sexist view, male-headed, nuclear, two-parent families were ideal. In his racist view, Black families statistically fell short of White families in fashioning this ideal.

This "disorganized family life" in Black neighborhoods was caused by racial discrimination, poverty, cultural pathology, and the introduction of the matriarchal Black family during slavery. Completely "stripped of his cultural heritage," the slave became a brute, Frazier argued. The slave's emergence "as a human being was facilitated by his assimilation" of his master's culture. And now, Black "assimilation of . . . the more formal aspects of white civilization" is ongoing in urban areas, Frazier concluded. "Intermarriage in the future will bring about a fundamental type of assimilation."[18]

E. Franklin Frazier was hardly alone in his assimilationist preference for becoming White. Psychologists Mamie Clark and Kenneth Clark found that the majority of the 253 Black children in their study in 1940 and 1941 preferred the white doll over the dark doll. Some junior high school students associated light to medium skin tones with intelligence and refinement, and dark tones with meanness and physical strength. The lighter, the better, paralleled the assimilationist idea of the straighter, the better. Since the 1920s and the craze of the *conk*—short for the recipe called *congalene*—Black men had joined Black women in straightening their hair. One teenager, "Shorty," gave his friend from Michigan his first conk in Boston in 1941 or 1942. "We both were grinning and sweating," Malcolm Little remembered. He stood there, looking in the mirror, "lost in admiration of my hair now looking 'white.'" Two decades later, Malcolm X reflected on his "first really big step toward self-degradation: when I endured all of that pain, literally burning my flesh to have it look like a white man's hair." Malcolm by then realized that he "had joined that multitude of Negro men and women in America who are brainwashed into believing that the black people are 'inferior'—and white people 'superior'—that they will even violate and mutilate their God-created bodies to try to look 'pretty' by white standards."[19]

THE SUDDEN WILLINGNESS to name and define racism did little to obliterate it, especially in popular culture. In 1939, MGM released *Gone with the Wind*, based on Margaret Mitchell's Pulitzer-winning 1936 novel. *Gone with the Wind* shared the story of the strong-willed daughter of a Georgia enslaver pursuing a married man. Scarlett O'Hara's lack of morality aside, the White enslavers are portrayed as noble and thoughtful; the slaves as loyal but shiftless, and unprepared for freedom.

African American protesters failed to stop the movie's success. It was almost universally praised by White film critics for its superb cast of actors and actresses, characters that seemed oh so real, bringing the old Georgia plantation to life before their eyes. The film smashed box-office records as hard as it smashed the truth of slavery, and it received ten Academy Awards. It supplanted *The Birth of a Nation* as a box-office leader, becoming the most successful film at the box office in Hollywood history. In the same way that *Tarzan* became the primary medium through which Americans learned about Africa, *Gone with the Wind* became the primary medium through which they learned about slavery. The only problem was that, in both cases, the depictions were woefully incorrect.[20]

The loyal, loving Mammy in *Gone with the Wind*, one of the most adored characters in Hollywood history, was played by the actress Hattie McDaniel. "By enjoying her servitude, [Mammy] acts as a healing salve for a nation ruptured by the sins of racism," political scientist Melissa Harris-Perry explained in a 2011 analysis of the film. McDaniel received an Oscar for Best Supporting Actress, a first for a Black person. After Hattie McDaniel, Hollywood producers loved to wrap bandanas around dark and hefty mammies in a parade of films in the mid-twentieth century. The stereotype masculinized Black femininity while emphasizing the ultra-femininity of their White counterparts on the screen. Light-skinned Black women saw either exotic or tragic mulattoes on movie screens. These characters failed to be assimilated into White womanhood, and failed to seduce White men.[21]

In the face of these racist caricatures, W. E. B. Du Bois clung to the promise of a group of young Black writers he met in Chicago in 1940. "One feels a certain sense of relief and confidence in meeting such sturdy pillars of the day to come," Du Bois glowed to *New York Amsterdam News* readers. It was his first time meeting the sturdiest pillar of all. Born and raised in Mississippi, the thirty-one-year-old pillar had migrated to Memphis and then had gone on to Chicago, where he acquainted himself with the work and students of assimilationist Robert Park. Richard Wright, who mused on the "cultural barrenness of black life" in his autobiography, *Black Boy* (1945), proved to be the novelistic equivalent of sociologist E. Franklin Frazier. Both gave the United States powerful exhibits into American discrimination. Both benefited from the North's intellectual march onto the assimilationist avenue during the Depression.[22]

Wright echoed Frazier's racist historical account of enslaved Africans being stripped of their culture and their "gradual dehumanization to the level of random impulse and hunger and fear and sex," as Wright said to a friend in 1945. Northwestern anthropologist Melville Herskovits disputed this theory in *The Myth of the Negro Past* in 1941, bringing on the critical wrath of E. Franklin Frazier. African culture was no less resilient than European culture, and the cultural exchange went two ways, Herskovits maintained. African Americans created a strong and complex culture of European "outward" forms "while retaining inner [African] values," he insightfully argued. Those who had consumed the myth of the Negro past were suffering from "race prejudice."[23]

Anthropologist Zora Neale Hurston was one of the few Black intellectuals writing for popular audiences who was not suffering from this race prejudice, this cultural assimilationism sweeping the academy in the 1930s and 1940s. Since her youthful days in Harlem's Niggerati, Hurston had struggled to make a living as a woman writer—and a Black woman writer at that. She had worked for a New Deal jobs program designed to put writers back to work, but had received less compensation than less qualified White writers. She had gone on to release *Mules and Men* (1935), the finest collection of Black folklore ever recorded. *Mules and Men* did not fit in the canon of media suasionist works that showed either harsh or stereotype-defying Black life, thus upsetting Howard University literary scholar Sterling Brown. Instead, Hurston's collection revealed the unique, varied, and imperfect humanity of southern Black folk.[24]

Mules and Men seemed almost like a nonfictional appetizer to the novel Hurston released in 1937. The new book carried the indelible title *Their Eyes Were Watching God*. In it, Hurston guided readers into the depths of rural Black culture in Florida through a protagonist named Janie Mae Crawford. After escaping the domineering confines of two well-off but domineering men, Janie marries and finds love in the much younger and much humbler Tea Cake, and finally feels her "soul crawl out of its hiding place." *Their Eyes Were Watching God* explores the precarious love life of a heterosexual Black woman at the intersection of sexism and racism. "Honey, de white man is de ruler of everything as fur as Ah been able tuh find out," Janie's grandmother tells her. "So de white man throw down de load and tell de nigger man tuh pick it up. He pick it up because he have to, but he don't tote it. He hand it to his womenfolks. De nigger woman is de mule uh de world so fur as Ah can see."

Hurston chose neither to glorify nor denigrate southern Black culture, probably knowing that media suasionists and assimilationists would be upset with her choices. But Hurston hardly cared. Instead, she took a revealing shot at the lunacy of Black assimilationists through her construction of Mrs. Turner, a friend of Janie's. "Anyone who looked more white folkish than herself was better than she was in her criteria," Hurston narrated. "Mrs. Turner, like all other believers had built an altar to the unattainable—Caucasian characteristics for all. Her god would smite her, would hurl her from pinnacles and lose her in deserts, but she would not forsake his altars."[25]

Hurston did not sell many copies, despite the largely positive (and racist) reviews from White critics. The novel reflects "normal" southern Negro life "with its holdovers from slave times, its social difficulties, childish excitements, and endless exuberances," according to one *New York Times* reviewer. *Their Eyes Were Watching God* is filled "with a limitless sense of humor, and a wild, strange sadness," hailed the *New York Herald Tribune*'s reviewer. While racist Whites enjoyed Hurston's depictions of every Negro "who isn't so civilized that he has lost the capacity for glory," to quote a reviewer from the *New York Herald Tribune*, Alain Locke, the godfather of media suasion, demanded that Hurston stop creating "these pseudo-primitives who the reading public still loves to laugh with, weep over, and envy." Richard Wright, drowning in all of his cultural racism, unable and unwilling to see her missives of antiracist feminism, and unable to see the politics of her love story, said the novel "carries no theme, no message, no thought." It only exploited the "quaint" aspects of Black life. It was like a minstrel show in a book, Wright maintained, satisfying the tastes of White readers.[26]

Hurston did not need to respond to these Black male critics. "I am not tragically colored," she had already told the world. "There is no great sorrow dammed up in my soul, nor lurking behind my eyes. I do not mind at all. I do not belong to the sobbing school of Negrohood who hold that nature somehow has given them a lowdown dirty deal and whose feelings are all hurt about it." But the sobbing school was selling out books. By the end of the decade, *Their Eyes Were Watching God* was out of print, and Hurston had to find work as a maid.[27]

Hurston was ahead of her time. When her time came in the 1970s, long after her death, and antiracist feminists rediscovered *Their Eyes Were Watching God*, they fittingly partook of their own self-defining love affair, like Janie. They self-defined the novel's greatness in a literary world rejecting it, unabashedly thrusting the once-rejected novel into the conversation as one of the finest—if not *the* finest—American novels of all time.[28]

IN CRITICIZING THE greatest antiracist novelist of the interwar era, Richard Wright made way for himself. When W. E. B. Du Bois first laid his eyes on Wright in 1940, he was laying his eyes on the author of *Native Son*, a novel Du Bois admired. *Native Son* received a Book-of-the-Month Club award, and it made Wright the toast of the literary world in the 1940s. The novel's main character, the bewildered (and bewildering) Bigger Thomas, represented "many" Negroes who "had become estranged from the religion and folk culture of his race" and lived "so close to the very civilization which sought to keep them out," Wright explained. Bigger Thomas "was hovering unwanted between two worlds." Thomas ended up killing both worlds—as embodied in the calculating rape and murder of his Black girlfriend and impulsive murder of a White girl. Through Bigger Thomas, Wright offered a gripping integration ultimatum in *Native Son*: if African Americans were not allowed into White civilization, then they would turn violent.[29]

By the end of March 1940, *Native Son* had sold 250,000 copies and garnered rave reviews from Whites and Blacks alike—more sold books and rave reviews than Hurston and Langston Hughes had received in two decades. Wright seemed untouchable until a twenty-four-year-old upstart Harlem writer began his literary coup with an essay, called "Everybody's Protest Novel," in 1949. This literary lightning bolt struck media suasion and the assimilationist underpinning of "social protest fiction," with its original cornerstone, Harriet Beecher Stowe's *Uncle Tom's Cabin*, and its latest cornerstone, *Native Son*. In "overlooking, denying, evading" the "complexity" of Black humanity for persuasion's sake, these protest novels were "fantasies, connecting nowhere with reality," wrote James Baldwin, five years before releasing his finest novel, *Go Tell It on the Mountain*. Like Stowe's Uncle Tom, Richard Wright's Bigger Thomas tragically "admits that possibility of his being sub-human, and feels constrained, therefore, to battle for his humanity." What Blacks needed to do was "infinitely more difficult": they had to accept their imperfectly equal humanity, Baldwin declared. "It is the peculiar triumph of society—and its loss—that it is able to convince those people to whom it has given inferior status of the reality of this decree."[30]

All these literary battles played out during and after the Second Great War. It was a war that ended with the global triumph of American power. It ended with the need to convince the decolonizing world of the reality of the newest American decree: that the United States should take its place as leader of the free world.

CHAPTER 28

Freedom Brand

LIKE MANY ACTIVISTS, W. E. B. Du Bois reeled from the height of the Nazi Holocaust of Jews and other non-Aryans. After the United States entered World War II in 1942, Du Bois felt energized by Black America's "Double V Campaign": victory against racism at home, and victory against fascism abroad. The Double V Campaign kicked the civil rights movement into high gear, especially up North, and the long-awaited comprehensive study of the Negro financed by the Carnegie Foundation kicked it into yet another gear, especially down South.

In 1936, Carnegie Foundation president Frederick P. Keppel had briefly considered some White American scholars when he had decided to heed Cleveland mayor Newton Baker's recommendation to sponsor a study on the "infant race." But there was almost no consideration of Zora Neale Hurston or the elder statesmen, W. E. B. Du Bois and Carter G. Woodson. Although White assimilationists and philanthropists were taking over the racial discourse in the academy, they were customarily shutting out Black scholars as being too subjective and biased to study Black people. It was amazing that the same scholars and philanthropists who saw no problem with White scholars studying White people had all these biased complaints when it came to Black scholars studying Black people. But what would racist ideas be without contradictions.[1]

Carnegie officials drew up a list of *only* foreign European scholars and White officials stationed in European colonies who they believed could complete the study "in a wholly objective and dispassionate

way." They ended up selecting the Swedish Nobel-laureate economist Gunnar Myrdal, bringing him to the United States in 1938. With
$300,000 in Carnegie funds, Myrdal employed a classroom of leading
Black and White scholars, including Frazier and Herskovits—seemingly everyone except Hurston, Du Bois, and Woodson.[2]

In his two-volume, nearly 1,500-page study, published in 1944,
Myrdal shined an optimistic light on what he termed, in his title, *An
American Dilemma*. He identified the racial problem as a "moral problem," as assimilationists long had since the days of William Lloyd Garrison. White Americans display an "astonishing ignorance about the
Negro," Myrdal wrote. Whites ignorantly viewed Negroes as "criminal," as having "loose sexual morals," as "religious," as having "a gift for
dancing and singing," and as "the happy-go-lucky children of nature."
Myrdal convinced himself—and many of his readers—that ignorance
had produced racist ideas, and that racist ideas had produced racist
policies, and therefore that "a great majority of white people in America would be prepared to give the Negro a substantially better deal if
they knew the facts." W. E. B. Du Bois probably shook his head when
he read this passage. "Americans know the facts," he may have thought
to himself, as he once wrote. Du Bois had been sharing the facts for
nearly fifty years, to no avail.[3]

Du Bois did enjoy most of the two volumes, including the devastating assault on the rationales of segregationists, the encyclopedic analysis of racial discrimination, and the fallacy of southerners'
separate-but-equal brand. "Never before in American history," Du
Bois admitted, had "a scholar so completely covered this field. The
work is monumental." E. Franklin Frazier agreed in his two glowing
reviews. He praised Myrdal's "objectivity" and willingness to describe
"the Negro community for what it was—a pathological phenomenon
in American life."[4]

And yet one of Myrdal's solutions to White racism was still Black
assimilation. "In practically all its divergences, American Negro culture is . . . a distorted development, or a pathological condition, of the
general American culture," Myrdal surmised. "It is to the advantage of
American Negroes as individuals and as a group to become assimilated

into American culture." *An American Dilemma* did for cultural assimilationists what Darwin's *Origin of Species* had done for Social Darwinists,
what Stowe's *Uncle Tom's Cabin* had done for abolitionists, what Samuel
Morton's *Crania Americana* had done for polygenesists, and what Robert
Finley's *Thoughts on Colonization* had done for colonizationists. The book
inspired a cadre of key politicians, lawyers, judges, preachers, scholars,
capitalists, journalists, and activists to power up the next generation of
racist ideas and the assimilationist wing of the civil rights movement.
To Myrdal, neither segregationist scholars, with their "preconceptions
about the Negroes' inherent inferiority," nor antiracist scholars, who
were "basically an expression of the Negro protest," could be objective
the way he and the new assimilationists could.[5]

AS WORLD WAR II neared its end in April 1945, W. E. B. Du Bois joined
representatives of fifty countries at the United Nations Conference on
International Organization in San Francisco. He pressed, unsuccessfully, for the new UN Charter to become a buffer against the political
racism of colonialism. Then, later in the year, Du Bois attended the
Fifth Pan-African Congress in Manchester, England, and was fittingly
introduced as the "Father of Pan-Africanism." A sense of determination
pervaded the Fifth Congress. In attendance were two hundred men
and women, some of whom would go on to lead the African decolonization movements, like Ghana's Kwame Nkrumah and Kenya's Jomo
Kenyatta. These delegates did not make the politically racist request
of past Pan-African congresses of gradual decolonization, as if Africans were not ready to rule Africans. The antiracist "Challenge to the
Colonial Powers" demanded immediate independence from European
colonial rule.[6]

The United States emerged from World War II, looked over at
the ravaged European and East Asian worlds, and flexed its unmatched
capital, industrial force, and military arms as the new global leader.
Only the Communist Soviet Union seemed to stand in America's way.
The Cold War between capitalism and communism to win the economic and political allegiances of decolonizing nations, and of their

markets and resources, had begun. In March 1946, Dean Acheson warned that the "existence of discrimination against minority groups in this country has an adverse effect on our relations with other countries." Acheson was a source as reliable as they came. He had headed the State Department's delegation at the 1944 Bretton Woods Conference, which rebuilt the international capitalist system. President Harry S. Truman, who took over after Roosevelt died in 1945, listened to Acheson's warning that globally circulating reports of discrimination, fanned by the flames of Russian media outlets, were harming US foreign policy and causing doors to shut on American businessmen, especially in the decolonizing non-White nations.[7]

President Truman was prepared to make some reforms, but southern segregationists fought tooth and nail to maintain the racial status quo. Mississippi's firebrand senator Theodore Bilbo, for one, did not get the memo from Acheson. "I call on every red-blooded white man to use any means to keep the niggers away from the polls," Bilbo said on a reelection campaign stop in 1946. Bilbo's call to arms ignited such a firestorm that when he won his election, the newly elected Republican majority blocked him from reentering the Senate in 1947. (His southern peers preaching "states' rights" to keep Blacks from the polls were allowed to take their seats.) Not to be silenced, Bilbo retired to his estate in southern Mississippi and self-published *Take Your Choice: Separation or Mongrelization* to rally the troops against egalitarians. "That the Negro is inferior to the Caucasian has been proved by six thousand years of world-wide experimentation," Bilbo claimed.[8]

Take Your Choice hit southern bookstores during a landmark publishing year, 1947. Howard historian John Hope Franklin's sweeping history of Black folk, *From Slavery to Freedom*, was a milestone, and pushed hard against the racist version of history promoted by Bilbo and Columbia's fading Dunning School. *From Slavery to Freedom* wasn't wholly antiracist, though. Franklin began with the racist historical conception that slavery had induced Black inferiority. This assertion did at least counteract Jim Crow historians' claims of enslavement as "a civilizing force." But both historical pictures were wrong and racist— one started Black people in inferiority before slavery, and the other ended Black people in inferiority after slavery. And Franklin cast Black women and poor people as impotent spectators in the Negro's "struggle for the realization of freedom." Prodded by Black feminist historians like Mary Frances Berry, Nell Irvin Painter, Darlene Clark Hine, and Deborah Gray White, John Hope Franklin—and the historically male-centered field of African American history—spent the rest of the century trying to correct these mistakes in subsequent editions and books.[9]

As Franklin set the new course of Black (male) historiography in 1947 (decades before Black women's history set a newer course), Columbia evolutionary biologist Theodosius Dobzhansky and anthropologist Ashley Montagu set the new course of Social Darwinism—away from eugenics. The Ukraine-born Dobzhansky had famously joined evolution and genetics by defining evolution as a "change in the frequency of an allele within a gene pool." The England-born Montagu had succeeded his mentor, Franz Boas, as America's most eminent anthropological opponent of segregation when Boas died in 1942. Montagu's *Man's Most Dangerous Myth: The Fallacy of Race* topped the charts that year, with Americans still shuddering from news of the Holocaust. Montagu exposed the dangerous myth of biological racial hierarchy and shared the antiracist concept that "all cultures must be judged in relation to their own history . . . and definitely not by the arbitrary standard of any single culture." Montagu did not always follow his own advice, however. In his "example of cultural relativity," he judged that in the past 5,000 years, while European cultures will have advanced, "the kingdoms of Africa have undergone comparatively little change."[10]

On June 6, 1947, these two commanding scholars published their groundbreaking article in the all-powerful *Science* journal. "Race differences," Dobzhansky and Montagu wrote, "arise chiefly because of the differential action of natural selection on geographically separate populations." They rejected eugenic ideas of fixed races, fixed racial traits, and a fixed racial hierarchy. Human populations (or races) were evolving, they argued, and changing genetically through two evolutionary processes: one biological, one cultural. It was not nature *or* nurture distinguishing humans, but nature *and* nurture. This formulation became known as the dual-evolution theory, or the modern evolutionary consensus. The consensus held as evolutionary biology grew over the course of the century. It was an area of growth that sometimes complemented the growth of molecular biology, particularly after American James Watson and Brits Francis Crick and Rosalind Franklin discovered the structure of deoxyribonucleic acid (DNA) in 1953.

Segregationists and assimilationists still found ways to adapt dual-evolution theory to suit their ideas about Black people. Segregationists could argue that African populations contained the lowest frequencies of "good" genes. Assimilationists could argue that European populations had created the most complex and sophisticated societies, and were the most culturally evolved populations. Dobzhansky and Montagu ended up dethroning the eugenicists in science but enthroning new racist ideas, as reflected in the globally reported United Nations Educational, Scientific, and Cultural Organization (UNESCO) Statements on Race in 1950 and 1951.[11]

UNESCO officials had assembled in 1950 an international dream team of scholars in Paris to draw up the final rebuttal to Nazism and eugenicists worldwide. Virtually all of the scholars, including Montagu, Dobzhansky, E. Franklin Frazier, and Gunnar Myrdal, had expressed assimilationist ideas—proof that even as the scientific establishment recognized segregationist ideas as racist, they still ensured that assimilationism endured and dominated the racial discourse. While claiming that no human populations had any biological evolutionary achievements, these assimilationists spoke of the "cultural achievements" of certain human populations in the 1950 UNESCO Race Statement. And then, in 1951, geneticists and physical anthropologists figured, in their revised statement: "It is possible, though not proved, that some types of innate capacity for intellectual and emotional responses are commoner in one human group than in another." Segregationist scholars set out to prove these innate racial differences in intelligence.[12]

Even before the UNESCO statements appeared on front pages from New York City to Paris, President Harry S. Truman had taken the initiative to improve race relations in the United States. Racial reform was a vital, though relatively unremembered facet of the "Truman Doctrine" that he presented to Congress on March 12, 1947. He branded the United States the leader of the free world and the Soviet Union the leader of the unfree world. "The free peoples of the world look to us for support in maintaining their freedoms," Truman proclaimed. Branding itself the leader of the free world opened the United States up to criticism about its myriad unfree racial policies (not to mention its unfree class, gender, and sexual policies). The harsh treatment of non-White foreigners, the string of nasty postwar lynchings of returning soldiers, the anti-lynching activism of the internationally renowned artist Paul Robeson, NAACP charges of human rights violations before the United Nations—suddenly these unfree racial policies and actions became a liability. Protecting the freedom brand of the United States became more important for northern politicians than sectional unity and securing segregationists' votes. In addition, exploiting foreign resources became more important for northern tycoons than exploiting southern resources. Cold War considerations and burgeoning activism suddenly forced civil rights onto the national agenda. But, of course, a recounting of these economic and political considerations was not the race relations story—or the history—that the Truman administration wanted consumed. Race relations, as Gunnar Myrdal wrote, were moral problems in need of morally based, persuasive solutions.[13]

In October 1947, Truman's Committee on Civil Rights issued its 178-page report, *To Secure These Rights*. The commission praised Myrdal's *An American Dilemma*, condemned the "moral dry rot" at the heart of America, and recommended civil rights legislation. "Our domestic civil rights shortcomings are a serious obstacle" in US foreign policy, the commission stated, using the now acting secretary of state Dean Acheson as a source. But Gallop pollsters found that only 6 percent of White Americans thought these rights should be secured immediately—only 6 percent, apparently, were antiracist in 1947.[14]

On February 2, 1948, Truman urged Congress to implement the recommendations of the President's Committee on Civil Rights, regardless of the lack of support among White Americans. "[The] position of the United States in the world today" made civil rights "especially urgent," Truman stressed. The backlash was significant. One Texas representative kicked off his winning US Senate campaign by rallying 10,000 supporters in Austin to view Truman's civil rights proposals as "a farce and a sham—an effort to set up a police state in the guise of liberty." Lyndon Baines Johnson did not, however, join the "Dixiecrats" who bolted from the Democratic Party on account of Truman's civil rights agenda. The Dixiecrats ran South Carolina's Strom Thurmond for president on a segregationist platform that read eerily like South Africa's apartheid Nationalist Party, which rose to power in 1948.[15]

Thanks in part to the support of Black voters, President Truman defeated both Thurmond and the runaway favorite, Republican Thomas E. Dewey, in the election that year. In voting for him, Black voters and civil rights activists were especially pleased with Truman's use of executive power in 1948 to desegregate the armed forces and the federal workforce. Civil rights activists had other reasons to be hopeful that year. Jackie Robinson desegregated Major League Baseball, and around the same time, the National Football League and the National Basketball Association were also desegregated. For decades thereafter, Black baseball, football, and basketball professionals were routinely steered into positions that took advantage of their so-called natural animal-like speed and strength (apparently, nonathletic Black folk were not really Black).[16]

Civil rights activists were also pleased when Truman's Justice Department filed a brief for *Shelley v. Kramer*. The case was decided on May 3, 1948, with the Supreme Court holding that the courts could not enforce all those Whites-only real estate covenants proliferating in northern cities to keep out migrants and stop housing desegregation. "The United States has been embarrassed in the conduct of foreign relations by acts of discrimination taking place in this country," the Justice Department's brief stated. It was the first time the US government had intervened in a case to vindicate Black civil rights. It would not be the last. Truman's Justice Department filed similar briefs for other successful desegregation cases in higher education during the 1940s and early 1950s, ever reminding the justices of the foreign implications of discrimination.[17]

The *Shelley v. Kraemer* decision was hardly popular. In 1942, 84 percent of White Americans told pollsters they desired separate Black sections in their towns. They apparently had little problem with the overcrowded conditions in those Black neighborhoods. But the 1948 decision did galvanize the open housing movement—and open the floodgates of White opposition to desegregation—in cities all over the postwar United States. The open housing movement featured a motley collection of folks. There were upwardly mobile Blacks and antiracist housing activists struggling for better housing options. There were racist Blacks who hated living in neighborhoods with inferior Black folks and dreamed of living next to superior White folks. And there were assimilationists who believed that integrated neighborhoods could facilitate uplift suasion, improve race relations, and solve the nation's racial problems. White real estate agents and speculators exploited everyone's racist ideas through blockbusting—the practice of convincing White owners to sell their homes at a reduced price, out of the fear that property values were on the verge of a steep drop due to Blacks moving in, only to resell at above-market value to Black buyers eager for better housing stock. Real estate agents and speculators easily scared White owners about the consequences of Blacks moving in, warning of "an immediate rise in crime and violence . . . of vice, of prostitution, of gambling and dope," as Detroit's most famous anti-open-housing activist put it. White neighborhoods became interracial and ended up almost all Black, and the changing demographics from White to Black quickly led to worsening conceptions of the same neighborhood. (By the end of the twentieth century, the opposite was occurring as Whites "gentrified" Black urban neighborhoods. Black neighborhoods became interracial and eventually ended up almost all White, with the changing demographics from Black to White quickly leading to improved conceptions of the same neighborhood. Apparently, the sight of White people marked a good neighborhood, whereas the sight of Black people in the same place marked a bad one, thus demonstrating the power of racist ideas.)[18]

When racist ideas and policies did not keep Blacks out, urban Whites sometimes turned to violence in the 1940s, 1950s, and 1960s. However, most urban Whites preferred "flight over fight." Real estate agents, speculators, and developers benefited, selling fleeing Whites new suburban homes. America experienced an unprecedented post-war boom in residential and new highway construction as White families moved to the suburbs and had to commute farther to their jobs. To buy new homes, Americans used wartime savings and the benefits of the GI Bill, passed in 1944. It was the most wide-ranging set of welfare benefits ever offered by the federal government in a single bill. More than 200,000 war veterans used the bill's benefits to buy a farm or start a business; 5 million purchased new homes; and almost 10 million went to college. Between 1944 and 1971, federal spending for former soldiers in this "model welfare system" totaled over $95 billion. As with the New Deal welfare programs, however, Black veterans faced discrimination that reduced or denied them the benefits. Combined with the New Deal and suburban housing construction (in developments that found legal ways to keep Blacks out), the GI Bill gave birth to the White middle class and widened the economic gap between the races, a growing disparity racists blamed on poor Black fiscal habits.[19]

While urban Black neighborhoods in postwar America became the national symbol of poverty and crime, the suburban White neighborhoods, containing the suburban White houses, wrapped by white picket fences, lodging happy White families, became the national symbol of prosperity and safety. All of the assimilationist chatter in the media, in science, and in popular culture hardly reined in the segregationist backlash to the open housing movement, but it did do wonders uniting historically oppressed European ethnic groups in White suburbia. Ethnic enclaves in cities transfigured into multiethnic suburbs, the land where the Italians, Jews, Irish, and other non-Nordics finally received the full privileges of Whiteness. "Neither religion nor ethnicity separated us at school or in the neighborhood," remembered Karen Brodkin, a University of California at Los Angeles anthropologist whose Jewish family moved to Long Island, New York, in 1949.[20]

NAACP chapters lent their support to the open housing movement. But engaging in activism was like walking a tightrope in postwar America. In 1950, Wisconsin senator Joseph McCarthy started leading a witch hunt for "Communists," meaning virtually anyone critical of the dominant ideas of the day, such as capitalism, America's pro-colonial policy abroad, northern assimilation, and southern segregation. Walter White and his right-hand man Roy Wilkins had to keep the NAACP's legal activism and uplift suasion carefully within the status quo of anti-communism and assimilation. "The Negro wants change in order that he may be brought in line with the American standard," Wilkins wrote in *The Crisis* in December 1951. Meanwhile, antiracists and socialists, and certainly antiracist socialists, were being threatened, fired, arrested, and jailed on trumped-up charges. An eighty-two-year-old Du Bois was arrested (and exonerated) in 1951. The US State Department revoked Du Bois's passport, as it did Paul Robeson's, and attempted to silence the St. Louis–born Black dancer Josephine Baker in France, all to manage the freedom brand of the United States abroad.[21]

But the State Department could not stop William Patterson, chairman of the short-lived Civil Rights Congress, from slipping into Geneva in 1951 and personally delivering a petition, entitled *We Charge Genocide*, to the United Nations Committee on Human Rights. Signed by Du Bois, Paul Robeson, Trinidadian journalist Claudia Jones (founder of England's first Black newspaper), and almost one hundred others, the petition—and documentation of nearly five hundred brutal crimes against African Americans in the late 1940s—blasted the credibility of the self-identified leader of the free world. The true "test of the basic goals of a foreign policy is inherent in the manner in which a government treats its own nationals," the antiracists boomed from Switzerland to Swaziland.[22]

Scurrying into damage control, the US State Department found some anti-communist, racist, unconditionally patriotic Blacks to go on speaking tours, such as Max Yergan, who became an outspoken defender of apartheid South Africa. In 1950 or 1951, a cadre of brilliant propagandists in what became known as the United States Information Agency (USIA)—the US foreign public relations agency—drafted and circulated a pamphlet around the world entitled *The Negro in American Life*. The pamphlet acknowledged the past failings of slavery and racism and declared that there had been racial reconciliation and redemption, made possible, of course, by the power of American democracy. These branders of the New America ingeniously focused on the history of racial progress (and not the racist present) and on Black elites (and not the Black masses) as the standards of measurement for American race relations. The question was not whether America had eliminated racial disparities. That was deemed impossible—just as the elimination of slavery was once deemed impossible. The question was whether the Talented Tenth were experiencing less discrimination today than yesterday. "It is against this background that the progress which the Negro has made and the steps still needed for the full solutions of his problems must be measured," the pamphlet read. Over the past fifty years, there had emerged more Black "large landowners," successful businessmen, and college students. Activism had not driven this "tremendous pace" of racial progress, but uplift and media suasion, *The Negro in American Life* imagined, evoking the imagination of Gunnar Myrdal. While fifty years ago, "the majority of whites, northern and southern, were unabashed in their estimate of the Negro as an inferior," the growing "number of educated Negroes, and their journalists and novelists, have made the white community keenly aware of the cruel injustice of prejudice." *The Negro in American Life* declared to the world that "today, there is scarcely a community where that concept has not been drastically modified."

In fact, there was scarcely a community in the early 1950s where prejudice was not fueling cruelly unjust White campaigns against open housing, desegregated education, equal job opportunities, and civil rights. *The Negro in American Life* displayed pictures of a desegregated classroom and community that few Americans would have recognized, while admitting "much remains to be done." The pamphlet asked, given how bad things were, is it not amazing how far we've come? With every civil rights victory and failure, this line of reasoning became the standard *past-future* declaration of assimilationists: we have come a long way, and we have a ways to go. They purposefully side-stepped the *present* reality of racism.[23]

The Negro in American Life attempted to win the hearts and minds—and markets and resources—of the decolonizing non-White world. Nothing would be better for our interests in Asia than "racial harmony in America," said the US ambassador to India, Chester Bowles, at Yale in 1952. However, after the illustrious World War II general Dwight D. Eisenhower entered the White House in 1953, he discontinued the Truman Doctrine on civil rights. Racial discrimination was not a societal problem, but a failure of individual feelings, Eisenhower lectured. The solution lay not in force, but in "persuasion, honestly pressed," and "conscience, justly aroused," Eisenhower added. This pipe dream allowed the shrewd Eisenhower to conciliate northern readers of *An American Dilemma* and southern readers of *Take Your Choice*.[24]

Before Truman left office, his Justice Department had submitted a brief for yet another desegregation case before the US Supreme Court, a combined case of five NAACP lawsuits against desegregated schools in Kansas, South Carolina, Virginia, Delaware, and Washington, DC. "It is in the context of the present world struggle between freedom and tyranny that the problem of race discrimination must be viewed," the brief stated in support of desegregation. The Court heard oral arguments in *Brown v. Board of Education of Topeka* for a second time on December 8, 1953. At a White House dinner, Eisenhower invited his newly appointed chief justice, Earl Warren, and grabbed a seat next to the eminent lawyer defending the segregationists, John Davis, someone the president repeatedly praised as "a great man." On a stroll to the coffee table, Eisenhower told Warren he could understand why southerners wanted to make sure "their sweet little girls are not required to sit in school alongside some big black buck."[25]

On May 17, 1954, Chief Justice Warren, in his opinion of the Supreme Court's unanimous decision, somehow agreed with the lower court's finding that southern schools had "been equalized, or are being equalized." Thus, for the Supreme Court, *Brown v. Board of Education* was about the psychological impact of separate schools on Black children.

Warren found the answer in the social science literature, the recent explosion of studies trying to figure out why Black people had not assimilated and why the racial disparities still persisted. With the slavery-deforming-Black-people theory no longer sustainable in the early 1950s, assimilationists conjured up the segregation-deforming-Black-people theory. They cited the famous doll tests of psychologists Kenneth Clark and Mamie Clark, as well as popular books on the subject, such as *The Mark of Oppression* (1951) by two psychoanalysts. Discrimination and the separation of the races, the assimilationists argued, had been having a horrible effect on Black personalities and self-esteem.[26]

In his *Brown* opinion, Chief Justice Warren footnoted the famous doll tests as evidence of the negative impact of segregation on Black people. He felt sure enough to write, "To separate [colored children] from others of similar age and qualification solely because of their race generates a feeling of inferiority as to their status in the community that may affect their hearts and minds in a way unlikely ever to be undone." In short, "segregation of white and colored children in public schools has a detrimental effect upon the colored children." It tended to retard their "education and mental development" and deprived "them of some of the benefits they would receive in a racial[ly] integrated school system," Warren surmised. "We conclude that, in the field of public education, the doctrine of 'separate but equal' has no place. Separate educational facilities are inherently unequal."[27]

Warren essentially offered a racist opinion in this landmark case: separate *Black* educational facilities were inherently unequal and inferior because Black students were not being exposed to White students. Warren's assimilationist problem led to an assimilationist solution over the next decade to desegregate American schools: the forced busing of children from Black schools to inherently superior White schools. Rarely were White children bused to Black schools. By the 1970s, segregationist White parents from Boston to Los Angeles were opposing forced busing, spitting on reformers all types of racist vitriol, while antiracist Black parents were demanding two-way busing or the reallocation of resources from the over-resourced White schools to the under-resourced Black schools. These antiracist plans were opposed by both assimilationists and segregationists, who seemed to assume, like the Court, that majority-Black schools could never be equal to majority-White schools.

Not many Americans immediately recognized the assimilationist reasoning behind the *Brown* decision. But Zora Neale Hurston did. She was then sixty-four and living in Florida, and she was as sharp as ever despite her recent literary descent. "If there are not adequate Negro schools in Florida, and there is some residual, some inherent and unchangeable quality in white schools, impossible to duplicate anywhere else, then I am the first to insist that Negro children of Florida be allowed to share this boon," wrote Hurston in the *Orlando Sentinel*. "But if there are adequate Negro schools and prepared instructors and instructions, then there is nothing different except the presence of white people. For this reason, I regard the ruling of the U.S. Supreme Court as insulting rather than honoring my race." Calling out civil rights leaders, she framed it a contradiction in terms to scream race pride and equality while at the same time spurning "Negro teachers and self-association." Hurston's widely reprinted letter was praised by segregationists and antiracists, but sparked only ire from assimilationists.[28]

Despite its basis in racist reasoning, for many—and of course many did not actually read Warren's opinion—the effect of the landmark decision overturning *Plessy v. Ferguson* honored Black people. "I have seen the impossible happen," wrote W. E. B. Du Bois. USIA propagandists were as elated as Black folk. Within an hour of the announcement, the Voice of America broadcast the news to Eastern Europe. Press releases were drawn up in multiple languages. The decision "falls appropriately within the Eisenhower Administration's many-frontal attack on global communism," the Republican National Committee had to state on May 21, 1954, since Eisenhower refused to endorse *Brown*.

In the Jim Crow South, Mississippi senator James Eastland vowed—rallying the troops—that the South "will not abide by or obey this legislative decision by a political court." And the segregationist resistance came so fast and so strong that when it came time for the Supreme Court to implement the *Brown* decision in 1955, for the first time in US history, the Court ended up vindicating a constitutional right and then "deferr[ing] its exercise for a more convenient time," sending Du Bois and other activists into a rage. Still, southern segregationists closed ranks and organized "massive resistance" through violence and racist ideas. Apparently, they cared more about defending their separate-but-equal brand before America than defending the American-freedom brand before the world.[29]

CHAPTER 29

Massive Resistance

THE MOST NOTORIOUS victim of what was to be called "massive resistance" to desegregation was fourteen-year-old Emmett Till on August 28, 1955. For hissing at a Mississippi White woman, hooligans beat Till so ruthlessly that his face was unrecognizable during his open casket funeral in his native Chicago. The gruesome pictures were shown around the enraged Black world. On March 12, 1956, nineteen US senators and seventy-seven House representatives signed a southern manifesto opposing the *Brown v. Board of Education* decision for planting "hatred and suspicion where there has been heretofore friendship and understanding." The Klan fielded new members, and elite segregationists founded White citizens councils. Southern schools ensured that their textbooks gave students "bedtime" stories, as historian C. Vann Woodward called them, that read like *Gone with the Wind*.

But the civil rights movement kept coming. W. E. B. Du Bois was stunned watching the unfolding Montgomery Bus Boycott during the 1956 election year. It was not the boycott's initial mobilizer, Alabama State College professor Jo Ann Robinson, nor the boycott's drivers, those walking Black female domestics, who surprised him. Any serious history student of Black activism knew that Black women were regularly driving forces. Du Bois was stunned by the twenty-seven-year-old figurehead of the boycott. A Baptist preacher as a radical activist? Du Bois had never thought his eighty-eight-year-old eyes would see a preacher like Martin Luther King Jr. Du Bois sent a message of encouragement, and King sent a grateful reply. King had read Du Bois's books, and he later characterized him as "an intellectual giant" who saw through the "poisonous fog of lies that depicted [Black people] as inferior." Du Bois also sent a proclamation to the Indian journal *Gandhi Marg*. King—in his strident commitment to nonviolent civil disobedience—could be the American Mahatma Gandhi.[1]

King's other favorite scholar penned the most controversial Black book of 1957, possibly of the entire decade. The gender racism of E. Franklin Frazier in *Black Bourgeoisie*, depicting White women as more beautiful and sophisticated than Black women, Black wives as domineering, and Black husbands as "impotent physically and socially," was as manifest as his historical racism. "Slavery was a cruel and barbaric system that annihilated the negro as a person," Frazier said. This theory resembled the racist thesis of historian Stanley Elkins in his smash hit *Slavery: A Problem in American Institutional and Intellectual Life* (1959). And yet Frazier had overcome his cultural racism. The popular social science literature about the psychological effects of discrimination that molded the *Brown* decision had remolded Frazier's old ideas of assimilation as psychological progress, and he now believed in assimilation as regression. No group of Black people held more firmly to assimilationist ideas, Frazier argued, than the Black bourgeoisie, who tried to "slough off everything . . . reminiscent of its Negro origin."[2]

Frazier sounded like the ministers of Elijah Muhammad's quickly growing Chicago-based Nation of Islam (NOI) in the late 1950s. "They won't let you be White and you don't want to be Black," the son of Garveyites, former convict, and the NOI's new Harlem minister liked to say. "You don't want to be African and you can't be an American. . . . You in bad shape!" CBS's Mike Wallace brought Malcolm X and the NOI to the attention of millions in the 1959 sensational five-part television series entitled *The Hate That Hate Produced: A Study of the Rise of Black Racism and Black Supremacy*. Elijah Muhammad and his ministers opposed assimilationists; instead, they preached racial separation (not Black supremacy), arguing that Whites were an inferior race of devils. Ironically, Black and White assimilationists, clothed in racism and hate for everything Black, condemned the Nation of Islam for donning racism and hate for everything White.[3]

In *Black Bourgeoisie*, Frazier delivered the most withering attack on the Black middle class in the history of American letters, commercializing a new class racism: the Black bourgeoisie as inferior to the White bourgeoisie, as more socially irresponsible, as bigger conspicuous consumers, as more politically corrupt, as more exploitative, and as sillier in their "politics of respectability," to use historian Evelyn Brooks Higginbotham's recent term. Despite, or rather because of, Frazier's overreach into class racism, *Black Bourgeoisie* had a significant effect on the civil rights movement, galvanizing Martin Luther King's generation of middle-class youngsters to break away from what Frazier termed their apathetic "world of make-believe."[4]

And this powerful force of youthful courage, growing more powerful by the day, was needed to resist the segregationist massive resistance that seemed to grow more massive with each passing day. Segregationists had stripped the Civil Rights Act of 1957 of its enforcement powers, making it practically a dead letter when it passed on August 29, 1957. On September 4, Arkansas governor Orval Faubus deployed the National Guard to block the Little Rock Nine from desegregating Central High School, defying a federal court order. With the globally circulating sights and sounds of government troops defending howling segregationist mobs, Little Rock harmed the American freedom brand.

"Our enemies are gloating over this incident," Eisenhower wailed in a nationally televised speech, "and using it everywhere to misrepresent our whole nation." Eisenhower and his aides agonized for two weeks, seeking solutions that could keep both his political image in the South and the American image abroad intact, to no avail. On September 24, in a decision he later regarded as "the most repugnant act in all his eight years in the White House," Eisenhower sent in federal troops to protect the Little Rock students as they entered the school. Some civil rights activists recognized the incredible power Cold War calculations had given them to embarrass America into desegregation. Still others believed and hoped that Gunnar Myrdal's dictum was coming true: that the civil rights movement was persuading away racist ideas.[5]

A NINETY-YEAR-OLD DU BOIS was hopeful, too, in another way. "Today, the United States is fighting world progress, progress which must be towards socialism and against colonialism," he said, speaking to seven hundred students and faculty at Howard University in April 1958. Later in the year, having gotten his passport back, Du Bois toured Eastern Europe, the Soviet Union, and Communist China, where he happily met Chairman Mao Tse-tung. When Mao started musing about the "diseased psychology" of African Americans, showing that he was attuned to the latest racist social science, Du Bois interjected. Blacks were not diseased psychologically; they lacked incomes, Du Bois explained, inciting a debate and a fusillade of questions from Mao. When Du Bois expressed some of his failures as an activist, Mao interjected. Activists only failed when they stopped struggling. "This, I gather," Mao said, "you have never done."[6]

Martin Luther King Jr. had not stopped struggling, either. But Du Bois had soured on King, deciding in late 1959 that he was not the American Gandhi after all. "Gandhi submitted [to nonviolence], but he also followed a positive [economic] program to offset his negative refusal to use violence," Du Bois said. At the time, Black critics were soundly blitzing King's philosophy of nonviolence, but some were also taking the civil rights movement figurehead to task on some of his lingering racist ideas. In 1957, King received a letter for his "Advice for the Living" column in *Ebony* magazine. "Why did God make Jesus white, when the majority of peoples in the world are non-white?" Jesus "would have been no more significant if His skin had been black," King responded. "He is no less significant because his skin was white." The nation's most famous Black preacher and activist prayed to a White Jesus? A "disturbed" reader ripped off a letter to *Ebony*. "I believe, as you do, that skin color shouldn't be important, but I don't believe Jesus was white," the reader stated. "What is the basis for your assumption that he was?" With only a basis in racist ideas, King did not respond.[7]

Du Bois and King had not let up on the pedal of struggle, and neither had college students. Four freshman at North Carolina A&T trotted into a Woolworths in Greensboro on February 1, 1960. They sat down at its restricted counter and remained until the store closed.

Within days, hundreds of students from area colleges and high schools were "sitting in." News reports of these nonviolent sit-ins flashed on screens nationally, setting off a sit-in wave to desegregate southern businesses. "Students at last to the rescue," rejoiced Du Bois, urging them on. By April, students were staging sit-ins in seventy-eight southern and border communities, and the Student Non-Violent Coordinating Committee (SNCC) had been established.[8]

If civil rights activists hoped that the attention they received would sway presidential candidates, they were disappointed. The Democratic nominee for president, a dashing Massachusetts senator, said as little about civil rights as possible, both on the campaign trail and in the first-ever televised presidential debates. John F. Kennedy excited activists by supporting the Democrats' civil rights plank, but disappointed them by naming a suspected opponent of civil rights, Texas senator Lyndon B. Johnson, as his running mate.

Kennedy and his GOP opponent, Richard Nixon, both tried not to take sides. The civil rights and massive resistance movements were stirring debates in many forums, including the scholarly and artistic communities, which in turned further stirred the civil rights and the resistance movements. An airline reservation agent in New York, who wrote fiction in her spare time, touched a chord among activists and sympathizers of the civil rights movement with a brilliantly crafted novel. Harper Lee did not expect the story of a young girl coming to terms with race relations in the South to become an instant and perennial best seller, or to win the Pulitzer Prize for Fiction in 1961. *To Kill a Mockingbird*—about a White lawyer defending a Black man wrongly accused of raping a White woman—became the *Uncle Tom's Cabin* of the civil rights movement, rousing millions of readers for the racial struggle through the amazing power of racist ideas. The novel's most famous homily, hailed for its antiracism, in fact signified the novel's underlying racism. "'Mockingbirds don't do one thing but make music for us to enjoy," a neighbor tells the lawyer's strong-willed daughter, Scout. "That's why it's a sin to kill a mockingbird." The mockingbird is a metaphor for African Americans. Though the novel was set in the 1930s, the teeming Black activism of that era was absent

from *To Kill a Mockingbird*. African Americans come across as spectators, waiting and hoping and singing for a White savior, and thankful
for the moral heroism of lawyer Atticus Finch. There had been no
more popular racist relic of the enslavement period than the notion
that Black people must rely on Whites to bring them their freedom.[9]

Civil rights activists waging sit-ins were hardly waiting on White
saviors. Then again, many of these students were expecting their
noble campaigns of nonviolent resistance to touch the moral conscience of White Americans, who in turn would save southern Blacks
from segregationist policies. That strategy sapped W. E. B. Du Bois's
pleasure with the civil rights movement. And activists desegregating southern businesses that low-income Blacks could hardly afford
did not seem like racial progress to Du Bois, who refused to measure
racial progress by the gains of Black elites. Du Bois had been waiting
for a political-economic program to arise. He had been waiting for
something like scholar Michael Harrington's shocking anti-poverty
best seller in 1962, *The Other America*. "A wall of prejudice is erected to
keep the Negroes out of advancement," Harrington wrote. "The more
education a Negro has, the more economic discrimination he faces."
Harrington used statistics to show that uplift suasion did not work.
Moreover, he pointed out that "the laws against color can be removed,
but that will leave the poverty that is the historic and institutionalized
consequence of color." By the time Harrington tossed a war on poverty onto the Democrats' agenda, Du Bois had left the country.[10]

On February 15, 1961, a few days short of his ninety-third birthday,
Du Bois received a note from President Kwame Nkrumah informing
him that the Ghana Academy of Learning would financially support
his long-desired *Encyclopedia Africana*. By the year's end, Du Bois had
arrived in Ghana. But within a few months, he suffered a prostrate
infection. Nkrumah later came to Du Bois's home for his ninety-fourth
birthday dinner in 1962. When Nkrumah rose to depart, Du Bois
reached for the president's hand and warmly thanked him for making
a way for him to end his years on African soil. Du Bois turned somber.
"I failed you—my strength gave out before I could carry out our plans

for the encyclopedia. Forgive an old man," said Du Bois. Nkrumah refused. Du Bois insisted. Du Bois's smile broke the somber silence, and Nkrumah departed in tears.[11]

IT WAS LEADERS of decolonized nations like Kwame Nkrumah, who were friendly to the Soviet Union and critical of American capitalism and racism, that US diplomats were trying to attract (if not undermine). But the viciously violent southern response to civil rights protests was embarrassing the United States around the non-White world. In 1961, President John F. Kennedy tried to shift the movement's energy from the humiliating direct-action protests to voter registration. He also established the Peace Corps, reportedly to "show skeptical observers from the new nations that Americans were not monsters." Northern universities were trying to show that they were not monsters, either, by gradually opening their doors to Black students. Down south, the Kennedy administration sent in troops to desegregate the University of Mississippi, receiving applause from the international community that was not lost on JFK.[12]

MOST AMERICANS DID not consider assimilationists to be racists. They did not consider northern segregation and racial disparities to be indicative of racist policies, and the avalanche of antiracist protests for jobs, housing, education, and justice from Boston to Los Angeles in 1963 hardly changed their views on the matter. The eyes of the nation, the world, and American history remained on the supposedly really racist region, the South. On January 14, 1963, George Wallace was inaugurated as the forty-fifth governor of Alabama. He had opposed the Klan as a politician and judge until he had lost to the Klan-endorsed candidate in the 1958 gubernatorial election. "Well boys," Wallace said to supporters after the defeat, "no other son-of-a-bitch will ever outnigger me again." Wallace joined the secret fraternity of ambitious politicians who adopted the popular racist rhetoric that they probably did not believe in private.[13]

The *New York Times, Time, Newsweek,* the major television stations, and a host of other media outlets came to cover what reporters expected to be a nastily polarizing speech. George Wallace did not disappoint, showing off his new public ideology. "It is very appropriate that from this cradle of the Confederacy, this very heart of the great Anglo-Saxon Southland, that today we sound the drum for freedom as have our generations of forebears before us time and again down through history," he said. He was sounding one of the two time-worn American freedom drums: not the one calling for freedom from oppression, but the one demanding freedom to oppress. "In the name of the greatest people that have ever trod this earth," he intoned, " . . . I say segregation now, segregation tomorrow, segregation forever."[14]

Wallace became the face of American racism, when he should have been rendered only as the face of segregation. Harper Lee should have reigned as the face of assimilation in the literary world, while sociologists Nathan Glazer and Daniel Patrick Moynihan should have reigned as the faces of assimilation in the scholarly world. In 1963, they published their best-selling book, *Beyond the Melting Pot: The Negroes, Puerto Ricans, Jews, Italians, and Irish of New York City.* Pulitzer Prize–winning Harvard historian Oscar Handlin, in his *New York Times* review of the book, hailed its treatment of Negroes as an "excellent" and "much-needed corrective to many loose generalizations." This assessment typified the wild affirmations the book received from northern academics.[15]

Native New Yorkers trained in postwar assimilationist social science, Glazer and Moynihan met one another while working in the Kennedy administration on poverty issues. *Beyond the Melting Pot* propagated a ladder of ethnic racism—that is, a hierarchy of ethnic groups within the racial hierarchy—situating the hard-working and intelligent Jews over the Irish, Italians, and Puerto Ricans, and West Indian migrants over the "Southern Negro" because of West Indians' emphasis on "saving, hard work, investment, [and] education." Glazer penned the chapter on the Negro, saying that "the period of protest" must be succeeded by "a period of self-examination and self-help." He claimed that "prejudice, low income, [and] poor education only explain so much" about "the problems that afflict so many Negroes." As an assimilationist, Glazer, citing Frazier, attributed the problems to both discrimination and Black inferiority, particularly the "weak" Black family, the "most serious heritage" of slavery. From historical racism, Glazer turned to the class racism of Frazier's *Black Bourgeoisie*. Unlike the other middle classes, "the Negro middle class contributes very little . . . to the solution of Negro social problems," he wrote. And from historical racism and class racism, he turned to cultural racism and political racism to explain why problems persisted in the Black community. "The Negro," he said, "is only an American, and nothing else. He has no values and culture to guard and protect." He criticized the Negro for insisting "that the white world deal with his problems because, he is so much the product of America." In Glazer's vivid imagination, the Negro insisted that "they are not *his* problems, but everyone's." And this, he said, was "the key to much in the Negro world," that Blacks were not taking enough responsibility for their own problems.[16]

Ironically, the actual "key to much in the Negro world" may have been the very opposite of Glazer's formulation—the Negro may have been taking too *much* responsibility for the Negro's problems, and therefore not doing enough to force the "white world" to end the discriminatory sources of the problems. Elite Blacks, raised on the strategy of uplift suasion and its racist conviction that every Negro represented the race—and therefore that the behavior of every single Black person was partially (or totally) responsible for racist ideas—had long policed each other. They had also policed the masses and the media portrayals of Blacks in their efforts to ensure that every single Black person presented herself or himself admirably before White Americans. They operated on the assumption that every single action before White America either confirmed or defied stereotypes, either helped or harmed the Negro race.

Beyond the Melting Pot saluted the leadership of the National Urban League, the NAACP, and the Congress of Racial Equality (CORE) for their lobbying and legal activism. Glazer and Moynihan neither saluted nor mentioned the many local groups that were fiercely confronting segregationists in the streets in 1963. Nor did they mention the youngsters of the Student Non-Violent Coordinating Committee in Mississippi, Malcolm X in Harlem, or Martin Luther King Jr.

On April 3, 1963, King helped kick off a spate of demonstrations in Birmingham, bringing on the wrath of the city's ruggedly segregationist police chief, "Bull" Conner. Nine days later, on Good Friday, eight White anti-segregationist Alabama clergymen signed a public statement requesting that these "unwise and untimely" street demonstrations cease and be "pressed in the courts." Martin Luther King Jr., jailed that same day, read the statement from his cell. Incited, he started doing something he rarely did. He responded to critics in his "Letter from the Birmingham Jail," published far and wide that summer. King attacked not only those Alabama preachers, but also the applauding audience of *Beyond the Melting Pot*. He confessed that he had "almost reached the regrettable conclusion that the Negro's great stumbling block in his stride toward freedom" was not the segregationist, "but the white moderate . . . who constantly says: 'I agree with you in the goal you seek, but I cannot agree with your methods of direct action'; who paternalistically believes he can set the timetable for another man's freedom." King explained that "injustice anywhere is a threat to justice everywhere."[17]

No one knows whether the sickly W. E. B. Du Bois read King's jail-house letter. But just as Du Bois had done in 1903, and later regretted, in his letter King erroneously conflated two opposing groups: the anti-racists who hated racial discrimination, and the Black separatists who hated White people (in groups like the Nation of Islam). King later distanced himself from both, speaking to a growing split within the civil rights movement. More and more battle-worn young activists had grown critical of King's nonviolence and disliked the pains he took to persuade away the racist ideas of Whites. More and more, they were listening to Malcolm X's sermons about self-defense, about persuading away the assimilationist ideas of Blacks, about mobilizing antiracists to force change. On May 3, 1963, these young people watched on television as Bull Connor's vicious bloodhounds ripped the children and teenagers of Black Birmingham to pieces; as his fire hoses broke limbs, blew clothes off bodies, and slammed bodies into storefronts; and as his officers clubbed marchers with nightsticks.

The world watched, too, and the United States Information Agency reported back to Washington about the "growing adverse local reactions" around the world to the "damaging pictures of dogs and fire hoses." Kennedy met with his top advisers to discuss this "matter of national and international concern." He dispatched an aide, Burke Marshall, to Birmingham to help negotiate the desegregation accord that stopped the protests. Kennedy also sent soldiers to ensure safety for the desegregation of the University of Alabama on May 21, 1963. Governor George Wallace put on a show for his voters, standing in the schoolhouse door, admonishing the "unwelcome, unwanted and force-induced intrusion . . . of the central government."

State Department officials had to put in overtime when agitated African leaders critical of the United States met in Ethiopia on May 22, 1963, to form the Organization of African Unity. Secretary of State Dean Rusk sent out a circular to American diplomats assuring them that Kennedy was "keenly aware of [the] impact of [the] domestic race problem on [the] US image overseas and on achievement [of] US foreign policy objectives." Rusk said Kennedy would take "decisive action."

On June 11, John F. Kennedy addressed the nation—or the world, rather—and summoned Congress to pass civil rights legislation. "Today we are committed to a worldwide struggle to promote and protect the rights of all who wish to be free," Kennedy said. "We preach freedom around the world, and we mean it." The eyes of the nation and the world turned to Washington's legislators, who kept their eyes on the world. When the new civil rights bill came before the Senate Commerce Committee, Kennedy asked Secretary of State Rusk to lead off the discussion. Racial discrimination had "had a profound impact on the world's view of the United States and, therefore, on our foreign relations," testified Rusk. Non-White newly independent peoples were "determined," he said, "to eradicate every vestige of the notion that the white race is superior or entitled to special privileges because of race." By August 1963, 78 percent of White Americans believed that racial discrimination had harmed the US reputation abroad. But not many inside (or outside) of the Kennedy administration were willing to admit that the growing groundswell of support in Washington for strong civil rights legislation had more to do with winning the Cold War in Africa and Asia than with helping African Americans. Southern segregationists cited those foreign interests in their opposition. South Carolina senator Strom Thurmond refused "to act on some particular measure, because of the threat of Communist propaganda if we don't," as he fired at Rusk.[18]

Kennedy's introduction of civil rights legislation did not stop the momentum of the long-awaited March on Washington for Jobs and Freedom. Though it had been organized by civil rights groups, the Kennedy administration controlled the event, ruling out civil disobedience. Kennedy aides approved the speakers and speeches, a lineup that did not include a single Black woman, or James Baldwin or Malcolm X. On August 28, approximately 250,000 activists and reporters from around the world marched to the area between the Lincoln Memorial and the Washington Monument. Before Kennedy officials happily read the USIA's report saying that numerous foreign newspapers contrasted the opportunity to march that had been "granted by a free society" with "the despotic suppression practiced by the USSR," and before King ended the round of approved speeches with his rousing and indelible antiracist dream of children one day living "in a nation where they will not be judged by the color of their skin, but by the content of their character," and before Mahalia Jackson sang into the blazing throng of approved placards and television cameras, the NAACP's Roy Wilkins came as the bearer of sad news.

W. E. B. Du Bois had died in his sleep the previous day in Ghana, Wilkins announced. "Regardless of the fact that in his later years Dr. Du Bois chose another path," Wilkins intoned, "it is incontrovertible that at the dawn of the twentieth century his was the voice calling you to gather here today in this cause." The well-trained journalist at the helm of the NAACP reported the truth. Indeed, the younger Du Bois had called for such a gathering, hoping it would persuade and endear millions to the lowly souls of Black folk. And yes, the older

Du Bois had chosen another path—the antiracist path less traveled—toward forcing millions to accept the equal souls of Black folk. It was the path of civil disobedience that the young marchers in the SNCC and CORE had desired for the March *on* Washington, a path a young woman from Birmingham's Dynamite Hill was already marching upon and would never leave. Roy Wilkins did not dwell on the different paths. Looking out at the lively March on Washington, he solemnly asked for a moment of silence to honor the ninety-five-year movement of a man.[19]

PART V

Angela Davis

CHAPTER 30

The Act of Civil Rights

SUMMER TOURISTS HAD already left the gaudy beachside casinos in Biarritz by the time she arrived for her Junior Year in France Program. She had come a long way from her hometown of Birmingham and her Brandeis University campus outside of Boston. On September 16, 1963, Angela Davis walked with classmates in Biarritz and skimmed a *Herald Tribune*. She noticed a headline about four girls dying from a church bombing. It did not hit her at first. Then, suddenly, it registered. She stopped, closing her eyes in disbelief as her puzzled companions looked on. She pointed to the article. "I know them," she spluttered out. "They're my friends." Avoiding her classmates and their perfunctory condolences, Davis kept staring at the familiar names in sadness and rage. Cynthia Wesley. Carole Robertson. Carol Denise McNair. Addie Mae Collins.

The only deceased girl Angela Davis did not know personally was Addie Mae. Angela's mother, Sallye, had taught Denise in the first grade. The Robertson and Davis families had been close friends as long as she could remember. The Wesleys lived around the block in the hilly Birmingham neighborhood where Angela grew up.[1]

Angela had been four years old when her parents, Sallye and B. Frank Davis, had desegregated that neighborhood in 1948. White families began moving out as Black families moved in. Some stayed and violently resisted. Because of White resisters' bombing of Black homes, the neighborhood was often called "Dynamite Hill."

But the bombings did not deter Angela's parents, especially her mother. Sallye Davis had been a leader in the Southern Negro Youth

Congress, an antiracist Marxist organization that protested against economic exploitation and racial discrimination in the late 1930s and 1940s, drawing the admiration of W. E. B. Du Bois. On Dynamite Hill, Sallye and her husband nurtured Angela on a steady diet of anticapitalist and antiracist ideas. And so, when Angela started the first grade, she was struck by the inequities at lunchtime: hungry children without enough food had to sit there and watch other children eat. Like her mother, she gave to the hungry children. She grew up detesting the poverty all around her. And she grew up detesting the poverty of the assimilationist ideas all around her, deciding, "very early, that I would never—and I was categorical about this—never harbor or express the desire to be white."[2]

She ventured north in the fall of 1959 to attend an integrated high school in Manhattan, where her history teachers nurtured her to socialism. She joined a youth organization, called "Advance," and picketed a Woolworths in solidarity with the rash of southern sit-ins in the spring of 1960. Davis stayed in the North for college, enrolling as one of the few Black students at Brandeis University in 1961. She wanted to continue her activism, but Brandeis's White campus activists alienated her. "It seemed as if they were determined to help the 'poor, wretched Negroes' become equal to them, and I simply didn't think they were worth becoming equal to," she remembered.[3]

Davis found other outlets. She attended the Eighth World Festival for Youth and Students in Helsinki, Finland, in the summer of 1962. When one of her favorite authors came for a lecture at Brandeis in October 1962, Davis captured a front-row seat. James Baldwin was nearing the publication of his luminous 1963 book for activists critical of the civil rights movement's integrationist, persuasion, and nonviolent thrusts. He titled the manifesto *The Fire Next Time*, with an epigraph quoting an African American spiritual to put the title in context: "God gave Noah the rainbow sign, / No more water, the fire next time!"[4]

News of the Cuban missile crisis prematurely ended Baldwin's lecture. But later he gave a powerful speech at a hastily organized antiwar rally on Brandeis's campus. Davis was there listening intently to Baldwin—and then to Brandeis's sophisticated Marxist philosopher, who would become her intellectual mentor and who was fast becoming the intellectual mentor of the rapidly organizing "New Left": Herbert Marcuse. Davis listened intently again when yet another towering mentor of 1960s youth came to speak at Brandeis. Davis could not relate to Malcolm X's religious deprecations of Whites. But she "was fascinated," she later said, "by his description of the way Black people had internalized the racial inferiority thrust upon us by a white supremacist society."[5]

By her junior year, Davis had gone to study in France, only to be thrust tragically back to Dynamite Hill by the murder of those four girls. Davis did not view the Birmingham church bombing on September 15, 1963, as an isolated incident carried out by southern White extremists. "It was this spectacular, violent event, the savage dismembering of four little girls, which has burst out of the daily, sometimes even dull, routine of racist oppression," in Davis's words. But Davis's classmates in France—indoctrinated by the mythology of the antiracist North and racist South—refused to accept her persisting analysis of "why the whole ruling stratum in their country, by being guilty of racism, was also guilty of this murder."[6]

The nineteen-year-old Angela Davis was hardly alone in the world in her analysis of American race relations. The Birmingham murders signified the massive resistance to the civil rights movement and the naked ugliness of American racism. As the brutality turned negative eyes to the United States in the decolonizing world, the stakes were raised for civil rights legislation to reassure the American freedom brand, forcing Kennedy's hand. President Kennedy announced his "deep sense of outrage and grief" over the Birmingham bombing. He launched an investigation, which caused his southern approval ratings to dip. Kennedy tried to boost his ratings two weeks later on a trip to Dallas. He never made it back to Washington.[7]

On November 27, 1963, two days after JFK's burial, the thirty-sixth president of the United States buried any lingering global fears that civil rights legislation had died with Kennedy. "No memorial oration or eulogy could more eloquently honor President Kennedy's memory than the earliest possible passage of the civil rights bill for which he fought so long," declared Lyndon Baines Johnson to Congress. Civil rights had hardly topped Kennedy's agenda, but activists and diplomats felt relieved.[8]

On March 26, 1964, Martin Luther King Jr. and Malcolm X came to watch the debate over the civil rights bill, meeting for the first and only known time at the US Capitol. Malcolm had recently been pushed out of the corrupted Nation of Islam. When he left Washington, he started warning American racists of the "ballot or the bullet." At a church in Detroit on April 12, 1964, Malcolm offered his plan for the ballot instead of the bullet: going before the United Nations to charge the United States with violating the human rights of African Americans. "Now you tell me how can the plight of everybody on this Earth reach the halls of the United Nations," Malcolm said, his voice rising, "and you have twenty-two million Afro-Americans whose churches are being bombed, whose little girls are being murdered, whose leaders are being shot down in broad daylight!" And America still had "the audacity or the nerve to stand up and represent himself as the leader of the free world . . . with the blood of your and mine mothers and fathers on his hands—with the blood dripping down his jaws like a bloody-jawed wolf."[9]

THE DAY AFTER the Detroit speech, Malcolm, who was Muslim, boarded a plane and embarked on his obligatory hajj to Mecca. After a lifetime in the theater of American racism that began with the lynching of his father, Malcolm X on this trip saw for the first time "all colors, from blue-eyed blonds to black-skinned Africans," interacting as equals. The experience changed him. "The true Islam has shown me that a blanket indictment of all white people is as wrong as when whites make blanket indictments against blacks," he said. From then on, he took on the racist wolves and devils, no matter their skin color. Though American media outlets reported his change, the narrative of Malcolm X as hating White people endured.[10]

Malcolm returned to the States on May 21 in the middle of the longest filibuster in the Senate's history—fifty-seven days. The senators who drove the filibuster were trying to stop the Civil Rights Act of 1964. Behind the scenes, supporters of the act agreed on outlawing future discrimination, but disagreed on what to do about past discrimination. Antiracists requested that the act's fair employment provisions eliminate the established seniority rights of White workers. Assimilationists balked at the idea, while segregationists tried to make the request into a wedge issue. Segregationists knew White Americans were commonly refusing to acknowledge the accumulated gains of past discrimination—and nothing signified those gains in the labor market better than seniority. But the bill's powerful assimilationist backers were adamant that it would not affect White seniority. "We don't think that one form of injustice can be corrected or should be corrected by creating another," AFL-CIO lawyer Thomas E. Harris said. Equating measures that healed inequities with measures that created inequities? It was as ridiculous as equating the harmful crime with the harmful punishment.[11]

Harris believed that taking away Whites' seniority "would be unjust to the white workers" who had been building seniority in their jobs for many years. However, *not* to do so would be unjust to the Negro workers who had been discriminated against for just as long. Not tackling the seniority question (and past discrimination) would be "akin to asking the Negro to enter the 100-yard dash forty yards behind the starting line," argued the general counsel for the Congress of Racial Equality (CORE), Carl Rachlin. But that was what the writers of the Civil Rights Act of 1964 were largely asking the Negro to do. And when the Negro lost the dashes and the racial disparities persisted, racists could blame the supposed slowness of the Negro, not the head starts of accumulated White privilege.[12]

And so, as much as the Civil Rights Act served to erect a dam against Jim Crow policies, it also opened the floodgates for new racist ideas to pour in, including the most racist idea to date: it was an idea that ignored the White head start, presumed that discrimination had been eliminated, presumed that equal opportunity had taken over, and figured that since Blacks were still losing the race, the racial disparities and their continued losses must be their fault. Black people must be inferior, and equalizing policies—like eliminating or reducing White seniority, or instituting affirmative action policies—would be unjust and ineffective. The Civil Rights Act of 1964 managed to bring on racial progress and progression of racism at the same time.

The most transformative verbiage of the 1964 act was the wording that legislated against clear and obvious "intention to discriminate," such as southern "Whites only" public policies. But what about those northern discriminators with private policies that had long kept Blacks out? What about those who were still blockbusting and segregating northern cities, and still creating, maintaining, and increasing racial inequities in wealth, housing, and education? If the northern backers of the act defined polices as racist by their public outcomes instead of their public intent, then they would be hard-pressed to maintain the myth of the antiracist North and the racist South. By not principally focusing on outcome, discriminators had to merely privatize their public policies to get around the Civil Rights Act. And that is precisely what they did.

Though the members of Congress were aware of these privatizing forces, they chose not to explicitly bar seemingly race-neutral policies that had discriminatory public outcomes through racial disparities. On the urgings of segregationists, in fact, Congress actually provided the means for the progression of racism. Section 703(h) of Title VII allowed employers "to give and to act upon the results of any professionally developed ability test." Though eugenicists had been discounted in mainstream America, members of Congress and their constituents had thoroughly embraced their standardized mental tests as having the capacity to assess what did not exist: general intelligence. In the job industry, in education, and in many other sectors of society, officials could justify their racial disparities by pointing to test scores and claiming they were not intending to discriminate. And to racist Americans, the racial gaps in the scores—the so-called achievement gap—said something was wrong with the Black test-takers—not the tests.[13]

The Civil Rights Act of 1964 was the first important civil rights legislation since the Civil Rights Act of 1875. It outlawed public, intentional discrimination on the basis of race, color, religion, sex, or national origin in government agencies and facilities, public accommodations, education, and employment; established a federal enforcement structure; and empowered victims of discrimination to sue and the government to withhold federal funds from violators. Hours after President Johnson signed it into law on July 2, 1964, he appeared before television cameras to play up the American "ideal of freedom" for cynics in Los Angeles and Lagos and Lhasa. "Today in far corners of distant continents," he proclaimed, "the ideals of those American patriots still shape the struggles of men who hunger for freedom."

Malcolm X had another take on the Civil Rights Act, echoing the thoughts of antiracist young minds like Angela Davis's. If the government could not enforce the existing laws, he asked the Organization of African Unity conference in 1964, "how can anyone be so naïve as to think all the additional laws brought into being by the civil-rights bill will be enforced?"[14]

THE PASSAGE OF the Civil Rights Act in 1964 hardly hurt Lyndon B. Johnson's commanding position for reelection during that election year. Johnson did face an improbable challenge for the Democratic nomination from Alabama governor George Wallace, however. After taking a public stand for segregation the year before, Wallace had received more than 100,000 approving letters, mostly from northerners. Wallace realized, as he told NBC's Douglas Kiker, "they all hate black people. . . . That's it! . . . The whole United States is southern!"[15]

During his campaign, George Wallace sounded more like the 1964 Republican nominee than LBJ. Arizona senator Barry Goldwater's nomination for president signified his star power over the escalating conservative movement in American politics, powered by his 1960 chart-topper, *The Conscience of a Conservative.* Inspiring millions of Democrats to turn Republican, including Hollywood movie star Ronald Reagan, Goldwater's tract deeply massaged those Americans who had outgrown (or never needed) government assistance. Welfare "transforms the individual from a dignified, industrious, self-reliant *spiritual* being into a dependent animal creature without his knowing it,"

Goldwater wrote without a shred of evidence. Many proud, dignified, industrious, self-reliant members of the White middle class, who had derived their wealth from the welfare of inheritance, the New Deal, or the GI Bill, accepted Goldwater's dictum as truth, despite the fact that parental or government assistance had not transformed them or their parents into dependent animal creatures. After looking at White mothers on welfare as "deserving" for decades, these Goldwater conservatives saw the growing number of Black mothers on welfare as "undeserving"—as dependent animal creatures.[16]

Barry Goldwater and his embryonic conservative movement hardly worried Johnson as he arrived on the beaches of Atlantic City for the Democratic National Convention in August 1964. But he was worried about those northern activists who had violently protested against police brutality and economic exploitation in urban summer rebellions from Harlem to Chicago. In the South, SNCC field agents had weathered Klan brutality during their "Mississippi Freedom Summer," which brought hundreds of northern college students to teach in antiracist "Freedom Schools" and assist in organizing the Mississippi Freedom Democratic Party (MFDP). The interracial MFDP came to Atlantic City and requested to be seated in place of the regular Mississippi delegation, which everyone knew had been elected through fraud and violence. The MFDP's electrifying vice chair, Fannie Lou Hamer, riveted the nation in her live televised testimony at the convention. "If the Freedom Democratic Party is not seated now, I question America. Is this America? The land of the free and the home of the brave? Where we have to sleep with our telephones off the hook, because our lives be threatened daily because we want to live as decent human beings."

President Johnson called an emergency press conference to divert the networks away from Hamer's transfixing testimony, and then later he offered the Freedom Party a "compromise": two nonvoting seats accompanying the segregationist delegation. "We didn't come all this way for no two seats!" bellowed Fannie Lou Hamer. MFDP and SNCC activists traveled home carrying a valuable lesson about power politics. Persuasion does not work. "Things could never be the same," SNCC's

Cleveland Sellers recalled. "Never again were we lulled into believing that our task was exposing injustices so that the 'good' people of America could eliminate them. . . . After Atlantic City, our struggle was not for civil rights, but for liberation." Malcolm X's empowerment philosophy of Black national and international unity, self-determination, self-defense, and cultural pride started to sound like music to the ears of the SNCC youths. At the end of 1964, Malcolm X returned from an extended trip to Africa to a growing band of SNCC admirers and a growing band of enemies.[17]

On February 21, 1965, Malcolm X was gunned down by some of those enemies at a Harlem rally. When James Baldwin heard the news in London, he was beside himself. "It is because of you," he shouted at London reporters, "the men that created this white supremacy, that this man is dead!" From his nationally watched voting registration campaign in Selma, Alabama, Martin Luther King Jr. was reflectively restrained. "While we did not always see eye to eye on methods to solve the race problem, I always had a deep affection for Malcolm and felt that he had a great ability to put his finger on the existence and root of the problem." On February 22, 1965, the *New York Times* banner headline read: "The Apostle of Hate Is Dead."[18]

Actor Ossie Davis christened Malcolm "our shining black prince" days later in his magnetic eulogy before the overflow crowd at Harlem's Faith Temple of the Church of God in Christ. "Many will say . . . he is of hate—a fanatic, a racist," Davis said. And the response would be, "Did you ever really listen to him? For if you did, you would know him. And if you knew him you would know why we must honor him."[19]

Antiracist Americans did honor him, especially after recordings and transcripts of his speeches began to circulate, and after Grove Press published *The Autobiography of Malcolm X*. Journalist Alex Haley had collaborated with Malcolm to write the autobiography, which was billed by Eliot Fremont-Smith of the *New York Times* as "a brilliant, painful, important book" upon its release in November 1965. Malcolm X's ideological transformation—from assimilationist, to anti-White separatist, to antiracist—inspired millions. Possibly no other American autobiography opened more antiracist minds than *The Autobiography of Malcolm X.* Malcolm condemned the half-truth of racial progress, bellowing that you don't stick a knife in a person's back nine inches, pull it out six inches, and say you're making progress. "The black man's supposed to be *grateful?* Why, if the white man jerked the knife *out,* it's still going to leave a *scar!*" He argued that White people were not born racist, but that "the American political, economic and social *atmosphere* . . . automatically nourishes a racist psychology in the white man." He encouraged antiracist Whites who had escaped racism to fight "on the battle lines of where America's racism really *is*—and that's in their own home communities." He ferociously attacked "the white man's puppet Negro 'leaders,'" who had exploited "their black poor brothers," and who did not want separation or integration, but only "to live in an open, free society where they can walk with their heads up, like men, and women!" But nothing was more compelling than Malcolm X's unstinting humanism: "I'm for truth, no matter who tells it. I'm for justice, no matter who it is for or against. I'm a human being first and foremost, and as such I'm for whoever and whatever benefits humanity as a whole."[20]

ANTIRACIST AMERICANS HAD some reason to hope for justice when Congress took up the voting rights bill after hundreds of marchers were bludgeoned on a bridge outside of Selma on March 7, 1965. Yet even with a voting rights bill, the United States would not be finished, President Johnson had the courage to declare in his commencement address to Howard University graduates in June. "You do not take a person who, for years, has been hobbled by chains[,] and liberate him, bring him up to the starting line of a race and then say, 'you are free to compete with all the others,' and still justly believe that you have been completely fair." It was quite possibly the most antiracist avowal ever uttered from the lips of a US president. And Johnson was just getting started. "We seek not just freedom but opportunity," he said. "We seek not just legal equity but human ability, not just equality as a right and a theory but equality as a fact and equality as a result." Racial progress had come primarily for "a growing middle class minority," while for poor Blacks, Johnson said, "the walls are rising and the gulf is widening."

In Johnson's time—in the midst of civil rights legislation—racial disparities in unemployment had grown, income disparities had grown, and disparities in poverty, in infant mortality, and in urban segregation had all grown—as he pointed out at Howard University. Why had all this happened? Johnson offered two "broad basic reasons": one anti-racist ("inherited poverty" and the "devastating" legacy of discrimination), and one racist (the devastation wrought by "the breakdown of the Negro family structure").[21]

Johnson's Howard address raised the hopes of civil rights leaders, and it delighted Johnson's assistant secretary of labor, Daniel Patrick Moynihan, whose Beyond the Melting Pot was still widely read in urban sociology. Moynihan in fact had composed Johnson's speech with the ideas still fresh in his mind from an unpublished government report he had just completed. Moynihan's "The Negro Family: The Case for National Action," which had reached Johnson's desk by May 1965, statistically demonstrated that civil rights legislation over the past ten years had not improved the living conditions of most African Americans. But then, after all these antiracist revelations about the progression of racism, Moynihan had rambled into assimilationist ideas. He argued that discrimination had forced the Negro family into "a matriarchal structure which, because it is so out of line with the rest of the American society, seriously retards the progress of the group as a whole, and imposes a crushing burden on the Negro male and, in consequence, on a great many Negro women as well." Moynihan ended up following E. Franklin Frazier—his main scholarly source—in judging female-headed families as inferior (in sexist fashion), and in judging the Black family as a "tangle of pathology" (in racist fashion). He portrayed Black men as emasculated by discrimination. And since they were overburdened from assuming their societal roles as heads of households, they were more oppressed than Black women. They needed, Moynihan pleaded, national action.[22]

On August 6, 1965, around the time the Moynihan report was leaked to the press, Johnson signed the momentous Voting Rights

392 STAMPED FROM THE BEGINNING

Act. Discriminators seeking a way around the Civil Rights Act of 1964 could have easily learned some lessons from voting discriminators, who had been hiding their intent for six or seven decades in their literacy tests, poll taxes, and grandfather clauses, which were all void of racial language. The Voting Rights Act of 1965 not only banned these seemingly race-neutral policies, which had almost totally disenfranchised southern Blacks, but also required that all changes to southern voting laws now be approved by a federal official, who would ensure that they would not "have the effect of denying or abridging the right to vote on account of race or color." The *intent-focused* Civil Rights Act of 1964 was not nearly as effective as the *outcome-focused* Voting Rights Act of 1965. In Mississippi alone, Black voter turnout increased from 6 percent in 1964 to 59 percent in 1969. The Voting Rights Act ended up becoming the most effective piece of antiracist legislation ever passed by the Congress of the United States of America. But the act was not without its loopholes. "We recognized that increased voting strength might encourage a shift in the tactics of discrimination," Attorney General Nicholas Katzenbach testified to Congress. "Once significant numbers of blacks could vote, communities could still throw up obstacles to discourage those voters or make it difficult for a black to win elective office." Katzenbach's recognition of the fact that racist policies could progress in the face of racial progress proved prophetic.[23]

CHAPTER 31

Black Power

IT DID NOT take long for the renewed progression of racism to show itself. On August 9, 1965, three days after Johnson signed the Voting Rights Act, *Newsweek* alarmed Americans by disclosing the findings of the leaked Moynihan report: "The rising rate of non-white illegitimacy," the "runaway curve in child welfare cases," and the "social roots" of the "American dilemma of race" were all from the "splintering Negro family." A photograph of Harlem kids tossing bottles contained the caption, "A time bomb ticks in the ghetto." The time bomb exploded two days later in the Watts neighborhood of Los Angeles, when a police incident set off six days of violence, the deadliest and most destructive urban rebellion in history. In its aftermath, the victimized mockingbird that had attracted so much paternalistic compassion in the past few years became the aggressive panther that needed to be controlled.[1]

As Watts burned, Angela Davis boarded a boat headed for Germany. She had come back from France, studied under philosopher Herbert Marcuse, and graduated from Brandeis. Now she was headed to Marcuse's intellectual home of Frankfurt to pursue her graduate studies in philosophy. She "felt again the tension of the Janus head—leaving the country at that time was hard for me," as she later said. But the antiracist struggle was globalizing, as she learned in France and would learn again in Germany. Shortly after she arrived, in September 1965, an international group of scholars gathered due north in Copenhagen for the Race and Colour Conference. Davis apparently did not attend. But if she had, she would have heard lectures on the racist role of language symbolism. Scholars pointed out everyday phrases like "black sheep," "blackballing," "blackmail," and "blacklisting," among others, that had long associated Blackness and negativity.[2]

The language symbolism was no less striking in two new American identifiers: "minority" and "ghetto." For centuries, racists had construed Black folk as minors to White majors, and that history could be easily loaded into their latest identifier of the supposed lesser peoples: minorities. The appellation only made sense as a numerical term, and as a numerical term, it only made sense indicating national population or power dynamics. But it quickly became a racial identifier of African Americans (and other non-Whites)—even in discussions that had nothing to do with national issues. It made no sense as another name for Black people, since most Black people lived, schooled, worked, socialized, and died in majority-Black spaces. The term only made sense from the viewpoint of Whites, who commonly related to Black people as the numerical minority in their majority-White spaces, and elite Blacks, who were more likely to exist as the numerical minority in majority-White spaces. And so, class racism—downgrading the lives of Black commoners in majority-Black spaces—became wrapped up in the term "minority," not unlike a term that psychologist Kenneth Clark had popularized after putting aside brown and light dolls.

In 1965, Clark published his seminal text, *Dark Ghetto*. The term "ghetto" was known as an identifier of the ruthlessly segregated Jewish communities in Nazi Germany. Though social scientists like Clark hoped the term would broadcast the ruthless segregation and poverty that urban Blacks faced, the word quickly assumed a racist life of its own. "Dark" and "Ghetto" would become as interchangeable in the racist mind by the end of the century as "minority" and "Black," and as interchangeable as "ghetto" and "inferior," "minority" and "inferior," "ghetto" and "low class," and "ghetto" and "unrefined." In these "dark ghettoes" lived "ghetto people" expressing "ghetto culture" who were "so ghetto"—meaning that the neighborhoods, the people, and the culture were inferior, low class, and unrefined. Class racists and some suburban Americans saw little distinction between impoverished Black urban neighborhoods, Black working-class urban neighborhoods, and Black middle-class urban neighborhoods. They were all ghettoes with dangerous Black hooligans who rioted for more welfare.[3]

On January 9, 1966, the *New York Times Magazine* contrasted these rioting "ghetto" Blacks with the "model minority": Asians. Some Asian Americans consumed the racist "model minority" title, which masked the widespread discrimination and poverty in Asian American communities and regarded Asian Americans as superior (in their assimilating prowess) to Latina/os, Native Americans, and African Americans. Antiracist Asian Americans rejected the concept of the "model minority" and fermented the Asian American movement in the late 1960s.[4]

Assimilationists were negatively loading the terms "model minority" and "ghetto" with racist associations in 1966. Meanwhile, antiracists were quickly extracting negative associations from the identifier "Black," foremost among them Stokely Carmichael. Carmichael had been born in Trinidad in 1941, and he had moved to the Bronx in 1952, the same year his idol, Malcolm X, was paroled from prison. In 1964, Carmichael graduated from Howard University. By then, Malcolm's disciples, Carmichael included, were loading the old identifier, "Negro," with accommodation and assimilation—and removing ugliness and evil from the old identifier, "Black." They were now passionately embracing the term "Black," which stunned Martin Luther King Jr.'s "Negro" disciples and their own assimilationist parents and grandparents, who would rather be called "nigger" than "Black."[5]

As the new chairman of the Student Non-Violent Coordinating Committee, Stokely Carmichael was one of the leaders of the Mississippi March Against Fear in the summer of 1966, alongside King and Floyd McKissick of the Congress of Racial Equality. The massive march careened through Mississippi towns, battling segregationist resisters, mobilizing and organizing locals, and registering the latter to vote. On June 16, 1966, the March Against Fear stopped in Greenwood, Mississippi, one of the buckles of the belt of majority Black southern counties still ruled by armed Whites. "We been saying freedom for six years and we ain't got nothing," Carmichael shouted at a Greenwood rally. "What we gonna start saying now is Black Power!"

"What do you want?" Carmichael screamed. "BLACK POWER!" the disempowered Greenville Blacks screamed back.[6]

Quickly blown by the fans of the American media, the maxim whisked through all the majority Black urban areas and rural counties that were politically controlled, economically exploited, and culturally denigrated by White assimilationists and segregationists. Antiracists, who would soon be reading Malcolm's autobiography, had been looking for a concept to wrap around their demands for Black control of Black communities. They latched onto Black Power as firmly in the North as they did in the South, and Martin Luther King Jr. learned why later in the summer. After an open housing march on August 5, 1966, through a fuming White neighborhood in Chicago, King told reporters he had "never seen as much hatred and hostility on the part of so many people."[7]

There was nothing more democratic than saying that the majority, in this case the disempowered Black majority, should rule their own local communities, should have Black power. But just as sexists could only envision male or female supremacy, northern and southern racists could only envision White or Black supremacy. And the twenty urban rebellions that ensued in the summer of 1966 only confirmed for many racists that Black Power meant Blacks violently establishing Black supremacy and slaughtering White folks. *Time*, the *Saturday Evening Post*, the *U.S. News and World Report*, the *New York Post*, and *The Progressive* are a few of the many periodicals that condemned the start of the Black Power movement.[8]

Even prominent Black leaders criticized Black Power. Roy Wilkins of the NAACP sang from the hymnal of assimilationist comebacks to antiracist ideas: he redefined the antiracist idea as segregationist and attacked his own redefinition. "No matter how endlessly they try to explain it, the term 'Black power' means anti-white power," Wilkins charged at the NAACP's annual convention on July 5, 1966. "It is a reverse Mississippi, a reverse Hitler, a reverse Ku Klux Klan." Vice President Hubert Humphrey added his two licks at the convention. "Yes, racism is racism—and there is no room in America for racism of any color." Riding the opposition to Black Power, Goldwater Republicans made substantial gains in the midterm elections of 1966.[9]

Carmichael did not stop promoting Black Power, however. He traveled around the nation in the final months of 1966 to build the movement. In October, he gave the keynote address at a Black Power conference at the University of California at Berkeley. In nearby Oakland that month, two community college students, incensed that their peers were not living up to Malcolm X's directives, had organized their own two-man Black Power conference. Huey P. Newton and Bobby Seale composed the ten-point platform for their newly founded Black Panther Party for Self Defense, demanding the "power to determine the destiny of our Black Community," "full employment," "decent housing," reparations, "an immediate end to POLICE BRUTALITY and MURDER of Black people," freedom for all Black prisoners, and "peace"— quoting Jefferson's Declaration of Independence. In the next few years, the Black Panther Party grew in chapters across the country, attracting thousands of committed and charismatic young community servants. They policed the police, provided free breakfast for children, and organized medical services and political education programs, among a series of other initiatives.[10]

The growth of the Black Panther Party and other Black Power organizations in 1967 reflected the fact that Black youngsters had realized that civil rights persuasion and lobbying tactics had failed to loosen the suffocating stranglehold of police brutalizers, tyrannical slumlords, neglectful school boards, and exploitive businessmen. But nothing reflected that realization, and that effort to release the stranglehold, more than the nearly 130 violent Black rebellions from coast to coast between March and September that year. And yet racist psychiatrists announced that these "rioters" suffered from schizophrenia, which they defined as a "Black disease" that manifested in rage. To Moynihan-Report-reading sociologists, the male rioters were raging from their emasculation. Meanwhile, racist criminologists suggested that the rioters were exuding urban Blacks' "subculture of violence," a phrase Marvin Wolfgang used in 1967 for his classic criminology textbook.[11]

A band of shrewd Goldwater politicians proclaimed that the "lazy" rioters demonstrated the need to reduce the welfare rolls and impose work requirements. But welfare mothers resisted. In September, the newly formed National Welfare Rights Association (NWRO) staged a sit-in in the chambers of the Senate Finance Committee, causing Louisiana senator Russell Long to blast the association as "Black Brood Mares, Inc." Congress still passed the first mandatory work requirement for welfare recipients.[12]

ANGELA DAVIS GREW restless in Frankfurt, Germany, reading about the surging Black Power movement, "being forced to experience it all vicariously." Davis decided to return to the United States during the summer of 1967. She arranged to finish her doctorate at the University of California at San Diego, where philosopher Herbert Marcuse was teaching after being politically muscled out of Brandeis. In late July on her way home, she stopped in London to attend the Dialectics of Liberation conference, where Marcuse and Carmichael were the featured speakers. Her natural hairstyle stood out like a signpost, and she quickly nestled in with the small Black Power contingent.[13]

When Davis arrived in southern California, she was itching to get involved in the Black Power movement. Like Black Power activists everywhere, she brought the movement to her backyard: she helped build UC San Diego's Black Student Union. That fall, wherever there were Black students, they were building BSUs or taking over student governments, requesting and demanding an antiracist and relevant education at historically Black *and* historically White colleges. "The Black student is demanding . . . a shaking, from-the-roots-up overhaul of their colleges," reported the *Chicago Defender*.[14]

In November, Davis took the short trip up to Watts to attend the Black Youth Conference. Walking into the Second Baptist Church, she noticed the colorful African fabrics on the energetic and smiling young women and men who were calling each other "sister" and "brother." It was her first real Black Power gathering in the United States. She felt exhilarated seeing Black as so beautiful.

Taking in the workshops, Davis learned that the minds of the attendees were as colorfully different as their adornments. Some activists were articulating Du Bois's old, antiracist socialism, delighting Davis. Other activists talked about their back-to-Africa, separatist, anti-White, community service, or revolutionary aspirations. Some FBI agents posing as activists aspired to collect notes and broaden the ideological fissures. Some activists aspired to ferment a cultural revolution, destroying assimilationist ideas and revitalizing African or African American culture. Black Power appealed to activists of many ideological stripes.[15]

Black Power even appealed to the face of the civil rights movement. Indeed, the civil rights movement was transforming into the Black Power movement in 1967, if not before. "No Lincolnian Emancipation Proclamation, no Johnsonian civil rights bill" could bring about complete "psychological freedom," boomed Martin Luther King Jr. at the annual convention of the Southern Christian Leadership Conference (SCLC) on August 16. The Negro must "say to himself and to the world . . . 'I'm black, but I'm black and beautiful.'" King brought on a chilling applause from SCLC activists, who waved signs that read, "Black Is Beautiful and It Is So Beautiful to Be Black."[16]

King made his way out of the good graces of assimilationist America that year. Assimilationists still wanted to keep him in the doubly conscious dreams of 1963, just as they had wanted to keep Du Bois in the doubly conscious souls of 1903. But King no longer saw any real strategic utility for the persuasion techniques that assimilationists adored, or for the desegregation efforts they championed. He now realized that desegregation had primarily benefited Black elites, leaving millions wallowing in the wrenching poverty that had led to their urban rebellions. King therefore switched gears and began planning the SCLC's Poor People's Campaign. His goal was to bring poor people to the nation's capital in order to force the federal government to pass an "economic bill of rights" committing to full employment, guaranteed income, and affordable housing, a bill that sounded eerily similar to the economic proposals on the Black Panther Party's ten-point platform.

The title of King's speech at the SCLC convention was the title of the book he released in the fall of 1967: *Where Do We Go from Here?*

"When a people are mired in oppression, they realize deliverance only when they have accumulated the power to enforce change," King wrote. "Power is not the white man's birthright; it will not be legislated for us and delivered in neat government packages." The road to lasting progress was civil disobedience, not persuasion, King maintained. He bravely critiqued the all-powerful Moynihan Report, warning about the danger that "problems will be attributed to innate Negro weaknesses and used to justify neglect and rationalize oppression." Moynihan assimilationists responded to King as firmly as they responded to segregationists, classifying the SCLC's Poor People's Campaign and King as extremist. King, they said, had become an anarchist. His own critique of antiracists as extremists and anarchists in his Birmingham Letter four years earlier had boomeranged back to hit him.

King's book seemed to complement Stokely Carmichael's coauthored *Black Power: The Politics of Liberation in America*, published shortly after *Where Do We Go from Here?* Carmichael and scholar Charles Hamilton gave innovative new names to two kinds of racism. They named and contrasted "individual racism," which assimilationists regarded as the principal problem, and which assimilationists believed could be remedied by persuasion and education; and "institutional racism," the institutional policies and collections of individual prejudices that antiracists regarded as the principal problem, and that antiracists believed only power could remedy.[17]

And White American power did not appear up to the task. On January 17, 1968, President Johnson submitted his State of the Union to Congress. Representatives and senators and their constituents were raging, raging not against discrimination, but against all the protests, whether nonviolent or violent, opposing the Vietnam War, racism, exploitation, and inequality. When Johnson thundered that "the American people have had enough of rising crime and lawlessness," the applause was deafening. After three straight summers of urban rebellions, some of those applauding the speech, both in the Capitol and around the country, actually feared that a violent Black revolution could be on the horizon. And their fears were reflected in a new blockbuster film that broke box-office records weeks after Johnson's address.[18]

When White astronauts land on a planet after a 2,000-year journey, apes enslave them. One astronaut escapes, and in one of the
iconic scenes in Hollywood history, at the end of the movie he comes
upon a rusted Statue of Liberty. The astronaut—Charlton Heston—
and the viewers realize with dismay that he is not light-years from
home, but back on Earth. *Planet of the Apes* took the place of *Tarzan* in
racist popular culture, inspiring four sequels between 1970 and 1973,
three more in the twenty-first century, a television series, and a host
of comic books, video games, and other merchandise—you name it,
the franchise produced it. While *Tarzan* put on America's screens the
racist confidence of conquering the dark world that prevailed in the
first half of the twentieth century, *Planet of the Apes* held up in full color
the racist panic during the second half of the twentieth century of the
conquered dark world rising up to enslave the White conqueror.

By 1968, both Democrats and Republicans had popularized the
call for "law and order." It became a motto for defending the Planet of
the Whites. "Law and order" rhetoric was used as a defense for police
brutality, and both the rhetoric and the brutality triggered urban
rebellions that in turn triggered more rhetoric and brutality. And no
one could explain all of this better in early 1968 than a giant of a man
and thinker and writer, the former convict turned Malcolm X disciple Eldridge Cleaver, who had become minister of information for the
Black Panther Party. "The police are the armed guardians of the social
order. The blacks are the chief domestic victims of the social order,"
Cleaver explained. "A conflict of interest exists, therefore, between the
blacks and the police."

Cleaver penned these words in what seemingly became the most
heralded literary response of the era to the mobilizing law-and-order
movement. In vividly angry, funny, disgusting, lucidly insightful
detail, Cleaver described "a black soul which has been 'colonized'" by
"an oppressive white society." Released in February 1968, 1 million
copies of *Soul on Ice* were sold in no time. The *New York Times* named the
part memoir, part social commentary one of the top ten books of the
year. *Soul on Ice* was timely and frigidly controversial. Cleaver mused
in the book on his bloodcurdling transformation from a "practice run"

rapist of Black women to an "insurrectionary" rapist of White women and finally to an optimistic human rights revolutionary. "If a man like Malcolm X could change and repudiate racism, if I myself and other former Muslims can change, if young whites can change, then there is hope for America," he concluded.

Cleaver's book became the manifesto of Black Power masculinity to redeem the tragic colonized male, whose soul was "on ice," whose being was the "Black Eunuch." The book demonstrated that Black Power masculinity had in fact accepted the racist idea of the emasculated Black man, an idea popularized by the ever-popular Moynihan Report of 1965. For all his antiracist strikes on assimilationist ideas, prisons, and policing, for all his antiracist Marxist strikes on White supremacist capitalism and the Black bourgeoisie, Cleaver's queer racism and gender racism were striking. Black homosexuals were doubly emasculated (and thus inferior to singularly emasculated White homosexuals): they were emasculated as Black men and emasculated through the "sickness" of homosexuality, Cleaver argued. In Cleaver's gender racism, the Black woman and the White man were "silent" allies; the White man placed the White woman "on a pedestal" and turned "the black woman into a strong self-reliant Amazon." And yet, Cleaver ended *Soul on Ice* with an impassioned love letter "To All Black Women, from All Black Men." "Across the naked abyss of negated masculinity, of four hundred years minus my Balls, we face each other today, my Queen," Cleaver wrote. "I have Returned from the dead."[19]

For all of his gender racism, Cleaver was still uniquely antiracist in his regal attraction to Black women, and especially to his new wife, Kathleen Cleaver, the Black Panther Party's national communications secretary. A product of a globetrotting military family, civil rights activism, and the SNCC, Kathleen was the first woman to enter the Panthers' Central Committee. To all those Black men refusing to date or appreciate Black women, and viewing White women as superior, Eldridge was unequivocal in his disdain. This new generation of Jack Johnsons were shrewdly understood by the Martinique-born psychiatrist Franz Fanon, who had married a French woman before becoming one of the godfathers of Black Power masculinity by authoring the anticolonial grenade *The Wretched of the Earth* (1961). "By loving me [the white woman] proves I am worthy of white love," Fanon wrote in *Black Skin, White Masks* (1952). "I am loved like a white man. I am a white man. . . . When my restless hands caress those white breasts, they grasp white civilization." And these Black assimilationist men—desiring to be White men, and constantly justifying that desire through imagining the wrongs of *Black* women—were quite numerous inside and outside of the Black Power movement in the late 1960s. Black men sought out White women because Black women's intense self-rejection caused them to stop seeking male attention and let themselves go, as Black psychiatrists William Grier (father of comedian David Alan Grier) and Price Cobbs argued in an influential 1968 text, *Black Rage*.[20]

Beliefs in pathological Black femininity and masculinity informed beliefs in the pathological Black family, which informed beliefs in pathological African American culture. They were like legs holding up the seat of America's racist ideas. Sociologist Andrew Billingsley was one of the first scholars to strike at those legs. His seminal study, *Black Families in White America*, broke the ground on antiracist Black family studies in 1968. He refused to analyze Black families from the criteria of White families. "Unlike Moynihan and others, we do not view the Negro as a causal nexus in a 'tangle of pathologies,' which feeds on itself," he wrote. Instead, he viewed the Black family as an "absorbing, adaptive, and amazingly resilient mechanism for the socialization of its children." Billingsley made the same case about African American culture. "To say that a people have no culture is to say that they have no common history which has shaped and taught them," Billingsley argued. "And to deny the history of a people is to deny their humanity."[21]

ON FEBRUARY 29, 1968, as Americans were reading *Soul on Ice*, the National Advisory Commission on Civil Disorders released its final report on the urban rebellions of 1967. Back in July, LBJ created the commission to answer the questions, "What happened? Why did it happen? What can be done to prevent it from happening again and again?" With the nine White and two Black investigators representing groups hostile to Black Power and touting the new status quo motto, "law and order," antiracists did not expect much from the Kerner Commission (named after its chair, Illinois governor Otto Kerner Jr.).

The conclusions of the Kerner Commission shocked the United States like the rebellions it investigated. The commission members unabashedly blamed racism for the urban rebellions. It said, "What white Americans have never fully understood—but what the Negro can never forget—is that white society is deeply implicated in the ghetto. White institutions created it, white institutions maintain it, and white society condones it." The racist mainstream media had failed America, the report concluded: "The press has too long basked in a white world looking out of it, if at all, with white men's eyes and white perspective." In the afterglow of the Civil Rights Act and the Voting Rights Act—as the United States proclaimed racial progress— the Kerner Commission proclaimed the progression of racism in its most famous passage: "Our nation is moving towards two societies, one black, one white—separate and unequal."[22]

Everyone seemed to have an opinion about the 426-page document, and it was purchased by more than 2 million Americans. Richard Nixon blasted the report for exonerating the rioters, as did the racists whom Nixon was attracting to his presidential campaign. Martin Luther King Jr., in the midst of organizing his Poor People's Campaign, christened the report "a physician's warning of approaching death, with a prescription for life." President Johnson felt that his own physicians had overblown White racism. And he was probably worried about the report's damaging effects on the half-truth of racial progress and the costs of its prescription for life. The report recommended the allocation of billions of dollars to diversify American policing, to provide new jobs, better schools, and more welfare to poor Black communities, and to eradicate housing discrimination and construct affordable, fresh, and spaced-out housing units for the millions of Black residents who had been forced to live in rat-infested and deteriorating houses and high-rise projects. Johnson and his bipartisan peers deployed the cost excuse, in the midst of more costly deployments for the hated war in Vietnam. Then again, Johnson did push through one recommendation: the creation of more police intelligence units to spy on Black Power organizations. The president created a second presidential commission on civil disorders later in the year, but this time, he selected the members more carefully. This commission recommended sharp increases in federal spending on police weapons, training, and riot preparation. Washington had no problem following through.[23]

ANGELA DAVIS SPENT the morning of April 4, 1968, at the new office of the SNCC in Los Angeles. The newly organized SNCC chapter was her new activist home as she shuffled back and forth between Los Angeles and her doctoral studies at UC San Diego. In the afternoon of April 4, she made a printing run. That evening, she heard someone scream, "Martin Luther King has been shot!" In disbelief at first, she felt an overwhelming sense of guilt when she confirmed the news. Like other Black Power activists, she had cast King aside as a harmless leader—harmless in his religious philosophy of nonviolence. "I don't think we had realized that his new notion of struggle—involving poor people of all colors, involving oppressed people throughout the world—could potentially present a greater threat to our enemy," Davis remembered. "Never would any of us have predicted that he would be struck down by an assassin's bullet." Apparently, King knew. The night before, he gave quite possibly the most bone-chilling, hope-inspiring, courage-inducing speech of his legendary speaking career at the Mason Temple in Memphis. He spoke of the "human rights revolution," of impoverished "colored peoples of the world" rising up demanding "to be free" in the Promised Land. "I may not get there with you," he said, his voice arresting. "But I want you to know tonight, that we, as a people, will get to the Promised Land!"[24]

Reeling from the assassination, Davis joined with the leaders of other local Black Power groups and organized a massive rally at the Second Baptist Church in Los Angeles. Attendees were urged to renew and escalate their fight against racism. As Davis saw it, "Racism was Martin Luther King's assassin, and it was racism that had to be attacked." She and her fellow rally organizers were intent on channel-ing the anger in Los Angeles away from physical confrontations with the well-equipped Los Angeles Police Department (LAPD), which had many officers who had been recruited from the Deep South. They succeeded. But the fire this time was elsewhere. In the week following King's assassination, more than 125 cities experienced another wave of urban rebellions, which led to another backlash of law and order from racist Americans. Aspiring presidents, including George Wallace and Richard Nixon, rode the backlash. Maryland governor Spiro T. Agnew quipped to Black leaders, "I call on you to publicly repudiate all black racists. This, so far, you have been unwilling to do." Agnew became such a celebrity that Nixon named him his running mate.[25]

King's death transformed countless doubly conscious activists into singly conscious antiracists, and Black Power suddenly grew into the largest antiracist mass mobilization since the post–Civil War period, when demands for land had been the main issue. The Godfather of Soul noticed Black America's brand new bag. With segregationists saying they should not be proud, with assimilationists saying they were not Black, James Brown began in August 1968 to lead the chant of millions: "Say It Loud—I'm Black and I'm Proud," a smash hit that topped the R&B singles chart for six weeks. All these Black Power chants caused some African Americans to trash their racist color hierarchies within Blackness (the lighter, the better). Some activists ominously inverted the color hierarchy, judging one's Blackness to be based on the darkness of the skin, the kinkiness of the hair, the size of the Afro, the degree of Ebonics fluency, or the willingness (of a light-skinned Black) to date a dark-skinned Black, or on whether someone wore Black leather or Afri-can garb or could quote Malcolm X. Antiracist Black Power activists engaged in the process of unearthing and trashing all of the deep-rooted assimilationist White standards. They were in the process of stopping Black people from looking at themselves and the world through what Du Bois had termed "the eyes of others" (and what the Kerner Commission had termed the "white perspective"). Antiracist Black Power compelled the controversial search for new standards, for Black perspectives, for Black people looking at themselves through their own eyes.

THE SEARCH FOR Black perspectives was especially taken up in schools and colleges, where Black student activists, educators, and parents were demanding the newest academic discipline, Black Studies. "When the focus in these classrooms is almost exclusively . . . white . . . and almost never black," Barbara Smith argued to the faculty at Mount Holyoke College, "dissatisfaction among those students with histori-cal and cultural roots which are not white and European is inevitable." From 1967 to 1970, Black students and their hundreds of thousands of non-Black allies compelled nearly 1,000 colleges and universities span-ning almost every US state to introduce Black Studies departments, programs, and courses. The demand for Black Studies filtered down into K–12 schools, too, where textbooks had presented African Amer-icans to "millions of children, both black and white, as . . . sub-human, incapable of achieving culture, happy in servitude, a passive outsider," as Hillel Black explained in *The American Schoolbook* in 1967. Early Black Studies intellectuals went to work on new antiracist textbooks. They weathered criticism from assimilationist and segregationist intellec-tuals of all races who looked down on Black Studies as separatist or inferior to the historically White disciplines. And they looked down on the new field for the same racist reasons they had looked down on historically Black colleges, institutions, businesses, groups, neighbor-hoods, and nations. Anything created by Black people, run by Black people, and filled by Black people, they thought, must be inferior. And if it was struggling to thrive, it must be the fault of those Black people. Racist ideas not only justified discrimination against Black people, but justified discrimination against Black establishments and against ideas promoted by Black activists, such as Black Studies.[26]

Nevertheless, Black Studies and Black Power ideas in general began to inspire antiracist transformations among non-Blacks. White members of the antiwar Students for a Democratic Society (SDS) and collectives of Hippies became sympathetic to Black Power and began pledging to "burn out the influence of racism from White Ameri-cans," as a White leader of the Communist Party of the United States urged in 1968. In founding the Young Lords Party in 1968, Puerto Rican antiracists recognized the "high degree of racism [that] existed between Puerto Ricans and Blacks, and between light-skinned and dark-skinned Puerto Ricans," as New York branch co-founder Pablo "Yoruba" Guzmán put it—a racist color hierarchy that existed within all the multicolored Latina/o and Chicana/o ethnicities. The emerging Brown Power movement challenged all these color hierarchies just as the emerging Black Power movement challenged the color hierarchies within all the multicolored Black ethnicities.[27]

THE LOS ANGELES SNCC survived its office being ransacked by the LAPD after King's assassination. But it could not survive the gender infighting that plagued many coed organizations. Black organizations had to contend with the popular theories of emasculated Black men from the Moynihan Report. Whenever Angela Davis and two other women asserted themselves, the group's racist patriarchs inevitably started reverberating the myths of Black womanhood, saying they were too domineering and were emasculating them. Kathleen Cleaver faced similar problems in the Black Panther Party, as did Frances Beal in her New York SNCC office.

Beal had become involved in civil rights and socialist activism in college before living in France in the early 1960s. By December 1968, she was back in the states and helping to found the Black Women's Liberation Committee in the SNCC. It was the first formal Black feminist collective of the Black Power movement. Beal provided Black feminists with one of their main ideological manifestoes, "Double Jeopardy: To Be Black and Female," a 1969 position paper that circulated further the next year when it appeared in Toni Cade Bambara's one-of-a-kind anthology, *The Black Woman*. "Since the advent of black power, Black men are maintaining that they have been castrated by society but that black women somehow escaped this persecution," Beal pointed out. Actually, "the black woman in America can justly be described as a 'slave of a slave'"—a victim of the double jeopardy of racial and gender discrimination. Beal cited labor statistics showing that non-White females accrued lower wages than White females, Black men, and White men—statistics that undermined the Frazier-Moynihan thesis that Black men were the most oppressed, a sensational thesis that had mobilized activists to defend the Black man. Beal's thesis of Black women having it the worst was no less effective in mobilizing activists to defend the Black woman. The rise of Black feminism and Black patriarchy led to ideological showdowns inside and outside of Black Power organizations over who had it the worst.[28]

In SNCC Los Angeles, the gender conflict—and then the Communist hunts—got so bad in 1968 that the chapter closed its doors by summer's end. Angela Davis then started seriously considering joining the Communist Party, a party she felt had not paid "sufficient attention to the national and racial dimensions of the oppression of Black people." But the CPUSA's new Che-Lumumba Club did. And this collective of Communists of color became Davis's entryway into the Communist Party in 1968, and her leap into campaign work for the first Black woman to run for the US presidency, CPUSA candidate Charlene Mitchell.[29]

In the 1968 presidential election, Mitchell squared off against Johnson's vice president, Hubert Humphrey. Across from the Democrats ran the Republican presidential hopeful, Richard Nixon. His innovative campaign unveiled the future of racist ideas.

CHAPTER 32

Law and Order

RICHARD NIXON AND his team of aides had carefully studied George Wallace's presidential campaigns. They realized that his segregationist banter made him attractive only to "the foam-at-the-mouth-segregationists." Nixon decided to appeal to these Wallace-type segregationists while also attracting all those Americans refusing to live in "dangerous" Black neighborhoods, refusing to believe that Black schools could be equal, refusing to accept busing initiatives to integrate schools, refusing to individualize Black negativity, refusing to believe that Black welfare mothers were deserving, and refusing to champion Black Power over majority-Black counties and cities—all those racists who refused to believe they were racist in 1968. Nixon framed his campaign, as a close adviser explained, to allow a potential supporter to "avoid admitting to himself that he was attracted by [the] racist appeal." How would he do that? Easy. Demean Black people, and praise White people, without ever saying *Black people* or *White people*.[1]

Historians have named this the "southern strategy." In fact, it was—and remained over the next five decades—the national Republican strategy as the GOP tried to unite northern and southern anti-Black (and anti-Latina/o) racists, war hawks, and fiscal and social conservatives. The strategy was right on time. In a 1968 Gallup poll, 81 percent of respondents said they believed Nixon's campaign slogan: "Law and order has broken down in the country." A Nixon television advertisement shrieked frightening music and frightening images of violent and bloodied activists. A deep voiceover says, "I pledge to you, we shall have order in the United States." The ad "hit it right on the nose. It's all about those damn Negro–Puerto Rican groups out there," Nixon reportedly said in private. In public, the tune was the same, save the racial lyrics. On September 6, 1968, before 30,000 applauding Texans, Nixon slammed the Supreme Court for having "gone too far in strengthening the criminal forces." Thirty years before, Theodore Bilbo would have said strengthening "the nigger forces." Campaign racism had progressed, and Nixon won the election.[2]

IN THE FALL of 1969, with Charlene Mitchell's campaign behind her, Angela Davis planned to quietly nestle into her first teaching position at the University of California at Los Angeles. The FBI had other plans. J. Edgar Hoover's agents had launched an all-out, unapologetic war to destroy the Black Power movement that year. The FBI's messenger at the *San Francisco Examiner*, Ed Montgomery, reported Davis's membership in the Communist Party (and Students for a Democratic Society, and the Black Panther Party). In the ensuing hubbub, California governor Ronald Reagan, eager to pick up points from the anti-Red, anti-student, anti-Black law-and-order voters, deployed an old anti-Communist regulation and fired the twenty-five-year-old Angela Davis. She appealed to the California courts, setting off a confrontation between the state's racists and antiracists, Communists and anti-Communists, academic emancipators and academic enslavers. Angela Davis had entered into the public light. Her detractors framed her as hate-filled and biased, hate mail started filling up her mailbox, she received threatening phone calls, and police officers started harassing her. On October 20, 1969, California Superior Court judge Jerry Pacht ruled that the anti-Communist regulation was unconstitutional. Davis resumed her teaching post, and Reagan began searching for another way to fire her.[3]

Sometime in February 1970, Davis's Che-Lumumba Club received word of the campaign to free three Black inmates at Soledad State Prison near San Jose. With evidence only that they were Black Power activists, George Jackson, John Clutchette, and Fleeta Drumgo had been indicted for the murder of a prison guard during a racially charged prison fight. In 1961, the eighteen-year-old George Jackson had been sentenced to serve one year to life for armed robbery; allegedly he had used a gun to steal $70 from a gas station. He had been transferred to Soledad in 1969, after experiencing a political transformation akin to Malcolm X's and Cleaver's, but his prison activism turned his $70 conviction into a life sentence. Davis became very close to George Jackson and his serious younger brother, Jonathan, who had dedicated his life to freeing his brother.[4]

Angela Davis spoke to a lively rally called "Free the Soledad Brothers" in Los Angeles within sight of the California Department of Corrections on June 19, 1970. It was the same day that Reagan's Board of Regents once again fired Davis from UCLA, this time on the grounds that her political speeches were "unbefitting a university professor." As evidence, Davis's terminators had cited, among other things, her rebuke of UC Berkeley educational psychologist Arthur Jensen, who represented the revival of segregationist scholars in the late 1960s. There was "an increasing realization" in psychology that the lower Black IQ scores could not be "completely or directly attributed to discrimination or inequalities in education," Jensen had written in the *Harvard Educational Review* in 1969. "It seems not unreasonable . . . to hypothesize that genetic factors may play a part in this picture." The Regents admonished Davis for not practicing the "appropriate restraint in the exercise of academic freedom" in soundly critiquing Jensen, who had engaged, according to the Regents, in "years of study" before publishing the "lengthy article." Academics, apparently, were only truly free to espouse racist ideas.[5]

As reporters peppered Davis for a response to her firing at the rally, she connected her academic enslavement to the judicial enslavement of political prisoners. A photographer snapped a shot of Davis carrying a sign. It read: "SAVE THE SOLEDAD BROTHERS FROM LEGAL LYNCHING." Jonathan Jackson stood behind her, holding another sign: "END POLITICAL REPRESSION IN PRISONS."[6]

On August 7, 1970, Jonathan Jackson walked into a courtroom in California's Marin County, holding three guns, and took the judge, the prosecutor, and three jurors hostage. Aided by three inmates, whom he freed in the courtroom, the seventeen-year-old younger brother of George Jackson led the hostages at gunpoint to a van parked outside. Police opened fire. The shootout took the lives of Jackson, the judge, and two inmates. Police traced the ownership of one of Jackson's guns to Angela Davis. A week later, Davis was charged with murder, kidnapping, and conspiracy, and a warrant was issued for her arrest. Still grieving Jackson's death, she saw the political repression on the wall—a death sentence if found guilty. She fled the massive woman-hunt, a fugitive trying to avoid slavery or worse, like so many of her political peers and ancestors had done before her. J. Edgar Hoover, months before his death, placed the "dangerous" Davis on the FBI's top ten most wanted list. The two pictures—one with shades, one without—on the "Wanted by the FBI" poster showcased the woman who became the iconic female activist of the Black Power movement.[7]

It showed her famous Afro, too. But the era's most popular Afro—the woman who really transformed the hairstyle from an anti-assimilationist political statement into a fashion statement—was the biggest, boldest, baddest, and Blackest woman, the movie star of *Foxy Brown* (1974) and *Coffy* (1973)—Pam Grier. The more African Americans let their Afros grow out like Grier's in the early 1970s, the more they faced the wrath of assimilationist parents, preachers, and employers, who called Afros ugly, "a disgrace"—like going "back to the jungle." African Americans were assimilationists not when they permed their own hair, but when they classified natural styles as unprofessional or aesthetically inferior to permed styles.[8]

The Afro was ever present in Hollywood's "Blaxploitation" genre of Black action-adventure films, a genre that peaked in popularity between 1969 and 1974. Facing economic ruin in the late 1960s, and mounting antiracist criticism of the Sidney Poitier–type characters prevalent in the integrationist film narratives of the 1960s, Hollywood decided to solve its economic and political woes by exploiting the popularity of Blackness. Blaxploitation's kingpin was Melvin Van Peebles. His *Sweet Sweetback's Baadasssss* in 1971 was the story of a *bad* Black stud who violently reacts to police repression, flees a massive police manhunt by using any weapon he can (including his penis), and escapes into the Mexican sunset. Along the way he is aided by Black children, preachers, gamblers, pimps, and prostitutes. The tornadoes of police repression over the past few years offscreen and the popular racist idea of the super-sexual, no-longer-emasculated Black male no doubt were factors helping the film become so enormously popular among African Americans.

But not all Blacks loved the film. In a literary explosion in *Ebony*, public intellectual Lerone Bennett Jr. judged it "neither revolutionary nor black" for romanticizing the poverty and misery of Black urban America. Bennett had a point. Whenever Black artists ordained financially deprived Black folk as the truest representatives of Black people, they were trekking through the back door into racist ideas. Too often, they regarded the world of poverty, hustling, prostitution, gambling, and criminality as the *Black* world, as if non-Blacks did not hustle, prostitute, deal drugs, gamble, and commit crimes at similar rates. And yet, whenever these artists humanized pimps, gangsters, criminals, and prostitutes, they were at their antiracist best. But those who made up the civil rights opposition to Blaxploitation films—in their unerring belief in media suasion—hardly looked for this humanist distinction. They simply saw unsavory stereotypes reinforcing Black characters offscreen. "The transformation from the stereotyped Stepin Fetchit to Super Nigger on screen is just another form of cultural genocide," the civil rights Coalition of Blaxploitation charged in 1972.[9]

THE WOMANHUNT CAUGHT up to Angela Davis in New York on October 13, 1970. Davis was jailed at the New York Women's House of Detention. It was there, surrounded by incarcerated Black and Brown women, that Davis began developing her "embryonic Black feminist consciousness," as she called it. It was that year, 1970, that the women's movement at last reached the mainstream consciousness of the United States. Norma L. McCorvey (under the alias Jane Roe) had filed suit in Texas to abort her pregnancy. When the Supreme Court legalized abortion in *Roe v. Wade* three years later, President Nixon professed there were only two "times when an abortion is necessary": "when you have a black and a white or a rape."[10]

On August 25, 1970, Frances Beal and her sisters in the newly renamed Third World Women's Alliance showed up with their placards ("Hands Off Angela Davis"), joining more than 20,000 feminists at the National Organization for Women (NOW) Strike for Equality in New York. Seeing the Beal poster, a NOW official rushed over and snapped, "Angela Davis has nothing to do with women's liberation." Beal snapped back, "It has nothing to do with the kind of liberation you're talking about. But it has everything to do with the kind of liberation we're talking about." As novelist Toni Morrison explained in the *New York Times Magazine* months later, Black women "look at White women and see the enemy for they know that racism is not confined to white men and that there are more white women than men in the country." Toni Morrison had just put out *The Bluest Eye*, an anti-assimilationist account of a Black girl's zealous pursuit of "beautiful" blue eyes. Morrison's debut novel was as moving fictionally as the real life account *I Know Why the Cage Bird Sings* (1969), Maya Angelou's award-winning autobiographical journey from the thorny woods of racist ideas (where she wished she could wake up from her "black ugly dream") into the clearing of antiracist dignity and resistance.[11]

IN DECEMBER 1970, Angela Davis was extradited back to California. She spent most of her jail time awaiting trial in solitary confinement, where she read and responded to letters from her thousands of supporters, studied her case, and thought about America. She sometimes heard the chants of "Free Angela," "Free all Political Prisoners." Two hundred defense committees in the United States and sixty-seven defense committees abroad were shouting the same words. The defense committees formed a broad interracial coalition of supporters who believed that Nixon's America had gone too far—too far in harassing, imprisoning, and killing hordes of antiracist, anticapitalist, antisexist, and anti-imperialist activists and condemning them for their ideas. Those ideas, at the moment, were wrapped up in the mind and body of Angela Davis, a mind and body that Nixon's and Reagan's law-and-order America wanted dead.[12]

The antiracist ideas that Davis embodied were argued in a different case before the Supreme Court around the time the police brought her back to California. In the 1950s, Duke Power's Dan River plant in North Carolina had publicly forced its Black workers into its lowest-paying jobs. After the passage of the Civil Rights Act, Duke Power adopted private discrimination—requiring high school diplomas and IQ tests—that produced the same outcome: Whites receiving the bulk of its high paying jobs. On March 8, 1971, the Supreme Court ruled in *Griggs v. Duke Power Co.* that Duke Power's new requirements had no bearing on job performance.

The Civil Rights Act "proscribes not only overt discrimination," opined Chief Justice Warren E. Burger, "but also practices that are fair in form, but discriminatory in operation." If the *Griggs* decision sounded too good for antiracists, then it was. It did not necessarily bar practices and policies that yielded racial disparities. Although Duke Power changed its policy on the day the Civil Rights Act took effect, the Supreme Court, astonishingly, upheld the appeals court supposition that there was no "discriminatory intent." And Chief Justice Burger gave employers a loophole for the progression of racism. "The touchstone is business necessity. If an employment practice which operates to exclude Negroes cannot be shown to be related to job performance, the practice is prohibited." Racist employers could then simply ensure that their discriminatory hiring and promotion practices were related to job performance, and therefore, to business necessity.[13]

The *Griggs* ruling hardly mattered to Black Power activists. They had no faith anyway that the US Supreme Court would outlaw the latest progression of institutional racism. Their attention was turned to their local struggles, the Davis case, and the largest Black convention in US history. Some 8,000 people attended the largest meeting of the six-year-old Black Power movement on March 10, 1972, in Gary, Indiana. The largest Black middle class in history was represented in that crowd—the New Black America. The emergence of these Black elites was the result of the activism and reforms of the civil rights *and*

Black Power movements as well as of the strong economy of the 1960s. By 1973, the rate of Black poverty would dip to its lowest level in US history. Black income levels were rising and political-economic racial disparities closing before the recession hit in 1973.[14]

By the opening of the Gary convention, Blacks had taken political control over many of the majority-Black cities and counties. But some Black voters had to learn the hard way that empowering a Black person in government did not automatically empower an antiracist. And so, the main demand of independents at the Gary convention—for an independent Black political party—would not have automatically been an antiracist upgrade over the current situation, marked by assimilationists in the Democratic Party. But self-serving Black politicians squashed the plan over the next few years anyway.[15]

DAYS BEFORE THE mammoth Gary convention opened, Angela Davis's trial finally began in California. "The evidence will show," said prosecutor Albert Harris, "that her basic motive was not to free political prisoners, but to free the one prisoner that she loved." The ownership of the gun, Davis's flight, and her words of love in her diary and letters for George Jackson were supposed to convict her of first degree murder, kidnapping, and conspiracy. All-White juries had convicted and meted out capital punishment for less. But not this jury, which acquitted Davis of all charges on June 4, 1972. She walked out of the clutches of the American penal system. But she walked out backward, looking at the women and men she left behind bars, and pledging the rest of her life to free them from slavery.[16]

Despite the law-and-order movement against activists, fewer than 350,000 people were held in prisons and jails nationwide in 1972. This was far too many for Davis and the nation's most well-respected criminologists, many of whom were predicting that the prison system would fade away. Sound anti-prison activism and ideas were having their effect. In 1973, the National Advisory Commission on Criminal Justice Standards and Goals called the prison system a "failure"—a creator of crime rather than a preventer. The commission recommended that "no new institutions for adults should be built and existing institutions for juveniles should be closed."[17]

After Davis's acquittal, the more than 250 Free Angela defense committees received a communiqué from Davis. "Stay with us as long as racism and political repression" kept human beings "behind bars." By May 1973, the defense committees had been organized into the National Alliance Against Racist and Political Repression. President Nixon's Watergate scandal heightened the contradictions on crime and prisons. All those Americans were serving prison terms, many of them for their political acts and views, while the champion of law and order, Richard Nixon, did not spend a day in prison for the Watergate scandal. When President Gerald Ford took office following Nixon's resignation, he pardoned and immunized Nixon from prosecution.[18]

In the fall of 1975, Davis returned to academia. It was five years later, but she was still the center of controversy. Alumni were irate when she joined the faculty of the Claremont Colleges Black Studies Center in southern California. She found that the marketplace of ideas was the same as when she had left: segregationists were still imagining genetic differences between the races, and assimilationists were still trying to ascertain why their only hope for Black uplift—integration—had failed. Assimilationist sociologist Charles Stember argued in *Sexual Racism* (1976) that the White man's sexual jealousy of the hypersexual Black man was the basis for the failure of integration. Sexual racism—the core of racism—was "largely focused" on the Black man, he maintained.[19]

At the same time, Stember downgraded the sexual racism faced by Black women and practically ignored the sexual racism faced by Black LGBTs. But LGBTs were hardly waiting on Stember. Since the interracial Stonewall rebellion in Manhattan's Greenwich Village in 1969, which had kicked off the gay liberation movement, Black LGBTs had two-stepped away from the margins of the women's liberation, Black Power, and White gay liberation movements, starting their own new integrative dance of queer antiracism in the 1970s. New York native and lesbian writer Audre Lorde brilliantly "gave name" to these "nameless" life dances in her poetry, essays, and speeches. Non-Whites, women, and LGBTs were "expected to educate" Whites, men, and heterosexuals to appreciate "our humanity," Lorde said in one of her most famous speeches. "The oppressors maintain their position and evade their responsibility for their own actions. There is a constant drain of energy which might be better used in redefining ourselves and devising realistic scenarios for altering the present and constructing the future."[20]

Black feminist Ntozake Shange used her creative antiracist energy to produce a play, *For Colored Girls Who Have Considered Suicide/When the Rainbow Is Enuf*, which debuted on Broadway on September 15, 1976. Seven Black women, named after colors of the rainbow, poetically and dramatically expressed their experiences of abuse, joy, heartbreak, strength, weakness, love, and longing for love. *For Colored Girls* emerged and reemerged as an artistic phenomenon over the next four decades on stages and screens as the "black feminist bible," to quote University of Pennsylvania professor Salamishah Tillet. At every stop, Shange stood strong under the naïve crosswinds of the Black portrayals debates. Some were vocal about their fear that the play would strengthen racist conceptions of Black women; others feared it would strengthen racist conceptions of Black men.[21]

The argument over *For Colored Girls* endured for the rest of the decade. The same record started playing again, but much louder, in 1982 when Alice Walker penned her novel *The Color Purple* (and again in 1985 over Steven Spielberg's blockbuster film adaptation, and again in 1995 over the film *Waiting to Exhale*, a film about four African American women). Set in rural Georgia, Walker's *The Color Purple* presents a Black woman negotiating (and finding) her way through the rugged confines of abusive Black patriarchs, abusive southern poverty, and abusive racist Whites. As the best-selling novel passed through thousands of hands, some readers (and probably more nonreaders) fumed at the portrayals of Black men. But if viewers of Shange's play or Walker's novel (or Spielberg's film) walked away from the theater or closed the book and generalized Black men as abusers, then they were faulty, not the play, the novel, or the film. There has always been a razor-thin line between the racist portrayer of Black negativity and the antiracist portrayer of imperfect Black humanity. When consumers have looked upon stereotypical Black portrayals as representative of Black behavior, instead of representative of those individual characters, then the generalizing consumers have been the racist problem, not the racist or antiracist portrayer. But this complex distinction, or the fact that positive Black portrayals hardly undermine racism, could never quite put an end to the senseless media portrayals arguments, which were inflamed yet again by the explosions of Hip Hop videos in the 1980s and 1990s and Black reality television in the twenty-first century.[22]

"WATCHING A PERFORMANCE of 'For Colored Girls' one sees a collective appetite for Black male blood," wrote sociologist Robert Staples in 1979 in "The Myth of Black Macho: A Response to Angry Black Feminists." However, the angriest Black feminist of the era was the twenty-seven-year-old Michele Wallace. *Ms.* magazine presented the young Wallace on its January 1979 cover, advertising her erupting *Black Macho and the Myth of the Superwoman* as "the book that will shape the 1980s." It certainly shaped the Black gender debate. Some hated her, some loved her for posing sexism as a greater concern than racism and for exposing the racist "myth of the black man's castration" and the racist myth of the Black woman as a "woman of inordinate strength." Wallace testified, "Even for me, it continues to be difficult to let the myth go" of the Black superwoman.[23]

But that's where her antiracism stopped and her racist attacks on both Black women and Black men took over. After tossing out the Black superwoman portrait, Wallace painted the opposite portrait for her readers, the portrait of a Black woman who "forced herself to be submissive and passive" during the 1960s—a pronouncement poet June Jordan blasted in the *New York Times* as "unsubstantiated, self-demeaning," and "ahistorical." Angela Davis set the record straight on the meaningful and aggressive activism in the 1960s of Black women and Black men in *Freedomways*. Davis included men because, according to Wallace, "the black [male] revolutionary of the sixties calls to mind nothing so much as a child who is acting for the simple pleasure of the reaction he will elicit from, the pain he will cause, his father"—"the White man." In the foreword to the new edition eleven years later, Wallace bravely admitted some mistakes, and she took back her thesis that Black machoism was *the* "crucial factor in the destruction of the Black Power Movement." To Wallace's credit, she had still brought awareness to patriarchal Black masculinity as *a* crucial factor in the demise of Black Power.[24]

Only one woman elicited more debate than Michele Wallace in Black communities in 1979—and it was a White woman, the White woman that many assimilationists saw as the most beautiful woman in the world. In the movie *10*, Bo Derek wore her hair in cornrows with beads, setting off a mad dash of elite White women flocking to salons to get their "Bo Braids." African Americans were angered reading the media coverage of the mad dash. Cornrows had arrived, media outlets announced, as if Whites were the sole carriers of culture. Around the same time, American Airlines fired ticket agent Renee Rogers for wearing cornrows. Racist Americans considered Afros, braids, locs, and other "natural" styles unprofessional. When Rogers sued for discrimination, the judge evoked "Bo Braids" in rejecting her claim that the style reflected her cultural heritage.[25]

Quite possibly the most passionate part of the furor over the Bo Braids was the widespread feeling that Bo Derek and her look-a-likes were appropriating from the storehouse of African American culture, a feeling that possibly stemmed from the dusty racist idea that European cultures could overpower African cultures. What was most amazing about the whole uproar—and similar White appropriation uproars that surrounded Eminem (rap music) and Kim Kardashian (bodily physique) decades later—was the hypocrisy of some Black people. Some of those Black people who had permed their hair—an appropriation of European culture—were now ridiculing Bo Derek and other White women for braiding their hair and appropriating African culture.

Bo Derek and her braided look-a-likes seemed to be everywhere in the early 1980s, annoying Black people. But the fashion trend did not nearly have the lasting power of the latest reinvention of ruling White masculinity. If *Planet of the Apes* epitomized racists' defeated sentiments in 1968, then the highest-grossing film of 1976, which won an Oscar for Best Picture, epitomized their fighting sentiment that year. *Rocky* portrayed a poor, kind, slow-talking, slow-punching, humble, hard-working, steel-jawed Italian journeyman boxer in Philadelphia facing off against the unkind, fast-talking, fast-punching, cocky African American World Heavy Champion. Rocky's opponent, Apollo Creed, with his amazing avalanche of punches, symbolized the empowerment movements, the rising Black middle class, and the real-life heavyweight champion of the world in 1976, the pride of Black Power masculinity, Muhammad Ali. Rocky Balboa—as played by Sylvester Stallone—came to symbolize the pride of White supremacist masculinity's refusal to be knocked out from the avalanche of civil rights and Black Power protests and policies.[26]

Weeks before Americans ran out to see *Rocky*, though, they ran out to buy Alex Haley's *Roots: The Saga of an American Family*. And those who did not want to slog through the 704-page tome that claimed the No. 1 spot on the *New York Times* Best Seller List watched the even more popular television adaptation that started airing on ABC in January 1977, becoming the most watched show in US television history. *Roots: The Saga of an American Family* shared the thrilling, tragic, and tumultuous story of Kunta Kinte, from his kidnapping in Gambia to his brutal crippling, which ended his incessant runaway attempts in Virginia. Claiming Kinte as his actual ancestor, Haley followed his life and the life of his descendants in US history down to himself. For African Americans in the radiance of Black Power's broadening turn to antiracist Pan-African ideas, and starved for knowledge about their life before and during slavery, *Roots* was a megahit, one of the most influential works of the twentieth century. *Roots* unearthed legions of racist ideas of backward Africa, of civilizing American slavery, of the contented slave, of stupid and imbruted slaves, of loose enslaved women, and of African American roots in slavery. The plantation genre of happy mammies and Sambos was gone with the wind.[27]

But the new plantation genre of lazy Black rioters who knocked down Whites' livelihoods—the poor through welfare, the upwardly mobile through affirmative action—remained in the wind in the late 1970s. Thus, as much as antiracist Black Americans loved their roots, racist White Americans loved—on and off screen—their other Rocky, with his unrelenting fight for the law and order of racism. And then, in 1976, their Rocky ran for president.

CHAPTER 33

Reagan's Drugs

IRONICALLY, IT WAS a former Hollywood star who came to embody Rocky Balboa in real life; and at the same time, to embody the racist backlash to Black Power in politics. This real-life Rocky decided to challenge incumbent Gerald Ford for the presidential seat on the Republican ticket in 1976. Ronald Reagan fought down all those empowerment movements fomenting in his home state of California and across the nation. Hardly any other Republican politician could match his law-and-order credentials, and hardly any other Republican politician was more despised by antiracists. When Reagan had first campaigned for governor of California in 1966, he had pledged "to send the welfare bums back to work." By 1976, he had advanced his fictional welfare problem enough to attract Nixon's undercover racists to his candidacy, gaining their support in cutting the social programs that helped the poor. On the presidential campaign trail, Reagan shared the story of Chicago's Linda Taylor, a Black woman charged with welfare fraud. "Her tax-free cash income is over $150,000," Reagan liked to say. Actually, Taylor had been charged with defrauding the state of $8,000, an exceptional amount for something that rarely happened. But truth did not matter to the Reagan campaign as much as feeding the White backlash to Black Power.[1]

Gerald Ford used every bit of his presidential incumbent power to narrowly stave off Ronald Reagan's challenge at the 1976 Republican National Convention. But Nixon's pardoner and the steward of a poor economy lost to the "untainted" and unknown former Democratic governor of Georgia, Jimmy Carter. Black hopes were high until the austere Carter administration, to boost the economy, started unprecedented cuts in social welfare, health care, and educational programs while increasing military spending. From the lowest Black poverty rate in US history in 1973, the decade ended with record unemployment rates, inflation, falling wages, rising Black poverty rates, and increasing inequality. At the local level, struggling activists and residents partially or totally blamed corporate-friendly Black politicians for the growing poverty. There was supposedly something wrong with *Black* politicians. Unsurprisingly, no one ever uncovered any evidence to substantiate this political racism of Black politicians. Black politicians and the Black elites they largely served were hardly different from the politicians and elites of other races, selling out to the highest bidders or sticking to their antiracist and/or racist principles.[2]

While racist Blacks blamed *Black* politicians—and increasingly *Black* capitalists—for their socioeconomic struggles, racist Whites blamed Black people and affirmative action for their struggles in the 1970s. Racist ideas put all of these Americans out of touch with reality—as out of touch as one White male aerospace engineer who wanted to be a doctor. Allan Bakke was over thirty-three when the medical school at the University of California at Davis turned him away a second time in 1973, citing his "present age" and lukewarm interview scores as the main factors in the rejection. By then, more than a dozen other medical schools had also turned him away, usually because of his age. In June 1974, Bakke filed suit against the University of California Regents—the body that had fired Angela Davis four years earlier. He did not allege age discrimination. He alleged that his medical school application had been rejected "on account of his race," because UC Davis set aside sixteen admissions slots out of one hundred for "disadvantaged" non-Whites. Agreeing, the California courts struck down the "quota" and ordered his admission.

The US Supreme Court decided to take *Regents v. Bakke*. Bakke's lawyers argued that the quota system had reduced his chances for admission by forcing him to compete for eighty-four slots instead of the full one hundred. The Regents' lawyers argued the state had a "compelling . . . interest" in increasing California's minuscule percentage of non-White doctors. Since they generally received inferior K–12 educations, non-Whites tended to have lower college grade point averages (GPAs) and test scores than Whites—thus the need to set aside sixteen seats. And despite their lower scores, these non-White students were indeed qualified, said the Regents' lawyers. Ninety percent of them graduated and passed their licensing exams, only slightly less than the White percentage.

The biggest irony and tragedy of the *Regents v. Bakke* case—and the affirmative action cases that followed—was not Allan Bakke's refusal to look in the mirror of his age and interviewing prowess. Instead, it was that no one was challenging the admissions factors being used: the standardized tests and GPA scores that had created and reinforced the racial disparities in admissions in the first place. The fact that UC Davis's non-White medical students had much lower Medical College Admission Test (MCAT) scores and college GPAs than their fellow White medical students, but still nearly equaled their graduation and licensing exam passage rates, exposed the futility of the school's admissions criteria. Since segregationists had first developed them in the early twentieth century, standardized tests—from the MCAT to the SAT and IQ exams—had failed time and again to predict success in college and professional careers or even to truly measure intelligence. But these standardized tests had succeeded in their original mission: figuring out an "objective" way to rule non-Whites (and women and poor people) intellectually inferior, and to justify discriminating against them in the admissions process. It had become so powerfully "objective" that those non-Whites, women, and poor people would accept their rejection letters and not question the admissions decisions.

Standardized exams have, if anything, predicted the socioeconomic class of the student and perhaps a student's first-year success in college or in a professional program—which says that the tests could be helpful for students *after* they are admitted, to assess who needs extra assistance the first year. And so, on October 12, 1977, a White male sat before the Supreme Court requesting slight changes in UC Davis's admissions policies to open sixteen seats for him—and not a poor Black woman requesting standardized tests to be dropped as an admissions criterion to open eighty-four seats for her. It was yet another case of racists v. racists that antiracists had no chance of winning.[3]

With four justices solidly for the Regents, and four for Bakke, the former Virginia corporate lawyer whose firm had defended Virginia segregationists in Brown decided Regents v. Bakke. On June 28, 1978, Justice Lewis F. Powell sided with four justices in viewing UC Davis's set-asides as "discrimination against members of the white 'majority,'" allowing Bakke to be admitted. Powell also sided with the four other justices in allowing universities to "take race into account" in choosing students, so long as it was not "decisive" in the decision. Crucially, Powell framed affirmative action as "race-conscious" policies, while standardized test scores were not, despite common knowledge about the racial disparities in those scores.[4]

The leading proponents of "race-conscious" policies to maintain the status quo of racial disparities in the late 1950s had refashioned themselves as the leading opponents of "race-conscious" policies in the late 1970s to maintain the status quo of racial disparities. "Whatever it takes" to defend discriminators had always been the marching orders of the producers of racist ideas. Allan Bakke, his legal team, the organizations behind them, the justices who backed him, and his millions of American supporters were all in the mode of proving that the earth was flat and the United States had moved beyond racism in 1978. These racists happily consumed the year's most prominent and acclaimed race relations sociological text, The Declining Significance of Race, and spun William Julius Wilson's arguments to proclaim that race no longer mattered. The University of Chicago sociologist attempted to solve the racial paradox of the late 1970s: the rise of the Black middle class and the fall of the Black poor. Wilson characterized the post–World War II era "as the period of progressive transition from racial inequalities to class inequalities." The "old barriers" of racial discrimination that restricted "the entire black population" had transformed into the "new barriers" restricting the Black poor. "Class has become more important than race in determining black access to privilege and power," Wilson wrote.

Wilson did not acknowledge the racial progress for some and the progression of racism for all. As Wilson's antiracist critics pointed out, he neglected the evidence showing the rising discrimination faced by rising middle-income Blacks—a point Michael Harrington's *The Other America* had already made in 1962. Wilson focused his scholarly lens on the economic dynamics that created an urban Black "underclass," a class made inferior, behaviorally, by its wrenching poverty.[5]

Assimilationist underclass scholarship in the late 1970s and early 1980s looked over at "ghetto ethnography," those assimilationist anthropologists reconstructing the supposed substandard cultural world of non-elite urban Blacks. "I think this anthropology is just another way to call me a nigger," complained a factory worker in the introduction to the classic antiracist ethnography of the era, *Drylongso* (1980). Syracuse anthropologist John Langston Gwaltney—who is blind—allowed his Black interviewees to construct their *own* cultural world. The *New York Times* characterized *Drylongso* as "the most expansive and realistic exposition of contemporary mainstream black attitudes yet published."[6]

On the thirty-third anniversary of *The Declining Significance of Race*, when scholars were once again pitting class over race to explain racial inequities, Wilson did what only the best scholars have found the courage to do: he admitted the book's shortcomings and confessed that he should have advanced "both race- and class-based solutions to address life chances for people of color."[7]

It was these race- and class-based solutions that Justice Thurgood Marshall had tried to will into existence in his separate dissenting opinion for *Regents v. Bakke*. The dissenting opinion of Harry Blackmun, the decider in *Roe v. Wade*, came last. Blackmun gave America a timeless lesson: "In order to get beyond racism, we must first take account of race. There is no other way. And in order to treat some persons equally, we must treat them differently. We cannot—we dare not—let the Fourteenth Amendment perpetuate racial supremacy." But that was exactly what racists intended to do. Supporters of affirmative action were "hard-core racists of reverse discrimination," argued Yale law professor and former solicitor general Robert Bork. In the *Wall Street*

Journal, Bork ridiculed the Supreme Court's decision to keep a limited form of affirmative action. Bork and others like him used the Four-teenth Amendment to attack antiracist initiatives over the next few decades, leaving behind only the wreckage of widening racial dispar-ities. Four years after *Regents v. Bakke*, White students were two and a half times more likely than Black students to enroll in highly selective colleges and universities. By 2004, that racial disparity had doubled.[8]

AS 1960S GAINS unraveled and poverty spread in the late 1970s, a grow-ing number of Black people grew alienated from the US political sys-tem. As their alienation grew, the racist ideas about them grew. Black voters looked down on Black nonvoters as inferior. The nonvoters, they believed, had callously disregarded the blood shed for Black vot-ing rights, had stupidly given up their political power, and as such were immoral and uncaring. Black nonvoters—or third-party Black voters like Angela Davis—clearly were not being driven to the polls by fear of Republican victories. They seemed to be only willing to vote *for* politicians, as Angela Davis began to realize.[9]

On November 19, 1979, the Communist Party announced its pres-idential ticket for the 1980 election. Sixty-nine-year-old Gus Hall, the longtime head of the CPUSA, was once again running for president. His newest running mate had reached the constitutionally required age of thirty-five on January 26. She had just joined the faculty at that historic campus where Black Studies had been born thirteen years ear-lier, San Francisco State University. Angela Davis agreed to partake in her first campaign for public office. But that does not mean Davis and other non-White members were totally happy with the CPUSA. The lack of diversity in the CPUSA leadership remained a source of con-flict within the party in the 1980s.[10]

Nor was Davis happy with the decline of antiracist activism, which was slowing in the midst of—or rather, because of—the growing pro-duction and consumption of racist ideas in the late 1970s. "In a racist society it is not enough to be non-racist, we must be antiracist," thun-dered Angela Davis in September 1979 at the Oakland Auditorium.

She joined with Bay Area politicians and activists in urging protests against the upcoming Nazi rally nearby. All decade long, Davis's National Alliance Against Racist and Political Repression had steadily challenged the growing Klan and Nazi groups. The Klan almost tripled its national membership between 1971 and 1980, unleashing its gun-toting terrorism in more than one hundred towns to try to destroy the gains of the 1960s. Lynchings were still occurring—at least twelve were committed in Mississippi in 1980, twenty-eight Black youngsters were killed in Atlanta from 1979 to 1982, and random street-corner executions took place in Buffalo in 1980. But Klan violence and lynchings by private citizens paled in comparison to the terror being perpetrated by gangs of policemen across the nation, from strip-searches and sexual abuse of Black women to pistol-whipping of Black males. By the early 1980s, one study showed that for every White person killed by police officers, police killed twenty-two Black people.[11]

"We can break this vicious cycle of racism, sexism, unemployment and inflation created by those who always put profits before people," Davis blared on posters announcing her campaign rallies in 1980. The Communist politicos had to get the word out about their campaign stops because their party received much less media attention than President Jimmy Carter, who was campaigning for reelection, and Ronald Reagan, who had finally secured the Republican nomination. In early August 1980, Angela Davis brought her "People Before Profits" campaign back to the place where her public life had begun: UCLA. She lamented about the poor turnout of the media. "It's part of a conspiracy to prevent us from getting our message to the people," she said, sitting at a table with undistributed press packets. "If Ronald Reagan were holding a press conference here you wouldn't have been able to see anything for blocks, there would have been so much press here."[12]

Days earlier, on August 3, 1980, the press did show up in full force when the former California governor more or less opened his presidential campaign at the Neshoba County Fair. The event was just a few miles from Philadelphia, Mississippi, where three civil rights activists had been killed in 1964. It was a clever strategy that improved on the tactics Nixon had mastered before him. Reagan never mentioned race when he looked out at some of the descendants of slaveholders and segregationists, people who had championed "states' rights" to maintain White supremacy for nearly two centuries since those hot days in the other Philadelphia, where the US Constitution had been written. Reagan promised to "restore to states and local governments the power that properly belongs to them." He then dodged Carter's charges of racism. Thanks in part to southern support, Reagan easily won the presidency.[13]

Reagan wasted little time in knocking down the fiscal gains that middle- and low-income people had made over the past four decades. Seemingly as quickly and deeply as Congress allowed and the poor economy justified, Reagan cut taxes for the rich and social programs for middle- and low-income families, while increasing the military budget. Reagan seemingly did offscreen what Sylvester Stallone had done on-screen, first knocking out elite Blacks the way Rocky had knocked out his opponent Apollo Creed in *Rocky II* (1979). And then, amazingly, Reagan befriended these Creeds—these racist or elite Blacks he had knocked down in previous fights—and used them to knock down the menacing low-income Blacks, as represented by Rocky's opponent in *Rocky III* (1982), Clubber Lang, popularly known as Mr. T.[14]

During Reagan's first year in office, the median income of Black families declined by 5.2 percent, and the number of poor Americans in general increased by 2.2 million. In one year, the *New York Times* observed, "much of the progress that had been made against poverty in the 1960s and 1970s" had been "wiped out."[15]

As the economic and racial disparities grew and middle-class incomes became more unstable in the late 1970s and early 1980s, old segregationist fields—like evolutionary psychology, preaching genetic intellectual hierarchies, and physical anthropology, preaching biological racial distinctions—and new fields, like sociobiology, all seemed to grow in popularity. After all, new racist ideas were needed to rationalize the newly growing disparities. Harvard biologist Edward Osborne Wilson, who was trained in the dual-evolution theory, published *Sociobiology: The New Synthesis* in 1975. Wilson more or less called on American scholars to find "the biological basis of all forms of social behavior in all kinds of organisms, including man." Though most sociobiologists did not apply sociobiology directly to race, the unproven theory underlying sociobiology itself allowed believers to apply the field's principles to racial disparities and arrive at racist ideas that blamed Blacks' social behavior for their plight. It was the first great academic theory in the post-1960s era whose producers tried to avoid the label "racist." Intellectuals and politicians were producing theories—like welfare recipients are lazy, or inner cities are dangerous, or poor people are ignorant, or one-parent households are immoral—that allowed Americans to call Black people lazy, dangerous, and immoral without ever saying "Black people," which allowed them to deflect charges of racism.[16]

Assimilationists and antiracists, realizing the implications of *Sociobiology*, mounted a spirited reproach, which led to a spirited academic and popular debate over its merits and political significance during the late 1970s and early 1980s. Harvard evolutionary biologist Stephen Jay Gould, who released *The Mismeasure of Man* in 1981, led the reproach in the biological sciences against segregationist ideas. Edward Osborne Wilson, not to be deterred, emerged as a public intellectual. He no doubt enjoyed hearing Americans say unproven statements that showed how popular his theories had become, such as when someone quips that a particular behavior "is in my DNA." He no doubt enjoyed, as well, taking home two Pulitzer Prizes for his books and a National Medal of Science from President Jimmy Carter. Wilson's sociobiology promoted but never proved the existence of genes for behaviors like meanness, aggression, conformity, homosexuality, and even xenophobia and racism.[17]

Angela Davis joined other antiracist scholars in fighting back against these segregationist claims inside (and outside) of the academy. Her most influential academic treatise, *Women, Race & Class*, appeared in 1981. It was a revisionist history of Black women as active historical agents despite the prevailing sexism and exploitation they had faced, and despite the racism they had faced from White feminists in the suffrage struggles and the recent reproductive and anti-rape struggles. Davis showcased the irony of the most popular pieces of anti-rape literature in the 1970s—Susan Brownmiller's *Against Our Will*,

Jean MacKeller's *Rape: The Bait and the Trap*, and Diana Russell's *Politics of Rape*—for reinvigorating the "myth of the Black rapist." This myth, Davis said, reinforced "racism's open invitation to white men to avail themselves sexually of Black women's bodies. The fictional image of the Black man as rapist has always strengthened its inseparable companion: the image of the Black woman as chronically promiscuous." Davis's wide-ranging account of Black women activists provided a powerful response to Michele Wallace's—and patriarchal historians'—racist pictures of Black women as "passive" during racial and gender struggles. Along with bell hooks's *Ain't I a Woman: Black Women and Feminism*, also published in 1981, Davis's *Women, Race & Class* helped forge a new method of study, an integrative race, gender, and class analysis, in American scholarship. As hooks indelibly penned, "racism has always been a divisive force separating black men and white men, and sexism has been a force that unites the two groups."[18]

But no great work of antiracist feminist scholarship—and *Ain't I a Woman* and *Women, Race & Class* were instant classics—stood any chance of stopping those producers of the segregationist ideas that were defending Reagan's racist and classist policies. In 1982, Reagan issued one of the most devastating executive orders of the twentieth century. "We must mobilize all our forces to stop the flow of drugs into this country" and to "brand drugs such as marijuana exactly for what they are—dangerous," Reagan said, announcing his War on Drugs. Criminologists hardly feared that the new war would disproportionately arrest and incarcerate African Americans. Many criminologists were publishing fairytales for studies that found that racial discrimination no longer existed in the criminal justice system.

"We can fight the drug problem, and we can win," Reagan announced. It was an astonishing move. Drug crime was declining. Only 2 percent of Americans viewed drugs as the nation's most pressing problem. Few considered marijuana to be a particularly dangerous drug, especially in comparison with the more addictive heroine. Substance-abuse therapists were shocked by Reagan's unfounded claim that America could "put drug abuse on the run through stronger law enforcement."[19]

REELING FROM THE ANNOUNCEMENT, Angela Davis ran again for vice president on the CPUSA ticket in 1984. "Bring to victory the defeat of Ronald Reagan," the "most sexist[,] . . . racist, anti–working class[,] . . . bellicose president in the history of this country," she charged at a Black women's conference in August. But the racial story of the 1984 elections was the stunning primary-campaign success of Martin Luther King Jr.'s former aide, the spellbinding orator and civil rights leader Rev. Jesse Jackson. Neither Jackson nor Davis garnered enough votes. Too many Americans fell for the myth of the good "morning in America" Reagan was selling them about the better economy.[20]

It may have been morning in America again in certain rich and White neighborhoods, which had awakened to prosperity repeatedly over the years. But it was not morning in America again in the communities where the CIA-backed Contra rebels of Nicaragua started smuggling cocaine in 1985. Nor was it morning in America for Black youths in 1985. Their unemployment rate was four times the rate it had been in 1954, though the White youth employment rate had marginally increased. Nor was it morning in America when some of these unemployed youths started remaking the expensive cocaine into cheaper crack to sell so they could earn a living. And the Reagan administration wanted to make sure that everyone knew it was not morning in America in Black urban neighborhoods, and that drugs—specifically, crack—and the drug dealers and users were to blame.

In October 1985, the US Drug Enforcement Administration (DEA) charged Robert Stutman, the special agent in charge of the DEA's New York City office, with drawing media attention to the spreading of crack (and the violence from dealers trying to control and stabilize drug markets). Stutman drew so much attention that he handed Reagan's slumbering War on Drugs an intense high. In 1986, thousands of sensationally racist stories engulfed the airwaves and newsstands describing the "predator" crack dealers who were supplying the "demon drug" to incurably addicted "crackheads" and "crack whores" (who were giving birth to biologically inferior "crack babies" in their scary concrete urban jungles). Not many stories reported on poor White crack sellers and users. In August 1986, *Time* magazine deemed crack "the issue of the year." But in reality, crack had become the latest drug addicting Americans to racist ideas.[21]

If Reagan's take on drugs was the overreported racist issue of the year, then the Free South Africa Movement (FSAM) made apartheid—and Reagan's fiscal and military support of it—the underreported antiracist issue of the year. The FSAM movement brought out into the open the long-standing ethnic racism between African Americans and African immigrants, an ethnic racism Eddie Murphy displayed in his box-office breaker of 1988, which became one of the most beloved Black comedies of all time. *Coming to America*, the love story of a rich African prince coming to Queens in search of a wife, hilariously mocked African Americans' ridiculously untrue racist ideas of animalistic, uncivilized, corrupt, and warlike people in Africa, racist ideas that *Roots* had not managed to fully expunge.

Weeks after passing the most antiracist bill of the decade over Reagan's veto—the Comprehensive Anti-Apartheid Act with its strict economic sanctions—Congress passed the most racist bill of the decade. On October 27, 1986, Reagan, "with great pleasure," signed the Anti-Drug Abuse Act, supported by both Republicans and Democrats. "The American people want their government to get tough and to go on the offensive," Reagan commented. By signing the bill, he put the presidential seal on the "Just say no" campaign and on the "tough laws" that would now supposedly deter drug abuse. While the Anti-Drug Abuse Act prescribed a minimum five-year sentence for a dealer or user caught with five grams of crack, the amount typically handled by Blacks and poor people, the mostly White and rich users and dealers of powder cocaine—who operated in neighborhoods with fewer police—had to be caught with five hundred grams to receive the same five-year minimum sentence. Racist ideas then defended this racist and elitist policy.[22]

The bipartisan act led to the mass incarceration of Americans. The prison population quadrupled between 1980 and 2000 due entirely to stiffer sentencing policies, not more crime. Between 1985 and 2000, drug offenses accounted for two-thirds of the spike in the inmate population. By 2000, Blacks comprised 62.7 percent and Whites 36.7

percent of all drug offenders in state prisons—and not because they were selling or using more drugs. That year, the National Household Survey on Drug Abuse reported that 6.4 percent of Whites and 6.4 percent of Blacks were using illegal drugs. Racial studies on drug dealers usually found similar rates. One 2012 analysis, the National Survey on Drug Use and Health, found that White youths (6.6 percent) were 32 percent *more* likely than Black youths (5 percent) to sell drugs. But Black youths were far more likely to get arrested for it.[23]

During the crack craze in the late 1980s and early 1990s, the situation was the same. Whites and Blacks were selling and consuming illegal drugs at similar rates, but the Black users and dealers were getting arrested and convicted much more. In 1996, when two-thirds of the crack users were White or Latina/o, 84.5 percent of the defendants convicted of crack possession were Black. Even without the crucial factor of racial profiling of Blacks as drug dealers and users by the police, a general rule applied that still applies today: wherever there are more police, there are more arrests, and wherever there are more arrests, people perceive there is more crime, which then justifies more police, and more arrests, and supposedly more crime.[24]

Since heavily policed inner-city Blacks were much more likely than Whites to be arrested and imprisoned in the 1990s—since more homicides occurred in their neighborhoods—racists assumed that Black people were actually using more drugs, dealing more in drugs, and committing more crimes of all types than White people. These false assumptions fixed the image in people's minds of the dangerous Black inner-city neighborhood as well as the contrasting image of the safe White suburban neighborhood, a racist notion that affected so many decisions of so many Americans, from housing choices to drug policing to politics, that they cannot be quantified. The "dangerous *Black* neighborhood" conception is based on racist ideas, not reality. There is such a thing as a dangerous "unemployed neighborhood," however. One study, for example, based on the National Longitudinal Youth Survey data collected from 1976 to 1989, found that young Black males were far more likely than young White males to engage in serious violent crime. But when the researchers compared only *employed* young males, the racial differences in violent behavior disappeared. *Certain* violent crime rates were higher in Black neighborhoods simply because unemployed people were concentrated in Black neighborhoods.[25]

But Reagan's tough-on-crime Republicans had no intention of committing political suicide among their donors and redirecting the blame for violent crime from the lawbreakers onto Reaganomics. Nor were they willing to lose their seats by trying to create millions of new jobs in a War on Unemployment, which would certainly have reduced violent crime. Instead, turning the campaign for law and order into a War on Drugs enriched many political lives over the next two decades. It hauled millions of impoverished non-White, nonviolent drug users and dealers into prisons where they could not vote, and later paroled them without their voting rights. A significant number of close elections would have come out differently if felons had not been disenfranchised, including at least seven senatorial races between 1980 and 2000, as well as the presidential election of 2000. What an ingeniously cruel way to quietly snatch away the voting power of your political opponents.[26]

Even the statistics suggesting that more violent crime—especially on innocent victims—was occurring in urban Black neighborhoods were based on a racist statistical method rather than reality. Drunk drivers, who routinely kill more people than violent urban Blacks, were not regarded as violent criminals in such studies, and 78 percent of arrested drunk drivers were White males in 1990. In 1986, 1,092 people succumbed to "cocaine-related" deaths, and there were another 20,610 homicides. That adds up to 21,702, still lower than the 23,990 alcohol-related traffic deaths that year (not to mention the number of serious injuries caused by drunk drivers that do not result in death). Drug dealers and gangsters primarily kill each other in inner cities, whereas the victims of drunk drivers are often innocent bystanders. Therefore, it was actually an open question in 1986 and thereafter whether an American was truly safer from lethal harm on the inner city's streets or on the suburban highways. Still, White Americans were far more likely to fear those distant Black mugshots behind their television screens than their neighborhoods' White drunk drivers, who were killing them at a greater rate.[27]

Since Reagan never ordered a War on Drunk Driving, it took a long and determined grassroots movement in the 1980s, forged by Mothers Against Drunk Driving (MADD), and countless horrible incidents—such as the drunk driver who killed twenty-seven schoolbus passengers in 1988—to force reluctant politicians to institute stronger penalties. But these new penalties for DUIs and DWIs still paled in comparison with the automatic five-year felony prison sentence for being caught for the first time with five grams of crack.

AS IT WAS, the media's attention in 1986 was not on the drunk drivers but focused narrowly on sensational crack crime stories and the subsequent effects on the Black family. In a CBS special report on "The Vanishing Family: Crisis in Black America," the network presented images of young welfare mothers and estranged fathers in a Newark apartment building, stereotypical images of Black female promiscuity, Black male laziness, and irresponsible Black parenting—the pathological Black family. It was these types of tales that prompted an aggravated Angela Davis to write an essay on the Black family in the spring of 1986. The percentage of children born to single Black women had risen from 21 percent in 1960 to 55 percent in 1985, Davis said. Black teenager birthrates could not explain this increase (those figures had remained *virtually unchanged* from 1920 to 1990). Davis explained that the "disproportionate number of births to unmarried teenagers" had been caused by the fact that older, married Black women had started having fewer children in the 1960s and 1970s. Therefore, it was the overall percentage of babies born to young and single Black mothers as opposed to married mothers—not the sheer number of babies born to single Black mothers—that dramatically rose.[28]

But to Reagan propagandists, welfare caused the nonexistent spike in single Black mothers, and the nonexistent spike had made the Black family disappear. "Statistical evidence does not prove those suppositions [that welfare benefits are an incentive to bear children]," admitted

Reagan's chief domestic policy adviser, Gary Bauer, in *The Family: Preserving America's Future* (1986). "And yet, even the most casual observer of public assistance programs understands there is indeed some relationship between the availability of welfare and the inclination of many young women to bear fatherless children." Evidence hardly mattered when convincing Americans that there was something wrong with Black welfare mothers—and therefore, with the Black family.[29]

Even the adored civil rights lawyer Eleanor Holmes Norton felt the need in 1985 to urge the restoration of the "traditional Black family." "The remedy is not as simple as providing necessities and opportunities," Norton explained in the *New York Times*. "The family's return to its historic strength will require the overthrow of the complicated predatory ghetto subculture." Norton provided no evidence to substantiate her class racism that "ghetto" Blacks were deficient in values of "hard work, education, respect for the Black family and . . . achieving a better life for one's children," in comparison to Black elites or any other racial class.[30]

This racist drug of the declining Black family was as addicting to consumers of all races as crack—and as addicting as the dangerous Black neighborhood. But many of the Black consumers hardly realized they had been drugged. And they hardly realized that the new television show they thought was so good at counteracting unsavory thoughts of Black people was just another racist drug.

CHAPTER 34

New Democrats

STAUNCH BELIEVERS IN uplift and media suasion looked to NBC's *The Cosby Show*, which premiered on September 20, 1984, to redeem the Black family in the eyes of White America. While many viewers enjoyed Bill Cosby's brilliant comedy and the show's alluring storylines, and many Black viewers delighted in watching a Black cast on primetime television for eight seasons, it was Cosby's racial vision that made *The Cosby Show* America's No. 1 show from 1985 to 1989 (and one of the most popular in apartheid South Africa). Cosby envisioned the ultimate uplift suasion show about a stereotype-defying family uplifted by their own striving beyond the confines of discriminated Blackness. He believed he was showing African Americans what was possible if they worked hard enough and stopped their antiracist activism. Cosby and his millions of loyal viewers actually believed that *The Cosby Show* and its spinoffs were persuading away the racist ideas of its millions of White viewers. And it did, for some. For other Whites, Cosby's fictional Huxtables were extraordinary Negroes, and the show merely substantiated their conviction—and Reagan's conviction, and racist Blacks' convictions—that racism could be found only in the history books. Some commentators understood this at the time. *The Cosby Show* "suggests that blacks are solely responsible for their social conditions, with no acknowledgement of the severely constricted life opportunities that most black people face," critiqued literary scholar Henry Louis Gates Jr. in the *New York Times* at the crest of the show's popularity in 1989.[1]

Like every attempt at uplift suasion before it, *The Cosby Show* did nothing to hinder the production and consumption of Reagan's racist drug war. Quite possibly the most sensationally racist crack story of the era was written by the Pulitzer Prize–winning, Harvard medical degree–holding *Washington Post* columnist Charles Krauthammer: "The inner-city crack epidemic is now giving birth to the newest horror: a bio-underclass, a generation of physically damaged cocaine babies," he wrote on July 30, 1989. These babies were likely a deviant "race of (sub) human drones" whose "biological inferiority is stamped at birth" and "permanent," he added. "The dead babies may be the lucky ones."[2]

The column triggered the second major round of horrendous crack stories. The *New York Times* told of how "maternity wards around the country ring with the high-pitched 'cat cries' of neurologically impaired crack babies." The *St. Louis Post-Dispatch* had one headline warning of a "Disaster in the Making: Crack Babies Start to Grow Up." Medical researchers validated these reports—and the racist ideas that inspired them—alongside pediatricians like UCLA's Judy Howard, who said crack babies lacked the brain function that "makes us human beings." Children's Hospital of Philadelphia neonatologist Hallam Hurt began following the lives of 224 "crack babies" born in Philadelphia between 1989 and 1992, and she fully anticipated "seeing a host of problems." In 2013, she concluded her study with a simple finding: poverty was worse for kids than crack. Medical researchers had to finally admit that "crack babies" were like the science for racist ideas: they never existed.[3]

BACKED BY SCIENCE or not, racist ideas persisted in American minds, and Reagan's vice president made sure to manipulate them when he ran for president in 1988. George H. W. Bush had been losing in the polls to the Democratic nominee, Massachusetts governor Michael Dukakis, until he released a television advertisement about a Black murderer and rapist of Whites, Willie Horton. "Despite a life sentence," the scary voiceover stated, "Horton received 10 weekend passes from prison. Horton fled, kidnapped a young couple, stabbing the man, and repeatedly raping his girlfriend. Weekend prison passes, Dukakis on crime."[4]

Setting himself apart from the "weak" Dukakis on crime, the "tough" Bush endorsed capital punishment and its rampant disparities. In 1987, the Supreme Court ruled in *McCleskey v. Kemp* that the "racially disproportionate impact" of Georgia's death penalty—Blacks were being sentenced to death four times more frequently than Whites— did not justify overturning the death sentence for a Black man named Warren McCleskey unless a "racially discriminatory purpose" could be demonstrated. If the Court had chosen to rule in McCleskey's favor, it would have opened the future to antiracist cases and to renovations of the criminal justice system, which was rotting in racism. But instead the justices disconnected racial disparities from racism, deemed racial disparities a normal part of the criminal justice system, and blamed these disparities on Black criminals, yet again producing racist ideas to defend racist policies. *McCleskey v. Kemp* turned out to be—as New York University lawyer Anthony G. Amsterdam predicted—"the *Dred Scott* decision of our time." The Supreme Court had made constitutional the rampant racial profiling that pumped up the inhumane growth of the Black executed and enslaved prison population.[5]

Like their ancestors, young urban Blacks resisted the law enforcement officials who condemned them to twentieth-century slavery. And they resisted sometimes to the beat. Hip Hop and rap blossomed in 1988 after a decade of growth from the concrete of the South Bronx. BET and MTV started airing their popular Hip Hop shows. *The Source* hit newsstands that year, beginning its reign as the world's longest-running rap periodical. It covered the head-slamming rhymes of Public Enemy—and "Fuck tha Police," the smashing hit of N.W.A., or Niggaz Wit Attitudes, from straight out of Compton.[6]

Hip Hop and Black Studies programs blossomed together in 1988. That year, professor Molefi Kete Asante established the world's first Black Studies doctoral program at Philadelphia's Temple University. Asante was the world's leading Afrocentric theorist, espousing a profound theory of cultural antiracism to counter the assimilationist ideas that continued their ascent after the demise of Black Power. Too many Black people—and too many Black Studies scholars—were "looking out" at themselves, at the world, and at their Black research subjects from the center and standards of Europeans, he argued in *The Afrocentric Idea* (1987). Europeans were masquerading their center as the finest, as sometimes the only, perspective. To Asante, there were multiple ways of seeing the world, being in the world, theorizing about the world, and studying the world—not just the Eurocentric worldviews, cultures, theories, and methodologies. He called for "Afrocentricity," by which he meant a cultural and philosophical center for African people based "on African aspiration, visions, and concepts."[7]

In 1989, Public Enemy recorded one of the most popular songs in Hip Hop history, "Fight the Power." The song headlined the soundtrack of Spike Lee's critically acclaimed 1989 urban rebellion flick, *Do the Right Thing*. "Fight the Power" tied together the commencement of the socially conscious age of Hip Hop and Black filmmaking and scholarship. *Do the Right Thing* was Lee's third feature film. His second, *School Daze* (1988), addressed assimilationist ideas related to skin tone and eye color (the lighter the better) and hair texture (the straighter the better), a theme suggested by the fact that Black Power's Afros were being cut or permed down. Some Blacks were even bleaching their skins White. The most known or suspected skin bleacher in the late 1980s and early 1990s was arguably the nation's most famous African American, singer Michael Jackson. It was rumored Jackson lightened his skin and thinned his nose and lips to boost his career. Indeed, light-skins still secured higher incomes and were preferred in adoptions, while dark-skins predominated in public housing and prisons and were more likely to report racial discrimination. Racists were blaming dark-skins for these disparities. Antiracists were blaming color discrimination. "The lighter the skin, the lighter the sentence," was a popular antiracist saying.[8]

SEVERAL DOZEN LEGAL scholars met at a convent outside of Madison, Wisconsin, on July 8, 1989, as Public Enemy's "Fight the Power" topped Billboard charts. They came together to forge an antiracist intellectual approach known as "critical race theory." Thirty-year-old UCLA legal scholar Kimberlé Williams Crenshaw organized the summer retreat the same year she penned "Demarginalizing the Inter-section of Race and Sex." The essay called for "intersectional theory," the critical awareness of gender racism (and thereby other intersec-tions, such as queer racism, ethnic racism, and class racism). "Although racism and sexism readily intersect in the lives of real people, they seldom do in feminist and antiracist practices," Crenshaw wrote three years later in another pioneering article in the *Stanford Law Review*. Der-rick Bell, Alan Freeman, and Richard Delgado, the early formulators of critical race theory in law schools, were also in attendance at the 1989 summer coming-out party for critical race theory. One of the greatest offshoots of the theory was critical Whiteness studies, investigating the anatomy of Whiteness, racist ideas, White privileges, and the tran-sition of European immigrants into Whiteness. Critical race theorists, as they came to be called, joined antiracist Black Studies scholars in the forefront of revealing the progression of racism in the 1990s.[9]

Angela Davis, a professor at San Francisco State University, work-ing from the same antiracist intellectual traditions, was also calling attention to the progression of racism. "African Americans are suffer-ing the most oppression since slavery," Davis thundered at California State University at Northridge in 1990. Her speech angered believers in racial progress. After all, African Americans possessed 1 percent of the national wealth in 1990, after holding 0.5 percent in 1865, even as the Black population remained at around 10 to 14 percent during that period. "Our country is now replete with many blacks in posi-tions of prestige and power," which was "certainly a far cry from the 'worst oppression since slavery,'" someone wrote in a miffed letter to the editor of the *Los Angeles Times*. It was not outside societal forces that were responsible for "impregnating unmarried girls" and forcing "young blacks to drop out of school and into drug-dealing, into gangs and into killing." No one had compelled Ugandans to "kill and oppress each other," or caused Ethiopia to make "such a mess of its econ-omy" that its citizens were "dependent on handouts from capitalists to survive." Apparently, in the United States and Africa, racists were imagining that it was Black-on-Black ethnic warfare and corruption, along with welfare handouts, that were causing global Black poverty and political instability and the lingering socioeconomic disparities between White and Black Americans and between Europe and Africa. In a much friendlier manner, Ronald Reagan echoed the letter writer's projection of global African incompetence when he spoke in England following the dissolution of the Soviet Union in December 1991. The end of the Cold War had "robbed much of the West of its common, uplifting purpose," Reagan declared. Americans and their allies should unite "to impose civilized standards of human decency" on the rest of the world.[10]

In the United States, it was poor, young Black women whom racists of all races supposed needed the greatest imposition of civilized standards of human decency. Producers and reproducers of racist ideas were saying that it was their loose sexual behavior—and not the actual declining number of Black children born to married Black couples—that was causing the increase in the *percentage* of children born to Black single mothers. Assimilationists argued that these young Black women could one day learn to discipline themselves sexually (like White women). Segregationists argued that they could not, advocating sterilization policies or long-term contraceptives. In December 1990, the US Food and Drug Administration approved the long-term contraceptive implant Norplant, despite its gruesome side effects. The *Philadelphia Inquirer* ran an editorial in support of it entitled "Poverty and Norplant: Can Contraception Reduce the Underclass?" The paper advocated Norplant—not an urban jobs bill—as a solution to the poverty of Black children.

While antiracists spit outrage at the editorial, Angela Davis emerged as one of the few voices condemning the ongoing denial of the sexual agency of young Black women. But Black and White racists rushed to the *Inquirer*'s defense. Louisiana legislator David Duke, the former KKK Grand Wizard, made a campaign out of it. He ran for Louisiana governor in 1991 on a pledge to reduce the number of Black welfare recipients by funding their implantations of Norplant. Duke's plan was shrewd. Even though most Blacks eligible for welfare did not utilize it, one study found that 78 percent of White Americans thought Blacks preferred to live on welfare. Duke lost the election even though the majority of Louisiana Whites voted for him. The next day, the *New York Times* printed a photo of a poor White welfare recipient who had voted for Duke because Blacks, she said, "just have those babies and go on welfare." The picture symbolized the power of racist ideas. Low-income Whites could be manipulated into voting for politicians who intended to slice their welfare, just as middle-income Whites were being manipulated into voting for politicians whose policies were increasing the socioeconomic inequities between the middle and upper classes.[11]

INSPIRED BY SOCIOLOGIST Patricia Hill Collins's 1990 volume *Black Feminist Thought*, Black feminists led the campaign to ban Norplant. The negative portrayals of young Black women in the Norplant debate never failed to leave them outraged. Some Black feminists were less outraged about the sexist portrayals of women in Hip Hop, viewing "sexism in rap as a necessary evil" or a reflection of sexism in American society, according to Michele Wallace's report in the *New York Times* on July 29, 1990. Wallace revealed the recent rise of women rappers, such as Salt-n-Pepa, M. C. Lyte, and the "politically sophisticated" Queen Latifah.[12]

Women rappers fared better than their sisters in Hollywood, because at least their art was in mass circulation. Aside from Julie Dash's pioneering *Daughters of the Dust*, Black men were the only ones producing major Black films in 1991. These included illustrious films like Mario Van Peebles's *New Jack City;* John Singleton's debut antiracist tragedy *Boyz N the Hood;* and Spike Lee's acclaimed *Jungle Fever. Jungle Fever* got people arguing about Black men cheating on Black women with White women; about interracial relations being "jungle fever," not love; about the discrimination that interracial couples faced; about whether anything was wrong with Black women (causing Black men to date White women); and about how "there ain't no good Black men out there," because all the Black men were "drug addicts, homos," or "dogs," to quote one character. Some moviegoers defended the antiracist truth: that there was nothing wrong with Black women or Black men as a group. Some consumed Spike Lee's satire at face value, probably not realizing that no good Black women plus no good Black men equaled no good Black people—equaled racist ideas.[13]

Black men produced more films in 1991 than during the entire 1980s. But a White man, George Holliday, shot the most influential racial film of the year on March 3 from the balcony of his Los Angeles apartment. He filmed ninety grueling seconds of four Los Angeles Police Department officers savagely striking Rodney King, a Black taxi driver. Holliday sent the footage to TV stations, and TV stations started broadcasting it across the country, from urban communities that had been suffering under the baton of aggressive policing for years to suburban and rural communities that had been cheering the aggressive policing of inner-city communities for years. Charges of assault with a deadly weapon and the use of excessive force were quickly filed against the four LAPD officers. In the emotional swing, N.W.A.'s "Fuck tha Police" reemerged with a social vengeance in thumping cars and on screaming televisions. President Bush condemned the beating, but he did not back down from the tough-on-crime mantra that he had ridden to the White House. It was a political mandate that the LAPD had executed on trampled and imprisoned Black bodies as efficiently as any department in the nation. Politicians created law-and-order America, but the police officers were the pawns carrying out the policies.[14]

Bush's political dancing on the King beating angered antiracists as spring turned into summer. He fanned the fury on July 1, 1991, when he nominated a Black jurist, Clarence Thomas, to replace civil rights icon Thurgood Marshall on the Supreme Court. Thomas saw himself as a paragon of self-reliance, even though he had needed antiracist activism and policies to get him into Holy Cross College and Yale Law School, and even though he had needed his racist Blackness to get him into the Reagan administration in 1981, first as assistant secretary of education for the Office of Civil Rights. He had been the backseat driver of antiracist and racist forces throughout his career. And now, Bush had called Thomas to the Supreme Court, claiming he was the "best qualified at this time," a judgment that sounded as ridiculous as those officers trying to justify the beating of Rodney King. The "best qualified" forty-three-year-old Thomas had served as a judge for all of fifteen months.[15]

During Thomas's formal confirmation hearings in the Senate that fall, Anita Hill, who had been his assistant at the Education Department and at the Equal Employment Opportunity Commission (EEOC), testified. She accused Thomas of sexual harassment and gender discrimination during their tenure in government employment. Thomas denied the allegations, framing it a "high-tech lynching for uppity blacks who in any way deign to think for themselves, to do for themselves." The frenzied Senate confirmation arguments that followed spilled out into the rest of America, making the summertime arguments over *Jungle Fever* seem mild. Again and again, Hill's defenders spoke out, arguing that the defamation of Black womanhood and the lack of awareness of sexual harassment was preventing Americans from believing her testimony. Thomas's defenders, meanwhile, argued that it was another case of the Black man being cut down. Gender racists generalized Thomas and Hill to weigh in on what was wrong with Black men or Black women. In the end, Thomas was narrowly confirmed on October 15, 1991. But the defenders of Hill and of Black women did not walk quietly into the night. "We cannot tolerate this type of dismissal of any one Black woman's experience," several hundred Black women wrote in a protest advertisement in the *New York Times* a month later.[16]

Clarence Thomas joined a US Supreme Court that had gutted the Civil Rights Act of 1964, compelling Congress to pass the Civil Rights Restoration Act over Reagan and Bush vetoes. The teeth of the bill bit down on provable "intentional discrimination," hardly touching the octopus arms of discrimination that had privately grown in the past three decades, causing very public racial disparities up and down the job market, from Black professionals receiving less pay than their White counterparts to Black workers being forced into the dead-end service industry. White workers and professionals had come to widely believe that they must secretly help their racial fellows in the job market, on the false assumption that government policies were helping Blacks more than Whites. Discriminating Whites had replaced the "old black-inferiority rationale for exclusion" by a more sophisticated affirmative action rationale for exclusion. It was a new racist theory to justify an old job discrimination. As for the racial disparities in unemployment rates, the newest racist theory was that African Americans' "refusal to lower their demands helps keep them jobless," as NYU political scientist Lawrence Mead stated. Racists cleverly avoided the question of whether jobless Whites were more willing to lower their demands. Instead, they dispatched their ethnic racism, regarding African Americans as less industrious, more welfare dependent, and less willing to lower their job demands than non-White immigrants.[17]

African Americans were making millions in the entertainment industry. But not all was well there, either. On November 7, 1991, HIV-positive Ervin "Magic" Johnson suddenly retired from the Los Angeles Lakers basketball team. Vowing to "battle this deadly disease," he became the overnight heterosexual face of the presumed White gay disease. After a long and torturous and murderously oppressive decade in the 1980s, HIV-positive men and women were finally starting to be seen as innocent victims of a disease by the early 1990s. But Johnson's public announcement, his face, and his admission of multiple sexual partners instigated a shift in perceptions of HIV and AIDS. The "gay White disease" affecting innocent victims—and necessitating protective politics—transformed into a "Black disease" affecting ignorant, hypersexual, callous marauders, and necessitating punitive policies to control them.[18]

FOR ANGELA DAVIS, 1991 began with outrage over the physical lashing of Rodney King and ended with outrage over the verbal lashing of Anita Hill. The year also ended for Davis in an unfamiliar place. She had taken a new professorship at the University of California at Santa Cruz, and she stepped away from the Communist Party after spending twenty-three years as the most recognizable Communist in the heartland of global capitalism. On the eve of the twenty-fifth CPUSA National Convention in Cleveland in December 1991, Davis joined with about eight-hundred other members to draft and sign an initiative critical of the party's racism, elitism, and sexism. In a punishing response, none of the signatories were reelected to office. They bolted the CPUSA.[19]

Although she was in the market for a new party, Davis did not join the Democratic Party, or rather, the newest force in US politics, the New Democrats. This group was espousing liberal fiscal policies but accepting Republican-style toughness on welfare and crime. A dazzling, well-spoken, and well-calculating Arkansas governor was now billing himself as the ultimate New Democrat. On January 24, 1992, weeks before the start of the Democratic primaries, Bill Clinton traveled back to Arkansas. The country had gone through Nixon's law and order, Reagan's welfare queens, and Bush's Willie Horton—and now Clinton made the execution of a mentally impaired Black man, Ricky Ray Rector, into a campaign spectacle to secure racist votes. "I can be nicked a lot," Clinton told reporters afterward, "but no one can say I'm soft on crime."[20]

By the time an all-White jury acquitted the four LAPD officers on April 29, 1992, for the Rodney King beating, Clinton had practically run away with the Democratic nomination. The millions of viewers of the beating were told that those officers had done nothing wrong. With justice denied them in the courts, Black and Brown residents rushed to claim justice in the Los Angeles streets. They had reached their own verdict: the criminal justice system, local business owners, and Reagan-Bush economic policies were guilty as charged of robbing the poor of livelihoods and assaulting them with the deadly weapon of racism. On April 30, 1992, Bill Cosby pleaded with the rebels to stop the violence and watch the final episode of The Cosby Show. Rodney King himself tearfully pleaded the next day, "Can we all get along?" It would take 20,000 troops to quell the six-day uprising and restore the order of racism and poverty in Los Angeles.[21]

Open-minded Americans seeking to understand the racist sources of rebellion and the progression of racism read Andrew Hacker's New York Times 1992 best seller, Two Nations: Black & White, Separate, Hostile, Unequal, and Derrick Bell's Faces at the Bottom of the Well: The Permanence of Racism—or, two years later, Cornel West's Race Matters. Or they entered theaters to watch Spike Lee's best-ever joint, a film Roger Ebert rated as the top film of 1992. In the opening scene of *Malcolm X*, Lee showed the beating of Rodney King and the burning of the American flag.[22]

"If you call it a riot it sounds like it was just a bunch of crazy people who went out and did bad things for no reason," argued South Central LA's new antiracist congresswoman, the walking powerhouse Maxine Waters. The rebellion, she said, "was [a] somewhat understandable, if not acceptable[,] . . . spontaneous reaction to a lot of injustice." To Vice President Dan Quayle, however, the rebels were not rebelling from economic poverty, but a "poverty of values." The New Democrat Bill Clinton blamed both political parties for failing urban America before blasting the "savage behavior" of "lawless vandals" who "do not share our values," whose "children are growing up in a culture alien from ours, without families, without neighborhood, without church, without support." On Clinton's racist note, Columbia University researchers began a five-year research study of *only* Black and Latino boys in New York to search for a connection between genetics and bad parenting and violence. (They did not find any connection.)[23]

About a month after the LA uprising, Bill Clinton took his campaign to the national conference of Jesse Jackson's Rainbow Coalition. Though Jackson was widely unpopular among those racist Whites whom Clinton was trying to attract to the New Democrats, when Jackson invited Hip Hop artist Sister Souljah to address the conference, the Clinton team saw its political opportunity. The twenty-eight-year-old Bronx poverty native had just released *360 Degrees of Power*, an antiracist album so provocative that it made Lee's films and Ice Cube's albums seem cautious. White Americans were still raging over her defense of the LA rebellion in the *Washington Post*: "I mean, if black people kill black people every day, why not have a week and kill white people?" It was clipped and circulated, but few racist Americans heard or understood—or wanted to understand—her point: she was critiquing the racist idea of occasional Black-on-White deaths mattering more to the government than Black people killing Black people every day.[24]

On June 13, 1992, Clinton took the podium at the Rainbow Coalition conference. "If you took the words 'white' and 'black' and reversed them, you might think David Duke was giving that speech," Clinton volleyed at Sister Souljah's post-rebellion comments. This dismissive assimilationist maneuver of equating antiracists with segregationists, this planned political stunt, thrilled racist voters nearly as much as Clinton's campaign pledge to "end welfare as we know it." Clinton gained a lead in the polls that he never lost.[25]

By the 1993 Christmas season, rappers were hearing criticism from all sides of the racist rainbow, not just from Bill Clinton. Sixty-six-year-old civil rights veteran C. Delores Tucker and her National Political Congress of Black Women took the media portrayals debate to a new racist level in their strong campaign to ban "Gangsta rap." Gangsta rap was not only making Black people look bad before Whites and reinforcing their racist ideas, she said. Gangsta rap lyrics and music videos were literally harming Black people, making them more violent, more sexual, more sexist, more criminal, and more materialistic (here she was sounding a sensational chord that would be replayed years later in response to Black reality shows). In short, Gangsta rap was making its urban Black listeners inferior (to say nothing of its greater number of suburban White listeners). It was a curious time for this well-meaning campaign, and not just because Queen Latifah had released her Grammy Award–winning feminist anthem "U.N.I.T.Y.," which headlocked and shouted at men, "Who you callin' a bitch?!" Political scientist Charles Murray was in the midst of reproducing racist ideas for the upcoming 1994 midterm elections, falsely connecting the "welfare system" to the rise in "illegitimacy" that, as he put it in the *Wall Street Journal* on October 29, "has now reached 68% of births to [single] black women." He repeated the claim on television shows in the final weeks of 1993.[26]

C. Delores Tucker could have campaigned against the anti-welfare ravings of Charles Murray, which were much more materially and socially devastating to poor Black people—especially women—than the lyrics of Gangsta rap. Instead, she became the dartboard for Hip Hop artists, especially the twenty-two-year-old new king of Gangsta rap, the son of Black Panthers, Tupac Shakur. In 1993, Tupac encouraged his fans to "Keep Ya Head Up," and connected to them with rhymes such as, "I'm tryin to make a dollar out of fifteen cents / It's hard to be legit and still pay tha rent."[27]

While Tucker remained focused on the scourge of Gangsta rap, Massachusetts Institute of Technology historian Evelyn Hammonds mobilized to defend against the defamation of Black womanhood. More than 2,000 Black female scholars from all across the country made their way to MIT's campus on January 13, 1994, for "Black Women in the Academy: Defending Our Name." It was the first-ever national conference of Black women scholars, whose academic lives and scholarship had been routinely cast aside by gender racism. In the cold of the Boston-area winter, these women came blazing about the public dishonor of Black welfare mothers, of Anita Hill, of Sister Souljah, of three of Clinton's failed appointments (Johnetta Cole, Lani Guinier, and Joycelyn Elders): of the Black woman. Some of the attendees had signed the *Times* advertisement defending Anita Hill in November 1991.

Angela Davis was honored as the conference's closing keynote speaker. She was certainly the nation's most famous African American woman academic. But more importantly, she had consistently, prominently, and unapologetically defended Black women over the course of her career, including those Black women that even some Black women did not want to defend. She had been arguably America's staunchest antiracist voice over the past two decades, unwavering in her search for antiracist explanations when others took the easier and racist way out of Black blame. Davis had looked into the eyes and minds and experiences of those young incarcerated Black and Brown women during her imprisonment in New York in 1970, and she had never stopped looking into their lives and defending them. Her career embodied the conference's title, like the careers of so many of those accomplished intellectuals who listened that day to her speech.

Davis opened her address by taking her audience back to the origins of the conference title, "Defending Our Name." She took them back to the moral policing of Black clubwomen in the 1890s, which, like the campaigns today "against teenage pregnancy," denied "sexual autonomy in young black women." Davis admonished the "contemporary law and order discourse" that was "legitimized" by both political parties and all the races. Black politicians were sponsoring "a deleterious anti-crime bill," and Black people were "increasingly calling for more police and more prisons," unaware that while African Americans constituted 12 percent of the drug users, they constituted more than 36 percent of the drug arrests. Davis called for her sisters to envision "a new abolitionism" and "institutions other than prisons to address the social problems that lead to imprisonment."[28]

Ten days later, in his first State of the Union Address, President Clinton called for the very opposite of "a new abolitionism." Congress, he said, should "set aside partisan differences and pass a strong, smart, tough crime bill." The president endorsed a federal "three strikes and you're out" law, bringing on wild applause from both Democrats and Republicans. Heeding Clinton's urging, Republicans and New Democrats sent him a $30 billion crime bill for his signature in August 1994. New Democrats hailed the bill as a victory for being "able to wrest the crime issue from the Republicans and make it their own." The Violent Crime Control and Law Enforcement Act, the largest crime bill in US history, created dozens of new federal capital crimes, instituted life sentences for certain three-times offenders, and provided billions for the expansion of police forces and prisons—and the net effect would be the largest increase of the prison population in US history, mostly on nonviolent drug offenses. Clinton fulfilled his campaign vow that no Republican would be tougher on crime than him—and crime in America was colored Black. As Tupac Shakur rhymed in "Changes," "Instead of war on poverty, they got a war on drugs so the police can bother me." (About two decades later, Hillary Clinton—in the thicket of a run for the White House—renounced the effects of her husband's signature anticrime bill, calling for the "end of the era of mass incarceration").[29]

Just as the discourse on the overblown welfare problem primarily defamed Black women, the discourse on the overblown crime problem in 1994 primarily defamed Black men. Media critic Earl Ofari Hutchinson passionately rebuked the defamers in *The Assassination of the Black Male Image,* his 1994 scorcher. The Queens-born rapper Nas released "One Love," a composition of letters to incarcerated friends, on his debut album, *Illmatic,* an instant classic, as revered that year— and in history—as "Juicy," the debut single of the Brooklyn-born Biggie Smalls. In Biggie's music video, one lyric is sung over the sight of a Black male behind bars: "Considered a fool 'cause I dropped out of high school / Stereotypes of a black male misunderstood / And it's still all good."[30]

Biggie Smalls had no idea he had released his debut single on the eve of the most spirited academic debate in recent history on whether Black people were natural or nurtured fools. It was an academic debate that had serious political repercussions for Clinton's tough-on-Blacks New Democrats and the newest force in American politics, which pledged to be even tougher.

CHAPTER 35

New Republicans

BY THE TIME Biggie Small's "Juicy" was released in 1994, a growing number of academics was accepting the truth that "intelligence" was so transient, so multifaceted, so relative, that no one could accurately measure it without being biased in some form or fashion. And these revelations were threatening the very foundation of racist ideas in education (as well as sexist and elitist ideas in education). These revelations were endangering the racist perceptions of the historically White schools and colleges as the most intelligent atmospheres; the contrived achievement gap (and actual funding gap); the privileged pipelines for Whites into the best-funded schools, colleges, jobs, and economic lives; and the standardized testing that kept those pipelines mostly White. Harvard experimental psychologist Richard Herrnstein and political scientist Charles Murray watched the growth of these endangering ideas in the 1980s and early 1990s. In response, they published *The Bell Curve: Intelligence and Class Structure in American Life*, a landmark book that gave standardized tests—and the racist ideas underpinning them—a new lease on life.

In the first sentence, Herrnstein and Murray took aim at the spreading realization that general intelligence did not exist, and as such, could not vary from human to human in a form that could be measured on a single weighted scale, such as a standardized test. "That the word *intelligence* describes something real and that it varies from person to person is as universal and ancient as any understanding about the state of being human," Herrnstein and Murray wrote at the beginning of their Introduction. They went on to dismiss as "radical" and "naïve" those antiracists who rejected standardized test scores as indicators of intelligence and thus the existence of the racial achievement gap. For Herrnstein and Murray, that left two reasonable "alternatives": "(1) the cognitive difference between blacks and whites is genetic" (as segregationists argued); "or (2) the cognitive difference between blacks and whites is environment" (as assimilationists argued). Actually, Herrnstein and Murray reasoned, "It seems highly likely to us that both genes and the environment have something to do with racial differences." They claimed that "cognitive ability is substantially heritable, apparently no less than 40 percent and no more than 80 percent."

The increasing genetically inferior "underclass" was having the most children, and as they had the most children, the great White and wealthy "cognitive elite" was slowly passing into oblivion. "Inequality of endowments, including intelligence, is a reality," Herrnstein and Murray concluded. "Trying to eradicate inequality with artificially manufactured outcomes has led to disaster."[1]

In fact, it was the resistance to egalitarian measures by those all-powerful beneficiaries of inequality and their producers of racist ideas, like Herrnstein and Murray, that had led to disaster. The book was well marketed, and initial reviews were fairly positive. It arrived during the final straightaway to the 1994 midterm elections, around the time the New *Republicans* issued their extremely tough "Contract with America" to take the welfare and crime issue back from Clinton's New Democrats. Charles Murray started the midterm election cycle whipping up voters about the "rise of illegitimacy," and ended by rationalizing the "Contract with America," especially the New Republicans' tough-on-crime "Taking Back Our Streets Act" and tough-on-welfare "Personal Responsibility Act."[2]

The term "personal responsibility" had been playing minor roles for some time. In 1994, Georgia representative Newt Gingrich and Texas representative Richard Armey, the main authors of the "Contract with America," brought the term to prime time—to the lexicon of millions of American racists—targeting not just Black welfare recipients. The mandate was simple enough: Black people, especially poor Black people, needed to take "personal responsibility" for their socioeconomic plight and for racial disparities, and stop blaming racial discrimination for their problems, and depending on government to fix them. The racist mandate of "personal responsibility" convinced a new generation of Americans that irresponsible Black people caused the racial inequities, not discrimination—thereby convincing a new generation of racist Americans to fight against irresponsible Black people.

It made sense to encourage a Black *individual* (or non-Black individual) to take more responsibility for his or her own life. It made racist sense to tell Black *people* as a group to take more personal responsibility for their lives and for the nation's racial disparities, since the irresponsible actions of Black individuals were always generalized in the minds of racists. According to this racist logic, Black people and their irresponsibility were to blame for their higher poverty and unemployment and underemployment rates, as if there were more dependent and lazy Black individuals than dependent and lazy White individuals. Slaveholders' racist theory of African Americans as more dependent had been dusted off and renovated for the 1990s, allowing racists to reside in the hollow mentality of thinking that African Americans were not taking enough personal responsibility, and that's why so many were dependent on government welfare, just as they used to be dependent on their masters' welfare.

It was a popular racist idea—even among Black people who were generalizing the individual actions of someone around them. In the 1994 midterm elections, voters handed Republicans and their dictum on personal responsibility control of Congress. After the New Democrats got tougher than the New Republicans by passing the toughest crime bill in history, New Republicans pledged to get even tougher than the New Democrats. Both angled to win over one of the oldest interest groups—the racist vote—which probably had never before been as multiracial as it was in 1994.

As 1995 began, the critical and affirming responses of *The Bell Curve* began to cross fire. It is hard to imagine another book that sparked such an intense academic war, possibly because the segregationists, in their think tanks, and the assimilationists, in universities and academic associations, and the antiracists, in their popular Black Studies and critical race theory collectives, were all so powerful. In his revised and expanded 1996 edition of *The Mismeasure of Man*, Stephen Jay Gould maintained that no one should be surprised that *The Bell Curve*'s publication "coincided exactly . . . with a new age of social meanness." *The Bell Curve*, said Gould, "must . . . be recording a swing of the political pendulum to a sad position that requires a rationale for affirming social inequalities as dictates of biology." He criticized the proponents of this new meanness for their calls to "slash every program of social services for people in genuine need . . . but don't cut a dime, heaven forbid, from the military . . . and provide tax relief for the wealthy." British psychologist Richard Lynn defended the social meanness and *The Bell Curve*, asking, in an article title, "Is Man Breeding Himself Back to the Age of the Apes?" The "underclass" was only "good" at "producing children," and "these children tend to inherit their parents' poor intelligence and adopt their socio-pathic lifestyle, reproducing the cycle of deprivation." The American Psychological Association (APA)—representing the originators and popularizers of standardized intelligence testing—convened a Task Force on Intelligence in response to *The Bell Curve*. "The differential between the mean intelligence test scores of Blacks and Whites does not result from any obvious biases in test construction and administration, nor does it simply reflect differences in socio-economic status," the assimilationist and defensive APA report stated in 1996. "Explanations based on factors of caste and culture may be appropriate, but so far there is little direct empirical support for them. There is certainly no such support for a genetic interpretation. At this time, no one knows what is responsible for the differential." No one will ever know what doesn't exist.[3]

While congratulating and lifting up Hernnstein and Murray for *The Bell Curve*, Republican politicians tried to unseat Angela Davis after UC Santa Cruz's faculty awarded her the prestigious President's Chair professorship in January 1995. "I'm outraged," California state senator Bill Leonard told reporters. "The integrity of the entire system is on the line when it appoints someone with Ms. Davis' reputation for racism, violence, and communism." Davis, he said, was "trying to create a civil war between whites and blacks." Southern segregationists had said that northern integrationists were trying to create a civil war between the races in the 1950s. Enslavers had said that abolitionists were trying to create a civil war between the races back in the 1800s. Both northern and southern segregationists had regarded Jim Crow and slavery as positively good and claimed that discrimination had ended or never existed. As much as segregationist theory had changed over the years, it had remained the same. Since the 1960s, segregationist theorists, like their predecessors, were all about convincing Americans that racism did not exist, knowing that antiracists would stop resisting racism, and racism would then be assured, only when Americans were convinced that the age of racism was over.[4]

After Hernnstein and Murray decreed that racial inequality was due not to discrimination, but to genetics, Murray's co-fellow at the American Enterprise Institute, almost on cue in 1995, decreed "the end of racism" in his challenging book, which used that phrase as its title. "Why should groups with different skin color, head shape, and other visible characteristics prove identical in reasoning ability or the ability to construct an advanced civilization?" asked the former Reagan aide Dinesh D'Souza. "If blacks have certain inherited abilities, such as improvisational decision making, that could explain why they predominate in certain fields such as jazz, rap, and basketball, and not in other fields, such as classical music, chess, and astronomy." These racist ideas were not racist ideas to D'Souza, who wrapped himself in his Indian ancestry on the book's first page in order to declare that his "inclinations" were "strongly antiracist and sympathetic to minorities." D'Souza, the self-identified antiracist, rejected the antiracist notion that racism was "the main obstacle facing African Americans today, and the primary explanation for black problems." Instead, he regarded "liberal antiracism" as African Americans' main obstacle, because it blamed "African American pathologies on white racism and opposes all measures that impose civilization standards."[5]

With D'Souza's incredible writing and speaking and marketing talents—and powerful backers—he had managed to get many Americans to ponder the issues discussed in *The End of Racism*. But discrimination was everywhere in 1995 for people who cared enough to open their eyes and look at the policies, disparities, and rhetoric all around them. How could anyone claim the end of racism during one of the most racially charged years in US history, with racist ideas swinging back and forth like Ping-Pong balls in the media coverage of the criminal trial of the century? From the opening statements on January 24 to the live verdict on October 3, 1995, the O. J. Simpson murder trial and exoneration became the epitome of softness on crime for upset racist Americans.[6]

The O.J. case was not the only evidence for the progression of racism that D'Souza wisely omitted. Florida's Don Black established one of the earliest White supremacist websites, Stormfront.org, in 1995. Informing the views of this new crop of "cyber racists," as journalist Jessie Daniels termed them, were segregationists like Canadian psychologist J. Phillippe Ruston, who argued that evolution had given Blacks different brain and genital sizes than Whites. "It's a trade-off; more brain or more penis. You can't have everything," Ruston told *Rolling Stone* readers in January 1995. In March, Halle Berry starred in *Losing Isaiah* as the spiraling debate over interracial adoptions hit theaters. The film was about a Black mother on crack whose baby is adopted by a White woman. And while the idea of Black parents adopting a White child was beyond the racist imagination, assimilationists were not only encouraging White savior parents to adopt Black children, but claiming that Black children would be better off in White homes than they were in Black homes.[7]

When asked in 1995 to "close your eyes for a second, envision a drug user, and describe that person to me," 95 percent of the respondents described a Black face, despite Black faces constituting a mere 15 percent of drug users that year. But racist Americans were closing their eyes to these studies, and opening them to pieces like "The Coming of the Super Predators" in the *Weekly Standard* on November 27, 1995.

Princeton University's John J. Dilulio—a fellow at the Manhattan Institute, where Charles Murray had resided in the 1980s—revealed the 300 percent increase in murder rates for Black fourteen- to seventeen-year-olds between 1985 and 1992, a rate six times greater than the White increase. He did not explain this surge in violence by revealing the simultaneous surge in unemployment rates among young Black males. Nor did Dilulio explain the violent surge by revealing that drug enforcement units were disproportionately mass incarcerating young Black drug dealers, in some cases knowing full well that the consequence of breaking up a drug ring was a violent struggle for control of the previously stabilized market. Dilulio explained this violent surge by sensationalizing the "moral poverty" of growing up "in abusive, violence-ridden, fatherless, Godless, and jobless settings." When we look "on the horizon," he said, there "are tens of thousands of severely morally impoverished juvenile super-predators" who "will do what comes 'naturally': murder, rape, rob, assault, burglarize, deal deadly drugs, and get high." What was Dilulio's solution to "super-predators"? "It's called religion."[8]

In the eyes of Dilulio, in the eyes of millions of people of all races, the baggy-clothes wearing, Ebonics-swearing, Hip Hop–sharing, "Fuck tha Police"–declaring young Black male did not have to wear a costume on Halloween in 1995. He was already a scary character—a "menace to society"—as a 1993 film had depicted (*Menace II Society*). And his young mother was a menace for giving birth to him. The main female and male prey of predatory racism were effectively stamped "super-predators." As an antiracist teacher in *Menace II Society* told young Black males, "The hunt is on and you're the prey!"[9]

In the midst of all of these proclamations about the end of racism in 1995, African Americans engaged in the largest political mobilization in their history, the bold Million Man March on Washington, DC. It had been proposed by Louis Farrakhan after the smoke cleared from the 1994 midterm elections. March fever quickly enraptured Black Americans. Antiracist feminists, Angela Davis included, ridiculed the gender racism of the march's unofficial organizing principle: Black men must rise up from their weakened state of emasculation to become heads of households and communities and uplift the race. "Justice cannot be served, by countering a distorted racist view of black manhood with a narrowly sexist vision of men standing 'a degree above women,'" Davis said at a Midtown Manhattan press conference on the eve of the march. But some critics went too far. As some Black feminists were erroneously calling march organizers sexist for mobilizing just Black *men*, some White assimilationists were erroneously calling march organizers racist for mobilizing just *Black* men.[10]

Some activists who split over the Million Man March did come together in the summer of 1995 to defend the life of the world's most famous Black male political prisoner, Mumia Abu-Jamal, who had been convicted of killing a White police officer in Philadelphia in 1982. "These are America's death row residents: men and woman who walk the razor's edge between half-life and certain death," Mumia said in *Live from Death Row*, a collection of his commentaries. "You will find a blacker world on death row than anywhere else. African-Americans, a mere 11 percent of the national population, compose about 40 percent of the death row population. There, too, you will find this writer."[11]

Weeks after *Live from Death Row* appeared to a shower of reviews in May 1995, and days before Mumia's lawyers filed an appeal for a new trial, law-and-order Pennsylvania governor Thomas Ridge, a Republican, signed Mumia Abu-Jamal's death warrant. His execution would be August 17, 1995. Protests erupted around the world that summer for Mumia's life and for the death of capital punishment. Among the protesters were graying activists, some of whom had screamed "Free Angela" decades ago, and younger ones, some of whom had helped to mobilize the Million Man March. But before the National Day of Protest was to take place, scheduled for August 12, Mumia was granted an indefinite stay of execution.[12]

At the end of that volcanic summer, the vast majority of African Americans were supportive of the doubly conscious Million Man March, doubly conscious of racist and antiracist ideas. Arguably, its most pervasively popular organizing principle was personal responsibility, the call for Black men to take more personal responsibility for their lives, their families, their neighborhoods, and their Black nation. Many of the roughly 1 million Black men who showed up on the National Mall on October 16, 1995, showed up believing the racist idea that something was wrong with Black men and Black teens and Black boys and Black fathers and Black husbands. But many of those marchers who stood there and listened to the fifty speakers also believed the antiracist idea that there was something wrong with rampant discrimination. As Louis Farrakhan thundered at the climax of his two-and-a-half-hour oration, "The real evil in America is not white flesh or black flesh. The real evil in America is the idea that undergirds the setup of the Western world, and that idea is called white supremacy."[13]

Bill Clinton did not greet the million Black men or hear their exclamations of racism's persistence on October 16. Instead he gave a racial progress speech at the University of Texas, pleading in the heart of evangelical America for racial healing, egging on the mass evangelical crusade for racial reconciliation in 1996 and 1997. Crusading evangelicals would go on to preach that the so-dubbed problem of mutual racial hate could be solved by God bringing about mutual love. Clinton, at least, did recognize in his Texas speech that "we must clean the house of white America of racism." But he surrounded one of the most antiracist statements of his presidency with two of the most racist statements of his presidency. Instead of relaying statistics that Whites usually suffered violence at the hands of Whites, Clinton legitimized the "roots of white fear in America" by saying that "violence for . . . white people too often has a black face." And then he went on the defensive: "It's not racist for whites to assert that the culture of welfare dependency, out-of-wedlock pregnancy, and absent fatherhood cannot be broken by social programs unless there is first more personal responsibility."[14]

Clinton officially declared himself a supporter of the racist idea of personal responsibility when he signed the Personal Responsibility and Work Opportunity Reconciliation Act (PRWORA) into law on August 22, 1996, with the next presidential election on the horizon. The bill was a compromise between Newt Gingrich's New Republicans and Clinton's New Democrats. It limited federal control of welfare programs, required work for benefits, and inserted welfare time limits. Even though programs for the poor represented only 23 percent of the non-defense budget, and had suffered 50 percent of the spending cuts over the past two years, welfare reform remained the leading domestic issue for the majority of White Americans. From Barry Goldwater's "animal creature" to Reagan's "welfare queen," producers of racist ideas had done their job on non-Black Americans. Republican congressman John L. Mica of Florida held up a sign that said it all during the congressional debate on the bill: "Don't Feed the Alligators / We post these warnings because unnatural feedings and artificial care creates dependency."[15]

The same producers of racist ideas had also done their job on Black Americans, averting a march against welfare reform, and causing some African Americans to hate irresponsible, dependent, violent "niggers" as much as racist non-Blacks did. "I love black people, but I hate niggers," jabbed a relatively unknown Black comedian, Chris Rock, on HBO's "Bring the Pain" on June 1, 1996. The unforgettable performance began with a litany of antiracist jabs at Blacks and Whites over their reactions to the O.J. verdict and catapulted Chris Rock into the pantheon of American comedy. It marked the beginning of a revolution in Black comedy and introduced the three main comedic topics for a new generation: relationships, the racism of White people, and what was wrong with Black people. Out of "Bring the Pain," doubly conscious Black comedy emerged as one of the most dynamic arenas of antiracist and racist ideas, with listeners laughing at, or with, the comedians.[16]

ANTIRACISTS SUFFERED A crushing loss in California on election night in 1996. California voters banned affirmative action, or "preferential treatment," in public employment, contracts, and education. Neither funding allocation policies for public colleges and K–12 schools nor standardized tests—both of which preferentially treated White, rich, and male students—were banned. The percentage of African Americans at University of California campuses began to decline.

The campaign for California's Proposition 209 ballot initiative displayed the progression of racist ideas in their full effect: its proponents branded antiracist affirmative action as discriminatory, named the campaign and ballot measure the "civil rights initiative," evoked the "dream" of Martin Luther King Jr. in an advertisement, and put a Black face on the campaign, University of California regent Ward Connerly. It was a blueprint Connerly would take on the road to eliminate affirmative action in other states, but not before receiving a public rebuke from the sixty-nine-year-old Coretta Scott King. "Martin Luther King, in fact, supported the concept of affirmative action," she said. "Those who suggest he did not support affirmative action are misrepresenting his beliefs and his life's work."[17]

On November 6, 1996, a day after passage of the proposition and the reelection of Clinton and a Republican Congress, quite possibly the most sophisticated, holistically antiracist thriller of the decade appeared in theaters. Directed by twenty-seven-year-old F. Gary Gray, who was already well known for *Friday* (1995), written by Kate Lanier and Takashi Bufford, and starring Jada Pinkett, Queen Latifah, Vivica A. Fox, and Kimberly Elise—*Set It Off* showcased just how and why four unique Black women could be motivated by Los Angeles's job, marital, and gender discrimination; class and sexual exploitation; and racist police violence to commit a violent crime—in their case, well-planned armed bank robberies—in an attempt to better their lives and get back at those who were trying to destroy them. *Set It Off* did what law-and-order and tough-on-crime racism refused to do: it humanized inner-city Black perpetrators of illegal acts, and in the process forced its viewers to reimagine who the real American criminals were. While Pinkett played an erudite, independent, sexually empowered heterosexual woman in all her normality among male lovers and abusers, Latifah portrayed a mighty butch lesbian in all her normality among poor Blacks. In the end, three women die, but the shrewd Pinkett escapes with the stolen money into the sunset away from American racism.

Critics and viewers fell in love with the tragedy and triumph of *Set It Off*. Even film critic Roger Ebert "was amazed how much I started to care about the characters." If only law-and-order America, seeing the structural racism, had started to care about the real characters. But the producers of racist ideas seemed determined to make sure that never, ever happened.[18]

BILL CLINTON WAS sadly mistaken about the root of the "problem of race" when he made a stunning announcement on the subject on June 14, 1997. In his commencement address at Angela Davis's alma mater, UC San Diego, Clinton pledged to lead "the American people in a great and unprecedented conversation on race." Racial reformers applauded Clinton for his willingness to condemn prejudice and discrimination and for his antiracist ambitions of building "the world's first truly multiracial democracy."[19]

Upward of 1 million Black women made sure to inject their ideas into the conversation, gathering in Philadelphia on October 25, 1997. Congresswoman Maxine Waters, Sister Souljah, Winnie Mandela, Attallah and Ilyasah Shabazz (daughters of Malcolm X), and Dorothy Height spoke to the Million Woman March. At one point, a helicopter flew down low to drown out their words. Thousands shot up their arms, trying to almost shoo the helicopter away like a fly. It worked. "See what we can do when we work together," intoned the passionate director of ceremonies, Brenda Burgess of Michigan.

The calls for Black unity resounded in Philadelphia as they had two years earlier among those million men in Washington, DC—as if Black people had a unity problem, as if this disunity was contributing to the plight of the race, and as if other races did not have sellouts and backstabbers. The nation's most unified race behind a single political party was never the most politically divided race. But, as always, racist ideas never needed to account for reality.[20]

"Racism will not disappear by focusing on race," House speaker Newt Gingrich argued in the wake of Clinton's national race conversation. This reaction to Clinton's conversation synthesized into a newly popular term: color-blind. "Color-blindness" rhetoric—the idea of solving the race problem by ignoring it—started to catch on as logical in illogical minds. "Color-blind" segregationists condemned public discussions of racism, following in the footsteps of Jim Crow and slaveholders. But these supposedly color-blind segregationists were much more advanced than their racist predecessors, announcing that anyone who engaged Clinton's national discussion in any antiracist way was in fact racist. In his 1997 book *Liberal Racism*, journalist Jim Sleeper argued that anyone who was not color blind—or "transracial"—was racist. In their runaway success of the same year, *America in Black & White*, Manhattan Institute Fellow Abigail Thernstrom and Harvard historian Stephan Thernstrom said that "race-consciousness policies make for more race-consciousness; they carry American society backward." "Few whites are now racists," and what dominates race relations now is "black anger" and "white surrender," the Thernstroms wrote, echoing the essays in *The Race Card*, an influential 1997 anthology edited by Peter Collier and David Horowitz. Criers of racial discrimination were playing the fake "race card," and it was winning because of liberal "white guilt."[21]

All this color-blind rhetoric seemed to have its intended effect. The court of public opinion seemed to start favoring the color-blind product nearly a century after the Supreme Court had ruled in favor of the product "separate but equal." The millennium was coming, and people were still being blinded to human equality by colors.

CHAPTER 36

99.9 Percent the Same

THE COLOR-BLIND IDEAL was reinforced by the propaganda of the arrival of American multiculturalism. "More than ever, we understand the benefits of our racial, linguistic, and cultural diversity," Clinton said in his speech at UC San Diego. The old assimilationist ideal of all Americans, no matter their cultural heritage, adopting Euro-American culture, had indeed suffered a devastating assault in schools, and especially colleges, from the new Ethnic Studies departments, the profusion of non-White immigrants, and Americans learning their native and foreign ancestral roots. Nathan Glazer, the coauthor of a book detailing the assimilationist standard of the 1960s, *Beyond the Melting Pot*, despondently confessed that things had changed. The title of his 1997 book was *We Are All Multiculturalists Now*. The book became a punching bag for assimilationists, who had spent the decade swinging at those increasingly popular Black Studies programs and departments.[1]

But Glazer again got it wrong on culture. A truly multicultural nation ruled by multiculturalists would not have Christianity as its unofficial standard religion. It would not have suits as its standard professional attire. English would not be its standard language or be assessed by standardized tests. Ethnic Studies would not be looked upon as superfluous to educational curricula. Afrocentric scholars and other multicultural theorists, lecturing on multiple cultural perspectives, would not be looked upon as controversial. No cultural group would be directly and indirectly asked to learn and conform to any other group's cultural norms in public in order to get ahead. A nation of different-looking people is not automatically multicultural or diverse if most of them practice or are learning to practice the same culture. The United States was maybe a multicultural nation in homes, behind closed doors, but certainly not in public in 1997. Racists in the United States were only embracing diversity and multiculturalism in name. In practice, they were enforcing cultural standards.

And this maintenance of the status quo became apparent in the critical reviews of Angela Davis's game-changing new book, *Blues Legacies and Black Feminism*, published in 1998. It had taken years for her to transcribe the entire body of Ma Rainey's and Bessie Smith's available blues recordings, the material basis of her analysis. Known for her integrative analysis of gender, race, and class, Davis quietly extended the analytical factors to include sexuality and culture. She looked at lyrics in light of lesbianism and bisexuality, and she examined African cultural retentions in the blues genre. Not many Americans had expressed antiracist ideas in the five major analytic categories: gender, race, class, sexuality, and culture. So the critiques came from all five sides, especially the side of culture. The *New York Times* reviewer rebuked Davis's cultural antiracism as "ingrained cultural nationalism," while the *Washington Post* ridiculed her "turgid academic jargon and rigid ideology." Apparently, scholars like Angela Davis who uncovered, studied, and articulated cultural differences in more than just name were ideologues and cultural nationalists.[2]

Davis continued her innovative integrative scholarship on Black women and remained focused on reviving the abolitionist movement as the new millennium arrived. "The two millionth prisoner entered the system in America on February 15, 2000 and half of those prisoners are Black," she said in early 2000 at the University of Colorado. Davis knew that most of these prisoners had been convicted of drug crimes. She also knew that Whites were found to be more likely to sell drugs than Blacks, as Human Rights Watch was reporting. Therefore, Davis was crossing the country and directing the attention of Americans to the unjust criminal justice system, which she viewed as the new slavery. Davis offered the natural abolitionist solution a few years later, asking the antiracist question of the age in 2003 in her new book title: *Are Prisons Obsolete?* She imagined "a world without prisons" in the 115-page manifesto for prison abolition. "Because of the persistent power of racism, 'criminals' and 'evildoers' are, in the collective imagination, fantasized as people of color," Davis wrote. And "the prison" relieved America "of the responsibility of thinking about the real issues afflicting those communities from which prisoners are drawn in such disproportionate numbers."[3]

A prominent Black linguist at UC Berkeley did not agree with Davis's assessment. The Black proportion of the prison population "neatly reflects the rate at which they commit crimes," maintained John McWhorter—without evidence—in *Losing the Race: Self-Sabotage in Black America.* This 2000 best seller catapulted him into the spotlight as America's best-known Black conservative intellectual. As a linguist, McWhorter of course had to spend a chapter commenting on the Ebonics debate, which had been tipped off four years earlier when word got out that the Oakland Unified School District had recognized Ebonics as a language derived from West Africa. Aside from a line saying that African Americans had a genetic predisposition to Ebonics (which was extracted in a future resolution), the 1996 Oakland resolution was amazingly antiracist and compassionate, equating Ebonics with more accepted English languages. Acknowledging those students as fluent in Ebonics, the school board wanted to maintain "the legitimacy and richness of such language" and "facilitate their acquisition and mastery of English language skills." They wanted to make sure these students were bilingual.[4]

Social psychologist Robert Williams had coined the term "Ebonics" back in 1973 to replace all the racist identifiers, like "Nonstandard Negro English." "We know that ebony means black and that phonics refers to speech sounds or the science of sounds," he explained then. "Thus, we are really talking about the science of black speech sounds or language." Ebonics remained a little-known linguistic term until the Oakland school board resolution set off a typhoon of assimilationist ire and antiracist defenses in the late 1990s. McWhorter made a name for himself as one of the few Black linguists opposing the Oakland resolution.[5]

Appearing on NBC's *Meet the Press* days after the resolution, Jesse Jackson bristled, "I understand the attempt to reach out to these children, but this is an unacceptable surrender, borderlining on disgrace. It's teaching down to our children." The Linguistic Society of America, on the other hand, issued a supportive statement in 1997. "Characterizations of Ebonics as 'slang,' 'mutant,' 'lazy,' 'defective,' 'ungrammatical,' or 'broken English' are incorrect and demeaning," the statement said. Evidence showed that people could "be aided in their learning of the standard variety by pedagogical approaches which recognize the legitimacy of the other varieties of a language. From this perspective, the Oakland School Board's decision to recognize the vernacular of African American students in teaching them Standard English is linguistically and pedagogically sound." When Jesse Jackson learned that Oakland planned to use Ebonics to teach, as he called it, "standard English," he backed off from his initial opposition. But Jackson's initial opposition—let alone the opposition of people of all races who continued to oppose the embrace of Ebonics—demonstrated that despite the lip service they gave it, many Americans despised multiculturalism.[6]

Assimilationists who came around to supporting the teaching of "Standard English" using Ebonics did not come around to discarding the racist hierarchy that places "standard" or "proper" English above Ebonics. And this linguistic hierarchy existed across the Western world. All the new languages that enslaved Africans had developed in the Spanish, French, Dutch, Portuguese, and British colonies were similarly denigrated in racist fashion as broken "dialects," or inferior varieties of the standard European language, which in the United States was "Standard English." Ebonics had formed from the trees of African languages and modern English, just as modern English had formed from the trees of the Latin and Germanic languages. Ebonics was no more "broken" or "nonstandard" English than English was "broken" or "nonstandard" German or Latin.[7]

To John McWhorter, those defending Oakland's decision to provide a bilingual education for their Ebonics speakers constituted yet another example of Black America's self-sabotaging. He argued in *Losing the Race: Self-Sabotage in Black America* that White people were better, and better off, than Blacks because they did not self-sabotage as much. With "white racism . . . all but obsolete," McWhorter argued, Black people's main obstacle was Black people: their "victimology" (or race cards), their separatism (or anti-assimilationist ideas), and their "Black anti-intellectualism," as revealed in the "Ebonics movement" and in the "acting White" putdown in schools that Black elites were raging about. McWhorter supplied his anecdotes as many other people were giving theirs. But he gave no proof that the Black children condemning other Black children for "acting White" were *always* relating intellectualism to "acting White." Some of these high-scoring students being scolded for "acting White" may have indeed been *looking down* on their lower-scoring classmates, which, from a political standpoint, would be "acting White" (*if* "acting White" is looking down on Black people). Some of these students may have indeed been "acting White" because they could not help but act out what their parents kept telling them: that they were not like those *other* Black kids. Some of these students may have indeed been "acting White" because they lacked a fluency in Black cultural forms (*if* "acting Black," from a cultural standpoint, is being fluent in Black cultural forms).[8]

Three years after the release of *Losing the Race,* John McWhorter submitted his *Essays for the Black Silent Majority.* According to this 2003 book, the silent Black majority believed that African Americans' own "culture-internal ideologies" had hobbled the group from "taking advantage of pathways to success." McWhorter wrote *Essays for the Black Silent Majority* from the half-truth of racial progress, ignoring the half-truth of the progression of racism. "Today, black success stories," he wrote, are "based on good old-fashioned hard work, ingenuity, and inner strength," with "residual racism . . . as a minor nuisance they overcame by keeping their eyes on the prize."[9]

McWhorter's "silent Black majority" was neither silent nor in the majority. But he was mobilizing a loud Black minority, and its expressions of cultural racism, of class racism, of struggling Black folk needing to take personal responsibility and work harder, may have been deeply personal. Some Black folks did not want to admit that they took advantage of extraordinary opportunities from their elite or even humble backgrounds—and that there are extremely hard-working poor people who never had the same opportunities. Like racist Whites, racist Blacks believed their "success" was due to their extraordinary God-given qualities and/or their extraordinary work ethic; that if they "made it," then any Black person could, if he or she worked hard enough. For many of these Black racists, their expressions may have been deeply political: they may have been cunningly reciting racist talking points in order to receive financial and occupational favor, whether they actually believed these racist ideas or not. Opportunities proliferated in political offices and think tanks and news mediums for Black racists willing to look down on African Americans in the twenty-first century. In 2003, McWhorter left academia for a posh position as a senior fellow at the Manhattan Institute. But if science mattered more than self-interest, then the Manhattan Institute's preeminent production of racist ideas would have ceased three years before McWhorter arrived.

REPORTERS CLAPPED AS Clinton walked into the East Room of the White House on June 26, 2000. He held the answer to one of the oldest questions of the modern world: whether there was some inherent biological distinction between the identifiable races. Flanking the presidential podium were two large screens that read: "Decoding the Book of Life / A Milestone for Humanity."

"We are here to celebrate the completion of the first survey of the entire human genome," Bill Clinton rejoiced to an audience of reporters and cameras. "Without a doubt, this is the most important, most wondrous map ever produced by humankind." It was a map that should "revolutionize" medicine by giving scientists information about the "genetic roots" of disease. It should also revolutionize racial science, Clinton announced. The map shows us "that in genetic terms, all human beings, regardless of race, are more than 99.9 percent the same."

One of the scientists responsible for sequencing the human genome, Craig Venter, was even more frank with reporters. "The concept of race has no genetic or scientific basis," Venter said. His research team at Celera Genomics had determined "the genetic code" of five individuals, who were identified as either "Hispanic, Asian, Caucasian or African American," and the scientists could not tell one race from another.[10]

When the press conference ceased and the reporters broadcast their stories, the old racist saying that a human book can be judged by its cover should have ceased. The refrain of "White blood" and "Black diseases" should have ceased, and the segregationist chorus saying that human beings were created unequal, that played for five centuries, should have also ceased. Science did not start the singing, though, and science would not stop it. Segregationists had too many racist policies to hide, racial disparities to justify, scientific and political careers to maintain, and money to make. The racial progress of Clinton's 99.9 percent announcement brought on the next segregationist theory: the 0.1 percent genetic difference between humans must be racial. First curse theory and then natural slave theory and then polygenesis and then Social Darwinism and now genes—segregationists had produced new ideas to justify the inequities of every era. "Scientists planning the next phase of the human genome project are being forced to confront a treacherous issue: the genetic differences between the human races," science reporter Nicholas Wade shared in the *New York Times*, just weeks after Clinton's press conference.[11]

Segregationist geneticists powered forward on their wild goose chase, trying to figure out something that did not exist: how the races differed genetically. In 2005, University of Chicago geneticist Bruce Lahn made the conjecture that there were two super-intelligence genes, and said they were least likely to exist in sub-Sahara Africans. When scientists demanded proof, Lahn had trouble providing it. Still no one had proven any association between genes and intelligence, let alone genes and race. "There is no such thing as a set of genes that belong exclusively to one [racial] group and not another," University of Pennsylvania bioethics scholar Dorothy Roberts explained in her 2011 book *Fatal Invention*, in which she exposes the unscientific basis of biological races, race-specific genes, and race-specific drugs for race-specific diseases. "Race is not a biological category that is politically charged," she added. "It is a political category that has been disguised as a biological one." But the biological ideas lived on comfortably. By 2014, Nicholas Wade had retired from the *New York Times* and released his own defense of biological racism, *A Troublesome Inheritance: Genes, Race, and Human History.* "The thesis presented here assumes . . . that there is a genetic component to human social behavior," Wade wrote. "Contrary to the central belief of multiculturalists, Western culture has achieved far more than other cultures in many significant spheres," he wrote, because of Europeans' genetic superiority. Craig Venter, the geneticist involved in mapping the genome, writing again in 2014, reassured his readers that "the results of genome sequences over the last thirteen years only prove my point more clearly": that there "are greater genetic differences between individuals of the same 'racial' group than between individuals of different groups."[12]

MONTHS AFTER CLINTON evoked that timeless phrase—"99.9 percent the same"—the United States Report to the United Nations Committee on the Elimination of Racial Discrimination pointed out what was now the broken US race record: there had been "substantial successes," but there were "significant obstacles" remaining. It was September 2000, and Texas governor George W. Bush was pledging to restore "honor and dignity" to the White House, while Vice President Al Gore was trying to distance himself from Bill Clinton's Monica Lewinsky scandal. The report's findings of discrimination and disparities across the American board did not become campaign talking points, as they reflected poorly on both the Clinton administration and the Republicans' color-blind America.

"U.S. law guarantees the right to participate equally in elections," the State Department had assured the United Nations. But on November 7, 2000, tens of thousands of Black voters in Governor Jeb Bush's Florida were barred from voting or had their votes destroyed, allowing George W. Bush to win his brother's state by fewer than five hundred votes and narrowly take the electoral college. It seemed ironically normal. After triumphantly proclaiming to the United Nations their commitment to eliminating racism, local officials, state officials, the Supreme Court, and the US Senate executed or validated the racism that won a presidential election. "The tactics have changed, but the goal remains depressingly the same," concluded *New York Times* columnist Bob Herbert. "Do not let them vote! If you can find a way to stop them, stop them."[13]

Funding evangelical race healers and personal responsibility advocates, once in office President Bush tried and failed to slow the antiracist momentum of the late 1990s. Trans-Africa executive director Randall Robinson accelerated that momentum in 2000 with his best-selling reparations manifesto, *The Debt: What America Owes to Blacks.* Robinson's reparations demands came on the heels of African nations demanding debt forgiveness and reparations from Europe. Meanwhile, the antiracist world was gearing up for one of the largest, most serious, most collaborative meetings in history. Nearly 12,000 women and men ventured to beautiful Durban, South Africa, for the United Nations World Conference Against Racism, Racial Discrimination, Xenophobia and Related Intolerance, held from August 31 to September 7, 2001. Delegates passed around a report on the prison-industrial complex and women of color that had been coauthored by Angela Davis. They also identified the Internet as the latest mechanism for spreading racist ideas, citing the roughly 60,000 White supremacist sites and the racist statements so often made in comments sections following online stories about Black people. The United States had the largest delegation, and antiracist Americans established fruitful connections with activists from around the world, many of whom wanted to ensure that the conference kicked off a global antiracist movement. As participants started venturing back to Senegal and the United States and Japan, Brazil, and France around September 7, 2001, they carried their antiracist momentum around the world.[14]

Then all this antiracist momentum smashed into a brick wall in the aftermath of September 11, 2001. After more than 3,000 Americans heartbreakingly lost their lives in attacks on the World Trade Center and the Pentagon, President Bush condemned the "evil-doers," the insane "terrorists," all the while promoting anti-Islamic and anti-Arab sentiments. Color-blind racists exploited the raw feelings in the post-911 moment, playing up a united, patriotic America where national defense had overtaken racial divides, and where antiracists and anti-war activists were threats to national security. But they could not exploit those feelings for long. Only 44 percent of African Americans endorsed the invasion of Iraq in 2003, far less than the 73 percent of Whites or 66 percent of Latina/os.[15]

By then, antiracists had regained their footing, inspired by California Newsreel's definitive three-part educational documentary, *Race: The Power of an Illusion*, released in April 2003. Months earlier, a comedian known for starring in *Half Baked* (1998) debuted his show on Comedy Central. Dave Chappelle performed a hysterical skit of a blind White supremacist, who thinks he is White, and who spits out anti-Black ideas like tobacco. In the end he tragically—or, for the viewer, comically—learns he is a Black man. Of all the notable antiracist sketches he did, that first sketch of the racist Black man may have been Chappelle's most clever and memorable. Millions replayed it on YouTube long after its original airing on January 22, 2003. The ever-popular *Chappelle's Show* aired for three seasons until 2006, routinely demonstrating the absurdity of the New Republicans' color-blind America.[16]

Many Republicans assumed, given the alleged "end of racism," that affirmative action would soon be on its way out. But shockingly, on June 23, 2003, Supreme Court Justice Sandra Day O'Connor issued a majority opinion upholding the University of Michigan's affirmative action policy, citing a "compelling interest in obtaining the educational benefits that flow from a diverse student body." Somewhat pleased, supporters of affirmative action reasoned that the Supreme Court had upheld affirmative action because having some Black students around benefited the interests of White students in the increasingly multiethnic nation and globalizing world. O'Connor's ruling added a time limit to the judgment, saying, "The Court expects that 25 years from now, the use of racial preferences will no longer be necessary to further the interest approved today." O'Connor's judgment was way off, according to United for a Fair Economy researchers. The racial "parity date" at the existing pace of gradual equality was not twenty-five years, but five-hundred years, and for some racial disparities, thousands of years from 2003. The defenders of affirmative action were still relieved that O'Connor had saved it, for now.[17]

That pace toward racial parity could be quickened if the racial preferences of standardized testing were eradicated. But the use of standardized testing grew exponentially in K–12 schooling when the Bush administration's bipartisan No Child Left Behind Act took effect in 2003. Under the act, the federal government compels states, schools, and teachers to set "high" standards and goals and to conduct regular testing to assess how well the students are reaching them. It then ties federal funding to the testing scores and progress to ensure that students, teachers, and schools are meeting those standards and goals. The bill professed that its purpose was to keep children from being left behind, but it simultaneously encouraged funding mechanisms that decrease funding to schools when students are not making improvements, thus leaving the neediest students behind. The No Child Left Behind Act was not supposed to make sense. It was the latest and greatest mechanism for placing the blame for funding inequities on Black children, teachers, parents, and public schools. And this victim blaming watered the growth of the quickening "No Excuses" charter school movement, which ordered *children* to rise above their difficult circumstances, and blamed (and expelled) these *children* if they could not.[18]

Scientists know that, developmentally, when children are sick or hurt, or confused or angry, one of the ways they express those feelings is through acting out, because children have difficulty identifying and communicating complex feelings (over things like hunger or parental incarceration or police harassment). While misbehaving White children have received compassion and tolerance—as they should— misbehaving Black children have been more likely to hear "No Excuses" and to be on the receiving end of zero tolerance and handcuffs. More than 70 percent of students arrested at school during the 2009–2010 school year were Black or Latina/o, according to Department of Education statistics.[19]

Assimilationists hailed the No Child Left Behind Act's explicit goal of narrowing the racial achievement gap, drowning out segregationists, who were saying that Black children were incapable of closing the achievement gap, and antiracists, who did not believe in the existence of an achievement gap, since it was predicated on standardized test scores, which they viewed as invalid. In the early 1970s, many Americans were imagining a world without prisons. In the early 1980s, many Americans were imagining a world without standardized tests. But racism had progressed since then. On the fiftieth anniversary of the *Brown* decision in 2004, a world without standardized testing seemed to many as unimaginable as a world without prisons, despite both keeping millions of Black young people behind bars.

And the anniversary of the *Brown* decision and discourse on Black education invariably brought out the racist ideas about what was wrong with Black parents. No one was better suited to that task than Bill Cosby, who had once been considered the model Black parent during the run of *The Cosby Show*. "The lower economic people are not holding up their end in this deal. These people are not parenting," Cosby said in Washington, DC, after being honored at an NAACP gala in May 2004. "They are buying things for kids. $500 sneakers for what? And they won't spend $200 for Hooked on Phonics. I am talking about these people who cry when their son is standing there in an orange suit."

Bill Cosby took his racist ideas on the road, causing a rash of debates between racists and antiracists. Sociologist Michael Eric Dyson shot back, knocking Cosby down from his high horse in his acclaimed 2005 book, *Is Bill Cosby Right? Or Has the Black Middle Class Lost Its Mind?* "All the self-help in the world will not eliminate poverty or create the number of good jobs needed to employ the African American community," historian Robin D.G. Kelley added.[20]

During Cosby's "blame-the-poor tour," as Dyson termed it, the rising star of the Democratic Party subverted Cosby's message during his keynote address at the Democratic National Convention in Boston on July 27, 2004. His star had appeared across the political landscape back in March, at the time of his stunning victory in the Illinois

Democratic primary for a US Senate seat. But it was his convention address before 9 million viewers that solidified his stardom. Working people of all kinds, from "small towns and big cities," were already taking responsibility, Barack Obama declared. "Go into any inner-city neighborhood, and folks will tell you that government alone can't teach kids to learn. They know that parents have to teach, that children can't achieve unless we raise their expectations and turn off the television sets and eradicate the slander that says a black youth with a book is acting white. They know those things." A booming applause interrupted Obama as his rebuke of the lecturing Cosby settled in. Also settling in were his affirmations of No Child Left Behind's high expectations, instead of high funding, and his pronouncement of the never-proven "acting white" achievement theory.

Barack Obama presented himself as the embodiment of racial reconciliation and American exceptionalism. He had had humble beginnings and a lofty ascent, and in him both native and immigrant ancestry and African and European ancestry came together. "I stand here knowing that my story is part of the larger American story . . . and that in no other country on Earth is my story even possible," he declared. "America, tonight, if you feel the same energy that I do, if you feel the same urgency that I do, if you feel the same passion that I do, if you feel the same hopefulness that I do, if we do what we must do, then I have no doubt that all across the country . . . the people will rise up in November, and John Kerry will be sworn in as president."[21]

Bush's Republicans, intent on stopping that rise, took their Black voter suppression techniques from Florida to Ohio in 2004. Kerry lost the election, of course, and Bush and his tactics seemed poised to embody the future of the Republican Party. But Barack Obama seemed poised to embody the future of the Democratic Party.

CHAPTER 37

The Extraordinary Negro

TWO WEEKS AFTER his exhilarating keynote address, Barack Obama's memoir, *Dreams from My Father: A Story of Race and Inheritance*, was republished. It rushed up the charts and snatched rave reviews in the final months of 2004. Toni Morrison, the queen of American letters, and the editor of Angela Davis's iconic memoir three decades earlier, deemed *Dreams from My Father* "quite extraordinary." Obama had written the memoir in the racially packed year of 1995 as he prepared to begin his political career in the Illinois Senate. In his most antiracist passage, Obama reflected on assimilated biracial Blacks like "poor Joyce," his friend at Occidental College. In Joyce and other Black students, he "kept recognizing pieces of myself," he wrote. People "like Joyce" spoke about "the richness of their multicultural heritage and it sounded real good, until you noticed that they avoided black people. It wasn't a matter of conscious choice, necessarily, just a matter of gravitational pull, the way integration always worked, a one-way street. The minority assimilated into the dominant culture, not the other way around. Only white culture could be 'neutral' and 'objective.' Only white culture could be 'nonracial.' . . . Only white culture had 'individuals.'"

Obama's antiracist litany continued in his critical revelation of the "extraordinary Negro" complex. "We, the half-breeds and the college-degreed, . . . [are] never so outraged as when a cabbie drives past us or the woman in the elevator clutches her purse, not so much because we're bothered by the fact that such indignities are what less fortunate coloreds have to put up with every single day of their lives—although that's what we tell ourselves—but because [we] . . . have somehow been mistaken for an ordinary nigger. Don't you know who I am? I'm an *individual!*"[1]

Ironically, racist Americans of all colors would in 2004 begin hailing Barack Obama, with all his public intelligence, morality, speaking ability, and political success, as the extraordinary Negro. The extraordinary-Negro hallmark had come a mighty long way from Phillis Wheatley to Barack Obama, who became the nation's only African American in the US Senate in 2005. Since Wheatley, segregationists had despised these extraordinary-Negro exhibits of Black capability and had done everything to take them down. But Obama—or rather Obama's era—was different. Segregationists turned their backs on their predecessors and adored the Obama exhibit as a proclamation of the end of racism. They wanted to end the discourse on discrimination.

But, to their dismay, the discourse would not quiet down. Segregationists hardly minded the animalistic Black Savior flicks, featuring physically supernatural Blacks saving Whites (*The Green Mile*, 1999); or the paternalistic White Savior flicks, featuring morally supernatural Whites saving Blacks (*The Blind Side*, 2009); or the flicks depicting amazing real-life stories of personal responsibility overcoming extreme adversity (*The Pursuit of Happyness*, 2006). But segregationists did mind Paul Haggis's 2005 Academy Award–winning Best Picture, *Crash*, a film that intertwined the racial experiences over a two-day period of characters from every racial group except Native Americans. Each character is shown as both prejudiced and the victim of prejudice, and the characters' prejudiced ideas and actions are depicted as stemming from both ignorance and hate. While segregationists over the years rebuked *Crash*'s explicit racial discourse, and assimilationists hailed the film's masterful portrayal of the pervasive, illogical, and oppressive effects of individual bigotry, antiracists argued that the film left much to be desired. They critiqued especially the lack of complexity on race relations in the film and the absence of any exploration of institutional racism. In *The Atlantic*, Ta-Nehisi Coates did not temper his antiracist review, calling it the "worst film of the decade." And for the color-blind segregationists, John McWhorter described *Crash* as "a melodrama, not a reflection of The Real America."[2]

But it was a devastating natural and racial disaster that summer that forced a tense debate about institutional and individual racism. During the final days of August 2005, Hurricane Katrina took more than 1,800 lives, forced millions to migrate, flooded the beautiful Gulf Coast, and caused billions in property damage. Hurricane Katrina blew the color-blind roof off America and allowed all to see—if they dared to look—the dreadful progression of racism.

For years, scientists and journalists had warned that if southern Louisiana took "a direct hit from a major hurricane," the levees could fail and the region would be flooded and destroyed, as the *New Orleans Times-Picayune* reported in 2002. Ignoring the warnings, it was almost as if politicians were hoping for a destructive hurricane to occur so that what Naomi Klein termed "disaster capitalism" could follow it. Politicians could award multimillion-dollar reconstruction contracts to corporations filling their campaign coffers, and New Orleans's Black residents locked on prime real estate could be cleared away to make room for gentrification. Whether they actually hoped for something like Hurricane Katrina hardly mattered, because politicos and disaster capitalists (Vice President Dick Cheney's Halliburton, for example) capitalized on the destruction. Even Klansmen got rich off their fake donation websites.[3]

It was rumored that the Bush administration directed the Federal Emergency Management Agency (FEMA) to delay its response in order to amplify the destructive reward for those who would benefit. Whether he actually did that is unknown, but it hardly mattered because FEMA did delay, and millions suffered because of it. While national reporters quickly reached the city and captured for their cameras thousands of residents of the predominantly Black Ninth Ward trapped on roofs and in the Superdome, federal officials made excuses for their delays. It took three days to deploy rescue troops to the Gulf Coast region, more time than it took to get troops on the ground to quell the 1992 Rodney King rebellion, and the result was deadly. "I believe it was racism," said a paramedic who witnessed the death spiral in New Orleans.[4]

But even this was not the full story of Hurricane Katrina. The extreme disaster story of racism became an extremely racist disaster story. The Associated Press dispatched a photograph of White people carrying "bread and soda from a local grocery store," and another photograph of a Black man who "loot[ed] a grocery store." As babies died of infections and hurt people waited for ambulances, reporters broadcasted sensational stories of "babies in the Convention Center who got their throats cut" in a crime-saturated city of "armed hordes" hijacking ambulances and "refugees" seeking shelter. Libertarian journalist Matt Welch did not mince words or the truth when he declared that the "deadly bigotry" of the media probably helped "kill Katrina victims." Federal officials and nearby emergency personnel used these media reports to justify their delays—citing the dangers of sending aid and personnel with so many people looting "gun stores" and shooting "at police, rescue officials and helicopters." Racist Americans actually reported, circulated, and believed the outrageous lies of those who were saying that Black people in a disaster zone would shoot at the very people coming to help them.

No one summed up the class racism of the government and media response to Hurricane Katrina victims better than Lani Guinier of Harvard Law School. "Poor Black people are the throw-away people. And we pathologize them in order to justify our disregard," she said. And no one summoned up the raw feelings of antiracist Blacks better than the superstar rapper who had just released his second studio album, *Late Registration*. "George Bush doesn't care about black people," Kanye West boldly stated, deviating from his script during a live hurricane relief concert on NBC on September 2, 2005. By mid-September 2005, the pollsters were rushing out to check the pulse of American racism. In one national poll, only 12 percent of White Americans— but 60 percent of African Americans—agreed that "the federal government's delay in helping the victims in New Orleans was because the victims were black." Presumably, the minds of 88 percent of White

Americans and 40 percent of Black Americans—if the poll was representative—had been flooded by racist ideas.

In the era of color-blind racism, no matter how gruesome the racial crime, no matter how much evidence was stacked against them, racists were standing up before the judge and claiming "not guilty." But how many criminals actually confess when they don't have to? From "civilizers" to standardized testers, assimilationists have rarely confessed to racism. Enslavers and Jim Crow segregationists went to their graves claiming innocence. George W. Bush will likely do the same. "I faced a lot of criticism as president," Bush mused in his post-presidency memoir. "I didn't like hearing people claim that I lied about Iraq's weapons of mass destruction or cut taxes to benefit the rich. But the suggestion that I was racist because of the response to Katrina represented an all-time low."[5]

Into the fall and winter of 2005, antiracist charges of racism in New Orleans were met with racist charges of "the irresponsible use of the race card," to quote Black media personality Larry Elder. Into 2006, the producers of racist ideas were arguing that the charges of widespread discrimination in New Orleans, and in the United States, were fabricated or overblown. The United States was color blind, and the Black people charging discrimination were lying—they were playing their race cards.[6]

It was in this polarized post-Katrina racial climate that Crystal Mangum stripped at a party for Duke University's White lacrosse team. After the party, in March 2006, the Black single mother and college student went to the Durham police. Team members had shouted racial epithets before forcing her into a room and gang-raping her, Mangum told police. Investigators then intercepted and released a post-party email. I wanted "to have some strippers over," Ryan McFadyen told his teammates. "I plan on killing the bitches" and cutting "their skin off while cumming in my duke issue spandex." As the Durham district attorney filed charges, the case became a national story. The national antiracist, anti-rape, and antisexist community rose up to support Crystal Mangum. "Regardless of the result of the police investigation," eighty-eight Duke professors said in a full-page advertisement in the *Duke Chronicle* on April 6, 2006, "what is apparent every day now is the anger and fear of many students who know themselves to be objects of racism and sexism."

By 2007, the case against the lacrosse players had fallen apart. Physical and DNA evidence had exonerated them of misconduct, and revelations of drug use, promiscuous sex, and mental health problems had smeared Crystal Mangum. When it was revealed that she had lied about being raped, everything seemed to turn upside down. The Durham district attorney was fired and disbarred. The players sued the city. Racists and sexists used her case to try to silence the post-Katrina discussion of racism as well as the discussion of rape culture that flowed from her allegation. It was said that Duke's antiracist, anti-sexist, antipoverty professors had exploited the case for propaganda.

Crystal Mangum's lies were generalized to all Black people, all women, and especially all Black women. Racists started waving their race cards, explaining that Black people had been fabricating and exaggerating the amount of racial discrimination all along. Sexists started waving "rape" cards, charging that women had been fabricating and exaggerating the amount of sexual violence all along. Gender racists combined the race and rape cards to dismiss the integrity of Black women claiming to be victims of racialized sexual violence. It was as if all Black women had done something wrong in Durham, North Carolina. And then the race and rape reformers felt betrayed—especially the men—and they started to belittle Crystal Mangum for setting the anti-rape and antiracist movements back, by giving rapists and racists more of the rape and race cards they loved to play. Her lies would make it more difficult for them to persuade away rapist and racist ideas, to convince Whites to acknowledge their racism, and to convince men to acknowledge their rape culture. Ironically, as these reformers condemned Mangum for her folly, foolish tactics of trying to persuade (instead of force) offenders to stop their crimes against humanity were setting rape culture and racism back.[7]

OUTSIDE THE MARX HOTEL in Syracuse, New York, antiwar activists were demonstrating against the US occupation of Iraq. Freezing rain dropped on their heads as they carried on. "You are not fair-weather activists!" Angela Davis proclaimed on October 20, 2006. Davis invited the demonstrators to hear her plenary speech at Syracuse University's "Feminism and War" conference. Many obliged. Davis lectured on how certain concepts had been "colonized" by the Bush administration, which had used "democracy," for example, in speeches about the need to "liberate" the women of Iraq and Afghanistan. "Diversity" had been used by the government, the military, and the prisons to present themselves as the most "diverse" institutions in history. But the oppressors were hiding behind their "diversity" and keeping their institutional racism intact, Davis proclaimed. It was a "difference that doesn't make a difference." Democracy and diversity were becoming as caustic to the antiracist cause as "race card" and "personal responsibility."[8]

Civil rights activists, however, remained fixated on the "N-word," especially after an N-word-laced rant went viral of *Seinfeld* actor Michael Richards confronting Black audience members during a standup at Hollywood's Laugh Factory on November 17, 2006. The outrage over Richards's "He's a nigger! He's a nigger! He's a nigger!" blended in the spring with the outrage over talk-show host Don Imus describing the dark-skinned members of the Rutgers University women's basketball team as "nappy-headed hos." The outrage did not just reflect on Richards and Imus. "It is us," Fox Sports journalist Jason Whitlock wrote in the *Pittsburgh Post-Gazette* on April 16, 2007. "At this time, we are our own worst enemies. We have allowed our youth to buy into a culture"—by which he meant Hip Hop—that "is anti-black, anti-education, pro-drug dealing and violent."[9]

At its annual convention in early July 2007, the NAACP held a public funeral and burial of the N-word. But "race card," "personal responsibility," "color blind," "no excuses," "achievement gap," and "it is us" were all allowed to live on in the dictionary of racism. "This was the greatest child that racism ever birthed," the Reverend Otis Moss III said in his eulogy for the N-word. All of the hurricane deaths in New Orleans from the womb of racism—and the N-word was the greatest child? Months earlier, on November 25, 2006, New

York police officers had slaughtered the twenty-three-year-old Sean Bell on his wedding night. Shortly thereafter, the excessive criminal charges against six Black high school students in Jena, Louisiana, were announced for their alleged crime of beating up a noose-hanging, racial-epithet-throwing White classmate. Days before the N-word funeral, Supreme Court Chief Justice John Roberts had struck down the efforts of three communities to desegregate their schools, saying that the "way to stop discriminating on the basis of race is to stop discriminating on the basis of race." And the N-word was the greatest child of racism? "Die N-word," Detroit mayor Kwame Kilpatrick ordered at the funeral. But nothing was said about racism's other, even more monstrous children.[10]

"HE'S THE FIRST mainstream African American who is articulate and bright and clean and a nice-looking guy." Presidential hopeful and Delaware senator Joe Biden might as well have labeled Barack Obama the extraordinary Negro. Biden's evaluations of his presidential rivals appeared in the *New York Observer* days before Obama stood in front of the Old State Capitol building in Springfield, Illinois, and formally announced his presidential candidacy on February 10, 2007. Obama stood on the spot where Abraham Lincoln had delivered his historic "House Divided" speech in 1858. Obama brimmed with words of American unity, hope, and change.

But Joe Biden's comments—which he later "deeply" regretted— became a sign of things to come. What was to come over the course of the campaign was a reflection of the audacity of racist minds—from President Bush to radio mega-personality Rush Limbaugh to Democratic stalwarts—all to view Obama as an extraordinary Negro. In February 2007, *Time* magazine speculated that African Americans were expressing greater support for New York senator Hillary Clinton because of questions over whether Obama was "black enough." It couldn't be because they saw Obama as a long shot. It had to be that they did not see Obama as ordinarily Black like them, meaning inarticulate and ugly and unclean and unintelligent.[11]

Pundits were dubbing Hilary Clinton the "inevitable" nominee until Barack Obama upset her on January 3, 2008, in the Iowa primary. By Super Tuesday on February 5, 2008, Americans had been swept up in the Obama "Yes We Can" crusade of hope and change, themes he embodied and spoke about so eloquently in his stump speeches that people started to hunger. In mid-February, his perceptive and brilliant wife, Michelle Obama, told a Milwaukee rally, "For the first time in my adult life, I am really proud of my country, and not just because Barack has done well, but because I think people are hungry for change." Suddenly, racist ridicule came down on her, smearing her "unpatri-otic" statements, slave ancestry, and brown skin, and tagging her the ultimate "angry Black woman." Later in the campaign, *The New Yorker* put an image of Michelle Obama on its cover. She was depicted in military gear and combat boots with an AK-47 across her back and a large Afro topping her head—it was the iconic, stereotypical image of the strong Black woman—and she was standing next to her husband in his Islamic apparel. Racist commentators became obsessed with Michelle Obama's body, her near-six-foot, chiseled, and curvy frame simultaneously semi-masculine and hyper-feminine. They searched for problems in her Black marriage and family, calling them extraordinary when they did not find any.[12]

When the dirt on the Obamas could not be found, investigative reporters started checking their associates. In early March 2008, ABC News released snippets of sermons from one of Black America's most revered liberation theologians, the recently retired pastor of Chicago's large Trinity United Church of Christ. Jeremiah Wright had married the Obamas and had baptized their two daughters. In an ABC News release, Wright was quoted proclaiming, in a sermon, "The govern-ment gives them the drugs, builds bigger prisons, passes a three-strike law and then wants us to sing 'God Bless America.' No, no, no . . . God damn America for treating our citizens as less than human." Wright had discarded the very old racist lesson that had first been taught to slaves: that African Americans were supposed to love the United States and consider it the world's greatest country no matter how they were treated. On top of his rejection of American exceptionalism,

Wright had the audacity to preach that American "terrorism" abroad had helped bring on the tragic events of 9/11. To put it lightly, Americans everywhere were livid.[13]

When Obama's flippant characterizations of Wright as a fraught "old uncle" did not calm Americans down, Obama decided to address the controversy on March 18, 2008. He stepped into the spotlight and gave a "race speech," entitled "A More Perfect Union," from Philadelphia's National Constitutional Center. Having taught constitutional law, worked in civil rights law, and overseen successful political campaigns (including his current campaign, which analysts were already regarding as masterful), Obama could easily be regarded as an expert on many things: constitutional law, civil rights law, Chicago politics, Illinois politics, campaigning, and race and politics. And just as racists presumed that all Black individuals represented the race, racists presumed that all articulate Black individuals were experts on Black people. They presumed, therefore, that Obama's Blackness made him an expert on Black people. And media outlets routinely brought on eloquent Black voices to pontificate on all sorts of "Black" issues they had not been trained in, making the actual interracial cast of experts squirm as they listened.

And so, in Philadelphia, many Americans did not see Obama as merely a politician saying what he needed to say to save his campaign. They listened to him—as his campaign aides had hoped they would— as an esteemed, knowledgeable, and sincere expert lecturer on race— as someone more credible on race relations than the supposedly angry and old Jeremiah Wright. Obama skillfully took advantage of this platform given to him by racist Americans—and who knows whether he expressed his actual beliefs or calculated that his most comfortable political space was to stand with assimilationists, the group that Robert M. Entman and Andrew Rojecki named the "ambivalent majority." These Americans believed that Blacks had some strikes against them, but sometimes used that as a crutch. And they were totally unaware that this viewpoint was not only racist, but hardly made much sense. It was like saying that the game was rigged, but Blacks should not let that stop them from winning, and that when they lost and complained about the game being rigged, they were "using that as a crutch."[14]

Obama dismissed Jeremiah Wright's "profoundly distorted view," but courageously refused to totally "disown" Wright. And then he opened his general lecture on race, explaining that socioeconomic racial inequities stemmed from the history of discrimination. From this firm antiracist opening, he rotated to the consensus racist theory of the "pervasive achievement gap," to the disproven racist theory of "the erosion of black families" that "welfare policies . . . may have worsened," and to the unproven racist theory that racial discrimination had bequeathed Blacks a "legacy of defeat."

According to Obama, this "legacy of defeat" explained why "young men and, increasingly, young women" were "standing on street corners or languishing in our prisons." He ignored the fact that this population was facing some of the nation's highest unemployment and policing rates. Obama added his "legacy of defeat" theory to the many racist folk theories circulating in classrooms and around dinner tables and in barbershops about slavery and discrimination—especially its trauma—making Black people biologically, psychologically, culturally, or morally inferior. Over the years, people had been using these folk theories—giving them names such as "post-traumatic slave syndrome," or the "slavery-hypertension thesis," or the "Hood Disease"—to walk away from the complete truth that discrimination had resulted in inferior opportunities and bank accounts for Black people, and not an inferior racial group.[15]

Those antiracist Jeremiah Wrights, their "anger is not always productive," Obama continued. "Indeed, all too often it distracts attention from solving real problems; it keeps us from squarely facing our own complicity within the African-American community in our condition." It was a classic assimilationist retort: calling antiracists "angry" for truly believing in racial equality, for not seeing anything wrong with Black people, and for seeing everything wrong with discrimination when squarely facing the African American condition. Like W. E. B. Du Bois and Martin Luther King Jr. before him, Obama lumped these "angry" antiracists with angry anti-White cynics to discredit them and distinguish himself from them. But when Du Bois and King ultimately arrived at antiracism, they had had to ward off the same "angry" and anti-White labels they had helped to produce. And now, Obama was doing the same thing, unaware that he was reproducing a label that his opponents would stamp onto him whenever and wherever he uttered another antiracist word—after this speech.

Obama uttered quite a few antiracist words in the speech—most profoundly, his analysis of how for "at least a generation" politicians had used "resentments," fears, and anger over welfare, affirmative action, and crime to distract White voters "from the real culprits of the middle class squeeze," the nation's "economic policies that favor the few over the many." But then, ever the politician, he refused to classify White "resentments" as "misguided or even racist"; amazingly, he "grounded" them "in legitimate concerns." Obama ended up following in the racist footsteps of every president since Richard Nixon: legitimizing racist resentments, saying those resentments were not racist, and redirecting those resentments toward political opponents.

The doubly conscious Obama encouraged African Americans to fight discrimination, take personal responsibility, be better parents, and end the "legacy of defeat." Obama did not offer any childrearing or psychological lessons for the presumably parentally and psychologically superior White Americans. He merely asked them to join him on the "long march" against racial discrimination—"not just with words but with deeds"—in a chillingly antiracist conclusion. He left the Philadelphia platform on March 18, 2008, as he began, expressing the half-truthful analogy of continuous racial progression. "This union may never be perfect," he said, "but generation after generation has shown that it can always be perfected."[16]

Segregationist and antiracist critiques were drowned out by the fawning eruption across the ideological isle. MSNBC political analyst Michelle Bernard framed it as "the best speech and most important speech on race that we have heard as a nation since Martin Luther King's 'I Have a Dream' speech." And it was not just Democrats who were fawning. Prominent Republicans—everyone from presidential candidates Mike Huckabee and John McCain to the Bush administration's Condoleezza Rice and Colin Powell and to the Clintons' old foe, Newt Gingrich—were also praising the speech. *The Bell Curve*'s author,

Charles Murray, called it "flat out brilliant—rhetorically, but also in capturing a lot of nuance about race in America."[17]

If Barack Obama hoped to transform *ABC News*'s roadblock into a springboard, then he succeeded, soaring into April and May away from Jeremiah Wright and Hillary Clinton and on to the Democratic nomination in early June. Meanwhile, Republican producers of racist ideas had gotten down to business, demanding to see Obama's birth certificate, questioning whether Barack *Hussein* Obama was really an American, and suggesting that only real Americans, who were White like McCain, could live in the White House of the United States. No other major-party candidate for the US presidency had ever been put under such a searing nativity microscope. Then again, no other major-party candidate for US president had ever been anyone other than a White male. The Obama campaign released a scanned copy of his US birth certificate, but the rumors of Obama being born in Kenya or some Islamic anti-American nation did not suddenly go away. They were not started out of ignorance, so why would they go away out of knowledge?

But the son of a single mother turned to other matters, like a Father's Day address on June 15, 2008. "If we are honest with ourselves, we'll admit that too many fathers are missing—missing from too many lives and too many homes," Obama said to a thunderous applause from Black hands at a Southside Chicago church. "They're acting like boys instead of men. And the foundations of our families are weaker because of it." The next day in *Time*, sociologist Michael Eric Dyson should have buried once and for all the racist exaggeration that Obama—and many other Americans—kept repeating on this issue of missing *Black* fathers. Dyson cited a study by Boston College's Rebekah Levine Coley finding that Black fathers not living in the home were more likely than fathers of every other racial group to keep in contact with their children. "Obama's words may have been spoken to black folk, but they were aimed at those whites still on the fence about whom to send to the White House," Dyson criticized.[18]

The legend of the "missing Black father" had become as popular as the legend that there are "no good Black men." Back in May 2008,

Tyra Banks had devoted an episode of her popular television talk show to the topic, calling it "Where Have All the Good Black Men Gone?" The nearly 1 million Black men in prison and the life expectancy of Black men being six years below White men did not make the discussion. Tyra Banks speculated, sounding the tune of racist Black women, that Black women were having trouble finding *good* Black men because so many were dogs or dating non-Black women or men. In no time, racist Black men were saying the same thing about Black women. The longest-running No. 1 R&B single of 2010, Alicia Keys's "I'm Ready," featured Hip Hop sensation Drake, who rapped: "Good women are rare too, none of them have come close." Few good Black men plus few good Black women equals few good Black people, equals racist ideas.[19]

ON NOVEMBER 4, 2008, a sixty-four-year-old recently retired professor cast a vote for a major political party for the first time in her voting life. She had retired from academia, but not from her very public activism of four decades. She was still traveling the country trying to rouse an abolitionist movement against prisons. In casting her vote for Democrat Barack Obama, Angela Davis joined roughly 69.5 million Americans. But more than voting for the man, Davis voted for the grassroots efforts of the campaign organizers, those millions of people demanding change. When the networks started announcing that Obama had been elected the forty-fourth president of the United States, happiness exploded from coast to coast, and from the United States around the antiracist world. Davis was in the delirium of Oakland. People whom she did not know came up and hugged her as she walked the streets. She saw people singing to the heavens, and she saw people dancing in the streets. People, in fact, were dancing on streets around the world. And the people Angela Davis saw and all the others around the world who were celebrating were not enraptured from the election of an individual; they were enraptured by the pride of the victory for Black people, by the success of millions of grassroots organizers, and because they had shown all those disbelievers, who had said that electing a Black president was impossible, to be wrong. Most of all, they were enraptured by the antiracist potential of a Black president.[20]

Behind the scenes of the exploding happiness that November night and over the next few weeks was the exploding fury of hate attacks on Black people. The producers of racist ideas were working overtime to take down some of their color-blind rhetoric that had blinded consumers from seeing discrimination for a decade. They were working to put up something better: a portrait of America conveying that there was no longer any need for protective or affirmative civil rights laws and policies—and no longer any need to ever talk about race. "Are we now in a post-racial America? . . . Is America past racism against black people?" John McWhorter asked in *Forbes* weeks after the election. "I say the answer is yes."[21]

Epilogue

SOME WHITE AMERICANS who voted for Barack Obama in the 2008 election were antiracist. Others probably dubbed Obama the extraordinary Negro, or set aside their racism. If antiracist Blacks could vote for racist Democrats as the "lesser of two evils" over the past few decades, then surely racist Whites could look at the Republican ticket and vote for Obama as the "lesser of two evils." To claim that a White Obama voter could not be racist would be as naïve (or manipulative) as assuming that a White person with Black friends could not be racist, or that a person with a dark face could not think that dark-faced people were in some way inferior. But White voters did not win the election for Obama, as the postracial headlines implied or declared. They gave him roughly the same percentage of votes (43 percent) they had given his Democratic predecessors after LBJ. Obama's 10 percent increase in non-White voters over John Kerry in 2004 and the record turnout of young voters won him the presidency of the United States.[1]

But racist ideas could have easily lost the election for him. What if Obama had been a descendant of American slaves? What if he had not been biracial? What if Obama's wife looked more like his mother? What if he had not started his lectures to Blacks on personal responsibility? What if Sarah Palin had not mobilized Democrats with her virtual Klan rallies where spectators shouted *"Kill him"*? What if the Bush Republicans had not had some of the worst approval ratings ever? What if Obama had not conducted what reportedly was the best presidential campaign in history? What if the Great Recession had not sent voters into a panic weeks before the election? Postracial theorists hardly cared about all those forces that had to come together to elect the first Black president of the United States. But when had producers of racist ideas ever cared about reality?[2]

The notion of a postracial America quickly became the new dividing line between racists and antiracists as Obama took office in 2009. University of Chicago political scientist Michael Dawson, speaking for antiracists, stated that the country had not yet "come close to achieving the status of 'post-racial.'" And the evidence was everywhere. The Great Recession reduced the median annual Black household income by 11 percent, compared to 5 percent for Whites. On January 1, 2009, an Oakland transit cop killed twenty-two-year-old Oscar Grant as he lay face down with his hands cuffed behind his back. All those geneticists, Klansmen, anonymous Internet racists, and of course members of the Tea Party—which formed on February 19, 2009—and other segregationists were organizing like there was no tomorrow after the election of Obama. Between 9/11 and that fateful June day in 2015 when Dylann Roof shot to death nine Bible-studying Charlestonians inside the oldest A.M.E. church in the south, White American Nazi-type terrorists had murdered forty-eight Americans—almost twice as many as were killed by anti-American Islamic terrorists. Law enforcement agencies were looking upon these White American terrorists as more dangerous to American lives than anti-American Islamic terrorists. But these White terrorists are not on the radar of the hawks who are endlessly waging their War on Terror. After Charleston, Americans merely engaged in a symbolic debate over the flying of the Confederate flag.[3]

Barack Obama had to notice this rising tidal wave of segregationism early in his presidency, years before he ever heard the name Dylann Roof. Or maybe he didn't. Or maybe he did, and thought that to point it out would have been divisive, like Jeremiah Wright. "There probably has never been less discrimination in America than there is today," Obama told the NAACP on July 16, 2009. "But make no mistake: The pain of discrimination is still felt in America." On that very day, someone in Cambridge, Massachusetts, called the police after seeing Harvard professor Henry Louis Gates Jr. trying to pry open the jammed front door of his home. When Obama commented that the responding White police officer had "acted stupidly in arresting somebody when there was already proof that they were in their own home," when he acknowledged the "long history" of racial profiling, the postracialists trounced to stop Obama's antiracism before it got out of hand. Obama's "angry" Jeremiah Wright construction had come back to bite him, as similar statements had for Martin Luther King Jr. and W. E. B. Du Bois before him. Obama has "over and over again" exposed himself as "a guy who has a deep-seated hatred for white people or the white culture," Tea Party darling Glenn Beck told his Fox News audience. "I'm not saying he doesn't like white people, I'm saying he has a problem. This guy is, I believe, a racist."[4]

It was a remarkable turn of events. During the NAACP speech, Obama lectured about African Americans needing a "new mind-set, a new set of attitudes," to free themselves from their "internalized sense of limitation," and rebuked Black parents for contracting out parenting. For this litany of rebukes of millions of Black people, Glenn Beck and the postracialists did not offer a critical word. Apparently, it was fine for Obama to critique millions of Black people. But as soon as he was critical of a single White discriminator, the postracialists pounced.

Months into Obama's presidency, the postracialists slammed down their new ground rules for race relations: Criticize millions of Black people whenever you want, as often as you want. That's not racialism or racism or hate. You're not even talking about race. But whenever you criticize a single White discriminator, that's race-speak, that's hate-speak, that's being racist. If the purpose of racist ideas had always been to silence the antiracist resisters to racial discrimination, then the postracial line of attack may have been the most sophisticated silencer to date.

All these postracialists had no problem rationalizing the enduring racial disparities, the enduring socioeconomic plight of Black people though blaming Black people, on *Fox News*, in the *Wall Street Journal*, on *The Rush Limbaugh Show*, on the Supreme Court, and from the seats of the Republican Party. Defending racist policy by belittling Black folk: that had been the vocation of producers of racist ideas for nearly six centuries, since Gomes Eanes de Zurara first produced these ideas to defend the African slave-trading of Portugal's Prince Henry. The postracial attacks triggered counterattacks from antiracists, pointing out racial discrimination from Twitter to Facebook, from Hip Hop to Black Studies scholarship, from shows on MSNBC to Sirius XM Progress, and from periodicals like *The Nation* to *The Root*, which then triggered counterattacks from postracialists, who called these antiracists divisive and racist. Assimilationists, stuck in the middle, considered themselves the voices of reasonable moderation. They kept up the drumbeat of the ill-conceived allegory of how far the nation had come and how far it still had to go. The actual American history of racial progress and the simultaneous progression of racism still did not suit their ideology.

Through it all, the postracialists and assimilationists failed to silence all those antiracists giving voice to racial discrimination or to make them conform. Antiracists joined the protest squatters representing the 99 percent in the "Occupy" uprising in 2011. They continue to demand reparations, one of the most notable examples being Ta-Nehisi Coates's feature story in *The Atlantic* in June 2014. They have fought the progression of racism in the stop-and-frisk policing practices in US cities and in the Republican-engineered disenfranchising policies. Antiracists helped power the unrelenting LGBT fight for equal rights. In the midst of that struggle, Black transgender activist Janet Mock released her memoir, *Redefining Realness*. Hailed by bell hooks and Melissa Harris-Perry and an all-star lineup of other antiracist voices, *Redefining Realness* debuted on February 1, 2014, on the *New York Times* Best-Seller List. Mock's thrilling and reflective personal quest for womanhood, identity, and love gave readers an opening into the lives and struggles and triumphs of transgender Americans, and especially Black transgender women. "Somewhere along the way, I grew weary of grasping at possible selves, just out of reach. So I put my arms down and wrapped them around me. I began healing by embracing myself through the foreboding darkness until the sunrise shone on my face." Mock wrote in closing. "Eventually, I emerged, and surrendered to the brilliance, discovering truth, beauty, and peace that was already mine."[5]

Antiracists seemed to be protesting everywhere, especially in front of prisons, struggling against what Angela Davis had struggled against for four decades: the racist criminal justice system (and the prison-industrial complex). In 2010, Ohio State University law professor Michelle Alexander entitled her bombshell best seller *The New Jim Crow: Mass Incarceration in the Age of Colorblindness*. She exposed racial discrimination at every stop in the criminal justice system, from law-making to policing practices, to who comes under suspicion, to who is arrested, prosecuted, judged guilty, and jailed. And when Black people leave those jails that are crowded with Black and Brown people, the slavery ends only so new forms of legal discrimination can begin. "A criminal record today authorizes precisely the forms of discrimination we supposedly left behind—discrimination in employment, housing, education, public benefits, and jury service," Alexander wrote. "Those labeled criminals can be denied the right to vote."[6]

Michelle Alexander exposed the lie of postracial America in *The New Jim Crow*. But nothing really jump-started the traveling exposition of the postracial lie better than what happened on February 26, 2012, when neighborhood watchman George Zimmerman stared down a trotting Black teen, Trayvon Martin, as if he'd stolen something in Sanford, Florida. Scared, the unarmed teen fled. Zimmerman defied a police dispatcher, chased after Trayvon, and ended the seventeen-year-old's life. A series of events followed—Zimmerman claiming self-defense, protests, Zimmerman's arrest, the murder case, the defense portraying Trayvon Martin as a scary thug, Zimmerman being exonerated, and finally, jurors airing their racist justifications as segregationists rejoiced over the verdict. Antiracists were upset, and assimilationists were of two minds. This emotional swing seemed to intensify with each police killing, including those of mentally ill Shereese Francis of New York, twenty-two-year-old Rekia Boyd of Chicago, and twenty-three-year-old Shantel Davis in Brooklyn, all within months of Trayvon Martin's assassination. On March 9, 2013, two New York police officers shot sixteen-year-old Kimani Gray seven times. The violent protests that followed Gray's death—and others—provoked another round of debates between the postracial segregationists, who condemned the violent "thugs"; the antiracists, who explained the racist source of the violence; and the assimilationists, who condemned the violent "thugs" and pointed out the discriminatory sources of the violence.

For many antiracists, the term "thug" had become "the accepted way of calling somebody the N-word nowadays." This was how Seattle Seahawks cornerback Richard Sherman explained it in early 2014 after he was subjected to the slur. When the Stanford-educated Sherman shouted into the camera, racist Americans did not see an athlete fired up minutes after his "Immaculate Deflection" that won his team the National Football Conference Championship. They saw a "thug," like the unarmed thugs officers were killing, and the thugs who were violently rebelling in 2013 for Kimani Gray; in 2014 for Staten Island's Eric Garner and Ferguson's Michael Brown; and in 2015 for Baltimore's Freddie Gray. "Thug" was one of many new acceptable ways of calling Black people inferior or "less than." Other widely used racist slurs and phrases included "ghetto," "minority," "personal responsibility," "achievement gap," "race card," "reverse discrimination," "good hair," "from the bottom," "no good Black . . . ," and "you see, that's what's wrong with Black . . ."[7]

Hearing the acquittal of George Zimmerman in 2013 punched Alicia Garza in the gut. Seeking relief, she pulled out her phone at an Oakland bar. She only got more upset as she read racist messages on her Facebook newsfeed "blaming black people for our own conditions." Garza, a domestic workers' advocate, composed a love note for Black people, pleading with them to ensure "that black lives matter." Her friend in Los Angeles, anti-police-brutality activist Patrisse Cullors, read Garza's impassioned love note on Facebook and tacked a hashtag in the front. Their tech-savvy friend, immigrant rights activist Opal Tometi, came in and built the online platform, and #Black Lives Matter was born. From the minds and hearts of these three Black women—two of whom are queer—this declaration of love intuitively signified that in order to truly be antiracists, we must also oppose all of the sexism, homophobia, colorism, ethnocentrism, nativism, cultural prejudice, and class bias teeming and teaming with racism to harm so many Black lives. The antiracist declaration of the era quickly leaped from social media onto shouting signs and shouting mouths at antiracist protests across the country in 2014. These protesters rejected the racist declaration of six centuries: that Black lives don't matter. #Black Lives Matter quickly transformed from an antiracist love declaration into an antiracist movement filled with young people operating in local BLM groups across the nation, often led by young Black women. Collectively, these activists were pressing against discrimination in all forms, in all areas of society, and from myriad vantage points. And in reaction to those who acted like Black male lives mattered the most, antiracist feminists boldly demanded of America to #Say Her Name. Say the names of Black women victims like Sandra Bland. "We want to make sure there is the broadest participation possible in this new iteration of a black freedom movement," Garza told *USA Today* in 2015. "We have so many different experiences that are rich and complex. We need to bring all of those experiences to the table in order to achieve the solutions we desire."[8]

WHEN WILL THE day arrive when Black lives will matter to Americans? It depends largely on what antiracists do—and the strategies they use to stamp out racist ideas.

The history of racist ideas tells us what strategies antiracists should stop using. *Stamped from the Beginning* chronicles not just the development of racist ideas, but the ongoing failure of the three oldest and most popular strategies Americans have used to root out these ideas: self-sacrifice, uplift suasion, and educational persuasion.

Racial reformers have customarily requested or demanded that Americans, particularly White Americans, sacrifice their own privileges for the betterment of Black people. And yet, this strategy is based on one of the oldest myths of the modern era, a myth continuously produced and reproduced by racists and antiracists alike: that racism materially benefits the majority of White people, that White people would lose and not gain in the reconstruction of an antiracist America. It has been true that racist policies have benefited White people *in general* at the expense of Black people (and others) *in general*. That is the story of racism, of unequal opportunity in a nutshell. But it is also true that a society of equal opportunity, without a top 1 percent hoarding the wealth and power, would actually benefit the vast majority of White people much more than racism does. It is not coincidental that slavery kept the vast majority of southern Whites poor. It is not coincidental that more White Americans thrived during the antiracist movements from the 1930s to the early 1970s than ever before or since. It is not coincidental that the racist movements that followed in the late twentieth century paralleled the stagnation or reduction of middle- and low-income Whites' salaries and their skyrocketing costs of living.

Antiracists should stop connecting selfishness to racism, and unselfishness to antiracism. Altruism is wanted, not required. Antiracists do not have to be altruistic. Antiracists do not have to be selfless. Antiracists merely have to have *intelligent self-interest*, and to stop consuming those racist ideas that have engendered so much unintelligent self-interest over the years. It is in the intelligent self-interest of middle- and upper-income Blacks to challenge the racism affecting the Black poor, knowing they will not be free of the racism that is slowing their socioeconomic rise until poor Blacks are free of racism. It is in the intelligent self-interest of Asians, Native Americans, and Latina/os to challenge anti-Black racism, knowing they will not be free of racism until Black people are free of racism. It is in the intelligent self-interest of White Americans to challenge racism, knowing they will not be free of sexism, class bias, homophobia, and ethnocentrism until Black people are free of racism. The histories of anti-Asian, anti-Native, and anti-Latina/o racist ideas; the histories of sexist, elitist, homophobic, and ethnocentric ideas: all sound eerily similar to this history of racist ideas, and feature some of the same defenders of bigotry in America. Supporting these prevailing bigotries is only in the intelligent self-interest of a tiny group of super rich, Protestant, heterosexual, non-immigrant, White, Anglo-Saxon males. Those are the only people who need to be altruistic in order to be antiracist. The rest of us merely need to do the intelligent thing for ourselves.

Historically, Black people have by and large figured the smartest thing we could do for ourselves is to partake in uplift suasion—a strategy as unworkable as White self-sacrifice. Beginning around the 1790s, abolitionists urged the growing number of free Blacks to exhibit upstanding behavior before White people, believing they would thereby undermine the racist beliefs behind slavery. Black people would acquire "the esteem, confidence and patronage of the whites, in proportion to your increase in knowledge and moral improvement," as William Lloyd Garrison lectured free Blacks in the 1830s.[9]

The history of racist ideas shows not only that uplift suasion has failed, but that, generally speaking, the opposite of its intended effect has occurred. Racist Americans have routinely despised those Black Americans the most who uplifted themselves, who defied those racist laws and theories that individuals employed to keep them down. So upwardly mobile Black folk have not persuaded away racist ideas or policies. Quite the contrary. Uplift suasion has brought on the progression of racism—new racist policies and ideas after Blacks broke through the old ones.

Everyone who has witnessed the historic presidency of Barack Obama—and the historic opposition to him—should now know full well that the more Black people uplift themselves, the more they will find themselves on the receiving end of a racist backlash. Uplift suasion, as a strategy for racial progress, has failed. Black individuals must dispose of it as a strategy and stop worrying about what other people may think about the way they act, the way they speak, the way they look, the way they dress, the way they are portrayed in the media, and the way they think and love and laugh. Individual Blacks are not race representatives. They are not responsible for those Americans who hold racist ideas. Black people need to be their imperfect selves around White people, around each other, around all people. Black is beautiful *and* ugly, intelligent *and* unintelligent, law-abiding *and* law-breaking, industrious *and* lazy—and it is those imperfections that make Black people human, make Black people equal to all other imperfectly human groups.

Aside from self-sacrifice and uplift suasion, the other major strategy that racial reformers have used is many forms of educational persuasion. In 1894, a youthful W. E. B. Du Bois believed "the world was thinking wrong about race because it did not know. The ultimate evil was stupidity. The cure for it was knowledge based on scientific investigation." Exactly fifty years later, in 1944, Swedish economist Gunnar Myrdal echoed Du Bois's teaching strategy in his landmark manifesto for the coming civil rights movement. But instead of teaching White Americans through science, Myrdal suggested teaching them through the media, saying: "There is no doubt, in the writer's opinion, that a great majority of white people in America would be prepared to give the Negro a substantially better deal if they knew the facts."[10]

Du Bois and Myrdal believed—like abolitionists before them, like racial reformers today—that racism could be persuaded away through presenting the facts. Educational persuasion came in many forms. Educators could teach the facts. Scientists could discover the facts. Lawyers could present the facts in cases for upstanding Black plaintiffs. Sitcoms and movies and novels could portray the facts of upstanding Black folk. At marches and rallies, Black folk could articulate the facts of their sufferings before viewers or listeners or readers. Networks and documentarians and reporters and scholars could present factual spectacles of agonizing Black folk in their own environments suffering under the brutal foot of discrimination.

These many forms of educational persuasion, like uplift suasion, have been predicated on the false construction of the race problem: the idea that ignorance and hate lead to racist ideas, which lead to racist policies. In fact, self-interest leads to racist policies, which lead to racist ideas leading to all the ignorance and hate. Racist policies were created out of self-interest. And so, they have usually been voluntarily rolled back out of self-interest. The popular and glorious version of history saying that abolitionists and civil rights activists have steadily educated and persuaded away American racist ideas and policies sounds great. But it has never been the complete story, or even the main story. Politicians passed the civil and voting rights measures in the 1860s and the 1960s primarily out of political and economic self-interest—not an educational or moral awakening. And these laws did not spell the doom of racist policies. The racist policies simply evolved. There has been a not-so-glorious progression of racism, and educational persuasion has failed to stop it, and Americans have failed to recognize it.

Ironically, W. E. B. Du Bois abandoned educational persuasion before Gunnar Myrdal's advocacy of the strategy appeared. In the midst of the Great Depression, Du Bois looked out at the United States from the peak of a colossal mountain of racial facts, partially filled with four decades of his books, essays, petitions, speeches, and articles. "Negro leaders" thought that "white Americans did not know of or realize the continuing plight of the Negro," he wrote in a 1935 essay. "Accordingly, for the last two decades, we have striven by book and periodical, by speech and appeal, by various dramatic methods of agitation, to put the essential facts before the American people. Today there can be no doubt that Americans know the facts; and yet they remain for the most part indifferent and unmoved."[11]

In the eight decades since Du Bois wrote his essay, antiracist Americans have continued to strive by similar methods to put the essential facts before the American people. There can be no doubt that the producers and defenders and ignorers of racist policies know the facts. And yet they remain for the most part indifferent and unmoved: indifferent to the need to pass sweeping legislation completely overhauling the enslaving justice system; unmoved in pushing for initiatives like fighting crime with more and better jobs; indifferent to calls to decriminalize drugs and find alternatives to prisons; unmoved in empowering local residents to hire and fire the officers policing their communities. They remain for the most part unwilling to pass grander legislation that re-envisions American race relations by fundamentally assuming that discrimination is behind the racial disparities (and not what's wrong with Black folk), and by creating an agency that aggressively investigates the disparities and punishes conscious and unconscious discriminators. This agency would also work toward equalizing the wealth and power of Black and White neighborhoods and their institutions, with a clear mission of repairing the inequities caused by discrimination.

Lawmakers have the power today to stamp out racial discrimination, to create racial "equality as a fact," to quote LBJ, if they want to. They have the ability to champion the antiracist cause of immediate equality, echoing those old chants of immediate emancipation. They have the ability to turn their back on the assimilationist cause of gradual equality and the segregationist cause of permanent inequality. But local and federal lawmakers fear the repercussions from campaign donors and voters. They know that the postracialists would reject any sweeping antiracism bill as discriminatory and hateful toward White people just as enslavers and segregationists did before them, even if such a bill would actually benefit nearly all Americans, including White people. If racism is eliminated, many White people in the top economic and political brackets fear that it would eliminate one of the most effective tools they have at their disposal to conquer and control and exploit not only non-Whites, but also both low-income and middle-income White people.

Those Americans who have the power to end racism as we know it, to become tough on racism, and to build the postracial society that the postracialists actually don't want to see—these people have known the facts throughout the storied lifetime of Angela Davis. Powerful Americans also knew the facts during the lifetimes of Cotton Mather, Thomas Jefferson, William Lloyd Garrison, and W. E. B. Du Bois. It is the primary job of the powerful to know the facts of America. So trying to educate knowledgeable people does not make much sense. Trying to educate these powerful producers or defenders or ignorers of American racism about its harmful effects is like trying to educate a group of business executives about how harmful their products are. They already know, and they don't care enough to end the harm.

History is clear. Sacrifice, uplift, persuasion, and education have not eradicated, are not eradicating, and will not eradicate racist ideas, let alone racist policies. Power will never self-sacrifice away from its self-interest. Power cannot be persuaded away from its self-interest. Power cannot be educated away from its self-interest. Those who have the power to abolish racial discrimination have not done so thus far, and they will never be persuaded or educated to do so as long as racism benefits them in some way.

I am certainly *not* stating that there are no Americans in positions of power who have ever self-sacrificed or been educated or persuaded by Black uplift or facts to end racial disparities in their sphere of influence. But these courageous antiracist powerbrokers are more the exception than the rule. I am certainly *not* stating that generations of consumers of racist ideas have not been educated or persuaded to discard those racist ideas. But as Americans have discarded old racist ideas, new racist ideas have constantly been produced for their renewed consumption. That's why the effort to educate and persuade away racist ideas has been a never-ending affair in America. That's why educational persuasion will never bring into being an antiracist America.

Although uplift and persuasion and education have failed, history is clear on what has worked, and what will one day eradicate racist ideas. Racist ideas have always been the public relations arm of the company of racial discriminators and their products: racial disparities. Eradicate the company, and the public relations arm goes down, too. Eradicate racial discrimination, then racist ideas will be eradicated, too.

To undermine racial discrimination, Americans must focus their efforts on those who have the power to undermine racial discrimination. Protesting against anyone or anything else is as much of a waste of time as trying to educate or persuade powerful people. History has shown that those Americans who have had the power to undermine racial discrimination have rarely done so. They have done so, however, when they realized on their own that eliminating some form of racial discrimination was in their self-interest, much as President Abraham Lincoln chose to end slavery to save the Union. They have also conceded to antiracist change as a better alternative than the disruptive, disordered, politically harmful, and/or unprofitable conditions that antiracist protesters created.

Antiracist protesters have commonly rejected those racist ideas of what's wrong with Black people that are used to justify the plight of majority-Black spaces and the paucity of Black people in majority-White spaces. The most effective protests have been fiercely local; they are protests that have been started by antiracists focusing on their immediate surroundings: their blocks, neighborhoods, schools, colleges, jobs, and professions. These local protests have then become statewide protests, and statewide protests have then become national protests, and national protests have then become international protests. But it all starts with one person, or two people, or tiny groups, in their small surroundings, engaging in energetic mobilization of antiracists into organizations; and chess-like planning and adjustments during strikes, occupations, insurrections, campaigns, and fiscal and bodily boycotts, among a series of other tactics to force power to eradicate racist policies. Antiracist protesters have created positions of power for themselves by articulating clear demands and making it clearer that they will not stop—and policing forces cannot stop them—until their demands are met.

But protesting racist policies can never be a long-term solution to eradicating racial discrimination—and thus racist ideas—in America. Just as one generation of powerful Americans could decide or be pressured by protest to end racial discrimination, when the conditions and interests change, another generation could once again encourage racial discrimination. That's why protesting against racist power has been a never-ending affair in America.

Protesting against racist power and succeeding can never be mistaken for seizing power. Any effective solution to eradicating American racism must involve Americans committed to antiracist policies seizing and maintaining power over institutions, neighborhoods, counties, states, nations—the world. It makes no sense to sit back and put the future in the hands of people committed to racist policies, or people who regularly sail with the wind of self-interest, toward racism today, toward antiracism tomorrow. An antiracist America can only be guaranteed if principled antiracists are in power, and then antiracist policies become the law of the land, and then antiracist ideas become the common sense of the people, and then the antiracist common sense of the people holds those antiracist leaders and policies accountable.

And that day is sure to come. No power lasts forever. There will come a time when Americans will realize that the only thing wrong with Black people is that they think something is wrong with Black people. There will come a time when racist ideas will no longer obstruct us from seeing the complete and utter abnormality of racial disparities. There will come a time when we will love humanity, when we will gain the courage to fight for an equitable society for our beloved humanity, knowing, intelligently, that when we fight for humanity, we are fighting for ourselves. There will come a time. Maybe, just maybe, that time is now.

Acknowledgments

I WOULD LIKE to acknowledge all of the people I know and do not know who assisted and supported me in composing this history. From my ever-loving family members and friends to my ever-supportive colleagues across academia, in the State University of New York system, and now at the University of Florida, and to the countless thinkers, dead and alive, inside and outside academia, whose works on race have shaped my thinking and this history—I thank you. Without a doubt, this book is as much by you as it is by me.

I initially had not planned to write this book. I intended to write a history of the origins of Black Studies in higher education in the late 1960s. I decided to write my first chapter on the history of scientific racism, to show what the founders of Black Studies were struggling against. When I finished, I had a ninety-page chapter and a heavy bag of new thoughts about the history of racist ideas. I started thinking I may have a book on my hands. I will never forget talking all of this over with my father-in-law. I'm not sure if he remembers that conversation, but I do. Afterward, I decided that I would write the book that you now hold in your hands. And so I would like to express my thanks to B. T. Edmonds.

I decided to write a scholarly history that could be devoured by as many people as possible—without shortchanging the serious complexities—because racist ideas and their history have affected all of us. While historians in academia have become more accepting in recent decades of historians who write histories *on* the masses of Americans, historians are not nearly as accepting of those who write histories *for* the masses of Americans. Hopefully this will change.

I would like to acknowledge my agent, Ayesha Pande, who from the beginning was one of the major champions of this book. Ayesha, I do not take for granted that you believed in my ability to produce this far-reaching work. And I must thank Nation Books, a press that saw the potential of this book even when I did not always see it. I would also like to thank my editors, who along with Ayesha urged me to expand my original proposal of a narrow history of scientific racism to this comprehensive history of racist ideas. I would especially like to thank Clive Priddle, Carl Bromley, Alessandra Bastagli, and Daniel LoPreto. To Katy O'Donnell at Nation Books, thank you for keeping me on track to achieve the book's vision and helping me to cross the finish line. To all of the people involved in the production and marketing of *Stamped from the Beginning*, I cannot thank you enough.

I must acknowledge that I had to compose this book during one of the most trying times of my life. These difficulties did not just stem from learning, nearly every week, about yet another tragic killing of an unarmed American by law enforcement. I also had to swallow my sadness in order to comfort and support two loved ones as they fought against the same debilitating disease. They experienced many personal struggles throughout these ordeals. As I am a very private person, I will not go into the details. But to all of those gracious family members, friends, and medical personnel who assisted my loved ones and helped them along the way, bringing a smile—or many smiles— and a sense of peace and healing to their faces and bodies, I thank you. When you brought them happiness and peace and healing, you brought me happiness and peace and healing. And when you brought me happiness and peace and healing, you enabled me to work on this book through those trying times.

I would like to give a special acknowledgment to my parents, the Reverends Carol and Larry Rogers; to my second mother, Nyota Tucker; and to my brothers, Akil and Macharia. Love is truly a verb, and I thank you for your love.

I saved one person, who is already joking about being the book's co-author, for last—my wife, Sadiqa. I cannot tell you how many times I was sitting in our office, writing this text, and she was sitting there, too, doing her own work, and I would interrupt her and ask, "Sadiqa, you have a second?" Inevitably, I would take more than a second to read her the passage and ask for her critical assessment. I cannot thank her enough for listening to me and giving me her critical love. I also cannot thank her enough for encouraging me through all those long, tiring days when I was researching and writing from the time it was dark in the morning to the time it was dark at night. Thank you, Sadiqa, and thank you everyone, for everything.

Notes

NOTES TO PROLOGUE

1. Ryan Gabrielson, Ryann Grochowski Jones, and Eric Sagara, "Deadly Force, in Black and White," *ProPublica*, October 10, 2014; Rakesh Kochhar and Richard Fry, "Wealth Inequality Has Widened Along Racial, Ethnic Lines Since End of Great Recession," December 12, 2014, Pew Research Center, www.pewresearch.org /fact-tank/2014/12/12/racial-wealth-gaps-great-recession; Sabrina Tavernise, "Racial Disparities in Life Spans Narrow, but Persist," *New York Times*, July 18, 2013, www.nytimes.com/2013/07/18/health/racial-disparities-in-life-spans-narrow-but -persist.html.

2. Leah Sakala, "Breaking Down Mass Incarceration in the 2010 Census: State-by-State Incarceration Rates by Race/Ethnicity," *Prison Policy Initiative*, May 28, 2014, www.prisonpolicy.org/reports/rates.html; Matt Bruenig, "The Racial Wealth Gap," *American Prospect*, November 6, 2013, http://prospect.org/article/racial -wealth-gap.

3. Senator Jefferson Davis, April 12, 1860, 37th Cong., 1st sess., *Congressional Globe* 106, 1682.

4. Gunnar Myrdal, *An American Dilemma*, vol. 2, *The Negro Problem and Modern Democracy* (New Brunswick, NJ: Transaction Publishers, 1996), 928–929.

5. Audre Lorde, "Age, Race, Class, and Sex: Women Redefining Difference," in *Sister Outsider: Essays & Speeches* (New York: Ten Speed, 2007), 115.

6. Columbia anthropologist and assimilationist Ruth Benedict was instrumental in defining racism. See Ruth Benedict, *Race: Science and Politics* (New York: Modern Age Books, 1940); Ruth Benedict, *Race and Racism* (London: G. Routledge and Sons, 1942).

7. Kimberlé Crenshaw, "Demarginalizing the Intersection of Race and Sex: A Black Feminist Critique of Antidiscrimination Doctrine, Feminist Theory, and Antiracist Politics," *University of Chicago Legal Forum* 140 (1989): 139–167.

CHAPTER 1: HUMAN HIERARCHY

1. Richard Mather, *Journal of Richard Mather: 1635, His Life and Death, 1670* (Boston: D. Clapp, 1850), 27–28; "Great New England Hurricane of 1635 Even Worse Than Thought," Associated Press, November 21, 2006.

2. Kenneth Silverman, *The Life and Times of Cotton Mather* (New York: Harper and Row, 1984), 3–4.

3. Samuel Eliot Morison, *The Founding of Harvard College* (Cambridge, MA: Harvard University Press, 1935), 242–243; Richard Mather et al., *The Whole Booke of Psalmes Faithfully Translated into English Metre* (Cambridge, MA: S. Daye, 1640); John Cotton, *Spiritual Milk for Boston Babes in Either England* (Boston: S. G., for Hezekiah Usher, 1656); Christopher J. Lucas, *American Higher Education: A History*, 2nd ed. (New York: Palgrave Macmillan, 2006), 109–110; Frederick Rudolph, *Curriculum: A History of the American Undergraduate Course of Study Since 1636* (San Francisco: Jossey-Bass, 1977), 29–30.

4. Francisco Bethencourt, *Racisms: From the Crusades to the Twentieth Century* (Princeton, NJ: Princeton University Press, 2013), 3, 13–15; David Goldenberg, "Racism, Color Symbolism, and Color Prejudice," in *The Origins of Racism in the West*, ed. Miriam Eliav-Feldon, Benjamin Isaac, and Joseph Ziegler (Cambridge, UK: Cambridge University Press, 2009), 88–92; Aristotle, edited and translated by Ernest Barker, *The Politics of Aristotle* (Oxford: Clarendon Press, 1946), 91253b; Peter Garnsey, *Ideas of Slavery from Aristotle to Augustine* (New York: Cambridge University Press, 1996), 114.

5. Hugh Thomas, *The Slave Trade: The Story of the Atlantic Slave Trade, 1440–1870* (New York: Simon and Schuster, 1997), 27, 30; Garnsey, *Ideas of Slavery from Aristotle to Augustine*, 75, 79.

6. Alden T. Vaughan, *Roots of American Racism: Essays on the Colonial Experience* (New York: Oxford University Press, 1995), 157. Unless otherwise noted, emphasis is in original.

7. Joseph R. Washington, *Anti-Blackness in English Religion, 1500–1800* (New York: E. Mellen Press, 1984), 232–235; Vaughan, *Roots of American Racism*, 157, 177–179; Lorenzo J. Greene, *The Negro in Colonial New England, 1620–1776* (New York: Columbia University Press, 1942), 15–17; Craig Steven Wilder, *Ebony & Ivy: Race, Slavery, and the Troubled History of America's Universities* (New York: Bloomsbury Press), 29.

8. John G. Jackson, *Introduction to African Civilizations* (Secaucus, NJ: Citadel Press, 1970), 196–231; Curtis A. Keim, *Mistaking Africa: Curiosities and Inventions of the American Mind*, 3rd ed. (Boulder: Westview Press, 2014), 38; Adrian Cole and Stephen Ortega, *The Thinking Past: Questions and Problems in World History to 1750*, instructor's ed. (New York: Oxford University Press, 2015), 370–371.

9. Ross E. Dunn, *The Adventures of Ibn Battuta, a Muslim Traveler of the Fourteenth Century* (Berkeley: University of California Press, 1986), 315–316.

10. Ibn Khaldūn, Franz Rosenthal, and N. J. Dawood, *The Muqaddimah: An Introduction to History*, Bollingen Series (Princeton, NJ: Princeton University Press, 1969), 11, 57–61, 117; Gary Taylor, *Buying Whiteness: Race, Culture, and Identity from Columbus to Hip Hop*, Signs of Race (New York: Palgrave Macmillan, 2005), 222–223.

11. Thomas, *Slave Trade*, 38–39.

CHAPTER 2: ORIGINS OF RACIST IDEAS

1. P. E. Russell, *Prince Henry "the Navigator": A Life* (New Haven, CT: Yale University Press, 2000), 6.

2. Ibid., 249; Gomes Eanes de Zurara, Charles Raymond Beazley, and Edgar Prestage, *Chronicle of the Discovery and Conquest of Guinea*, 2 vols. (London: Printed for the Hakluyt Society, 1896), 1, 6, 7, 29.

3. William McKee Evans, *Open Wound: The Long View of Race in America* (Urbana: University of Illinois Press, 2009), 17–18.

4. Thomas, *Slave Trade*, 22–23.

5. Zurara et al., *Chronicle*, 81–85; Russell, *Prince Henry "the Navigator,"* 240–247, 253, 257–259.

6. Thomas, *Slave Trade*, 74; Zurara et al., *Chronicle*, xx–xl; Russell, *Prince Henry "the Navigator,"* 246.

7. Zurara et al., *Chronicle*, lv–lviii; Bethencourt, *Racisms*, 187.

8. Thomas, *Slave Trade*, 71, 87.

9. Lawrence Clayton, "Bartolomé de Las Casas and the African Slave Trade," *History Compass* 7, no. 6 (2009): 1527.

10. Thomas, *Slave Trade*, 50, 104, 123; Bethencourt, *Racisms*, 177–178; David M. Traboulay, *Columbus and Las Casas: The Conquest and Christianization of America, 1492–1566* (Lanham, MD: University Press of America, 1994), 58–59.

11. Lawrence A. Clayton, *Bartolomé de Las Casas: A Biography* (Cambridge, UK: Cambridge University Press, 2012), 349–353, 420–428; Bethencourt, *Racisms*, 233; Peter N. Stearns, *Sexuality in World History* (New York: Routledge, 2009), 108.

12. Leo Africanus, John Pory, and Robert Brown, *The History and Description of Africa*, 3 vols. (London: Hakluyt Society, 1896), 130, 187–190.

13. Washington, *Anti-Blackness*, 105–111; Thomas, *Slave Trade*, 153–159.

CHAPTER 3: COMING TO AMERICA

1. Charles de Miramon, "Noble Dogs, Noble Blood: The Invention of the Concept of Race in the Late Middle Ages," in *The Origins of Racism in the West*, ed. Miriam Eliav-Feldon, Benjamin H. Isaac, and Joseph Ziegler (Cambridge, UK: Cambridge University Press, 2009), 200–203; Stearns, *Sexuality in World History*, 108; Winthrop D. Jordan, *White over Black: American Attitudes Toward the Negro, 1550–1812* (Chapel Hill: University of North Carolina Press, 1968), 28–32.

2. Taylor, *Buying Whiteness*, 222–223; Washington, *Anti-Blackness*, 113–114.

3. Edmund S. Morgan, *American Slavery, American Freedom: The Ordeal of Colonial Virginia* (New York: W. W. Norton, 1975), 14–17; Washington, *Anti-Blackness*, 146–154.

4. Everett H. Emerson, *John Cotton* (New York: Twayne, 1965), 18, 20, 37, 88, 98, 100, 108–109, 111, 131; Washington, *Anti-Blackness*, 174–182.

5. Washington, *Anti-Blackness*, 196–200.

6. Taylor, *Buying Whiteness*, 224.

7. Anthony Gerard Barthelemy, *Black Face, Maligned Race: The Representation of Blacks in English Drama from Shakespeare to Southerne* (Baton Rouge: Louisiana State University Press, 1987), 72–73, 91–93; Bethencourt, *Racisms*, 98–99.

8. Jordan, *White over Black*, 37–40.

9. Tim Hashaw, *The Birth of Black America: The First African Americans and the Pursuit of Freedom at Jamestown* (New York: Carroll and Graf, 2007), 3–11.

10. Paul Lewis, *The Great Rogue: A Biography of Captain John Smith* (New York: D. McKay, 1966), 57–150; Wilder, *Ebony & Ivy*, 33.

11. Ronald T. Takaki, *A Different Mirror: A History of Multicultural America* (Boston: Little, Brown, 1993), 26–29.

12. Lewis, *Great Rogue*, 2, 244–257; Vaughan, *Roots of American Racism*, 304–305.

13. Jordan, *White over Black*, 33; Tommy Lee Lott, *The Invention of Race: Black Culture and the Politics of Representation* (Malden, MA: Blackwell, 1999), 9; Takaki, *Different*

Mirror, 51–53; Washington, *Anti-Blackness*, 15, 154–157; Vaughan, *Roots of American Racism*, 164; Taylor, *Buying Whiteness*, 221–229.

14. Jackson, *Introduction to African Civilizations*, 217–218.

15. Hashaw, *Birth of Black America*, xv–xvi.

16. Jon Meacham, *Thomas Jefferson: The Art of Power* (New York: Random House, 2012), 5.

17. Vaughan, *Roots of American Racism*, 130–134; Paula Giddings, *When and Where I Enter: The Impact of Black Women on Race and Sex in America* (New York: W. Morrow, 1984), 35.

18. Cedric B. Cowing, *The Saving Remnant: Religion and the Settling of New England* (Urbana: University of Illinois Press, 1995), 18–19; Washington, *Anti-Blackness*, 191–196, 240–241; Francis D. Adams and Barry Sanders, *Alienable Rights: The Exclusion of African Americans in a White Man's Land, 1619–2000* (New York: HarperCollins, 2003), 8–9.

19. Morgan, *American Slavery, American Freedom*, 225, 319.

20. Taunya Lovell Banks, "Dangerous Woman: Elizabeth Key's Freedom Suit—Subjecthood and Racialized Identity in Seventeenth Century Colonial Virginia," *Akron Law Review* 41, no. 3 (2008): 799–837; Warren M. Billings, "The Cases of Fernando and Elizabeth Key: A Note on the Status of Blacks in Seventeenth Century Virginia," *William and Mary Quarterly* 30, no. 3 (1973): 467–474; Anthony S. Parent, *Foul Means: The Formation of a Slave Society in Virginia, 1660–1740* (Chapel Hill: University of North Carolina Press, 2003), 110–111.

21. Thomas, *Slave Trade*; Thomas C. Holt, *Children of Fire: A History of African Americans* (New York: Hill and Wang, 2010), 60–61.

22. Warren M. Billings, ed., *The Old Dominion in the Seventeenth Century: A Documentary History of Virginia, 1606–1689* (Chapel Hill: University of North Carolina Press, 1975), 172; Morgan, *American Slavery, American Freedom*, 311; Parent, *Foul Means*, 123.

23. Morgan, *American Slavery, American Freedom*, 334–336.

24. Derek Hughes, *Versions of Blackness: Key Texts on Slavery from the Seventeenth Century* (Cambridge, UK: Cambridge University Press, 2007), vii–xi, 5–17.

25. Sharon Block, "Rape and Race in Colonial Newspapers, 1728–1776," *Journalism History* 27, no. 4 (2001–2002): 146, 149–152.

26. Greene, *The Negro in Colonial New England*, 165; Stephan Talty, *Mulatto America: At the Crossroads of Black and White Culture: A Social History* (New York: HarperCollins, 2003), 52–53.

27. Richard Ligon and Karen Ordahl Kupperman, *A True and Exact History of the Island of Barbados* (Indianapolis: Hackett, 2011), vi; Cotton Mather, Samuel Mather, and Edmund Calamy, *Memoirs of the Life of the Late Reverend Increase Mather* (London: J. Clark and R. Hett, 1725), 66; Taylor, *Buying Whiteness*, 270–273.

28. Taylor, *Buying Whiteness*, 271–294.

29. Ibid., 296–300.

CHAPTER 4: SAVING SOULS, NOT BODIES

1. Washington, *Anti-Blackness*, 455–456; Greene, *The Negro in Colonial New England*, 275; Jeffrey Robert Young, "Introduction," in *Proslavery and Sectional Thought in the Early South, 1740–1829: An Anthology*, ed. Jeffrey Robert Young (Columbia: University of South Carolina Press, 2006), 19–21; Brycchan Carey, *From Peace to Freedom:*

Quaker Rhetoric and the Birth of American Antislavery, 1657–1761 (New Haven, CT: Yale University Press, 2012), 7–8.

2. Richard Baxter, *A Christian Directory* (London: Richard Edwards, 1825), 216–220.

3. Morgan, *American Slavery, American Freedom*, 311–312; Adams and Sanders, *Alienable Rights*, 10; Billings, *Old Dominion in the Seventeenth Century*, 172–173.

4. Ann Talbot, *"The Great Ocean of Knowledge": The Influence of Travel Literature on the Work of John Locke* (Leiden: Brill, 2010), 3–4; Taylor, *Buying Whiteness*, 334.

5. R. S. Woolhouse, *Locke: A Biography* (Cambridge, UK: Cambridge University Press, 2007), 98, 276; Young, "Introduction," 18.

6. Charles F. Irons, *The Origins of Proslavery Christianity: White and Black Evangelicals in Colonial and Antebellum Virginia* (Chapel Hill: University of North Carolina Press, 2008), 28–29; David R. Roediger, *How Race Survived U.S. History: From Settlement and Slavery to the Obama Phenomenon* (London: Verso, 2008), 10; Taylor, *Buying Whiteness*, 313–323; Hughes, *Versions of Blackness*, 344–348; Parent, *Foul Means*, 240–241.

7. Washington, *Anti-Blackness*, 460–461; Hildegard Binder-Johnson, "The Germantown Protest of 1688 Against Negro Slavery," *Pennsylvania Magazine of History and Biography* 65 (1941): 151; Katharine Gerbner, "'We Are Against the Traffik of Men-Body': The Germantown Quaker Protest of 1688 and the Origins of American Abolitionism," *Pennsylvania History: A Journal of Mid-Atlantic Studies* 74, no. 2 (2007): 159–166; Thomas, *Slave Trade*, 458; "William Edmundson," *The Friend: A Religious and Literary Journal* 7, no. 1 (1833): 5–6.

8. Wilder, *Ebony & Ivy*, 40.

9. Takaki, *Different Mirror*, 63–68; Parent, *Foul Means*, 126–127, 143–146; Roediger, *How Race Survived U.S. History*, 19–20; Morgan, *American Slavery, American Freedom*, 252–270, 328–329.

10. Silverman, *Life and Times of Cotton Mather*; Tony Williams, *The Pox and the Covenant: Mather, Franklin, and the Epidemic That Changed America's Destiny* (Naperville, IL: Sourcebooks, 2010), 34.

11. Robert Middlekauff, *The Mathers: Three Generations of Puritan Intellectuals, 1596–1728* (New York: Oxford University Press, 1971), 198–199; Ralph Philip Boas and Louise Schutz Boas, *Cotton Mather: Keeper of the Puritan Conscience* (Hamden, CT: Archon Books, 1964), 27–31.

12. Greene, *The Negro in Colonial New England*, 237; Silverman, *Life and Times of Cotton Mather*, 31, 36–37, 159–160.

13. Silverman, *Life and Times of Cotton Mather*, 15–17.

14. Morgan, *American Slavery, American Freedom*, 314; Taylor, *Buying Whiteness*, 269.

15. Silverman, *Life and Times of Cotton Mather*, 41.

16. Slep Stuurman, "Francois Bernier and the Invention of Racial Classification," *History Workshop Journal* 50 (2000): 1–2; Francois Bernier, "A New Division of the Earth," *History Workshop Journal* 51 (2001): 247–250.

CHAPTER 5: BLACK HUNTS

1. Silverman, *Life and Times of Cotton Mather*, 55–72.

2. Ibid., 53–79.

3. Washington, *Anti-Blackness*, 273; Silverman, *Life and Times of Cotton Mather*, 84–85.

4. Taylor, *Buying Whiteness*, 306–307; Thomas, *Slave Trade*, 454; Hughes, *Versions of Blackness*, xi–xii; Jordan, *White over Black*, 9, 27–28; Washington, *Anti-Blackness*, 228–229.

5. Philip Jenkins, *Intimate Enemies: Moral Panics in Contemporary Great Britain* (New York: Aldine de Gruyter, 1992), 3–5; Silverman, *Life and Times of Cotton Mather*, 84–85.

6. Edward J. Blum and Paul Harvey, *The Color of Christ: The Son of God & the Saga of Race in America* (Chapel Hill: University of North Carolina Press, 2012), 20–21, 27, 40–41; Silverman, *Life and Times of Cotton Mather*, 88–89.

7. Charles Wentworth Upham, *Salem Witchcraft; with an Account of Salem Village, a History of Opinions on Witchcraft and Kindred Subjects*, vol. 1 (Boston: Wiggin and Lunt, 1867), 411–412; Blum and Harvey, *The Color of Christ*, 27–28; Boas and Boas, *Cotton Mather*, 109–110.

8. Silverman, *Life and Times of Cotton Mather*, 94; Williams, *The Pox and the Covenant*, 38; Boas and Boas, *Cotton Mather*, 89.

9. Boas and Boas, *Cotton Mather*, 119.

10. Silverman, *Life and Times of Cotton Mather*, 83–120; Thomas N. Ingersoll, "'Riches and Honour Were Rejected by Them as Loathsome Vomit': The Fear of Leveling in New England," in *Inequality in Early America*, ed. Carla Gardina Pestana and Sharon Vineberg Salinger (Hanover, NH: University Press of New England, 1999), 46–54.

11. Washington, *Anti-Blackness*, 185–186, 257, 280–281; Daniel K. Richter, "'It Is God Who Had Caused Them to Be Servants': Cotton Mather and Afro-American Slavery in New England," *Bulletin of the Congregational Library* 30, no. 3 (1979): 10–11; Greene, *The Negro in Colonial New England*, 265–267.

12. Washington, *Anti-Blackness*, 184–185, 273–277.

13. Cotton Mather, *Diary of Cotton Mather, 1681–1724*, 2 vols., vol. 1 (Boston: The Society, 1911), 226–229; Silverman, *Life and Times of Cotton Mather*, 262–263; Parent, *Foul Means*, 86–89.

14. Samuel Clyde McCulloch, "Dr. Thomas Bray's Trip to Maryland: A Study in Militant Anglican Humanitarianism," *William and Mary Quarterly* 2, no. 1 (1945): 15; C. E. Pierre, "The Work of the Society for the Propagation of the Gospel in Foreign Parts Among the Negroes in the Colonies," *Journal of Negro History* 1, no. 4 (1916): 350–351, 353, 357; Wilder, *Ebony & Ivy*, 42.

15. Morgan, *American Slavery, American Freedom*, 348–351; Parke Rouse, *James Blair of Virginia* (Chapel Hill: University of North Carolina Press, 1971), 16–22, 25–26, 30, 37–38, 40, 43, 71–73, 145, 147–148; Albert J. Raboteau, *Slave Religion: The "Invisible Institution" in the Antebellum South* (New York: Oxford University Press, 1978), 100.

16. Silverman, *Life and Times of Cotton Mather*, 241–242.

CHAPTER 6: GREAT AWAKENING

1. Samuel Sewall and Sidney Kaplan, *The Selling of Joseph: A Memorial* (Northampton, MA: Gehenna Press, 1968).

2. Greene, *The Negro in Colonial New England*, 22.

3. Albert J. Von Frank, "John Saffin: Slavery and Racism in Colonial Massachusetts," *Early American Literature* 29, no. 3 (1994): 254.

4. Greene, *The Negro in Colonial New England*, 259–260, 296–297; Lawrence W. Towner, "The Sewall-Saffin Dialogue on Slavery," *William and Mary Quarterly* 21, no. 1 (1964): 40–52.

5. Parent, *Foul Means*, 120–123; Morgan, *American Slavery, American Freedom*, 330–344; Greene, *The Negro in Colonial New England*, 171.

6. Adams and Sanders, *Alienable Rights*, 39–40.

7. Cotton Mather, *The Negro Christianized* (Boston: Bartholomew Green, 1706), 1–2, 14–16.

8. Silverman, *Life and Times of Cotton Mather*, 264–265; Wilder, *Ebony & Ivy*, 85.

9. Towner, "The Sewall-Saffin Dialogue," 51–52; Juan González and Joseph Torres, *News for All the People: The Epic Story of Race and the American Media* (London: Verso, 2011), 20, 24; Greene, *The Negro in Colonial New England*, 33.

10. A. Judd Northrup, *Slavery in New York: A Historical Sketch*, State Library Bulletin History (Albany: University of the State of New York, 1900), 267–272; Pierre, "Work of the Society," 356–358; Herbert Aptheker, *American Negro Slave Revolts* (New York: International Publishers, 1963), 172–173.

11. Greene, *The Negro in Colonial New England*, 23–30, 73.

12. Williams, *The Pox and the Covenant*, 2–4, 25, 29, 33–34.

13. Arthur Allen, *Vaccine: The Controversial Story of Medicine's Greatest Lifesaver* (New York: W. W. Norton, 2007), 36–37.

14. Silverman, *Life and Times of Cotton Mather*, 197, 254; Cotton Mather, *Diary of Cotton Mather, 1681–1724*, 2 vols., vol. 2 (Boston: The Society, 1911), 620–621; Williams, *The Pox and the Covenant*, 42–43.

15. Williams, *The Pox and the Covenant*, 73–74, 81–82, 117–118.

16. David Waldstreicher, *Runaway America: Benjamin Franklin, Slavery, and the American Revolution* (New York: Hill and Wang, 2004), 40–43; John B. Blake, *Public Health in the Town of Boston, 1630–1822* (Cambridge, MA: Harvard University Press, 1959), 53–61; Williams, *The Pox and the Covenant*, 102.

17. Adams and Sanders, *Alienable Rights*, 25; Williams, *The Pox and the Covenant*, 190–191.

18. Irons, *Origins of Proslavery Christianity*, 30; Greene, *The Negro in Colonial New England*, 260–261; Thomas, *Slave Trade*, 474.

19. Parent, *Foul Means*, 159–162, 236–237, 249–250; Wilder, *Ebony & Ivy*, 43; Irons, *Origins of Proslavery Christianity*, 31–32; Rouse, *James Blair of Virginia*, 32–36.

20. Greene, *The Negro in Colonial New England*, 275–276; Jon Sensbach, "Slaves to Intolerance: African American Christianity and Religious Freedom in Early America," in *The First Prejudice: Religious Tolerance and Intolerance in Early America*, ed. Chris Beneke and Christopher S. Grenda (Philadelphia: University of Pennsylvania Press, 2011), 208–209; Kenneth P. Minkema, "Jonathan Edwards's Defense of Slavery," *Massachusetts Historical Review* 4 (2002): 23, 24, 40; Adams and Sanders, *Alienable Rights*, 40–41.

21. Silverman, *Life and Times of Cotton Mather*, 372–419.

22. Samuel Mather, *The Life of the Very Reverend and Learned Cotton Mather* (Boston: Applewood Books, 2009), 108.

CHAPTER 7: ENLIGHTENMENT

1. Parent, *Foul Means*, 169–170.

2. Benjamin Franklin, "A Proposal for Promoting Useful Knowledge Among the British Plantations in America," *Transactions of the Literary and Philosophical Society of New York* 1, no. 1 (1815): 89–90.

3. Benjamin Franklin, *Observations Concerning the Increase of Mankind, Peopling of Countries* (Tarrytown, NY: W. Abbatt, 1918), 10.

4. Thomas, *Slave Trade*, 319, 325–327.

5. Malachy Postlethwayt, *The African Trade, the Great Pillar* (London, 1745), 4.

6. Dorothy E. Roberts, *Fatal Invention: How Science, Politics, and Big Business Re-Create Race in the Twenty-First Century* (New York: New Press, 2011), 29–30; Bethencourt, *Racisms*, 252–253.

7. Harriet A. Washington, *Medical Apartheid: The Dark History of Medical Experimentation on Black Americans from Colonial Times to the Present* (New York: Harlem Moon, 2006), 83; Thomas C. Holt, *Children of Fire: A History of African Americans* (New York: Hill and Wang, 2010), 21.

8. Holt, *Children of Fire*, 19–21; Thomas, *Slave Trade*, 399–402.

9. Voltaire, *Additions to the Essay on General History*, trans. T. Franklin et al., vol. 22, *The Works of M. De Voltaire* (London: Crowder et al., 1763), 227–228, 234.

10. Thomas, *Slave Trade*, 464–465.

11. Bethencourt, *Racisms*, 165–166, 172–173, 178; Roberts, *Fatal Invention*, 31–32.

12. Georges Louis Leclerc Buffon, *Natural History of Man*, new ed., vol. 1 (London: J. Annereau, 1801), 78–79, 83–94; Georges Louis Leclerc Buffon, *Natural History, General and Particular*, trans. William Smellie, 20 vols., vol. 3 (London: T. Cadell et al., 1812), 440–441; Johann Joachim Winckelmann, *History of the Art of Antiquity*, trans. Harry Francis Mallgrave (Los Angeles: Getty Research Institute, 2006), 192–195.

13. Thomas Jefferson, "To John Adams," in *The Writings of Thomas Jefferson*, ed. H. A. Washington (Washington, DC: Taylor and Maury, 1854), 61.

14. Silvio A. Bedini, *Thomas Jefferson: Statesman of Science* (New York: Macmillan, 1990), 12–13.

15. Thomas Jefferson, *Notes on the State of Virginia* (London: J. Stockdale, 1787), 271.

16. Samuel Davies, "The Duty of Christians to Propagate Their Religion Among the Heathens," in *Proslavery and Sectional Thought in the Early South, 1740–1829: An Anthology*, ed. Jeffrey Robert Young (Columbia: University of South Carolina Press, 2006), 113; Peter Kalm, "Travels into North America," in *A General Collection of the Best and Most Interesting Voyages and Travels in All Parts of the World*, ed. John Pinkerton (London: Longman, Hurst, Rees, and Orme, 1812), 503; Landon Carter, *The Diary of Colonel Landon Carter of Sabine Hall, 1752–1778*, 2 vols., vol. 2 (Charlottesville: University Press of Virginia, 1965), 1149.

17. Thomas P. Slaughter, *The Beautiful Soul of John Woolman, Apostle of Abolition* (New York: Hill and Wang, 2008), 94–133.

18. John Woolman, *Some Considerations on the Keeping of Negroes* (Philadelphia: Tract Association of Friends, 1754), 4.

19. Geoffrey Gilbert Plank, *John Woolman's Path to the Peaceable Kingdom: A Quaker in the British Empire* (Philadelphia: University of Pennsylvania Press, 2012), 105–109.

20. Ibid., 110; Slaughter, *Beautiful Soul*, 194–196; John Woolman, "The Journal of John Woolman," in *The Journal and Major Essays of John Woolman*, ed. Phillips P. Moulton (New York: Oxford University Press, 1971), 63.

21. Slaughter, *Beautiful Soul*, 231–236; Plank, *John Woolman's Path*, 175–177.

22. John Woolman, *Considerations on Keeping Negroes: Part Second* (Philadelphia: B. Franklin and D. Hall, 1762), 24, 30.

23. Slaughter, *Beautiful Soul*, 173; Plank, *John Woolman's Path*, 133, 149–153; Woolman, *Journal and Major Essays*, 53–57, 75–78.

24. Jon Meacham, *Thomas Jefferson: The Art of Power* (New York: Random House, 2012), 11–12.

25. Ibid., 39, 44–45; Bedini, *Thomas Jefferson*, 34, 39, 49.

26. Henry Wiencek, *Master of the Mountain: Thomas Jefferson and His Slaves* (New York: Farrar, Straus, and Giroux, 2012), 24–26; Meacham, *Thomas Jefferson*, 47–49.

CHAPTER 8: BLACK EXHIBITS

1. Henry Louis Gates, *The Trials of Phillis Wheatley: America's First Black Poet and Her Encounters with the Founding Fathers* (New York: Basic Civitas, 2010), 14.

2. Vincent Carretta, *Phillis Wheatley: Biography of a Genius in Bondage* (Athens: University of Georgia Press, 2011), 4–5, 7–8, 12–14; Kathrynn Seidler Engberg, *The Right to Write: The Literary Politics of Anne Bradstreet and Phillis Wheatley* (Lanham, MD: University Press of America, 2010), 35–36.

3. Carretta, *Phillis Wheatley*, 1–17, 37–38.

4. Ibid., 46–47, 58–59, 66–67, 82–83.

5. Gates, *Trials of Phillis Wheatley*, 27–29.

6. Edward Long, *The History of Jamaica*, 3 vols., vol. 2 (London: T. Lowndes, 1774), 476, 483.

7. David Hume, "Of Natural Characters," in *Essays and Treatises on Several Subjects*, ed. David Hume (London: T. Cadell, 1793), 206n512.

8. Silvia Sebastiani, *The Scottish Enlightenment: Race, Gender, and the Limits of Progress* (New York: Palgrave Macmillan, 2013), 103–104.

9. Adams and Sanders, *Alienable Rights*, 26–29.

10. Ignatius Sancho and Joseph Jekyll, *Letters of the Late Ignatius Sancho, an African*, 2 vols. (London: J. Nichols, 1782).

11. Ukawsaw Gronniosaw, *A Narrative of the Most Remarkable Particulars in the Life of James Albert, Ukawsaw Gronniosaw* (Newport, RI: S. Southwick, 1774); Olaudah Equiano, *The Interesting Narrative of the Life of Olaudah Equiano, or Gustavus Vassa, the African*, 2 vols. (New York: W. Durell, 1791).

12. Benjamin Rush, *An Address to the Inhabitants of the British Settlements in America, on the Slavery of Negroes in America* (Philadelphia: John Dunlap, 1773), 2, 3, 8, 15, 16, 26.

13. Carretta, *Phillis Wheatley*, 91, 95–98; Gates, *Trials of Phillis Wheatley*, 33–34; Phillis Wheatley, *Poems on Various Subjects, Religious and Moral* (London: A. Bell, 1773).

14. Peter N. Stearns, *Sexuality in World History* (New York: Routledge, 2009), 108; Lester B. Scherer, "A New Look at Personal Slavery Established," *William and Mary Quarterly* 30 (1973): 645–646; Richard Nisbet, *Slavery Not Forbidden by Scripture, or, a Defence of the West-India Planters* (Philadelphia: John Sparhawk, 1773), 23.

15. Wiencek, *Master of the Mountain*, 26–27, 33–34; Meacham, *Thomas Jefferson*, 69–70, 90–91.

16. Holt, *Children of Fire*, 104; Vincent Harding, *There Is a River: The Black Struggle for Freedom in America* (New York: Harcourt, Brace, Jovanovich, 1981), 43.

17. Long, *History of Jamaica*, 2:356, 364, 371, 475–478.

18. Henry Home of Kames, *Sketches of the History of Man*, 4 vols., vol. 1 (Edinburgh: W. Creech, 1807), 15.

19. Johann Friedrich Blumenbach, "On the Natural Variety of Mankind," in *The Anthropological Treatises of Johann Friedrich Blumenbach*, ed. Thomas Bendyshe (London: Longman, Green, Longman, Roberts, and Green, 1865), 98–100n4.

20. Emmanuel Chukwudi Eze, ed., *Race and the Enlightenment: A Reader* (Cambridge, MA: Blackwell, 1997), 38–64.

21. González and Torres, *News for All the People*, 28–29; Meacham, *Thomas Jefferson*, 97.

22. Waldstreicher, *Runaway America*, 211–212; Samuel Johnson, *Taxation No Tyranny: An Answer to the Resolutions and Address of the American Congress* (London: T. Cadell, 1775), 89.

CHAPTER 9: *CREATED EQUAL*

1. Meacham, *Thomas Jefferson*, 103.

2. Wiencek, *Master of the Mountain*, 27–29 (emphasis added).

3. Jacqueline Jones, *A Dreadful Deceit: The Myth of Race from the Colonial Era to Obama's America* (New York: BasicBooks, 2013), 64.

4. Roediger, *How Race Survived U.S. History*, 31–32, 41–42.

5. Robert L. Hetzel, "The Relevance of Adam Smith," in *Invisible Hand: The Wealth of Adam Smith*, ed. Andres Marroquin (Honolulu: University Press of the Pacific, 2002), 25–29; Adam Smith, *An Inquiry into the Nature and Causes of the Wealth of Nations*, 2 vols., vol. 1 (London: W. Strahan and T. Cadell, 1776), 25; Adam Smith, *An Inquiry into the Nature and Causes of the Wealth of Nations*, 9th ed., 3 vols., vol. 2 (London: A. Strahan, T. Cadell, and W. Davies, 1799), 454.

6. Thomas Jefferson, "Jefferson's 'Original Rough Draught' of the Declaration of Independence," in *The Papers of Thomas Jefferson*, vol. 1, *1760–1776*, ed. Julian P. Boyd (Princeton, NJ: Princeton University Press, 1950), 243–247.

7. Samuel Hopkins, *A Dialogue, Concerning the Slavery of the Africans* (Norwich, CT: Judah P. Spooner, 1776).

8. Joseph J. Ellis, *American Sphinx: The Character of Thomas Jefferson* (New York: Alfred A. Knopf, 1997), 27–71; Meacham, *Thomas Jefferson*, 106.

9. Jefferson, *Notes on the State of Virginia*, 229.

10. Roediger, *How Race Survived U.S. History*, 46.

11. Jefferson, *Notes on the State of Virginia*, 229.

12. Ibid., 232–234.

13. Herbert Aptheker, *Anti-Racism in U.S. History: The First Two Hundred Years* (New York: Greenwood Press, 1992), 47–48.

14. Jefferson, *Notes on the State of Virginia*, 231–232.

15. Ibid., 100, 239; Thomas Jefferson, "To General Chastellux, June 7, 1785," in *The Papers of Thomas Jefferson*, 8:186.

16. Meacham, *Thomas Jefferson*, xxvi, 144, 146, 175, 180.

17. Adams and Sanders, *Alienable Rights*, 88–89; Meacham, *Thomas Jefferson*, 188–189; Thomas Jefferson, "To Brissot de Warville, February 11, 1788," in *The Papers of Thomas Jefferson*, 12:577–578.

18. Fawn McKay Brodie, *Thomas Jefferson: An Intimate History* (New York: W. W. Norton, 2010), 287–288; Constantin-Francois Volney, *Travels Through Syria and Egypt: The Years 1783, 1784, and 1785*, vol. 1 (London: G. G. J. and J. Robinson, 1788), 80–83.

19. Meacham, *Thomas Jefferson*, 208.

20. James Bowdoin, "A Philosophical Discourse Publickly Addressed to the American Academy of Arts and Sciences," *Memoirs of the American Academy of Arts and Sciences* 1 (1785): 8–9; John Morgan, "Some Account of a Motley Colored, or Pye Negro Girl and Mulatto Boy," *Transactions of the American Philosophical Society* 2 (1784): 393.

21. Samuel Stanhope Smith, *An Essay on the Causes of the Variety of Complexion and Figure in the Human Species: To Which Are Added Strictures on Lord Kaim's Discourse, on the Original Diversity of Mankind* (Philadelphia: Robert Aitken, 1787), 17, 32, 58, 72, 111.

22. Ayana D. Byrd and Lori L. Tharps, *Hair Story: Untangling the Roots of Black Hair in America* (New York: St. Martin's Press, 2001), 19–21.

23. Bruce R. Dain, *A Hideous Monster of the Mind: American Race Theory in the Early Republic* (Cambridge, MA: Harvard University Press, 2002), 43; Samuel Stanhope Smith, *Strictures on Lord Kaim's Discourse, on the Original Diversity of Mankind* (Philadelphia: Robert Aitken, 1787), 2, 20.

24. David O. Stewart, *The Summer of 1787: The Men Who Invented the Constitution* (New York: Simon and Schuster, 2007), 68–81.

25. Roediger, *How Race Survived U.S. History*, 47; Adams and Sanders, *Alienable Rights*, 50–66, 78, 80–81.

26. Meacham, Thomas Jefferson, xxvi, 144, 146, 175, 180, 209–210.

27. Ibid., 216–217.

28. Adams and Sanders, *Alienable Rights*, 90–93.

29. Meacham, *Thomas Jefferson*, 216–223.

30. Ibid., 231–235, 239, 241, 249, 254.

CHAPTER 10: UPLIFT SUASION

1. Aptheker, *Anti-Racism in U.S. History*, 15–16; Henry E. Baker, "Benjamin Banneker, the Negro Mathematician and Astronomer," *Journal of Negro History* 3 (1918): 104.

2. Joanne Pope Melish, "The 'Condition' Debate and Racial Discourse in the Antebellum North," *Journal of the Early Republic* 19 (1999): 654–655, 661; Stewart, *Summer of 1787*, 25–27.

3. Roediger, *How Race Survived U.S. History*, 56–57, 142–143; Adams and Sanders, *Alienable Rights*, 28–29.

4. Jordan, *White over Black*, 447–449, 531.

5. Benjamin Banneker, "To Thomas Jefferson, August 19, 1791," in *The Papers of Thomas Jefferson*, 22:49–54.

6. Thomas Jefferson, "To Benjamin Banneker, August 30, 1791," in ibid., 97–98; Thomas Jefferson, "To Condorcet," August 30, 1791," in ibid., 98–99.

7. C. L. R. James, *The Black Jacobins: Toussaint L'ouverture and the San Domingo Revolution*, 2nd ed. (New York: Vintage Books, 1963), 88.

8. Thomas Jefferson, "St. Domingue (Haiti)," *Thomas Jefferson Encyclopedia, Monticello*, www.monticello.org/site/research-and-collections/st-domingue-haiti.

9. Leon F. Litwack, *North of Slavery: The Negro in the Free States, 1790–1860* (Chicago: University of Chicago Press, 1961), 18–19; Melish, "'Condition' Debate," 651–657, 661–665.

10. Melish, "'Condition' Debate," 660–661; Jones, *Dreadful Deceit*, 131.

11. Gary B. Nash, *Forging Freedom: The Formation of Philadelphia's Black Community, 1720–1840* (Cambridge, MA: Harvard University Press, 1988), 127–132.

12. Bedini, *Thomas Jefferson*, 247–248; Meacham, *Thomas Jefferson*, 262–263, 275.

13. Peter Kolchin, *American Slavery*, 1619–1877, rev. ed. (New York: Hill and Wang, 2003), 94–96; Holt, *Children of Fire*, 125.

14. Charles D. Martin, *The White African American Body: A Cultural and Literary Exploration* (New Brunswick, NJ: Rutgers University Press, 2002), 37; Jordan, *White over Black*, 533–534; Joanne Pope Melish, *Disowning Slavery: Gradual Emancipation and "Race" in New England, 1780–1860* (Ithaca, NY: Cornell University Press, 1998), 145.

15. Bethencourt, *Racisms*, 167; Benjamin Rush, *The Autobiography of Benjamin Rush* (Princeton, NJ: Princeton University Press, 1948), 307; Martin, *The White African American Body*, 19–24; Jefferson, *Notes on the State of Virginia*, 118–119.

16. Benjamin Rush, "To Thomas Jefferson, February 4, 1797," in *The Papers of Thomas Jefferson*, 29:284.

17. Benjamin Rush, "Observations Intended to Favour a Supposition That the Black Color (as It Is Called) of the Negroes Is Derived from the Leprosy," *Transactions of the American Philosophical Society* 4 (1799): 289–297.

18. Jordan, *White over Black*, 502–503; Meacham, *Thomas Jefferson*, 299.

19. *Richmond Recorder*, September 1, 1802.

20. Meacham, *Thomas Jefferson*, 378–380, 418–419, 454.

21. Kimberly Wallace-Sanders, *Skin Deep, Spirit Strong: The Black Female Body in American Culture* (Ann Arbor: University of Michigan Press, 2002), 15–16.

22. Larry E. Tise, *Proslavery: A History of the Defense of Slavery in America, 1701–1840* (Athens: University of Georgia Press, 1987), 36–37; Meacham, *Thomas Jefferson*, 348–350.

23. Jordan, *White over Black*, 349, 368, 375, 379, 385, 401, 403, 410, 425.

24. Meacham, *Thomas Jefferson*, 386–387, 392.

25. Jordan, *White over Black*, 531; Dain, *Hideous Monster*, 58–60.

26. Wilder, *Ebony & Ivy*, 209; Charles White, *An Account of the Regular Gradation in Man, and in Different Animals and Vegetables; and from the Former to the Latter* (London, 1799), iii, 11–40, 61.

27. Jordan, *White over Black*, 505–506, 531.

28. Samuel Stanhope Smith, *An Essay on the Causes of the Variety of Complexion and Figure in the Human Species*, 2nd ed. (New Brunswick, NJ: J. Simpson, 1810), 33, 48, 93–95, 252–255, 265–269, 287–296, 302–305.

CHAPTER 11: BIG BOTTOMS

1. Thomas Jefferson, "To Pierre Samuel Du Pont de Nemours, March 2, 1809," *Founders Online*, National Archives, http://founders.archives.gov/documents/Jefferson/99-01-02-9936; Meacham, *Thomas Jefferson*, 428–432, 468; Bedini, *Thomas Jefferson*, 396–397.

2. Jordan, *White over Black*, 442; Clement Clarke Moore, *Observations upon Certain Passages in Mr. Jefferson's Notes on Virginia* (New York: 1804), 19–32; Bedini, *Thomas Jefferson*, 379–380, 416, 429–430.

3. Henri Grégoire, *An Enquiry Concerning the Intellectual and Moral Faculties and Literature of Negroes. Followed with an Account of the Life and Works of Fifteen Negroes and Mulattoes*

Distinguished in Science, Literature, and the Arts (College Park, MD: McGrath, 1967), 128, 131, 134, 155–157.

4. Angela Y. Davis, *Women, Race & Class* (New York: Vintage Books, 1983), 7; Thomas, *Slave Trade*, 551–552, 568–572; Kolchin, *American Slavery*, 93–95; Thomas Jefferson, "To John W. Eppes, June 30, 1820," in *Thomas Jefferson's Farm Book: With Commentary and Relevant Extracts from Other Writings*, ed. Edwin Morris Betts (Princeton, NJ: Princeton University Press, 1953), 46.

5. Holt, *Children of Fire*, 105; Jedidiah Morse, *A Discourse, Delivered at the African Meeting-House* (Boston: Lincoln and Edmands, 1808), 18.

6. Thomas Jefferson "To Henri Grégoire, February 25, 1809," *Founders Online*, National Archives, http://founders.archives.gov/documents/Jefferson/99-01-02-9893.

7. Beverly Guy-Sheftall, "The Body Politic: Black Female Sexuality and the Nineteenth-Century Euro-American Imagination," in *Skin Deep, Spirit Strong: The Black Female Body in American Culture*, ed. Kimerbly Wallace-Sanders (Ann Arbor: University of Michigan Press, 2002), 18.

8. Clifton C. Crais and Pamela Scully, *Sara Baartman and the Hottentot Venus: A Ghost Story and a Biography* (Princeton, NJ: Princeton University Press, 2009), 8–10, 24, 25, 37, 40, 50–57, 64, 66, 70, 71, 74, 78–81, 100, 101, 105, 107, 111–113, 124, 126–141.

9. Barbara Krauthamer, *Black Slaves, Indian Masters: Slavery, Emancipation, and Citizenship in the Native American South* (Chapel Hill: University of North Carolina Press, 2013), 17–23, 26, 32, 34–35.

10. Herbert Aptheker, *American Negro Slave Revolts* (New York: International Publishers, 1963), 249–251; Daniel Rasmussen, *American Uprising: The Untold Story of America's Largest Slave Revolt* (New York: Harper, 2011), 1–3.

11. James Kirke Paulding, *Letters from the South by a Northern Man*, new ed., 2 vols., vol. 1 (New York: Harper and Brothers, 1835), 96–98; Kolchin, *American Slavery*, 93–95.

12. Tise, *Proslavery*, 42–52, 142–143, 384; Robert Walsh, *Appeal from the Judgements of Great Britain Respecting the United States of America*, 2nd ed. (Philadelphia, 1819), 397, 409–411.

13. Meacham, *Thomas Jefferson*, xix.

14. Randall, *Thomas Jefferson*, 585; Bedini, *Thomas Jefferson*, 396; Meacham, *Thomas Jefferson*, 446–448.

15. Bedini, *Thomas Jefferson*, 379–380, 402, 403, 416, 429–432, 437.

16. Adams and Sanders, *Alienable Rights*, 107–108.

CHAPTER 12: COLONIZATION

1. Aptheker, *American Negro Slave Revolts*, 222–223.

2. Tise, *Proslavery*, 58.

3. Philip Slaughter, *The Virginian History of African Colonization* (Richmond: Macfarlane and Fergusson, 1855), 1–8; Eric Burin, *Slavery and the Peculiar Solution: A History of the American Colonization Society* (Gainesville: University Press of Florida, 2005), 10–11.

4. Charles Fenton Mercer, *An Exposition of the Weakness and Inefficiency of the Government of the United States of North America* (n.p., 1845), 173, 284.

5. Douglas R. Egerton, "'Its Origin Is Not a Little Curious: A New Look at the American Colonization Society," *Journal of the Early Republic* 4 (1985): 468–472.

6. Robert Finley, "Thoughts on the Colonization of Free Blacks," *African Repository and Colonial Journal* 9 (1834): 332–334.

7. Scott L. Malcomson, *One Drop of Blood: The American Misadventure of Race* (New York: Farrar, Straus, and Giroux, 2000), 191; Finley, "Thoughts on the Colonization of Free Blacks," 332–334.

8. Tibebu Teshale, *Hegel and the Third World: The Making of Eurocentrism in World History* (Syracuse, NY: Syracuse University Press, 2011), 74–76, 79, 80, 83, 87, 89, 171, 174, 178–179.

9. Egerton, "'Its Origin Is Not a Little Curious,'" 476, 480.

10. Burin, *Slavery and the Peculiar Solution*, 15–16; Douglas R. Egerton, "Averting a Crisis: The Proslavery Critique of the American Colonization Society," *Civil War History* 42 (1997): 143–144.

11. Litwack, *North of Slavery*, 34–39.

12. Myron O. Stachiw, "'For the Sake of Commerce': Slavery, Antislavery, and Northern Industry," in *The Meaning of Slavery in the North*, ed. David Roediger and Martin H. Blatt (New York: Garland, 1998), 35.

13. David Robertson, *Denmark Vesey* (New York: Alfred A. Knopf, 1999), 4–5, 41–42, 47–48, 98, 123; Aptheker, *American Negro Slave Revolts*, 81, 115, 268–275; Adams and Sanders, *Alienable Rights*, 142–143; Tise, *Proslavery*, 58–61.

14. Burin, *Slavery and the Peculiar Solution*, 15–16.

15. Ellis, *American Sphinx*, 314–326; Meacham, *Thomas Jefferson*, 475, 77.

16. Thomas Jefferson, *Autobiography of Thomas Jefferson, 1743–1790* (New York: G. P. Putnam's Sons, 1914), 77.

17. Edward J. Blum and Paul Harvey, *The Color of Christ: The Son of God & the Saga of Race in America* (Chapel Hill: University of North Carolina Press, 2012), 78–83, 93–100; Meacham, *Thomas Jefferson*, 473.

18. Tise, *Proslavery*, 52–54, 302–303; James Brewer Stewart, "The Emergence of Racial Modernity and the Rise of the White North, 1790–1840," *Journal of the Early Republic* 18, no. 2 (1998): 193–195; Adams and Sanders, *Alienable Rights*, 112–113.

19. Melish, "'Condition' Debate," 667–668.

20. Hosea Easton, "An Address," in *To Heal the Scourge of Prejudice: The Life and Writings of Hosea Easton*, ed. George R. Price and James Brewer Stewart (Amherst: University of Massachusetts Press, 1999), 62.

21. *Freedom's Journal*, March 16, 1827.

22. Frederick Cooper, "Elevating the Race: The Social Thought of Black Leaders, 1827–50," *American Quarterly* 24, no. 5 (1972): 606–608.

23. González and Torres, *News for All the People*, 109–113; Stewart, "The Emergence of Racial Modernity," 193–195.

24. Albert Ebenezer Gurley, Charles Rogers, and Henry Porter Andrews, *The History and Genealogy of the Gurley Family* (Hartford, CT: Press of the Case, Lockwood, and Brainard Company, 1897), 72; Melish, "'Condition' Debate," 658.

25. Thomas Jefferson to Jared Sparks Monticello, February 4, 1824, *The Letters of Thomas Jefferson, 1743–1826*, American History, www.let.rug.nl/usa/presidents/thomas-jefferson/letters-of-thomas-jefferson/jefl276.php.

26. "American Colonization Society," *African Repository and Colonial Journal* 1 (1825): 1, 5; T.R., "Observations of the Early History of the Negro Race," *African Repository and Colonial Journal* 1 (1825): 7–12.

27. Meacham, *Thomas Jefferson*, 488.

28. Bedini, *Thomas Jefferson*, 478–480; Meacham, *Thomas Jefferson*, 48, 492–496.

CHAPTER 13: GRADUAL EQUALITY

1. Ellis, *American Sphinx*, 298.

2. Wilder, *Ebony & Ivy*, 255, 256, 259, 265–266.

3. Henry Mayer, *All on Fire: William Lloyd Garrison and the Abolition of Slavery* (New York: St. Martin's Press, 1998), 3–13; John L. Thomas, *The Liberator: William Lloyd Garrison, a Biography* (Boston: Little, Brown, 1963), 7–20, 27–42.

4. Mayer, *All on Fire*, 51–55.

5. Ibid., 62–68.

6. Ibid., 68–70.

7. William Lloyd Garrison, "To the Public," *Genius of Universal Emancipation*, September 2, 1829.

8. David Walker, *David Walker's Appeal* (Baltimore: Black Classic Press, 1993), 36, 37, 39–42, 70, 91, 95.

9. Mayer, *All on Fire*, 77–78, 83–88, 91–94; Litwack, *North of Slavery*, 233–235.

10. Alexis de Tocqueville, *Democracy in America*, trans. Henry Reeve, 3rd American ed., vol. 1 (New York: G. Adlard, 1839), 340–356, 374.

11. William Lloyd Garrison, "To the Public," *The Liberator*, January 1, 1831.

12. William Lloyd Garrison, *An Address, Delivered Before the Free People of Color, in Philadelphia*, 2nd ed. (Boston: S. Foster, 1831), 5–6; Thomas, *The Liberator*, 152.

13. *Minutes and Proceedings of the Second Annual Convention, for the Improvement of the Free People of Color in These United States* (Philadelphia, 1832), 34.

14. Alexander Saxton, "Problems of Class and Race in the Origins of the Mass Circulation Press," *American Quarterly* 36, no. 2 (1984): 212, 213, 217, 231; Litwack, *North of Slavery*, 113, 119, 126, 131, 168–170; Tise, *Proslavery*, 294–302; Mayer, *All on Fire*, 117–118, 169; González and Torres, *News for All the People*, 50–51.

15. Bruce A. Glasrud and Alan M. Smith, *Race Relations in British North America, 1607–1783* (Chicago: Nelson-Hall, 1982); Litwack, *North of Slavery*, 162–164.

16. Washington, *Medical Apartheid*, 86–90, 94–98; David R. Roediger, *The Wages of Whiteness: Race and the Making of the American Working Class*, rev. ed. (London: Verso, 2007), 115–116.

17. Leonard Cassuto, *The Inhuman Race: The Racial Grotesque in American Literature and Culture* (New York: Columbia University Press, 1997), 139–143; Paula T. Connolly, *Slavery in American Children's Literature, 1790–2010* (Iowa City: University of Iowa Press, 2013), 53, 56–57; David Kenneth Wiggins, *Glory Bound: Black Athletes in a White America* (Syracuse, NY: Syracuse University Press, 1997), 14–15; John Pendleton Kennedy, *Swallow Barn, or, a Sojourn in the Old Dominion*, 2 vols. (Philadelphia: Carey and Lea, 1832).

18. Aptheker, *American Negro Slave Revolts*, 293–295, 300–307; Blum and Harvey, *The Color of Christ*, 123; Nat Turner and Thomas R. Gray, *The Confessions of Nat Turner* (Richmond: T. R. Gray, 1832), 9–10.

19. Mayer, *All on Fire*, 117, 120–123, 129–131; Thomas, *The Liberator*, 131–132, 136–137; Aptheker, *American Negro Slave Revolts*, 313.

20. Mayer, *All on Fire*, 131–134.

21. William Lloyd Garrison, *Thoughts on African Colonization* (New York: Arno Press, 1968), xix, 151; Mayer, *All on Fire*, 134–139, 140.

22. Garrison, *Thoughts on African Colonization*, ix–xi; Thomas R. Dew, *Review of the Debate in the Virginia Legislature of 1831 and 1832* (Bedford, MA: Applewood Books, 2008), 5, 93.

23. Litwack, *North of Slavery*, 153–158.

24. Chancellor Harper, *Memoir on Slavery* (Charleston: James S. Burges, 1838), 55; Ralph Gurley, "Garrison's Thoughts on African Colonization," *African Repository and Colonial Journal* 8, no. 8 (1832): 277; González and Torres, *News for All the People*, 42–44; Tise, *Proslavery*, 64–74, 267–268; Mayer, *All on Fire*, 139–145, 148, 157, 166–167.

25. Aptheker, *Anti-Racism in U.S. History*, 129; Mayer, *All on Fire*, 170–176.

26. Mayer, *All on Fire*, 195; Russel B. Nye, *William Lloyd Garrison and the Humanitarian Reformers*, Library of American Biography (Boston: Little, Brown, 1955), 81–82.

CHAPTER 14: IMBRUTED OR CIVILIZED

1. George M. Fredrickson, *The Black Image in the White Mind: The Debate on Afro-American Character and Destiny, 1817–1914* (Middletown, CT: Wesleyan University Press, 1987), 103–104; Connolly, *Slavery in American Children's Literature*, 26–30.

2. Ronald Bailey, "'Those Valuable People, the Africans': The Economic Impact of the Slave(ry) Trade on Textile Industrialization in New England," in *The Meaning of Slavery in the North*, ed. David Roediger and Martin H. Blatt (New York: Garland, 1998), 13; Christine Stansell, *City of Women: Sex and Class in New York, 1789–1860* (Urbana: University of Illinois Press, 1987), 83–100; Jones, *Dreadful Deceit*, 107; Bertram Wyatt-Brown, "The Abolitionists' Postal Campaign of 1835," *Journal of Negro History* 50, no. 4 (1965): 227–238; González and Torres, *News for All the People*, 39–40, 46–47; Mayer, *All on Fire*, 196–199; Adams and Sanders, *Alienable Rights*, 146–147, 149; Tise, *Proslavery*, 279, 308–310.

3. John C. Calhoun, "Speech on Slavery," US Senate, *Congressional Globe*, 24th Cong., 2nd sess. (February 6, 1837), 157–159.

4. Mayer, *All on Fire*, 218.

5. *Colored American*, June 1, 1839.

6. Calvin Colton, *Abolition a Sedition* (Philadelphia: G. W. Donohue, 1839), 126; William Ragan Stanton, *The Leopard's Spots: Scientific Attitudes toward Race in America, 1815–59* (Chicago: University of Chicago Press, 1960), 24–25.

7. Samuel George Morton, *Crania Americana* (Philadelphia: J. Dobson, 1839), 1–7.

8. Ann Fabian, *The Skull Collectors: Race, Science, and America's Unburied Dead* (Chicago: University of Chicago Press, 2010), 24, 81–82, 90; "Crania Americana," *Boston Medical and Surgical Journal* 21, no. 22 (1840): 357; "Review," *American Journal of Science and Arts* 38, no. 2 (1840): 341; Sven Lindqvist, *The Skull Measurer's Mistake: And Other Portraits of Men and Women Who Spoke Out Against Racism* (New York: New Press, 1997), 44–47.

9. Edward Jarvis, "Statistics of Insanity in the United States," *Boston Medical and Surgical Journal* 27, no. 7 (1842): 116–121.

10. "Vital Stastitics of Negroes and Mulattoes," *Boston Medical and Surgical Journal* 27, no. 10 (1842); Stanton, *The Leopard's Spots*, 65–68.

11. Edward Jarvis, "Insanity Among the Coloured Population of the Free States," *American Journal of Medical Sciences* 6, no. 13 (1844): 71–83.

12. Mayer, *All on Fire*, 326; Nye, *William Lloyd Garrison*, 148–149.

13. Stanton, *The Leopard's Spots*, 45–53, 60–65; Fredrickson, *The Black Image in the White Mind*, 74–75; H. Shelton Smith, *In His Image: But . . . Racism in Southern Religion, 1780–1910* (Durham, NC: Duke University Press, 1972), 144; Litwack, *North of Slavery*, 46.

14. Fergus M. Bordewich, *Bound for Canaan: The Underground Railroad and the War for the Soul of America* (New York: Amistad, 2005), 224–226.

15. Frederick Douglass, *Narrative of the Life of Frederick Douglass, an American Slave* (New Haven, CT: Yale University Press, 2001), 3, 4, 6, 8, 9; Mayer, *All on Fire*, 350–352.

16. Connolly, *Slavery in American Children's Literature*, 35, 38; Stanton, *The Leopard's Spots*, 68–72, 97–99; Josiah Clark Nott, *Two Lectures on the Natural History of the Caucasian and Negro Races* (Mobile: Dade and Thompson, 1844), 38; E. G. Squier, "American Ethnology," *American Review* 9 (1849): 385–398.

17. Michael T. Bernath, *Confederate Minds: The Struggle for Intellectual Independence in the Civil War South*, Civil War America (Chapel Hill: University of North Carolina Press, 2010), 83–84; González and Torres, *News for All the People*, 138.

18. Samuel A. Cartwright, "Report on the Diseases and Physical Peculiarities of the Negro Race," *De Bow's Review* 7 (1851), 692–696.

19. Washington, *Medical Apartheid*, 55, 57, 61–68.

20. González and Torres, *News for All the People*, 118–119.

21. Litwack, *North of Slavery*, 47–48; James D. Bilotta, *Race and the Rise of the Republican Party, 1848–1865* (New York: P. Lang, 1992), 83–99.

22. Patricia A. Schechter, "Free and Slave Labor in the Old South: The Tredegar Ironworkers' Strike of 1847," *Labor History* 35, no. 2 (1994): 165–186.

23. William Lloyd Garrison, "Complexional Prejudice," in *Selections from the Writings and Speeches of William Lloyd Garrison* (New York: Negro Universities Press, 1968), 286–288.

24. Mayer, *All on Fire*, 393.

25. John Bachman, *The Doctrine of the Unity of the Human Race Examined on the Principles of Science* (Charleston, SC: C. Canning, 1850), 91, 212.

26. Peter A. Browne, *The Classification of Mankind, by the Hair and Wool of Their Heads* (Philadelphia, 1850), 1, 8, 20; M. H. Freeman, "The Educational Wants of the Free Colored People," *Anglo-African Magazine*, April 1859.

27. Henry Clay, "Remark in Senate," in *The Papers of Henry Clay: Candidate, Compromiser, Elder Statesman, January 1, 1844–June 29, 1852*, vol. 10, ed. Melba Porter Hay (Lexington: University Press of Kentucky, 2015), 815.

28. Henry Clay, "Remark in Senate," in ibid., 815.

CHAPTER 15: SOUL

1. Joan D. Hedrick, *Harriet Beecher Stowe: A Life* (New York: Oxford University Press, 1994), 202–205.

2. Giddings, *When and Where I Enter*, 54–55, 132–133.

3. Hedrick, *Harriet Beecher Stowe*, 206–207.

4. Harriet Beecher Stowe, *Uncle Tom's Cabin* (London: George Bell and Sons, 1889), iii, 193.

5. *A Key to Uncle Tom's Cabin: Presenting the Original Facts and Documents upon Which the Story Is Founded* (London: Sampson Low, Son and Company, 1853), 52; Stowe, *Uncle Tom's Cabin*, 327.

6. Stephan Talty, *Mulatto America: At the Crossroads of Black and White Culture. A Social History* (New York: HarperCollins, 2003), 22–24.

7. Stowe, *Uncle Tom's Cabin*, 80, 473; Millard Fillmore, "Mr. Fillmore's Views Relating to Slavery," in *Millard Fillmore Papers*, vol. 1, ed. Frank H. Severance (Buffalo: Buffalo Historical Society, 1907), 320–324.

8. William Lloyd Garrison, "Review of Uncle Tom's Cabin; or, Life Among the Lowly," *The Liberator*, March 26, 1852.

9. Frederick Douglass, *The Life and Times of Frederick Douglass: From 1817–1882* (London: Christian Age Office, 1882), 250.

10. Martin Robison Delany, *The Condition, Elevation, Emigration, and Destiny of the Colored People of the United States, Politically Considered* (Philadelphia, 1852), 10, 24–27.

11. Giddings, *When and Where I Enter*, 60–61; Christian G. Samito, *Changes in Law and Society During the Civil War and Reconstruction: A Legal History Documentary Reader* (Carbondale: Southern Illinois University Press, 2009), 17.

12. Connolly, *Slavery in American Children's Literature*, 69–76; "Southern Slavery and Its Assailants: The Key to Uncle Tom's Cabin," *De Bow's Review*, November 1853.

13. Franklin Pierce, "Address by Franklin Pierce, 1853," Joint Congressional Committee on Inaugural Ceremonies, www.inaugural.senate.gov/swearing-in/address/address-by-franklin-pierce-1853; Mayer, *All on Fire*, 425–427.

14. Josiah Clark Nott and George R. Gliddon, *Types of Mankind*, 7th ed. (Philadelphia: J.B. Lippincott, Grambo, 1855), v, 60.

15. John H. Van Evrie, *Negroes and Negro "Slavery": The First an Inferior Race: The Latter Its Normal Condition*, 3rd ed. (New York: Van Evrie, Horton, 1963), 221; Thomas F. Gossett, *Race: The History of an Idea in America*, new ed. (New York: Oxford University Press, 1997), 342–346; Stanton, *The Leopard's Spots*, 174–175.

16. Carolyn L. Karcher, "Melville's 'the 'Gees': A Forgotten Satire on Scientific Racism," *American Quarterly* 27, no. 4 (1975): 425, 430–431.

17. Waldo E. Martin, *The Mind of Frederick Douglass* (Chapel Hill: University of North Carolina Press, 1984), 229.

18. James McCune Smith, "On the Fourteenth Query of Thomas Jefferson's Notes on Virginia," *The Anglo-African Magazine*, August 1859.

19. Frederick Douglass, *The Claims of the Negro, Ethnologically Considered* (Rochester, NY: Lee, Mann, 1854); Wilson Jeremiah Moses, *Afrotopia: The Roots of African American Popular History* (Cambridge, UK: Cambridge University Press, 1998), 111–113.

20. William Lloyd Garrison, "Types of Mankind," *The Liberator*, October 13, 1854.

21. "Frederick Douglass and His Paper," *The Liberator*, September 23, 1853.

22. Mayer, *All on Fire*, 431–434.

CHAPTER 16: THE IMPENDING CRISIS

1. Eric Foner, *The Fiery Trial: Abraham Lincoln and American Slavery* (New York: W. W. Norton, 2010), 65–67.

2. Mayer, *All on Fire*, 424–425.

3. Foner, *Fiery Trial*, 5, 11, 12, 31, 60–62.

4. James Buchanan, "Inaugural Address," March 4, 1857, at Gerhard Peters and John T. Woolley, The American Presidency Project, www.presidency.ucsb.edu/ws/?pid=25817.

5. *Dred Scott v. John F. A. Sanford*, March 6, 1857, Case Files 1792–1995, Record Group 267, Records of the Supreme Court of the United States, National Archives.

6. Harding, *There Is a River*, 195, 202–204.

7. Abraham Lincoln and Stephen A. Douglas, *Political Debates Between Hon. Abraham Lincoln and Hon. Stephen A. Douglas, in the Celebrated Campaign of 1858, in Illinois* (Columbus, OH: Follett, Foster, 1860), 71, 154, 232, 241.

8. Foner, *Fiery Trial*, 101–111.

9. Mayer, *All on Fire*, 474–477.

10. Hinton Rowan Helper, *The Impending Crisis of the South: How to Meet It* (New York: Burdick Brothers, 1857), 184.

11. Fredrickson, *The Black Image in the White Mind*, 113–115.

12. Adams and Sanders, *Alienable Rights*, 178; Mayer, *All on Fire*, 494–507.

13. William C. Davis, *Jefferson Davis: The Man and His Hour* (Baton Rouge: Louisiana State University Press, 1996), 277–279.

14. Charles Darwin, *On the Origin of Species by Means of Natural Selection, or the Preservation of Favoured Races in the Struggle for Life*, 3rd ed. (London: J. Murray, 1861), 4, 6, 18, 24, 35, 413, 524.

15. Richard Hofstadter, *Social Darwinism in American Thought* (Boston: Beacon Press, 1992), 5, 13, 22, 29, 31–41.

16. Francis Galton, *Hereditary Genius: An Inquiry into Its Laws and Consequences* (New York: D. Appleton, 1891), 338; Gossett, *Race*, 155–158.

17. Carl N. Degler, *In Search of Human Nature: The Decline and Revival of Darwinism in American Social Thought* (New York: Oxford University Press, 1991), 59–61.

18. Charles Darwin, *The Descent of Man, and Selection in Relation to Sex* (New York: D. Appleton, 1872), 163, 192–193, 208.

19. "Free Negro Rule," *De Bow's Review* 3, no. 4 (1860): 440.

20. "Review 2," *De Bow's Review* 3, no. 4 (1860): 490–491; John Tyler Jr., "The Secession of the South," *De Bow's Review* 3, no. 4 (1860): 367.

21. Mayer, *All on Fire*, 508–509; Foner, *Fiery Trial*, 139–142.

22. Mayer, *All on Fire*, 513–514; Litwack, *North of Slavery*, 269–276.

23. Abraham Lincoln, "To John A. Gilmer," in *Collected Works of Abraham Lincoln*, vol. 4 (Ann Arbor: University of Michigan Press, 2001), 152; Apotheker, *American Negro Slave Revolts*, 357–358; Bernard E. Powers Jr., "'The Worst of All Barbarism': Racial Anxiety and the Approach of Secession in the Palmetto State," *South Carolina Historical Magazine* 112, nos. 3–4 (2011): 152–156.

CHAPTER 17: HISTORY'S EMANCIPATOR

1. "Declaration of the Immediate Causes Which Induce and Justify Secession of South Carolina from the Federal Union," The Avalon Project: Documents in Law, History and Diplomacy, Lillian Goldman Law Library, Yale Law School, http://avalon.law.yale.edu/19th_century/csa_scarsec.asp; Roediger, *How Race Survived U.S. History*, 70–71; Eric Foner, *Reconstruction: America's Unfinished Revolution, 1863–1877* (New York: Perennial Classics, 2002), 25; Foner, *Fiery Trial*, 146–147; Myron O. Stachiw, "'For the Sake of Commerce': Slavery, Antislavery, and Northern Industry," in *The Meaning of Slavery in the North*, ed. David Roediger and Martin H. Blatt (New York: Garland, 1998), 33–35.

2. Abraham Lincoln, "First Inaugural Address," March 4, 1861, The Avalon Project: Documents in Law, History, and Diplomacy, Lillian Goldman Law Library, Yale Law School, http://avalon.law.yale.edu/19th_century/lincoln1.asp; Alexander

H. Stephens, "'Corner Stone' Speech," Teaching American History, http://teaching americanhistory.org/library/document/cornerstone-speech.

3. Connolly, *Slavery in American Children's Literature*, 76, 77, 80, 81, 83, 84; Bernath, *Confederate Minds*, 13; William C. Davis, *Look Away!: A History of the Confederate States of America* (New York: Free Press, 2002), 142–143.

4. Mayer, *All on Fire*, 525–526.

5. See *Weekly Anglo-African*, April 27, 1861.

6. Davis, *Look Away*, 142–143.

7. Andrew Johnson, "Proclamation on the End of the Confederate Insurrection," April 2, 1866, Miller Center, University of Virginia, http://millercenter.org /president/johnson/speeches/proclamation-on-the-end-of-the-confederate -insurrection; Washington, *Medical Apartheid*, 149–150.

8. "The President's Proclamation," *New York Times*, September 26, 1862; Abraham Lincoln, "First Annual Message," December 3, 1861, Messages and Papers of the Presidents, at Gerhard Peters and John T. Woolley, The American Presidency Project, www.presidency.ucsb.edu/ws/?pid=29502; William Lloyd Garrison, "To Oliver Johnson, December 6, 1861," *The Letters of William Lloyd Garrison: Let the Oppressed Go Free, 1861–1867* (Cambridge, MA: Harvard University Press, 1979), 47.

9. Aptheker, *American Negro Slave Revolts*, 359–367; Foner, *Reconstruction*, 15–17.

10. Foner, *Fiery Trial*, 215–220.

11. Ibid., 221–227; William Lloyd Garrison, "The President on African Colonization," *The Liberator*, August 22, 1862; Mayer, *All on Fire*, 531–539; Paul D. Escott, "*What Shall We Do with the Negro?*" Lincoln, *White Racism, and Civil War America* (Charlottesville: University of Virginia Press, 2009), 53–55; Litwack, *North of Slavery*, 277–278.

12. Horace Greeley, "The Prayer of Twenty Millions," *New York Tribune*, August 20, 1862.

13. Abraham Lincoln, "A Letter from the President," *National Intelligencer*, August 23, 1862.

14. Abraham Lincoln, "Preliminary Emancipation Proclamation," September 22, 1862, National Archives and Records Administration, www.archives.gov/exhibits /american_originals_iv/sections/transcript_preliminary_emancipation.html.

15. Foner, *Fiery Trial*, 227–232; Peter S. Field, "The Strange Career of Emerson and Race," *American Nineteenth Century History* 2, no. 1 (2001): 22–24; Mayer, *All on Fire*, 537–543.

16. Abraham Lincoln, "Second Annual Message," December 1, 1862, Messages and Papers of the Presidents, at Gerhard Peters and John T. Woolley, The American Presidency Project, University of California at Santa Barbara, www.presidency .ucsb.edu/ws/?pid=29503.

17. Foner, *Fiery Trial*, 238–247; Escott, "*What Shall We Do with the Negro*," 62–63.

18. Mayer, *All on Fire*, 544–547; Thomas, *The Liberator*, 419–420.

19. Escott, "*What Shall We Do with the Negro*," 62–64.

CHAPTER 18: READY FOR FREEDOM?

1. Henry Villard, *Memoirs of Henry Villard, Journalist and Financier, 1863–1900*, 2 vols., vol. 2 (Boston: Houghton, Mifflin, 1904), 14–24, 52–55.

2. Escott, "*What Shall We Do with the Negro*," 42–50; Fredrickson, *The Black Image in the White Mind*, 233–235.

3. Foner, *Fiery Trial*, 52–53; James Brooks, *The Two Proclamations* (New York: Printed by Van Evrie, Horton, 1862), 6.

4. Forrest G. Wood, *Black Scare: The Racist Response to Emancipation and Reconstruction* (Berkeley: University of California Press, 1968), 40–52.

5. Foner, *Fiery Trial*, 251.

6. Orestes Augustus Brownson, "Abolition and Negro Equality," in *The Works of Orestes A. Brownson*, vol. 17, ed. Henry F. Brownson (Detroit: Thorndike Nourse, 1885), 553.

7. Foner, *Fiery Trial*, 258–260.

8. Foner, *Reconstruction*, 35–37, 46–50, 63–64; Mayer, *All on Fire*, 562–563.

9. William Lloyd Garrison, "To Oliver Johnson," in *The Letters of William Lloyd Garrison: Let the Oppressed Go Free, 1861–1867*, vol. 10, ed. Walter M. Merrill (Cambridge, MA: Harvard University Press, 1979), 201.

10. Abraham Lincoln, "Address at Sanitary Fair, Baltimore, Maryland," in *Collected Works of Abraham Lincoln*, 7:302–303.

11. Foner, *Fiery Trial*, 275–277.

12. Samuel G. Howe, *The Refugees from Slavery in Canada West, Report to the Freedmen's Inquiry Commission* (Boston: Wright and Potter, 1864), 1, 33; Robert Dale Owen, *The Wrong of Slavery: The Right of Emancipation, and the Future of the African Race in the United States* (Philadelphia: J. B. Lippincott, 1864), 219–222.

13. Escott, *"What Shall We Do with the Negro,"* 73–93.

14. William Lloyd Garrison, "To Francis W. Newman," in *The Letters of William Lloyd Garrison*, 10:228–229.

15. Foner, *Fiery Trial*, 302–311.

16. "Account of a Meeting of Black Religious Leaders in Savannah, Georgia, with the Secretary of War and the Commander of the Military Division of the Mississippi," in *Freedom: A Documentary History of Emancipation, 1861–1867*, series 1, vol. 3, ed. Ira Berlin et al. (New York: Cambridge University Press, 1982), 334–335.

17. Nicholas Guyatt, "'An Impossible Idea?': The Curious Career of Internal Colonization," *Journal of the Civil War Era* 4, no. 2 (2014): 241–244.

18. Foner, *Reconstruction*, 59; Guyatt, "'An Impossible Idea?'" 241–244; Foner, *Fiery Trial*, 320–321; Horace Greeley, "Gen. Sherman and the Negroes," *New York Tribune*, January 30, 1865.

19. Foner, *Fiery Trial*, 313, 317–320; Mayer, *All on Fire*, 572–576.

20. Samuel Thomas, "To General Carl Schurz," in *Senate Executive Documents for the First Session of the Thirty-Ninth Congress of the United States of America* (Washington, DC: US Government Printing Office, 1866,) 81; General O. O. Howard, *Report of the Brevet Major General O. O. Howard, Commissioner Bureau of Refugees, Freedmen, and Abandoned Lands, to the Secretary of War* (Washington, DC: US Government Printing Office, 1869), 8; Josiah C. Nott, "The Problem of the Black Races," *De Bow's Review*, new ser., vol. 1 (1866): 266–270.

21. Foner, *Reconstruction*, 73.

22. Ibid., 31, 67–68; Foner, *Fiery Trial*, 330–331.

23. Terry Alford, *Fortune's Fool: The Life of John Wilkes Booth* (New York: Oxford University Press, 2015), 257.

24. Blum and Harvey, *The Color of Christ*, 131.

25. Foner, *Reconstruction*, 67; Adams and Sanders, *Alienable Rights*, 196–197; Hans L. Trefousse, *Andrew Johnson: A Biography* (New York: W. W. Norton, 1989), 183; Clifton R. Hall, *Andrew Johnson: Military Governor of Tennessee* (Princeton, NJ: Princeton University Press, 1916), 102.

CHAPTER 19: RECONSTRUCTING SLAVERY

1. Foner, *Reconstruction*, 103–106, 110, 132–133, 138, 153–155, 198–205, 209–210, 215.

2. Ibid., 235–237; "The Negro's Claim to Office," *The Nation*, August 1, 1867.

3. James D. Anderson, *The Education of Blacks in the South, 1860–1935* (Chapel Hill: University of North Carolina Press, 1988), 6–7, 11–12.

4. William Lloyd Garrison, "Official Proclamation," *The Liberator*, December 22, 1865; William Lloyd Garrison, "Valedictory: The Last Number of the Liberator," *The Liberator*, December 29, 1865.

5. Mayer, *All on Fire*, 594–603; Foner, *Reconstruction*, 180–181.

6. Matt Wray and Annalee Newitz, *White Trash: Race and Class in America* (New York: Routledge, 1997), 2–3.

7. Adam I. P. Smith, *No Party Now: Politics in the Civil War North* (New York: Oxford University Press, 2006), 54–55; Andrew Johnson, "Veto of the Freedmen's Bureau Bill," February 19, 1866, http://teachingamericanhistory.org/library/document/veto-of-the-freedmens-bureau-bill/.

8. Andrew Johnson's Veto of the Civil Rights Bill, March 27, 1866, America's Reconstruction: People and Politics After the Civil War, www.digitalhistory. uh.edu/exhibits/reconstruction/section4/section4_10veto2.html.

9. Foner, *Reconstruction*, 241–251; C. Vann Woodward, *American Counterpoint: Slavery and Racism in the North-South Dialogue* (Boston: Little, Brown, 1971), 168–171; Roediger, *How Race Survived U.S. History*, 130.

10. Howard N. Rabinowitz, *Race Relations in the Urban South, 1865–1890* (Athens: University of Georgia Press, 1996), 24–182; Foner, *Reconstruction*, 261–264.

11. Wood, *Black Scare*, 120–123, 141–143.

12. Text of Fourteenth Amendment, Cornell University Law School, https://www.law.cornell.edu/constitution/amendmentxiv.

13. Foner, *Reconstruction*, 255, 261.

14. Elizabeth Cady Stanton, Susan B. Anthony, and Matilda Joslyn Gage, eds., *History of Woman Suffrage, 1861–1876*, vol. 2 (Rochester, NY: Charles Mann, 1887), 188, 214; Frances Ellen Watkins Harper, "We Are All Bound Up Together," in *Proceedings of the Eleventh Women's Rights Convention* (New York: Robert J. Johnston, 1866); Giddings, *When and Where I Enter*, 65–67; Davis, *Women, Race & Class*, 64–65, 70–75, 80–81.

15. Gerda Lerner, ed., *Black Women in White America: A Documentary History* (New York: Pantheon Books, 1972), 569–570.

16. Foner, *Reconstruction*, 253–271, 282–285, 288–291, 308–311.

17. Paul D. Moreno, *Black Americans and Organized Labor: A New History* (Baton Rouge: Louisiana State University Press, 2006), 24–26.

18. Ibram H. Rogers, *The Black Campus Movement: Black Students and the Racial Reconstitution of Higher Education, 1965–1972* (New York: Palgrave Macmillan, 2012), 13–15;

National Freedman's Relief Association of New York Annual Report of 1865/66 (New York: Holman, 1866), 22; Anderson, *Education of Blacks in the South*, 28–63.

19. Kathy Russell-Cole, Midge Wilson, and Ronald E. Hall, *The Color Complex: The Politics of Skin Color Among African Americans* (New York: Harcourt, Brace, Jovanovich, 1992), 26–29.

20. Woodward, *American Counterpoint*, 172–176; Andrew Johnson, "Third Annual Message," December 3, 1867, at Gerhard Peters and John T. Woolley, The American Presidency Project, www.presidency.ucsb.edu/ws/?pid=29508.

21. Foner, *Reconstruction*, 340–345; Adams and Sanders, *Alienable Rights*, 211; Wood, *Black Scare*, 116–117, 120, 123–129.

22. Foner, *Reconstruction*, 446–447; Fredrickson, *The Black Image in the White Mind*, 185–186; Woodward, *American Counterpoint*, 177–179.

23. Louise Michele Newman, *White Women's Rights: The Racial Origins of Feminism in the United States* (New York: Oxford University Press, 1999), 65.

24. Giddings, *When and Where I Enter*, 68–70; Moreno, *Black Americans and Organized Labor*, 27–32; Roediger, *How Race Survived U.S. History*, 103–104.

25. Davis, *Women, Race & Class*, 82–86; Giddings, *When and Where I Enter*, 67–71.

26. Wood, *Black Scare*, 102.

CHAPTER 20: RECONSTRUCTING BLAME

1. Mayer, *All on Fire*, 613–614; Foner, *Reconstruction*, 448–449.

2. William A. Sinclair, *The Aftermath of Slavery: A Study of the Condition and Environment of the American Negro* (Boston: Small, Maynard, 1905), 104.

3. Wood, *Black Scare*, 143–153.

4. Adams and Sanders, *Alienable Rights*, 212–215; Woodward, *American Counterpoint*, 179–182.

5. Foner, *Reconstruction*, 316–331, 346–365, 379–390.

6. Fionnghuala Sweeney, *Frederick Douglass and the Atlantic World* (Liverpool: Liverpool University Press, 2007), 175.

7. Adams and Sanders, *Alienable Rights*, 215–217.

8. Henry Ward Beecher, *The Life of Jesus, the Christ* (New York: J. B. Ford, 1871), 134–137.

9. Stetson Kennedy, *After Appomattox: How the South Won the War* (Gainesville: University Press of Florida, 1995), 220–221; Jack B. Scroggs, "Southern Reconstructions: A Radical View," in *Reconstruction: An Anthology of Revisionist Writings*, ed. Kenneth M. Stampp and Leon F. Litwack (Baton Rouge: Louisiana State University Press, 1969), 422–423; Foner, *Reconstruction*, 499–504.

10. LeeAnna Keith, *The Colfax Massacre: The Untold Story of Black Power, White Terror, and the Death of Reconstruction* (New York: Oxford University Press, 2008); Peter H. Irons, *A People's History of the Supreme Court* (New York: Viking, 1999), 202–205.

11. Irons, *A People's History of the Supreme Court*, 197–201; *Slaughterhouse Cases*, 83 US 36, see https://www.law.cornell.edu/supremecourt/text/83/36.

12. Foner, *Reconstruction*, 512–517, 525, 531–532, 537–539; Adams and Sanders, *Alienable Rights*, 219.

13. Foner, *Reconstruction*, 393–411, 536–538.

14. Rabinowitz, *Race Relations in the Urban South*, 237–238, 243–248.

15. Mayer, *All on Fire*, 616; James S. Pike, *The Prostrate State: South Carolina Under*

Negro Government (New York: D. Appleton, 1874), 12.

16. Adams and Sanders, *Alienable Rights*, 219–220; Foner, *Reconstruction*, 525–527, 554; González and Torres, *News for All the People*, 151–153; Mayer, *All on Fire*, 615–616.

17. Irons, *A People's History of the Supreme Court*, 206–207; Foner, *Reconstruction*, 532–534, 563, 590.

18. Foner, *Reconstruction*, 565; Mayer, *All on Fire*, 617.

19. Foner, *Reconstruction*, 571–573; Adams and Sanders, *Alienable Rights*, 223–224.

20. Mary Gibson, *Born to Crime: Cesare Lombroso and the Origins of Biological Criminology*, Italian and Italian American Studies (Westport, CT: Praeger, 2002), 43–44, 249–250; Degler, *In Search of Human Nature*, 35–36; Giddings, *When and Where I Enter*, 79; Washington, *Medical Apartheid*, 247; Cesare Lombroso and William Ferrero, *The Female Offender* (New York: D. Appleton, 1895), 111–113.

21. Moreno, *Black Americans and Organized Labor*, 45–67.

22. Adams and Sanders, *Alienable Rights*, 222–227; Irons, *A People's History of the Supreme Court*, 206–209; Foner, *Reconstruction*, 575–596.

23. George B. Tindall, *South Carolina Negroes, 1877–1900* (Columbia: University of South Carolina Press, 1952), 12; Wade Hampton, "Ought the Negro to Be Defranchised? Ought He to Have Been Enfranchised?" *North American Review* 168 (1879): 241–243.

24. Isabel Wilkerson, *The Warmth of Other Suns: The Epic Story of America's Great Migration* (New York: Random House, 2010), 39.

25. Adams and Sanders, *Alienable Rights*, 228; Foner, *Reconstruction*, 598–602; Mayer, *All on Fire*, 624–626.

CHAPTER 21: RENEWING THE SOUTH

1. W. E. B. Du Bois, *Black Reconstruction in America: An Essay Towards a History of the Part Which Black Folk Played in the Attempt to Reconstruct Democracy in America, 1860–1880* (New York: Atheneum, 1971), 30.

2. David Levering Lewis, *W. E. B. Du Bois: Biography of a Race, 1868–1919* (New York: Henry Holt, 1993), 11–37.

3. Washington, *Medical Apartheid*, 152–153.

4. Lewis, *W. E. B. Du Bois, 1868–1919*, 31–40.

5. Irons, *A People's History of the Supreme Court*, 209–215.

6. Henry W. Grady, *The New South* (New York: Robert Bonner's Sons, 1890), 146, 152; Atticus G. Haygood, *Pleas for Progress* (Cincinnati: M. E. Church, 1889), 28; *Our Brother in Black: His Freedom and His Future* (New York: Phillips and Hunt, 1881).

7. Thomas U. Dudley, "How Shall We Help the Negro?" *Century Magazine* 30 (1885): 273–280; George Washington Cable, *The Silent South, Together with the Freedman's Case in Equity and the Convict Lease System* (New York: Scribner's, 1885); Henry W. Grady, "In Plain Black and White: A Reply to Mr. Cable," *Century Magazine* 29 (1885), 911.

8. "Two Colored Graduates," *Philadelphia Daily News*, February 22, 1888.

9. Robert L. Dabney, *A Defense of Virginia* (New York: E. J. Hale and Son, 1867); Thomas Nelson Page, *In Ole Virginia; or, Marse Chan and Other Stories* (New York: Charles Scribner's Sons, 1887); Philip Alexander Bruce, *The Plantation Negro as a Freeman: Observations on His Character, Condition, and Prospects in Virginia* (New York: G. P. Putnam's Sons, 1889), 53–57.

10. Lewis, *W. E. B. Du Bois, 1868–1919*, 51–76.

11. "Review of *History of the Negro Race in America from 1619 to 1880*, by George W. Williams," *Magazine of American History* 9, no. 4 (1883): 299–300.

12. George W. Williams, *History of the Negro Race in America from 1619 to 1880* (New York: G. P. Putnam's Sons, 1885), 1:60, 2:451, 548.

13. Lewis, *W. E. B. Du Bois, 1868–1919*, 76–78; W. E. B. Du Bois, *The Autobiography of W. E. B. Du Bois: A Soliloquy on Viewing My Life from the Last Decade of Its First Century* (New York: International Publishers, 1968), 142.

14. Benjamin Harrison, "First Annual Message," December 3, 1889, in Gerhard Peters and John T. Woolley, The American Presidency Project, www.presidency.ucsb.edu/ws/?pid=29530.

CHAPTER 22: SOUTHERN HORRORS

1. Fredrickson, *The Black Image in the White Mind*, 262–268.

2. Edward Wilmot Blyden, "The African Problem, and the Method of Its Solution," *African Repository* 66, no. 3 (1890): 69; Henry M. Stanley, *Through the Dark Continent* (New York: Harper and Brothers, 1878); Joseph Conrad, *Heart of Darkness* (New York: Penguin, 2007), 41.

3. Thomas Adams Upchurch, *Legislating Racism: The Billion Dollar Congress and the Birth of Jim Crow* (Lexington: University Press of Kentucky, 2004), 23–45; Keim, *Mistaking Africa*, 47–53.

4. Mary Frances Berry, *My Face Is Black Is True: Callie House and the Struggle for Ex-Slave Reparations* (New York: Alfred A. Knopf, 2005), 33–49, 75–80.

5. Lewis, *W. E. B. Du Bois, 1868–1919*, 100–102.

6. Albert Bushnell Hart, *The Southern South* (New York: D. Appleton, 1910), 99–105, 134; Lewis, *W. E. B. Du Bois, 1868–1919*, 111–113.

7. Lewis, *W. E. B. Du Bois, 1868–1919*, 116.

8. Upchurch, *Legislating Racism*, 85–128.

9. August Meier, *Negro Thought in America, 1880–1915* (Ann Arbor: University of Michigan Press, 1963), 192.

10. Giddings, *When and Where I Enter*, 123–125; Moreno, *Black Americans and Organized Labor*, 68–81, 93–96, 99–100.

11. Giddings, *When and Where I Enter*, 18; Ida B. Wells, *Southern Horrors: Lynch Law in All Its Phases* (New York: New York Age, 1892), www.gutenberg.org/files/14975/14975-h/14975-h.htm; Adams and Sanders, *Alienable Rights*, 231–232.

12. Giddings, *When and Where I Enter*, 81–83; Anna Julia Cooper, *A Voice from the South* (Xenia, OH: Aldine, 1892), 34, 134.

13. Wells, *Southern Horrors*.

14. Deborah Gray White, *Too Heavy a Load: Black Women in Defense of Themselves, 1894–1994* (New York: W. W. Norton, 1999), 22–27, 71, 78, 109.

15. Geoffrey C. Ward, *Before the Trumpet: Young Roosevelt* (New York: Harper and Row, 1985), 215–216.

16. Lewis, *W. E. B. Du Bois, 1868–1919*, 144–149.

17. W. E. B. Du Bois, "My Evolving Program for Negro Freedom," in *What the Negro Wants*, ed. Rayford W. Logan (New York: Agathon, 1969), 70.

18. For Washington's private civil rights activism, see David H. Jackson, *Booker T. Washington and the Struggle Against White Supremacy: The Southern Educational Tours*,

1908–1912 (New York: Palgrave Macmillan, 2008); David H. Jackson, *A Chief Lieutenant of the Tuskegee Machine: Charles Banks of Mississippi* (Gainesville: University Press of Florida, 2002).

19. Booker T. Washington, "Atlanta Compromise Speech," 1895, http://history matters.gmu.edu/d/39/.

20. Lewis, *W. E. B. Du Bois, 1868–1919*, 174–175.

21. Paula Giddings, *Ida: A Sword Among Lions—Ida B. Wells and the Campaign Against Lynching* (New York: Amistad, 2009), 366–367.

22. Irons, *A People's History of the Supreme Court*, 219–232; Woodward, *American Counterpoint*, 230–232.

23. See Robert H. Wiebe, *The Search for Order, 1877–1920* (New York: Hill and Wang, 1967).

CHAPTER 23: BLACK JUDASES

1. Havelock Ellis, *Studies in the Psychology of Sex*, vol. 1 (London: Wilson and Macmillan, 1897), x.

2. Siobhan Somerville, "Scientific Racism and the Emergence of the Homosexual Body," *Journal of the History of Sexuality* 5, no. 2 (1994): 244–259.

3. Frederick L. Hoffman, *Race Traits and Tendencies of the American Negro* (New York: Macmillan, 1896), 311–312.

4. W. E. B Du Bois, "Review of Race Traits and Tendencies, by Frederick L. Hoffman," *Annals of the American Academy of Political and Social Science* 9 (1897): 130–132; Khalil Gibran Muhammad, *The Condemnation of Blackness: Race, Crime, and the Making of Modern Urban America* (Cambridge, MA: Harvard University Press, 2010), 61–65, 78.

5. W. E. B. Du Bois, "The Conservation of Races," in *W. E. B. Du Bois: A Reader*, ed. David Levering Lewis (New York: Henry Holt, 1995), 20–27.

6. W. E. B. Du Bois, *The Philadelphia Negro: A Social Study* (Philadelphia: University of Pennsylvania Press, 1899), 68, 387–389; "Review of *The Philadelphia Negro*, by W. E. B. Du Bois," *American Historical Review* 6, no. 1 (1900): 162–164.

7. Lewis, *W. E. B. Du Bois, 1868–1919*, 238–239.

8. González and Torres, *News for All the People*, 157–160; W. Fitzhugh Brundage, "The Darien 'Insurrection' of 1899: Black Protest During the Nadir of Race Relations," *Georgia Historical Quarterly* 74, no. 2 (1990): 234–253; W. E. B. Du Bois, *Dusk of Dawn* (New York: Oxford University Press, 2007), 34; Du Bois, "My Evolving Program," 70.

9. W. E. B. Du Bois, "To the Nation of the World," in *W. E. B. Du Bois: A Reader*, 639–641.

10. Rudyard Kipling, "The White Man's Burden," *McClure's Magazine*, February 1899.

11. Fredrickson, *The Black Image in the White Mind*, 305–310; González and Torres, *News for All the People*, 178–179.

12. Roediger, *How Race Survived U.S. History*, 141–142, 156–158, 160; Douglas S. Massey and Nancy A. Denton, *American Apartheid: Segregation and the Making of the Underclass* (Cambridge, MA: Harvard University Press, 1993), 29.

13. George H. White, "Farewell Speech," in Benjamin R. Justesen, *George Henry White: An Even Chance in the Race of Life* (Baton Rouge: Louisiana State University Press, 2001), 441.

14. Howard K. Beale, "On Rewriting Reconstruction History," *American Historical Review* 45, no. 4 (1940): 807; William Archibald Dunning, *Reconstruction, Political and Economic, 1865–1877* (New York: Harper and Brothers, 1907), 212.

15. Ulrich Bonnell Phillips, *American Negro Slavery* (New York: D. Appleton, 1929), 8; John David Smith, *Slavery, Race, and American History: Historical Conflict, Trends, and Method, 1866–1953* (Armonk, NY: M. E. Sharpe), x–xii, 28, 29.

16. Joseph Moreau, *Schoolbook Nation: Conflicts over American History Textbooks from the Civil War to the Present* (Ann Arbor: University of Michigan Press, 2003), 163–174; Will Kaufman, *The Civil War in American Culture* (Edinburgh: Edinburgh University Press, 2006), 28–29.

17. Booker T. Washington, *Up from Slavery: An Autobiography* (New York: Doubleday, Page, 1901).

18. Lewis, *W. E. B. Du Bois, 1868–1919*, 262–264.

19. William Hannibal Thomas, *The American Negro: What He Was, What He Is, and What He May Become* (New York: Macmillan, 1901), 129, 195, 296, 410; John David Smith, *Black Judas: William Hannibal Thomas and the American Negro* (Athens: University of Georgia Press, 2000), 161–164, 177–178, 185–189.

20. Addie Hunton, "Negro Womanhood Defended," *Voice* 1, no. 7 (1904): 280; Smith, *Black Judas*, xxvi, 206–209; Muhammad, *Condemnation of Blackness*, 79–81.

21. Clarence Lusane, *The Black History of the White House*, Open Media Series (San Francisco: City Lights Books, 2011), 225–233; Seth M. Scheiner, "President Theodore Roosevelt and the Negro, 1901–1908," *Journal of Negro History* 47, no. 3 (1962): 171–172; Stephen Kantrowitz, *Ben Tillman and the Reconstruction of White Supremacy* (Chapel Hill: University of North Carolina Press, 2000); 259; Charles Carroll, *The Negro a Beast; Or, In the Image of God* (Miami: Mnemosyn, 1969).

22. Aptheker, *Anti-Racism in U.S. History*, 25; James Weldon Johnson, *Along This Way: The Autobiography of James Weldon Johnson* (Boston: Da Capo, 2000), 203; W. E. B. Du Bois, *The Souls of Black Folk: Essays and Sketches* (Chicago: A. C. McClurg, 1903), 11–12.

23. Ibid., 3–4, 11.

24. Ibid., 53.

25. W. E. B. Du Bois, "The Talented Tenth," in *The Negro Problem: A Series of Articles by Representative American Negroes of Today* (New York: James Pott, 1903), 43–45.

26. Lewis, *W. E. B. Du Bois, 1868–1919*, 291–294; Carl Kelsey, "Review of *The Souls of Black Folk*, by W. E. B. Du Bois," *Annals of the American Academy of Political and Social Science* 22 (1903): 230–232.

CHAPTER 24: GREAT WHITE HOPES

1. Sander Gilman, *Jewish Frontiers: Essays on Bodies, Histories, and Identities* (New York: Palgrave Macmillan, 2003), 89.

2. W. E. B. Du Bois, ed., *The Health and Physique of the American Negro* (Atlanta: Atlanta University Press, 1906).

3. Michael Yudell, *Race Unmasked: Biology and Race in the Twentieth Century* (New York: Columbia University Press, 2014), 48–49; W. E. B. Du Bois, *Black Folk Then and Now: An Essay in the History and Sociology of the Negro Race* (New York: Henry Holt, 1939), vii.

4. Lewis, *W. E. B. Du Bois, 1868–1919*, 331–333; Theodore Roosevelt, "Sixth Annual Message," December 3, 1906, at Gerhard Peters and John T. Woolley, American Presidency Project, www.presidency.ucsb.edu/ws/?pid=29547.

5. Lester Frank Ward, *Pure Sociology: A Treatise on the Origin and Spontaneous Development of Society* (New York: Macmillan, 1921), 359; James Elbert Cutler, *Lynch Law: An Investigation into the History of Lynching in the United States* (New York: Longman, Green, 1905), 269; W. E. B. Du Bois, "Some Notes on Negro Crime," Atlanta University Publications (Atlanta: Atlanta University Press, 1904), 56.

6. Lewis, *W. E. B. Du Bois, 1868–1919*, 332.

7. Geoffrey C. Ward, *Unforgivable Blackness: The Rise and Fall of Jack Johnson* (New York: Alfred A. Knopf, 2004), 98–100, 130–133, 137–139, 144–145, 422–424.

8. John Gilbert, *Knuckles and Gloves* (London: W. Collins Sons, 1922), 45; González and Torres, *News for All the People*, 209–211; Ward, *Unforgivable Blackness*, 115–116.

9. Keim, *Mistaking Africa*, 48; Emily S. Rosenberg, *Financial Missionaries to the World: The Politics and Culture of Dollar Diplomacy, 1900–1930* (Durham, NC: Duke University Press, 2003), 201–203.

10. Du Bois, *Autobiography*, 227–229.

11. Lewis, *W. E. B. Du Bois, 1868–1919*, 386–402.

12. Charles Benedict Davenport, *Heredity in Relation to Eugenics* (New York: Henry Holt, 1911), 1; Yudell, *Race Unmasked*, 31–40; Dorothy E. Roberts, *Killing the Black Body: Race, Reproduction, and the Meaning of Liberty* (New York: Pantheon Books, 1997), 61–62, 66–68.

13. Lewis, *W. E. B. Du Bois, 1868–1919*, 413–414.

14. Franz Boas, *The Mind of Primitive Man* (New York: Macmillan, 1921), 127–128, 272–273; Lee D. Baker, *Anthropology and the Racial Politics of Culture* (Durham, NC: Duke University Press, 2010), 24.

15. Giddings, *Ida*, 479–480.

16. *The Crisis*, June 1911.

17. W. E. B. Du Bois, "Hail Columbia!" in *W. E. B. Du Bois: A Reader*, 295–296.

18. Nannie H. Burroughs, "Not Color but Character," *Voice of the Negro* 1 (1904), 277–278.

19. Giddings, *When and Where I Enter*, 122–123; N. H. Burroughs, "Black Women and Reform," *The Crisis*, August 1915.

20. Lewis, *W. E. B. Du Bois, 1868–1919*, 419–424; Woodrow Wilson, *Division and Reunion, 1829–1909* (New York: Longman, Green, 1910).

21. Blum and Harvey, *The Color of Christ*, 141–142.

22. Louis R. Harlan, *Booker T. Washington: The Wizard of Tuskegee, 1901–1915* (New York: Oxford University Press, 1983), 431–435; Lewis, *W. E. B. Du Bois, 1868–1919*, 460–463, 501–509; Ed Guerrero, *Framing Blackness: The African American Image in Film* (Philadelphia: Temple University Press, 1993), 10–17; W. E. B. Du Bois, *The Negro* (New York: Cosimo, 2010), 82.

CHAPTER 25: THE BIRTH OF A NATION

1. W. E. B. Du Bois, "'Refinement and Love,'" *The Crisis*, December 1916.

2. Wilkerson, *The Warmth of Other Suns*, 8–15, 36–46, 160–168, 177–179, 217–221, 237–241, 249–251, 348–350; Carter G. Woodson, *A Century of Negro Migration* (Washington, DC: Association for the Study of Negro Life and History, 1918), 180.

3. David Levering Lewis, *W. E. B. Du Bois: The Fight for Equality and the American Century, 1919–1963* (New York: Henry Holt, 1993), 50–55.

4. Edward Byron Reuter, *The Mulatto in the United States* (Boston: Gorham Press, 1918), 58.

5. Somerville, "Scientific Racism and the Emergence of the Homosexual Body," 256–263.

6. Madison Grant, *The Passing of the Great Race; Or, The Racial Basis of European History* (New York: Charles Scribner's Sons, 1918), 16, 193, 226.

7. Jonathan Peter Spiro, *Defending the Master Race: Conservation, Eugenics, and the Legacy of Madison Grant* (Lebanon, NH: University Press of New England, 2009), 356–357.

8. Lewis M. Terman, *The Measure of Intelligence: An Explanation of and a Complete Guide for the Use of the Standard Revision and Extension of the Binet-Simon Intelligence Scale* (New York: Houghton Mifflin, 1916), 92.

9. Gossett, *Race*, 374–377.

10. W. E. B. Du Bois, "Reconstruction and Africa," *The Crisis*, February 1919; Du Bois, *Dusk of Dawn*, 137.

11. Ira Katznelson, *When Affirmative Action Was White: An Untold History of Racial Inequality in Twentieth-Century America* (New York: W. W. Norton, 2005), 84–86.

12. Cameron McWhirter, *Red Summer: The Summer of 1919 and the Awakening of Black America* (New York: Henry Holt, 2011), 10, 12–17, 56–59; Claude McKay, "If We Must Die," Poetry Foundation, www.poetryfoundation.org/poem/173960.

13. Giddings, *When and Where I Enter*, 184.

14. Davis, *Women, Race & Class*, 123–125; Moreno, *Black Americans and Organized Labor*, 107–111; Timothy Johnson, "'Death for Negro Lynching!': The Communist Party, USA's Position on the African American Question," *American Communist History* 7, no. 2 (2008): 243–247.

15. Earl Ofari Hutchinson, *Blacks and Reds: Race and Class in Conflict, 1919–1990* (East Lansing: Michigan State University Press, 1995).

16. W. E. B. Du Bois, *Darkwater: Voices from Within the Veil* (New York: Harcourt, Brace, and Howe, 1920), 39, 73.

17. Ibid., 166, 168, 185–186.

18. White, *Too Heavy a Load*, 125–128.

19. Lewis, *W. E. B. Du Bois, 1919–1963*, 20–23.

20. Ibid., 62–67; Edmund David Cronon, *Black Moses: The Story of Marcus Garvey and the Universal Negro Improvement Association* (Madison: University of Wisconsin Press, 1969), 64–67.

21. Russell-Cole et al., *The Color Complex*, 26, 30–32; Giddings, *When and Where I Enter*, 178; Lewis, *W. E. B. Du Bois, 1919–1963*, 66–71.

22. Lewis, *W. E. B. Du Bois, 1919–1963*, 70–76.

23. Ibid., 77–84, 118–128, 148–152.

24. I. A. Newby, *Jim Crow's Defense: Anti-Negro Thought in America, 1900–1930* (Baton Rouge: Louisiana State University Press, 1965), 55; Gossett, *Race*, 407.

25. Robert E. Park, "The Conflict and Fusion of Cultures with Special Reference to the Negro," *Journal of Negro History* 4, no. 2 (1919): 129–130; W. E. B. Du Bois, *The Gift of Black Folk: The Negro in the Making of America* (Millwood, NY: Kraus-Thomson, 1975), iv, 287, 320, 339.

CHAPTER 26: MEDIA SUASION

1. Lewis, *W. E. B. Dubois, 1919–1963*, 153–159, 161–166; Alain Locke, "The New Negro," in *The New Negro: Voices of the Harlem Renaissance*, ed. Alain Locke (New York: Simon and Schuster, 1992), 15.

2. Rogers, *The Black Campus Movement*, 19, 23, 35–47.

3. Valerie Boyd, *Wrapped in Rainbows: The Life of Zora Neale Hurston* (New York: Simon and Schuster, 1997), 116–119; Wallace Thurman, *The Blacker the Berry* (New York: Simon and Schuster, 1996).

4. Langston Hughes, "The Negro Artist and the Racial Mountain," *The Nation*, June 1926.

5. David L. Lewis, *When Harlem Was in Vogue* (New York: Penguin, 1997), 180–189; W. E. B. Du Bois, "On Carl Van Vechten's *Nigger Heaven*," in *W. E. B. Du Bois: A Reader*, 516; Carl Van Vechten, *Nigger Heaven* (Urbana: University of Illinois, 2000), 50.

6. Van Vechten, *Nigger Heaven*, 89, 90.

7. John Martin, *John Martin Book of the Dance* (New York: Tudor, 1963), 177–189.

8. Wiggins, *Glory Bound*, 183–184.

9. Angela Davis, *Blues Legacies and Black Feminism: Gertrude "Ma" Rainey, Bessie Smith, and Billie Holiday* (New York: Vintage, 1998); Giles Oakley, *The Devil's Music: A History of the Blues* (New York: Da Capo, 1976).

10. Lewis, *W. E. B. Du Bois, 1919–1963*, 214–220.

11. Donald Young, "Foreword," *Annals of the American Academy of Political and Social Science* 140 (1928): vii–viii.

12. Thorsten Sellin, "The Negro Criminal: A Statistical Note," in ibid., 52–64.

13. Walter White, "The Color Line in Europe," in ibid., 331.

14. Moreno, *Black Americans and Organized Labor*, 141–143; Johnson, "'Death for Negro Lynching,'" 247–254; Hutchinson, *Blacks and Reds*, 29–40.

15. Claude G. Bowers, *The Tragic Era: The Revolution After Lincoln* (Cambridge, MA: Riverside, 1929), vi.

16. Lewis, *W. E. B. Du Bois, 1919–1963*, 320–324; W. E. B. Du Bois, *Black Reconstruction*, 700, 725; Roediger, *Wages of Whiteness*.

17. Lewis, *W. E. B. Du Bois, 1919–1963*, 349–378.

18. Ibid., 284–285; Vanessa H. May, *Unprotected Labor: Household Workers, Politics, and Middle-Class Reform in New York, 1870–1940* (Chapel Hill: University of North Carolina Press, 2011), 123.

19. Washington, *Medical Apartheid*, 194–202; Degler, *In Search of Human Nature*, 148–151, 202; Roberts, *Killing the Black Body*, 72–86.

20. Earnest Albert Hooton, *Up from the Ape* (New York: Macmillan, 1931), 593–594.

21. Roberts, *Fatal Invention*, 85–87; Elazar Barkan, *The Retreat of Scientific Racism: Changing Concepts of Race in Britain and the United States Between the World Wars* (Cambridge, UK: Cambridge University Press, 1992), 100–108.

22. Lott, *The Invention of Race*, 10–13; "Monster Ape Pack Thrills in New Talkie," *Chicago Tribune*, April 23, 1933; Blum and Harvey, *The Color of Christ*, 186–188.

23. González and Torres, *News for All the People*, 250–254; Melissa V. Harris-Perry, *Sister Citizen: Shame, Stereotypes, and Black Women in America* (New Haven, CT: Yale University Press, 2011), 88.

CHAPTER 27: OLD DEAL

1. Lewis, *W. E. B. Du Bois, 1919–1963*, 256–265, 299–301, 306–311.

2. Ibid., 310–311; Davis, *Women, Race & Class*, 69; W. E. B. Du Bois, "Marxism and the Negro Problem," *The Crisis*, May 1933; Du Bois, *Dusk of Dawn*, 103.

3. Lewis, *W. E. B. Du Bois, 1919–1963*, 295–297, 300–314; Anderson, *The Education of Blacks in the South*, 276–277; Carter G. Woodson, *The Miseducation of the Negro* (Mineola, NY: Dover, 2005), 55.

4. Robin D. G. Kelley, *Hammer and Hoe: Alabama Communists During the Great Depression* (Chapel Hill: University of North Carolina Press, 1990), 107–109, 116.

5. Jacqueline Jones, *American Work: Four Centuries of Black and White Labor* (New York: W. W. Norton, 1998), 344.

6. Katznelson, *When Affirmative Action Was White*, 36–61.

7. Degler, *In Search of Human Nature*, 167.

8. W. E. B. Du Bois, "On Being Ashamed," *The Crisis*, September 1933; W. E. B. Du Bois, "Pan-Africa and New Racial Philosophy," *The Crisis*, November 1933; W. E. B. Du Bois, "Segregation," *The Crisis*, January 1934.

9. W. E. B. Du Bois, "A Free Forum," *The Crisis*, February 1934.

10. W. E. B. Du Bois, "Segregation in the North," *The Crisis*, April 1934; Lewis, *W. E. B. Du Bois, 1919–1963*, 330–331, 335–349.

11. Lewis, *W. E. B. Du Bois, 1919–1963*, 395–396.

12. Chris Mead, *Joe Louis: Black Champion in White America* (Mineola, NY: Dover, 1985), 68.

13. "Adolf Hitler, Jesse Owens, and the Olympics Myth of 1936," History News Network, July 8, 2002, http://historynewsnetwork.org/article/571; M. Dyreson, "American Ideas About Race and Olympic Races in the Era of Jesse Owens: Shattering Myths of Reinforcing Scientific Racism?," *International Journal of the History of Sport* 25, no. 2 (2008): 251–253.

14. Dean Cromwell and Al Wesson, *Championship Techniques in Track and Field* (New York: Whittlesey House, 1941), 6; W. Montague Cobb, "Race and Runners," *Journal of Health and Physical Education* 7 (1936): 3–7, 52–56; Patrick B. Miller, "The Anatomy of Scientific Racism: Racialist Responses to Black Athletic Achievement," *Journal of Sport History* 25, no. 1 (1998): 126–135.

15. Lewis, *W. E. B. Du Bois, 1919–1963*, 422–423; Robert L. Fleeger, "Theodore G. Bilbo and the Decline of Public Racism, 1938–1947," *Journal of Mississippi History* 68, no. 1 (2006): 8–11; Degler, *In Search of Human Nature*, 203–204.

16. Ruth Benedict, *Race: Science and Politics* (New York: Viking, 1940), v–vi.

17. W. E. B. Du Bois, ed., *The Negro American Family* (Atlanta: Atlanta University Press, 1908), 41; E. Franklin Frazier, *The Negro Family in the United States* (Chicago: University of Chicago Press, 1939), xix.

18. Frazier, *Negro Family*, 41, 331, 355, 487–488.

19. Russell-Cole et al., *The Color Complex*, 51–54, 66; Byrd and Tharps, *Hair Story*, 44–47; Malcolm X and Alex Haley, *The Autobiography of Malcolm X* (New York: Ballantine Book, 1999), 55–57.

20. Guerrero, *Framing Blackness*, 17–31.

21. Harris-Perry, *Sister Citizen*, 76–77; Patricia Morton, *Disfigured Images: The Historical Assault on Afro-American Women* (Westport, CT: Greenwood, 1991), 6–7.

22. Lewis, *W. E. B. Du Bois, 1919–1963*, 471–472; Richard Wright, *Black Boy* (New York: HarperPerennial, 1998), 37.

23. Richard H. King, *Race, Culture, and the Intellectuals: 1940–1970* (Baltimore: Johns Hopkins University Press, 2004), 139; Melville J. Herskovits, *The Myth of the Negro Past* (Boston: Beacon Press, 1990), 1, 298.

24. Zora Neale Hurston, *Mules and Men* (New York: HarperPerennial, 2008).

25. Zora Neale Hurston, *Their Eyes Were Watching God: A Novel* (New York: Perennial Library, 1990), 14, 98–99, 144–145.

26. Mary Helen Washington, "Foreword," in ibid., ix–xvii; Ralph Thompson, "Books of the Times," *New York Times*, October 6, 1937; Sheila Hibben, "Book Review," *New York Herald Tribune*, September 26, 1937.

27. Zora Neale Hurston, "How It Feels to Be Colored Me," *World Tomorrow*, May 1928.

28. Washington, "Foreword," ix–xvii.

29. King, *Race, Culture, and the Intellectuals*, 138–144.

30. Boyd, *Wrapped in Rainbows*, 345; James Baldwin, "Everybody's Protest Novel," *Partisan Review* 16 (1949): 578–585.

CHAPTER 28: FREEDOM BRAND

1. Jerry Gershenhorn, *Melville J. Herskovits and the Racial Politics of Knowledge* (Lincoln: University of Nebraska Press, 2004), 142–152; Lewis, *W. E. B. Du Bois, 1919–1963*, 435–436.

2. Ibid., 448–449.

3. Gunnar Myrdal, *An American Dilemma: The Negro Problem and Modern Democracy*, vol. 1 (New York: Harper and Brothers, 1944), 48.

4. Lewis, *W. E. B. Du Bois, 1919–1963*, 451–452; King, *Race, Culture, and the Intellectuals*, 132–133.

5. Gunnar Myrdal, *An American Dilemma: The Negro Problem and Modern Democracy*, vol. 2 (New York: Harper and Brothers, 1944), 751–752, 928–929.

6. Lewis, *W. E. B. Du Bois, 1919–1963*, 510–515.

7. Fleeger, "Theodore G. Bilbo and the Decline of Public Racism," 2–3.

8. Ibid., 1–4, 8, 13–27; Theodore G. Bilbo, *Take Your Choice: Separation or Mongrelization* (Poplarville, MS: Dream House, 1947), 7–8.

9. Morton, *Disfigured Images*, 90–91.

10. M. F. Ashley Montagu, *Man's Most Dangerous Myth: The Fallacy of Race* (New York: Columbia University Press, 1945), 150–151; Degler, *In Search of Human Nature*, 80, 216–218; Zoë Burkholder, *Color in the Classroom: How American Schools Taught Race, 1900–1954* (New York: Oxford University Press, 2011), 4–11, 39–95; Yudell, *Race Unmasked*, 132–137.

11. Theodosius Dobzhansky and Ashley Montagu, "Natural Selection and the Mental Capacities of Mankind," *Science* 105, no. 2736 (1947): 587–590; Hamilton Cravens, "What's New in Science and Race Since the 1930s? Anthropologists and Racial Essentialism," *The Historian* 72, no. 2 (2010): 315–318; Yudell, *Race Unmasked*, 111–132, 201–202.

12. UNESCO, *Four Statements on the Race Question*, UNESCO and Its Programme (Paris: UNESCO, 1969), 30–43; Yudell, *Race Unmasked*, 148–167; Roberts, *Fatal Invention*, 43–45.

13. Harry S. Truman, "Address Before a Joint Session of Congress," March 12, 1947, The Avalon Project: Documents in Law, History, and Diplomacy, Lillian Goldman Law Library, Yale Law School, http://avalon.law.yale.edu/20th_century /trudoc.asp; Mary L. Dudziak, *Cold War Civil Rights: Race and the Image of American Democracy* (Princeton, NJ: Princeton University Press, 2000), 26–46.

14. President's Committee on Civil Rights, *To Secure These Rights*, 1947, 139, 147, Harry S. Truman Library and Museum, www.trumanlibrary.org/civilrights/srights1 .htm#contents; Lewis, *W. E. B. Du Bois, 1919–1963*, 529.

15. Harry S. Truman, "Special Message to the Congress on Civil Rights," February 2, 1948, at Gerhard Peters and John T. Woolley, The American Presidency Project, www.presidency.ucsb.edu/ws/?pid=13006; Robert A. Caro, *Means of Ascent: The Years of Lyndon Johnson*, vol. 2 (New York: Vintage, 1990), 125; Francis Njubi Nesbitt, *Race for Sanctions: African Americans Against Apartheid, 1946–1994* (Bloomington: Indiana University Press, 2004), 9–10.

16. Lewis, *W. E. B. Du Bois, 1919–1963*, 522–524, 528–534; Hutchinson, *Betrayed*, 62–70; Dudziak, *Cold War Civil Rights*, 43–46, 79–86.

17. Dudziak, *Cold War Civil Rights*, 91–102.

18. Thomas J. Sugrue, *The Origins of the Urban Crisis: Race and Inequality in Postwar Detroit*, Princeton Studies in American Politics (Princeton, NJ: Princeton University Press, 1996), 181–258; Massey and Denton, *American Apartheid*, 49–51.

19. Massey and Denton, *American Apartheid*, 44–49; Katznelson, *When Affirmative Action Was White*, 113–141.

20. Karen Brodkin, *How Jews Became White Folks and What That Says About Race in America* (New Brunswick, NJ: Rutgers University Press, 1998), 35–36; Burkholder, *Color in the Classroom*, 137–170; Nell Irvin Painter, *The History of White People* (New York: W. W. Norton, 2010), 366–372.

21. Lewis, *W. E. B. Du Bois, 1919–1963*, 545–554; Dudziak, *Cold War Civil Rights*, 6, 11–15, 28–29, 88–90.

22. Dudziak, *Cold War Civil Rights*, 63–66.

23. Ibid., 47–77.

24. Ibid., 77–78.

25. Ibid., 79, 90–91; Hutchinson, *Betrayed*, 75–76.

26. Abrahm Kardiner and Lionel Ovesey, *The Mark of Oppression* (New York: W. W. Norton, 1951).

27. *Brown v. Board of Education of Topeka*, 347 U.S. 483 (1954), https://supreme.justia .com/cases/federal/us/347/483/case.html#T10.

28. Zora Neale Hurston, "Court Order Can't Make Races Mix," *Orlando Sentinel*, August 11, 1955; Boyd, *Wrapped in Rainbows*, 423–425.

29. Dudziak, *Cold War Civil Rights*, 102–114; Lewis, *W. E. B. Du Bois, 1919–1963*, 557; Giddings, *When and Where I Enter*, 261.

CHAPTER 29: MASSIVE RESISTANCE

1. Lewis, *W. E. B. Du Bois, 1919–1963*, 557; Lewis V. Baldwin, *There Is a Balm in Gilead: The Cultural Roots of Martin Luther King, Jr.* (Minneapolis, MN: Fortress Press, 1991), 45.

2. E. Franklin Frazier, *Black Bourgeoisie* (New York: Free Press, 1962), 4, 221; E. Franklin Frazier, "The Failure of the Negro Intellectual," in *On Race Relations: Selected Writings of E. Franklin Frazier*, ed. G. Franklin Edwards (Chicago: University of Chicago Press, 1968), 270, 277; Stanley M. Elkins, *Slavery: A Problem in American Institutional and Intellectual Life* (Chicago: University of Chicago Press, 1959).

3. Malcolm X. "The Root of Civilization," Audio Clip, http://shemsubireda.tumblr .com/post/55982230511/africa-is-a-jungleaint-that-what-they-say.

4. Evelyn Brooks Higginbotham, *Righteous Discontent: The Women's Movement in the Black Baptist Church, 1880–1920* (Cambridge, MA: Harvard University Press, 1994); Frazier, *Black Bourgeoisie*, 25.

5. Hutchinson, *Betrayed*, 84–87, 93; Dudziak, *Cold War Civil Rights*, 115–151; Adams and Sanders, *Alienable Rights*, 277–278.

6. Lewis, *W. E. B. Du Bois, 1919–1963*, 558–566.

7. Ibid., 557–558; Blum and Harvey, *The Color of Christ*, 205–213.

8. Lewis, *W. E. B. Du Bois, 1919–1963*, 566.

9. Isaac Saney, "The Case Against *To Kill a Mockingbird*," *Race & Class* 45, no. 1 (2003): 99–110.

10. Michaal Harrington, *The Other America* (New York: Simon and Schuster, 1997), 72, 76.

11. Lewis, *W. E. B. Du Bois, 1919–1963*, 565–570.

12. Adams and Sanders, *Alienable Rights*, 281–283; Dudziak, *Cold War Civil Rights*, 155–166.

13. Dan T. Carter, *The Politics of Rage: George Wallace, the Origins of the New Conservatism, and the Transformation of American Politics* (Baton Rouge: Louisiana State University Press, 2000), 96.

14. "The Inaugural Address of Governor George C. Wallace," January 14, 1963, http://media.al.com/spotnews/other/George%20Wallace%201963%20Inauguration%20Speech.pdf.

15. Oscar Handlin, "All Colors, All Creeds, All Nationalities, All New Yorkers," *New York Times*, September 22, 1963.

16. Nathan Glazer and Daniel P. Moynihan, *Beyond the Melting Pot: The Negroes, Puerto Ricans, Jews, Italians, and Irish of New York City* (Cambridge, MA: M.I.T. Press, 1963), 11, 35, 50–53, 84–85.

17. Martin Luther King Jr., "Letter from a Birmingham Jail," April 16, 1963, https://www.africa.upenn.edu/Articles_Gen/Letter_Birmingham.html.

18. Dudziak, *Cold War Civil Rights*, 169–187.

19. Ibid., 187–200, 216–219; Du Bois, *W. E. B. Du Bois, 1868–1919*, 2.

CHAPTER 30: THE ACT OF CIVIL RIGHTS

1. Angela Y. Davis, *Angela Davis: An Autobiography* (New York: International Publishers, 1988), 128–131.

2. Ibid., 77–99.

3. Ibid., 101–112.

4. James Baldwin, *The Fire Next Time* (New York: Vintage, 1963).

5. Davis, *Autobiography*, 117–127.

6. Ibid., 128–131.

7. John F. Kennedy, "Statement by the President on the Sunday Bombing in Birmingham," September 16, 1963, Gerhard Peters and John T. Woolley, The American Presidency Project, www.presidency.ucsb.edu/ws/?pid=9410.

8. Lyndon B. Johnson, "Address to a Joint Session of Congress," November 27, 1963, *Public Papers of the Presidents of the United States: Lyndon B. Johnson, 1963–64*, vol. 1, entry 11 (Washington, DC: US Government Printing Office, 1965), 8–10.

9. Ossie Davis, "Eulogy for Malcolm X," in *Say It Loud: Great Speeches on Civil Rights and African American Identity*, ed. Catherine Ellis and Stephen Smith (New York: New Press, 2010).

10. Malcolm X and Alex Haley, *The Autobiography of Malcolm X* (New York: Ballantine, 1999), 369.

11. Adams and Sanders, *Alienable Rights*, 290.

12. Moreno, *Black Americans and Organized Labor*, 252–258.

13. Michael K. Brown et al, *Whitewashing Race: The Myth of a Color-Blind Society* (Berkeley: University of California Press, 2003), 168–174.

14. Dudziak, *Cold War Civil Rights*, 208–214, 219–231; Malcolm X, "Appeal to African Heads of State," in *Malcolm X Speaks: Selected Speeches and Statements*, ed. George Breitman (New York: Grove Press, 1965), 76.

15. Carter, *The Politics of Rage*, 344.

16. Adams and Sanders, *Alienable Rights*, 287–291; Barry M. Goldwater, *The Conscience of a Conservative* (Washington, DC: Regnery, 1994), 67.

17. Chana Kai Lee, *For Freedom's Sake: The Life of Fannie Lou Hamer*, Women in American History (Urbana: University of Illinois Press, 1999), 89, 99; Cleveland Sellers and Robert L. Terrell, *The River of No Return: The Autobiography of a Black Militant and the Life and Death of SNCC* (Jackson: University Press of Mississippi, 1990), 111.

18. "Baldwin Blames White Supremacy," *New York Post*, February 22, 1965; Telegram from Martin Luther King Jr. to Betty al-Shabazz, February 26, 1965, The Martin Luther King Jr. Research and Education Institute, Stanford University, http://kingencyclopedia.stanford.edu/encyclopedia/documentsentry/telegram _from_martin_luther_king_jr_to_betty_al_shabazz/.

19. Ossie Davis, "Eulogy for Malcolm X," 29.

20. Eliot Fremont-Smith, "An Eloquent Testament," *New York Times*, November 5, 1965; Malcolm X and Haley, *Autobiography*.

21. Lyndon B. Johnson, "Commencement Address at Howard University: 'To Fulfill These Rights,'" in *Public Papers of the Presidents of the United States: Lyndon B. Johnson, 1965*, vol. 2, entry 301 (Washington, DC: US Government Printing Office, 1966), 635–640.

22. Daniel Patrick Moynihan, *The Negro Family: The Case for National Action* (Washington, DC: Office of Policy Planning and Research, US Department of Labor, 1965), 29–30, http://web.stanford.edu/~mrosenfe/Moynihan's%20The%20 Negro%20Family.pdf.

23. US House of Representatives, "Voting Rights Act of 1965," House Report 439, 89th Cong., 1st sess. (Washington, DC: US Government Printing Office, 1965), 3.

CHAPTER 31: BLACK POWER

1. "New Crisis: The Negro Family," *Newsweek*, August 9, 1965; James T. Patterson, *Freedom Is Not Enough: The Moynihan Report and America's Struggle over Black Family Life—from LBJ to Obama* (New York: Basic Books, 2010), 65–70.

2. Davis, *Autobiography*, 133–139; Russell-Cole et al. *The Color Complex*, 59–61.

3. Massey and Denton, *American Apartheid*, 3, 18–19, 167; Kenneth Clark, *Dark Ghetto: Dilemmas of Social Power* (New York: Harper and Row, 1965).

4. "Success Story, Japanese-American Style," *New York Times Magazine*, January 9, 1966; "Success Story of One Minority Group in the U.S.," *US News and World Report*, December 26, 1966; Daryl J. Maeda, *Chains of Babylon: The Rise of Asian America* (Minneapolis: University of Minnesota Press, 2009).

5. Byrd and Tharps, *Hair Story*.

6. Peniel E. Joseph, *Waiting 'Til the Midnight Hour: A Narrative History of Black Power in America* (New York: Henry Holt, 2006), 141–142.

7. "Dr. King Is Felled by Rock: 30 Injured as He Leads Protesters: Many Arrested in Race Clash," *Chicago Tribune*, August 6, 1966.

8. Joseph, *Waiting 'Til the Midnight Hour*, 146.

9. Roy Wilkins, "Whither 'Black Power'?" *The Crisis*, August–September 1966, 354; "Humphrey Backs N.A.A.C.P. in Fight on Black Racism," *New York Times*, July 7, 1966.

10. Joshua Bloom and Waldo E. Martin, *Black Against Empire: The History and Politics of the Black Panther Party* (Berkeley: University of California Press, 2013), 70–73.

11. Malcolm McLaughlin, *The Long, Hot Summer of 1967: Urban Rebellion in America* (New York: Palgrave Macmillan, 2014), 6–9, 12; Jonathan M. Metzl, *The Protest Psychosis: How Schizophrenia Became a Black Disease* (Boston: Beacon Press, 2010); Marvin E. Wolfgang and Franco Ferracuti, *The Subculture of Violence: Toward an Integrated Theory in Criminology* (London: Tavistock, 1967).

12. Premilla Nadasen, *Welfare Warriors: The Welfare Rights Movement in the United States* (New York: Routledge, 2005), 135–138.

13. Davis, *Autobiography*, 149–151.

14. "New Black Consciousness Takes Over College Campus," *Chicago Defender*, December 4, 1967.

15. Davis, *Autobiography*, 156–161.

16. Martin Luther King Jr., "Where Do We Go from Here?" in *Say It Loud*, 41.

17. Joseph, *Waiting 'Til the Midnight Hour*, 197–201.

18. Lyndon B. Johnson, "Annual Message to the Congress on the State of the Union, January 17, 1968," in *Public Papers of the Presidents of the United States: Lyndon B. Johnson, 1968–1969* (Washington, DC: US Government Printing Office, 1970), 30.

19. Eldridge Cleaver, *Soul on Ice* (New York: Dell, 1968), 101–111, 134, 159–163, 181, 187–188, 205–206.

20. Franz Fanon, *Black Skin, White Masks* (New York: Grove Press, 2008), 45; William H. Grier and Price M. Cobbs, *Black Rage* (New York: BasicBooks, 1968).

21. Andrew Billingsley, *Black Families in White America* (New York: Simon and Schuster, 1968), 33, 37.

22. *Report of the National Advisory Commission on Civil Disorders* (New York: New York Times Publications, 1968), 1–2, 389.

23. Report of the Select Committee on Assassinations of the US House of Representatives, Findings in the Assassination of Dr. Martin Luther King Jr., 277, National Archives, www.archives.gov/research/jfk/select-committee-report/part-2-king-findings.html; Adams and Sanders, *Alienable Rights*, 299–300; Hutchinson, *Betrayed*, 136–137, 144–145; González and Torres, *News for All the People*, 303–304.

24. Martin Luther King Jr., "Mountaintop Speech," April 3, 1968, video, https://vimeo.com/3816635.

25. Davis, *Autobiography*, 160–178; Spiro T. Agnew, Opening Statement of Conference with Civil Rights and Community Leaders," April 11, 1968, http://msa.maryland.gov/megafile/msa/speccol/sc2200/sc2221/000012/000041/pdf/speech.pdf.

26. Rogers, *The Black Campus Movement*, 114; Hillel Black, *The American Schoolbook* (New York: Morrow, 1967), 106; Moreau, *Schoolbook Nation*.

27. Pablo Guzman, "Before People Called Me a Spic, They Called Me a Nigger," in *The Afro-Latin@ Reader: History and Culture in the United States*, ed. Miriam Jimenez Roman and Juan Flores (Durham, NC: Duke University Press), 235–243; Hutchinson, *Blacks and Reds*, 257–258.

28. Frances Beale, "Double Jeopardy: To Be Black and Female," in *The Black Woman: An Anthology*, ed. Toni Cade Bambara (New York: Washington Square Press, 2005), 109–122.

29. Davis, *Autobiography*, 180–191.

CHAPTER 32: LAW AND ORDER

1. Dan T. Carter, *From George Wallace to Newt Gingrich: Race in the Conservative Counterrevolution* (Baton Rouge: Louisiana State University Press, 1996), 27; John Ehrlichman, *Witness to Power: The Nixon Years* (New York: Simon and Schuster, 1982), 223.

2. Carter, *From George Wallace to Newt Gingrich*, 27; Ehrlichman, *Witness to Power*, 223.

3. Davis, *Autobiography*, 216–223; Hutchinson, *Betrayed*, 145–149.

4. Davis, *Autobiography*, 250–255, 263–266.

5. "Academic Freedom and Tenure: The University of California at Los Angeles," *AAUP Bulletin* 57, no. 3 (1971): 413–414; Arthur R. Jensen, "How Much Can We Boost IQ and Scholastic Achievement," *Harvard Educational Review* 39, no. 1 (1969): 82.

6. Davis, *Autobiography*, 270–273.

7. Ibid., 3–12, 277–279.

8. Byrd and Tharps, *Hair Story*, 60–63.

9. Guerrero, *Framing Blackness*, 69–111.

10. Cheryll Y. Greene and Marie D. Brown, "Women Talk," *Essence*, May 1990; "President Nixon Said It Was 'Necessary' to Abort Mixed-Race Babies, Tapes Reveal," *Daily Telegraph*, June 24, 2009.

11. Giddings, *When and Where I Enter*, 304–311; Toni Morrison, "What the Black Woman Thinks of Women's Lib," *New York Times Magazine*, August 1971; Toni Morrison, *The Bluest Eye* (New York: Penguin, 1970); Maya Angelou, *I Know Why the Caged Bird Sings* (New York: Random House, 1969).

12. Joseph, *Waiting 'Til the Midnight Hour*, 273–275.

13. Brown et al., *Whitewashing Race*, 164–192.

14. Massey and Denton, *American Apartheid*, 60–62.

15. Joseph, *Waiting 'Til the Midnight Hour*, 283–293.

16. Davis, *Autobiography*, 359.

17. Michelle Alexander, *The New Jim Crow: Mass Incarceration in the Age of Colorblindness* (New York: New Press, 2010), 8; National Advisory Commission on Criminal Justice Standards and Goals, *Task Force Report on Corrections* (Washington, DC: US Government Printing Office, 1973), 358.

18. "15000 at NY Angela Davis Rally," *The Militant*, July 14, 1972.

19. Charles Herbert Stember, *Sexual Racism: The Emotional Barrier to an Integrated Society* (New York: Elsevier, 1976).

20. Audre Lorde, "Age, Race, Class, and Sex: Women Redefining Difference," in *Sister Outsider: Essays and Speeches*, ed. Audre Lorde (Berkeley, CA: Crossing Press, 2007), 115.

21. Salamishah Tillet, "Black Feminism, Tyler Perry Style," *The Root*, November 11, 2010, www.theroot.com/articles/culture/2010/11/a_feminist_analysis_of_tyler _perrys_for_colored_girls.html.

22. Alice Walker, *The Color Purple: A Novel* (New York: Harcourt, Brace, Jovanovich, 1982).

23. Robert Staples, "The Myth of Black Macho: A Response to Angry Black Feminists," *The Black Scholar* 10, no. 6/7 (March/April 1979): 24–33; Michele Wallace, *Black Macho and the Myth of Superwoman* (New York: Verso, 1990), 23, 107.

24. June Jordan, "To Be Black and Female," *New York Times*, March 18, 1979; Angela Y. Davis, "Black Writers' Views of America," *Fredomways* 19, no. 3 (1979): 158–160; Wallace, *Black Macho and the Myth of Superwoman*, xxi, 75.

25. Byrd and Tharps, *Hair Story*, 100–107.

26. Guerrero, *Framing Blackness*, 113–138.

27. Alex Haley, *Roots: The Saga of an American Family* (Garden City, NY: Doubleday, 1976).

CHAPTER 33: REAGAN'S DRUGS

1. "'Welfare Queen' Becomes Issue in Reagan Campaign," *New York Times*, February 15, 1976; "The Welfare Queen," *Slate*, December 19, 2013, www.slate.com/articles /news_and_politics/history/2013/12/linda_taylor_welfare_queen_ronald_reagan_ made_her_a_notorious_american_villain.html.

2. Massey and Denton, *American Apartheid*, 61, 83–114; Manning Marable, *Race, Reform, and Rebellion: The Second Reconstruction and Beyond in Black America, 1945–2006* (Jackson: University Press of Mississippi, 2007), 151–154.

3. Brown et al., *Whitewashing Race*, 164–192.

4. *Regents of Univ. of California v. Bakke*, 438 U.S. 265 (1978).

5. Phyllis Ann Wallace, Linda Datcher-Loury, and Julianne Malveaux, *Black Women in the Labor Force* (Cambridge, MA: MIT Press, 1980), 67; William J. Wilson, *The Declining Significance of Race: Blacks and Changing American Institutions*, 2nd ed. (Chicago: University of Chicago Press, 1980), 2–3; Michael Harrington, *The Other America: Poverty in the United States* (New York: Simon and Schuster, 1997), 76.

6. John Langston Gwaltney, *Drylongso: A Self-Portrait of Black America* (New York: Random House, 1980), xix; Mel Watkins, "Books of the Times: Blacks Less 'Hateful' Enlightened Interviews," *New York Times*, September 2, 1980.

7. William Julius Wilson, "The Declining Significance of Race: Revisited & Revised," *Daedalus* 140, no. 2 (2011): 67.

8. *Regents of Univ. of California v. Bakke*; Robert Bork, "The Unpersuasive Bakke Decision," *Wall Street Journal*, July 21, 1978; Sean F. Reardon, Rachel Baker, and Daniel Klasik, *Race, Income, and Enrollment Patterns in Highly Selective Colleges, 1982–2004* (Stanford, CA: Center for Education Policy Analysis, 2012), https://cepa.stanford .edu/sites/default/files/race%20income%20%26%20selective%20college%20 enrollment%20august%203%202012.pdf.

9. Marable, *Race, Reform, and Rebellion*, 165–171.

10. "Gus Hall and Angela Davis Lead Communist Party's Ticket for '80," *New York Times*, November 20, 1979; Hutchinson, *Blacks and Reds*, 297–298.

11. Marable, *Race, Reform, and Rebellion*, 171–175; "Angela Davis Says Get Tough with E. Bay Nazis," *Sun Reporter*, September 20, 1979.

12. "Angela Davis Brings Vice Preisdential Campaign to UCLA—Where It All Began," Los Angeles Times, August 7, 1980; Poster, "People Before Profits: A Campaign Rally Featuring Angela Davis," 1980, Oakland Museum of California Collection, http://collections.museumca.org/?q=collection-item/201054471.

13. "Transcript of Ronald Reagan's 1980 Neshoba County Fair Speech," Neshoba Democrat, November 15, 2007, http://web.archive.org/web/20110714165011/http://neshobademocrat.com/main.asp?SectionID=2&SubSectionID=297&ArticleID=15599&TM=60417.67.

14. Guerrero, Framing Blackness, 113–138.

15. Adams and Sanders, Alienable Rights, 311–312; Moreno, Black Americans and Organized Labor, 276–279; Marable, Race, Reform, and Rebellion, 179–181.

16. Edward O. Wilson, "What Is Sociobiology?," Society, September/October 1978, 10; Edward O. Wilson, Sociobiology: The New Synthesis (Cambridge, MA: Harvard University Press, 1975).

17. Yudell, Race Unmasked, 179–200.

18. Davis, Women, Race & Class, 14, 18–19, 23, 31, 178–182; bell hooks, Ain't I a Woman: Black Women and Feminism, 2nd ed. (New York: Routledge, 2014), 99.

19. Brown et al., Whitewashing Race, 136–137; Alexander, The New Jim Crow, 5–7, 49; Julian Roberts, "Public Opinion, Crime, and Criminal Justice," in Crime and Justice: A Review of Research, vol. 16, ed. Michael Tonry (Chicago: University of Chicago Press, 1992); Ronald Reagan, "Remarks on Signing Executive Order 12368, Concerning Federal Drug Abuse Policy Functions," June 24, 1982, Gerhard Peters and John T. Woolley, The American Presidency Project, www.presidency.ucsb.edu/ws/?pid=42671.

20. "Davis Addresses Women's Confab," Washington Informer, August 22, 1984.

21. Alexander, The New Jim Crow, 5–7, 51–53, 86–87, 206.

22. "Reagan Signs Anti-Drug Measure; Hopes for 'Drug-Free Generation,'" New York Times, October 28, 1968, www.nytimes.com/1986/10/28/us/reagan-signs-anti-drug-measure-hopes-for-drug-free-generation.html.

23. Marc Mauer, Race to Incarcerate, 2nd rev. ed. (New York: New Press, 2006), 30–36; Human Rights Watch, Punishment and Prejudice: Racial Disparities in the War on Drugs, vol. 12, HRW Reports (New York: Human Rights Watch, 2000); Christopher Ingraham, "White People Are More Likely to Deal Drugs, But Black People Are More Likely to Get Arrested for It," Washington Post, September 30, 2014, www.washingtonpost.com/news/wonkblog/wp/2014/09/30/white-people-are-more-likely-to-deal-drugs-but-black-people-are-more-likely-to-get-arrested-for-it/.

24. The Sentencing Project, "Crack Cocaine Sentencing Policy: Unjustified and Unreasonable," April 1997.

25. William Julius Wilson, When Work Disappears: The World of the New Urban Poor (New York: Vintage Books, 1997), 22.

26. Gail Russell Chaddock, "U.S. Notches World's Highest Incarceration Rate," Christian Science Monitor, August 18, 2003; Christopher Uggen and Jeff Manza, "Democratic Contradiction? Political Consequences of Felon Disenfranchisement in the United States," American Sociological Review 67 (2002): 777.

27. Craig Reinarman, "The Crack Attack: America's Latest Drug Scare, 1986–1992," in Images of Issues: Typifying Contemporary Social Problems (New York: Aldine de Gruyter, 1995), 162; Marc Maeur, Race to Incarcerate, 150–151; National Institute

on Drug Use, *Data from the Drug Abuse Warning Network: Annual Data 1985*, Statistical Series I, #5 (Washington, DC: National Institute on Drug Abuse, 1986); US Census Bureau, "Table 308: Homicide Trends," https://www.census.gov/compendia /statab/11s0308.xls; "Deaths from Drunken Driving Increase," *New York Times*, October 29, 1987, www.nytimes.com/1987/10/29/us/deaths-from-drunken-driving -increase.html; Alexander, *The New Jim Crow*, 200–201.

28. CBS News, "The Vanishing Family: Crisis in Black America," first aired in January 1986, https://www.youtube.com/watch?v=6VHMHmhUdHs; Angela Y. Davis, *Women, Culture & Politics* (New York: Vintage Books, 1990), 75–85.

29. Gary Bauer, *The Family: Preserving America's Future* (Washington, DC: US Department of Education, 1986), 35.

30. Eleanor Holmes Norton, "Restoring the Traditional Black Family," *New York Times*, June 2, 1985.

CHAPTER 34: NEW DEMOCRATS

1. Henry Louis Gates Jr., "TV's Black World Turns—but Stays Unreal," *New York Times*, November 12, 1989.

2. Charles Krauthammer, "Children of Cocaine," *Washington Post*, July 30, 1989.

3. Washington, *Medical Apartheid*, 212–215; "'Crack Baby' Study Ends with Unexpected but Clear Result," *Philadelphia Inquirer*, July 22, 2013, http://articles.philly.com/2013-07-22/news/40709969_1_hallam-hurt-so-called -crack-babies-funded-study.

4. Marable, *Race, Reform, and Rebellion*, 212–213; Hutchinson, *Betrayed*, 189–190.

5. *McCleskey v. Kemp*, 481 U.S. 279, 1981; "New Look at Death Sentences and Race," *New York Times*, April 29, 2008, www.nytimes.com/2008/04/29/us/29bar .html.

6. Jeffrey O. G. Ogbar, *Hip-Hop Revolution: The Culture and Politics of Rap*, CultureAmerica (Lawrence: University Press of Kansas, 2007), 105–109, 146–155.

7. Molefi Kete Asante, *Afrocentricity*, new rev. ed. (Trenton, NJ: Africa World Press, 1988), 1, 104–105.

8. Russell-Cole et al., *The Color Complex*, 37–39, 51–54, 90–101, 107–109, 166; Byrd and Tharps, *Hair Story*, 112; J. Randy Taraborrelli, *Michael Jackson: The Magic, the Madness, the Whole Story, 1958–2009* (New York: Grand Central, 2009), 351.

9. Crenshaw, "Demarginalizing the Intersection of Race and Sex"; Kimberlé Crenshaw, "Mapping the Margins: Intersectionality, Identity Politics, and Violence Against Women of Color," *Stanford Law Review* 43, no. 6 (1991): 1242; Mari J. Matsuda, *Where Is Your Body? And Other Essays on Race, Gender, and the Law* (Boston: Beacon Press, 1996), 47; Richard Delgado and Jean Stefancic, *Critical Race Theory: An Introduction*, 2nd ed. (New York: New York University Press, 2012), 7–10.

10. Dalton Conley, *Being Black, Living in the Red: Race, Wealth, and Social Policy in America* (Berkeley: University of California Press, 1999), 25; Robert S. Ellyn, "Angela Davis' Views," *Los Angeles Times*, March 10, 1990; *Sunday Times*, December 6, 1992.

11. "Poverty and Norplant: Can Contraception Reduce the Underclass?" *Philadelphia Inquirer*, December 12, 1990; Roberts, *Killing the Black Body*, 17–18, 106–110, 116, 122, 244–245; Washington, *Medical Apartheid*, 206–212; Angela Davis, "Black Women and the Academy," *Callaloo* 17, no. 2 (1994): 425–426.

12. Patricia Hill Collins, *Black Feminist Thought: Knowledge, Consciousness, and the Politics of Empowerment* (Boston: Unwin Hyman, 1990); Michele Wallace, "When Black Feminism Faces the Music, and the Music Is Rap," *New York Times*, July 29, 1990.

13. Guerrero, *Framing Blackness*, 157–167.

14. Hutchinson, *Betrayed*, 192–198.

15. Jeffrey Toobin, "The Burden of Clarence Thomas," *New Yorker*, September 27, 1993; Nancy Langston, "Clarence Thomas: A Method in His Message?" *Holy Cross Journal of Law and Public Policy* 1 (1996): 10–11; Clarence Thomas, *My Grandfather's Son: A Memoir* (New York: Harper, 2007).

16. Marable, *Race, Reform, and Rebellion*, 216–217; Earl Ofari Hutchinson, *The Assassination of the Black Male Image* (New York: Simon and Schuster, 1996), 63–70; Duchess Harris, *Black Feminist Politics from Kennedy to Clinton*, Contemporary Black History (New York: Palgrave Macmillan, 2009), 90–98; White, *Too Heavy a Load*, 15–16.

17. Adams and Sanders, *Alienable Rights*, 314; Brown et al., *Whitewashing Race*, 184–185; Lawrence M. Mead, *The New Politics of Poverty: The Nonworking Poor in America* (New York: Basic Books, 1992), 142.

18. Washington, *Medical Apartheid*, 330–332, 337–346.

19. Joy James, "Introduction," in *The Angela Y. Davis Reader*, ed. Joy James (Malden, MA: Blackwell, 1998), 9–10.

20. Alexander, *The New Jim Crow*, 55; Adams and Sanders, *Alienable Rights*, 316–317.

21. Marable, *Race, Reform, and Rebellion*, 223; "'Cosby' Finale: Not All Drama Was in the Streets," *Los Angeles Times*, May 2, 1992, http://articles.latimes.com/1992-05-02/entertainment/ca-1105_1_cosby-show.

22. Andrew Hacker, *Two Nations: Black and White, Separate, Hostile, Unequal* (New York: Scribner's, 1992); Hutchinson, *Assassination*, 55–60; Guerrero, *Framing Blackness*, 197–208; Derrick Bell, *Faces at the Bottom of the Well: The Permanence of Racism* (New York: Basic Books, 1992); Cornel West, *Race Matters* (Boston: Beacon Press, 1993).

23. "Was It a 'Riot,' a 'Disturbance,' or a 'Rebellion'?," *Los Angeles Times*, April 29, 2007; Aldore Collier, "Maxine Waters: Telling It Like It Is in LA," *Ebony*, October 1992; "Excerpts from Bush's Speech on the Los Angeles Riots: 'Need to Restore Order,'" *New York Times*, May 2, 1992; David M. Newman and Elizabeth Grauerholz, *Sociology of Families*, 2nd ed. (Thousand Oaks, CA: Pine Forge Press, 2002), 18; "Clinton: Parties Fail to Attack Race Divisions," *Los Angeles Times*, May 3, 1992; Washington, *Medical Apartheid*, 271–277.

24. "Sister Souljah's Call to Arms," *Washington Post*, May 13, 1992.

25. Marable, *Race, Reform, and Rebellion*, 217.

26. Ibid., 226–227; Charles Murray, "The Coming White Underclass," *Wall Street Journal*, October 29, 1993.

27. Tupac Shakur, "Keep Ya Head Up," 1994, www.songlyrics.com/tupac/keep-ya-head-up-lyrics/.

28. Angela Y. Davis, "Black Women and the Academy," in *The Angela Y. Davis Reader*, ed. Joy James (Malden, MA: Blackwell, 1998), 222–231.

29. Alexander, *The New Jim Crow*, 55–59; Marable, *Race, Reform, and Rebellion*, 218–219; Bill Clinton, "1994 State of the Union Address," January 25, 1994, www.washingtonpost.com/wp-srv/politics/special/states/docs/sou94.htm; Ben Schreckinger and Annie Karni, "Hillary's Criminal Justice Plan: Reverse Bill's Policies,"

Politico, April 30, 2014, www.politico.com/story/2015/04/hillary-clintons-criminal
-justice-plan-reverse-bills-policies-117488.html.

30. Hutchinson, *Assassination*; The Notorious B.I.G., "Juicy," 1994, www.songlyrics
.com/the-notorious-b-i-g/juicy-clean-lyrics/.

CHAPTER 35: NEW REPUBLICANS

1. Richard J. Herrnstein and Charles A. Murray, *The Bell Curve: Intelligence and Class Structure in American Life* (New York: Free Press, 1994), xxv, 1–24, 311–312, 551; Roberts, *Killing the Black Body*, 270.

2. "Republican Contract with America," 1994, see http://web.archive.org/web /19990427174200/http://www.house.gov/house/Contract/CONTRACT.html.

3. Richard Lynn, "Is Man Breeding Himself Back to the Age of the Apes?," in *The Bell Curve Debate: History, Documents, Opinions*, ed. Russell Jacoby and Naomi Glauberman (New York: Times Books, 1995), 356; Ulrich Neisser, Gwyneth Boodoo, Thomas J. Bouchard Jr., A. Wade Boykin, Nathan Brody, Stephen J. Ceci, Diane F. Halpern, John C. Loehlin, Robert Perloff, Robert J. Sternberg, and Susana Urbina, "Intelligence: Knowns and Unknowns," *American Psychologist* 51 (1996): 77–101.

4. Marina Budhos, "Angela Davis Appointed to Major Chair," *Journal of Blacks in Higher Education* 7 (1995): 44–45; Manning Marable, "Along the Color Line: In Defense of Angela Davis," *Michigan Citizen*, April 22, 1995.

5. Dinesh D'Souza, *The End of Racism: Principles for a Multiracial Society* (New York: Free Press, 1995), vii–viii, 22–24, 441.

6. Hutchinson, *Assassination*, 152–161.

7. "Professors of Hate: Academia's Dirty Secret," *Rolling Stone*, October 20, 1994; Jessie Daniels, *Cyber Racism: White Supremacy Online and the New Attack on Civil Rights*, Perspectives on a Multiracial America (Lanham, MD: Rowman and Littlefield, 2009), 41–53, 61–63, 96, 159–167, 174–182.

8. B. W. Burston, D. Jones, and P. Roberson-Saunders, "Drug Use and African Americans: Myth Versus Reality," *Journal of Alcohol and Drug Education* 40 (1995), 19–39; Alexander, *The New Jim Crow*, 122–125; John J. Dilulio Jr., "The Coming of the Super Predators," *Weekly Standard*, November 27, 1995.

9. Allen Hughes and Albert Hughes, *Menace II Society*, May 26, 1993.

10. "Black Women Are Split over All-Male March on Washington," *New York Times*, October 14, 1995.

11. Mumia Abu-Jamal, *Live from Death Row* (New York: HarperCollins, 1996), 4–5.

12. "August 12 'Day of Protest' Continues Despite Mumia's Stay of Execution," *Sun Reporter*, August 10, 1995; Kathleen Cleaver, "Mobilizing for Mumia Abu-Jamal in Paris," in *Liberation, Imagination, and the Black Panther Party: A New Look at the Panthers and Their Legacy*, ed. Kathleen Cleaver and George N. Katsiaficas (New York: Routledge, 2001), 51–68.

13. Marable, *Race, Reform, and Rebellion*, 228–231.

14. Michael O. Emerson and Christian Smith, *Divided by Faith: Evangelical Religion and the Problem of Race in America* (Oxford: Oxford University Press, 2000), 63–133; Bill Clinton, "Remarks at the University of Texas at Austin, October 16, 1995," in *Public Papers of the Presidents of the United States: William J. Clinton, 1995*, bk. 2 (Washington, DC: National Archives and Records Administration, 1996), 1600–1604.

15. John Mica and Barbara Cubin, "Alligators and Wolves," in *Welfare: A Documentary History of U.S. Policy and Politics*, ed. Gwendolyn Mink and Rickie Solinger (New York: New York University Press, 2003), 622.

16. Randall Kennedy, *Nigger: The Strange Career of a Troublesome Word* (New York: Pantheon, 2002), 41–43.

17. Marable, *Race, Reform, and Rebellion*, 220–221; "Prop. 209 Backer Defends Use of King in Ad," *Los Angeles Times*, October 24, 1996.

18. Roger Ebert, "Set It Off," November 8, 1996, www.rogerebert.com/reviews /set-it-off-1996.

19. William J. Clinton, "Commencement Address at the University of California San Diego in La Jolla, California," June 14, 1997, Gerhard Peters and John T. Woolley, The American Presidency Project, www.presidency.ucsb.edu /ws/?pid=54268.

20. "At Million Woman March, Focus Is on Family," *New York Times*, October 26, 1997.

21. Jim Sleeper, *Liberal Racism* (New York: Viking, 1997); Brown et al., *Whitewashing Race*, 5–17, 21, 153–160; Peter Collier and David Horowitz, *The Race Card: White Guilt, Black Resentment, and the Assault on Truth and Justice* (Rocklin, CA: Prima, 1997); Stephan Thernstrom and Abigail M. Thernstrom, *America in Black and White: One Nation, Indivisible* (New York: Simon and Schuster, 1999), 494, 500, 539.

CHAPTER 36: 99.9 PERCENT THE SAME

1. Nathan Glazer, *We Are All Multiculturalists Now* (Cambridge, MA: Harvard University Press, 1997).

2. Angela Y. Davis, *Blues Legacies and Black Feminism: Gertrude "Ma" Rainey, Bessie Smith, and Billie Holiday* (New York: Pantheon Books, 1998); David Nicholson, "Feminism and the Blues," *Washington Post*, February 12, 1998; Francis Davis, "Ladies Sing the Blues," *New York Times*, March 8, 1998.

3. "Angela Davis, Still Carrying the Torch in 2000," *Lesbian News*, April 2000; Angela Y. Davis, *Are Prisons Obsolete?* (New York: Seven Stories Press, 2003), 7–8, 15–16.

4. John H. McWhorter, *Losing the Race: Self-Sabotage in Black America* (New York: Free Press, 2000), 13; "Original Oakland Resolution on Ebonics," December 18, 1996, http://linguistlist.org/topics/ebonics/ebonics-res1.html.

5. Robert Williams, "Ebonics as a Bridge to Standard English," *St. Louis Post-Dispatch*, January 28, 1997.

6. "Black English Is Not a Second Language, Jackson Says," *New York Times*, December 23, 1996, www.nytimes.com/1996/12/23/us/black-english-is-not-a-second-language-jackson-says.html; "LSA Resolution on the Oakland 'Ebonics' Issue," 1997, Linguistic Society of America, www.linguisticsociety.org/resource /lsa-resolution-oakland-ebonics-issue.

7. Albert C. Baugh and Thomas Cable, *A History of the English Language*, 5th ed. (Upper Saddle River, NJ: Prentice-Hall, 2002).

8. McWhorter, *Losing the Race*, x, 124–125, 195.

9. John H. McWhorter, *Authentically Black: Essays for the Black Silent Majority* (New York: Gotham Books, 2003), xii–xiii, 33–35, 262–264.

10. "Remarks Made by the President, Prime Minister Tony Blair of England (via satellite), Dr. Francis Collins, Director of the National Human Genome Research

Institute, and Dr. Craig Venter, President and Chief Scientific Officer, Celera Genomics Corporation, on the Completion of the First Survey of the Entire Human Genome Project," June 26, 2000, https://www.genome.gov/10001356.

11. Nicholas Wade, "For Genome Mappers, the Tricky Terrain of Race Requires Some Careful Navigating," *New York Times*, July 20, 2001.

12. Reanne Frank, "Forbidden or Forsaken? The (Mis)Use of a Forbidden Knowledge Argument in Research on Race, DNA, and Disease," in *Genetics and the Unsettled Past: The Collision of DNA, Race, and History*, ed. Alondra Nelson, Keith Wailoo, and Catherine Lee (New Brunswick, NJ: Rutgers University Press, 2012), 315–316; Roberts, *Fatal Invention*, 4, 50–54; Nicholas Wade, *A Troublesome Inheritance: Genes, Race, and Human History* (New York: Penguin, 2014); Yudell, *Race Unmasked*, ix–xi.

13. United States, *Initial Report to the Committee on the Elimination of Racial Discrimination*, September 2000, www1.umn.edu/humanrts/usdocs/cerdinitial.html; Bob Herbert, "In America; Keep Them Out!" *New York Times*, December 7, 2000, www.nytimes.com/2000/12/07/opinion/in-america-keep-them-out.html; Marable, *Race, Reform, and Rebellion*, 236–237.

14. Ibid., 249–250; Randall Robinson, *The Debt: What America Owes to Blacks* (New York: Dutton, 2000).

15. Marable, *Race, Reform, and Rebellion*, 240–243.

16. Dave Chappelle, "Black White Supremacist," Comedy Central, https://www.youtube.com/watch?v=rQtysS7fB4k.

17. Roediger, *How Race Survived U.S. History*, 215; Marable, *Race, Reform, and Rebellion*, 243–246.

18. Marable, *Race, Reform, and Rebellion*, 247.

19. Donna Lieberman, "School to Courthouse," *New York Times*, December 8, 2012, www.nytimes.com/2012/12/09/opinion/sunday/take-police-officers-off-the-school-discipline-beat.html?_r=0; P. L. Thomas, *Ignoring Poverty in the U.S.: The Corporate Takeover of Public Education* (Charlotte, NC: Information Age Pub, 2012), 186–187.

20. Marable, *Race, Reform, and Rebellion*, 247–248; Michael Eric Dyson, *Is Bill Cosby Right? Or Has the Black Middle Class Lost Its Mind?* (New York: BasicCivitas, 2005); Micheal E. Dyson, "The Injustice Bill Cosby Won't See," *Washington Post*, July 21, 2006.

21. "Transcript: Illinois Senate Candidate Barack Obama," *Washington Post*, July 27, 2004.

CHAPTER 37: THE EXTRAORDINARY NEGRO

1. Barack Obama, *Dreams from My Father: A Story of Race and Inheritance* (New York: Three Rivers Press, 2004), 98–100.

2. Ta-Nehisi Coates, "Worst Movie of the Decade," *The Atlantic*, December 30, 2009, www.theatlantic.com/entertainment/archive/2009/12/worst-movie-of-the-decade/32759/; John McWhorter, "Racism in America Is Over," *Forbes*, December 30, 2008, www.forbes.com/2008/12/30/end-of-racism-oped-cx_jm_1230mcwhorter.html.

3. "Washing Away," *New Orleans Times-Picayune*, June 23–27, 2002; Daniels, *Cyber Racism*, 117–155; Naomi Klein, *The Shock Doctrine: The Rise of Disaster Capitalism* (New York: Metropolitan Books / Henry Holt, 2007).

4. "'Racist' Police Blocked Bridge and Forced Evacuees Back at Gunpoint," *Independent* (London), September 11, 2005.

5. George W. Bush, *Decision Points* (New York: Crown, 2010), 325–326; Marable, *Race, Reform, and Rebellion*, 251–256.

6. Larry Elder, "Katrina, The Race Card, and the Welfare State," *WND*, September 8, 2005, www.wnd.com/2005/09/32236/.

7. Harris-Perry, *Sister Citizen*, 157–179.

8. Angela Locke, "Angela Davis: Not Just a Fair-Weather Activist," *Off Our Backs* 37, no. 1 (2007): 66–68.

9. "Imus Isn't the Real Bad Guy," *Kansas City Star*, April 11, 2007.

10. "NAACP Symbolically Buries N-Word," *Washington Post*, July 9, 2007.

11. "Biden's Description of Obama Draws Scrutiny," CNN, February 9, 2007, www.cnn.com/2007/POLITICS/01/31/biden.obama/; Roediger, *How Race Survived U.S. History*, 216; H. Samy Alim and Geneva Smitherman, *Articulate While Black: Barack Obama, Language, and Race in the U.S.* (Oxford: Oxford University Press, 2012), 31–44.

12. Harris-Perry, *Sister Citizen*, 273–277; *The New Yorker*, July 21, 2008.

13. "Obama's Pastor: God Damn America, U.S. to Blame for 9/11," ABC News, March 13, 2008, http://abcnews.go.com/Blotter/DemocraticDebate/story?id=4443788.

14. Robert M. Entman and Andrew Rojecki, *The Black Image in the White Mind: Media and Race in America* (Chicago: University of Chicago Press, 2000), 33–60.

15. Joy DeGruy, *Post Traumatic Slave Syndrome: America's Legacy of Enduring Injury and Healing* (Portland: Joy DeGruy, 2005); Jay S. Kaufman and Susan A. Hall, "The Slavery Hypertension Hypothesis: Dissemination and Appeal of a Modern Race Theory," *Epidemiology* 14, no. 1 (2003): 111–118; "Doctors Claim 'Hood Disease' Afflicts Inner-City Youth," NewsOne, May 17, 2014, http://newsone.com/3010041/doctors-claim-hood-disease-afflicts-inner-city-youth/.

16. Barack Obama, "Transcript: Barack Obama's Speech on Race," NPR, March 18, 2008, www.npr.org/templates/story/story.php?storyId=88478467.

17. "What Should Obama Do About Rev. Jeremiah Wright?" *Salon*, April 29, 2008, www.salon.com/2008/04/29/obama_wright/; "Huckabee Defends Obama . . . and the Rev. Wright," *ABC News*, March 20, 2008, http://blogs.abcnews.com/politicalpunch/2008/03/huckabee-defend.html; Michelle Bernard, "Hardball with Chris Mathews," MSNBC, March 21, 2008; John McCain, "Hardball College Tour at Villanova University," MSNBC, April 15, 2008; Charles Murray, "Have I Missed the Competition?" *National Review Online*, March 18, 2008; Newt Gingrich, "The Obama Challenge: What Is the Right Change to Help All Americans Pursue Happiness and Create Prosperity," speech at the American Enterprise Institute, Washington, DC, March 27, 2008, transcript, https://web.archive.org/web/20080404112807/http://newt.org/tabid/102/articleType/ArticleView/articleId/3284/Default.aspx.

18. "Text of Obama's Fatherhood Speech," *Politico*, June 15, 2008, www.politico.com/story/2008/06/text-of-obamas-fatherhood-speech-011094; Michael Eric Dyson, "Obama's Rebuke of Absentee Black Fathers," *Time*, June 19, 2008.

19. "Life Expectancy Gap Narrows Between Blacks, Whites," *Los Angeles Times*, June 5, 2012, http://articles.latimes.com/2012/jun/05/science/la-sci-life-expectancy-gap-20120606; "Michelle Alexander: More Black Men Are in Prison Today Than

Were Enslaved in 1850," *Huffington Post*, October 12, 2011, www.huffingtonpost
.com/2011/10/12/michelle-alexander-more-black-men-in-prison-slaves-1850_n
_1007368.html; Alexander, *The New Jim Crow*, 174–176.

20. "On Revolution: A Conversation Between Grace Lee Boggs and Angela
Davis," March 2, 2012, University of California, Berkeley, video and transcript,
www.radioproject.org/2012/02/grace-lee-boggs-berkeley/.

21. John McWhorter, "Racism in America Is Over," *Forbes*, December 30, 2008,
www.forbes.com/2008/12/30/end-of-racism-oped-cx_jm_1230mcwhorter.html.

EPILOGUE

1. "Dissecting the 2008 Electorate: Most Diverse in U.S. History," Pew Research
Center, April 30, 2009, www.pewhispanic.org/2009/04/30/dissecting-the
-2008-electorate-most-diverse-in-us-history/; "Youth Vote May Have Been Key in
Obama's Win," NBC News, November 5, 2008, www.nbcnews.com/id/27525497
/ns/politics-decision_08/t/youth-vote-may-have-been-key-obamas-win/#
.VgyfvstVhBc.

2. "Obama Hatred at McCain-Palin Rallies: 'Terrorist!' 'Kill Him!'" *Huffington Post*,
November 6, 2008, www.huffingtonpost.com/2008/10/06/mccain-does-nothing
-as-cr_n_132366.html.

3. Michael C. Dawson, *Not in Our Lifetimes: The Future of Black Politics* (Chicago:
University of Chicago Press, 2011), 91; Jones, *Dreadful Deceit*, 290–292; Jill Lep-
ore, *The Whites of Their Eyes: The Tea Party's Revolution and the Battle over American History*, Public Square Book Series (Princeton, NJ: Princeton University Press, 2010),
3–4; Daniels, *Cyber Racism*, 3–5; "White Supremacists More Dangerous to America Than Foreign Terrorists," *Huffington Post*, June 24, 2015, www.huffingtonpost
.com/2015/06/24/domestic-terrorism-charleston_n_7654720.html.

4. Barack Obama, "Remarks by the President to the NAACP Centennial Convention," July 16, 2009, https://www.whitehouse.gov/the-press-office/remarks
-president-naacp-centennial-convention-07162009; "Obama: Police Who
Arrested Professor 'Acted Stupidly,'" CNN, July 23, 2009, www.cnn.com/2009/US
/07/22/harvard.gates.interview/; Glenn Beck, "Fox Host Glenn Beck: Obama Is a
'Racist,'" July 28, 2009, www.huffingtonpost.com/2009/07/28/fox-host-glenn-beck
-obama_n_246310.html.

5. Ta-Nehisi Coates, "The Case for Reparations," *The Atlantic*, June 2014; Janet
Mock, *Redefining Realness: My Path to Womanhood, Identity, Love & So Much More* (New
York: Atria Books, 2014), 258.

6. Alexander, *The New Jim Crow*, 6–7, 138, 214–222.

7. "Richard Sherman: Thug Is Now 'The Accepted Way of Calling Somebody the
N-Word,'" *Huffington Post*, January 22, 2014, www.huffingtonpost.com/2014/01/22
/richard-sherman-thug-n-word-press-conference_n_4646871.html.

8. "Meet the Woman Who Coined #BlackLivesMatter," *USA Today*, March 4,
2015, www.usatoday.com/story/tech/2015/03/04/alicia-garza-black-lives-matter
/24341593/.

9. Garrison, *An Address, Delivered Before the Free People of Color*, 5–6.

10. Du Bois, "My Evolving Program for Negro Freedom," 70; Myrdal, *An American Dilemma*, 1:48.

11. W. E. B. Du Bois, "A Negro Nation Within the Nation," *Current History* 42
(1935): 265–270.

Index

Ibram X. Kendi is a #1 *New York Times* bestselling author, professor of history and international studies, and the Director of the Boston University Center for Antiracist Research. He is an Ideas Columnist at *The Atlantic* and a correspondent with CBS News. He is the author of four books, including *Stamped from the Beginning: The Definitive History of Racist Ideas in America*, which won National Book Award for Nonfiction, the *New York Times* bestsellers *How to Be an Antiracist* and *STAMPED: Racism, Antiracism, and You*, co-authored with Jason Reynolds, and *Antiracist Baby*.